Sociology of Constitutions

This collection brings together some of the most influential sociologists of law to confront the challenges of current transnational constitutionalism. It shows the constitution appearing in a new light: no longer as an essential factor of unity and stabilisation but as a potential defence of pluralism and innovation.

The first part of the book is devoted to the analysis of the concept of constitution, highlighting the elements that can contribute from a socio-legal perspective, to clarifying the principle meanings attributed to the constitution. The study goes on to analyse some concrete aspects of the functioning of constitutions in contemporary society. In applying Luhmann's General Systems Theory to a comparative analysis of the concept of constitution, the work contributes to a better understanding of this traditional concept in both its institutionalised and functional aspects.

Defining the constitution's contents and functions both at the conceptual level and by taking empirical issues of particular comparative interest into account, this study will be of importance to scholars and students of sociology of law, sociology of politics and comparative public law.

Alberto Febbrajo is Professor of Sociology of Law at the Department of Law, University of Macerata, Italy.

Giancarlo Corsi is Associate Professor of Sociology at the Department of Communication and Economics, University of Modena-Reggio Emilia, Italy.

Studies in the Sociology of Law
Series Editor
Alberto Febbrajo, University of Macerata, Italy

The objectives of Studies in the Sociology of Law are threefold. Firstly, the series aims to deepen the analysis of the sociolegal problems related to the enlarged European Union and the different paths of its constitutional process and policy. Secondly, it examines the many facets of legal cultures within and outside the European context in comparative perspective and in an open debate with extra European scholarship. Thirdly, it reconsiders the historical legacy of sociolegal thought while dealing with the broader dynamic and the new challenges of contemporary societies.

Law and Intersystemic Communication
Understanding 'Structural Coupling'
Edited by Alberto Febbrajo and Gorm Harste
ISBN 9781409421108

Sociology of Constitutions

A paradoxical perspective

Edited by Alberto Febbrajo and Giancarlo Corsi

Routledge
Taylor & Francis Group
LONDON AND NEW YORK

First published 2016
by Routledge
2 Park Square, Milton Park, Abingdon, Oxon OX14 4RN

and by Routledge
711 Third Avenue, New York, NY 10017

First issued in paperback 2017

Routledge is an imprint of the Taylor & Francis Group, an informa business

British Library Cataloguing in Publication Data
A catalogue record for this book is available from the British Library

Library of Congress Cataloging-in-Publication Data
Sociology of constitutions: a paradoxical perspective / by Alberto Febbrajo and Giancarlo Corsi.
pages cm. — (Studies in the sociology of law)
Includes bibliographical references and index.
ISBN 978-1-4724-7959-4 (hardback) 1. Constitutional law—Social aspects. I. Febbrajo, Alberto, editor. II. Corsi, Giancarlo, editor.
K3165.S63 2016
342—dc23
2015034043

ISBN 13: 978-1-138-49756-6 (pbk)
ISBN 13: 978-1-4724-7959-4 (hbk)

Typeset in Times New Roman
by Apex CoVantage, LLC

Contents

Tables

Contributors

Ino Augsberg, Professor of Legal Philosophy and Public Law, Christian-Albrechts-University Kiel.

Michele Carducci, Professor of Comparative Constitutional Law, University of Salento.

Giancarlo Corsi, Professor of Sociology, University of Modena-Reggio Emilia.

Matías Dewey, Researcher, Max-Planck-Institut für Gesellschaftsforschung, Cologne.

Alberto Febbrajo, Professor of Sociology of Law and Anthropology of Law, University of Macerata.

Bogdan Iancu, Associate Professor (Comparative Constitutional Law and Constitutional Theory), Faculty of Political Science, University of Bucharest.

Karl-Heinz Ladeur, Professor (Emeritus), University of Hamburg.

Aldo Mascareño, Professor at the School of Government in the Adolfo Ibáñez University, Santiago de Chile.

Hans-Georg Moeller, Professor of Philosophy and Religious Studies Programme, University of Macau.

Marcelo Neves, Professor of Public Law, University of Brasilia.

Cesare Pinelli, Professor of Public Law, Department of Law, University of Rome 1, La Sapienza.

Johannes F.K. Schmidt, Researcher, University of Bielefeld.

Gunther Teubner, Professor (Emeritus) of Private Law and Sociology of Law, Goethe University, Frankfurt.

Chris Thornhill, Professor of Public Law, University of Manchester.

Introduction

Alberto Febbrajo and Giancarlo Corsi

The fundamental concept of the constitution is changing rapidly. On the basis of the general formula one state, one constitution, the constitution used to be seen as the sole and indisputable mother of the legal order, i.e. as the 'norm of the norms', on which the individual legal decisions could ultimately be grounded, as the benchmark for sustainable and coherent solutions to the problems of a differentiated society, and as a safe harbour, where the certainty of law could be protected successfully. Due to its privileged relations with civil society on the one side, and with political power on the other, the constitution was consequently applied in many convergent ways: by judges as the main tool for granting identity to their legal decisions, by political actors as the main criterion for defining the limits of legal interventions, and by the public as the main institutionalised norm for defending the abstract recognition of new rights or the elimination of previous constraints.

Many parts of these legal and sociological narratives have now come to be regarded as outdated. Criticism has focused on the main images of law and state on which the traditional concept of the constitution was based. Both sociologists and jurists no longer consider it a case of blasphemy to admit that constitutions have lost their strategic role, and even among the public there is a more widespread perception of the profound social distance between the constitution and everyday life – with complex effects on the politically-based democratic order itself.

There are plenty of reasons for these changes of image. Transnational organisations, economic interests that transcend state borders and emerging calls for greater autonomy from local communities, all require regulations of such a scope that single states are coming to accept significant limitations to their own autonomy. Here some questions arise: is it possible to imagine a reliable constitution without a clear reference to a sovereign state? Can a plurality of states agree reciprocally to downscale their own political roles, even in the absence of a corresponding meta-state and of a fully institutionalised new order?

Although several theoretical attempts have been made to find an answer to these questions, the specific contents and functions of the concept of 'constitution' still seem to lack a clear definition in this phase of transition. It is actually easier to say what the constitution *was* rather than what the constitution *is*. The absence of a clear positive definition is an important reason for the increased ambiguity that the concept of constitution now shares with other leading concepts of traditional dogmatics. As a matter of fact, this may easily lead to the constitution's role being overestimated or underestimated.

The constitution may be overestimated, insofar as it now appears – even more than in the past – to lack the instruments necessary for effectively innovating the legal order. In today's new transnational perspective, the constitution tends to act as a factor of hope, rather than a factor of change, and often does not succeed in effectively implementing even the rights that are broadly considered to be constitutionally inalienable in our societies.

It is also possible to underestimate the value of the constitution. In spite of the individual state's reduced autonomy, it may control many important regulations, such as the legal rules internal to the state organisation, the procedures related to the administration of justice, and the internal harmonisation of legal orders. An under-evaluated constitution is not perceived to be responsible for possible failures of the legal order and for the delusions that the consequent disorder can provoke.

From a legal point of view, it could be imagined that a better interpretation of the same constitution might be able to improve its degree of success significantly. From a sociological point of view, it could be suggested that an adequate legal order depends not so much on the constitution, as on the positive effects of intervening social factors. On the one hand, constitutions tend to be immunised against visible dysfunctions, on the other they convey the impression of not being responsible for the achievement of a wide spectrum of expectations.

All these perceptions contain elements of truth that are hard to rebut. Constitutions are legitimised by the interests mediated by politics, but in their turn the same interests have to be legitimised by the constitution. Constitutions are *explanans* and *explanandum*. In general in such cases, the sociologist records a complex circular relationship, which is construed as the dependence of the phenomena under study on reciprocally interrelated factors. This opens up the door to circular explanations, which makes relations of cause and effect not unequivocally determinable, but reciprocally invertible.

A causal analysis in which the same element is not only the cause, but also the effect, may reveal some at least apparently paradoxical contradictions. Paradoxes, in the case of the constitution, are capable of defining a certain problem and also a possible solution. Especially with the eclipse of a centralistic vision of the state, paradoxes provide us with a useful vantage point for observing the constitution as a flexible element that cannot be defined unequivocally in a causal perspective, as in Baron von Münchhausen's claim to be able to raise himself from the ground by pulling on his own hair. While the analysis of constitutional paradoxes is incapable of avoiding current constitutional contradictions, it can at least define the area where possible solutions can be found. That is the very reason why the constitution is nowadays an increasingly relevant crossroad for socio-legal thinking.

The aim of this book is to suggest a possible definition of the constitution underlining its paradoxical aspects. For this purpose, leading experts were invited to contribute to a constructive debate open to scholars from European and non-European countries in an attempt to understand how certain paradoxical aspects of the constitution can be made visible in today's new transnational scenario.[1] Their contributions are arranged in order to examine the paradoxical aspects of the constitution through the problems of its conceptual definition and its concrete functions.

The volume is thus divided in two parts. The first part, devoted to the analysis of the concept of constitution, highlights the elements that can clarify from a socio-legal perspective, the principal meanings attributed to the constitution. In the opening chapter, Giancarlo Corsi offers an overview of the main reasons why the constitution is a paradoxical concept. A sophisticated approach like that of the general systems theory, in particular of its self-referential variant, is capable not only of revealing the constitution's paradoxes, but also of suggesting corresponding solutions. Constitution is a self-constituting set of norms which furnishes a sense to the legal system as a whole. This can be achieved by distinguishing between two different parts of the constitution: a general part containing the basic values indicated by the constitution's fundamental point of reference, and an instrumental part that identifies certain basic procedures for translating those values into reality. This dichotomy is also related to the ambiguous role of the fundamental rights that cannot be specified in a constitution because they are connected to case-by-case definitions handed down by the administration of justice. One example of circular self-reference that underpins paradoxes is the transfer from political to legal systems and vice versa: these systems are supported by constitutions, and are open to constant revisions and self-critical adjustments whose purpose is to communicate acceptable criteria of rationality to other systems and to define the constitutional/unconstitutional dichotomy.

Gunther Teubner develops a systemic analysis of the constitution in the second chapter, where he sets out to establish a link between four really problematic aspects of modern law: judge-made law, renewed interest in natural law, the role of protest movements and the process of constitutionalisation that is not limited to the state, but can also be observed in other social subsystems. Teubner argues that this link is provided in the way that every subsystem deals with its 'foundational paradox'. In the case of the legal system, the paradox has to be externalised, i.e. the law must rely on politics if it is to legitimise the production of laws, while politics must rely on the law to legitimise the use of power. This is the main function of the state constitution. But the question then arises as to whether modern law bypasses political systems, giving birth to 'highly specialised legal regimes', which are 'detached from public international law and now coupled closely with the inner rationality of the social fields'. This leads to the rise of other constitutional forms, in economics, in the sciences and in every other subsystem, breaking politics' monopoly in the deparadoxisation of the legal system. This process may cause new problems, such as the risk that subsystems will be delivered up to extraneous structural logic or to further external paradoxes.

Analysing the constitution from the point of view of semiotics, Ino Augsberg points out that constitutions are texts and, as such, linguistic phenomena. They constitute themselves while describing themselves as constitutions and have to put themselves into practice by exercising this role. In other words, the constitutional document [*Urkunde*] is no primeval document [*Ur-Kunde*] and, as a normative text, it contains something more than the text itself, an 'unavailable Other that must underpin every normative act'. Developing this premise, Augsberg then underlines the inherent double perspective of every text that, in a paradoxical way, is at the same time performative and constative. Every statement contained in the text, including constitutional texts, has a specific reference, while at the same time being open-ended and capable of incorporating additional threads, some of which may be unknown. This 'genealogical dimension' of linguistic analysis gives constitutions a double 'autopoietic' dimension, on which their specific character as a promise depends: something that 'must be presumed in the act of giving to be already given and accepted as such'.

Hans-Georg Moeller bases his reasoning on the philosophy of Kant, setting out to illustrate the foundation of the idea of the constitution in the German-speaking area. The categorical imperative as the basic law of the metaphysics of moral in Kant in its turn provides the basis for developing a scientific jurisprudence. In this context, the state constitution is situated 'between jurisprudence, which brings legal practices to expression *a priori*' and rights intended as the actual or 'empirical' legal practice. Being founded on reason, the whole Kantian system seems to be explicitly detached from any form of paradox, but, when observed from the point of view of modern philosophy and social sciences, constitutions can formulate principles performatively, as they only become real and effective through the process of their formulation. The binding force of constitutions is thus based on 'the success of a performative communication' which is, paradoxically, self-generated.

Concluding this section, Alberto Febbrajo sets out to reconstruct some of the different models of constitution implicitly or explicitly proposed by socio-legal studies. Starting from the not state-centred perspective they adopt to criticise the role of legal propositions produced artificially by the state, he reconstructs different forms of constitution respectively connected with an *asymmetric* pluralism, characterised by the prevalence of historically-based constitutions produced spontaneously by social associations (Ehrlich), a *statistical* pluralism, which rejects the proclamatory norms contained in formal constitutions and only considers norms that are defended by means of sanctions (Geiger), a *relativistic* pluralism based on a complex set of decision-making criteria embedded in constitutions capable of combining internal and external legal cultures with the functional requirements of the different sectors of society (Weber), and a *systemic* pluralism that considers the constitution to be an instrument of structural coupling, capable of connecting legal and political systems (Luhmann). In continuity with the past, this more comprehensive approach highlights the possibility to reconsider the limits of a hierarchical perspective for the purpose of grasping the current, profoundly heterogeneous normative situation, which is still based on the circular, and thus paradoxical, combinations of normativity and cognitivity, of order and disorder.

The second part of the volume is devoted to analysing the main issues that crop up whenever a concrete attempt is made to study how the constitutions of different countries operate. In this context, scholars who start out from legal and sociological standpoints represent complementary aspects of the tendencies towards generalisation and diversification, which paradoxically jurisprudence is called on to interpret simultaneously in the framework of the emerging global constitutionalism.

In the chapter that opens this second section, Chris Thornhill underlines that sociology fails to grasp the origin and meaning of the transformations in modern law. A number of processes can be observed that produce law with constitutional character in the confused and paradoxical interaction between national constitutional courts and international courts, application of international jurisprudence and 'adaptation to international norms' which characterise local political systems trying to address internal national problems. At the same time, a 'transnational judicial democracy' is developed through 'a shift in power from legislatures and executives to judiciaries'. Arguing that the lack of an adequate sociological inquiry in this field is due to the persistent focus on legalistic perspectives, Thornhill uses several examples to illustrate that the distinction between international and domestic law is fictitious and underlines that a fruitful sociological analysis of the interaction between international and national courts should take into account that global constitutional law is not imposed on national institutions externally, but is rather the expression 'of a reflexive and adaptive dimension within these institutions'.

Cesare Pinelli focuses his attention on the 'disputed relationship' between constitutionalism and globalisation, emphasising that the pluralistic roots of constitutionalism can offer 'an alternative meaning' to the often discussed 'constitution beyond state hypothesis'. He underlines how the increase in 'constitutionalisation' outside the traditional channels of international law set a process of fragmentation in motion, which has rendered the construction of a global order on a constitutional basis increasingly problematic, and affirms that today's fragmentation could become not an obstacle, but an opportunity 'for redefining the constitutional problems of world society' on a pluralistic basis. Analysing the apparently paradoxical opposition of contemporary constitutionalism to pluralism, he then observes that this opposition appears to be 'a caricature of constitutionalism', because what now seems to be important – as demonstrated by the EU's weak reaction to the financial crisis – is to find 'heterarchical, rather than hierarchical, criteria' for an 'ordered pluralism' capable of assuring 'a fair equidistance between citizens and public powers'. Given the role of private as well as public institutions, it might be thus possible to deal 'both with the growing complexity and fragmentation of legal and political orders and with the forced uniformity pursued by the global financial market'.

Michele Carducci adopts a comparative perspective to discuss the problems connected with the development of a semantics of global constitutionalism. One particularly crucial problem for comparison is what we call the 'judicial dialogue', based on a process of 'communication about the pluralism of rights, but not necessarily of information about the plurality of constitutional conceptions'. In this context, particular importance is attributed to the role played by a variety of constitutional conceptions disseminated in several parts of the world, with such specific features as individualistic interpretations of pluralism, connections 'between sustainable development, human development and constitutional development', the 'global supermarket' where empty rules are 'made available to any operation of "constitutional borrowing"'. In this confused, often contradictory and paradoxical context it is more realistic to speak not so much about 'global constitutionalism', but about a 'cross-constitutionalism' whose matrix is still European and North American. This kind of constitutionalism is fundamentally oriented towards 'a democratic and eco-systemic equilibrium' that could be analysed in a general perspective and with the support of a new semantics, without 'making a complete break away from the state approach'.

In the following chapter, Karl-Heinz Ladeur adopts an evolutionary perspective in his attempt to identify some changes in the nature of constitution. After illustrating the distinction between 'society of individuals', 'society of organisations' and 'society of networks', he recognises the centrality of individuals for the 'liberal' idea of the constitution. He observes that this differentiation has, paradoxically enough, produced a 'trans-subjective acentric order', whose function is to distribute subjective rights. Individuality based on social norms protects individuals through social control, but when organisations come about as central legal actors, 'social norms and the law go their increasingly separate ways'. The case of freedom of opinion shows that professional and deontological rules, which were originally determined within the borders of public law, are now blurring the classical distinctions between public and private, as well as between market and organisation, when networks come into play. As a consequence, high-tech companies do not rely on external judges to construe and settle conflicts, but prefer a form of 'self-adjustment', while the law is further fragmented, both in its structure and in its function, especially when juridification is called into play. But even though basic rights are 'historicised' as values, the question arises: what relevance do they still have for a 'society of networks'?

Bogdan Iancu analyses the legal system at work in Romania in order to describe the emergence of a new frontier of global constitutionalism that is clearly independent of traditional constitutional values, focusing attention on the good governance. The combination of efficiency and effectiveness – a universal requirement of good governance practices – is actually applicable to a wide variety of situations in the interest of transnational homogeneity of the rules of the legal game. In these cases, as for instance in the case of the danger of a serious global epidemic, the independence of national regulations is significantly restricted. Listing the strategic fields where the criteria of good governance have been applied successfully, particular attention is reserved to the anti-corruption measures in the European Union. In this context a closer analysis reveals, paradoxically, profound contradictions and apparent convergences. They are produced by an emerging global constitutionalism which masks national practices because of the resistance of local constitutionalism. It is therefore plausible to wonder whether this fragmentation 'will not produce, in time, generous possibilities for manipulation, and thus open avenues for, albeit more insidious, equally detrimental forms of corruption'.

Matías Dewey presents a case study of an illegal market in Buenos Aires, arguing that a peculiar paradox can be observed there: a socio-economic sphere where 'the law [is] decoupled from the economy', but normal economic forms, such as contracts and property rights, are recognised and actually work. Given the presence of clientelism, criminal organisations and widespread illegality, the state has been in these cases replaced by third parties who apply an informal tax system that structures the expectations of both buyers and sellers. Dewey argues that this case illustrates a blind spot in sociology, particularly in the systems theory: when Luhmann defines legitimation as the acceptance of decisions motivated through legal procedures, he neglects the presence and the importance of other kinds of legitimacy, produced on the 'silent' side of social exclusion, which remains 'unexplored' in the systems theory. In this way it 'loses its ability to capture phenomena' that produce economic structures outside the constitution and without legal legitimation, but are nevertheless capable of attaining legitimacy on the basis of an informal policy that successfully enforces contracts and property.

Aldo Mascareño analyses how Latin American constitutions have developed in their recent history. He uses Venezuelan and Chilean constitutions as case studies, analysing how in these contexts particularistic norms collide with universalistic expectations in domestic political projects, as well as in transnational constitutionalism. Paradoxically, insofar as it aims at harmonising the functional autonomy of social subsystems with environmental concerns, the process of constitutionalisation in Latin America would actually call for the deconstitutionalisation of local constitutional particularisms. While collisions between transnational normative orders on the one side and domestic policy and interests on the other are processed and decided through intermediate mechanisms, in the Latin American region a 'normative particularism' has prevailed that has barred the way to achieving a 'liberal constitutionalism' of the kind familiar in Europe, leading instead to the formation of political elites and to an 'instrumentalisation of the state's apparatus by particular interests and groups'.

In the final chapter of this second section, Marcelo Neves addresses the problem of 'transconstitutionalism'. Starting from the two central problems that gave birth to modern constitutions, namely the 'emergence of demands for fundamental or human rights' and the question of the 'limitation of power and its internal and external control', he sets out to illustrate how Latin American – and especially Brazilian – jurisprudence tackles these problems, adopting a perspective that cuts across existing legal orders. Using a rich array of legal cases, Neves describes the complexity of the relationships between public international law, supranational law, state law and even extra-state legal orders. He devotes particular attention to the emerging conflict between the universalism of human rights and the controversial legitimacy of local, in particular 'native' laws. In this context, he underlines the emergence of a paradox, that is extremely hard to conceal in the current situation: that of a jurisprudential approach with transnational – even universal – ambitions, which has to be implicitly transformed and reinterpreted when particularisms are recognised. The reason for this paradox lies in an internal contradiction, as transconstitutionalism requires methods rather than authority and aims to promote a generalised inclusion rather than an ideal constitutional identity.

In an additional section Giancarlo Corsi and Johannes Schmidt explore Luhmann's methodology of his famous card index in search of references to the specific issue of the constitution. Luhmann conceived the card index as a huge amount of notes with a numbered fixed location, each related to a previous note and with no specific or predetermined order. Schmidt's research clearly demonstrates that the meaning of each note in this filing system derives from its references to other notes, in an often fragmented connection. In this context, Luhmann's card index sheds light on the character of a difficult tool that drives its user towards unexpected results, almost inevitably leading to ideas that cannot be deduced directly from the filing system itself. Luhmann wrote notes and then put them in what he called his *Zettelkasten* in order to surprise himself. And it comes as no surprise from a scholar who had a sense of self-irony and a particular sensitivity for paradoxes.

The theses discussed in all these chapters underline, from different standpoints, that today's multiplication of normative sources, below and above the state, reinforces the ambiguity and the paradoxical character of the traditional concept of constitution. They are also converging towards a definition of the constitution which, in a centreless society, has to be open to a multidimensional legal order and to an increasingly complex environment. In this context, now even more so than in the past, constitutional paradoxes suggest that sociology of law adopt a renewed critical, commitment towards sociological definitions and functional justifications of the constitution.

Note

1 All the chapters collected in this volume were presented in two meetings organised by the University of Modena-Reggio Emilia (2013) and in Fermo, by the University of Macerata (2014) with the participation of sociologists and comparatists of law.

Part I

1 On paradoxes in constitutions

Giancarlo Corsi

Foreword

If sociology is the science that studies the improbability of social structures at the very moment when they have become thoroughly familiar and normal, then the constitution, given its ambiguous role in the legal order, should be an ideal terrain for socio-legal research. Constitutions are a very recent invention that have spread across the world, asserting themselves with surprising speed and acquiring a quasi-sacred status that defies explanation, but we have not to forget that they are an artificial normative instrument produced by decisions and whose every part is – at least in principle – subject to amendment.[1]

Despite this the constitution is a topic that is not sufficiently analysed. It is only in recent years that studies have been published that refer constitution not only to legal theory or to politology, but also to sociology. Those of these studies that are more widely known and discussed focus primarily on the constitution's function, in particular on the issue of the legitimation of the political power,[2] on the foundations of the law and on the role played by the constitution in regulating relations between the law and other sectors of society.[3] Many of these studies share doubts about the role of the state and the relevance that it assumes in international or transnational organisations, going well beyond the classical territorial borders established by nation states and local jurisdictions.[4]

The specific nature of these phenomena is often observed starting out not from the normative orientation typical of legal approaches in the strict sense of the term, or from the central role played by the institutions and the organisational apparatuses for more typically politological analyses, but from unquestioned ideological approaches that are not justified for their empirical scope.[5] That is why it is advisable to underline that a sociology of constitution does not have the task of providing the judge or political action with indications about how to operate. Legal theory is ultimately no more than a part of the system of law, which is where its meaning can be found, just as politology is ultimately no more than a part of the system of politics. This is therefore a question of differentiating society, which involves distinct functions for the various subsystems, implies also different problems, concepts and theoretical constructions. In terms of research, then, we can stress the interdisciplinarity or 'transdisciplinarity' of a study of the constitution that takes the form of a rather clear case of research that necessarily involves different perspectives.[6]

This diversity becomes apparent in the way that the constitution's form is analysed.

The constitution is a self-legitimising text that establishes its own pre-eminent position (paramount law) over ordinary law. Starting out from this position, then, the constitution also has to talk about itself, about its own validity and about how it was constructed. It has to establish the criteria governing its own amendment and make due provision for exceptions that it imposes on itself, should the political situation require it (e.g. in the case of a state of emergency). It has to establish fundamental rights that are not just an historically recent invention, but are also the product of decisions, so contingent like any other decision. At closer sight this means that they are fundamental *because* they are not necessary. On the political side, the constitution provides that the power to decide who will govern is vested in those who are governed and establishes criteria for legitimising political action, so also itself. This calls for a non-material sovereign, with no communicative address, such as the people. The list could continue: these are just the most evident and more frequently studied cases.

I shall here attempt to analyse the constitution, starting from the structure of its text, its internal articulation and the contents that make it one of the more typical structures of modern systems of law and of politics. Starting from the premise of systems theory, which holds that the constitution's function is not to provide foundations or to 'constitute', but to 'regulate' the relations between law and politics, the thesis that I shall propose is that this can only be achieved in an openly circular, tautological and thus inherently paradoxical manner. That is, in fact, the only way that the constitution allows both legal and political systems to face towards the future and not back towards the past, i.e. to operate on the basis of their own contingency and so *not to identify with any specific structure*. And that is the only way that law and politics can provide *a foundation in the absence of existing foundations*.

Why paradoxes?

Paradoxes are of interest to sociology not only because of the logical problems they generate. As has been demonstrated by abstract disciplines, such as systems theory, cybernetics and mathematics,[7] paradoxes always come about when an observer is self-referential; in other words, when he can observe himself. This is always the case of social systems. Paradoxes can come about when texts take themselves into consideration, as is of course the case of constitutions.[8] In general, a paradox is found when a distinction is made for itself. If a distinction is drawn between good and evil, for example, it is – or ought to be – inevitable that we ask ourselves whether drawing such a distinction is in itself good or evil. And that is a question to which no answer can be given.

One of this argument's underlying premises is that every distinction, without exception, is always the construct of an observer.[9] The observer cannot come across his own distinctions 'in nature', but has to elaborate them on the basis of the resources and the structures he has available.[10] For this reason, no observer can avoid asking himself what unit of distinction he is using, a question that is fated to end up in a short circuit. When that happens, the observer can do one of two things: he can drop it and observe something else, or he can become creative[11] – for example by inventing the constitution, if the old structures, such as natural law, have ceased to be functional. But whatever solution he chooses, it naturally postpones the paradox: it is just another paradoxical form that will have to be managed in a new form, so as to avoid being blocked by the short circuit, for example by replacing natural law with fundamental rights.

This is an important point that is not stressed enough in the literature:[12] paradoxes cannot be avoided, as any solution sought will bring them up again in any case, just in a different form. The problem is how to find forms that are *compatible* with existing structures, ultimately with the given societal context, and 'compatible' means that they succeed in concealing the paradox that would otherwise continuously block the communication's development.

What this means is particularly clear in the case of a constitution. Let's take the classical case of the constituent power. The constituent power's paradox goes beyond the traditional paradox of political theory, which asks whether the person who holds the power is subject to the same limitations that he imposes on others. The problem here is how to justify a power that arrogates the right to constitute the state and so also itself: gone are the days when the solution could be that of an investiture whose origin is natural or divine, since modernity has explicitly set such yardsticks aside. The best solution for achieving a functional differentiation of society[13] is therefore to distinguish between the constituent power and the constituted power. And yet this is clearly a sleight of hand: the difference only comes about after the constituent process, and it really ought to be admitted that the only true sovereign is the constituent power itself – i.e. the power that asserts that it is power without any additional adjectives.[14] This in turn means that everything that can be said about how the power is exercised is a consequence of a short circuit. Then we can be creative and invent democracy, i.e. a form of government where the sovereign people choose whom they want to govern them.[15] One paradox replaces another paradox, but in a way that is compatible with the requirements of modern politics, even though in democracy we can chose a dictatorship (see Europe's twentieth-century fascisms) or we can choose not to choose at all, with the result of a statistically improvable, but not impossible, parity (such as the US presidential elections in 2000).

On the strictly legal side, we come across another typical paradox when we ask on the basis of what law it is that the law distinguishes between right and wrong.[16] Once again, the problem is relatively simple: both sides of the distinction are products of the same system. It is not possible to be in the right unless someone else is in the wrong. This is probably one of the reasons why there exists such a concept as the prohibition of justice denied: the judge is obliged to decide, even when the information available to him is not sufficient to enable him to do so. An observer could ask whether an obliged decision is still a decision.[17] But that is how the courts operate and it is to this that we can connect if we want to understand under what conditions we can be in the right or the wrong in a dispute. Once again in this case, the solution is both a paradox and at the same time a stimulus to construct structures that are more or less flexible and compatible with society's evolution.

To summarise: paradoxes are inherent in every kind of observation and so in every kind of structure. Those who go in search of the essence, the fundament, the prime element, find a paradox, and paradoxes block observation, because they do not allow us to indicate anything without also indicating its opposite. The observer – every observer – always comes up against 'hard cases' or 'tragic choices' with no solution.[18]

In the next two paragraphs, I intend to analyse two aspects typical of any constitution, so as to demonstrate that their paradoxical formulation is actually the condition for the constitution to function and that they can only become a benchmark for the law and for politics if they are paradoxical. These two aspects are fundamental rights and legitimacy.

The aspecificity of fundamental rights

Constitutional texts typically comprise at least two parts. While the second of these is usually devoted to the 'form of the state' and the procedures for amending the constitution (and here it is clear that the constitution is talking about itself), the first groups together references to values and to fundamental rights. If we consider what the two parts refer to, we can say that the constitution distinguishes between referring to itself (in the second part) and referring to factors that it does not determine and that are placed (we ought to say: that the constitution places) outside and above itself (in the first part). In this sense, there is a demarcation towards the inside and towards the outside: towards the inside on the level of decision-making and procedural structures, for which the constitution takes on responsibility; towards the outside in reference to factors that evade decisions and are proposed as 'quasi' natural yardsticks that legitimate themselves and are referred to without being questioned.

This demarcation towards the outside shows some interesting idiosyncrasies. In fact, the first formulations of the rights that were in due course to become constitutional rights are still to a certain extent connected to traditional, pre-modern societal structures. Such terms as 'subjects' or 'individuals' originally referred to those who took part in society freely, above all as landowners: certain rights, such as franchise, were formulated primarily with them in mind (Stourzh 1989b). Similarly, such values as freedom and equality were devised for those who can and must exploit chances that are only equal within the same social class. In other words, the equality in question is conditional and based on the premise of differences in social, moral and status terms.

But when we reach the modern constitution, at the end of the eighteenth century in North America and, albeit in a different manner, in France, these last 'incrustations' of the old order disappear.[19] In the form they take on today, values and fundamental rights are formulated to be substantially generic or even aspecific. In the case just mentioned of the classical constitutional values of equality and freedom, it is easy to see where the difference lies compared to previous eras: it is impossible to state who is equal to whom and who is free from what, because that would introduce discriminations that would be incompatible with the fundamental law's general nature. These values' universalism thus seems to oblige to be semantically empty.[20] How they should be specified in concrete terms is left up to ordinary law, to the legislator, to the courts, to procedures and to the organisational criteria of decision-making, which can change with ordinary proceedings and so be receptive to the changes that are constantly taking place in society.[21]

In this sense, fundamental rights change above all in terms of how they relate to passing time. While in traditional formulations they may appear to certify what happened in the past, since they guarantee those who possess them by right of birth or of acquisition, in constitutions they are imposed *against* the past.[22] Rights and values now apply to everyone and any discrimination or restriction on rights must be compatible with this 'universalism'. As we have seen, fundamental rights, like any structure, do not determine the contents of potential future norms, but are limited to ruling out certain possibilities, and that explains why they have to be semantically aspecific.[23] This is not intended to mean that they are not effective from a point of view of constructing the abstract situations that provide for them, of denouncing their breaches or of repercussions in ordinary law. Suffice to consider the interpretations of the continuously changing concept of equality, which impact on the legal concept of the family, of sexuality, of how people are treated in the workplace and so on. But the fact that these new degrees of awareness can develop is in itself attributable to the difference between a constitutional value and its definitions in ordinary law. In other words, constitutional values are generic not only for practical reasons, i.e. so as to avoid having to amend the constitution every time that a value is vested with new concrete expressions, but also because that is how they keep future options open for situations that may one day turn out to be significant. Establishing in the constitution that a value is 'natural', without saying what that means in practice, is a way of obliging the law to interpret and reinterpret it continuously, so that these interpretations are subjected to interpretation in their turn (for example in the case of a state of emergency). This is one way of generating uncertainty in decision-making, which can be 'absorbed', i.e. translated into effective decisions, according to the circumstances or to the Zeitgeist.

The meaning of values and of fundamental rights is different from the political point of view. Here it is a case of how to reconcile them if they find themselves on a collision course. To stick with the more classical case, that of the relationship between freedom and equality: implementing equality means restricting freedom and it is no coincidence that nineteenth-century ideologies parted company primarily over this issue. In other cases, for example when more recent values are inserted into constitutions, new conflicts may be created that the law propose, leaving to politics the difficult (or impossible) task of finding a way to create harmony between the new values and the ones that already existed previously.[24] In this case, too, however, the fact that the value is aspecific enables politics to expand its possibilities (of planned opposition and of construction of convergences). Precisely because it does *not* say how those values should be programmed, then, the aspecificity of values is the premise for specifying political programmes, with all the freedom that parliaments manage to arrogate to themselves and, if they do not manage to do so, the reasons may be only political, not legal or constitutional.

In some cases, fundamental values are so generic as to have no specification that can be generalised, whether in the legal sense or in the political sense as a government or opposition agenda. Such is the case of human rights and human dignity, which are only recognised when they are subjected to gross breach, since that is when they become a matter of discussion by public opinion.[25] It is this exposure to public opinion that often leads to judgements being subjected to moralism: this can become a problem for the law when it has to judge cases when these rights are breached, often in courts that were established specifically for that purpose and so are afflicted by the difficulties involved in legitimising their own proceedings. For politics, breaches of these rights cannot become the subject matter of party manifestos or coalition agendas, simply because politics itself is nearly always the root cause, especially when the situation degenerates to the level of open conflict and no alternative is left but the recourse to violence.

The thesis that the constitution's paradoxes serve the purpose of underpinning the constitution's own lack of foundations is thus clearly emerging in fundamental rights. These rights declare themselves to be unalterable, because that is the only way that they can claim to legitimise the future, while at the same time waiving the right to define it in advance.[26] These rights are recognised, not instituted: 'politics began to articulate its legitimacy as bound to the recognition, through constitutions, of rights'.[27] And they can only be defined if, when binding a future they cannot know, they leave their own concrete specification to the ordinary law on the one hand and to contingent political awareness (and the oppositions it involves) on the other. This generates a decision-making potential that must be exploited in the circumstances that arise as time goes by, enabling new issues and situations to be 'incorporated' into fundamental rights without too much difficulty. Suffice to consider the issue of privacy, which has to be reviewed radically in the light of today's new communication technologies, or that of risk-taking, which has always been extremely hard for the law to regulate.[28]

Legitimacy as self-legitimation

Paradoxes of very different kinds meet when the time comes to tackle the classical problem of both politics and law: that of legitimacy, and of providing legitimacy.[29] When the problem occurs, it is almost banal: decisions cannot be legitimised arbitrarily, i.e. by means of a tautology. Like every other organised decision-making body, law and politics have to justify what they are and what they do. We cannot say: the state decides how it decides and that is its legitimacy. Or, to put it another way: the tautology of power that legitimises itself by simply stating its own legitimacy would generate something of a *horror vacui*. Since it is a tautology, in fact, such an arbitrary whim would block the quest for alternatives. No objection can be raised when we are faced with the tautological statement 'I decide how I decide because

I decide how I decide'. So the problem of arbitrary whim is not found in the fear that, in the absence of external references, decision-makers would end up deciding in their own interest or that of a select few (someone would say that they do this anyway). Instead, the problem is the typical one of every form of paradoxical circular argument: if the circle is too small, and risks short-circuiting or becoming a vicious circle, every activity is blocked and no further argument is possible.

That is why decisions of all kinds of organisations have to seek external justification that does not coincide with the decisions themselves. The problem becomes acute in the case of politics, because the decisions in question are destined to be binding on an entire population and not only on the interested parties. How to structure the power and how to justify its highest echelons remains one of the most serious issues facing political theory – maybe I should even describe it as an impossible task.

The problem was solved in ancient traditions by quoting natural or divine investiture. In those days, the paradox would take the form of a sovereign who was both of this earth and, at the same time, divine, deriving his legitimacy directly from God.[30] The problem that the sovereign might abuse his prerogatives was solved with equally paradoxical institutions, such as the right of resistance or the possibility to transform the king into a tyrant.[31] Juridical and political forms of this kind were possible in a society that gave the past a binding meaning, against which every novelty had to be measured and evaluated, since the novelty's meaning had to be in harmony with the prevailing order. No other alternative to that order was considered to be practicable: only barbarity or chaos.[32] In modern society, this guarantee of stability has disappeared and the past has lost its determinative strength. To clarify this mutation, which is important for the topic under discussion here, let's take a look at some of the main arguments that are used in this context:

a the past certainly cannot be changed, but that does not mean that we can deduce instructions for how to act in the present. On the contrary: conformity with past models now gets a negative press, while novelty, deviance and change are considered in a positive light. Compared to traditional societies, we can no longer rely on the idea that the state, organisations in general and also mere citizens are inclined to put their virtues on show, to seek perfection or to achieve a destiny that has already been written. These days, we take it for granted that it is possible *to make a break with the past* and that *the future*, whatever it will be, *depends on our decisions*;

b this does not mean that the past is irrelevant, however. It could be said that, instead of giving instructions, these days the past *excludes possibilities generically*. In times of crisis, for example, government will be forced to cut investments and keep its spending down, but that general trend does not determine which sectors should be promoted with the scant resources available. Another singular example for an era like ours is that of the election of the president of the United States: all we can say is that no one born outside the country can be a candidate, but that says nothing at all about other sources of legitimation. Or again, if scandals and abuses of power end up putting certain political forces out of the running, there is no way of forecasting what will replace them, as experience in Europe in recent decades has illustrated extensively. The effect of the limitation imposed by the past (i.e. by the structures given, the decisions made and the norms that have accumulated in the course of time, also in terms of opportunities seized or missed and risks run, not always successfully) may therefore lead to a marked reduction in perspectives, but it is actually that very *limitation* that enables us to imagine possibilities and alternatives and to construct decision-making *potential*;[33]

c that is what happens in the law and in how it elaborates its knowledge, not just through the philosophy or theory of law, but also through juridical arguments: this produces a marked redundancy, as connections are generated between different decisions and different interpretations that open up a space of possibilities and contingency, within which we then have to make our way forward with more decisions or interpretations. Possibilities of combinations do not make sense only because they offer guarantees of continuity or 'fidelity' with the past, then, but also because they enable us to innovate and to *introduce unpredictable novelty*;

d going back to the expression coined by Kelsen and already mentioned before,[34] the past *only has the capacity of negative determination* of the present: it rules out possibilities, but provides no unequivocal and generalisable indications about what ought to be done in the present. These days, no decision could be considered to be a mere consequence of the past, even though such concepts as rationality, reason, objectivity and others may lead us to think it may be so.[35] It is hard for jurists to accept, as the legal decision is represented typically as something of a 'deduction' that starts out from facts and norms; it is actually the increasing incongruence of current jurisprudence in many sectors that demonstrates that this idea is no longer plausible;

e in many respects, the past seems to be represented in modern society primarily as a *combinatory potential*. What can be remembered is presented in communication as a set of data that can be compared with one another and recombined in the light of the perspectives adopted. Just consider the significance that has come to be attributed to statistics in constructing generalisable expectations starting from data and correlations that enable us to measure different degrees of probability of future scenarios.[36] That is why deciding means giving a different meaning to the past, according to the decision-maker's perspective, presenting more or less surprising combinations in the form of practicable alternatives. Decisions are thus distanced from the past and take on the semblance of creative, arbitrary, unpredictable actions:[37] that is why they are vested with the responsibility for what eventually happens;

f this dependence on decisions is correlated to the central role and importance that *organisations* have acquired for modern society: it is only through organisations that decision-making processes can be stimulated and co-ordinated with each other. Traditional corporative formations have been transformed into organisational structures. Royal courts have mutated into parliaments, while the mystery and secrecy of the court have been replaced by the complexity of political and administrative structures and exposure to public opinion, which produces constant uncertainty about what can be decided. In the place of the rivalry that once surrounded the crowned head, we now find the difference between government and opposition, which obliges us to take part in discussions, often in polemics and in long drawn-out negotiations that illustrate just how great can be the distance between the different positions held by those who must in any case reach a decision. On the one hand, this is a fundamental change that enormously expands the decision-making power of modern society and its subsystems, including laws and politics. But, on the other, it is right here that new problems arise, directly concerned with the issue of legitimacy and the constitution.

The theory and the sociology of organisations have highlighted a crucial aspect of decision-making processes. Deciding always entails excluding possibilities that are no less plausible and legitimate than the ones that are chosen.[38] When the decision is made, in fact, it transforms the past – no longer binding – into an alternative that cannot encompass preferences within itself, as it would otherwise be no true alternative. The decision-maker's act therefore appears to be arbitrary precisely because it depends on factors that cannot be derived from the context: if we want to understand why a certain decision has been made, we have to observe the decision-maker, not the context in which he finds himself deciding. Communicating a decision in the strict sense of the term therefore means also communicating the fact that a different decision might have been made.[39] Whoever it is that decides, whether it is a parliament or a court, always communicates both of these aspects: the decision's contents, but also, at least implicitly, the alternatives that have been discarded *despite being thoroughly plausible*. In this sense, every decision has to be legitimised *ex novo*.

These arguments, which have been developed above all by systems theory, are essential for approaching the issue of the constitution's political legitimacy. The state, in all its forms, is a decision-maker and, as such, always says that it could also have decided differently. It contradicts itself and denies itself.[40] It is 'deconstructing' itself. It can be presumed that this is the real problem in a society that depends on decisions. In fact, the decision's contents always refer to other possibilities that have been excluded, thus inducing the possibility of refusing to accept it. This goes much further than what is already provided for in the form of political opposition *internal* to the state as, for a highly argumentative public opinion, the decision may not be convincing for the very reason that it is internal. In public discussion, state institutions rely on political and legal semantics, referring to such positive values as ethics and morals, authority and justice, the common weal and so on, and in this way not only do they not solve the problem, but they risk making it worse, because it is values that construct the indeterminacy that stimulates the search for alternatives:[41] we can think of anything in the name of a value, but that is why we can always also say something.

Starting out from these premises, systems theory maintains that legitimacy is paradoxical because it is in any case a product of the system that needs it, like politics. It is the state that says that it is legitimised. That is why *legitimacy is always self-legitimation*.[42] At the same time, however, we have to avoid the short-circuit of a system that justifies itself, of a decision that decides to give itself the necessary grounding. In other words, legitimacy must be externalised.[43] Being 'externalised' means that the communication of political decisions must always relate to a yardstick that does not coincide with the decision itself, without being obliged to fall back on the decision-maker's arbitrary free will. This must be done both on the level of everyday political communications, i.e. in the statements made by politicians, in the motions passed by majorities in parliament, in the criticisms voiced by the opposition, and on the formal level of the premises for decision-making, so primarily on the level of the constitution.

If we analyse how constitutions are written from this point of view, looking at the structures that they have given themselves, we can discern certain peculiarities.

The first and most important in relation to the question of legitimacy concerns the typical sub-division of constitutional texts, as we already saw above. The first part deals with values and fundamental freedoms, while the second tackles the premises for decision-making (the division of powers, the form of the state, electoral laws, etc.). Politics exploits both sides: from the point of view of public opinion, the reference to values remains the most important source of legitimacy. Everything that the state builds, in terms of services, of bureaucracy, of administration, but also of the use of violence through the police or the armed forces, must be capable of relying on some form of value or be perceivable as the achievement of some fundamental right. This does not remove the paradox of decisions' 'self-deconstruction', but it enables 'the other player to be put back onto the defensive'. A large part of the public debate about political issues is based on this kind of virtual fencing match, which on the one hand always enables some argument to be found to wield against one's political adversaries, while on the other continuously confirming the impression that it is ultimately just a question of partisan interests. But that is how democracy functions, although there is no guarantee that the public will always remain interested in the questions thus raised.

Nevertheless, for the very reason that anything can be done in the name of values and of fundamental rights and that public debate may end up becoming exceedingly moralist, the constitution provides for the second part of the text, which defines the formal procedures for decision-making. We could say that this is actually the real legitimacy that is guaranteed by the constitution. The merits of any single provision in the constitution can be discussed, but the threshold that draws the line between legitimate and illegitimate is the one that is laid down by the procedural norms.[44] And this is where we find the paradox: values can legitimise because they are 'eternal', 'non-negotiable', but they *cannot control* what can be decided in their name. Procedures can legitimise because they are premises for decision-making, but *they pay the price* of being contingent, so constantly negotiable. In the end, legitimacy comes about on a dual plane: the plane of values and of rights, which must always be taken into consideration when establishing procedures (consideration of minorities, the division of powers etc.), and the plane of those procedures, which must always be taken into consideration when thinking of how to plan the values.

The state cannot escape the obligation to live with the 'precariousness' that it generates itself, in a society, among other things, that probably no longer considers it to be the same central institution that was represented during the first phase of the modern era. These days, equal importance is attributed to transnational organisations and to decision-making organisms that no longer refer directly to the nation state from the legal standpoint.[45]

But we can also ask ourselves whether all this is a symptom of crisis and of problems related to specific situations, or whether it depends on how the relationships between law and politics are regulated in functional differentiation.

Structural coupling

We started with the thesis that the constitution's function is not to provide a foundation for the exercise of power on the one hand and of the law on the other. If anything, the problem that is tackled by the constitution is precisely the opposite: to provide a benchmark structure for both systems, once functional differentiation has enabled them to become not only autonomous, but also thoroughly contingent, so bereft of any possibility of extra-societal foundation. This can only be achieved by means of a composed text that can be defined in a circular manner, in the language of 'cybernetic sociology', so by means of an autological[46] and inherently paradoxical text.

This characteristic of being circular derives from the historical and evolutionary context in which the constitution first came about, especially in North America, as a result of having to tackle the issues of settling and redesigning the normative apparatus raised by independence from Great Britain. From the point of view of the law, as the wealth of literature on this topic illustrates,[47] it became clear for the first time that the old difference between natural law and positive law no longer held and that what was needed instead was a criterion capable of regulating the normative apparatus *from inside*, i.e. making use of the normative apparatus itself. The difference between natural law and positive law is often replaced these days by the difference between constitutional law and ordinary law.[48] The law's applicability is not only established by the law itself, but is thus established on the basis of a text that, paradoxically, has to be subject to its own criteria of enforceability.

In operational terms, this innovation leads us to draw two distinctions: the distinction between compliance and non-compliance with the law and the distinction between constitutional and unconstitutional. A decision or a norm may comply with the law and yet also be unconstitutional: both things at the same time.[49] As America's founding fathers noted, law as a whole continuously comes within the scope of the law from the point of view of its constitutionality, for example creating a need for collision rules that reverse the principle whereby *lex posterior derogat legi priori*. Translated into terms pertinent to the issue at stake here, we can say that the constitution is the only past to which the law can be oriented legitimately – a past oriented towards the future, that makes all law contingent, and a future in which there is also the past, i.e. the constitutional limitation itself, which can be changed.

The constitution also provides something of a double circle from the point of view of politics, in this case to legitimise the exercise of power. On the one hand, the sovereign takes on a formless form,[50] the people, which for this reason can only express itself through very selective procedures, in particular elections, and only in this way conceals the political paradox of the governed choosing those who govern them. Once again, as in the case of the law, no structure that is elaborated to conceal the paradox can escape being contingent, so it should come as no surprise if the evolution of society sooner or later makes state institutions obsolete, giving the impression of a 'crisis of the state', of an erosion of authority or of a loss of legitimacy. In fact, a state that has to legitimise itself is potentially always in a crisis.[51]

That is why the constitution's function cannot be to constitute: it has to betray its own etymology. Neither modern law nor modern politics can or must be founded. From a sociological standpoint, we ought to draw a distinction between function and structure: in a regime of functional differentiation, the function remains constant, while the structures as such are contingent. That is why we ought to say that law and politics are founded on their function, leaving to evolution the task of producing and destroying the structures that enable it to perform that task. From other vantage points, this might be seen as a problem, for example because the developments of modern law take us a long way away from classical institutions and traditional guarantees: when tackling juridical forms that are no longer restricted to the state, we can ask ourselves what happens to the hierarchy of legal sources, local jurisdictions and also the relationship between the production of the law and state legislation if global legislation and global jurisdictions start coming into play at world level, replacing state and territorial legislations and jurisdictions.[52] But it is actually developments of this very kind that imply that the constitution's function is not to guarantee structures and institutional forms of the law and of politics.

If we ask ourselves what the constitution's function is, the latest literature puts major emphasis on a proposal that once again comes from systems theory. The idea is that the constitution was invented to regulate the relationships between law and politics, once these two systems are differentiated once and for all and there remains no possibility of polyfunctionality.[53] The concept employed by systems theory to clarify the function of the constitution is that of *structural coupling*.[54]

The concept of structural coupling was in fact coined to solve a theoretical problem that arose from the diffusion of another concept, to which it is complementary and which has also been applied to legal studies: that of autopoiesis.[55] The main thesis sustained by the concept of autopoiesis is that it is possible to talk about a system only when the system's operations connect to one another and are closed to the outside world in the process. The law, in this sense, is an autopoietic system because every legal communication can only be connected to other legal communications and in this way can contribute to building structures (for example norms, procedures and specific forms of organisation) that only mean anything inside the legal system. Regardless of whether it is a question of interpretations, of judgements, of arguments or of the elaboration of a doctrine, the law can only produce communication within itself. Outside its own confines, the law is only one yardstick among others, albeit an important one.

But it can neither import nor export its operations. It cannot determine economic exchanges, nor even construct political agendas. In the same way, of course, no other system can intervene operatively in the law: traditional legal disputes cannot be solved by new elections or relying on the 'law of the market'.

But this raises a question: how can a system start from such an operative closure, i.e. from its autopoiesis, and take what happens in its surrounding environment into consideration, so as to avoid ending up with a short circuit, a cyclic self-reference without any external connections? Autopoiesis, in other words, is a concept that tells us nothing relevant to the structures that become necessary to distinguish between what may be of relevance in the environment and what is of no relevance: it only tells us that if a system exists, then it is autopoietic. But how it may be 'influenced' by its own surrounding environment cannot be clarified by the concept of autopoiesis. That is why another concept is introduced: the concept of structural coupling.

This concept indicates the capacity – and the necessity – on the part of a system to develop specific kinds of awareness towards sectors in its environment, while remaining indifferent to all the rest.[56] The systems theory defines these kinds of awareness as 'irritations', in the sense of disturbances or interferences, so as to underline that they are not cases of input coming in from outside, but of points of contact inside the system itself that generate effects that depend on its own structures and not on those of the irritating factor.[57] The law, for example, is indifferent to everything that happens in the economy, with the exception of those forms that are common to both systems, that have a meaning both for the economy and for the law, such as contract and the institution of property. When a contract is drawn up, it produces information in both systems simultaneously, but in ways that are completely different in the one and in the other. It is a structure that enables the two systems to irritate one another reciprocally.

What systems theory proposes is seeing the constitution as a form of structural coupling between law and politics:[58] that part of the law that may be politically relevant and, vice versa, that part of politics that may be of relevance to the law, passes through the constitution. Despite appearances, if we observe what actually happens in many parts of the world today, law and politics can only influence one another reciprocally in this way: law cannot be practised directly with politics and politics cannot be practised directly with the law. Concretely, that means that politics can decide what it believes, it can build alliances and conflicts, compromises and agreements, but always and only on the basis of the procedures provided in the constitution. In the same manner, law delegates legislation to politics, if I may be allowed to put it that way, but also here only through the filter of procedural legitimacy, and that is the only way that lawgiving can also be a juridical act with a juridical meaning.[59] Since the common reference to the constitution is the medium whereby the relationships between the law and politics are regulated, the production of laws must in any case be based on a political agreement and every political interest must in any case pass the test of constitutional control. In this way, the two systems are found to be on the one hand limited by a textual form, which may sometimes be very rigid and from which no derogations can be made, although on the other hand this limitation constitutes the precondition for a freedom of decision-making that neither of the two has ever enjoyed in previous eras.[60] Precisely because politics can do whatever it succeeds in imagining, as long as it does not breach constitutional restrictions, modern parliaments are left a very free hand – although it could then be objected that it is that self-same freedom that can create problems so serious as to make it impossible for the parliaments to make their decisions.

In the same way, the law finds the extensive limitation imposed by constitutions to be an impressive source of novelty and of opportunities for amending norms. These days it is hard to start out from our constitutions to select what could become a juridical acquisition, a relevant situation or an opening in jurisprudence. And here, too, it could be objected that this is exactly what creates new problems that cast doubt on the existence of what used to be described as the certainty of the law or justice.[61] From the point of view of systems theory, this is also a consequence of the new relationship with politics mediated by the constitution.

The constitution and its organised form, the state, have to fulfil this decisive function: to guarantee that the two coupled systems – law and politics – can develop decision-making potentials compatible with the condition of their reciprocal operative closure.[62] The constitution must enable the law to open the way to possibilities of change in the normative apparatus and in jurisprudence which politics can then use when wielding its democratic tools; and it must enable politics to open the way to decision-making possibilities in the exercise of power which the law can then use when intervening in its own structures. This can only be achieved if the decision-making circumstances in both systems are capable of not grinding to a halt when they are the first ones that have to submit to their own conditions.

To be sure, once law is positive law and politics is democratic politics, structural coupling achieved by means of the constitution leads to a vigorous decision-making pressure being exercised on both systems. This may be the subject of attention paid by certain observers, such as public opinion, towards whom politics must be oriented if it is to construct its own chances of decision-making.[63] But, as we have seen, public opinion not only enables construction: it constructs and at the same time deconstructs everything that is produced as the underlying or legitimising structure, because it focuses attention on decision-makers rather than on the 'nature of things'. Decision-makers can and must try to assert themselves in an extremely unstable, turbulent context, but they can only do so by declaring their readiness to contemplate change. In other words, from a reflexive, somewhat paradoxical perspective, to deny themselves.

Notes

1 On the improbability of this normation, see Grimm 2010: 3; Luhmann 1990a: 176ff.

2 See the works of Chris Thornhill (2008, 2011a, 2011b).

3 The key concept here is structural coupling (about which more later): see Febbrajo and Harste 2013 and Luhmann 1990a, who was the first to use this concept in a sociological framework. On the possibility of considering the constitution to be a form of foundation and at the same time a limitation and regulation of the relations between the law and other subsystems, see the works of Teubner (2002, 2011).

4 In addition to the authors quoted above, see Ladeur 2003 and Febbrajo and Gambino 2013.

5 One rather obvious example is found in critical theory. See, among others, Habermas 1973, with his well-known idea that consent obtained by means of free discussion is the only source of legitimacy – but this idea cannot be legitimised in this way in itself. See also the more recent example of Christodoulidis 2003, who stresses the political potential of protest movements against capitalist economic hegemony – but without justifying his argument *sociologically*. Maybe statistical sociological research should also be added as a case of a normative approach, which takes for granted that only numbers can constitute an empirical reference – but this assumption cannot of course be justified in itself by using numbers. Clearly, the problem is self-implication, which cannot be solved with a simple a priori.

6 On the issue of interdisciplinarity, see Kirste 2015; on the relationship between sociology and law in particular my own Corsi 2015.

7 Among many others, see Wormell 1958, who already then considered paradoxes to be constituent of any self-referential context and not mere contradictions. On this, see also Gumbrecht and Pfeiffer 1990, and above all the works of Luhmann and Esposito.

8 With obviously unpredictable consequences. See the classic Watzlavick et al. 1971: 184ff.

9 There is plentiful literature about reality as a construct, most of which was published in the 1980s. I shall refer here only to von Foerster (1984: 1–22, 257–71) and to Luhmann et al. (1990).

10 This also happens when the observer cites distinctions drawn by other observers. In our case, for example, the observer is a sociologist who is interested in how law and politics construct their

benchmark reality, i.e. in the distinctions the two systems elaborate. But the meaning that these distinctions take on in sociology is obviously quite unlike the meaning they have in their original context. For the sociologist, they are empirical data to be analysed, while for law and politics they are the underlying premise of their modus operandi.

11 Thus Luhmann 1990c: 104.

12 See for example Perez, who distinguishes between 'system' and 'sentences': 'The notion of paradox . . . does not apply to law as such . . . This has to do with the fact that paradoxes are properties of sentences' (2006: 13).

13 A concept that is now common and a given in the literature. See Luhmann 1997: 743ff.

14 Thus Portinaro 1996. See also Zagrebelsky 1996b and Tushnet 2013: 1986ff. See also Dogliani 1995 about the difference between the constituent power and the power of constitutional amendment, a difference that can easily become paradoxical.

15 On the paradox of the people who are both sovereign and at the same time governed, see Galligan, although he is sceptical about the explanatory capacity of the paradox, arguing: 'without rules it is hard to see how popular sovereignty could be exercised' (2008: 348). Certainly, but those rules have to come before the administration of sovereignty. If you like, the problem is typically theological, the problem of the beginning that is only solved because, when the problem arises, a start has already been made. This demonstrates that paradoxes explain nothing: they only call attention to the fact that the way out has to be 'created', not deduced. For example, the expression 'popular sovereignty' is decidedly creative.

16 In other words, it calls for an additional element that shifts the insoluble problem of coincidence (*Recht* is *Unrecht*) to the soluble problem of the alternative (*Recht* or *Unrecht*). About this see, in addition to the many writings of Niklas Luhmann, Ladeur 2000 about Luhmann 2000a. It is also possible to refute the radical nature of systems theory about this, when it uses such concepts as autopoiesis, operative closure and paradoxes of observation, for example making explicit use of metaphors, but at the cost of 'pulling out' of the 'game', i.e. of withdrawing unilaterally from reality. See De Kerchove and Ost 1992, 1993.

17 The conclave is a similar case, when the cardinals are shut in until the new pope has been elected. This, too, is a constriction, as though the decision in itself were impossible. To tell the truth, the theory of organisation now takes it for granted that decisions have to be made for the very reason that they cannot be made. See for example Weick 2007 and von Foerster 1989: 30.

18 The expression 'hard cases' comes from Twining and Miers 1976: 91ff. (about the possibility of having 'legal' recourse to torture).

19 In France, the reference to contents remained predominant compared to the procedural aspects central to the US constitution, this being one reason why a method for verifying that laws are constitutional was only introduced at a later stage in France (see Stourzh 1989a). On the difference between rights focused on contents (motives, aims, etc.) and rights focused on know-how, see Ladeur 1995: 206.

20 The expression comes from Podlech 1971. On this point, see also Corsi 2001a.

21 In this sense, fundamental rights 'present' the future in the form of a circular relationship between their relative indeterminacy, the central role played by the individual as the 'development of the personality' (*Persönlichkeitsentfaltung*) and the state (Häberle 1962).

22 Mohnhaupt 2004.

23 In this sense, Kelsen talks about 'negative certainty' (*negative Bestimmtheit*) (Kelsen 1985: 75f.). On the other hand, it is worth noting that this aspecific generalisation of rights also calls for changes in the lexicon we use: certain terms of constitutional significance, for example, become collective singulars, as in the case of freedom, which mutates from the concept of the plural freedoms of the privileged classes to the freedom (singular) of everyone; while other terms related to a use that is no longer entirely compatible with the constitutionalisation of the law disappear, as in the case of the German word *Herrschaft* (meaning mastery or dominion). See Koselleck 1983.

24 One recent case concerns health: if it is declared to be an inalienable right of the individual, what else can a court do but order the responsible institutions (local government and hospital administrations) to respect it in every single case? And if that ends up being financially impossible, what then? See on the discussion in Brazil, Pandolfo et al. 2012 and on the problem of the relationship between medicine, the economy, law and politics Luhmann 1983.

25 Luhmann 1993: 580. See also Fischer-Lescano 2002: if this kind of rights only becomes juridically evident when public anger is unleashed, this raises the question of whether a 'global constitution of world society' (*globale Verfassung der Weltgesellschaft*) is possible and necessary. But we should

also ask ourselves what purpose it may serve: if it is a question of making these rights formal, then maybe it is enough to use the mass media – a global constitution could only quote and repeat what is already stipulated by 'local' constitutions. Or its purpose may be to illustrate even more clearly that segmentation into nation states in practice means that every convention, every agreement and every ratification of treaties is deprived of all enforceability.

26 Hence the authors of the first constitutions took care of the possible consequences of such a self-imposed restriction on the freedom of future decision-makers: no constitution should prejudge future generations, as it was said at the time. See Webster's decided objection to the idea of an unalterable constitution, attributed to Jefferson: 'The contest for perpetual bills of rights against a future tyranny, resembles Don Quixote's fighting windmills; and I never can reflect on the declamation about an unalterable constitution to guard certain rights, without wishing to add another article, as necessary as those that are generally mentioned, viz. "that no future Convention or Legislature shall cut their own throats, or those of their constituents". While the habits of the Americans remain as they are, the people will choose their Legislature from their own body; that Legislature will have an interest inseparable from that of the people, and therefore an act to restrain their power in any article of legislation, is as unnecessary as an act to prevent them from committing suicide' (Webster 1790: 67). About this concern, which can already be found in Locke and the French constitution of 1793 and was then repeated in the discussion in America, see Holmes 1988: 172ff. and Zagrebelsky 1996a: 53, where constitutional norms are defined as a 'preventive accumulation of the future' – a collapse of the dimension of time. See also Tushnet 2013: 2002: 'Preambles consisting primarily of general principles are almost entirely forward-looking. More typically, preambles are both backward and forward-looking'; Cuypers 1993: 258: 'The legal system principally is oriented to the past. Although it decides about a part of the future of an individual or a situation, it nevertheless basically is engaged in facts situated earlier on the time scale.'

27 But that does not make the problem disappear: they still have to be declared – and that contradicts the passiveness of their recognition. See also Birtsch, who defines human rights as 'pre- and suprastate rights . . . pre-constitutional . . . as such rooted in nature or in the order of creation' (*vor- und überstaatliche Rechte . . . vorkonstitutionell . . . als solche in der Natur oder in der Schöpfungsordnung verwurzelt*, 1981: 16).

28 On the compatibility between fundamental rights and the 'risk society', a very hot topic, see Häberle 1972. On how time is construed in modern law and how not only the past, but also the future, can be taken into consideration, see Häberle 1996, who quotes a distinction drawn by Gerhart Husserl: the legislator is the man of the future, the administrator the man of the present and the judge the man of the past.

29 On the history of the problem of political legitimacy, see Thornhill 2011a, construed as a theory of political legitimacy and of limiting and controlling power.

30 On the history of the paradox (yet without describing it by this name) of how law is created, see Dilcher 1988. On the divine legitimation of the prince, see De Mattei 1982: 33ff., with various references to sources in sixteenth-century Italy.

31 See Stourzh 1989b. Are these possibilities maybe still available today? 'Behind every constitutional structure lies the possibility of revolutionary overthrow' (Tushnet 2013: 2006).

32 There is a rich literature about the dimension of pre-modern time. I refer here only to Le Goff 1960 (note 3/2: 428), because in that essay he refers explicitly to Max Weber's celebrated thesis about the relationship between Calvinism and the birth of the modern economy; his purpose is to contradict it, arguing that both are the product of a new form of differentiation and not of a reciprocal stimulus. In sociological terms, he is talking about functional differentiation, which involves the need to construct relationships between religion and the economy, because they have now become completely reciprocally differentiated.

33 It is very fashionable these days to talk about this in terms of 'liquidity', especially in connection with Zygmunt Bauman. But it should be remembered that the only liquidity permissible is this potential, but there is no way that anything can be done about it. Nobody can place himself on this plane. To stay with this terminology, all there is is solid: the observer, the decision-maker and the commenter are always on the real side of reality, the only side from which it is possible to imagine, i.e. to construct possibilities. Bauman's books, too, are solid.

34 See note 23.

35 Just consider education, which provides individuals with premises for constructing life chances, yet without determining their future. Or money, maybe the most fluid of media from this point of view: the very fact that it preserves no memory of its past enables it to be capitalised in view of possible, maybe even indeterminate, transactions.

36 Although the reference is to quite different contexts, see Cevolini 2014.
37 'Decision . . . is creative and is able to be so through the freedom which uncertainty gives for the creation of unpredictable hypotheses' (Shackle 1969: 4).
38 Deciding and constructing alternatives are simultaneous processes, even though the perspectives may be very different before or after the decision. See March: 'Our current thinking pushes us strongly in the direction of theories of adaptation, theories that treat the premises and constraints of action as changing at the same time and the same arena as the action does' (1996: 203).
39 'The decision must then inform about itself, but then also about the alternatives, so about the paradox that the alternative is both one (as the decision would otherwise be no decision) and at the same time none (as the decision would otherwise be no decision)' (Luhmann 2000b: 142).
40 Ivi: 143. Luhmann again: 'Every collectively binding decision . . . is marked in such a way that, however it is concealed, points at other possibilities. It thus reproduces . . . the possibility of other decisions . . . maybe the state is a result of this self-mystification' (Luhmann 1995: 106–7).
41 About this combination of the indeterminacy of values and decision-making potential, see Corsi 2001b.
42 Luhmann 1981: 68.
43 Ibid.
44 This is the celebrated thesis expounded by Luhmann 1969.
45 About this consequence of globalisation, see the discussion launched especially by Teubner 1997 and Ladeur 2003.
46 Luhmann 1990a: 187.
47 See Grimm 1991, who makes distinct analyses of developments in France, North America and England, and Luhmann 1992. About the history of the term 'constitution', see Stourzh 1988 and Mohnhaupt 1998.
48 The reference to natural law does not disappear in the American debate, however. But, since nature cannot be referred to in the historical sense, its meaning is now sought in the original intent of the founders: 'we can consider parts of the Constitution as meant to protect natural rights when we find something in the historical record to confirm that understanding of the founders. But the rule itself . . . that very rule is not itself in the positive law of the Constitution' (Arkes 2013: 973–4). Even so, there is still a risk that references to natural law only serve to justify the speaker's own preferences (Kozinsky 2013: 982).
49 On the improbability of this articulation from a sociologist's point of view, see Luhmann 2005: 231–2.
50 Carl Schmitt calls it a 'formless forming' (*formlose Formende*), as quoted by Holmes 1988.
51 It certainly cannot rely on ultimate foundations any more, as a recent empirical case demonstrates. In the European debate in the 1990s about the possibility of a European constitution and a European state, attempts were made to insert references to natural law or to necessary ultimate principles, for example the roots of Europe (both religious in nature, such as Christianity and Judaism, and with a historical and cultural matrix, such as the Enlightenment). We all know the consequences: a very heated discussion that ended up producing precisely nothing. Not only was the 'crisis' of the European institution not halted by the sacredness of these issues, therefore: it was actually accelerated.
52 See Thornhill 2010: 319–20; Teubner 1997, 2002. This is also discussed in terms of fragmented law: see Febbrajo and Gambino 2013. Similarly, Cassese 2002 talks about the crisis of the state when discussing independent authorities and economic sovereignty.
53 This is how Thornhill defines the constitution: 'the constitution is defined here as a distinctively political structure, originally and enduringly typified by its function in producing, restricting and refining power utilized by states' (2011a: 11). That is why he argues that the constitution is nothing new to history and evolution, in the sense of systems theory. It still remains to be seen, however, why it is necessary to construct a text with the characteristics that we have seen, especially if this is one of the consequences of its invention: 'constitutions bring the crucial benefit to societies that they allow political systems in modern societies positively to produce power and internally to multiply the reserves of power that they contain' (2011b: 372). But how can this be possible without radically reconfiguring the relationships between politics and law?
54 This concept comes from biology (Maturana and Varela 1987: 85ff.). About its application in sociology, see volume 7 (2001) of *Soziale Systeme*: *Begriff und Phänomen der strukturellen Kopplung*.
55 On its application in the field of sociology of law, see Teubner, especially the introduction (1988: 1–10) and the essay by Luhmann (12–35).
56 So it is not a question of 'relationships' between different systems, but of the difference between irritation and indifference. The literature is not always clear about this and it is not unusual to come

across references to the concept of structural coupling as a way of indicating any form of reciprocal influence. On other occasions, diluting the radical nature of the concepts of autopoiesis and of structural coupling is suggested as a way of making them compatible with the idea of 'interdiscursive relations' (Teubner 2013: 347). But in that case we can also ask whether it is actually necessary or even just useful to adopt these concepts . . .

57 The examples quoted by the concept's inventor, Maturana, are familiar: the force of gravity, for example, with its consequences on the musculature and bone structure of many animals, including mankind. Or language, in an example somewhat closer to sociology, for its relationship between conscience and communication, without which children would not be able to socialise nor even produce behaviour deviant from what is normal for communication.

58 For the original formulation, see Luhmann 1990a and 1993: 440ff.

59 The application of the law obviously remains primarily the preserve of the law itself – albeit with the not inconsiderable number of exceptions noted, such as parliamentary committees vested with the right to sit in judgement.

60 This is another point that can be defined as absolutely typical of Luhmann's theoretical construction: the *limitation of possibilities* is the condition for *increasing what is possible*.

61 Or also that there is still something like a system of law that is capable of managing and controlling its structures through the traditional forms of the state, of hierarchies and of sources. On this, see Febbrajo and Gambino 2013.

62 Doubts about this proposal of seeing the constitution as the form of structural coupling between law and politics are expressed by Hasso Hofmann (2009: 84–5). The argument is that the relationships between law and politics are in any case not symmetrical, as the hypothesis of structural coupling would have us believe, because the constitution is a juridical text and juridical arguments take precedence over political arguments. This objection is not very clear, however: there is no question that the constitution is *also* a juridical text – in fact it is not at all understandable how it could be otherwise. But it is empirically difficult to maintain that this sanctions the law taking precedence in constitutional matters: suffice to observe how politics is oriented towards the constitution everywhere. For politics, it is just a question of understanding on the basis of what legal conditions political agendas can be built – and so also contrasts and divergences of opinion between parties and coalitions. If necessary, articles of the constitution can also be amended or formulated in such a way as to mediate with the 'requirements' of public opinion or of the law itself, without truly changing social relationships in the process. In this sense, Marcelo Neves talks about a 'symbolic constitution' typical of Latin America (Neves 1994).

63 Law cannot avoid this exposure, either: if the law's applicability is the result of decisions, i.e. if the law is positive law, then we must observe its decision-makers if we want to understand its meaning. On the relevance of public opinion not only to a constitution's legitimacy, but also to its concrete feasibility, see the celebrated discussion between Dieter Grimm and Jürgen Habermas about the European Union (Grimm 1995; Habermas 1996).

References

Arkes, Hadley. 'The Natural Law Challenge'. *Harvard Journal of Law & Public Policy* 36/3 (2013): 961–75.

Birtsch, Günter. 'Einleitung: Die Geschichte der Grund- und Freiheitsrechte als Gegenstand der Forschung'. In *Grund- und Freiheitsrechte im Wandel von Gesellschaft und Geschichte*, edited by Günter Birtsch, 11–21. Göttingen: Vandenhoeck & Ruprecht, 1981.

Cassese, Sabino. *La crisi dello stato*. Roma-Bari: Laterza, 2002.

Cevolini, Alberto, ed. *Die Ordnung des Kontingenten*. Wiesbaden: VS Verlag, 2014.

Christodoulidis, E., 'Constitutional Irresolution: Law and the Framing of Civil Society'. *European Law Journal* 9/4 (2003): 401–32.

Corsi, Giancarlo. 'Sociologia da constituição'. *Revista da Faculdade de Direito da UMFG* 39 (2001a): 169–89.

———. 'Valores y derechos fundamentales en perspectiva sociológica'. *Metapolitica* 5/20 (2001b): 159–69.

———. '"Inkongruente Perspektiven". Interdisziplinarität aus soziologischer Sicht'. In *Interdisziplinarität in den Rechtswissenschaften. Innen- und Außenperspektiven*, edited by Stephan Kirste. Berlin: Duncker & Humblot, 2015, in press.

Cuypers, Christel. 'The Social Construction of Time in the Legal System'. In *Laws and Rights. Proceedings of the International Congress of Sociology of Law for the Ninth Centenary of the University of Bologna (May 30–June 3, 1988)*, edited by Vincenzo Ferrari and Carla Faralli, 251–62. Milano: Giuffrè, 1993.

De Mattei, Rodolfo. *Il pensiero politico italiano nell'età della Controriforma*. Milano: Ricciardi, 1982.

Dilcher, Gerhard. 'Vom ständischen Herrschaftsvertrag zum Verfassungsgesetz'. *Der Staat* 27 (1988): 161–93.

Dogliani, Mario. 'Potere costituente e revisione costituzionale'. *Quaderni costituzionali* 15/1 (1995): 7–32.

Febbrajo, Alberto, and Francesco Gambino, eds. *Il diritto frammentato*. Milano: Giuffrè, 2013.

Febbrajo, Alberto, and Gorm Harste, eds. *Law and Intersystemic Communication, Understanding 'Structural Coupling'*. Aldershot: Ashgate, 2013.

Fischer-Lescano, Andreas. 'Globalverfassung: Los Desaparecidos und das Paradox der Menschenrechte'. *Zeitschrift für Rechtssoziologie* 23/2 (2002): 217–49.

von Foerster, Heinz. *Observing Systems*. Seaside: Intersystems Publications, 1984.

———. 'Wahrnehmen wahrnehmen'. In *Ars Electronica. Philosophien der neuen Technologie*, edited by Jean Baudrillard, Vilém Flusser, Friedrich Kittler, Hannes Böhringer, Heinz von Foerster and Peter Weibel, 27–40. Berlin: Merve, 1989.

Galligan, Denis. J. 'The Paradox of Constitutionalism or the Potential of Constitutional Theory?' *Oxford Journal of Legal Studies* 28/2 (2008): 343–67.

Grimm, Dieter. *Die Zukunft der Verfassung*. Frankfurt: Suhrkamp, 1991.

———. *Braucht Europa eine Verfassung?* Munich: Carl Friedrich von Siemens Stiftung, 1995.

———. 'The Achievement of Constitutionalism and Its Prospects in a Changed World'. In *The Twilight of Constitutionalism?*, edited by Petra Dobner and Martin Loughlin, 3–22. Oxford: Oxford University Press, 2010.

Gumbrecht, Hans U., and K. Ludwig Pfeiffer, eds. *Paradoxien, Dissonanzen, Zusammenbrüche. Situationen offener Epistemologie*. Frankfurt: Suhrkamp, 1990.

Häberle, Peter. *Die Wesensgehaltsgarantie des Art. 19 Abs. 2 Grundgesetz. Zugleich ein Beitrag zum institutionellen Verständnis des Grundrechte und zur Lehre vom Gesetzesvorbehalt*. Karlsruhe: Müller, 1962.

———. 'Grundrechte im Leistungsstaat'. *VVDSZRL* 30 (1972): 43–141. Also in *Die Verfassung des Pluralismus. Studien zur Verfassungstheorie der offenen Gesellschaft*, by Peter Häberle, 163–247. Kökigstein/Ts: Athenäum, 1980.

———. 'Zeit und Verfassung'. In *Verfassung als öffentlicher Prozeß. Materialien zu einer Verfassungstheorie der offenen Gesellschaft*, by Peter Häberle, 59–92. Berlin: Duncker & Humblot, 1996.

Habermas, Jürgen. *Legitimationsprobleme im Spätkapitalismus*. Frankfurt: Suhrkamp, 1973.

———. 'Braucht Europa eine Verfassung? Eine Bemerkung zu Dieter Grimm'. In *Die Einbeziehung des Anderen*, 185–91. Frankfurt: Suhrkamp, 1996.

Hofmann, Hasso. *La libertà nello Stato moderno. Saggi di dottrina della Costituzione*. Napoli: Guida, 2009.

Holmes, Stephen. 'Precommitment and the Paradox of Democracy'. In *Constitutionalism and Democracy*, edited by Jon Elster and Rune Slagstad, 19–58. Cambridge: Cambridge University Press, 1988.

Kelsen, Hans. *Reine Rechtslehre. Einleitung in die rechtswissenschaftliche Problematik*. Aalen: Scientia Verlag, 1985.

van de Kerchove, Michel, and François Ost. *Le droit ou le paradoxes du jeu*. Paris: PUF, 1992. Italian translation: *Il diritto ovvero i paradossi del gioco*. Milano: Giuffrè, 1995.

———. 'En quel sens le systèmes juridiques sont-ils autonomes?' In *Laws and Rights. Proceedings of the International Congress of Sociology of Law for the Ninth Centenary of the University of Bologna (May 30–June 3, 1988)*, edited by Vincenzo Ferrari and Carla Faralli, 355–69. Milano: Giuffrè, 1993.

Kirste, Stephan, ed. *Interdisziplinarität in den Rechtswissenschaften. Innen- und Außenperspektiven*. Berlin: Duncker & Humblot, 2015, in press.

Koselleck, Reinhart. 'Begriffsgeschtliche Probleme der Verfassungsgeschichtsschreibung'. In *Gegenstand und Begriffe der Verfassungsgeschichtsschreibung. Der Staat*, Beiheft 6, 7–21. Berlin: Duncker & Humblot, 1983.

Kozinsky, Alex. 'Natural Law Jurisprudence: A Skeptical Perspektive'. *Harvard Journal of Law & Public Policy* 36/3 (2013): 977–82.

Ladeur, Karl-Heinz. *Postmoderne Rechtstheorie. Selbstreferenz-Selbstorganisation-Prozedualisierung.* Berlin: Duncker & Humblot, 1995.

———. 'Das selbstreferentielle Kamel. Die Emergenz des modernen autonomen Rechts'. *Zeitschrift für Rechtssoziologie* 21/1 (2000): 177–88.

———. 'Globalisation and the Conversion of Democracy to Polycentric Networks: Can Democracy Survive the End of the Nation State?' EUI Working Paper Law 2003/4. Florence: European University Institute, 2003.

Le Goff, Jacques. 'Temps de l'Eglise et temps du marchand'. *Annales* 15/3 (1960): 417–33.

Luhmann, Niklas. *Legitimation durch Verfahren*. Neuwied-Berlin: Luchterhand, 1969. Reprint Frankfurt: Suhrkamp, 1983.

———. 'Selbstlegitimation des Staates'. In *Legitimation des modernen Staates*, Supplement 15 of *Archiv für Rechts- und Sozialphilosophie*, edited by Norbert Achterberg and Werner Krawietz (1981): 65–83.

———. 'Anspruchsinflation im Krankheitssystem: Eine Stellungnahme aus gesellschaftstheoretischer Sicht'. In *Die Anspruchsspirale*, edited by Philipp Herder-Dorneich and Alexander Schuller, 28–49. Stuttgart: Kohlhammer, 1983.

———. 'Verfassung als evolutionäre Errungenschaft'. *Rechtshistorisches Journal* 9 (1990a): 176–220.

———. 'Sthenographie und Euryalistik'. In *Paradoxien, Dissonanzen, Zusammenbrüche. Situationen offener Epistemologie*, edited by Hans U. Gumbrecht and K. Ludwig Pfeiffer, 58–82. Frankfurt: Suhrkamp, 1990b.

———. 'Gleichzeitigkeit und Synchronisation'. In *Soziologische Aufklakrung 5: Konstruktivistische Perspektiven*, by Niklas Luhmann, 95–130. Opladen: Westdeutscher Verlag, 1990c.

———. *Das Recht der Gesellschaft*. Frankfurt: Suhrkamp, 1993.

———. 'Metamorphosen des Staates'. In *Gesellschaftsstruktur und Semantik. Studien zur Wissenssoziologie der Moderne*. Vol. 3., by Niklas Luhmann, 101–37. Frankfurt: Suhrkamp, 1995.

———. *Die Gesellschaft der Gesellschaft*. Frankfurt am Main: Suhrkamp, 1997.

———. 'Die Rückgabe des zwölften Kamels: Zum Sinn einer soziologischen Analyse des Rechts'. *Zeitschrift für Rechtssoziologie* 21/1 (2000a): 3–60.

———. *Organisation und Entscheidung*. Opladen: Westdeutscher Verlag, 2000b.

———. *Einführung in die Theorie der Gesellschaft*. Heidelberg: Carl-Auer, 2005.

Luhmann, Niklas, Humberto Maturana, Mikio Namiki, Volker Redder and Francisco J. Varela. *Beobachter. Konvergenz der Erkenntnistheorien?* Munich: Fink, 1990.

March, James G. 'Ambiguity, Endogeneity and Intelligence'. In *The Logic of Organizational Disorder*, edited by Massimo Warglien and Michael Masuch, 199–205. Berlin and New York: W. de Gruyter, 1996.

Maturana, Humberto, and Francisco J. Varela. *Der Baum der Erkenntnis: Die biologischen Wurzeln des menschlichen Erkennens*. Munich: Scherz-Verlag, 1987.

Mohnhaupt, Heinz. 'Von den "Leges fundamentales" zur modernen Verfassung in Europa. Zum begriffs- und dogmengeschichtlichen Befund (16.-18. Jahrhundert)'. *Ius Commune* 25 (1998): 121–58. Also in *Historische Vergleichung im Bereich von Staat und Recht*, by Heinz Mohnhaupt, 36–72. Frankfurt: Vittorio Klostermann, 2000.

———. 'Der Entwicklungsgang von der wohlerworbenen, konzessionierten Rechten und Privilegien zu den dem Menschen zugehörigen Grundrechte'. *Europäische Grundrechte Zeitschrift* 31 (2004): 604–11.

Neves, Marcelo. *A constitutionalização simbólica*. São Paulo: Editoria Academica 1994.

Pandolfo, Mércia, Maria C. Delduque and Rita Goreti Amaral. 'Aspectos jurídicos e sanitários condicionantes para o uso da via judicial no acesso aos medicamentos no Brasil'. *Revista de salud pública* 14 (2012): 340–49.

Perez, Oren. 'Law in the Air: A Prologue to the World of Legal Paradoxes'. In *Paradoxes and Inconsistencies in the Law*, edited by Oren Perez and Gunter Teubner, 3–39. Portland: Hart, 2006.

Podlech, Adalbert. *Gehalt und Funktionen des allgemeinen verfassungsrechtlichen Gleichheitssatzes*. Berlin: Duncker & Humblot, 1971.

Portinaro, Pier Paolo. 'Il grande legislatore e il custode della costituzione'. In *Il futuro della costituzione*, edited by Gustavo Zagrebelsky, Pier Paolo Portinaro and Jorg Luther, 5–34. Torino: Einaudi, 1996.

Shackle, George L.S. *Decision, Order and Time in Human Affairs*. Cambridge: Cambridge University Press, 1969.

Stourzh, Gerald. '*Constitution*: Changing Meanings of the Term from the Early Seventeenth to the Late Eighteenth Century'. In *Conceptual Change and the Constitution*, edited by Terence Ball and John G.A. Pocock, 35–54. Lawrence: University Press of Kansas, 1988.

———. 'Vom Widerstandsrecht zur Verfassungsgerichtsbarkeit: Zum Problem der Verfassungswidrigkeit im 18. Jahrhundert'. In *Wege zur Grundrechtsdemokratie. Studien zur Begriffs- und Institutionengeschichte des liberalen Verfassungsstaates*, edited by Gerald Stourzh, 37–74. Wien-Köln: Böhlau, 1989a.

———. 'Zur Konstitutionalisierung der Individualrechte in der Amerikanischen und Französischen Revolution'. In *Wege zur Grundrechtsdemokratie. Studien zur Begriffs- und Institutionengeschichte des liberalen Verfassungsstaates*, edited by Gerald Stourzh, 155–74. Wien-Köln: Böhlau, 1989b.

Teubner, Gunther. *Autopoietic Law: A New Approach to Law and Society*. Berlin and New York: de Gruyter, 1988.

———. 'Breaking Frames: The Global Interplay of Legal and Social Systems'. *The American Journal of Comparative Law* 45 (1997): 149–69.

———. 'Hybrid Laws: Constitutionalizing Private Governance Networks'. In *Legality and Community*, edited by R.A. Kagan, Martin Kryger and K. Winston, 311–31. Berkeley: Public Policy Press, 2002.

———. 'Das Projekt der Verfassungssoziologie'. *Zeitschrift für Rechtssoziologie* 32 (2011): 189–204.

———. 'Legal Pluralism as a Form of Structural Coupling'. In *Law and Interesystemic Communication*, edited by Alberto Febbrajo and Gorm Harste, 343–60. Farnham: Ashgate, 2013.

Thornhill, Chris. 'Towards a Historical Sociology of Constitutional Legitimacy'. *Theory and Society* 37/2 (2008): 161–97.

———. 'Niklas Luhmann and the Sociology of the Constitution'. *Journal of Classical Sociology* 10 (2010): 315–37.

———. *A Sociology of constitutions: Constitutions and State Legitimacy in Historical-Sociological Perspective*. Cambridge: Cambridge University Press, 2011a.

———. 'The Future of the State'. In *The Financial Crisis in Constitutional Perspective*, edited by Poul Kjaer, Gunther Teubner and Alberto Febbrajo, 357–93. Oxford: Hart, 2011b.

Tushnet, M. 'Constitution-Making: An Introduction'. *Texas Law Review* 91 (2013): 1983–2013.

Twining, William, and David Miers. *How to do Things With Rules: A Primer of Interpretation*. London: Weindenfeld & Nicholson, 1976. Italian translation: *Come fare cose con regole. Interpretazione e applicazione del diritto*. Milano: Giuffrè, 1988.

Watzlavick, Paul, Don D. Jackson and H. Janet Beavin. *Pragmatics of Human Communication: A Study of Interactional Patterns, Pathologies, and Paradoxes*. New York and London: Norton & Company, 1962. Italian translation: *Pragmatica della comunicazione umana*. Roma: Astrolabio, 1971.

Webster, Noah. 'Government, Mr. Jefferson's Argument in Favor of an Unalterable Constitution, Considered'. *American Magazine* 1 (1788). Reprinted in *A Collection of Essays and Fugitive Writings on Moral, Historical, Political and Literary Subjects*, 59–71. Boston: Thomas & Andrews, 1790.

Weick, Karl E. 'Nowhere Leads to Somewhere'. *The Conference Board Review* 44 (2007): 14–15.

Wormell, C.P. 'On the Paradoxes of Self-Reference'. *Mind* 67 (1958): 267–71.

Zagrebelsky, Gustavo. 'Storia e costituzione'. In *Il futuro della costituzione*, edited by Gustavo Zagrebelsky, Pier Paolo Portinaro and Jorg Luther, 35–82. Torino: Einaudi, 1996a.

———. 'I paradossi della riforma costituente'. In *Il futuro della costituzione*, edited by Gustavo Zagrebelsky, Pier Paolo Portinaro and Jorg Luther, 293–314. Torino: Einaudi, 1996b.

2 Exogenous self-binding

How social subsystems externalise their foundational paradoxes in the process of constitutionalisation

Gunther Teubner

Four remarkable phenomena

I aim to establish a link between four remarkable, yet mutually rather distant, phenomena, whose interpretation is subject to considerable uncertainty. The first remarkable phenomenon is that judge-made law is now expanding drastically also in transnational contexts. It was already offensive enough in the nation state that the courts – which after all are supposed to be no more than '*la bouche de la loi*'– produced more and more legal norms on their own, even in the presence of a dominant political legislature, thus diametrically contradicting the basic principles of the separation of powers and of democratic legitimacy.[1] Yet now we find that this trend is continuing unfettered and even accelerating in transnational regimes. In a secondary analysis of empirical data, the sociologist of law Chris Thornhill comes to the conclusion that:

> international courts and other appellate actors have assumed a remit that substantially exceeds conventional arbitrational functions. They now increasingly focus on objectives of 'norm-advancement': that is, they invoke rights to shape acts of national legislation and, without a clear constitutional mandate, to construct a supra- or transnational normative order.[2]

Critical observers, such as Ran Hirschl, trace this back to power and interest configurations that favour the illegitimate claims to power of a 'global juristocracy'.[3] Apologist observers, such as Josef Esser, on the other hand, consider and maintain that judicial law-making is more rational than its legislative counterpart.[4] Neither interpretation is satisfactory.

Secondly, it has recently been possible to observe a striking return of natural law. While philosophers, historians and legal theorists have been diagnosing the demise of natural law, jurisprudence scholars from both progressive and conservative backgrounds – but also judges in their decision-making practices – have been celebrating the resurrection of arguments grounded in natural law.[5] And not only in the sustained boom of fundamental and human rights. Even here, satisfactory explanations are few and far between. These are either hegemonic tendencies in legal culture, supported by power and interest groups, as diagnosed in Gramsci's tradition, or, as Lon Fuller maintains prominently, they are powers that work in the arcanum of the law, silently operating an 'inner morality of law' that opposes the principle of legal positivism that holds sway politically and legally.[6]

A third remarkable phenomenon is a change in direction among protest movements, which some observers interpret as the implementation of a new political quality.[7] The conflicts in which these changes can be found today are Brent Spar, the World Social Forum, Gorleben, animal rights protests against universities, companynamesucks.com, Stuttgart 21, Wikileaks, the *indignados* and Occupy Wall Street. The common denominator is that these civil society protests are addressed not (only) against the state, but also selectively and purposefully against the organised professional institutions of the economy and of other functional systems that they hold responsible for seriously distorted development.

The last remarkable phenomenon is the greatly different status of various types of constitution: the state constitution, the economic constitution and the constitution of science. The dominance, if not exactly the monopoly, of state constitutions is obvious, both in practice and in theory. The status of economic constitutions is already more precarious. Nobody would now deny the actual existence of different economic constitutions and their foundational role for the economy, politics and law. And radical changes to the existing global economic constitution, as laid down in the Washington Consensus, are being advanced with normative bravura at this very moment.[8] But whether these are actually constitutions in the strict sense of the term and who then acts as the constituent power – the economy? politics? the law? society? – is extremely controversial. The existence of a constitution of science, in its turn, is only really maintained in a metaphorical sense.[9] Why do social subsystems have such a different constitutional status?

How a constitution deals with its foundational paradox – this is the *pointe* that links these four reciprocally separate phenomena together. This *pointe* is not restricted to the state constitution alone, but is also and pertinently applicable to the constitutions of other social systems.[10] The starting point is Luhmann's argument that the law, with the aid of the state constitution, externalises its original paradox towards politics, while politics externalises its own towards the law. Over and above this, the question needs to be raised about whether – and if so, how – the law also pursues a comparable deparadoxisation vis-à-vis other social subsystems. Meanwhile, the same question is asked, but now in the opposite direction, about whether other social systems also behave like politics, externalising their paradoxes towards the law with the aid of a constitution, or whether they employ alternative deparadoxisations. Both of these lead to the concluding question, regarding which subsequent problems are generated by those externalisations. The differences between various approaches to deparadoxisation may possibly clarify the four original questions, so: why is judge-made law developing new prominence transnationally? Under what conditions will a particular kind of natural law make headway again against positivism even today? Why is it that protest movements are shifting the sights of their protests? And for what reasons do social subsystems constitutionalise not in accordance with a standard pattern, but with clear differences of intensity?

Reciprocal paradox externalisation in law and politics

The starting point here is Niklas Luhmann's theory of the state constitution, which gives a central role to how law and politics deal with their original paradox.[11] As the law is founded on the binary code of legal and illegal, it gets into a tangle with the paradoxes of self-reference when the code is inevitably applied to itself. This foundational paradox exposes law to the suspicion of arbitrariness, undermines its quest for legitimacy and paralyses decisions. The escape routes only lead to the familiar Münchhausen trilemma of the law: infinite regress (religious natural law), arbitrary interruption (Hans Kelsen) or the circularity of the foundation of norms (Herbert Hart). As none of these three offers a satisfactory way out, in the end only one strategy of deparadoxisation has been found to be successful in the past. Law externalises its paradox towards politics with the aid of the state constitution. In this way, the law seeks its ultimate legitimation in democratic politics, is thus disburdened of its own problem of paradox and no longer needs to concern itself with how politics comes to terms with this externalisation.

Politics, on the other hand, has to struggle with an internally insoluble paradox – 'the paradox of the binding of necessarily unbound authority'.[12] How could one bind the sovereign to rational rules and above all to its own promises? This was only facilitated when it was externalised towards the law, which once again was accomplished by the state constitution. The constitution commits politically unconstrained sovereignty to the process of the law. The state constitution, as a structural coupling between the law and politics, is thus characterised by the fact that *there is a reciprocal externalisation of the original paradoxes of politics and law*. Law and politics develop complex forms of an exogenous self-constraint that are – not coincidentally – reminiscent of freedom through self-constraint and of the artful conjunction between self-constraint and externally imposed constraint found in the myth of Odysseus.

Is it possible to generalise this theory of the political constitution? Do other social systems externalise their paradoxes towards the law and vice versa, in such a way that, alongside the state constitution, other subsystem constitutions – an economic constitution, a media constitution, an organisational constitution – also act as instruments of practical paradox management? Luhmann did not pursue this question explicitly. Luhmann, like many state-centred constitutional lawyers, is rather sceptical towards an economic constitution, third-party effects of fundamental rights, societal constitutionalism and also transnational constitutional phenomena.[13] And yet due to the inner logic of systems theory it is virtually compulsory to pursue the question of whether the generalisation of constitutional issues, as they have become visible in politics, and their respecification are indicated in other social systems.[14] Since not only politics and law, but every, truly every, functional system based on binary coding is enmeshed with paradoxes of self-reference that, if there is no way to circumvent them, end up in paralysis.[15] There is no way to avoid the generalisation. The unanswered question only concerns how deparadoxisation is respecified in other contexts. Is it also successful in other social systems to externalise the relevant original paradox towards the legal system with the aid of the constitution – and vice versa? Or are other methods of deparadoxisation applied in non-political subsystems?

Deparadoxisations of law

The state constitution

Externalising the legal paradoxes towards the political system of the nation state was such a runaway success story in the past that, until the end of the twentieth century, it was advanced not only in constitutional law, but across the board in all fields of law. In the state constitution, in the procedural guarantees of the state governed by the rule of law, in the division of power between legislation and the administration of justice and in the constitutional jurisdiction, law-making was ascribed coherently to the political-parliamentary process. Customary law – an evident exception to this – was increasingly marginalised in the nation state. To cap it all, the still-unruly area of private law was constitutionalised, just as the original paradoxes of contract and of private organisations based on private autonomy were 'rerouted' into the state constitution.[16] Technically speaking, this was achieved by means of more or less plausible fictions: the comprehensive hierarchy of legal norms, which also incorporated contracts and associations understood as delegation to private individuals, the state's reception of social norms and/or their relegation into the purely factual domain.[17]

It already became obvious in the nation state that the total externalisation of legal paradoxes towards the political system would end up overburdening both the law and politics. The (over) politicisation of law thus unleashed demonstrated its most extreme disintegrating effects in the national socialist and real-socialist regimes, but was also painfully perceptible in the post-war welfare state. 'Legislation failure' is how this was criticised by jurists, who targeted both how the production of legal norms was instrumentalised by the party-political system and also how politics was not ready to react with legislative activities which were responsive to the needs of the legal system.[18] Externalisation became almost impossible when transnational regimes began to create their own law, as there is no transnational counterpart to the nation state constitution as the structural link between law and politics, within which externalisation could take place. Rule making outside the framework of international law that occurs so massively all over the globe reopens all the problems of the legal paradox which had been encountered in the nation state before they had been successfully transferred to politics.[19] This leads legal doctrine to lose its orientation drastically so that leading jurists describe a '*contrat sans loi*', i.e. a contract that is not founded in the law of a nation state, as logically impossible and pernicious for the law.[20]

Social constitutions

In the quest for alternative ways to cope with the legal paradox, the law seems to react by forcing an internal differentiation into subsectors, but then, instead of orienting these subsectors on criteria internal to the law, it bypasses the political system and bases its norm production on other social systems. This is already apparent in the nation state, when semi-autonomous subsectors of the law, such as economic law, labour law, social law, medical law, media law and science law, evolve vigorously – undermining the traditional separation of public law and private law.[21] Although these special legal fields officially preserve the externalisation towards politics, they actually reduce it progressively in a surreptitious manner, shifting the paradox of forming norms into the regulated social system.[22]

The law's internal differentiation is promoted even more radically at the transnational level. Diverse social fields are governed by highly specialised legal regimes that are to a considerable extent detached from public international law and now coupled closely with the inner rationality of the social fields.[23] 'Public regimes', such as the World Trade Organization, that have come into being as treaties in international law, marginalise the paradox externalisation to politics that had been initially present. They assert far-reaching autonomy vis-à-vis the nation states and establish themselves as 'self-contained regimes', generating new forms of structural coupling with the regulated social fields. In 'private' regimes, such as the *lex mercatoria*, the *lex sportiva* or the *lex digitalis*, which are formed from the very start independently of national law and state treaties, the question of externalising the legal paradox towards politics does not even arise. Instead, the original paradoxes of these transnational legal orders are displaced from the very outset into the social fields with which they have entered into a close symbiosis.

If the law no longer externalises its paradox to politics, but diverts it to other social systems, this means much more than a simple change of law's self-description. Since the application of the legal code to itself not only introduces the abstract question of the law's legitimation, which is no longer answered with the 'legislator's will', but more probably with the inner rationality of the social subsystems involved. The law not only changes the founding myth where it conceals its paradoxes, but looks for a different constitutional foundation of its norm production. If it is now no longer the state constitution that is enlisted for externalising paradoxes, but the constitutions of social subsectors, so of the economy, the media, science and healthcare, then there are immediate, tangible consequences. To say it with Robert Cover, who sees the jurisgenerative force of a plurality of legal orders in the interaction between nomos and narrative,[24] the narrative is not the only one to change when the way that paradoxes are tackled is altered: the nomos itself is converted. When the legal paradox is transformed, other processes of norm production move into the foreground and a different kind of substantive legal norms comes into force.

The once-dominant law-making process, which translates collective political decisions into legal norms, is to a considerable extent being replaced in transnational regimes by social norm production that is transformed into applicable law.[25] Contract, formal organisation and standardisation are the three great jurisgenerative processes whereby the self-made rules of the economy, but also of science, education, the media and healthcare, becomes valid law. The role played by the political lawmaker with regard to the legislative authorities at work in international politics is then restricted increasingly to merely reformulating this law created within society.

Protest movements

This is where we find the explanation why protest movements are changing their addressees, as described above. Protest movements react to the change of externalising the paradoxes of law. They no longer address state authorities as the targets of their protests, but transnational corporations or other social institutions. Protest movements change the direction of their attacks whenever the legal system engages political legislation only for its formal legitimation and turns to contract, formal organisation and standardisation. Protest movements exert social pressure on the points where they believe they detect the causes of distorted social development and, even more so, real chances to bring change about. This explains why protest movements are perceiving stronger potential for a repoliticisation, a re-regionalisation and a re-individualisation of the processes of law-making, which are no longer concentrated in the political system, but can be found in various different social subsectors.[26] Some authors see in these direct contacts of protest movements a new quality of political struggles.[27]

'Constitutionalism from below' – this is the headline under which the protest movements' contribution to constitutionalism is discussed today. A series of authors – James Tully, Antonio Negri, Gavin Anderson – have observed that the transnational *pouvoir constituant* cannot be found in the political institutions but is now manifested in social movements, i.e. in the multitude, in a variety of protest movements, in NGOs and in transnational segments of the public.[28] Anderson identifies such a 'transnational constitutionalism from below' in the new 'constituent powers found both within and outside the structures of representative democracy, the latter comprising decolonisation and internationalist movements, alternative NGOs and bodies which escape traditional categorisation, such as the World Social Forum'.[29]

However exaggerated it may sound to identify protest movements completely with the *pouvoir constituant*, serious consideration must be given to one suggestion from these authors. What they mean by *pouvoir constituant* is no longer the all-embracing demos, but just fragmented processes. In transnational relations, it is crystal-clear that there is no such thing as a constitutional dynamic that embraces world society as whole, but that what we have at the most is a series of heterogeneous processes of constitutionalisation. This gives up on the traditional notion, in which the political constitution provides the collective energies of a society as a whole with the form that encapsulates it – in the past as a nation and now as the international community. Instead, modern society's collective potential is no longer available as a unity, but is increasingly compartmentalised in a multiplicity of social potentials, energies and strengths. And if the law alters the way it externalises its paradoxes, targeting social subsectors instead of politics, then the quality of the *pouvoir constituant* necessarily also changes. Law will then no longer seek its legitimation primarily through the political constitution, but through sectorial constitutions. These derive from the communicative potentials that cluster around society's various specialised communication media.[30]

Judge-made law

This now also illustrates how the expansion of judge-made law – as indicated above – relates to externalising paradoxes. Judge-made law is now beginning to play an unprecedented role: it is not just self-referentially producing the rules of 'case law' in litigation so as to solve individual conflicts;[31] it now also takes on board the social norms produced by contract, organisation and standardisation, deriving from this a different form of legitimation that is no longer legal, nor political, but social. This upgrades judge-made law vis-à-vis law-making, and not only in quantitative terms. Its new quality comes from the fact that case law takes over a genuine constitutional function; however, it does not derive its norms from the state constitution, but from the constitutions of various social subsystems.[32] It needs to be stressed that these constitutions cannot just mirror their subsystemic rationality but need to find their legitimation in a society wide *ordre public transnational*.[33]

This comes across most clearly in one of the most important twentieth-century institutions of private law, in the legal control of standard contracts.[34] Under the guise of contracting, markets have developed authoritative private regulations that no longer govern an individual contractual relationship, but have practically all the characteristics of general legislation. There is no genuine contractual consensus any more: instead, enterprises and business associations establish norms unilaterally, on the basis of asymmetric power relations, comparable to those between state and citizens. Judge-made law has reacted to these privately-imposed norms by taking on a dual constitutional role. On the one hand, it legitimates this form of one-sided norm production backed by economic power, whose problems it downplays by labelling it 'contractual', and uses secondary rules to regulate private norm production. The political legislature then does no more than incorporate the norms drawn up by judge-made law into the civil code. On the other hand, the courts intervene wholesale with strict judicial review in the economy's self-made law, whose intensity is on a par with the constitutional review exercised on political legislation. Shielded by such traditional formulae as 'good faith' and '*boni mores*', judge-made law has pieced together a new constitutional control hierarchy, in which the lower-ranking norms of the standard contracts are controlled by higher-ranking constitutional norms. Yet these higher-ranking norms are produced by the principles not of the political constitution, but of the economic constitution.

Judge-made law plays a comparable role in other social areas, when it subjects norm production in all sorts of social organisations based on private law – hospitals, universities, trade unions, professional associations, media concerns and recently, internet intermediaries – to a comprehensive legal review. Here, too, it fulfils the dual constitutional function just mentioned, on the one hand, normalising the procedures of social normation, on the other checking the substantive norms of internal organisational law for unconstitutionality. Similarly, judge-made law legitimates and controls processes of standardisation that are either laid down in private standardisation organisations or are pushed through naturally in so-called spontaneous communication processes. Here, too, it is not the state constitution, but the respective sectorial constitution – in healthcare, the system of education, the information media or the Internet – that furnishes the review criteria.

On the global scale, emerging transnational regime laws deal similarly with the problems of their original paradoxes. Here it is only possible to externalise towards politics within extremely narrow confines. Instead, various transnational regimes' own constitutions cause the regime laws' original paradoxes to disappear, as they relocate them into their respective social systems. The paradigm here is the *lex mercatoria*, which gives force to '*contrats sans loi*', i.e. to free-floating contracts without any extra-contractual foundations. This evident paradox can no longer be accommodated in the law of nation states. In a remarkable circularity, it relies on courts of arbitration that it has created itself to produce higher-ranking norms, which in turn find the narrative and nomos of the *lex mercatoria* in economic contractual practice.[35]

Natural law

There is a clear connection between alternative ways of externalising paradoxes and natural law, long believed to be moribund, which is now celebrating its resurrection in specialised fields of law and in transnational legal regimes. When judge-made law gives force to higher-ranking constitutional norms, it derives its criteria from the internal rationality of social subsystems. Efficiency as a legal principle, the functionality of social organisations, the self-definition of art, the neutrality and objectivity of science, the educational mission of schools and universities and the network adequacy of Internet norms – under legal positivism, social rationality formulae of these kinds could only become valid legal principles if the legislative made explicit provision. Yet such formulae are constantly flowing into legal practice from the various different social systems and are transformed into legal principles by judge-made law, then given force as concrete legal norms.[36]

We have long been aware from state constitutions of this inflow of substantive principles. The state constitution is construed as a material constitution, because it contains not only formal procedural norms, but also substantive norms and principles. There is only one way to explain their highly problematic 'natural law' character today. It is not the legal system, but the political system that decides, in the course of lengthy conflicts, about certain fundamental principles of politics, which are then constructed juridically by constitutional law and at the same time altered for legal purposes. The rule of law, the separation of powers, democracy, the welfare state and today environmental protection are examples of such reflexive decisions within the political system that flow into the law via the state constitution. Similarly, other social subsystems in their own reflection processes, develop fundamental principles that are legally reconstructed in the economic constitution, in the constitution of science, etc. and are used as criteria for the judicial review of norms. The legal principles of the economic constitution, for example, include the classical liberal principles of property, freedom of contract and competition, but also restrictions on contractual freedom, social obligations of property, fundamental rights vis-à-vis economic power and nowadays ecological sustainability and corporate social responsibility.[37]

The continuity of natural law thinking is perceptible here. Natural law has always been used to make the paradoxes of self-reference in the legal code disappear.[38] And this formula has always provided a smooth path for substantive principles to make their way into legal practice: from religion in the Middle Ages, from moral philosophy in the Age of Reason, from the political constitution in the nation state and from multiple societal constitutions in the postmodern era. Unlike the old natural law whose origins were religious, rationalist or political, it is now feasible to talk in terms of a sociological natural law, because it uses societal constitutions to reconstruct the rationalities of diverse subsystems within the legal system and transform them into binding principles. And the law does not care whether or not the democratically legitimated legislator has ordered it.

Deparadoxisation in other social systems

If the law, in the course of its development, has broken politics' monopoly on externalisation and become internally differentiated in such a way that special legal regimes shift the legal paradox into the social areas under their care, how do things look in the opposite direction? Do other social areas also experience reciprocal externalisation, so that they in turn cede their original paradoxes to the law?

The state constitution

As discussed above, the original paradox of politics became visible when the ruler's power becomes reflexive. When power is forced by power, when hierarchies of power are constructed, then politics is also exposed to an infinite regress – much like the law in the Münchhausen trilemma: the regress of overpowering power. And much as in the law, religious solutions to the problem of *ultima potestas* were convincing in mediaeval unitary cosmology. But if politics has become independent since the Renaissance, if it has broken free of religious bonds, if it has ultimately become sovereign and declared itself to be *legibus absoluta*, then the sovereignty paradox, the paradox of the binding of necessarily unbound authority, comes to the fore in all its poignancy. Within politics it is insoluble.[39]

It is the state constitution that enables politics to master this paradox, by displacing it outwards. Politics transfers to the law the task of constraining unconstrained sovereignty by means of legal procedures – by means of organisation as the inner bond and of fundamental rights for constraining arbitrariness towards the outside. This takes the edge off the paradox of politics. Admittedly, it implies a loss of sovereignty, as politics is henceforth tangled up in lasting, legally binding relationships. Yet this is compensated for, since binding acts of power by transforming them into acts of law puts political decisions on a permanent footing, so strengthens their efficacy. In this respect, the secret affinity between the communication of power and the normativity of the law shows itself to be more than productive. But politics' bond with the law only becomes bearable when the law-making machinery in turn guarantees politics a decisive influence on law-making. Only then can the state constitution drive the intricate relation between law and politics so far that a legal secondary codification of politics emerges. The rule of law is extended to cover all political events and thus treat every act of power as an act of law. State constitutions get their unique lustre from this externalisation of paradoxes executed in complete symmetry – from politics towards the law and from the law towards politics. This lustre induced Dieter Grimm to speak about the 'completeness' of state constitutions and Neil Walker to define their 'holistic' character. It is here that we can find the more profound reason why they deny the honorary title of constitution to the fundamental orders of other functional systems.[40]

The economic constitution

What role does the law play when the economy has to cope with its own fundamental paradox – the paradox of scarcity? This paradox paralyses economic action in such a way that acquisition of finite goods does away with scarcity, while at the same time generating scarcity. In the past, the only way to overcome this blockage was by replacing the scarcity paradox with the clear-cut binary code of property/non-property. But that presumes that every act of economic acquisition is sufficiently strict about 'condensing' vaguely understood positions of having/not having into durable positions of property/non-property. According to Luhmann, this condensation has played a key role in rendering the economy autonomous:

> Condensation means that structures of meaning are available for repetition from situation to situation; and this happens despite their paradoxical origins and despite their exposition to the opposition of the counter-value. Condensing is repeating the same . . . so that expectations of the future take shape and acquire certainties with regard to fulfilling needs and compensating privations.[41]

Condensing social positions into binding certainties cannot be achieved by acts of economic acquisition alone, however. At the most, such acts can generate diffuse social expectations in this direction, but cannot shape them strictly enough to achieve a precarious deparadoxisation in three dimensions. In the temporal dimension, property expectations must establish solid bonds that will last for a long time; in the social dimension they must establish the unambiguous inclusion/exclusion of the group of people concerned, which causes considerable difficulties, especially in the case of collective ownership; and in the substantive dimension they must generate clearly defined clusters of expectations with regard to rights of use, rights of exclusivity, rights of exploitation and rights of acquisition and their respective borderlines. This can only be achieved by a highly developed legal system. So it is the constitution of property that generates a close structural coupling between the economy and the law and in practice externalises the scarcity paradox in the law of property.

The property constitution only constitutes the first phase of an economic constitution. As soon as a highly developed monetary economy takes shape, and especially as soon as banks specialise in credit activities, the economic constitution enters a second phase, in which the scarcity paradox takes on a completely different form. Deparadoxisation then correspondingly runs on different tracks. And here the economy once again externalises the paradox, which threatens to paralyse monetary transactions, towards the law. In the banking sector, both the ability and the inability to pay are generated simultaneously. The banking system is based on the paradox of self-reference, on the unity of the ability and the inability to pay. 'The banks have the crucial privilege of being able to sell their debts at a profit.'[42] This paradox can be mitigated to a certain extent if the payment operations take on a reflexive mode, i.e. if operations involving quantities of money are applied to money operations in daily transactions. However, these reflexive economic operations remain unstable until an internal hierarchy is created within the banking sector, the hierarchy of central banks in their relation to commercial banks.

Yet the banking hierarchy cannot be institutionalised exclusively via self-regulation, and this applies in particular to the institutionalisation of the central bank. It needs to be supported from outside by legal rules, in order to constitute the unique position of the central bank with binding regulations. The parallels with the hierarchies in the political system and the role of the state constitution are evident. The economy, too, only copes with its monetary paradox with the help of the law, which uses the financial constitution, i.e. norms of procedure, of competence and of organisation, to regulate the establishment and operating methods of the central banks vis-à-vis the commercial banks. As an economic corollary to the different branches of government, the executive, the legislature and the judiciary, the 'monetative' of the central banks is established by the economic constitution.[43]

The way that the economic constitution deparadoxises money circulation is always precarious, however: it is always threatened by the danger of a return of the paradox. The hierarchy underpinned by the economic constitution in the relationship between the central banks and the commercial banks has not eliminated the paralysis of the financial system for good:

> The logical and empirical possibility that the entire system will collapse, of a return of the paradox and a complete blockage of all operations by the original equivalence capable of payment = incapable of payment cannot be ruled out, but is made sufficiently improbable.[44]

The recent financial crisis demonstrated that this is anything but 'sufficiently improbable'. The excessive growth compulsion in global financial transactions gave us all a glimpse of a possible default of the banking sector. This was followed immediately by recent initiatives to reform the financial constitution, which set out to readjust the hierarchy of the banks all over again. Without these reforms, the central banks would have difficulties exercising sufficient control over the money markets: they would only be able to stimulate or destimulate them indirectly by intervening singly. They would only be able to guide the money supply indirectly via the prime rate, which makes credit more or less expensive. With reforms that strengthen the role played by the central banks vis-à-vis the commercial banks, the law embraces the limitative function of the economic constitution, prevents the return of paradoxes and total blockage and at the same time stabilises the self-reflexive relations in payment operations, which would disintegrate if they were not fixed on a legal basis.

The fact that politics externalises the sovereignty paradox, while in parallel the economy externalises the scarcity paradox, both towards the law, and that in this way the state constitution and the economic constitution fulfil the same function, is quite astonishing. And yet, major differences are conspicuous. As for monetary operations within the economy, there is no sign of the complete secondary coding that forces the political system to apply the binary code legal/illegal to all political operations. There are basically three reasons for this. Firstly: there is no doubt that economic transactions are regulated by legal norms and also checked by the courts, but it is notable that the intense relation between political and legal operations has no counterpart in the relation between monetary and legal operations. An administrative act can be construed without further ado as the implementation of existing legal norms, in many cases even as a strictly conditional programme. Yet things follow a different course in economic transactions. To be sure, economic transactions are valid only under certain contractual conditions, yet in practice, economic transactions are the diametric opposite of the implementation of existing norms. Secondly: while the juridification of political decisions further strengthens their collectively binding character, it would be simply counterproductive for economic action if individual transactions were collectively binding for the whole economy. The legally guaranteed binding nature of transactions comes about only on the micro-level of contractual relations and economic organisations. Only on the micro-level is it possible to talk in terms of a secondary legal coding of economic transactions in the form of contractual acts or corporate acts. Unlike in the political system, where the collective is bound by political decisions, the macro-level in the economy remains unconstrained. The privity principle in Common Law forbids extending a binding nature to third parties, to say nothing of extending it to the economic order as a whole. Thirdly: the ongoing concatenation of political and economic operations differs one fundamentally from the other. Political decisions have precedential effects on subsequent decisions: if it intends to deviate from them, politics has to go through the entire legal procedure once again and the deviating decision must be rendered positive with an explicit *actus contrarius*. Future monetary transactions, on the contrary, are by no means bound normatively by previous transactions. Instead, the individual act of payment generates nothing but cognitive expectations for subsequent acts of payment.

These three reasons explain why, despite the parallels with which the economy and politics externalise their paradoxes towards the law, there are weighty differences in the intensity of their constitutionalisation. The decentralisation of decision-making that is prevalent in the economy, the intended restriction of contractual commitments to the contracting partners and the exclusively cognitive style of expectation that binds economic transactions to one another, in practice rule out the possibility of completing the symmetry of reciprocal externalisations, as they come about between politics and law, in relation to the economy and law. Unlike the state constitution, the economic constitution exhibits a remarkable degree of asymmetry. While it is true, as illustrated above, that law externalises the legal paradox to a considerable extent towards economic norm production – contract, organisation and standardisation – it is nevertheless also true that, if it is to avoid damaging its structural integrity, the economy can only pursue its legal constitutionalisation to a limited extent.

The constitution of science

This asymmetry of externalisations is even more marked in the constitution of science. To be sure, science also has its paradox of self-foundation: only scientific operations can determine reflexively what actually constitutes science. The Cretan paradox, which derives from applying cognitive operations to cognitive operations, is probably the best-known case of a self-referential paradox. But unlike politics and the economy, it is mostly impossible to externalise the scientific paradox towards the law. Normative stipulations which are legally or constitutionally binding and which can be changed only with difficulty, are self-destructive for science. It would actually be absurd to interpret cognitive acts as the implementation of rules. Admittedly, even though it portrays itself as undogmatic, science too is no stranger to extensive norm production. Methods are binding; theories are immunised normatively against a change of paradigm; neutrality, objectivity and immunity to interest are accepted professional norms.[45] And yet the juridification of such social norms would generate a paralysis irreconcilable with the cognitive style. It is no coincidence that the state constitution leaves science the right to self-definition, limiting itself to second order observation.[46] Nor is it any coincidence that the constantly repeated proposals for scientific courts, whose remit would be to issue binding decisions about the validity of the results of new research, have had no success whatsoever. Only a normative style that is always open to being reversed, of a flexibility quite unknown to the law, is at all permissible in science.[47]

Unlike politics and the economy, science cannot pass its paradox on to the law, but has to seek out other ways to achieve deparadoxisation.[48] It finds them mainly in processes internal to science itself. Temporalising the paradox, creating a hierarchy of different levels of analysis, enduring contradictions, antinomies and incommensurabilities, tolerating uncertainty, relinquishing the compulsion to decide, creating a constructivist worldview: these are some of the tools used by science in the attempt to make its paradoxes more bearable.

That does not mean, however, that there can be no such thing as a constitution of science, in which scientific and legal reflexions are coupled together structurally. It is just that the internal asymmetry of their coupling is extremely strongly developed. As illustrated above, when the law regulates scientific activities it externalises its paradox to scientific processes without further ado and uses the underlying principles of scientific cognition to legitimate legal norms that impact on science. Science in its turn keeps the integrity of its cognitive operations largely free of legal constraints. Only its external borders should be protected by legal norms. Freedom of science as a guarantee that the cognitive process remains open thus becomes the sole norm of the scientific constitution. The law provides a binding guarantee that science may be bound to nothing but its own freedom. A pertinent part of this is its legal protection against being corrupted by politics, by the economy and by the law itself. The most important task of the constitution of science is 'to stabilise the epistemological difference between the knowledge of science, of politics and of the law itself'.[49] It guarantees this with the aid of 'mechanisms that . . . help stop science being colonised by other, alien system rationalities – in particular by the economy and by politics, but also by the law itself'. Dedifferentiation tendencies whose aim is to 'replace relevances internal to science with values and norms external to science are to be averted'.[50] Yet the law must also guarantee a sufficient plurality of processes within science, so that it is always possible to break down roadblocks that hinder development by adopting a fundamental change of perspective. The requirement for pluralism and for the protection of scientific minorities thus becomes a binding principle of the scientific constitution. And, of course, the external organisational framework of universities, research institutes and professional organisations is also furnished with a legally binding guarantee.[51]

Constitutionalisation with differing intensity

Altogether, then, societal constitutionalism – as exemplified here by politics, the economy and science – paints a picture of constitutional pluralism, although one that is anything but uniform, since it realises different degrees of intensity of constitutionalisation. It follows that the model of the state constitution cannot be transferred lock, stock and barrel to other social constitutions. It is true that the issues raised by the state constitution need to be generalised, since all functional systems have to cope with the paradoxes of self-reference, whether they will follow the path of externalising completely towards the law, as politics chose to do with the legal secondary codification of its operations, or whether they will opt, like the economy, for only a partial externalisation towards the law, or whether, like science, they will rule out a juridification of their operations and adopt other possible methods of deparadoxisation. However, this choice depends on the affinity between their own structures and the specific normativity developed within the legal system.

This clearly shows why the state constitution occupies a unique position among social constitutions. This position certainly does not derive from the state's constitutional monopoly, as state-centric constitutional lawyers would have us believe, since other disciplines – historiography, economics, sociology and international relations – have long demonstrated the existence of non-state constitutions.[52] Neither is this unique position derived from a hierarchical superiority of the state constitution over the so-called sub-constitutions, as many authors maintain, who certainly admit to constitutional pluralism, but are not prepared to forego the dominant position of the state constitution.[53] Nor again, lastly, does it derive from the state constitutions being the only ones to have a legal character, while other social constitutions – including transnational regimes – are only 'constituted' de facto, or only contain social fundamental values, or are constitutions only in a metaphorical sense. Instead, the reciprocal externalisation of politics towards the law and of law towards politics is totally symmetrical – this is responsible for the unique position of state constitutions. While the law, in its diverse legal fields, pursues a variegated approach to externalising paradoxes in all sorts of different social systems and so derives its normative contents from the various constitutions of different social areas, in the opposite direction there are drastic differences in the juridification of social systems' original paradoxes. Structural couplings are generally misunderstood – and social constitutions in particular – when it is said that structural couplings only exist as reciprocal relations. Indeed, it is quite possible for one social system to be closely coupled to another, while the latter system, in its operations, is only partly coupled or largely forgoes a structural coupling. It is like love: it is often only experienced on one side and only in a handful of lucky cases is it truly reciprocated by the person who is loved.

Consequent problems

In conclusion, let us take a brief look at the consequences of externalisation. What happens after the constitutional paradox has been externalised? As we have seen, externalising brings major advantages for the system in question, sometimes even making autopoiesis at all possible, but it simultaneously entails some serious costs. The system that outsources its paradox is now delivered up to an extraneous structural logic. As illustrated above, the differences between the constitutionalisation of politics, the economy and science can be explained by the incompatibilities that a complete juridification of their paradoxes can generate. Constitutions would then drive social systems systematically in a wrong juridical direction if the extent of externalisation towards the law were incompatible with their own structures. The fact that their operations at the same time also have to be subjected to the conditions for legal operations explains why many social systems adopt routes to deparadoxisation alternative to passing them to the law.

Another aspect is even more problematic: externalisation delivers the system up to the extraneous paradox itself. The law is delivered up to the political paradox, politics to the legal paradox. Formulated in general terms, the law is delivered up to the paradox of the constituted social system, while the social system is delivered up to the legal paradox. There is a danger that the constitution, as a structural coupling of the law with another social system, does not differentiate sufficiently between including and excluding the extraneous, unlike what is found typically in successful structural couplings.[54] This then becomes fatal at the latest when the externalisation also embraces the system's contingency formula, so for example when the principle of legal justice is thoroughly politicised or economised. A fair number of authors argue in favour of politicising the contingency formula of justice, whose operative nucleus lies in the equal treatment of similar cases and the unequal treatment of dissimilar cases, in the direction of democracy and the common weal, or of economising it in the direction of reducing scarcity and increasing efficiency. Yet the desired gain in precision fails to materialise, as one contingency formula is only replaced by the other, so one high degree of uncertainty is replaced by another comparably high degree of uncertainty. Even worse: the process of determination, which in all cases ends up in a self-transcendence and calls for creative solutions under the dominance of the respective contingency formula, manoeuvres in the wrong direction. The parties to a legal conflict are offered solutions oriented towards achieving efficiency or policy effectiveness, rather than a fair decision of their conflict: they are offered stone when they want bread. Whenever possible, a clear distinction should be drawn here between the original paradox and the paradox of decision. The unavoidable externalisation of the legal original paradoxes should not be allowed to cause the legal process to be delivered up to the political or economic decision-making paradox. And the same applies to the contrary.

Notes

1 The formulae ('legal cognition', judge-made law as 'customary law') offered by contemporary legal theory to describe the issue of judge-made law are typically awkward, see Klaus F. Röhl and Hans C. Röhl (2008) *Allgemeine Rechtslehre: Ein Lehrbuch*, 3rd edn, Köln: Heymann, 571ff.

2 Chris Thornhill (2013) 'A Sociology of Constituent Power: The Political Code of Transnational Societal Constitutions', 20 *Indiana Journal of Global Legal Studies*, 551–603, 568; Yuval Shany (2009)

'No Longer a Weak Department of Power? Reflections on the Emergence of a New International Judiciary', 20 *The European Journal of International Law*, 81–91.

3 Ran Hirschl (2004) *Towards Juristocracy: The Origins and Consequences of the New Constitutionalism*, Cambridge, MA: Harvard University Press.

4 *Locus classicus*: Josef Esser (1956) *Grundsatz und Norm in der richterlichen Fortbildung des Privatrechts: Rechtsvergleichende Beiträge zur Rechtsquellen- und Interpretationslehre*, Tübingen: Mohr Siebeck.

5 For an overview of recent natural law theories, see Kenneth Einar Himma, 'Natural Law', in the Internet Encyclopaedia of Philosophy: www.iep.utm.edu/natlaw/. For a transnational human rights as natural law, Matthias Mahlmann (2009) 'Varieties of Transnational Law and the Universalistic Stance', 10 *German Law Journal*, 1325–36.

6 On the contemporary discussion about Gramsci, see Sonja Buckel and Andreas Fischer-Lescano (eds) (2007) *Hegemonie gepanzert mit Zwang: Zivilgesellschaft und Politik im Staatsverständnis Antonio Gramscis*, Baden-Baden: Nomos. For Fuller's concept of natural law, see Lon Fuller (1969) *The Morality of Law*, New Haven: Yale University Press.

7 Robert O'Brien, Anne Marie Goetz, Jan A. Scholte and Marc Williams (2002) *Contesting Global Governance: Multilateral Economic Institutions and Global Social Movements*, Cambridge: Cambridge University Press, 2.

8 For example David Schneiderman (2008) *Constitutionalizing Economic Globalization: Investment Rules and Democracy's Promise*, Cambridge: Cambridge University Press.

9 More extensively, although with due caution, Ino Augsberg (2011) 'Wissenschaftsverfassungsrecht', in: Thomas Vesting and Stefan Korioth (eds) *Der Eigenwert des Verfassungsrechts: Was bleibt von der Verfassung nach der Globalisierung?* Tübingen: Mohr Siebeck, 203–23, 223.

10 On the debate about societal constitutions, particularly in the transnational realm, see Grahame Thompson (2015) 'The Constitutionalisation of Everyday Life', in: Poul Kjaer and Eva Hartmann (eds) *The Evolution of Intermediary Institutions in Europe: From Corporatism to Governance*, London: Palgrave; Poul F. Kjaer (2014) *Constitutionalism in the Global Realm: A Sociological Approach*, London: Routledge; Gunther Teubner and Anna Beckers (eds) (2013) Symposium 'Transnational Societal Constitutionalism', 20 *Indiana Journal of Global Legal Studies*.

11 Niklas Luhmann (1990) 'Verfassung als evolutionäre Errungenschaft', 9 *Rechtshistorisches Journal*, 176–220; Niklas Luhmann (1989) 'Zwei Seiten des Rechtsstaates', in: The Institute of Comparative Law in Japan (ed.) *Conflict and Integration: Comparative Law in the World Today*, Tokyo: Chuo University Press, 493–506; Niklas Luhmann (1973) 'Politische Verfassungen im Kontext des Gesellschaftssystems', 12 *Der Staat*, 1–22, 165–82.

12 Niklas Luhmann (2004) *Law as a Social System*, Oxford: Oxford University Press, 408.

13 Niklas Luhmann (1965) *Grundrechte als Institution: Ein Beitrag zur politischen Soziologie*, Berlin: Duncker & Humblot, 115f.; 205, Fn. 9; Luhmann (Fn. 12) 487f.

14 On the method of generalising and respecifying, see Talcott Parsons and Charles Ackerman (1966) 'The Concept of "Social System" as a Theoretical Device', in: Gordon J. DiRenzo (ed.) *Concepts, Theory and Explanation in the Behavioral Sciences*, New York: Random House, 19–40.

15 Niklas Luhmann (2013) *Theory of Society*, Palo Alto: Stanford California Press, Ch. 2, XI.

16 On the constitutionalisation of the legal order as a whole, see Hans C. Röhl (2008) 'Verfassungsrecht als wissenschaftliche Strategie?', in: Hans-Heinrich Trute, Thomas Gross, Hans C. Röhl and Christoph Möllers (eds) *Allgemeines Verwaltungsrecht: Zur Tragfähigkeit eines Konzepts*, Tübingen: Mohr Siebeck, 821–36.

17 For the current discussion about the status of customary law and private law, see Röhl and Röhl (Fn. 1) 541ff., 554ff.

18 For example, Matthias Ruffert (2001) *Vorrang der Verfassung und Eigenständigkeit des Privatrechts: Eine verfassungsrechtliche Untersuchung zur Privatrechtswirkung des Grundgesetzes*, Tübingen: Mohr Siebeck, 223.

19 In detail, see Gunther Teubner (1998) 'The King's Many Bodies: The Self-Deconstruction of Law's Hierarchy', 33 *Law and Society Review*, 763–87.

20 Frederick A. Mann (1968) 'Internationale Schiedsgerichte und nationale Rechtsordnung', 130 *Zeitschrift für das Gesamte Handelsrecht*, 97–129, 197.

21 The significance of this internal differentiation of the law is acknowledged, albeit in connection with a scarcely plausible polemic, as a loss of unity of private law, by Wolfgang Zöllner (1996) 'Regelungsspielräume im Schuldvertragsrecht: Bemerkungen zur Grundrechtsanwendung im Privatrecht und zu den sogenannten Ungleichgewichtslagen', 196 *Archiv für die civilistische Praxis*, 1–36. On

the latest discussion, see Tanja Domej (ed.) (2008) *Einheit des Privatrechts, komplexe Welt: Herausforderungen durch fortschreitende Spezialisierung und Interdisziplinarität. Jahrbuch Junger Zivilrechtswissenschaftler*, Stuttgart: Boorberg.

22 This comes close to the 'constitutional law of law' by Rudolf Wiethölter (2005) 'Just-ifications of a Law of Society', in: Oren Perez und Gunther Teubner (eds) *Paradoxes and Inconsistencies in the Law*, Oxford: Hart, 65–77, 71ff.

23 On this, see Martti Koskenniemi (2012) 'Hegemonic Regimes', in: Margaret Young (ed.) *Regime Interaction in International Law: Facing Fragmentation*, Cambridge: Cambridge University Press, 305–24; Andreas Fischer-Lescano and Gunther Teubner (2004) 'Regime-Collisions: The Vain Search for Legal Unity in the Fragmentation of Global Law', 25 *Michigan Law Journal of International Law*, 999–1045.

24 Robert M. Cover (1983) 'The Supreme Court, 1982 Term – Foreword: Nomos and Narrative', 97 *Harvard Law Review*, 4–68.

25 See for example Richard Nobles and David Schiff (2012) 'Using Systems Theory to Study Legal Pluralism: What Could Be Gained?', 46 *Law & Society Review*, 265–95; Leon E. Trakman (2011) 'A Plural Account of the Transnational Law Merchant', 2 *Transnational Legal Theory*, 309–45; James Harrison (2009) 'Regime Pluralism and the Global Regulation of Oil Pollution Liability and Compensation', 5 *International Journal of Law in Context*, 379–91.

26 See Gavin W. Anderson (2009) 'Corporate Constitutionalism: From Above and Below (but Mostly Below)', *The Constitutionalization of the Global Corporate Sphere?* Paper presented at Copenhagen Business School, Copenhagen, September 17–18, 1–14.

27 Colin Crouch (2011) *The Strange Non-Death of Neoliberalism*, Cambridge: Polity Press; O'Brien et al. (Fn. 7) 2.

28 James Tully (2007) 'The Imperialism of Modern Constitutional Democracy', in: Neil Walker and Martin Loughlin (eds) *The Paradox of Constitutionalism: Constituent Power and Constitutional Form*, Oxford: Oxford University Press, 315–38, 319, 323ff.; Michael Hardt and Antonio Negri (2009) *Commonwealth*, Cambridge, MA: Harvard University Press; Gavin W. Anderson (2013) 'Societal Constitutionalism, Social Movements and Constitutionalism from Below', 20 *Indiana Journal of Global Legal Studies*, 881–906.

29 Anderson (Fn. 28) 902.

30 Gunther Teubner (2012) *Constitutional Fragments: Societal Constitutionalism and Globalization*, Oxford: Oxford University Press, 61ff.

31 Wolfgang Fikentscher (1977) *Methoden des Rechts in vergleichender Darstellung*, Bd.IV. Tübingen: Mohr Siebeck, 199ff., 201.

32 For details, Gunther Teubner (2004) 'Societal Constitutionalism: Alternatives to State-Centred Constitutional Theory?', in: Christian Joerges, Inger-Johanne Sand and Gunther Teubner (eds) *Transnational Governance and Constitutionalism*, Oxford: Hart, 3–28.

33 For an elaboration, Teubner (Fn. 30) 87f., 157f. See also Pablo Holmes (2014) 'The Politics of Law and the Law of Politics: The Political Paradoxes of Transnational Constitutionalism', 21 *Indiana Journal of Global Legal Studies*, 553–83, 569ff.

34 A recent excellent analysis is Pasquale Femia (2013) 'Desire for Text: Bridling the Divisional Strategy of Contract', 76 *Law and Contemporary Problems*, 150–68.

35 About this, see Gunther Teubner (1997) 'Breaking Frames: Economic Globalization and the Emergence of Lex Mercantoria', 45 *The American Journal of Comparative Law*, 149–69.

36 On the law's recourse to social standards, see Thomas Vesting (2007) *Rechtstheorie: Ein Studienbuch*, München: Beck, 95ff.

37 For greater detail about this, see Teubner (Fn. 30) 172ff.

38 Niklas Luhmann (1988) 'The Third Question: The Creative Use of Paradoxes in Law and Legal History', 15 *Journal of Law and Society*, 153–65.

39 Luhmann (Fn. 11).

40 Dieter Grimm (2010) 'The Achievement of Constitutionalism and Its Prospects in a Changed World', in: Petra Dobner and Martin Loughlin (eds) *The Twilight of Constitutionalism?* Oxford: Oxford University Press, 3–22; Neil Walker (2010) 'Beyond the Holistic Constitution?', in: Petra Dobner and Martin Loughlin (eds) *The Twilight of Constitutionalism?* Oxford: Oxford University Press, 291–308.

41 Niklas Luhmann (1988) *Die Wirtschaft der Gesellschaft*, Frankfurt: Suhrkamp, 188.

42 Luhmann (Fn. 41) 145.

43 More specifically about this, see Gunther Teubner (2011) 'A Constitutional Moment? The Logics of "Hit the Bottom"', in: Poul F. Kjaer, Gunther Teubner and Alberto Febbrajo (eds) *The Financial*

Crisis in Constitutional Perspective: The Dark Side of Functional Differentiation, Oxford: Hart, 9–52, 21ff.

44 Luhmann (Fn. 41) 146.

45 John Ziman (2000) *Real Science: What It Is, and What It Means*, Cambridge: Cambridge University Press.

46 Epistemological insights go into the legal determination of scientific freedom, see Eberhard Schmidt-Assmann (1989) 'Wissenschaftsrecht im Ordnungsrahmen des öffentlichen Rechts', 45 *Juristenzeitung*, 205–11, 207.

47 Niklas Luhmann (1990) *Die Wissenschaft der Gesellschaft*, Frankfurt: Suhrkamp, 93ff.

48 Luhmann (Fn. 47) 172ff.

49 Augsberg (Fn. 9) 217

50 Ino Augsberg (2012) 'Subjektive und objektive Dimensionen der Wissenschaftsfreiheit', in: Friedemann Voigt (ed.) *Freiheit der Wissenschaft. Beiträge zu ihrer Bedeutung, Normativität und Funktion*, Berlin: De Gruyter, 65–89, 82.

51 Isabell Hensel (2009) 'Grundrechtskollisionen in der Stiftungsuniversität: Überwältigte Einheit oder organisierte Vielfalt', in: Gralf-Peter Calliess, Andreas Fischer-Lescano, Dan Wielsch and Peer Zumbansen (eds) *Soziologische Jurisprudenz: Festschrift für Gunther Teubner zum 65. Geburtstag*, Berlin: De Gruyter, 509–30.

52 For political science, Thompson (Fn. 10); for social history, Reinhart Koselleck (2006) 'Begriffsgeschichtliche Probleme der Verfassungsgeschichtsschreibung', in: Reinhart Koselleck (ed.) *Begriffsgeschichten: Studien zur Semantik und Pragmatik der politischen und sozialen Sprache*, Frankfurt: Suhrkamp, 365–401; for economics, James M. Buchanan (1991) *Constitutional Economics*, Oxford: Blackwell; for sociology, Thornhill (Fn. 2); for international relations, Joel P. Trachtman (2006) 'The Constitutions of the WTO', 17 *European Journal of International Law*, 623–46.

53 Christian Joerges and Florian Rödl (2009) 'Zum Funktionswandel des Kollisionsrechts II: Die kollisionsrechtliche Form einer legitimen Verfassung der postnationalen Konstellation', in: Gralf-Peter Calliess, Andreas Fischer-Lescano, Dan Wielsch and Peer Zumbansen (eds) *Soziologische Jurisprudenz: Festschrift für Gunther Teubner zum 65. Geburtstag*, Berlin: De Gruyter, 765–78.

54 Neves identifies transversal paradoxes here, which in themselves come about as a result of the constitutional procedure and can be controlled only insufficiently by constitutional courts, Marcelo Neves (2013) *Transconstitutionalism*, London: Hart, 51ff.

References

Anderson, Gavin W. 'Corporate Constitutionalism: From Above and Below (but Mostly Below)'. In *The Constitutionalization of the Global Corporate Sphere?* Paper presented at Copenhagen Business School, Copenhagen, 17–18 September 17–18 2009.

———. 'Societal Constitutionalism, Social Movements and Constitutionalism from Below'. *Indiana Journal of Global Legal Studies* 20 (2013): 881–906.

Augsberg, Ino. 'Wissenschaftsverfassungsrecht'. In *Der Eigenwert des Verfassungsrechts: Was bleibt von der Verfassung nach der Globalisierung?* edited by Thomas Vesting and Stefan Korioth, 203–23. Tübingen: Mohr Siebeck, 2011.

———. 'Subjektive und objektive Dimensionen der Wissenschaftsfreiheit'. In *Freiheit der Wissenschaft. Beiträge zu ihrer Bedeutung, Normativität und Funktion*, edited by Friedemann Voigt, 65–89. Berlin: De Gruyter, 2012.

Buchanan, James M. *Constitutional Economics*. Oxford: Blackwell, 1991.

Buckel, Sonja, and Andreas Fischer-Lescano. *Hegemonie gepanzert mit Zwang: Zivilgesellschaft und Politik im Staatsverständnis Antonio Gramscis*. Baden-Baden: Nomos, 2007.

Cover, Robert M. 'The Supreme Court, 1982 Term – Foreword: Nomos and Narrative'. *Harvard Law Review* 97 (1983): 4–68.

Crouch, Colin. *The Strange Non-Death of Neoliberalism*. Cambridge: Polity Press, 2011.

Domej, Tanja (ed.). *Einheit des Privatrechts, komplexe Welt: Herausforderungen durch fortschreitende Spezialisierung und Interdisziplinarität. Jahrbuch Junger Zivilrechtswissenschaftler*. Stuttgart: Boorberg, 2008.

Esser, Josef. *Grundsatz und Norm in der richterlichen Fortbildung des Privatrechts: Rechtsvergleichende Beiträge zur Rechtsquellen- und Interpretationslehre*. Tübingen: Mohr Siebeck, 1956.

Femia, Pasquale. 'Desire for Text: Bridling the Divisional Strategy of Contract'. *Law and Contemporary Problems* 76 (2013): 150–68.

Fikentscher, Wolfgang. *Methoden des Rechts in vergleichender Darstellung*, Bd.IV. Tübingen: Mohr Siebeck, 1977.

Fischer-Lescano, Andreas, and Gunther Teubner. 'Regime-Collisions: The Vain Search for Legal Unity in the Fragmentation of Global Law'. *Michigan Law Journal of International Law* 25 (2004): 999–1045.

Fuller, Lon. *The Morality of Law*. New Haven: Yale University Press, 1969.

Grimm, Dieter. 'The Achievement of Constitutionalism and Its Prospects in a Changed World'. In *The Twilight of Constitutionalism?* edited by Petra Dobner and Martin Loughlin, 3–22. Oxford: Oxford University Press, 2010.

Hardt, Michael, and Antonio Negri. *Commonwealth*. Cambridge, MA: Harvard University Press, 2009.

Harrison, James. 'Regime Pluralism and the Global Regulation of Oil Pollution Liability and Compensation'. *International Journal of Law in Context* 5 (2009): 379–91.

Hensel, Isabell. 'Grundrechtskollisionen in der Stiftungsuniversität: Überwältigte Einheit oder organisierte Vielfalt'. In *Soziologische Jurisprudenz: Festschrift für Gunther Teubner zum 65. Geburtstag*, edited by Gralf-Peter Calliess, Andreas Fischer-Lescano, Dan Wielsch and Peer Zumbansen, 509–30. Berlin: De Gruyter, 2009.

Himma, Einar: 'Natural Law'. In *The Internet Encyclopaedia of Philosophy*. Available at: www.iep.utm.edu/natlaw/.

Hirschl, Ran. *Towards Juristocracy: The Origins and Consequences of the New Constitutionalism*. Cambridge, MA: Harvard University Press, 2004.

Holmes, Pablo. 'The Politics of Law and the Law of Politics: The Political Paradoxes of Transnational Constitutionalism'. *Indiana Journal of Global Legal Studies* 21 (2014): 553–83, 569ff.

Joerges, Christian, and Florian Rödl. 'Zum Funktionswandel des Kollisionsrechts II: Die kollisionsrechtliche Form einer legitimen Verfassung der postnationalen Konstellation'. In *Soziologische Jurisprudenz: Festschrift für Gunther Teubner zum 65. Geburtstag*, edited by Gralf-Peter Calliess, Andreas Fischer-Lescano, Dan Wielsch and Peer Zumbansen, 765–78. Berlin: De Gruyter, 2009.

Kjaer, Poul F. *Constitutionalism in the Global Realm: A Sociological Approach*. London: Routledge, 2014.

Koselleck, Reinhart. 'Begriffsgeschichtliche Probleme der Verfassungsgeschichtsschreibung'. In *Begriffsgeschichten: Studien zur Semantik und Pragmatik der politischen und sozialen Sprache*, 365–401. Frankfurt: Suhrkamp, 2006.

Koskenniemi, Martti. 'Hegemonic Regimes'. In *Regime Interaction in International Law: Facing Fragmentation*, edited by Margaret Young, 305–24. Cambridge: Cambridge University Press, 2012.

Luhmann, Niklas. *Grundrechte als Institution. Ein Beitrag zur politischen Soziologie*. Berlin: Duncker & Humblot, 1965.

———. 'Politische Verfassungen im Kontext des Gesellschaftssystems'. *Der Staat. Zeitschrift für Staatslehre, Öffentliches Recht und Verfassungsgeschicte* 12 (1973): 1–22, 165–82.

———. *Die Wirtschaft der Gesellschaft*. Frankfurt: Suhrkamp, 1988.

———. 'The Third Question: The Creative Use of Paradoxes in Law and Legal History'. *Journal of Law and Society* 15 (1988): 153–65.

———. 'Zwei Seiten des Rechtsstaates'. (1988). In *Conflict and Integration. Comparative Law in the World Today: The 40th Anniversary of The Institute of Comparative Law in Japan*, 493–506. Tokyo: Chuo University Press, 1989.

———. *Die Wissenschaft der Gesellschaft*. Frankfurt: Suhrkamp, 1990.

———. 'Verfassung als evolutionäre Errungenschaft'. *Rechtshistorisches Journal* 9 (1990): 176–220.

———. *Law as a Social System*. Oxford: Oxford University Press, 2004.

———. *Theory of Society*. Palo Alto: Stanford California Press, 2013.

Mahlmann, Matthias. 'Varieties of Transnational Law and the Universalistic Stance', *German Law Journal* 10 (2009): 1325–36.

Mann, Frederick A. 'Internationale Schiedsgerichte und nationale Rechtsordnung'. *Zeitschrift für das Gesamte Handelsrecht* 130 (1968): 97–129.

Neves, Marcelo. *Transconstitutionalism*. London: Hart, 2013.

Nobles, Richard, and David Schiff. 'Using Systems Theory to Study Legal Pluralism: What Could Be Gained?' *Law & Society Review* 46 (2012): 265–95.

O'Brien, Robert, Anne Marie Goetz, Jan A. Scholte and Marc Williams. *Contesting Global Governance: Multilateral Economic Institutions and Global Social Movements*. Cambridge: Cambridge University Press, 2002.

Parsons, Talcott and Charles Ackerman. 'The Concept of "Social System" as a Theoretical Device'. In *Concepts, Theory and Explanation in the Behavioral Sciences*, edited by Gordon J. DiRenzo, 19–40. New York: Random House, 1966.

Röhl, Hans C. 'Verfassungsrecht als wissenschaftliche Strategie?' In *Allgemeines Verwaltungsrecht: Zur Tragfähigkeit eines Konzepts*, edited by Hans-Heinrich Trute, Thomas Gross, Hans C. Röhl and Christoph Möllers, 821–36. Tübingen: Mohr Siebeck, 2008.

Röhl, Klaus F., and Hans C. Röhl. *Allgemeine Rechtslehre: Ein Lehrbuch*, 3rd edition. Köln: Heymann, 2008.

Ruffert, Matthias. *Vorrang der Verfassung und Eigenständigkeit des Privatrechts: Eine verfassungsrechtliche Untersuchung zur Privatrechtswirkung des Grundgesetzes*. Tübingen: Mohr Siebeck, 2001.

Schmidt-Assmann, Eberhard. 'Wissenschaftsrecht im Ordnungsrahmen des öffentlichen Rechts'. *Juristenzeitung* 45 (1989): 205–11.

Schneiderman, David. *Constitutionalizing Economic Globalization: Investment Rules and Democracy's Promise*. Cambridge: Cambridge University Press, 2008.

Shany, Yuval. 'No Longer a Weak Department of Power? Reflections on the Emergence of a New International Judiciary'. *The European Journal of International Law* 20 (2009): 81–91.

Teubner, Gunther. 'Breaking Frames: Economic Globalization and the Emergence of Lex Mercatoria'. *The American Journal of Comparative Law* 45 (1997): 149–69.

———. 'The King's Many Bodies: The Self-Deconstruction of Law's Hierarchy'. *Law and Society Review* 33 (1998): 763–87.

———. 'Societal Constitutionalism: Alternatives to State-centred Constitutional Theory?' In *Transnational Governance and Constitutionalism*, edited by Christian Joerges, Inger-Johanne Sand and Gunther Teubner, 3–28. Oxford: Hart, 2004.

———. 'A Constitutional Moment? The Logics of "Hit the Bottom"'. In *The Financial Crisis in Constitutional Perspective: The Dark Side of Functional Differentiation*, edited by Poul F. Kjaer, Gunther Teubner and Alberto Febbrajo, 9–52. Oxford: Hart, 2011.

———. *Constitutional Fragments: Societal Constitutionalism and Globalization*. Oxford: Oxford University Press, 2012.

Teubner, Gunther, and Anna Beckers (eds). Symposium 'Transnational Societal Constitutionalism'. *Indiana Journal of Global Legal Studies* 20 (2013).

Thompson, Grahame. 'The Constitutionalisation of Everyday Life'. In *The Evolution of Intermediary Institutions in Europe: From Corporatism to Governance*, edited by Poul Kjaer and Eva Hartmann, 177–98. London: Palgrave, 2015.

Thornhill, Chris. 'A Sociology of Constituent Power: The Political Code of Transnational Societal Constitutions'. *Indiana Journal of Global Legal Studies* 20 (2013): 551–603.

Trachtman, Joel P. 'The Constitutions of the WTO'. *European Journal of International Law* 17 (2006): 623–46.

Trakman, Leon E. 'A Plural Account of the Transnational Law Merchant'. *Transnational Legal Theory* 2 (2011): 309–45.

Tully, James. 'The Imperialism of Modern Constitutional Democracy'. In *The Paradox of Constitutionalism: Constituent Power and Constitutional Form*, edited by Neil Walker and Martin Loughlin, 315–38. Oxford: Oxford University Press, 2007.

Vesting, Thomas. *Rechtstheorie: Ein Studienbuch*. München: Beck, 2007.

Walker, Neil. 'Beyond the Holistic Constitution?' In *The Twilight of Constitutionalism?* edited by Petra Dobner and Martin Loughlin, 291–308. Oxford: Oxford University Press, 2010.

Wiethölter, Rudolf. 'Just-ifications of a Law of Society'. In *Paradoxes and Inconsistencies in the Law*, edited by Oren Perez and Gunther Teubner, 65–77. Oxford: Hart, 2005.

Ziman, John. *Real Science: What It Is, and What It Means*. Cambridge: Cambridge University Press, 2000.

Zöllner, Wolfgang. 'Regelungsspielräume im Schuldvertragsrecht: Bemerkungen zur Grundrechtsanwendung im Privatrecht und zu den sogenannten Ungleichgewichtslagen'. *Archiv für die civilistische Praxis* 196 (1996): 1–36.

3 Promise as premise

Rewriting the paradox of constitutional reasoning

Ino Augsberg

Introduction

Die Verfassung verspricht (sich).[1] A constitution is a dual promise (*Versprechen*) in both the Kantian and the Freudian sense,[2] a linguistic act missing its own performative objective with structurally determined inevitability. Yet, as such an ostensibly sheer slip, this *Versprechen* is not simply meaningless. It has a peculiar meaning of its own.[3] The constitution as slippery promise is always already ahead of itself and therefore non-identical with itself; it generates an excess with which its own method and aspirations cannot catch up. This hyperbolic structure of the constitution is the premise for what can be described as its paradox: its fundamental problem to serve as the solid base for legal reasoning while lacking any foundation of its own.

My intention is to expand in three steps on this thesis of the linguistic background of the *constitutional* paradoxes. In the first step, I shall start with the constitution's apparently dual empirical-normative character. I will show how this dichotomy – presented as semantic evidence – is subverted by the constitution as a necessarily linguistic phenomenon. A second step investigates from a historical perspective why the constitution's textual form is not merely a superficial phenomenon largely contingent on its 'substantial core'. I argue that, on the contrary, the constitution is determined predominantly by its textuality. Therefore, modern expansions on the constitutional concept which aim to extend beyond the narrow context of the state must also be measured by this yardstick. The third step looks into the constitution's character as a promise. This characterisation does not equate the constitution with contractual constructions – be they strongly idealised or acknowledged as fictional – but addresses its autopo(i)etic dimension and thus makes expansions in the light of hitherto contradictory legal traditions possible. A brief conclusion summarises these considerations with a last look at the paradoxes of the constitution.

Constitution as language

Verfassung as well as the Latin equivalent *constitutio* and its derivatives in many European languages, is a homonym, a word pronounced and spelled the same way while conveying two apparently divergent meanings. 'The term', Dieter Grimm summarises, 'has two different meanings. In the first sense, the word "constitution" means the condition of a country in relation to its political circumstances. In the second sense, "constitution" means a statute that deals with the task of establishing and executing a political regime. Thus the first meaning refers to an empirical or descriptive term, while the second meaning is a normative or prescriptive one'.[4] Grimm goes on to emphasise his point as follows: 'Every political unit *is* in a constitution.

But not every one *has* a constitution. The term "constitution" encompasses both conditions.'[5] With this, Grimm – probably unconsciously – takes up a phrase of Ernst Bloch, although leaving out its evolutionary punchline. Unlike Bloch's dictum ('I am. But I don't have myself. Therefore we're only just becoming'[6]), Grimm does not interpret the tension between the two variants as a possible impetus for further development of the concept. Instead, the contrast is encoded into the well-known is–ought dichotomy and dropped as a subject of further argument. Without delving deeper into the equivocation's potential inner logic and utilising it to analyse the constitutional concept, a historical narrative unfolds, which focuses almost exclusively on the success story of its normative elements of meaning.

Hence, despite all its other merits, Grimm's story remains insufficient at one crucial point. It ignores any commonality and familiarity between the normatively based order and the order that is, ostensibly, to be merely taken as an empirical phenomenon. Thus, it misjudges the relevance of this connection for the concept as a whole. This connection can best be formulated ex negativo: neither the alleged empiricism of the is-condition nor the normative ought-perspective are comprehensible as the simple thing-in-itself. The former constitutes no ontological data independent from its observer. Just like the prescriptive constitution, its descriptive counterpart – *nomen est omen* – also requires an act of scripture, of writing. Construed as object-related, the 'condition of a country in relation to its political circumstances' is the result of a descriptive process compelled to use a specific medium. The alleged thing-in-itself is a linguistically communicated thing-for-itself, thereby constituting the foundation of social reflection: a society describes itself in its constitution, without that sense of 'self' already preceding the act of description. Society is constituted in the process of describing itself in its constitution. This mediating description unravels the is–ought dichotomy from the inside out, not by reuniting the opposites at a higher level but by revealing the correlating subject to be necessarily split by linguistic practice.[7] With this description, the constitution, even in its supposedly merely descriptive dimension, already takes part in the imperative and normative character of language which compels to use reference, mediation and generalisation, and in its patterns of representation.[8] There is no pure 'natural' order of society that has not already passed through a symbolic order and has been influenced by it.[9]

This applies even more so to the normative understanding of constitution. If the essential evolutionary achievement of the constitutional notion is construed as the self-reflexivity of law established and highlighted in the process,[10] then this ability rests on the constitution's linguistic constitution which subverts the seemingly dual form of the constitutional concept by creating and reproducing it in the first place. The constitution only occupies its status as a medium of social reflection by participating in the originally specular process of language, which not only facilitates but also practises the first fundamental juxtaposition underlying every self-contemplation.

Constitution as text

The historical process of the constitutionalisation of the state also ties in with the equivocation surrounding the concept of constitution as mentioned by Grimm. In said process the normative variant of the constitutional notion is linked to its written codification. From this point of view, only a constitution that has been written down, in other words a constitutional document, constitutes a sufficiently binding foundation for the normatively charged constitution of a country.[11] The contrast of the positions adopted by Hegel and his disciple Eduard Gans is exemplary for the debate about the need for a constitutional document. Within this debate, Hegel takes a rather defensive stand, sidestepping the central question whether the constitution needs to be written down by referring to its descriptive variant. Since he defines a constitution as 'something simply existent in and by itself . . . and so as exalted above the sphere of things that are made',[12] the notion no longer connotes a constitutional document guaranteeing specific rights. As something that is not made, but has come into being in time, it is not the object of any kind of poietology or – in reference to its linguistic construction – poetology. This removes the constitution from the environs of immediate political discussion: it does not form an 'ought'-, but an 'is'-term. Therefore Hegel comes down on the side of description (which, of course, also has a political and in this sense a prescriptive function, even in this context). By contrast, Gans, who took over Hegel's Berlin lectures in philosophy of law, adopts a clear stance in favour of the prescriptive understanding of the term: 'Whether the constitution takes the form of a constitutional monarchy or a republic, there is always a demand for reasonable governing, for active participation of citizens and for an irremovable status of the judiciary. The state needs to be constituted, not organised arbitrarily.'[13] The written specification of the constitutional intentions is to ensure this form of freedom from despotism, together with its aforementioned specific substantive demands.

Under modern circumstances, the question may at first seem to be largely obsolete since, concerning the state, it has been decided predominantly in favour of the written form. States without a complete constitutional document (such as Israel or the United Kingdom) are the blatant exceptions calling for an explanation. However, in view of alleged new forms of the process of constitutionalisation beyond the state, the question has acquired new relevance.[14] Given such processes exist: can they then dispense with the need of a written form, that is with a textual form of the constitution? Or do these changed circumstances mean that the time has come for *textuality* to be stressed once again as a characteristic of the constitution – a textuality which as such might differ from the simple notion of a written document?

The answer to this question is already implied in defining the constitution as a linguistically mediated reflection and representation. This definition emphasises the necessarily poetological dimension present in the analysis of the constitutional concept; an interpretation which, at least in the German language, can also be supported from an etymological point of view.[15] The Grimm brothers' German Dictionary expressly records the link between the activity of constituting (*Verfassen*) and textual practices. In the German original, the relevant passage reads as follows: 'aus der bedeutung "zusammenfassen" entwickelt sich die allgemeinere "herrichten, herstellen", stets mit der nebenbedeutung, dasz daraus ein wohlgeordnetes ganzes entsteht, vergl. das lat. componere. in dieser bedeutung ist das wort heute besonders üblich . . . ganz besonders ist in neuerer zeit die fügung ein buch, eine schrift, ein werk verfassen geläufig: verfassen ist so viel als ab-fassen eine schrifft, concipere, mandare literis'.[16] Accordingly, a *Verfasser* (i.e. author) is an *auctor, scriptor alicujus rei*.[17]

This reference to the genealogical dimension of the constitutional concept not only shows that a Grimm loves company. What is more, it indicates that the notion of the 'constituter' (*Verfasser*) as 'author' has a reflexive structure: the constitutional subject pursuing authoritative postulations is always already split and thus doubled. As a reflexive-specular occurrence allowing for no differentiation between prototype and copy, it presupposes itself. This once again illustrates the extent to which the German *Verfassung*, like its Latin counterpart (which highlights the active aspect of constitution even more explicitly), expresses a fundamentally ambiguous concept. In this sense, 'constitution as text' no longer describes a particular state of language, as it still did in the debate about the 'constitutional document'; rather, it describes precisely this medially structured ambiguity of the constitutional process. Instead of representing just one of many subforms of linguistic practice, text – in this perspective – possesses a singular quality: therewith, linguistic mediation is made explicit. In this context, 'text' serves as a cipher for an act of representation whose referentiality does not denote a secondary phenomenon in contrast to an intrinsically relevant 'original' which is merely referred to. The constitutional document (in German: *Urkunde*) is no *Ur-Kunde*, that is to say, it does not refer to an original message later on expressed in written form. The 'strict mediacy' of the textual occurrence, which appears in the form of the law, does not constitute a form of deviance from the allegedly preferable immediacy. Rather, it marks the finite and therefore only possible manner of understanding the world, constituted exclusively by and in juxtapositions.[18] In contrast to fantasies of immediacy looking for a direct access to the phenomenon without regard for its necessarily medially determined presentation, text interrupts the apparent identity between the speaker/author and the way meaning is construed.[19] Text introduces an element of otherness and difference, which does not allow linguistic mediation to withdraw behind the object of reference; instead, linguistic mediation is emphasised specifically as an occurrence. This specific character is made explicit when dealing with texts: 'the act of reading . . . (this text we write as we are reading) shatters and scatters'.[20] It is only against the background of this first experience of otherness that such a thing as identity can be constituted.

This identifies a first function of textuality in the context of constitutional theory. Constitution as text not only functions as a mean to make the self-commitment of the sovereign (a self-commitment that in itself already constitutes a double-bind-phenomenon, as it can – and even must – be presupposed as a pre-existing social phenomenon on the one hand; and that on the other hand not only imposes boundaries on itself, but is also only constituted in the process of constitutionalisation[21]) more recognisable or to establish it in a more explicit form. Nor is this function of textuality just about the fact that the hierarchical organisation of the law, that is the reflexive permeation of law in the sense that 'norms of a higher rank enable, justify and limit norms of a lower rank', could first be portrayed only by the completely codified constitution.[22] Rather, constitution as text describes the linguistic constitution of the constitution as the unavailable Other necessarily underlying every normative act. It thus constitutes (*verfasst*) a commonwealth not only in the sense of an organizing conclusion, in which the prefix *con-* (as well as the German *ver-*) once more stresses the underlying operation and highlights its abstract character. In fact, *verfassen* can also be understood in the sense of a negation indicated by the prefix *ver-*, which fails at a comprehensive conclusion, because it takes into account the inconceivable dimension of the constitution (*das Unfassbare an der Verfassung*).[23]

In this perspective 'text' does not denote closed totality of meaning, but a 'differential network, a fabric of traces endlessly signifying something else, referring to other differential traces'.[24] This does not only address a horizontal form of innumerable possible connections. The reference to etymology rather shows that the textual character also implies a vertical dimension of the dispersed traces. The constitutional concept has to be understood as a palaeonym, which addresses the treatment of traditional notions as a process of continuous updating and overwriting.[25]

Understanding the constitution can in this sense only be realized as a reading of the constitutional text, which is receptive to the aim of a thorough hermeneutic comprehension, and yet at the same time eludes it by defying its comprehensive character. Jewish legal tradition has captured this form of inextricable entanglement of giving and withdrawing in which the legal text presents itself, the convolution of immanence and transcendence, in the formula: the Torah is 'from heaven, but not in heaven'.[26] Inside of the text, this corresponds to the tension between the text's referentiality and its grammaticality, that is, the tension between its internal claims of consistency and its – according to its intention – singular external reference. These two aspects cannot be pitted against each other, but together constitute the textuality.[27] Thus fantasies of immediacy, for example in the form of a 'secondary orality' as practised by balancing as a specific technique in constitutional law, which aims at an unmediated and therefore just decision of the individual case but at the same time only focuses on the referential aspect of the legal text, are put in their place.[28]

This already broaches the second subject concerning the constitution's textuality. Textuality no longer places the constitution exclusively in the context of a pyramidal structure, but identifies it as a construct imagined in a horizontal network. Rather than advocating the pyramid as a symbol of comprising completion – and thus ultimately as a king's tomb – and rather than postulating the constitutional document as a symbol for of a finite, self-contained unit functioning as a default, text in this context literally emerges as a fabric which continues to weave itself in accordance with established, yet at the same time constantly evolving and varying, patterns, without reference to any central authority: 'Text means fabric; but while this fabric has hitherto always been perceived as a product, as a finished veil, behind which meaning (truth) resides in a more or less concealed fashion, we now stress the generative notion that text is created by an ongoing act of weaving and that it edits itself in the process; lost in this fabric – this texture – the subject dissolves like a spider merging with the constructive secretions of its own web.'[29] Considering the common classification of speech acts as either performative or constative,[30] the textual structure is unique in the sense that it subverts this distinction in a dual movement of opening and closing itself. Paul de Man makes this finding explicit: 'We call *text* any entity that can be considered from such a double perspective: as a generative, open-ended, non-referential grammatical system and as a figural system closed off by a transcendental signification that subverts the grammatical code to which the text owes its existence. . . . A text is defined by the necessity of considering a statement as performative and at the same time constative.'[31]

Put negatively, the task of guaranteeing the unity of law, which has found its emblematically condensed shape in the pyramidal form, thereby becomes precarious. Put positively, however, the fabric thus designed allows for the incorporation of additional threads, that is a stronger connection to the rationale of other fields outside the law or at least outside a particular legal tradition.[32] Instead of locating the task of connecting different fields at a structural and institutional level,[33] the respective function is conceived of as modus operandi typical of the textual practice.[34]

Finally, the constitution as a textual phenomenon holds a third relevance, an aspect of textuality already alluded to in the remarks about the palaeonymic character of the constitution: it elucidates the structure of the constitution in its genealogical dimension. The fact that every constitution is realized as a description tells us, among other things, that each description does not start all over again; rather, it enters a history of previous descriptions. Textuality always implies intertextuality: 'no texts . . . are organic, self-contained unities, created out of the spontaneous, freely willed act of a self-identical subject. . .. every text is constrained by the literary system of which it is part and . . . every text is ultimately dialogical in that it cannot but record the traces of its contentions and doubling of earlier discourses.'[35] The constitutional text, which is constitutive for social order, is itself already constituted: it operates as its own successor and doppelgänger. With reference to a suggestion made by Pierre Legendre, the constitutional text can therefore be understood as a palimpsest in which each current form can only be rendered legible on the basis of earlier texts which may have been diligently scraped off, but which were not completely erased in the process.[36] Aspects such as the secularisation of political events have to be situated in this context, since they do not cause their religious heritage to disappear, but continue to carry it along in the form of a more or less well concealed 'political theology'.[37]

Constitution as promise

The constitution as promise is not a social contract in the sense of classical contractualism in the Western tradition which presupposes self-conscious, autonomous subjects as contractors. The constitution as promise not only subverts this concept by referring to the need for a reflexive split and doubling of the subject. What is more, it also undermines the usual objection to all contractualist constructions that they presuppose a particular form of normativity as the basis of a binding conclusion of the contract. The promise designates a process preceding every explicit linguistic act of commitment. In Werner Hamacher's words, it is not only a performative, which requires an already existing network of conventions to function, but a pre-performative, an occurrence which first enables the performative:[38] an afformative.[39] 'A promise . . . is the legislation of reason itself, a speech act in which language gives itself a law and thus constitutes itself as language in the first place. This act does not have a merely empirical character but is constitutive of every will and every language – a transcendental speech act.'[40] This law-giving is in itself without fundament, unable to refer to another normative authority that could explain its act of giving by way of an explicit justification (*Recht-Fertigung*). Since applying the law means more than responding to a rule in the sense of a trivial cause-reaction-scheme, the promise as law of the law (*Gesetz des Gesetzes*) is at the same time a 'law-without-law', indicating that by 'dictating a non-existent rule as an imperative, the law marks an unlawfulness inherent in the law itself'.[41]

This basic paradox of auto-legislation[42] does not constitute a destructive deconstruction of the concept of law. Rather, it denotes a transcendental figure which raises the issue of what has necessarily already been considered in that context. A promise is the autopoietic-autopoetic act *par excellence*: 'In every promise, the promise makes a promise to itself to be a promise. Only insofar as a promise is an a priori autosynthesis and thus autonomous can it also be the discursive synthesis that binds any given word with a future one, any word with an act, each word and each act with every other.'[43] What is originally and primarily promised in a promise is not merely the result of a performative occurrence made possible and kept stable by pre-existing linguistic conventions. It always already precedes the act of promising. It not only refers to the promise as premise, but also to the premise of the promise, thus introducing into every individual act of promising an unavoidable element of otherness: 'Those who assign a law to their will by making a promise can no longer recognize in this law a self-assigned goal of action; they can only recognize a still heterogeneous demand before which their will must falter.'[44]

Accordingly, a promise (*Versprechen*) contains a *Versagen* in both senses of the German word: as a failure and as a limit. As law of the law, a promise – and therefore also the constitution as promise – cannot be given, but must be presumed to be already given and accepted in the act of giving. In the act of promising, language does not merely promise something: it promises itself to itself and thus performs a movement that precedes every reflexive act of self-identification. A promise constitutes an inaccessibly excessive act of self-positioning not preceded by a previously consolidated self. The constitution as promise promises to be more than merely a constitution. It promises something else than the law. The constitutional promise conveys the otherness of the law.

In this sense, the constitution as promise constitutes not only a 'minimal social contract', that is a contract that the will concludes with itself.[45] Rather, the promise as an act of acknowledging the otherness of the prescribed law is reminiscent of the alternative to the founding myth of the social contract: the law handed over and received on Mount Sinai.[46] The autopoetic autonomy of the promise (*Sich-Versprechen*) refers to a form of heteronomy, yet without being able to assign it to an authority that is, or at least could be, defined as a concrete entity, as something other than the self. Taking the Sinai analogy one step further, it is the anonymity of the God who established the covenant that constitutes the proximity to the promise.[47] Further attempts to specify this faceless Other, by substituting the anonymous reference with something else, like 'objective values', misconstrue the autopo(i)etic character of the promise.

Paradoxes of the constitution

Die Verfassung verspricht (sich). In its act of reflexive auto-legislation, the primary thing to be given is law itself; only this law then makes the act of giving possible. *Sich-Versprechen* thus denotes a quasi-transcendental dimension of the constitution's autopoietic-autopoetic occurrence. Hence the self always already succeeds or – and it is specifically in this uncertainty of direction that the problem lies – always already precedes itself. The transcendental pattern cannot be reduced to a linear relation of dependence. Therefore, the self never reaches the ostensible equilibrium of congruence with itself. This set of problems is expressed in concepts such as Kelsen's basic norm. Here, the transcendental occurrence is not phrased as the postmodern paradox of an impossibility as possibility's precondition;[48] rather, it is phrased – in the tradition of the philosophy of mind – as a positive, but at the same time expressly fictional and therefore paradoxical, postulation.[49] A paraphrase of this process can be found in the figure of the latency of the *pouvoir constituant* in modern constitutional states, which only serves as a signifier for different manifestations of the *pouvoir constitué*.[50] Lastly, the figure of the circular constitution, which contains the criteria for its own legitimation and modification, can be understood in this context. A concept of beginning that excessively surpasses everything that follows and enforces its repetition by virtue of this unsurpassability[51] is substituted by a nexus between beginning and end of a movement. This nexus attempts to compensate for the irritating figure of an occurrence non-identical with itself by overstressing the aspects concerning identity, thus replacing the paradox of the constitution by a tautology.

Notes

1 In the style of Paul de Man's dictum '*Die Sprache verspricht (sich)*'; see Paul de Man, 'Promises (Social Contract)', in: Paul de Man, *Allegories of Reading. Figural Language in Rousseau, Nietzsche, Rilke, and Proust*, New Haven and London 1979, pp. 246ff. (277). De Man then continues: 'to the extent that it is necessarily misleading, language just as necessarily conveys the promise of its own truth'. See also Werner Hamacher, 'Unlesbarkeit', in: *Paul de Man, Allegorien des Lesens*, Frankfurt/M. 1988, esp. pp. 7ff. (21).

2 See Immanuel Kant, *Grundlegung zur Metaphysik der Sitten*, in: *Werke*, ed. Weischedel, vol. IV: *Schriften zur Ethik und Religionsphilosophie*, Darmstadt, 5th edition 1998, pp. 7ff.; Sigmund Freud, *Zur Psychopathologie des Alltaglebens (Über Vergessen, Versprechen, Vergreifen, Aberglaube und Irrtum)*, *Gesammelte Werke*, vol. IV, Frankfurt/M., 8th edition 1983, pp. 61ff.

3 See Sigmund Freud, 'Vorlesungen zur Einführung in die Psychoanalyse', *Gesammelte Werke*, vol. XI, Frankfurt/M., 3rd edition 1961, pp. 25ff.

4 Dieter Grimm, 'Ursprung und Wandel der Verfassung', in: Dieter Grimm, *Die Zukunft der Verfassung II. Auswirkungen von Europäisierung und Globalisierung*, Berlin 2012, pp. 11ff. (11).

5 Grimm, 'Ursprung und Wandel der Verfassung', p. 11.

6 Ernst Bloch, *Spuren*, *Gesamtausgabe* vol. 1, Frankfurt/M. 1969, p. 3 (leading into the book as a sort of motto, with the title *Zuvor*); also Ernst Bloch, *Tübinger Einleitung in die Philosophie*, *Gesamtausgabe* vol. 13, Frankfurt/M. 1977, p. 13.

7 See Pierre Legendre, *Über die Gesellschaft als Text. Grundzüge einer dogmatischen Anthropologie*, Wien/Berlin 2012, pp. 15f.

8 On this normative aspect see Legendre, *Über die Gesellschaft als Text*, pp. 28f.; on imperative character, see Werner Hamacher, '"Lectio": de Mans Imperative', in: Werner Hamacher, *Premises: Essays on Philosophy and Literature fomr Kant to Celan*, Stanford 1996, pp. 181ff. (201): 'Language

is imperative. It is imperative because its referential function gives the directions for possible reference, even if no referential answers to it and even though it corresponds to no referent.'

9 For a somewhat different perspective on the connection between constitution and symbolic order, see Thomas Vesting, 'Ende der Verfassung? Zur Notwendigkeit der Neubewertung der symbolischen Dimension der Verfassung in der Postmoderne', in: Thomas Vesting and Stefan Korioth (eds), *Der Eigenwert des Verfassungsrechts. Was bleibt von der Verfassung nach der Globalisierung?*, Tübingen 2011, pp. 71ff.

10 See e.g. Dieter Grimm, 'Die Verfassung im Prozess der Entstaatlichung', in: Grimm, *Die Zukunft der Verfassung II*, pp. 67ff. (76); the essential idea is developed in Niklas Luhmann, 'Verfassung als evolutionäre Errungenschaft', *Rechtshistorisches Journal* 9 (1990), pp. 176ff.; Niklas Luhmann, 'Politische Verfassungen im Kontext des Gesellschaftssystems', *Der Staat* 12 (1973), pp. 1ff. (Part 1) and pp. 165ff. (Part 2).

11 See Dieter Grimm, 'Der Verfassungsbegriff in historischer Entwicklung', in: Dieter Grimm, *Die Zukunft der Verfassung*, Frankfurt/M., 2nd edition 1994, pp. 101ff. (esp. pp. 126ff.).

12 Georg Wilhelm Friedrich Hegel, *Philosophy of Right*. Translated by T.M. Knox, Oxford 1967, § 273.

13 Eduard Gans, *Naturrecht und Universalrechtsgeschichte. Vorlesungen nach G.W.F. Hegel*. Edited and introduced by Johann Braun, Tübingen 2005, p. 374.

14 See Gunther Teubner, *Constitutional Fragments: Societal Constitutionalism and Globalisation*, Oxford 2012.

15 On the etymology of 'etymology', see Stefan Willer, *Poetik der Etymologie. Texturen sprachlichen Wisens in der Romantik*, Berlin 2003, pp. 1ff.

16 Jacob Grimm and Wilhelm Grimm, *Deutsches Wörterbuch*, entry on *Verfassen* (a rough translation into English could be: 'from the meaning "*zusammenfassen*" (i.e. to summarise or resume) derives the more general meaning "*herrichten, herstellen*" (i.e. to arrange, to produce), always with the secondary meaning that there with is established a well ordered whole, see the Latin *componere*. In this meaning the word is most common nowadays . . . In particular in modern times the connotation of writing a book, a scripture, a work is quite familiar: *verfassen* (to constitute) means to write down something, *concipere, mandare literis*'). See *Etymologisches Wörterbuch* (by Pfeifer), where, with reference to Luther, *verfassen* is explained as 'einen Text entwerfen und niederschreiben' (to draft a text and write it down).

17 Grimm and Grimm, *Deutsches Wörterbuch*, entry on *Verfasser*.

18 On this perspective, cf. Friedrich Hölderlin, *Pindar-Fragmente: Das Höchste*, in: Friedrich Hölderlin, *Sämtliche Werke*. Stuttgart Hölderlin edition, edited by Friedrich Beißner, vol. 5: *Übersetzungen*, Stuttgart 1954, pp. 305ff. (309); see also Thomas Schestag, *Parerga: Friedrich Hölderlin/Carl Schmitt/Franz Kafka/Platon/Friedrich Schleiermacher/Walter Benjamin/Jacques Derrida. Zur literarischen Hermeneutik*, Munich 1991, pp. 15ff.

19 See Roland Barthes, 'Das Lesen schreiben', in: Roland Barthes, *Das Rauschen der Sprache (Kritische Essays IV)*, Frankfurt/M. 2006, pp. 29ff.

20 Barthes, 'Das Lesen schreiben', p. 30.

21 On this dual movement in constitutionalisation, see Grimm, 'Die Verfassung im Prozess der Entstaatlichung', pp. 76f.

22 See Gerd Roellecke, 'Das Paradox der Verfassungsauslegung. Eine Einführung', in: Gerd Roellecke, *Das Paradox der Verfassungsauslegung*, Paderborn 2012, pp. 7ff. (9).

23 On this see Grimm and Grimm, *Deutsches Wörterbuch*.

24 Sarah Kofman, *Derrida lesen*, Wien 1987, p. 156 (an implicit reference to Jacques Derrida, *Überleben*, in: Jacques Derrida, *Gestade*, Wien 1994, pp. 119ff. [130]). A similar approach is adopted from a legal theory standpoint as a distinction from the traditional understanding of a 'book's unit of meaning' by Friedrich Müller and Ralph Christensen, *Juristische Methodik*. Vol. I: *Grundlegung für die Arbeitmethoden der Rechtspraxis*, 10th edition Berlin 2009, pp. 381f.

25 On the relevance of Paleonymy see Jacques Derrida, 'Outwork, Prefacing', in: Jacques Derrida, *Dissemination*, translated by Barbara Johnson, Chicago 1981, pp. 1ff. (3ff.).

26 See e.g. Eliezer Berkowitz, *Not in Heaven: The Nature and Function of Halakha*, New York 1983. Also Daniel Boyarin, *Intertextuality and the Reading of Midrash*, Bloomington and Indianapolis 1994, p. 34: 'Meaning is not in heaven, not in a voice behind the text, but in the house of midrash, in the voices in front of the text.'

27 See de Man, 'Promises'.

28 See Karl-Heinz Ladeur, ' "Finding Our Text . . . ". Der Aufstieg des Abwägungsdenkens als ein Phänomen der "sekundären Oralität" und die Wiedergewinnung der Textualität des Rechts in

der Postmoderne', in: Ino Augsberg and Sophie-Charlotte Lenski (eds), *Die Innenwelt der Außenwelt der Innenwelt des Rechts. Annäherungen zwischen Rechts- und Literaturwissenschaft*, München 2012, pp. 173ff.

29 Roland Barthes, *Die Lust am Text*, Frankfurt/M. 1974, p. 94. In this extended sense, Luhmann's file card system could also be described in its textual idiosyncrasy; in general about this file card system, see also Chapter 15, in this volume.

30 See John L. Austin, *How to Do Things with Words*, Oxford 1976; also, from a legal theory standpoint, see Ralph Christensen and Kent D. Lerch, 'Performanz. Die Kunst, Recht geschehen zu lassen', in: Kent D. Lerch (ed.), *Die Sprache des Rechts*, Vol. 3: *Recht vermitteln. Strukturen, Formen und Medien der Kommunikation im Recht*, Berlin and New York 2005, pp. 55ff.; Ino Augsberg, *Die Lesbarkeit des Rechts. Texttheoretische Lektionen für eine postmoderne juristische Methodologie*, Weilerswist 2009, pp. 55ff.

31 de Man, 'Promises', p. 270.

32 This is further expounded in Augsberg, *Die Lesbarkeit des Rechts*, pp. 143ff.

33 See Niklas Luhmann, *Das Recht der Gesellschaft*, Frankfurt/M. 1993, pp. 470ff.

34 For a corresponding conversion of the perspective from vertical to horizontal rationales, see also Chapter 9, in this volume.

35 Boyarin, *Intertextuality and the Reading of Midrash*, p. 14, in reference to Julia Kristeva's fundamental accomplishments in intertextuality. On the relationship between textuality and intertextuality from a juridical perspective, see also Christensen and Lerch, 'Performanz', pp. 105ff.

36 See Legendre, *Über die Gesellschaft als Text*, p. 47: 'By regarding society as palimpsest, I propose that we venture to undertake what is actually at stake in this framework and do so by tackling the sedimentary consistency of the text, i.e. the deleted substrata of the societal constitution, and by observing the discourse that is currently being written, but on the basis of a negative stance, i.e. by virtue of the impact of the process of deletion itself.'

37 See Clemens Pornschlegel, *Hyperchristen. Brecht, Malraux, Mallarmé, Brinkmann, Deleuze. Studien zur Präsenz religiöser Motive in der literarischen Moderne*, Wien and Berlin 2011, pp. 13ff.

38 See Werner Hamacher, 'The Promise of Interpretation: Remarks on the Hermeneutic Imperative in Kant and Nietzsche', in: Hamacher, *Premises*, pp. 81ff. (97): 'Performative acts defined by conventional rules are not therefore under discussion here: rather, the discussion concerns a fundamental linguistic operation.'

39 See Werner Hamacher, 'Afformative, Strike', 13 *Cardozo Law Review* (1991), pp. 1133, 1139: '*Afformative* is not *aformative*; afformance "is" the event of forming, itself formless, to which all forms and all performative acts remain exposed. (The Latin prefix *ad-* and accordingly *af-*, marks the opening of an act, and of an act of opening, as in the very appropriate example of affor, meaning "addressing", *e.g.* when taking leave). But of course, in affirmative one must also read *aformative*, as determined by *afformative*.'

40 Hamacher, 'The Promise of Interpretation', p. 97, with reference to Kant and the 'hermeneutic imperative'.

41 Hamacher, 'The Promise of Interpretation', p. 90.

42 About this, with reference primarily to Kant, see the essays in Thomas Khurana and Christoph Menke (eds), *Paradoxien der Autonomie. Freiheit und Gesetz I*, Berlin 2011, especially Terry Pinkard, 'Das Paradox der Autonomie: Kants Problem und Hegels Lösung', pp. 25ff.

43 Hamacher, 'The Promise of Interpretation', p. 97.

44 Hamacher, 'The Promise of Interpretation', p. 101.

45 See Hamacher, 'The Promise of Interpretation', p. 97.

46 About these two alternative foundation myths, see Robert Cover, 'Obligation: A Jewish Jurisprudence of the Social Order', in: Martha Minow, Michael Ryan and Austin Sarat (eds), *Narrative, Violence, and the Law: The Essays of Robert Cover*, Ann Arbor 1993, pp. 239ff. About the modern myth of the constitution – in the dual meaning of a *genitivus subjectivus* and *objectivus* – see also Karl-Heinz Ladeur, 'Mythos als Verfassung – Verfassung als Mythos', in: Otto Depenheuer (ed.), *Mythos als Schicksal. Was konstituiert die Verfassung?*, Wiesbaden 2009, pp. 185ff.

47 About the relationship between autonomy and heteronomy in the light of Kant's moral philosophy, see Ino Augsberg, '"The Moral Feeling Within Me". On Kant's Concept of Human Freedom and Dignity as Auto-Heteronomy', in: Dieter Grimm, Christoph Möllers and Alexandra Kemmerer (eds), *Human Dignity in Context*, Oxford 2016 (forthcoming).

48 See Hamacher, 'The Promise of Interpretation', pp. 100f., who in this context refers to Heidegger's concept of being-toward-death.

49 See Hans Kelsen, *Allgemeine Theorie der Normen*, Vienna 1979, pp. 206f.
50 See Dieter Grimm, *Souveränität. Herkunft und Zukunft eines Schlüsselbegriffs*, Berlin 2009, pp. 69ff.
51 About this kind of conception in the context of his thinking about being, see Martin Heidegger, 'Beiträge zur Philosophie (Vom Ereignis)', *Gesamtausgabe* vol. 65, edited by Friedrich-Wilhelm von Herrmann, Frankfurt/M., 2nd edition, 1994, p. 55.

References

Augsberg, Ino. *Die Lesbarkeit des Rechts. Texttheoretische Lektionen für eine postmoderne juristische Methodologie*. Weilerswist: Velbrück Wissenschaft, 2009.

———. '"The Moral Feeling Within Me". On Kant's Concept of Human Freedom and Dignity as Auto-Heteronomy'. In *Human Dignity in Context*, edited by Dieter Grimm, Christoph Möllers, and Alexandra Kemmerer. Oxford: Hart, 2016 (forthcoming).

Austin, John L. *How to Do Things with Words*. Oxford: *Oxford* University Press, 1976.

Barthes, Roland. *Die Lust am Text*. Frankfurt am Main: Suhrkamp, 1974.

———. 'Das Lesen schreiben'. In *Das Rauschen der Sprache (Kritische Essays IV)*, 29–32. Frankfurt am Main: Suhrkamp, 2006.

Berkowitz, Eliezer. *Not in Heaven: The Nature and Function of Halakha*. New York: Ktav Pub Inc, 1983.

Bloch, Ernst. *Spuren*, *Gesamtausgabe* vol. 1. Frankfurt am Main: Suhrkamp, 1969.

———. *Tübinger Einleitung in die Philosophie*, *Gesamtausgabe* vol. 13. Frankfurt am Main: Suhrkamp, 1977.

Boyarin, Daniel. *Intertextuality and the Reading of Midrash*. Bloomington and Indianapolis: Indiana University Press, 1994.

Christensen, Ralph and Kent D. Lerch. 'Performanz. Die Kunst, Recht geschehen zu lassen'. In *Die Sprache des Rechts*. Vol. 3: *Recht vermitteln. Strukturen, Formen und Medien der Kommunikation im Recht*, 55–132. Berlin and New York: Walter de Gruyter, 2005.

Cover, Robert. 'Obligation: A Jewish Jurisprudence of the Social Order'. In *Narrative, Violence, and the Law: The Essays of Robert Cover*, edited by Martha Minow, Michael Ryan and Austin Sarat, 239–49. Ann Arbor: University of Michigan Press, 1993.

de Man, Paul. 'Promises (Social Contract)'. In *Allegories of Reading. Figural Language in Rousseau, Nietzsche, Rilke, and Proust*, 246–77. New Haven and London: Yale University Press, 1979.

Derrida, Jacques. 'Outwork, Prefacing'. In *Dissemination*, translated by Barbara Johnson, 1–66. Chicago: University of Chicago Press, 1981.

Etymologisches Wörterbuch (founded by Pfeifer) (available online at www.dwds.de).

———. *Überleben*. In *Gestade*, 1–65. Wien: Passagen Verlag, 1994.

Freud, Sigmund. 'Vorlesungen zur Einführung in die Psychoanalyse'. In *Gesammelte Werke*. Vol. XI, 313–30. Frankfurt am Main: S. Fischer Verlag, 1961.

———. *Zur Psychopathologie des Alltagslebens (Über Vergessen, Versprechen, Vergreifen, Aberglaube und Irrtum)*. In *Gesammelte Werke*. Vol. IV. Frankfurt am Main: S. Fischer Verlag, 1983.

Gans, Eduard. *Naturrecht und Universalrechtsgeschichte. Vorlesungen nach G.W.F. Hegel*. Edited and introduced by Johann Braun. Tübingen: Mohr-Siebeck, 2005.

Grimm, Dieter. 'Der Verfassungsbegriff in historischer Entwicklung'. In *Die Zukunft der Verfassung*, 101–55. Frankfurt am Main: Suhrkamp, 2nd edition, 1994.

———. *Souveränität. Herkunft und Zukunft eines Schlüsselbegriffs*. Berlin: Berlin University Press, 2009.

———. 'Ursprung und Wandel der Verfassung'. In *Die Zukunft der Verfassung II. Auswirkungen von Europäisierung und Globalisierung*, 11–66. Berlin: Suhrkamp, 2012.

———. 'Die Verfassung im Prozess der Entstaatlichung'. In *Die Zukunft der Verfassung II. Auswirkungen von Europäisierung und Globalisierung*, 67–91. Berlin: Suhrkamp, 2012.

Grimm Jacob, and Wilhelm Grimm. *Deutsches Wörterbuch*. Leipzig: Hirzel, 1854–1954 (available online at www.dwb.uni-trier.de).

Hamacher, Werner. 'Unlesbarkeit'. In *Paul de Man, Allegorien des Lesens*, 7–26. Frankfurt am Main: Suhrkamp, 1988.

———. 'Afformative, Strike'. 13 *Cardozo Law Review* (1991): 1133–57.

———. '"Lectio": de Mans Imperative'. In *Premises: Essays on Philosophy and Literature from Kant to Celan*, 181–221. Stanford: Stanford University Press, 1996.

———. 'The Promise of Interpretation. Remarks on the Hermeneutic Imperative in Kant and Nietzsche'. In *Premises: Essays on Philosophy and Literature from Kant to Celan*, 81–142. Stanford: Stanford University Press, 1996.

Hegel, Georg Friedrich Wilhelm. *Philosophy of Right*. Translated by T.M. Knox. Oxford: Oxford University Press, 1967.

Heidegger, Martin. 'Beiträge zur Philosophie (Vom Ereignis)'. In *Gesamtausgabe*. Vol. 65, edited by Friedrich-Wilhelm von Herrmann. Frankfurt am Main: Vittorio Klostermann, 2nd edition, 1994.

Hölderlin, Friedrich. *Pindar-Fragmente: Das Höchste*. In *Sämtliche Werke*. Vol. 5: *Übersetzungen*, edited by Friedrich Beißner. Stuttgart: Stuttgart Hölderlin Edition, 1954.

Kant, Immanuel. *Grundlegung zur Metaphysik der Sitten*. In *Werke*. Vol. IV: *Schriften zur Ethik und Religionsphilosophie*, edited by Wilhelm Weischedel. Darmstadt: Wissenschaftliche Buchgesellschaft, 1998.

Kelsen, Hans. *Allgemeine Theorie der Normen*. Wien: Manz, 1979.

Khurana, Thomas, and Christoph Menke, eds. *Paradoxien der Autonomie. Freiheit und Gesetz I*. Berlin: August Verlag, 2011.

Kofman, Sarah. *Derrida lesen*. Wien: Passagen, 1987.

Ladeur, Karl-Heinz. 'Mythos als Verfassung – Verfassung als Mythos'. In *Mythos als Schicksal. Was konstituiert die Verfassung?*, edited by Otto Depenheuer, 185–206. Wiesbaden: VS Verlag für Sozialwissenschaften, 2009.

———. '"Finding our text . . . ". Der Aufstieg des Abwägungsdenkens als ein Phänomen der "sekundären Oralität" und die Wiedergewinnung der Textualität des Rechts in der Postmoderne'. In *Die Innenwelt der Außenwelt der Innenwelt des Rechts. Annäherungen zwischen Rechts- und Literaturwissenschaft*, edited by Ino Augsberg and Sophie-Charlotte Lenski, 173–206. München: Wilhelm Fink, 2012.

Legendre, Pierre. *Über die Gesellschaft als Text. Grundzüge einer dogmatischen Anthropologie*. Wien and Berlin: Turia & Kant, 2012.

Luhmann, Niklas. 'Politische Verfassungen im Kontext des Gesellschaftssystems'. *Der Staat* 12 (1973): 1ff. (Part 1) and 165ff. (Part 2).

———. 'Verfassung als evolutionäre Errungenschaft'. *Rechtshistorisches Journal* 9 (1991): 176–220.

———. *Das Recht der Gesellschaft*. Frankfurt am Main: Suhrkamp, 1993.

Müller, Friedrich, and Ralph Christensen. *Juristische Methodik*. Vol. I: *Grundlegung für die Arbeitmethoden der Rechtspraxis*. Berlin: Duncker & Humblot, 2009.

Pinkard, Terry. 'Das Paradox der Autonomie: Kants Problem und Hegels Lösung'. In *Paradoxien der Autonomie. Freiheit und Gesetz I*, edited by Thomas Khurana and Christoph Menke, 25–59. Berlin: August Verlag, 2011.

Pornschlegel, Clemens. *Hyperchristen. Brecht, Malraux, Mallarmé, Brinkmann, Deleuze. Studien zur Präsenz religiöser Motive in der literarischen Moderne*. Wien and Berlin: Turia & Kant, 2011.

Roellecke, Gerd. 'Das Paradox der Verfassungsauslegung. Eine Einführung'. In *Das Paradox der Verfassungsauslegung*, 7–14. Paderborn: Ferdinand Schöningh, 2012.

Schestag, Thomas. *Parerga: Friedrich Hölderlin/Carl Schmitt/Franz Kafka/Platon/Friedrich Schleiermacher/Walter Benjamin/Jacques Derrida. Zur literarischen Hermeneutik*. München: Boer, 1991.

Teubner, Gunther. *Constitutional Fragments: Societal Constitutionalism and Globalisation*. Oxford: Oxford University Press, 2012.

Vesting, Thomas. 'Ende der Verfassung? Zur Notwendigkeit der Neubewertung der symbolischen Dimension der Verfassung in der Postmoderne'. In *Der Eigenwert des Verfassungsrechts. Was bleibt von der Verfassung nach der Globalisierung?*, edited by Thomas Vesting and Stefan Korioth, 71–93. Tübingen: Mohr Siebeck, 2011.

Willer, Stefan. *Poetik der Etymologie. Texturen sprachlichen Wisens in der Romantik*. Berlin: Walter de Gruyter, 2003.

4 On the binding nature of constitutions

Hans-Georg Moeller

The constitution and its binding nature in Kant's philosophical system

In the German-speaking area, the modern notion of constitution has been influenced substantially by Immanuel Kant. Although he actually made no particularly extensive comments about it, the relevant writings can be found in his later works: on the one hand, in his celebrated 1795 essay *On Perpetual Peace* and, on the other, in a handful of paragraphs in his *Metaphysics of Morals*, first published in 1797. In keeping with Kant's philosophical methodology, these two essays and the toolkit of notions used and developed in them should be understood in the framework of his overall system, whose basic tenets he had presented in the Critiques and other writings he had completed during the previous decade.

As Kant puts it himself, his overall philosophical system can be construed as a comprehensive attempt at guiding philosophy to the 'sure path of science'.[1] This undertaking in turn takes place in the history of thought against a background of two closely related processes discussed by Kant himself, i.e. the rise of natural sciences, being achieved by their increasing detachment from philosophy, and the demise, linked to the Protestant Reformation, of the 'dogmatic' religiousness characteristic of the European Middle Ages. Philosophy found itself in a remarkable position between these two parallel processes: on the one hand, it considered itself set free of its purely service role as 'theology's handmaiden' and was prepared to establish itself as 'pure reason', but on the other hand, with regard to its significance as a social force actually endowing knowledge, it was increasingly overtaken by natural sciences. One of Kant's basic purposes was to remedy this 'scandal of philosophy' once and for all, since it seemed 'almost ridiculous, while every other science is continually advancing, that in this [philosophy, HGM], which pretends to be Wisdom incarnate, for whose oracle every one inquires, we should constantly move round the same spot, without gaining a single step'.[2] Accordingly, Kant was concerned to render philosophy scientific, so as to enable it to regain its due place as the most fundamental of all possible forms of knowledge, underlying all the others and, at the same time, showing humanity the way out of the 'self-imposed immaturity'[3] in which it had been making itself at home with an irrational religious attitude for far too long.

For Kant, the way to rehabilitate philosophy as the discipline 'for whose oracle everyone inquires' was primarily one of *method*. In order to regain its status as the most fundamental of all sciences, philosophy had on the one hand so to speak to exorcise its inherited religious spirit and at last stop fantasising about the afterlife and, on the other, learn to speak really scientifically, i.e. in the form of fundamentals, principles and laws that are considered to be necessary and proven and so must be acknowledged as *binding*. Unlike the natural sciences, however, philosophy cannot derive its fundamentals from the field of experience. After all, Kant's transcendental about-turn ultimately consists of his acknowledgement that the laws that metaphysics recognises – more precisely both the ones that concern taking note of nature and the practical ones related to moral laws – are ultimately not 'conditioned' by things or by experiencing phenomena, but precede every experience. That is why metaphysics is the only philosophical science that operates with 'purity', i.e. on the basis only of reason and not of the principles grounded in experience that underlie all other scientifically ascertainable laws – the laws of nature and practical laws that the law ultimately has to determine.

The key question that must be answered by every 'metaphysics capable of appearing as a science' is therefore primarily methodical in nature: 'how is such a science at all possible?'. In concrete terms, that means how it should express itself linguistically or what form its sentences and laws should take. As we know, Kant answered this question by stating that philosophy as a science or metaphysics speaks primarily in the form of *synthetic a priori propositions*: 'this part of metaphysics however is precisely what constitutes its essential end'.[4]

Synthetic *a priori* propositions are axiomatic of philosophy. As they apply *a priori*, it follows by definition that they do not derive from the observation of experience. These are propositions of pure reason that cannot be limited, refuted or proved by any experience. On the contrary, they are certain by virtue of pure reason and as such apodictically or necessarily true. As synthetic sentences, their truth is at the same time not merely 'analytical', in that this is not a mere consistent dissection of expressions that are ultimately only tautologically true. Synthetic sentences actually say something *extra* about a topic, something that is not already included in their concept. These are therefore necessarily accurate judgements that add something extra to our knowledge about what is being judged. In the field of traditional ontology and epistemology, such judgements constitute the actual content of the *Critique of Pure Reason* as reason's judgements of its own structure. This self-awareness on the part of reason is expanded in the *Critique of Pure Reason*, where synthetic *a priori* propositions are also formulated in practical terms, which for Kant means *normatively binding propositions* about the correct or reasonable application of reason in the 'real life' of all rational beings, which in concrete terms means all people, who are considered to be rational.

As a science, practical metaphysics is reason's normative self-regulation. It is how reason recognises what it has to do and how it can play a major role in shaping the life of all rational beings, and so conduct them towards their true purpose: that of a rational form of existence that is conducive to them. This makes practical metaphysics the normative adjunct of the pure metaphysics that refers to the metaphysical foundations of the laws of nature, which it complements by dealing with the foundations of the laws of freedom as the laws of the free exercise of reason. The science that recognizes these laws and gives them a binding formulation is ethics or, to use Kant's terminology, the metaphysics of morals.

Kant's entire philosophical and scientific ethics consists of his insight into a single practically and apodictically binding synthetic *a priori* proposition – into the celebrated and into the 'categorical imperative' that can be formulated in various different forms, which need concern us no further here. The categorical imperative is thus the essential *basic law* of moral science. Every additional scientific and moral judgement must agree with it and may not contradict it. At the same time, it is purely formal and 'is not concerned with what results *from* the conduct, or even what will happen *in* the conduct (its matter), but only with the form and principle from which the conduct follows'.[5] In this respect, the categorical imperative is for the science of morals – and so for moral regulation – what the constitution is for social regulation/legislation and so for the law and politics. With its universal 'binding nature', which is stated to be a 'duty',[6] this imperative underlies the binding nature of all moral judgements and acknowledgements positively suitable to it: to a certain extent, it is the Holy Ghost that saturates the entire moral sphere from the roots up. The binding nature established by the categorical imperative (as by the constitution) thus has a dual meaning: it is binding on the one hand in the sense of a basic tenet that may not be circumvented, so must be *obeyed without exception*, and on the other in the sense of a supreme principle that binds together into a unity everything that corresponds to or agrees with it, and so also – regardless of whether explicitly or implicitly – excludes everything that is declared to be incompatible with it.

In Kant, the categorical imperative has the function of a basic law of scientific ethics. In its turn, the scientific ethics, or metaphysics of morals, prepares the 'metaphysical foundations' of a scientific philosophy of law.[7] Finally, valid conclusions can be drawn from the insight into the original ground of the philosophy of law or into the *law as such*, always to be considered *a priori*, in relation to legal practice as actually encountered or considered in experience and thus formed, as can *rights* themselves. In relation to such reasonable legal knowledge, which is necessary as a foundation for reasonable legislation, certain legal questions and legal concepts can and must now be explained. This also includes the relationship between the law and the state and, in this context, also the concept of the constitution, in the tangible sense of the state constitution.

As mentioned above, this kind of *localisation* of the concept of the state constitution within Kant's overall scientific and philosophical system is crucially important to understanding it. According to Kant, a (state) constitution is the foundation for every 'populations' process of legislation'.[8] It is therefore situated between the philosophy of law, which brings legal principles to expression *a priori*,[9] and *rights* as the actual or 'empirical' legal practice. If a constitution 'derives from the legal concept'[10] and so is 'legitimate',[11] it can thus correspond to the philosophy of law, or not, as the case may be, in which case it would underlie an illegitimate state. Kant tells us that there are many such illegitimate constitutions, while on the other hand there is only 'one completely legitimate constitution':[12] the republican constitution. The republican constitution incorporates the principle of (man's) freedom, the basic tenet of the rule of law and the law of equality (of citizens), while the principle of the republic expressed in the constitution at the same time guarantees the 'segregation of the executive power (of the government) from the legislative'.[13]

In terms of its system architecture, then, the position of the republican constitution turns out to be the only one reasonable, the only one that can enable the 'absolutely legal condition of civic society':[14] the generally binding foundation of a scientific ethics is provided by the irrevocable and incontrovertible categorical imperative. In its turn, the scientific ethics provides the foundation for a scientific philosophy of law, which thus bases the principles of the law on moral principles. Finally, law that derives from legal principles enables a tangible legitimate state to be established, since the 'executive power', or government, working together with a 'legislative power',[15] practises concrete legislative and political processes, so applies the rule of law. In this edifice, the constitution furnishes the floor for the legitimate state that combines politics with judicial practice, on the one hand *underpinning* it and on the other *linking* it to the underlying stories of legal and moral principles. As the 'sole remaining state constitution', the republican constitution ensures that the law 'is self-governing and depends on no particular person',[16] so establishes a self-stabilising structure that stops Kant's moral and legal edifice from collapsing in the long term.

In addition to this internal structure that stops it collapsing, it should also be noted that Kant's moral and legal edifice also has an external protection. It has clearly defining and segregating inner and outer walls that separate it from all irrational brutes or 'savages', as Kant calls them.[17] A state shielded by a constitution has two remedies against these: it can either oblige them to assimilate and, as we might say these days, 'integrate' them, or it can tackle the risk for the state's security constituted by potential enemies of the constitution by aiming at exclusion and driving them out or finding some other way of rendering them harmless. As Kant himself put it: 'Man (or the people) in the pure state of nature takes this security away from me and already harms me by this very condition, since he is next to me, despite not being active (*facto*), yet by virtue of the lawlessness of his condition (*statu injusto*), so that I am always threatened by him, and I can give him notice, either to enter into a legal condition with me, or to remove himself from my vicinity.'[18]

Paradoxes of the constitution

Kant's scientific system is built on reason, necessity and the exclusion of aporias. To this extent, it is inimical to paradox. The principles to be established will brook no inconsistency. This applies in general, so also to the 'only legitimate constitution' that must express 'the binding nature of the constituent power'[19] in accordance with the principle of law. This binding nature, which here has the dual meaning of always being applicable, without exception, and an effectiveness of the kind that generates a sense of community, must avoid all paradoxes. The claim to be free of paradoxes that is related implicitly to the concept of the constitution in Kant, and as a consequence to any constitution that sets out to guarantee the 'legitimate condition of civic society' in the Kantian sense, has certainly proved to be susceptible to deconstruction by external observers.

There are two paradoxes here: the first is when the text of the constitution legitimises a society's entire legal order, although it is itself a part of that same legal order. To that extent, its legitimation is circular. Secondly, the constitution – paradoxically – establishes how it can be amended, so in practice can be circumvented. As a rule, constitutions establish a certain number of binding legal principles or 'core values', which are supposed to apply universally and *a priori*, so have to remain unspecified. Yet when these values are called upon to have an impact in concrete law – which after all is what the constitution is supposed to provide the foundations for – this self-same non-specificity is the reason why the question of how they should be specified often remains open. The paradox of non-specificity is found regularly in the decisions handed down by constitutional courts or supreme courts, since the judges usually disagree about what the constitution demands in practice. Time and again, the result is a majority decision that has more to do with the more or less random choice of the constitutional court judges and their 'subjective' interpretations of the constitution (or their ideological and political convictions, or maybe also their mood that day), than with the constitution's hardly transmittable 'objective' spirit.

Two further paradoxes of constitutions are described by U.K. Preuß. On the one hand, he states, the constitution expresses the 'paradoxical idea of a fundamental, basic or highest law that is even binding on the sovereign'.[20] For example, it may proclaim that all power emanates 'from the people', although in practice it ensures that this power actually derives from itself and not from the people. On the other hand, Preuß points to an 'oft-quoted sentence' of E.-W. Bockenförde, who implies that a state based on the rule of law and founded on a constitution 'lives on precepts that it is often itself incapable of guaranteeing without questioning its own freedom'.[21] Put in another way, the constitution admits freedoms that can also be used for the purpose of rendering the same constitution inoperative, which in turn obliges the constitution to link the freedoms it guarantees fundamentally – and so unconditionally – to conditions that in practice hem them in.

Furthermore, one paradox can be recognised as deriving from the constitution's integrating effect as postulated. As a document that institutes the state or the nation, the constitution binds its legal and political subjects together into a societal unity. As a result, it is geared to include everyone. At the same time, however, as we already saw in Kant, it also draws clear demarcation lines that identify internal and external 'others'. The 'constitution's ground' is necessarily restricted by the constitution itself and thus generates a differentiation between those who are located on that ground and those who are not. As a consequence of binding some together, the constitution at the same time also separates others. Already in Kant, the constitution not only establishes civic society, it also in the process differentiates between essentially reasonable citizens and unreasonable 'not quite citizens', which may be taken to mean 'savages' or people with no property, or women and children, or these days religious fundamentalists or right-wing radicals.

In conclusion, I would like to call attention to yet another paradox, which I find to be particularly notable: I shall call this one a performative paradox. In Kant and thereafter, the constitution implicitly or explicitly expresses principal, inalienable and universal legal principles, which in turn are derived from moral principles. In Kant's terminology, these principles constitute the *transcendental* foundation of the subsequently empirical basic constitution. Unlike in pre-Enlightenment times, human rights are no longer founded on transcendent divine law, but on rational, comprehensible and accessible true principles. Yet in reality, as must be admitted by the impartial external observer, these principles actually exist precisely as little as did the divine laws beforehand. While it is true that the conversion from transcendence to transcendentality secularised the illusion of the existence of absolute, generally valid moral values and legal tenets, it did nothing to make it less of an illusion. The binding nature that is postulated by a constitution evidently does not derive from an effectively complete and rationally achieved accord between all rational human beings about necessarily true principles, but is actually generated 'performatively', since the constitution speaks in the vein of the binding nature. To put it another way: just as at one time we knew what we knew about God because we had read it about him in the religious texts we had written, so we now know what we know about the moral and legal principles laid down in the constitution because we can read about them in the moral and legal texts that we have written. The constitution generates principles performatively, since it constructs communicatively and so makes them real and effective in society. As a result, prior to that communication these principles do not exist or, as the case may be, they remain exactly as unobservable as God or things in themselves were for Kant.

In the eighteenth century, for example in Kant and in the United States of America, the constitution took the form, as I believe U.K. Preuß is very right in saying, of 'a secularised expression of the Protestant belief in the written word'.[22] Kantian and American Protestantism no longer sought the truth in the institutions, but in the texts on which they appeared to depend. Just as Holy Writ was supposed to be the sole authentic formulation of divine truth, so were Kant's philosophical and scientific texts now expected to apply apodictically as 'the Wisdom incarnate, for whose oracle every one inquires', or as the foundations, for example, of 'a future metaphysics of morals' and of an 'indispensable'[23] metaphysics of morals – and practically bear the onus of the 'sole remaining state constitution'. In accordance with this claim, Kant's texts, like today's constitutional texts, establish their own binding nature performatively. Their binding nature is an effect of their mode of speaking, their way of communicating, so is a binding nature that is merely asserted and to a certain extent groundless – or it is one that is empirically non-binding, that can only be made societally binding by being communicated successfully.

Binding nature and functional differentiation

The constitution's binding nature is thus demonstrated to be non-binding or, to put it more precisely, to be based not on the real existence of transcendental principles, but on the success of a performative communication of a binding nature or mode of speaking. In practice, then, what constitutions maintain is, as a rule, simply not correct: for example, all power does not emanate from the people and human dignity is not truly inalienable. And yet, in their favour, it must be admitted that constitutions function well societally, so in concrete terms of law and politics. It is legitimate to ask ourselves why this should be so: why is it then that, despite actually being 'semantically empty', citing Adalbert Podlech, constitutional texts are nevertheless highly prestigious and influential?

One possible answer to this question is that the reason why they function is because they do not occupy the position in society that is attributed to them by Kant's system architecture, and because modern society itself in no way reflects the image of it depicted by Kant's system. The Kantian model of society and its foundation is linear and integrative. An 'enlightened' society, or the political and legal organisation that makes it what it is, i.e. a civic society in a condition of legality, is constructed on the foundation of the scientifically and philosophically recognised metaphysically, politically and juridically binding nature of principles described and prescribed in fundamental texts. The complete societal edifice comprises the superimposition, on a metaphysical, moral and juridical substructure of rational principles and the floor of the 'sole remaining state constitution' that has been installed on it, of a superstructure of 'empirical' political and juridical institutions that provide the state's population with a shared living space, into which it then inserts and combines that population. According to this model, modern society with all its institutions and its environment is both founded on universally valid principles of reason and morals and also integrated by them.

Yet reality looks somewhat different. Kant's Utopia of a scientific investigation of moral principles, which must then necessarily be agreed to by all rational beings, has not come true. There is no scientific or any other form of consensus about such principles and – which is possibly more significant – there is no moral that integrates society as a whole. If we start from the theory of social systems (in the form given to it by Niklas Luhmann), then society's construction is anything but linear and united or supported by any kind of universal principles, but is far more of a complex interaction between functional systems, each of which is related to the others and none of which occupies a central or fundamental place. Rather than a binding moral or rationality, we have a multiplicity of each time systematically different and evolutionarily dynamic moral discourses and system rationalities.

In concrete terms, this means that what is moral or reasonable when observed from a medical, economic, political, religious or legal standpoint, for example, is different and changeable every time, and above all that none of these moralities and rationalities constructed and communicated inside the system can be binding on the others, as there is no common denominator that would enable what is moral and rational in one system to be translated correctly and transferred into another system. The various different normative communications that are generated to be specific to each respective system are neither led by any moral science that precedes them all *a priori*, nor programmed by means of a universal, transcendent logic of reason. In the light of the empirical lack of any such substructure, the complexity of society's morals and reason cannot be reduced or generalised across all systems by any one system.

If we understand constitutional texts as generating a structural coupling between politics and law, then on the one hand we can understand how they can use a feedback mechanism to bestow legal legitimacy on politics and political legitimacy on the law, while on the other hand at the same time seeing that this functions 'autologically', so that this legitimacy is constructed communicatively and not drawn from extra-societal or alien sources, and that this legitimacy therefore cannot be extended to apply to society as a whole. In concrete terms, the constitution cannot tell medicine what it can and cannot describe as healthy, or science what it will determine to be true or false, or the mass media what they should or should not select as informative. The constitution can only observe medicine, science and the mass media respectively in their societal environments and so transcodify their communications legally and politically. For example, it may describe certain medical procedures, such as abortion or euthanasia, as not complying with the constitution, but it can hardly describe them as 'ill'.

On the other hand, it is perfectly possible for science, for example, to observe the constitution scientifically and to transcodify it accordingly, as is taking place in this lecture and constantly throughout this conference. Admittedly, the constitution can observe everything in its environment and communicate it in the characteristic style of its binding nature, but at the same time this also makes it observable by all other societal systems, which can now communicate about it in their turn. As Niklas Luhmann has indicated, all societal communication systems have 'system-specific universalism',[24] i.e. they can communicate whatever they want in a binding manner, but they can only ever do so in their own way and with their own normativity, generated within their own system. Just as medical texts can speak in a medically binding manner, so a constitution can speak in a legally and politically binding manner, but the price of this binding nature is the fact that each of these statements is not binding on other systems. The constitution must leave a medically binding nature to medicine and a philosophically binding nature to philosophy, while medicine and philosophy must do likewise in return. This causes the Kantian vision of binding talk about the constitution itself to end up in a paradox. If the constitution speaks in a binding manner, its binding nature cannot be derived from Kant's constitutional philosophy, but must itself generate it performatively.

The reason why the constitution does not function accordingly is not because of a transcendental foundation – which does not exist in any case – or because of an equally non-existent single moral or single reason spanning the system, but because it produces a 'symbiosis' of politics and law that enables both systems to stabilise reciprocally on a communications basis and construct internal complexity. 'Real' sociologists are better able to describe exactly how that happens than I am. The actual 'binding nature' of the constitution that could make it societally successful – and this I believe I can state in the light of what has been said so far – would be a binding effect that is generated between law and politics.

Notes

1 Immanuel Kant in the Preface to the second edition (1787) of the *Critique of Pure Reason.*
2 Immanuel Kant, *Prolegomena to Any Future Metaphysics that Will be Able to Present Itself as a Science.* Stuttgart: Reclam, 1989. 6.
3 Immanuel Kant, 'An Answer to the Question: What is Enlightenment?' in Immanuel Kant, *Perpetual Peace and Other Essays.* Frankfurt/Main: Fischer, 2008. 25.
4 *Prolegomena*, 25.
5 Immanuel Kant, *Groundwork for the Metaphysic of Morals.* Stuttgart: Reclam, 1991. 61.
6 Kant, *Groundwork*, 94. Emphasis in the original.
7 Immanuel Kant, *The Metaphysics of Morals.* Berlin: de Gruyter, 1968. 205.
8 Immanuel Kant, 'Towards Perpetual Peace', in Immanuel Kant, *Towards Perpetual Peace and Other Writings.* Frankfurt/Main: Fischer, 2008. 160.
9 The 'general principle of law', which underlies everything that is right, states: 'A treatment is right if it enables the free will of each individual to coexist with the freedom of every other individual according to a general law, either directly or according to its maxims.' Kant, *The Metaphysics of Morals*, 230.

10 Kant, 'Towards Perpetual Peace', 161.
11 Kant, *The Metaphysics of Morals*, 340.
12 Kant, 'Towards Perpetual Peace', 163.
13 Kant, 'Towards Perpetual Peace', 159–60.
14 Kant, *The Metaphysics of Morals*, 341.
15 Kant, 'Towards Perpetual Peace', 162.
16 Kant, *The Metaphysics of Morals*, 341.
17 Kant, *The Metaphysics of Morals*, 339.
18 Kant, 'Towards Perpetual Peace', 159, Comment 1.
19 Kant, *The Metaphysics of Morals*, 340.
20 U.K. Preuß, *Verfassung* (Constitution), in Joachim Ritter, Karlfried Gründer and Gottfried Gabriel (eds), *Historisches Wörterbuch der Philosophie*. Vol. 11. Darmstadt: Wissenschaftliche Buchgesellschaft, 2001. 637.
21 Preuß, *Verfassung* (Constitution), 639; E.-W. Bockenförde, 'Das Grundrecht der Gewissensfreiheit', in *Staat, Gesellschaft, Freiheit. Studien zur Staatstheorie und zum Verfassungsrecht*. Frankfurt am Main: Suhrkamp, 1976. 93–111.
22 Preuß, *Verfassung*, 638.
23 Kant, *Groundwork for the Metaphysic of Morals*, 22–3.
24 Niklas Luhmann, *Die Realität der Massenmedien*. Opladen: Westdeutscher Verlag, 1996. 49–52.

References

Bockenförde, Ernst-W. 'Das Grundrecht der Gewissensfreiheit'. In *Staat, Gesellschaft, Freiheit. Studien zur Staatstheorie und zum Verfassungsrecht*, 93–111. Frankfurt am Main: Suhrkamp, 1976.

Kant, Immanuel. *Critique of Pure Reason*. 1787.

———. *The Metaphysics of Morals*. Berlin: de Gruyter, 1968.

———. *Prolegomena to Any Future Metaphysics that Will be Able to Present Itself as a Science*. Stuttgart: Reclam, 1989.

———. *Groundwork for the Metaphysic of Morals*. Stuttgart: Reclam, 1991.

———. 'An Answer to the Question: What is Enlightenment?' In *Perpetual Peace and Other Essays*, 25–33. Frankfurt am Main: Fischer, 2008.

———. 'Towards Perpetual Peace'. In *Towards Perpetual Peace and Other Writings*, 152–204. Frankfurt am Main: Fischer, 2008.

Luhmann, Niklas. *Die Realität der Massenmedien*. Opladen: Westdeutscher Verlag, 1996.

Preuß, Ulrich K. *Verfassung* (Constitution), 639. In 'Das Grundrecht der Gewissensfreiheit', edited by E.-W. Bockenförde in *Staat, Gesellschaft, Freiheit. Studien zur Staatstheorie und zum Verfassungsrecht*, 93–111. Frankfurt am Main: Suhrkamp, 1976.

———. 'Verfassung' (Constitution). In *Historisches Wörterbuch der Philosophie*, edited by Joachim Ritter, Karlfried Gründer and Gottfried Gabriel, vol. 11, 636–43. Darmstadt: Wissenschaftliche Buchgesellschaft, 2001.

5 Constitutionalism and legal pluralism

Alberto Febbrajo

Introductory remarks

This chapter's title suggests a paradoxical connection.[1] If constitution is oriented towards the uniqueness of the legal order, whereas legal pluralism is oriented towards the many possible normative orders that co-exist in the same society, how can the two be combined? How can the idea of the homogeneity of the legal order, embodied by a constitution, be compatible with the pluralist idea that every society admits different binding orders? In other words, in which way can a hierarchically organised normative world be reconciled with the idea of a poliarchy of different sets of norms?

These problems are obviously not only theoretical, but also practical. In many countries, the pragmatic side of law, supported by a state-centred approach, has inspired the image of law disseminated by universities among legal professionals. According to this approach, legal orders are generally perceived as both coherent and complete. When deciding what is right and what is wrong in given situations, a judge needs to find the norm that best suits the case. In this context, the presupposition of a legal order based on a unique constitution becomes essential for avoiding contradictions and arbitrary decisions. State constitutions are regarded not only as the highest point of reference for the legal order, but also as an emergency pool of general criteria used for filling gaps in written regulations.

The image of constitutions that derives from a socio-legal perspective assumes a profoundly different standpoint.[2] When seen from the top of the legal order, the constitution seems to be its unifying element; when seen from its social basis, the constitution shows its external roots and appears to be the outcome of a plurality of cultural elements.[3] Constitutions regulate this complex chain of elements, but are also profoundly conditioned by them. The reassuring architecture of norms, characterised by hierarchical internal relations, is thus rejected in favour of a polycentric representation of the interactions between social and legal factors.[4]

From a socio-legal perspective, the legal order is presented as compatible with other organised social norms. Being provided by a superior complexity, law is able to adapt its *content* to previous social norms, its *structure* to other normative organisations and its *function* to the needs of various social sectors. From this point of view law takes on a 'subsidiary' role. A decision based on legal rules is an *extrema ratio* that provides the ultimate response to conflicts in which no other solution, proposed by different normative orders, seems to be acceptable. The constitution could thus be considered as the bridge that connects legal and social orders in a dual perspective: as the most social element of a positive legal order, as well as the most legal element of society.

This strategic position, at least implicitly recognised to legal orders and to their constitutions, is not always visible and real. We can thus speak of a 'silent' constitution[5] when the presence of a fundamental norm is not declared but just presupposed, or when a new legal order is established by political power without the official proclamation of a new constitution. We can also speak of a 'symbolic' constitution when the formal recognition of the set of general norms, values and principles, collected by a constitution and used to legitimise a legal order, is officially maintained, regardless of the low level of implementation really achieved in legal praxis.[6]

A constitution can be considered a milestone in the internal evolution of a legal order, as well as in the external processes of the legitimation of law. These internal and external orientations, present in every constitution, might be defined as the constitution's 'formal' and 'material' aspects.[7] The task of the formal constitution is to describe how the legal machine has to work according to its 'instruction manual'; the task of the material constitution is to represent a concrete legal order conceived as the result of a continuous process of constitutional adjustment to changing social situations. In short, a formal constitution could be considered an instrument of internal continuity and stability; a material constitution an instrument of external adaptation and innovation.

In order to face the problems raised by a constitution that somewhat paradoxically combines both the problems of the identity of legal order and the problem of its evolution[8] sociology of law has to presuppose a specific sociology of the constitution. The duality of formal and material constitutions does not rule out the possibility of their mutual presuppositions, but implies it. As ideal-typical expressions of a 'conceptual' opposition within a pluralistic context of social and legal norms, stability and innovation appear as two complementary sides of the same sociologically comprehensive concept of the constitution.[9] To have a formal constitution without a material one is no more possible than to eliminate the last carriage from a train. Formal constitutions need the support of the socially-rooted norms that contribute externally to the development of material constitutions, while material constitutions need the support of the legally-rooted norms that contribute internally to interpreting formal constitutions.

These dual aspects combined in every constitution could avoid unilateral interpretations of the constitution and ensure a socio-legal approach based on a circular movement from stabilisation to innovation and vice versa. Constitutions influence, and are influenced by, the work of legal professionals whose internal culture *of* law is mainly oriented to technical knowledge and skills, as well as by the culture *about* law of normal citizens presented as the rulers and at the same time as the ruled in a modern legal order.[10] Social norms can be introduced into a formal constitution not only by open-minded judges but also by innovative legislators; legal norms can be introduced into a material constitution by citizens or other political actors who participate in shaping a new *communis opinio* in relation to constitutionally-relevant issues.[11]

In this context, various combinations of internal and external legal cultures, of social and legal norms, have the potential to instil the flexibility called for by a variety of sociological issues into the concept of the constitution. These may correct models of the constitution

Table 5.1 Internal and external legal cultures

Legal cultures	*Actors*	*Instruments*	*Effects*
Internal legal culture (culture of law)	Legal actors	Transformation from social to legal norms	From innovation to stabilisation (legal selection)
External legal culture (culture about law)	Political actors	From legal to social norms	From stabilisation to innovation (social selection)

presented unilaterally either as shields against unjustified restrictions imposed by arbitrary legislation (freedom 'from'), or as instruments for recognising the area of individual rights (freedom 'of'). Both aspects are equally important for a modern constitution. This flexibility may also offer a solution to a question of particular relevance for sociology of law: how can the constitution be applied not only to the first generation of citizens, who are presumed to share its basic values and norms, but also to an indefinite series of future generations, who feel probably culturally distant from its original positions?[12]

In the following pages, we will briefly present some socio-legal authors who have started out from the common critical attempt to underline the limits of a hierarchical state-centred structure, and have developed the basic elements of a sociology of the constitution based on an interplay between internal and external legal cultures, legal and social norms, stabilising and innovative requirements.

These authors demonstrate that it is impossible to understand the real functioning of a legal order and of its pluralistic context without explicitly or implicitly adopting a certain idea of the constitution. In particular, they share the following presuppositions: (a) that, in order to be combined with a pluralistic approach, the idea of the constitution has to avoid rigid, unilateral interpretations; (b) that these flexible interpretations have to be oriented towards formally stabilising functions as well as towards materially innovative functions; (c) that the combination of these different functions may produce paradoxical consequences.

Further convergences among the authors examined also emerge at the methodological level. They have inserted formal and material aspects of constitutions both in a *structural* process of institutionalisation which, through a bottom-up orientation towards legal norms, shapes the gradual reception of social norms into legal orders, and in a *functional* process of mutual adaptation which, through a horizontal orientation towards other sectors of society, determines the production of effects external to the legal order. These two complementary processes form a sort of 'T junction', whose upright reproduces a self-referential perspective that can be recognised as the basis of formal constitutions, while its horizontal element reproduces a perspective oriented towards external society that can be recognised as the basis of material constitutions. In other words, structural and functional perspectives represent a dual process capable of combining the specificity of the legal order and its pluralistic context.

In the next paragraphs, after having pointed out the fundamental continuity that links classical sociology of law and contemporary sociology of law, attention will be focused on some new forms of 'constitutional pluralism' that, despite evident innovations due to the so-called 'globalisation of law', may justify a constructive reconsideration of the socio-legal legacy with its implicit or explicit paradoxes, and suggest further articulations of the traditional semantic.

Three classical models of pluralism

Starting from a common anti-normativistic and anti-hierarchical approach, three classical sociologists of law have tried to combine different models of *pluralism* and *constitution* with the specific support of society-oriented elements respectively definable as *traditions*, *practices* and *meanings*.

(A) The most radical representative of an anti-hierarchical pluralism based on traditions is Eugen Ehrlich, whose work deserves particular attention here.[13] Ehrlich's pluralism is 'asymmetric', since it gives absolute priority to the material constitutions of social associations over the formal constitution of the state. He stresses that the living law (*lebendes Recht*) produced spontaneously by ethnically homogeneous social associations (*Verbände*), normally linked to a given territory where they have developed their customs and traditions in the course of history, constitutes an autonomous legal order.[14] The living law of associations is culturally closer to their single members than the legal propositions formally imposed by a distant state, perceived as the most extensive 'association of associations'.

Living law can overstep the bounds to which state law is subject and become strong enough to exert a bottom-up influence on the judges and their decisions. This is clearly expressed in the frequently-quoted preface to Ehrlich's most important work, considered the first manifesto of sociology of law, where he states that 'the centre of gravity of legal development lies not in legislation, nor in juristic science, nor in judicial decision, but in society itself'.[15]

On this basis, a socio-legal treatment of law has to take the spontaneous order of social associations and their social constitutions as its primary field of research. The family, as a social aggregation based on autonomous constitutions, is considered by Ehrlich to be the genetic group in every society. Families, and in general social associations, are made up of binding norms rooted in a tried-and-tested past of shared customs. The living law that regulates such associations is defined by unwritten constitutions produced by gradually consolidating customary laws directly inspired by the human species' primary needs.

In this context, only an oversimplification enables living law to be understood as merely the product of the general principle *ex facto oritur jus*.[16] A closer look reveals that living law is the result, not of an 'empirical', but of a hidden 'normative' process. In other words, the 'living' constitution of associations depends on a socially immanent normative principle: that of the selection of the best norm produced through anonymous adjustments. The basic rule of this process obliges social groups to select those norms that have proved historically more 'efficient', i.e. capable, in an 'evolutionist' perspective, of achieving their aims and meeting social needs at the lowest social costs. Norms that pass this test are destined to assert themselves. Otherwise, they will be replaced, spontaneously, by more efficient norms, without any explicit intervention on the part of the legislator but with the possible support of judges in individual cases.

It is this basic principle that shapes the material constitution of every society. Ensuring constant compliance with the criteria of efficiency, it successfully combines the supply and demand of social norms[17] and guarantees a gradual evolution of law.[18] Social rules become 'living' constitutional norms if they are consolidated by efficient normative solutions and traditions. As a result, associations not only *have* constitutions, but *are* constitutions, in the sense that they are born and raised together with their living law.

It should be stressed here that what enabled this to happen was the tolerant attitude adopted by the Austro-Hungarian Empire. Its constitution traditionally left ample room to regulations implemented by the different nationalities that at that time co-existed peacefully in its territory, and in particular in Bucovina, the province of the Empire where Ehrlich lived.[19] According to Ehrlich's example, this explains why the community of property between spouses was the form of property most often chosen by German Austrian peasants, even though it was completely different from the community of property accurately described by the written norms of the Austrian Civil Code. As in many other cases, this enabled Ehrlich to state that 'the regulations in the Civil Code' are not generally applied in the different regions of the Austro-Hungarian Empire, because of the overwhelming presence of a plurality of concurrent living social orders.[20]

The living law complied with spontaneously by a certain population is legally recognised. In order to avoid open conflicts between living and state-oriented normative orders, judges create socially acceptable interpretations of positive law. It is this constant adaptation that renders a material constitution substantially different from the formal constitution. Only in Vienna could the formal constitution be realistically considered 'a unitary legal basis to all independent social associations'; in reality, it remained external to the living law in many regions of the Empire.

Since it is supported by social acceptance, living law is capable of adjusting official legal propositions to their cultural environment. Recognising different levels of normativity, practitioners are interested in interpreting law according to a general theory that takes the reality of living law and actors' successful expectations into consideration,[21] and sociology of law could actually provide a theoretical background and useful indicators for practical operators, as it happens in other fields (e.g. medicine, engineering).

For Ehrlich, the 'facts of the law' (*Tatsachen des Rechts*) are the core of a socially oriented legal theory.[22] From a comparative perspective, they are the legal relations present in every legal order: in addition to usage (*Übung*), considered to be the fundamental fact of the law, they also include domination over other subjects (*Herrschaft*), possession of things (*Besitz*) and declarations of will (*Willenserklärungen*), especially contracts and testaments. On the common basis of these 'facts of the law', Ehrlich tried to open his socio-legal conception up to an ambitious project: to carry out anthropological comparisons in order to contribute to an empirical 'morphology' of the constitutions that support legal life in different cultural contexts.[23]

Although this project was never achieved, the specific character of the principle of efficiency led Ehrlich to focus principally on one social sector: the economy. Adopting the horizontal approach that connects law functionally to other social sectors, Ehrlich states that jurists and economists 'are concerned everywhere with the same social phenomena', and that 'it would be difficult to find a single object that the science of the law is concerned with as much as economics'.[24] Efficiency and close links to the economy explain why 'living' material constitutions of specific associations cannot accept a meta-order, such as that of a natural law, which tends to stabilise constitutions rigidly. This would render their legal order basically untouchable, while it needs variability in order to take the social factors into account that may gain the upper hand in different situations. Consequently Ehrlich focuses his idea of justice on the alternation between individualism and collectivism: both are destined to prevail cyclically in a process that does not lead to the definitive victory of one over the other, but enables humanity to progress 'almost as though it were following the thread of a screw', because 'these two ideas of justice have been drawing the human race upward alternately'.[25]

'Living' constitutions are inserted by Ehrlich into a general process that involves the following elements: (a) customs and traditions are based on historically-established living law; (b) judges are not considered as neutral interpreters of state law, but as intermediaries between state law and living law; (c) the state is not the strongest, but the weakest link in this constitutional process, since every community has its living constitution, in a material more than in a formal sense. This means that every official legal order must necessarily be completed and/or replaced by a plurality of living legal orders independent of the state, and based on social norms.

Ehrlich's sociology of law represents, and here is the reason for its importance in this context, one of the most radical counterparts to Kelsen's normative approach and, more in general, to every hierarchical explanation of the role of constitutions in a modern state. Historical traditions and efficiency are the impersonal factors that substantially condition formal and material constitutions. Law, in its highest form, is for Ehrlich *fusis* more than *nomos*, natural more than artificial regulation; it reflects society in its historically-based order, and refuses the vain attempts to bring about change in societal reality through single decisions.

In particular, Ehrlich constructs his model of the constitution on the basis of the following anthropological presuppositions: (a) that the subject to whom the spontaneous production of social norms is attributed is a collective organism, capable of regulating itself autonomously and impersonally; (b) that the criteria of this production entail a fundamentally utilitarian approach; (c) that the strength of institutionalised customs and their living constitutions prevails over the decisions of any central legislator and its pale constitution, because of the living law's close functional bonds with the economy and with the fundamental, implicit rule of efficiency.[26]

Yet Ehrlich fails to come to grips sufficiently with the fundamental paradox of its socio-legal construction: unity not in spite of plurality, but because of plurality. As a consequence, he makes an insufficient analysis of such questions as: How can a plurality of local constitutions, co-existing in the same state, be co-ordinated? How can a law, that can be traced back to 'living' and not official constitutions, assert itself against deviant behaviours?[27]

(B) Deviance and sanctions, which do not attract sufficient attention from Ehrlich's spontaneous pluralism, are actually the concepts on which the 'statistical' model of constitution elaborated by Theodor Geiger mostly focuses. Geiger tries to counter the normativistic representation of formal law and its constitutions from a behaviouristic point of view, concentrated not on valid norms, but on real practices. Starting from the premises of legal realism, Geiger considers written law to be sociologically irrelevant if not 'effective', that is if it is not protected by institutionalised sanctions in case of infringements. Paraphrasing Ehrlich's celebrated introduction to his *Grundlegung*, Geiger criticises the normative approach from a different perspective and clarifies his pluralist conception of the sources of law: 'Neither the legislator, nor the judge, neither custom nor legal science can be considered, each one in isolation, as the source of validity of legal norms. The source of validity is always the entire dynamically structured system of legal life, in which legal society achieves its characteristic social interdependence.'[28]

In this context, only those norms that are destined to become 'real' by virtue of an apparatus that reacts to disobediences with legal sanctions belong to a sociologically relevant concept of law. Sanctions are thus a useful empirical criterion for defining both the borders and the contents of law. Correspondingly, the lack of reactions to the infringement of some formal norms may demonstrate that these norms are perceived as socially irrelevant or potentially harmful, and therefore sociologically to be ignored.[29]

If a sanction is the only visible indicator of the existence of legal norms, a norm constantly obeyed could be invisible, and thus, paradoxically, of less interest for a sociologist of law than a norm sometimes *not* applied, and for this reason capable of producing visible reactions to its infringements. In 'ideal' societies with neither conflicts nor courts, neither victims nor criminals, law and constitution could thus become superfluous, and their place could easily be taken by morals or universally accepted customs. But in normal societies, sanctions are a selective way of reconstructing, in an evolutionary perspective, the passage from a formal constitution, seen merely as a set of officially-proclaimed language units, to a material constitution, suitable for social actors' expectations and defended by more or less institutionalised reactions to unexpected, deviant behaviours.

The institutionalisation of reactions is important for distinguishing effective law from merely written law and for defining the empirical basis of the material constitution. For Geiger, this process of institutionalisation is linked to a spontaneous social order characterised by three essential aspects: a *social interdependence*, based on the instinctive cohesion produced by the individual's need to survive with the help of others; a *vital interrelation*, in which people identify with other people, assuming that it is possible to interpret and understand (or believe to understand) their attitudes; a *conjectural interrelation*, in which the practical moment of adaptation to the behaviour of others is based on intuitive hypotheses relative to their possible reactions.

These various aspects affect personal interrelations guided by single individuals and by a sort of constant adjustment of the *ego–alter* relationship.[30] An advanced concept of order emerges when social evolution abandons the 'natural' level of interdependence (*Interdependenz*) and enters into the 'artificial' level of co-ordination (*Koordination*) of social behaviours.

This kind of order marks the transition from archaic to civilised societies. It is oriented towards norms provided by institutionalised sanctions and is based on 'predictability'. In this 'artificial' order, the institutionalisation of sanctions passes, according to Geiger, through different phases: a phase that tends to address all the members *MM* of the integrated social group Σ indiscriminately with respect to the sanctions requested; a phase that is characterised by specific sanctions used in defence not only of particular, but also of general interests; finally, a phase characterised by the creation of a specific judicial organ Δ.

This last phase ensures not only that 'the individual can predict with reasonable certainty how others will behave in recurrent typical situations',[31] but also which effective reactions will respond to specific deviant behaviours. The characteristic of legal orders in this phase is that every norm implies a second level, oriented against those who fail to react to infringements of a first-level norm.[32] Therefore Geiger's approach presupposes a higher, material constitution behind this 'second-level norm' that reflects the ways and the limits of the sanctions applied in individual cases.

This additional order records not only what should happen from a formalistic perspective, but, from a material perspective, in what 'percentage' it actually happens. In other words, Geiger does not recognise formal constitutions that, as intended by legal positivism, adopt a rigid 'yes or no' alternative, and distinguishes unequivocally legal from merely social norms. He believes that it is impossible to hold to the idea, dominant in traditional legal science, of a clear-cut functional separation between the norm's enactment and its application, between the legislator and the judge. The legislator Θ can typically produce 'proclamatory' normative propositions, or politically recognise already consolidated subsistent, effective norms.[33] The judicial organ Δ, on the other hand, is decisive for providing certain norms with the stigma of obligation *v*, but is far from having a completely discretionary range. A judge cannot fail to consider the extension of the semantic area of the norms as it is established by jurisprudential practices and linguistic conventions.

This area 'has a maximum and a minimum radius of reference', and in 'the zone delimited by these two radii is located the fluid boundary of the validity of the norm, such as it is legally administered'.[34] The contents of every legal norm, including constitutional norms, will thus be encompassed within this area of oscillation. Geiger holds that it is possible to speak of a 'material' legal error if the judge makes a distorted reconstruction of the concrete circumstances, and of a 'formal' legal error if the judge's attempt to modify the statistically consolidated area of application of a given normative proposition fails to obtain an effective affirmation, i.e. the supportive intervention of a superior organ.

Lawyers operating in their everyday practice constantly notice how difficult it is to find consolidated nuclei in the field of jurisprudence. They tend to dissimulate this truth, emphasising the ideas of unity and coherence generally connected to the legal order and its formal constitution. In Geiger's 'realistic' perspective, the contents of a legal order emerge neither from normative propositions, nor from the conceptual schemes of an 'ideally correct law', but from a sort of material constitution, i.e. from the law that is 'really applied', without asking whether its contents are just or unjust, good or bad.[35]

The basic elements of Geiger's construction are clearly focused on the realistic principle of eliminating 'unreal' elements from the analysis of law, including the legally supposed *ex ante* superiority of formal constitutions. The refusal of traditional premises, such as the homogeneity of jurisprudence and the predominance of formal constitutions, transforms the normative concept of the certainty of law into a 'statistical' concept. Geiger bypasses the limits of the legal order's capacity to produce certainty through the 'rule of law', by introducing a statistical '*calculation of obligation*'.[36] This calculation is based not on logical presuppositions, legislative norms or general principles, but on the simple statistical evaluation of the stability of certain jurisprudential trends in the interpretation of every legal norm, including constitutional norms.

In the case of a new law, about which no jurisprudence has yet been formed, a series of indications about the probability of its future application can be deduced from sociological elements, such as the effective social influence of the beneficiaries of the new norm. In the case of a norm that has been left in abeyance for a long time, the calculation can work on the basis of the functions already fulfilled by the norm in the period of its application. In particular, Geiger speaks about a '*calculation*' made by the judge in attempting to defend his own image against the risk of seeing his decisions corrected by other organs of jurisdiction.[37] This calculation is based on the level of conformity effectively practised by the other judges[38] and on the widespread necessity to avoid unbearable excesses in the everyday production of material constitutions.

According to a vision concentrated on the reality of law, and on the concrete possibility to react to infringements of norms, Geiger's behaviouristic model chooses unequivocally the point of view of material constitutions in order to verify *ex post* the written norms considered compatible with social relations. In this perspective, the function of legal science in advanced societies becomes purely cognitive for Geiger, while his approach points out the transformation of illusory formal constitutions into concrete material constitutions, really defended by institutionalised sanctions.

(C) A 'relativistic', not simply 'realistic', definition of pluralism, capable of considering the different meanings ascribed to historical legal orders and their constitutions in a comparative perspective, can be found in the work of Max Weber. The ambitious scope of Weber's programme clearly emerges in his definition of the concept of law proposed in *Economy and Society*.[39] This definition adopts a subject-oriented perspective, *à la* Ehrlich, when Weber states that law is an 'order' that is valid because it is 'regarded by the actor as in some way obligatory or exemplary for him', and a sanction-oriented perspective, similar to that later adopted by Geiger, when he states that law 'is externally guaranteed by the probability that "coercion" (physical or psychological), to bring about conformity or avenge violation, will be applied by a staff of people holding themselves especially ready for that purpose'.[40] The combination of these two elements (respectively subject-oriented and sanction-oriented), is based on both external and internal legal cultures, innovative and stabilising perspectives, material and formal constitutions.[41]

The context through which legal and social norms, traditional and new meanings can be combined is discussed explicitly by Weber in one of his more complex methodological writings.[42] In this work, he refines his definition of the relations between legal and social norms with recourse to the metaphor of the *game*. Every game, including the game of law, has a constitution whose purpose is, at least implicitly, to define its possible contents and borders. In analysing games, particular attention has to be devoted to different kind of rules: '*regulative*' rules, which attribute the qualities of 'prohibited', 'permitted' or 'obligatory' to certain social behaviours, and '*constitutive*' rules, which have the property of creating new behaviours within the legal game that would otherwise not be conceivable.[43] In the game of law this second type of rules is clearly connected with legal constitution which can be considered a set of rules that gives meaning to the entire legal game.

Not all constitutive rules are concentrated in legal constitutions. They are widespread in private and in public law and, in particular, in the institutions that create previously non-existent roles that would be quite meaningless outside their respective games. Taking as example the card game of *Skat*, traditionally embedded in German culture, Weber underlines that, like the game of law, this game can be considered from multiple vantage points: from the quasi-constitutional perspective of a *Skat* convention, from the quasi-jurisprudential perspective of the interpreters who discuss whether a match has to be considered 'lost' if a player makes a mistake, whether someone has played 'correctly' (i.e. in compliance with the norm), or 'well' (i.e. in compliance with his purposes), or 'morally' (i.e. according to the specific moral of *Skat*, which admits an understanding between two players against the third).[44]

The metaphor of the game[45] has an important consequence: when the constitutive rule of a social game, in particular of a legal game, is broken, the behaviour in question is not 'deviant', as it is when a regulative rule is broken, but merely 'irrelevant'. In these cases, the actor ends up in a position not against the game, but outside it. A further distinction needs to be drawn between the game and its contingent milieu, i.e. between the multiple behaviours that are relevant or not relevant to the game.[46]

Like every social game, the game of law is characterised by a sort of 'constitution', whose main purpose is to preserve the game's identity. The constitution can provide the normative 'presupposition' of all possible behaviours and the criteria for defining the virtual borders of the game. The players' strategies are normally defined by presuming that each other player will make the best use of the rules of the game for his own ends. In this context, the rules of the game contribute to the interpretation of the formal constitution required for understanding how the players had to proceed, and to the empirical recognition of the material constitution designed by the real decisions of the players. As a matter of fact, the interplay between internal and external legal cultures may make the reality of material constitutions quite different from the original abstract principles of formal constitutions.

Relevant to Weber's complex perception of constitution is the close attention he pays to the fundamental distinction between the legal and the sociological point of view. When we speak about 'law', 'legal order' and 'legal proposition', he observes, the legal problem is: 'What is intrinsically valid as law? That is to say: What significance, or in other words what *normative* meaning, ought to be attributed, in correct logic, to a verbal pattern having the form of a legal proposition? But if we take the sociological point of view, we can ask: What *actually* happens in a community owing to the probability that persons participating in the communal activity . . . subjectively consider certain norms as valid and practically act according to them?'[47]

Weber develops this basic distinction through an articulated typology of the different legal cultures. In modern societies, legal cultures are based on two fundamental dimensions, that of 'rationality' and that of 'formality'.[48] In particular, formality, opposed to materiality, entails a more 'technical' perspective, while rationality opposed to irrationality presumes a more 'intersubjective' perspective. This means that law's 'formal' dimension is connected to the criteria of decision-making that are perceived as typically legal, while the 'rational' dimension is connected to the predictions made by those who do not belong to the professional apparatus.

The combination of these internal and external aspects represents a major achievement of legal evolution. A modern legal order may be not only technical but intersubjective, not only closed but open to requests from different sectors of society, not only rigid but flexible. Weber's approach is oriented to a comparative analysis of different cultural models, including the normativistic one, which was widespread in German universities in his day, in order to ensure the level of predictability generally associated with the rule of law. Here lies one important paradox of Weber's concept of constitution: to maintain a pluralistic approach, even if the prevalent formalistic legal culture appears to be strictly connected to the recognition of the centrality of the state.[49] This means that for Weber the self-representation of internal legal culture, mostly connected to formal constitutions, and the legal perceptions of normal actors, mostly connected to material constitutions, belong to different cultural perspectives that can be combined in several ways, especially according to particular interests

Of particular importance are the functional relations provided by a horizontal link between rational-formal law and different social sectors typically oriented towards the need for predictability.[50] These relations are important for better understanding the functional compatibility of the legal order and of its constitution with other social sectors. From this point of view Weber emphasises the advantages of a formal rationality for the market and for the predictability its exchanges require.

For Weber, this variety of functional relations cannot be reconstructed unilaterally. It is basically governed by three principles: the principle of the 'plurality of interests', which underlines that law guarantees not only economic interests, but also interests of a different nature;[51] the principle of the 'relative autonomy' of the economic order vis-à-vis the legal order, which underlines that legal coercion comes up against significant limits when it tries to regulate economic activity, as generally demonstrated by the failure of price-calming measures;[52] the principle of 'reciprocal indifference', which underlines that a legal order can remain unchanged, even when economic relations change radically, and vice versa.[53]

The relations between formal rationality and the capitalist economy, which should be reconstructed referring to the constitutional principle of the 'freedom of contract', can actually be limited in the most advanced Western legal orders and in their constitutions by apparently contrasting perspective.[54] Commercial law, which is strictly formalistic as far as the 'exchange' is concerned, may become non-formalistic in the interests of the will of the parties and of 'good commercial practice', interpreted in the sense of an 'ethical minimum'. Furthermore, it may be driven in an anti-formal direction by all those factors, such as aspirations to material justice, that claim to make legal practice into a tool of equity, rather than a tool for achieving neutral solutions to conflicts of interests.

For Weber, Western legal orders are pluralistic in the sense that they may include areas where different types of rationality are asserted. A law 'can be rational in several different senses, depending on which of several possible courses legal thinking takes toward rationalisation'.[55] In particular, formal rational law is closely linked not only to the management of economic risks, but also to the modern state and its bureaucratic organisation.[56] Bureaucracy should be capable *in abstracto* of combining rapidity and impersonality of decisions, but this does not rule out the possibility *in concreto* of a significant distance between ideal type and reality.[57]

In summary, all the authors examined underline different points of convergence between social and legal rules, material and formal constitutions. Focusing attention respectively on *traditions*, *practices* and *meanings*, they refer in particular to the defence of established customs (Ehrlich), the regular implementation of sanctions (Geiger), and the compatibility of different criteria of rationalisation in legal and social domains (Weber). These perspectives emphasise complementary levels of analysis to describe different aspects of the material constitution: the *asymmetric* level (Ehrlich) concentrates historically on the norms produced by anonymous forces according to specific traditions; the *realistic* level (Geiger) concentrates statistically on the norms applied by individuals and enforced by professionals according to specific practices; the *relativistic* level (Weber) concentrates on the possibility of perceiving social expectations through the specific meanings suggested by the different cultural lenses provided by different ideas and interests.

On each of these levels, classical sociology of law implicitly suggests specific models of constitution, characterised by corresponding ways to connect their formal and material aspects. In general we cannot speak of law without considering, directly or indirectly, that constitutions absorb a number of social norms into a legal order and give them unity; that the distinction between the formal and the material constitution is strictly connected with the distinction between the constitution as it is declared and the constitution as it is socially implemented; that a socio-legal approach has to define the structural differences, and the possible functional complementarities, between the state normative order and the many normative orders co-existing in a given society.

A systemic model of pluralism

Despite using a different terminology, contemporary sociology of law, especially in its most important strand inspired by the general systems theory, demonstrates a fundamental continuity with the models applied by the classics. Niklas Luhmann, without any doubt the most articulate author to adopt this approach, devoted many of his works to an in-depth analysis of legal systems. This analysis was grounded on many of the elements underlined by classical theories in order to reinterpret them in ways better suited to the complexity of the present situation.

Luhmann still considers constitutions to be the result of a double process of structural institutionalisation and of functional connection, but the accent in his work is on the plurality of normative strategies used to defend the internal order from an increasingly complex environment.[58] In this context, the constitution acquires greater visibility within the legal order and is presented as a sort of intersystemic structure that, at the most abstract level, controls the borders of the legal system and its relations with the environment.

Luhmann explicitly emphasises the fundamental paradox that, in order to communicate with the rest of the world, every constitution has to combine such conflicting qualities as rigidity and adaptability, closure and opening, normativity and cognitivity, change and identity.[59] Analysing these apparently opposite aspects from a systemic standpoint, attention focuses on two questions connected with the role of constitutions in modern societies: how can the legal system achieve unity through a constitution? How can the constitution translate external social stimuli into its own borders? Answering these questions, Luhmann concentrates basically on two fundamental features of constitutions: the *self-referentiality* of formal constitutions, and the *intersystemic character* of material constitutions.

(A) According to Luhmann, legal structures are connected with processes of normative experience, generalisation and abstraction.[60] In particular, norms provide: continuity of social actors' expectations, regardless of the fact that they are disappointed in individual cases; generalisation of possible standard 'expectations of expectations';[61] abstraction of their contents that may alternatively refer to concrete persons, roles, programmes and values.[62] Since it is capable of combining all these different aspects, law is represented as an advanced normative structure that, in a pluralistic context, takes on the task of ensuring the 'congruent generalisation of normative behavioural expectations'.[63]

In order to fulfil this task, advanced legal systems produce a *positive* law that is based on contingent decisions. This means that law can be changed at any moment by norms that enable other norms to be created.[64] In an evolutionary perspective, positive law can become self-critical, making decisions that change what was defined by previous decisions. Reproducing a circle like the myth of Sisyphus, the more complex is the system, the more external complexity it can perceive and control, and the more internal complexity it has to produce in response to the overwhelming complexity of its environment. With the introduction of the concept of *autopoietic* law, which claims to exercise internally all the functions required by the essential moments of stabilisation, innovation and selection, Luhmann considers a legal system to be self-sufficient that is capable of facing up to the challenges of the external world, while maintaining its own stability.

In general, any analysis of law's evolution must consider not only the moments of stabilisation and innovation, but also the moment of selection. An excess of possibilities of decision is indeed the crucial premise of every attempt at reducing complexity on the part of the legal system. This moment implies the potential recycling of possibilities of decisions that, for cultural reasons, are not used at a given time (*redundancies*). The constitutionally compatible possibility of decisions, eliminated in a first phase, thus remains available and can be recuperated whenever changing circumstances call for them. This normative heritage is often preserved in the collective memory and can be drawn upon in every democracy, designing different combinations of formal and material constitutions, innovation and stabilisation, identity and change, reduction and extension of complexity.[65]

Revealing in this point a partial proximity to Kelsen's vision, Luhmann depicts law as a 'self-referential' social system capable of using legal decisions to produce other legal decisions. The identity of legal systems is defined by applying a typical binary code: lawful/unlawful, licit/illicit, legal/illegal.[66] The legal system has to observe itself. Without reflexivity and self-referentiality it would be impossible to establish whether and to what extent certain acts, including legislative or judicial decisions, are in- or outside the legal order. A formal constitution should ensure internal consistency at the highest level of the legal order, reducing the range of possible decisions, or producing new possibilities of decisions.

Yet formal constitutions are not able to fulfil this important task on their own. They have to be supported by an instrument – the procedure – that is both inside and outside the legal system. In this strategic position, it can be decisive for creating a set of positive norms adequate to the challenges of a complex environment and for transforming formal into material constitutions.

Being itself a social system, every procedure has a normative structure that selects what is relevant and what is not relevant, what is inside and what is outside the legal system, allowing for stabilised innovations at the level of material constitutions.[67] Through legal procedures, social facts that are legally relevant are selected without causing loss of identity for the legal system. The selective entrance into the legal system of social elements filtered by procedures is important not only to procedural law, in particular to trials, but also to every legally relevant sequence of acts to be concluded by legal decisions.

Since procedures are capable of connecting in a selective way external factors to normative structures for the purpose of producing contingent results, they are, for Luhmann, the functional equivalent of what customs are for Ehrlich, sanctions for Geiger and games for Weber. For Luhmann, in particular, procedures are an instrument for producing not an improbable legitimation of legal decisions, but merely a 'delegitimation of delegitimation', which denies external support to possible resistances against the procedure's outcomes performed by the disappointed parts.[68]

Learning from the outside world is necessary for the legal system. Formal constitutions gradually produce material constitutions better suited to their social environment, and more capable of learning from it. Material constitutions could be attributed with the function of inserting potential cognitive variation into the normative structures stabilised by formal constitutions.[69] In other words, somewhat paradoxically, constitutions have to regulate *normatively* their capacity for learning. In this context legal procedures can significantly augment the law's capacity to evolve in advanced societies, defining how and through which channels normatively selected social elements can be learned.

Criticising old European traditions, Luhmann rules out that such normative criteria of selection can be found within fundamental rights if they are associated with a sort of 'civic religion' indifferent to the costs requested and to the consequences produced in different 'systemic' contexts.[70] The implementation of the constitutional culture of human rights must take the limits of their material implementation's sustainability into account, and has to be compatible, at intersystemic level, with the functioning of the different systems involved. We have to find the bounds – not always clearly perceived because of ideological curtains – of the possibility to translate the constitutional norms into reality, and vice versa.[71]

(B) The selective inclusion of external elements into social systems is so important for Luhmann that he elaborates specific concepts, so as to designate different ways of mapping the borders of the legal system. Constitutions are specifically defined as tools of 'structural coupling' because they connect the legal system to the political system.[72] In this context, constitutions occupy an essential, ambiguous position, and are presented explicitly as the most legal part of the political system and as the most political part of the legal system.

But at the intersystemic level of a structural coupling, constitutions have to be compatible with the functioning of more than just the political and the legal systems.[73] When a payment – i.e. an economic operation – produces an obligation, the legal system selects certain economic behaviours and recognises that they are capable of producing legal effects. This could happen in relation to every communicative connection which, by defining the borders of social systems, also absorbs external complexity through increasing internal complexity.[74]

According to an autopoietic circuit, constitutions combine stabilisation and variation, selecting the possibilities of stabilisation offered by internal legal cultures, the possibilities of variation offered by social rules and the possibilities of self-representation offered by dogmatics (Table 5.2).[75]

Constitutions take the form of instruments of intersystemic interactions that reflexively connect different and apparently contradictory aspects of the social functioning of law. Here lies the basic paradox manifested by constitutions in Luhmann's work, and presupposed by classical sociology of law: the ability to maintain, in every legal system, a fundamental connection between normativity and cognitivity, between conservation and change.[76] As we have seen, this calls both for a duplication of the constitution's functions and the circular connection of its material and formal aspects. Legitimised by society when it comes into force, a formal constitution in its turn legitimises the innovations inspired by society as soon as it is transformed into a material constitution. The flexible borders of material constitutions, which recognise and legitimise aspects of society that are not explicitly regulated by a formal constitution, are perceived as constantly ready to switch on to a normatively-selected cognitivity and/or to a cognitively-selected normativity.

To sum up, for the classics, as well as for the sophisticated systemic approach, the constitution is inserted into a pluralistic context and absorbs the risks of social evolution for the entire legal order. Table 5.3 represents these general visions as characterised by different, in principle complementary, types of social order, connections between legal order and society, models of constitution.

All the authors examined are not referring exclusively to formal constitutions, and are concentrating, at least implicitly, on the material aspects of constitutions. In order to defend norms inherited from the past, determined by the present and directed to the future, these reconstructions of legal and social orders focus on different temporal aspects. In particular for Ehrlich, the material constitution is the fundamental cultural orientation of integrated communities based on reliable traditions oriented to the past; for Geiger, it is a constantly-changing statistical

Table 5.2 Internal autopoietic circuit

	Variation provided by external social rules
Constitutions *select* possibilities of	*Stabilisation* provided by internal legal cultures
	Self-representation provided by dogmatics

Table 5.3 Socio-legal models of pluralism and constitution

Model of pluralism	*Basis of the social order*	*Basis of the legal order*	*Social criteria*	*Model of constitution*
Asymmetric (Ehrlich)	Associations	Custom	Efficiency	Tolerant
Realistic (Geiger)	Calculation of obligations	Sanction	Effectiveness	Statistical
Relativistic (Weber)	Reciprocal orientations	Game	Rationality	Bureaucratic
Systemic (Luhmann)	Generalisation of expectations	Procedure	Reduction of complexity	Explicitly paradoxical

series of behaviours clearly embedded in the present; for Weber, it is a set of criteria of decisions oriented basically to their future effects on the different sectors of advanced societies; for Luhmann, finally, it is connected with the reflexive mechanisms of a normativity that combines three typical moments: a stabilisation oriented to the past, a selection oriented to the present and an innovation oriented to the future.

New forms of constitutional pluralism

Sociology of law has constantly set out to criticise a rigidly state-based model of law, which probably never existed in these terms (*pars destruens*), and to recognise the social norms and external legal cultures relevant to its development (*pars construens*). This programme was maintained combining the more static level of formal constitutions with the changing legal praxis of material constitutions more oriented to innovative interpretations. Under the presupposition of a pluralism internal to the state, in the previous reconstructions, pluralism and the constitution were linked by structural and functional connections. They ensure that the admission of external inputs into legal structures is selectively regulated and that the functional impact of legal structures on different social sectors is generally sustainable.

Now, at a time when increasing numbers of normative orders interfere with the decisions made by individual states and a so-called 'global' framework is producing increasing quantities of legally relevant rules outside the state, new forms of constitutional pluralisms are emerging. Problems, such as the defence of natural resources, the fight against organised crime, the control of financial investments, the protection of individuals, the circulation of data, are de facto inserted in a perspective that is not confined to individual states and to national constitutions.

We have thus to ask whether the critical legacy of socio-legal studies directed against a unilaterally state-oriented law is still of significance. The answer to this question cannot be reduced to a simple yes or no alternative. Since sociology of law is no longer accompanied by the challenging presence of an apparently powerful state, it sometimes seems to approximate to a political party that has been deprived of its regular adversary, so has to redefine its critical targets by passing through an inevitable phase of semantic confusion and possible refoundation.

In this new context, constitutions need a perspective open to a multilevel pluralism not only within the state, but also outside it.[77] Moreover, traditional collectivities, such as families, organised parties and professional associations, which in the past produced social rules recognised by material constitutions of single states, no longer seem to be capable of maintaining their role in the face of competition from national and extra-national movements, with closer relations to new media and more flexible organisations.

This panorama of potentially globalising factors challenges not only the state's constitution, but also the state's most important pillars, which seem to be miles away from their traditional representations: a *sovereignty* frustrated by the intrusive presence of supra-national entities is substantially reduced by these external pressures; a more mobile *demos* is increasingly oriented towards norms produced by the larger horizon of a world society; a *territory* inhabited by multinational interests and organisations is more and more showing that its borders are inadequate for efficient controls without the collaboration of other states.

These elements could prevent even the most convinced supporters of the formula *ubi* state *ibi* constitution from speaking about a truly state-oriented constitution. It may seem to be necessary for the legal order either to absorb external pressures through a large variety of international norms and agreements, or to construct additional storeys over the legal order for supra-state authorities. In other words, in the present situation new constitutions could be produced either by horizontal connections among states, functionally involved in resolving specific problems, or by new forms of vertical institutionalisation, structurally inserted in meta-national hierarchies higher than in the past, on which the state constitution nowadays depends.

In addition a third solution is emerging with particular evidence. This is characterised by a neo-constitutionalism based on communications among new centres of constitutional aggregation. Significant examples of this transnational constitutionalism are: (a) the dialogue between judges of different constitutional courts, in order to create a self-imposed law on the basis of judge-to-judge relations, according to an emerging formal rationality still vaguely perceived beyond a given territory; (b) the increasing attention devoted by many legislators to new definitions of legally relevant concepts, such as that of citizenship or family, according to a material, value-oriented rationality recognised beyond the traditional demos; (c) the pressures exercised on state governments for defining mainly economic regulations according to transnational criteria of purposive rationality beyond national sovereignty.

Also for jurists, the production of new norms (*nomogenesis*) without the umbrella of nation-states and their formal constitutions is becoming a problem. They can no longer find adequate solutions in traditional legal theories and have in particular to admit that territory offers a setting to legal relations that are not limited by national borders, that demos is not a homogeneous entity, but a cluster of heterogeneous concepts of citizenship, and that sovereignty is limited by powerful external factors, especially connected with the economic and financial world. Moreover, given the increasing external influences exercised on constitutions at spatial (*territory*), social (*demos*) and substantial (*sovereignty*) level, transplants of parts of constitutions between different states become an easily admissible routine.[78]

These connections, which respectively overcome the territory, the demos and the sovereignty traditionally attributed to individual states, have important side effects on the role of a Eurocentric legal culture. The pluralistic approach external to the state has the potential to enhance, on the one hand, a more relativistic perspective of European values in a globalised

Table 5.4 Emerging forms of constitutionalism outside the state

Instruments	*Actors*	*Criteria*	*New type of constitution*
Dialogue oriented	Judge	Formal rationality	Constitution beyond territory
Value oriented	Legislator	Material rationality	Constitution beyond demos
Economics oriented	Government	Purposive rationality	Constitution beyond sovereignty

vision and, on the other, a more radical defence of these values, as a reaction against the dangerous threats to which they seem to be exposed in this context. This ambivalent cultural attitude is capable of stimulating the expansion of material constitutions inspired either by an emerging cosmopolitan vocation or by a reinforced sense of cultural identity.[79]

In a global – or transnational – context, the concept of state, which international law still considers to be sufficiently homogeneous, would appear to be profoundly articulated by new sources of stratification and oligarchy. At least four types of state define their positions in the transnational arena, on the basis of their relations with differentiated sources of constitutional principles. In addition to states, oriented towards the construction of material constitutions founded on the basic principles proclaimed in formal constitutions, we can register the presence of *imperialistic* states, which try to interpret their constitutions in order to follow, with varying degrees of success, the strategies of older empires oriented towards expanding outside their borders the area of cultural, economic and political influence;[80] of *emerging* states, which try to use the possibilities offered by their constitutions to compete with the former states, concentrating more on economic expansion,[81] and of *spectator* states, which constantly struggle for survival within the community of states in order to defend the level of autonomy proclaimed by their formal constitutions.[82]

A new constitutionalism for a new pluralism?

Given the diffuse revisions of the traditional concept of 'state', the fundamental socio-legal critique of the state-centred model of constitution may be oriented against a more abstract target. Socio-legal studies have thus to develop the idea of a constitution *also* outside the state, using not only the basic criticisms expressed by classical sociology of law against a state incapable of fulfilling its ambitious promises, but the reflexive strategies suggested by Luhmann's self-referential approach.

A *first* reflexive strategy is offered by the possibility to consider the use of *regulation of regulations*. Constitutions have to regulate not only the regulations of the politico-legal order, but also the mutual regulations of different sectors of society, in a transnational perspective. A more extensive use of this reflexive mechanism is necessary in those situations of crises that are produced by self-reinforcing instabilities of intersystemic borders and by negative feedbacks between different systems. At present, state regulations are far from reaching a level suitable for controlling international crises, and this task can only be approached by processes of trial and error.[83]

A *second* reflexive strategy is suggested by the possibility to consider the use of *communication of communications*. In order to reflect on the sustainable level of opening and closure of autonomous systems a transnational perspective may require a more articulated awareness of the intersystemic communications. This could be provided not only by new strategies of communication articulated with the form of networks, but also by new combinations of cognitive and normative communications, so as to avoid a counterproductive systemic isolation and to explore the adjustments required by increasingly complex intersystemic connections.

A *third* reflexive strategy is finally offered by the possibility to consider the use of *differentiation of differentiations*. This reflexive mechanism is already used by Luhmann to differentiate specific intersystemic mechanisms. Luhmann's recognition of the role played by the constitution as the structural coupling between political and legal systems[84] cannot be considered a *Grenzfall*, a borderline case, but could be applied generally, creating further differentiations between systemic differentiations. The constitution may thus appear to be a form of structural coupling, focusing not only on how legal and political systems overlap, but also on the possible interrelations of law and politics with other systems as economy or religion.[85] Consequently, the attempt to clarify what is *inside* and what is *outside* a politico-legal system at transnational level can open up this system to new differentiations of their relations with the outside world.

From this standpoint the widely accepted and consolidated functionalism of distinctions could be corrected by means of an emerging functionalism of connections.[86] Moreover, even if we consider the constitution merely as an intermediary element between legal and political systems, this does not necessarily mean that the constitution occupies a position midway between both systems. The perfect balance of these systems achieved by means of the constitution is an ideal-typical simplification. In every conceptual – or human – couple, the concrete relations generally leans towards one side or the other. It is thus possible to imagine a constitution that is more politically oriented or more legally oriented.[87]

Without having recourse to the hypothesis of a radical disappearance of the state,[88] these reflexive strategies could clarify the role of the various supra-national factors that are largely independent of the state and of its formal constitution.[89] The reconstruction of the material constitution, studied by sociologists of law at local and national level, is now in progress at a transnational level, where jurists have still to transform 'a hitherto uncodified constitution into a codified one'.[90]

Conclusions

All the possible ways out of the present cultural gap between the level of complexity of the emerging constitutional problems and the level of complexity of available theoretical solutions converge towards the quest for a new semantics. In a society that is acquiring a global perspective and losing sight of the role once played by states, the resulting multi-dimensional pluralism might affect the legal as well as the social role of constitutions, their formal as well their material aspects.

One fundamental question has to be raised here: is it still possible to use the old concept of 'constitution' in this new context? In the present, confused scenario, one thing is sure: that the role played by the concept of the constitution has changed significantly, and that the formula *ubi* state *ibi* constitution tends gradually to be replaced by a radical institutionalism, based on the formula *ubi* institution *ibi* constitution, which explicitly bypasses the state and the centrality of its political dimension.[91] The use of the term 'constitution' has no longer to be restricted in the present context to a fully recognisable formal constitution or its counterpart, a fully-fledged material constitution, but also encompasses still insufficiently defined signals of pluralistic orders, such as the new material constitutions emerging independently from the state at transnational level.[92]

Traditional state constitutions could thus be perceived, especially in Europe, as a portrait gallery of ancestors wearing very elegant ceremonial clothing, reflecting a hierarchically organised legal order. If we really want constitutions to face up to the concrete normative problems of today's social context, they must shed those uniforms and adopt a more fashionable dress. To the extent that the state is no longer recognised as the supreme controller of social relations and turns out to be largely controlled by external factors, the most important step for a better understanding of recent forms of constitutional pluralism would thus be to develop a more differentiated conceptual framework.[93]

For this purpose, some of the distinctions that have been implicitly suggested by sociology of law in different phases of its own history could be useful. In order to differentiate the now widespread pan-constitutionalism, we have, firstly, to distinguish between state-constitutions (SC) and living constitutions (LC), created spontaneously in various sectors of society; between formal living constitutions (fLC), stabilised and institutionalized, and material living constitutions (mLC), constantly adapted by customs and traditions to emerging social needs; between formal state constitutions (fSC), i.e. officially-proclaimed state constitutions, and material state constitutions (mSC), i.e. state constitutions produced by the constant adjustment of formal state constitutions to their social environment. In analogous way it is useful to differentiate the emerging category of transnational-constitutions (TC), connected to the normative orders created by collective actors in areas not restricted by the borders of a single state. As a matter of fact, TC reproduce either formal aspects (fTC), which may be institutionalised by means of international agreements among states, or material aspects (mTC), which may be produced informally, for instance by a constitutional dialogue among international courts. In this context the grey area characterised by cross-cutting relationships between material transnational constitutions (mTC) and formal transnational constitutions (fTC), is still a fragmented source of regulation for private and public legal institutions.[94]

These regulations could be better defined, starting from the anti-hierarchical hypothesis that does not consider constitutions to be the apex of legal orders, the guardians of their borders. In different situations these borders have to be defended according to different strategies against the pressure of social norms and external cultures. Constitutions could thus be seen not so much as an example of bilateral structural coupling, but as genuine *sub-systems* that assume a more explicit learning *and* normative character, and are involved in a constant confrontation with the external world.

This suggests a new paradox: not only that of stabilisation *because of* change, but that of order *because of* disorder. We should not forget that disorder is a contingent category.[95] If we consider that disorder encompasses what is extraneous to the current self-representations of legal sciences and is produced by our inability to find categories for describing and understanding the current situation, the apparent paradox is just the result of the present ambiguity of the concept of the constitution.

While in a state-centric vision of law and society the constitution was pluralist in the sense that it could use the various social norms and legal cultures existing within states' borders as its wheels towards preservation or change, its present pluralist dimension is produced by a larger range of factors outside states' borders. To overcome this new source of disorder sociology of law could introduce, as we have seen, reflexive distinctions in order to achieve a better understanding of the relations between formal and material aspects of constitutions.

In this context the *process* of constitutionalisation multiplies the possible causes of normative disorder by multiplying the criteria of selection of norms. Here the old socio-legal teaching surfaces again that decreed that long-term historical processes are more important for the evolution of law, especially of constitutions, than single events.[96] The main challenge that now faces sociology of law is that it must continue its long fight against the model of a state-centred society,[97] adapting, in a situation explicitly characterised by the reduced role of the state, the traditional anti-hierarchical awareness to new cultural factors such as an emerging transnational pluralism and a prevalently institutions-oriented constitutionalism, both based on a sort of constitution of constitutions.

Notes

1 I wish to thank Denis Galligan, Pedro Rubim Borges Fortes and Aldo Mascareño who have offered comments on this chapter.

2 Neil MacCormick defines the constitution as 'a body of higher-order norms establishing and conditioning governmental powers' (Neil MacCormick, *Questioning Sovereignty: Law, State and Nation in the European Commonwealth*, Oxford: Oxford University Press, 1999, 119). The same author

refers to political power, focusing attention on a plurality of partly independent normative structures capable of interacting with the constitution.

3 The pluralistic problem is often stressed by recent socio-legal studies. See e.g. Anne Griffith, 'Legal Pluralism', in Reza Banakar and Max Travers (eds), *An Introduction to Law and Social Theory*, Oxford: Hart Publishing, 2002, 289–310; John Griffith, 'What is a Legal Pluralism?' *Journal of Legal Pluralism and Unofficial Law* (1986): 1–55; Nico Krisch, *Beyond Constitutionalism: The Pluralistic Structure of Postnational Law*, Oxford: Oxford University Press, 2010; Nico Krisch, 'Who Is Afraid of Radical Pluralism? Legal Order and Political Stability in the Postnational Space', *Ratio Juris* 24 (2011): 386–412; Neil Walker, 'The Idea of Constitutional Pluralism', *Modern Law Review* 65 (2002): 317–59.

4 As a matter of fact, the fundamental source of this circular approach is the ambitious positivistic project, sustained by Comte, to renounce external 'metaphysic' factors or hierarchical perspectives and to exclusively explain society in terms of society. See Alberto Febbrajo, *From Hierarchical to Circular Models in the Sociology of Law: Some Introductory Remarks*, Milano: Giuffrè, 1988, 3–21; Reza Banakar, *Merging Law and Sociology: Beyond the Dichotomies of Socio-Legal Research*, Berlin and Wisconsin: Galda and Wilch, 2003.

5 For an overview of some silent, or 'pre-constitutional', constitutions, see Chris Thornhill, *A Sociology of Constitutions: Constitutions and State Legitimacy in Historical-Sociological Perspective*, Cambridge: Cambridge University Press, 2011. As Joseph de Maistre put it, constitutions have to remain at least partially unwritten. Constitutions with 'neither author nor date' may rely on the deeply-rooted will of the nation and 'must be left behind a dark and impenetrable cloud on pain of overturning the state'. As in music, 'there is something in all governments that is impossible to write' (see Joseph de Maistre, *The Works of Joseph de Maistre*, New York: Schocken Books, 1971, 162).

6 The constitution often provides a legal order with legitimation, regardless of the results actually achieved, as if it were a sort of political manifesto. The fact that the results are often inadequate compared to the objectives set out in the text of the constitution does not exclude that various countries' constitutions continue to be legitimised by the reproduction of their general promises at a political level. On this point, see Marcelo Neves, 'The Symbolic Force of Human Rights', *Philosophy & Social Criticism* XXXIII (2007): 411–44; Marcelo Neves, *A Constitucionalização Simbólica*, 3rd edn. São Paulo: Martins Fontes, 2007.

7 The distinction between a 'formal' constitution and a 'material' constitution has been highlighted starting from a sociologically-oriented approach to constitutional studies. See Costantino Mortati, *La costituzione in senso materiale*, Milano: Giuffrè, 1940.

8 If the common distinction between 'law in the books' and 'law in action' is used as a parallel for the distinction between the formal constitution and the material constitution, some specific features of each distinction may not be grasped. The first distinction is normally drawn between what ought to be real, but for many reasons is not, and what is real; the second distinction is drawn between two empirical aspects of the constitution, oriented towards different social aims, respectively stabilisation and innovation, and supported by different cultural factors.

9 A formal constitution can be considered something like a legal order's official identity card. The original photo taken when the ID card holder was younger has thus to be interpreted. Who is then authorised to proceed to such a recognition: an expert such as a judge, who can probably perceive continuities that are invisible to others? The people, who are supposed to comply with the constitution and legitimise it every day through their social behaviour? A legislator, who has constantly to produce new norms in conformity with the current constitution? A special body as a Constitutional Court that has to draw the line between what is constitutional and what is not? As a matter of fact, different ways of applying constitutional texts according to countless legal cultures and sources of 'legal' meanings can lead to innovative and/or stabilising results. For an overview of the possible role of legal cultures in this context D. Nelken (ed.), *Comparing Legal Cultures*, Dartmouth: Ashgate, 1997. Among contemporary constitutionalists with a particular affinity to this approach, it is worth mentioning Peter Häberle (see *Der kooperative Verfassungsstaat- aus Kultur und als Kultur. Vorstudien zu einer universalen Verfassungslehre*, Berlin: Duncker & Humblot, 2013).

10 In the West's oldest constitution the ambiguous concept '*the People*' is explicitly the abstract 'author' of the text of the constitution and at the same time its real 'recipient'. See A. de Tocqueville, *Democracy in America*, Chicago: University of Chicago Press, 2000. This ambiguity is, as we will see, an important source of constitutional paradoxes.

11 One particularly enlightening example of the ample margin of flexibility allowed by constitutions can be found in the Italian constitution, where the different possible interpretations of the delicate role

played by the President of the Republic smooth the way for a transition from a parliamentary system to a system that tends to be presidential. For an analysis of the material constitution produced in relation to this crucial issue, see Serio Galeotti and Barbara Pezzini, *Il Presidente della Repubblica nella Costituzione italiana*, Torino: UTET, 2003.

12 The question of how and to what extent the freedom of action of future generations can be restricted when it has been awarded to past generations is always a thorny one to solve. Constitutional democracy paradoxically tends on the one hand to limit future generations, on the other to leave them free. It is no coincidence that Tom Ginsburg (*The Endurance of National Constitutions*, Cambridge: Cambridge University Press, 2009, edited with Z. Elkins and J. Melton), working on the basis of a wide-ranging empirical analysis, calculated the average life expectancy of a constitution at 19 years, i.e. about the cycle of a generation. But a constitution can be also an obstacle more than a spring-board, a source of different interpretations and confusion more than of certainty. See Maurizio Fioravanti, 'Costituzione, amministrazione e trasformazioni dello Stato', in Aldo Schiavone (ed.), *Stato e cultura giuridica in Italia dall'Unità alla Repubblica*, Bari: Laterza, 1990.

13 See Eugen Ehrlich, *Fundamental Principles of the Sociology of Law,* with an introduction by Roscoe Pound, New York: Russell & Russell, 1962. The original German work was first published in 1912; the same translation, with an introduction by Klaus Ziegert, was recently republished (New Brunswick: Transaction, 2002).

14 In this sense, Ehrlich can be seen as a forerunner of the pluralism that considers every institution to be a bearer of a homogeneous law of its own, capable of successfully competing with the more abstract law of the state.

15 See Ehrlich, *Fundamental Principles of the Sociology of Law*, XV.

16 This is one of Kelsen's main criticisms about Ehrlich's work. See Hans Kelsen, 'Eine Grundlegung der Rechtssoziologie', *Archiv für Sozialwissenshaft und Sozialpolitik* XXXIX (1915): 839–76.

17 Here Ehrlich's construction refers implicitly to pre-sociological, especially historical, traditions. See R. Treves, *Introducción a la sociología del derecho*, Madrid: Taurus, 1978; A. Febbrajo, 'E. Ehrlich: Dal diritto libero al diritto vivente', *Sociologia del diritto* 3 (1982): 137–59; R. Cotterrell, *The Sociology of Law: An Introduction*, London: Butterworth, 1992.

18 It is not the mere repetition of a given model of behaviour that makes a norm, but the intrinsically normative criterion of efficiency that sociologically justifies this repetition. Kelsen seems not to realise the hidden presence of this normative criterion when he reproves Ehrlich for the logical fallacy of relating facts directly to norms. About the answer of Ehrlich to Kelsen's critiques and the resulting debate, see A. Febbrajo, 'Introduction', in E. Ehrlich, H. Kelsen and M. Weber, *Verso un concetto sociologico di diritto*, Milano: Giuffrè, 2010.

19 Ehrlich observes that 'by creating constitutional and administrative law, the state has created its own law for its own needs', *Fundamental Principles of the Sociology of Law*, 388. On the other side 'the individual, in an association, lives his own life, having his own ends in view', 394.

20 From a sociological point of view, Kelsen's position, that a judge always has to apply the laws of the state, is hardly applicable to sectors like family, which as such are profoundly disconnected from state law. 'No two marriages and no two families will ever be found in which the same order obtains, for the simple reason that in the whole wide world there are no two married couples that are exactly alike, nor two sets of parents and children that are exactly alike' (Ehrlich, *Fundamental Principles of the Sociology of Law*, 392).

21 'It is the tragic fate of juristic science that, though at the present time it is an exclusively practical science of law, it is at the same time the only science of law in existence' (Ehrlich, *Fundamental Principles of the Sociology of Law*, 6).

22 Ehrlich, *Fundamental Principles of the Sociology of Law*, 83ff.

23 See my introduction to the Italian translation of *Grundlegung der Soziologie des Rechts* (Eugen Ehrlich, *I fondamenti della sociologia del diritto*, Milano: Giuffrè, 1976).

24 In other words, 'the jurist and the economist are dealing with different aspects of the same social phenomena'; the former 'with their legal regulation and their legal consequences', the latter 'with their economic significance and scope' (Ehrlich, *Fundamental Principles of the Sociology of Law*, 503–4).

25 Ehrlich, *Fundamental Principles of the Sociology of Law*, 241.

26 It is worth noting that there is a close economic connection in Ehrlich's work between the concept of 'interest' used for interpreting individual behaviours, and the 'autonomy' recognised to collective behaviours.

27 The role played by the concept of 'sanction' is reduced significantly. The focus for Ehrlich is on the (single or collective) actor's voluntary compliance with a normative order capable of ensuring the

convergence of individual and general interests. Therefore, Ehrlich attributes more importance to the 'spontaneous' reactions of the members of an association when they are confronted by a visible disobedience of social rules, than to 'institutionalised' sanctions (Ehrlich, *Fundamental Principles of the Sociology of Law*, 63–4).

28 Theodor Geiger, *Vorstudien zu einer Soziologie des Rechts*, Neuwied: Luchterhand, 1964, 171. See Treves, *Introducción a la sociología del derecho*; A. Febbrajo, *Sociologia del diritto*, Bologna: Il Mulino, second edition, 2013.

29 The fundamental formula *s→g* states that, in a given integrated social group Σ, 'the behaviour g usually occurs in the case of s'. This empirical part of the 'real order' is transformed into a subsistent norm only if it is reinforced by a binding obligation expressed by the stigma (*v*). This means that every actor A 'who becomes involved in s, must face the alternative of either putting the *s→g* into practice, or else of exposing himself to a reaction *r* against a deviant behaviour'. See Geiger, *Vorstudien zu einer Soziologie des Rechts*, 51.

30 Geiger, *Vorstudien zu einer Soziologie des Rechts*, 46.

31 Geiger, *Vorstudien zu einer Soziologie des Rechts*, 48.

32 Geiger, *Vorstudien zu einer Soziologie des Rechts*, 132.

33 Geiger, *Vorstudien zu einer Soziologie des Rechts*, 86.

34 Geiger, *Vorstudien zu einer Soziologie des Rechts*, 262.

35 Geiger's constant concern with avoiding non-empirical elements explains why he rules values and subjective purposes out of the social factors relevant to the evolution of law. See Geiger, *Vorstudien zu einer Soziologie des Rechts*, 105, 313.

36 Geiger, *Vorstudien zu einer Soziologie des Rechts*, 277.

37 Geiger, *Vorstudien zu einer Soziologie des Rechts*, 157.

38 For Geiger, the concept of 'imitation' (*mimesis*) is essential.

39 See in particular the collection of various sections of Max Weber, *Wirtschaft und Gesellschaft* edited by Max Rheinstein, *Max Weber on Law in Economy and Society*, Cambridge, MA: Harvard University Press, 1954.

40 Weber, *Max Weber on Law in Economy and Society*, 5.

41 One point worth mentioning in this context is that the same dual function, of stabilisation and change, is for Weber exercised by natural law in constitutional history (see *Max Weber on Law in Economy and Society*, 284ff.)

42 Max Weber, 'R. Stammler's "Overcoming" of the Materialist Conception of History', in Hans H. Bruun and Sam Whimster (eds), *Collected Methodological Writings*, London and New York: Routledge, 2012, 185–226.

43 Weber, *Collected Methodological Writings*, 203ff. On the 'constitutive rules', John Rawls, 'Two Concepts of Rules', *The Philosophical Review* LXIV (1955): 3–32; John R. Searle, 'How to Derive "Ought" from "Is" ', *The Philosophical Review* LXXIII (1964): 43–58.

44 Weber, *Collected Methodological Writings*, 212ff.

45 See Johan Huizinga, *Homo Ludens: A Study of the Play-Element in Culture*, London: Routledge & Kegan Paul, 1949; from a different perspective Douglas G. Baird, Robert H. Gertner and Randal C. Picker, *Game Theory and the Law*, Cambridge, MA: Harvard University Press, 1998.

46 Weber, *Collected Methodological Writings*, 214ff.

47 Weber, *Max Weber on Law in Economy and Society*, 11.

48 Weber, *Max Weber on Law in Economy and Society*, 224.

49 About this apparent contradiction, recently A. Febbrajo, 'Dall'unità alla pluralità del diritto', in *Ripensare Max Weber nel centocinquantesimo dalla nascita, Atti dei convegni Lincei*, Rome: Scienze e Lettere, 2015, 171–92.

50 See Reinhard Bendix, *Max Weber: An Intellectual Portrait*, Berkeley: University of California Press, 1977.

51 Weber, *Max Weber on Law in Economy and Society*, 35.

52 Weber, *Max Weber on Law in Economy and Society*, 35–6.

53 Weber, *Max Weber on Law in Economy and Society*, 36.

54 Weber, *Max Weber on Law in Economy and Society*, 125.

55 Weber, *Max Weber on Law in Economy and Society*, 60.

56 Weber, *Max Weber on Law in Economy and Society*, 334.

57 Weber, *Max Weber on Law in Economy and Society*, 336.

58 It should be noted here that Luhmann's sociology of law did not maintain a unique framework, but gradually enriched its contents by importing concepts from a variety of fields, such as cybernetics,

biology, cognitive and communicative sciences. For a recent presentation of the basic elements of Luhmann's theory see Michael King, 'The Radical Sociology of Niklas Luhmann', in Reza Banakar and Max Travers (eds), *Law and Social Theory*, second edition, Oxford: Hart, 2013.

59 As a matter of fact, the concept of identity is hardly compatible with continuous processes of evolution in every social system. The borders of legal systems are constantly under pressure because social rules could become so powerful as to impose on constitutions adapting strategies for balancing the increasing levels of complexity of the outside world. Niklas Luhmann, *A Sociological Theory of Law*, London: Routledge, 1985, 370.

60 Niklas Luhmann, *A Sociological Theory of Law*, 40.

61 Luhmann, *A Sociological Theory of Law*, 49.

62 Luhmann, *A Sociological Theory of Law*, 66.

63 Luhmann, *A Sociological Theory of Law*, 82.

64 Luhmann, *A Sociological Theory of Law*, 159ff. In advanced societies time has a different relevance because the newer legal norm prevails over the older one, and not vice versa.

65 In practice, Luhmann holds that, in a democratic system, the same mechanism applies to the legislator, who does not eliminate discarded possibilities, but leaves them at the disposal of future decision-makers. No continuous progress can be thus found in the legal order and its constitution, but only a greater ability to choose, from time to time, whatever solutions are structurally and functionally most suitable. On this point Jean Clam, 'What is Modern Power?', in M. King and C. Thornhill (eds), *Luhmann on Law and Politics: Critical Appraisals and Applications*, Oxford: Hart, 2006.

66 This issue is touched upon in several places of Luhmann's work. See in particular Niklas Luhmann, 'The Coding of the Legal System', in G. Teubner and A. Febbrajo (eds), *State, Law and Economy as Autopoietic Systems: Regulation and Autonomy in a New Perspective*, Milano: Giuffré, 1992, 145–86.

67 The second-order level of observation is easily reached here. In this case, for Luhmann, 'we observe how the system observes and how it, in so doing, operationalises the distinction between self-reference and external reference'. See N. Luhmann, *Law as a Social System*, Oxford: Oxford University Press, 2004, 106.

68 See N Luhmann, *Legitimation durch Verfahren*, Frankfurt a.M.: Suhrkamp, 2001.

69 See N. Luhmann, *Rechtssystem und Rechtsdogmatik*, Stuttgart: Kohlhammer, 1982.

70 See N. Luhmann, 'Grundwerte als Zivilreligion', *Archivio di Filosofia* 46 (1978): 51–71.

71 See Luhmann, *Legitimation durch Verfahren*.

72 For the concept of structural coupling see, in this context, N. Luhmann, 'Operational Closure and Structural Coupling: The Differentiation of the Legal System', *Cardozo Law Review* 13 (1992): 1419–41; N. Luhmann, *Law as a Social System*, Oxford: Oxford University Press, 2004, 440ff.

73 Through the concept of structural coupling Luhmann no longer adopts the logic of the isolated system which reproduce itself through a sort of parthenogenesis. In case of a collaboration of two or more systems, each system can refer to the other in a circular manner.

74 This evolutive approach can be found in Luhmann's first socio-legal writings. Law is here inserted in a process whose aim is to tackle the world's complexity and contingency, increasing at the same time the internal and external complexity of the legal system. See Niklas Luhmann, 'Normen in soziologischer Perspektive', *Soziale Welt* XX (1969): 28–48.

75 Luhmann, *Law as a Social System*, 25. In this and other cases, for Luhmann 'the conditions for evolution' produce further social evolution, because every change of social structures creates the conditions for new legal and social change (*Law as a Social System*, 243).

76 In relation to the paradoxical connection 'conservation because change', Luhmann, on several occasions, observes that a true conservative strategy must be open to change, because it is only by changing that it is possible to conserve. Change can defend stability, and produce constant adjustments. This is required by the endless expansion of the complexity of the environment, which is destined to increase as a consequence of the increase in the complexity of the systems. The source of this self-reproductive approach is for Luhmann W.R. Ashby, 'Principles of the Self-Organizing System', in Heinz von Foerster and Georg W. Zopf (eds), *Principles of Self-Organization*, New York: Pergamon Press, 1962.

77 Analyses of the new constitutionalism beyond the state are highly differentiated. See Joseph Weiler, *The Constitution of Europe: Do the New Clothes have an Emperor?*, Cambridge: Cambridge University Press; 1998; Mattias Kumm, 'Who is the Final Arbiter of Constitutionality in Europe? Three Conceptions of the Relationship Between the German Federal Constitutional Court and the European Court of Justice', *Common Market Law Review* 36 (1999): 351–86; Neil Walker, 'The Idea of Constitutional Pluralism', *Modern Law Review* 65 (2002): 317–59; Neil Walker, 'Post-Constituent Constitutionalism? The Case of the European Union', in Martin Laughlin and Neil Walker (eds),

The Paradox of Constitutionalism: Constituent Power and Constitutional Form, Oxford: Oxford University Press, 2007, 247–67; Joseph Weiler and Marlene Wind (eds), *European Constitutionalism Beyond the State*, Cambridge: Cambridge University Press, 2003; Sousa Santos de Boaventura and César Rodriguez-Garavito, *Law and Globalization from Below: Towards a Cosmopolitan Legality*, Cambridge: Cambridge University Press, 2005; Dieter Grimm, *Die Zukunft der Verfassung* II, Berlin: Suhrkamp, 2012. The process of harmonisation required by these transitional problems suggests sometimes musical analogy. See Miguel P. Maduro, 'Contrapunctual Law: Europe's Constitutional Pluralism in Action', in Neil Walker (ed.), *Sovereignty in Transition*, Oxford: Hart Publishing, 2003, 501–37; Jan Winczoreck, 'Making Law Together? On Some Intersystemic Conditions of Judicial Cooperation', in A. Febbrajo and G. Harste (eds), *Law and Intersystemic Communication, Understanding 'Structural Coupling'*, Aldershot: Ashgate, 2013, 229–54.

78 See Alan Watson, *Legal Transplants: An Approach to Comparative Law*, second edition, University of Georgia Press, 1993. For this author, the strategy of transplant is more widespread than admitted for the upper hand of legal professionals in constitutional processes and the reduced possibility of a real participation of the population. Starting from a different point of view it is possible to underline that 'cross-cultural transplantation of constitutional provisions is always dangerous, as an unreflected generalization from experience in a single culture is always likely to be wrong' (see Michel Rosenfeld, 'Modern Constitutionalism as Interplay between Identity and Diversity', in Michel Rosenfeld (ed.), *Constitutionalism, Identity, Difference and Legitimacy: Theoretical Perspectives*, Durham, NC: Duke University Press, 1994, 35). These different evaluations are clearly grounded on the different aspects of the constitution they take into consideration: the first seems concentrated on the formal, the second on the material constitution. An interesting debate in D. Nelken and J. Feest (eds), *Adapting Legal Cultures*, Oxford: Hart, 2001, with contributions of P. Legrand, 'What "Legal Transplants"?', R. Cotterrell, 'Is There a Logic of Legal Transplants', L. Friedman, 'Some Comments on Cotterrell and Legal Transplants'.

79 For this second approach see Weiler, *The Constitution of Europe*.

80 Russia can easily be identified with this type of state, being more aware than other comparable states not only of its global role, but also of its past at the head of an empire. The lack of historical experience affect the apparently parallel role of the United States.

81 With the exception of Russia, this seems to be the case of the countries normally identified as the BRICS, which are now developing a global role. Also the nuclear weapons divide is relevant in this context, even if not always decisive.

82 The limited size of some states, or institutionalised territorial divisions, could be a precondition for playing this role, with at least one significant exception: the Vatican City, which can exercise a much stronger cultural, and in some circumstances even political, influence than that of a normal spectator.

83 See P.F. Kjaer, G. Teubner and A. Febbrajo (eds), *The Financial Crisis in Constitutional Perspective: The Dark Side of Functional Differentiation*, Oxford: Hart, 2011.

84 On the large field of possible applications of this concept, see A. Febbrajo and G. Harste (eds), *Law and Intersystemic Communication, Understanding 'Structural Coupling'*, Aldershot: Ashgate, 2013.

85 Among the classical authors, Weber is the most committed to developing a potentially intersystemic, historically-based, perspective. See Max Weber, *The Protestant Ethic and the Spirit of Capitalism*, London and Boston: Unwin Hyman, 1930.

86 See A. Febbrajo, 'Introduction', in A. Febbrajo and G. Harste (eds), *Law and Intersystemic Communication, Understanding 'Structural Coupling'*, Aldershot: Ashgate, 2013.

87 Europe and Latin America are two good examples. In Latin America the use of constitutions seems to be more flexible. Constitutions appear more oriented towards material effectiveness than towards formal stability. They are thus less able to absorb delusions and every government is considered directly responsible for fulfilling or not fulfilling constitutionally relevant expectations. The idea of order has thus to be combined, somewhat paradoxically, with the idea of progress, as announced by the Brazilian flag which, starting from positivistic presuppositions, suggests a continuous production of *ordem e progresso*. This means that the concept of order is not static, but every order has to be transformed into a new, more complex order, with the potential for being adequate to the complexity of the environment. In this context, the level of popular tolerance for political delusions seems to be much lower than in Europe, where constitutional continuity is considered a positive factor because it assures both more certainty to the legal order and more independence to the political system.

88 Like a solar eclipse, the twilight of state law is more visible from some parts of the world than from others. It is at present particularly visible from Europe, where the EU is a political reality and the

multi-dimensional government imposed by the EU shows up significant limitations of the sovereignty of the single states.

89 The profound structural and functional transformation of the state and its politics represents one of the dominant themes in recent literature. See in this context, G. Teubner (ed.), *Global Law without a State*, Aldershot: Ashgate, 1997.

90 This could happen 'in a piecemeal and ad hoc way', without 'any degree of consensus as to what the final resting place should be'. See Vernon Bogdanor, 'The Conflict between Government and the Judges' (Working paper of the Foundation for Law, Justice and Society, Centre for Socio-legal Studies, Oxford, 2).

91 Institutionalism, seen as the attribution to every spontaneous social organisation of the ability to produce law as an alternative to, or as a replacement for, what the state actually decides, represents the strongest element of continuity linking Ehrlich's sociology of law to the critiques expressed today with regard to the centrality of the state in a global society. Among the old interpretations of institutionalism that straddle the borderline between legal and sociological sciences, see Santi Romano, *Lo Stato moderno e la sua crisi*, Milano: Giuffrè, 1910; Santi Romano, *L'ordinamento giuridico*, Firenze: Sansoni, 1918. For an articulated reformulation of institutionalism, see Neil MacCormick and Ota Weinberger, *An Institutional Theory of Law: New Approaches to Legal Positivism*, Dordrecht: D. Reidel, 1986.

92 I use the term 'transnational' very generally here. For an attempt to discover the connections between constitution and society in the current situation by means of a neo-institutional approach, see David Sciulli, *Theory of Societal Constitutionalism: Foundations of a Non-Marxist Critical Sociology*, Cambridge: Cambridge University Press, 1992; Gunther Teubner, *Constitutional Fragments: Societal Constitutionalism and Globalization*, Oxford: Oxford University Press, 2012.

93 At present, models of constitutions are concentrated not so much on structural restrictions of political power as on functionally acceptable, normative orders rendered even more pluralistic by the eclipse of a strong state. According to a 'back to the future' perspective, the concept of community, which was central for Ehrlich and for the birth of sociology of law, is now considered to offer a potential benchmark for a *new* pluralistic approach. See Roger Cotterrell, 'Transnational Communities and the Concept of Law', *Ratio Juris* 21 (2008): 1–18.

94 See A. Febbrajo and F. Gambino (eds), *Il diritto frammentato*, Milano: Giuffrè, 2014.

95 A reference to the important contributions by Edgar Morin concerning the theory of disorder is obligatory here. In fact, if disorder is construed as the inability to find a rule capable of explaining and forecasting (Wittgenstein), this latter paradox appears to be the contingent product of a defect of cognitive *and* normative complexity in the current models of constitution. See Mireille Delmas-Marty, *Ordering Pluralism: A Conceptual Framework for Understanding the Transnational Legal World*, Oxford: Hart, 2009.

96 In fact, there is still a widespread tendency of internal legal culture to overestimate the importance of formal decisions compared to gradual and less visible processes, not only because of the persistent influence of the role attributed to decisions by normativism, but also because of the general weakening of the relations between sociology and history. One largely documented critique of the normative approach from a socio-legal standpoint can be found in Bruno Leoni, *Freedom and the Law*, expanded third edition, Indianapolis: Liberty Fund, 1991.

97 In this context, there is scope for further developing Ehrlich's critique against a state-centred vision of law. It is no coincidence that illustrious scholars of Roman law recently revived the main leitmotivs espoused by Ehrlich, who was a scholar of Roman law himself. These interpretations of the current situation are based on the cognitive-normative combination that provides the inspiration for an adaptive law, similar to that produced by Roman jurists. Even in advanced legal orders, it is possible to overcome law's apparent disorder using flexible and adaptive tools like that invented by Roman jurisprudence, which these days would be described as tools of intersystemic connection. Cf. Rémi Brague, *Europe, la voie romaine*, Paris: Criterion, 1992; Marie T. Fögen, *Römische Rechtsgeschichten. Über Ursprung und Evolution eines sozialen Systems*, Göttingen: Vandenhoeck & Ruprecht, 2002, where the judge is represented as the 'thermostat of law'.

References

Ackerman, Bruce. 'The Rise of World Constitutionalism', *Virginia Law Review* 83 (1997): 771–97.

Alexy, Robert. *A Theory of Constitutional Rights*, Oxford: Oxford University Press, 2002.

Ashby, W.R. 'Principles of the Self-Organizing System', in Heinz von Foerster and George W. Zopf (eds), *Principles of Self-Organization*, New York: Pergamon Press, 1962, 255–78.

Baird, Douglas G., Robert H. Gertner and Randal C. Picker. *Game Theory and the Law*, Cambridge, MA: Harvard University Press, 1998.

Banakar, Reza. *Merging Law and Sociology: Beyond the Dichotomies of Socio-Legal Research*, Berlin and Wisconsin: Galda and Wilch, 2003.

———. *Normativity in Legal Sociology: Methodological Reflections on Law and Regulation in Late Modernity*, Switzerland: Springer, 2015

Banakar, Reza, and Max Travers (eds). *Law and Social Theory*, second edition, Oxford: Hart, 2013.

Bendix, Reinhard. *Max Weber: An Intellectual Portrait*, Berkeley: University of California Press, 1977.

Brague, Rémi. *Europe, la voie romaine*, Paris: Criterion, 1992.

Calvo-Garcia, Manuel, and William L.F. Felstiner. *Federalismo Federalism*, Madrid: Dykinson, 2008.

Carducci, Michele, and Anna S. Bruno. 'The Brics Countries between Justice and Economy: Methodological Challenges on Constitutional Comparison', *Sociology and Anthropology* 2 (2014): 46–58.

Clam, Jean. 'What is Modern Power?', in M. King and C. Thornhill (eds), *Luhmann on Law and Politics: Critical Appraisals and Applications*, Oxford: Hart, 2006, 145–62.

Corsi, Giancarlo, and Elena Esposito (eds). *Reform und Innovation in einer unstabilen Gesellschaft*, Stuttgart: Lucius & Lucius, 2005.

Cotterrell, Roger. *The Sociology of Law: An Introduction*, second edition, London: Butterworth, 1992.

———. 'Is There a Logic of Legal Transplants', in D. Nelken and J. Feest (eds), *Adapting Legal Cultures*, Oxford: Hart, 2001, 70–92.

———. 'Transnational Communities and the Concept of Law', *Ratio Juris* 21 (2008): 1–18.

Deflem, Mathieu, *Sociology of Law: Visions of Scholarly Tradition*, Cambridge: Cambridge University Press, 2008.

Delmas-Marty, Mireille. *Ordering Pluralism: A Conceptual Framework for Understanding the Transnational Legal World*, Oxford: Hart Publishing, 2009.

de Maistre, Joseph. *The Works of Joseph de Maistre*, New York: Schocken Books, 1971.

Ehrlich, Eugen. *Fundamental Principles of the Sociology of Law*, edited by Roscoe Pound, New York: Russell & Russell, 1962 (new edition, with a new introduction by Klaus A. Ziegert, London: Transaction Publishers, 2002).

Esposito, Elena. 'Paradoxien als Unterscheidungen von Unterscheidungen', in Hans U. Gumbrecht, and K. Ludwig Pfeiffer (eds), *Paradoxien, Dissonanzen, Zusammenbrüche. Situationen offener Epistemologie*, Frankfurt am Main: Surkhamp, 1991, 35–57.

Febbrajo, Alberto. *Funzionalismo strutturale nell'opera di Niklas Luhmann*, Milano: Giuffré, 1975.

———. Introduzione to Eugen Ehrlich, *I fondamenti della sociologia del diritto*, Milano: Giuffrè, 1976, V–XLIX.

———. 'E. Ehrlich: Dal diritto libero al diritto vivente', *Sociologia del diritto* 3 (1982): 137–59.

———. *From Hierarchical to Circular Models in the Sociology of Law: Some Introductory Remarks*, Milano: Giuffrè, 1988.

———. 'Introduction', in E. Ehrlich, H. Kelsen and M. Weber (eds), *Verso un concetto sociologico di diritto*, Milano: Giuffrè, 2010.

———. *Sociologia del diritto. Concetti e problemi*, second edition, Bologna: il Mulino, 2013.

———. 'Dall'unità alla pluralità del diritto', in *Ripensare Max Weber nel centocinquantesimo dalla nascita, Atti dei convegni Lincei*, Rome: Scienze e Lettere, 2015, 171–92.

Febbrajo, Alberto, and Francesco Gambino (eds). *Il diritto frammentato*, Milano: Giuffré, 2014.

Febbrajo, Alberto, and Gorm Harste (eds). *Law and Intersystemic Communication, Understanding 'Structural Coupling'*, Aldershot: Ashgate, 2013.

Fioravanti, Maurizio. 'Costituzione, amministrazione e trasformazioni dello Stato', in Aldo Schiavone (ed.), *Stato e cultura giuridica in Italia dall'unità alla repubblica*, Bari: Laterza, 1990, 3–87.

Fischer-Lescano, A., and Gunther Teubner. *Regime-Kollisionen: zur Fragmentierung des globalen Rechts*, Frankfurt am Main: Suhrkamp, 2006.

Fögen, Marie T. *Römische Rechtsgeschichten. Über Ursprung und Evolution eines sozialen Systems*, Göttingen: Vandenhoeck & Ruprecht, 2002.

Friedman, Lawrence, 'Some Comments on Cotterrell and Legal Transplants', in D. Nelken and J. Feest (eds), *Adapting Legal Cultures*, Oxford: Hart, 2001, 93–8.

Frishman, Olga. 'Transnational Judicial Dialogue as an Organizational Field', *European Law Journal* 19 (2013): 739–58.

Galeotti, Serio, and Barbara Pezzini. *Il Presidente della Repubblica nella Costituzione italiana*, Torino: UTET, 2003.

Galligan, Denis. 'The Paradox of Constitutionalism or the Potential of Constitutional Theory?' *Oxford Journal of Legal Studies* 28/2 (2008): 343–67.

——— (ed.). *Constitutions and the Classics: Patterns of Constitutional Thought from Fortescue to Bentham*, Oxford: Oxford University Press, 2014.

Galligan, Denis, and Mila Versteeg (eds). *Social and Political Foundations of Constitutions*, Cambridge: Cambridge University Press, 2013.

Gawron, Thomas, and Ralf Rogowski. *Die Wirkung des Bundesverfassungsgerichts. Rechtssoziologische Analysen*, Baden-Baden: Nomos, 2007.

Geiger, Theodor. *Vorstudien zu einer Soziologie des Rechts*, Neuwied: Luchterhand, 1964.

Ginsburg, Tom, Zachary Elkins and James Melton (eds). *The Endurance of National Constitutions*, Cambridge: Cambridge University Press, 2009.

Griffith, Anne. 'Legal Pluralism', in Reza Banakar and Max Travers (eds), *An Introduction to Law and Social Theory*, Oxford: Hart Publishing, 2002, 289–310.

Griffith, John. 'What is Legal Pluralism?', *Journal of Legal Pluralism and Unofficial Law* 24 (1986): 1–55.

Grimm, Dieter. *Die Zukunft der Verfassung II*, Berlin: Suhrkamp, 2012.

Häberle, Peter. *Der kooperative Verfassungsstaat- aus Kultur und als Kultur Vorstudien zu einer Universalen Verfassungslehre*, Berlin: Duncker & Humblot, 2013.

Hasebe, Y. and C. Pinelli. 'Constitutions', in M. Tushnet, T. Fleiner and C. Saunders (eds), *Routledge Handbook of Constitutional Law*, London and New York: Routledge, 2013, 9ff.

Huizinga, Johan. *Homo Ludens: A Study of the Play-Element in Culture*, London: Routledge & Kegan Paul, 1949.

Kelsen, Hans. 'Eine Grundlegung der Rechtssoziologie'. *Archiv für Sozialwissenschaft und Sozialpolitik* 39 (1915): 839–76.

King, Michael, 'The Radical Sociology of Niklas Luhmann', in Reza Banakar and Max Travers (eds), *Law and Social Theory*, second edition, Oxford: Hart, 2013.

King, Michael, and Chris Thornhill. *Luhmann on Law and Politics: Critical Appraisals and Applications*, Oxford: Hart, 2006, 59–74.

Kjaer, Poul F. *Constitutionalism in the Global Realm: A Sociological Approach*, London: Routledge, 2014.

Kjaer P.F., G. Teubner and A. Febbrajo. *The Financial Crisis in Constitutional Perspective: The Dark Side of Functional Differentiation*, Oxford: Hart, 2011.

Koselleck, Reinhart. *Die Zukunft der Verfassung*, Frankfurt am Main: Suhrkamp, 1991.

———. 'Begriffsgeschichtliche Probleme der Verfassungsgeschichtsschreibung', in Reinhart Koselleck (ed.), *Begriffsgeschichten: Studien zur Semantik und Pragmatik der politischen und sozialen Sprache*, Frankfurt: Suhrkamp, 2006, 365–401.

Krisch, Nico. *Beyond Constitutionalism: The Pluralistic Structure of Postnational Law*, Oxford: Oxford University Press, 2010.

———. 'Who Is Afraid of Radical Pluralism? Legal Order and Political Stability in the Postnational Space', *Ratio Juris* 24 (2011): 386–412.

Kumm, Mattias. 'Who is the Final Arbiter of Constitutionality in Europe? Three Conceptions of the Relationship Between the German Federal Constitutional Court and the European Court of Justice', *Common Market Law Review* 36 (1999): 351–86.

Legrand, Pierre, 'What "Legal Transplants"?', in D. Nelken and J. Feest (eds), *Adapting Legal Cultures*, Oxford: Hart, 2001, 55–69.

Leoni, Bruno. *Freedom and the Law*, expanded third edition, Indianapolis: Liberty Fund, 1991.

Loughlin, Martin. *The Idea of Public Law*, Oxford: Oxford University Press, 2004.

———. 'In Defence of *Staatslehre*', *Der Staat* 48 (2009): 1–27.
———. 'What is Constitutionalisation?', in Petra Dobner and Martin Loughlin (eds), *The Twilight of Constitutionalism?* Oxford: Oxford University Press, 2010, 47–69.
Luhmann, Niklas. 'Normen in soziologisher Perspektive', *Soziale Welt* XX (1969): 28–48.
———. 'Grundwerte als Zivilreligion', *Archivio di Filosofia* 46 (1978): 51–71.
———. *Rechtssystem und Rechtsdogmatik*, Stuttgart: Kohlhammer, 1982.
———. 'Reflexive Mechanismen', in Niklas Luhmann (ed.), *Soziologische Aufklärung 1: Aufsätze zur Theorie sozialer Systeme*, Opladen: Westdeutscher Verlag, 1984, 92–112.
———. *A Sociological Theory of Law*, London: Routledge, 1985.
———. 'Verfassung als evolutionäre Errungenschaft', *Rechtshistorisches Journal* 9 (1990): 176–220.
———. 'The Coding of the Legal System', in Gunther Teubner and Alberto Febbrajo (eds), *State, Law and Economy as Autopoietic Systems: Regulation and Autonomy in a New Perspective*, Milano: Giuffrè, 1992, 145–86.
———. *Legitimation durch Verfahren*, Frankfurt am Main: Suhrkamp, 2001.
———. *Law as a Social System*, Oxford: Oxford University Press, 2004.
MacCormick, Neil. *Questioning Sovereignty: Law, State and Nation in the European Commonwealth*, Oxford: Oxford University Press, 1999.
———. *Institutions of Law: An Essay in Legal Theory*, Oxford: Oxford University Press, 2007.
MacCormick, Neil, and Ota Weinberger. *An Institutional Theory of Law: New Approaches to Legal Positivism*, Dordrecht: D. Reidel, 1986.
Maduro, Miguel P. 'Contrapunctual Law: Europe's Constitutional Pluralism in Action', in Neil Walker (ed.), *Sovereignty in Transition*, Oxford: Hart Publishing, 2003, 501–37.
Mellisaris, Emmanuel. *Ubiquitous Law: Legal Theory and the Space for Legal Pluralism*, Aldershot: Ashgate, 2009.
Mortati, Costantino. *La costituzione in senso materiale*, Milano: Giuffrè, 1940.
Nelken, David (ed.). *Comparing Legal Cultures*, Dartmouth: Ashgate, 1997.
Nelken, David, and Johannes Feest (eds). *Adapting Legal Cultures*, Oxford: Hart Publishing, 2001.
Neves, Marcelo. *A Constitucionalização Simbólica*, São Paulo: Martins Fontes, 2007.
———. 'The Symbolic Force of Human Rights', *Philosophy & Social Criticism* XXXIII (2007): 411–44.
Nicolis, Pierre, and Ilya Prigogine. *Die Erforschung des Komplexen*, München: Piper, 1987.
Nobles, Richard, and David Schiff. 'Using Systems Theory to Study Legal Pluralism: What Could Be Gained?' *Law & Society Review* 46 (2012): 265–95.
———. *Observing Law through Systems Theory*, Oxford: Hart, 2013.
Parsons, Talcott, and Charles Ackerman. 'The Concept of "Social System" as a Theoretical Device', in Gordon J. DiRenzo (ed.), *Concepts, Theory and Explanation in the Behavioral Sciences*, New York: Random House, 1966, 19–40.
Pernice, Ingolf. 'Multilevel Constitutionalism in the European Union', *European Law Review* 27 (2002): 511–29.
Rawls, John. 'Two Concepts of Rules', *The Philosophical Review* LXIV (1955): 3–32.
———. *The Law of Peoples*, Cambridge, MA: Harvard University Press, 1999.
Romano, Santi. *Lo Stato moderno e la sua crisi*, Milano: Giuffrè, 1910.
———. *L'ordinamento giuridico*, Firenze: Sansoni, 1918.
Rosenfeld, Michel. 'Modern Constitutionalism as Interplay between Identity and Diversity', in Michel Rosenfeld (ed.), *Constitutionalism, Identity, Difference and Legitimacy: Theoretical Perspectives*, Durham, NC: Duke University Press, 1994, 3–38.
———. 'The Identity of the Constitutional Subject', in Peter Goodrich and David G. Carlson (eds), *Law and the Postmodern Mind: Essays on Psychoanalysis and Jurisprudence*, Ann Arbor: The University of Michigan Press, 1998, 143–74.
Schauer, Frederick. 'On the Migration of Constitutional Ideas', *Connecticut Law Review* 37/4 (2005): 907–19.
Schelsky, Helmut. 'Über die Stabilität von Institutionen, besonders Verfassungen. Kulturanthropologische Überlegungen zu einem rechtssoziologischen Thema', *Jahrbuch für Sozialwissenschaften* 3/1 (1952): 1–21.

Sciulli, David. *Theory of Societal Constitutionalism: Foundations of a Non-Marxist Critical Sociology*, Cambridge: Cambridge University Press, 1992.

Searle, John R. 'How to Derive "Ought" from "Is"', *The Philosophical Review* 73 (1964): 43–58.

Sousa Santos de, Boaventura. *Towards a New Legal Common Sense*, London: Butterworth, 2002.

Sousa Santos de, Boaventura, and César Rodriguez-Garavito. *Law and Globalization from Below: Towards a Cosmopolitan Legality*, Cambridge: Cambridge University Press, 2005.

Supiot, Alain. 'The Public-Private Relation in the Context of Today's Refeudalization', *International Journal of Constitutional Law* 11 (2013): 129–45.

Tebbe, N., and R.L. Tsai. 'Constitutional Borrowing', *Michigan Law Review* 108 (2010): 459–522.

Teubner, Gunther (ed.). *Global Law without a State*, Aldershot: Ashgate, 1997.

———. 'Societal Constitutionalism: Alternatives to State-Centred Constitutional Theory?' in Christian Joerges, Inger-Johanne Sand and Gunther Teubner (eds), *Transnational Governance and Constitutionalism*, Oxford: Hart, 2004, 3–28.

———. *Constitutional Fragments: Societal Constitutionalism and Globalization*, Oxford: Oxford University Press, 2012.

Thornhill, Chris. *A Sociology of Constitutions: Constitutions and State Legitimacy in Historical-Sociological Perspective*, Cambridge: Cambridge University Press, 2011.

Tönnies, Ferdinand. *Gemeinschaft und Gesellschaft: Grundbegriffe der reinen Soziologie*, Darmstadt: Wissenschaftliche Buchgesellschaft, 1979.

Tocqueville de, Alexis. *Democracy in America*, Chicago: University of Chicago Press, 2000.

Treves, Renato. *Introducción a la sociología del derecho*, Madrid: Taurus, 1978.

Trubek, David M., and Alvaro Santos (eds). *The New Law and Economic Development*, Cambridge: Cambridge University Press, 2006.

Tully, James. 'The Imperialism of Modern Constitutional Democracy', in Neil Walker and Martin Loughlin (eds), *The Paradox of Constitutionalism: Constituent Power and Constitutional Form*, Oxford: Oxford University Press, 2007, 315–38.

Twining, William, and David Miers. *How to do Things With Rules: A Primer of Interpretation*, London: Weidenfeld & Nicolson, 1976.

Von Foerster, Heinz. 'On Constructing Reality', in Heinz Von Foerster (ed.), *Observing Systems*, Seaside: Intersystems Publications, 1981, 288–309.

Walker, Neil. 'The Idea of Constitutional Pluralism', *Modern Law Review* 65 (2002): 317–59.

———. 'Post-Constituent Constitutionalism? The Case of the European Union', in Martin Loughlin and Neil Walker (eds), *The Paradox of Constitutionalism: Constituent Power and Constitutional Form*, Oxford: Oxford University Press, 2007, 247–67.

Walter, Christian. *Religionsverfassungsrecht*, Tübingen: Mohr, 2006.

Watson, Alan. *Legal Transplants: An Approach to Comparative Law*, second edition, Athens, GA: University of Georgia Press, 1993.

Weber, Max. *The Protestant Ethic and the Spirit of Capitalism*, London and Boston: Unwin Hyman, 1930.

———. *Max Weber on Law in Economy and Society*, translated by Edward Shils and Max Rheinstein, edited with introduction and annotations by Max Rheinstein, Cambridge, MA: Harvard University Press, 1954.

———. 'R. Stammler's "Overcoming" of the Materialist Conception of History', in Hans H. Bruun and Sam Whimster (eds), *Collected Methodological Writings*, London and New York: Routledge, 2012, 185–226.

Weiler, Joseph. *The Constitution of Europe: Do the New Clothes have an Emperor?* Cambridge: Cambridge University Press, 1998.

Weiler, Joseph, and Marlene Wind (eds). *European Constitutionalism Beyond the State*, Cambridge: Cambridge University Press, 2003.

Weinberger, Ota. *Law, Institution and Legal Politics: Fundamental Problems of Legal Theory and Social Philosophy*, Dordrecht: Kluwer, 1991.

Winczoreck, Jan. 'Making Law Together? On Some Intersystemic Conditions of Judicial Cooperation', in Febbrajo Alberto and Gorm Harste (eds), *Law and Intersystemic Communication: Understanding 'Structural Coupling'*, Aldershot: Ashgate, 2013, 229–54.

Zagrebelsky Gustavo, Pier Paolo Portinaro and Jorg Luther (eds). *Il futuro della costituzione*, Torino: Einaudi, 1996.

Zumbansen, Peer. 'Transnational Legal Pluralism', *Transnational Legal Theory* 1 (2010): 141–89.

———. 'Comparative, Global and Transnational Constitutionalism: The Emergence of a Transnational Legal-Pluralist Order', *Global Constitutionalism* 1 (2012): 16–52.

Part II

6 The sociological origins of global constitutional law

Chris Thornhill

What is global constitutional law?

There is currently much debate about global law, and in particular about global constitutional law.[1] In very general terms, the defining outlooks in this debate can be aligned to two distinct camps. Observers in one category define global constitutional law as an intensification of classical international law. From this perspective, global constitutional forms an overarching hierarchy of norms, which has its origins in principles of international law seen as having *erga omnes* standing, and it determines basic rules for the different actors or *subjects*, be these states, persons, international organisations, or even corporations, that populate the international arena.[2] On the other hand, a rival set of observers now conceive of global constitutional law as a legal order emanating mainly from private law, or at least from a confluence between private and public international law. These observers argue that this law is formed through relatively spontaneous engagement between different norm providers and the specific exigencies of different transnational social exchanges. On this account, the various functional domains of world society engender their own particular regulatory structures, often combining elements of classical public law and elements of private law, which are reproduced across the boundaries between national jurisdictions, and which acquire quasi-constitutional character both for national states and for actors locating within different functional domains. Broadly speaking, observers in the first category still work within the monism/dualism paradigm of late positivism, and they perceive the rise of global constitutional law as the final triumph of *classical monism*. Interpreters in the second category accept a *hybrid monism* as a basic fact of global legal order. Both outlooks, however, argue that global society now possesses a distinct constitutionality.[3] Whilst owing great appreciation to the above theoretical camps, this chapter offers an account of global constitutional law that differs in certain respects from both these constructions. On one hand, first, it opposes the international-law perspective in these debates, as it claims that we can identify a body of global constitutional law which, although doubtless in part attributable to norms assuming sanction as international law, is not reducible to international law, and it does not originate, or it only very obliquely originates, in inter-state acts. Global constitutional law is in fact engendered, in relatively fluid adaptive fashion, by actors moving quite freely between the national and the international domain. In this respect, my view of global constitutional law has a certain proximity both to Philip Jessup's original idea of transnational law,[4] and to the theory of *dédoublement functionnel* proposed by Georges Scelle.[5] Then, second, in contrast to the alternative or transnationalist view outlined above, this chapter differentiates global constitutional law quite strictly from private law. Some emerging accounts of transnational constitutional law opt for radical fragmentation and deeply hybridised pluralism over hierarchy and normative structure as principles of legal form.[6] Although I agree with Gunther Teubner that we can observe autogenetic legal forms in different subsystems of transnational society, my approach is underscored by the claim that we do not need to abandon the more conventional plane of public law to identify a corpus of transnational or global constitutional law. On my approach, we can observe a number of processes in contemporary society which clearly produce law with de facto constitutional rank at a global or transnational level. This occurs in a fashion which clearly differentiates such law from international conventions or inter-state agreements, so that, to agree with theorists of transnational as a hybrid form, transnational law retains a distinct autonomy against international law. Yet, this also occurs in a fashion which means that the constituent subjects of transnational constitutional law are still identifiably and in fact categorically *public*.

To substantiate this, I wish to suggest that global constitutional law is generated through complex interactions between courts and other judicial bodies (i.e. between bodies with clear public standing), which are positioned at different points in the global political system, and which radiate norms of original international provenance through and across jurisdictional boundaries. As a result of these interactions, legal norms migrate quite spontaneously across limits between formally distinct jurisdictions, they are often proportioned to objectives far removed from the principles of international law that first shaped their formation, and they generate constitutional norms, in often unpredictable fashion, both within and for national states. To this degree, a network of transnational judicial interactions gives rise to a corpus of global constitutional law, but this legal corpus is marked by a distinct public character.

On my account, this judicial production of global constitutional law takes place, typically and primarily, through three distinct lines of interaction between international law and national law. Two of these are easily observable, but one is somewhat less immediately evident.

Line of interaction 1: direct interaction between national constitutional courts and international courts

This process will normally be visible in the acceptance of principles of deference, comity, margin of appreciation, and use of local remedies by courts occupying distinct positions in world society.[7] By organising their relations to each other through such principles, courts create a setting in which norms originally prescribed at an international level enter, permeate and shape national jurisdictions, and the interaction between courts creates a constitutional form both for national states and global society as a whole. Constitutional law is formed through complex co-operation, often semi-conflictual, between different tiers of a transnational judicial order, and interaction and contest over jurisdiction between courts creates a half-pluralistic, but also half-unified legal system, reaching across national boundaries. In such cases, courts usually dispute and mark out their spheres of competence by adherence to overriding obligations defined by international human rights conventions. Rights form a grammar by which different spheres of judicial discretion define both their independence from, and their basic compatibility with, other components of the judicial system, and rights underpin a transnationally constructed judicial constitution. This can be seen in the way that the local remedies doctrine is practised by the International Court of Justice (ICJ).[8] However, the controversies between the European Court of Justice (ECJ) and the German *Bundesverfassungsgericht*, expressed in the rulings *Solange I* and *Solange II*, are the most illuminating example of how rights punctuate the grammar of inter-judicial relations.[9]

Line of interaction 2: judicial borrowing

This process will normally be visible in the citation of rulings of one national court in a different national court, or, more typically, through the application of the jurisprudence of international courts in domestic courts. This is now an almost global phenomenon, which, as one observer has declared, means that 'the rampart of state sovereignty is breached'. It creates a situation in which, independently of international law *sensu stricto*, norms and judicial decisions are able laterally 'to pass from the international legal order into the municipal legal order'.[10] This is usually characteristic either of cases relating to problems emanating from the international arena or, most notably, of cases with implications regarding human rights. In this respect, courts produce an informal, yet quasi-constitutional, nexus by sharing legal norms, and they stabilise cross-boundary principles and expectations by so doing. However, this is some distance from the simple vertical imposition of a global constitutional structure. Through judicial borrowing, which is often implicit, international norms undergo context-dictated transformation, and they are often proportioned to nationally specific questions. Through this process a 'transjudicial model' of norm production is established, which blurs conventional boundaries between domestic comparative and international law.[11]

Line of interaction 3: constructive adaption of international norms to address problems embedded in structure of national societies

This process is rather more difficult to exemplify. To make it intelligible, we need to think of situations in which national states are afflicted by structural pressures or endemic instability within their own national setting or institutional substance. In such contexts, international law is often assimilated, typically via actors in the high judiciary, to mollify the exposure of the national political system to deep-rooted conflicts and challenges. In particular, we can link this to the *differentiation and functional abstraction* of the political system. We can observe a number of cases, historical and contemporary, in which the legal interaction between national and international courts gains relevance for the position of the political system in a national society at large, especially in circumstances where the political system is marked only by precarious levels of differentiation and has only been able to abstract itself weakly and uncertainly against other organisations in society. In many such cases, the national political system utilises international law to harden its stability in relation to actors, which are otherwise able to pull against its formal/differentiated abstraction or autonomy.

To illuminate this, we can think (1) of cases in which states have weak authority for legislation, perhaps operating in divided or factionalised societal landscapes, and they require additional legitimacy to gain compliance for law or even to legislate at all. In such instances, courts often stand alongside and provide backstopping for legislatures by using norms based in international law to authorise legislation and to enforce laws against highly entrenched factions. An example of this could be Hungary or Poland in the democratic transitions after 1989. We can think (2) of cases in which a state is required to address a high volume of legislation surviving from a previous regime, which obstruct its functions and perceived legitimacy. Courts are then able to use norms based in international law to clear away legal debris. One example of this is Italy in the 1950s and beyond. We can think (3) of cases in which a state is beset by rival factions seeking to gain control of power and needs to stabilise its basic structure. In such circumstances, courts might use international law to solidify principles that are above challenge by rival parties. Post-apartheid South Africa provides an example of this. We can think (4) of cases in which state is affected by a lateral, divisive pull caused by residues of structural privatism, patron–client linkages and/or patrimonialism. Under such circumstances, courts might use international law to stabilise an inclusionary structure against private actors, and to make visible the distinction between law of state and power of private persons. Post-1992 Ghana would seem to furnish an example of this. We can think (5) of cases in which the state is marked by deep and debilitating intersection with trade unions, or rendered unstable by volatile patterns of corporatism, which impede the formation of the state as a relatively autonomous centre of policy-making. As discussed below, Argentina after 1983 is a key example of this. We can think (6) of cases where the state is marked by a high politicisation of ethnicity. In settings of this kind, courts intervene to apply international norms to separate basic substance of state from ethnic monopoly. This is exemplified by Kenya. We can think (7) of cases in which the state has difficulty separating public power from private power, especially in geographically extensive national environments. Recent developments in China, Russia and Argentina provides examples of this. In such cases, the absorption of international law in national contexts is often used to bring consistency to judicial rulings, and to detach legal offices from manifestly local/private authority. We can think (8) of cases where a state is only notionally centralised and in fact marked by high local power monopolies. Post-Franco Spain offers a complex illustration of this phenomenon. In such cases, international law is applied by courts, often in conjunction with processes of decentralisation, to construct the legal system as a relatively uniform inclusionary order. We can think (9) of cases in which the state is incapable of producing law with any degree of public reliability. Russia under and after Yeltsin looks like the most obvious example of this. In such cases, the assimilation of international law acts as a source of constitutional law *faute de mieux*.

In each of these cases, we encounter situations in which political actors located within national states assimilate international law, and in which they actively and strategically impose international-legal norms on the fabric of a national state and a national society. They do this, typically, in order to remedy, or at least to diminish the consequences of, phenomena that have historically brought acute crisis to domestic institutions and which countervail the abstraction of the political system as a reliable and moderately autonomous centre of inclusionary legislation. In such cases, normally, this process is promoted by, or at least channelled through, judicial bodies, whether acting autonomously or under immediate political pressure, and the articulation between superior domestic courts and courts with international jurisdiction becomes a vital source of law, legitimacy and stability for the national political system. In such cases, the norms borrowed from international law are usually norms referring to, or derived from, human rights conventions, and internationally defined rights norms are applied to authorise legislation or to stabilise the legitimacy of institutions in contexts where resources of legitimacy are otherwise lacking, volatile or unmanageably contested. In many instances, therefore, national courts construct *transnational legitimacy* through their engagement with international judicial organs – normally, regional human rights courts, but perhaps also the ICJ, or UN human rights treaty bodies. Through their filtration of international norms into national societies, courts create reserves of legitimacy which national states themselves struggle to generate, and they construct an internal foundation for the political system on which it can legislate in relatively insulated manner, even in the teeth of high levels of social polarisation, political resistance, or institutional fragmentation. In each case, international law is employed as a basis for, or at least as a dimension of, national constitutional law, and national constitutional law is rigidified through its assimilation of international law. In observing these processes, notably, it is difficult to argue that international law remains strictly *international*: that is, it does not assume constitutional standing because of the external limits that it places on state institutions. On the contrary, international law is modified and transformed by actors who utilise it in order to react to long-standing inner-societal problems, especially problems regarding the inclusionary capacities of the national political system. In such cases, the application of international law is usually highly selective, and certain specified norms of international law are proportioned to the need to resolve quite localised problems of systemic structure. In particular, in all these cases, international law is used to harden the existing constitutional structure of the state, and to bring additional normative support to the national state and its inclusionary functional within its daily functional domains.

The point that I wish to make, therefore, is that in analysing global constitutional law our horizon need not be constrained by an emphasis on relatively conventional models of international law. We can observe global constitutional law as distinctively global or transnational, as produced by multiple actors, and as evolving in a sphere of legal production that cannot be tied either to a hierarchy of national norms or to simple inter-state agreements. Despite this, however, we can still approach global constitutional law as constitutional in an eminent sense: that is, as applied by, and binding on, public actors, and as serving to consolidate distinctively *public* functions and institutions. Global constitutional law typically arises from complex overlapping relations between domestic and extra-national pressures. This law in fact functions in direct analogy to classical constitutional law. Like classical constitutional law, it reacts to problems of systemic abstraction in national societies, and it distils original non-reducible normative residues which facilitate the construction of political legitimacy and the inclusionary transmission of law. In this light, transnational constitutional law stands in for, or at least reinforces, the classical functions of constituent power, and it generates default supplies of constituent power in national societies which have not been able to construct a sustainable national constitutional order.

The transformation of classical constitutionalism

In whatever way we wish to define the current post-national trends in constitutional law, it seems clear that, in recent decades, classical patterns of constitutional foundation and norm setting have undergone a substantial transformation. Most societies are marked – to different degrees – by a constitutional order which is connected immediately to the global legal system, and which imposes a transnational normative form on national polities. This has given rise to a widespread model of constitutional formation, which, with distinctions, has become visible in most national settings. Most contemporary constitutional polities, admittedly with high levels of variance, are marked by the following features:

An increase in judicial power, and a shift in emphasis to the judicial branch

In most contemporary polities, the judicial branch has assumed unprecedented importance, as a check on, or filter for, acts of legislation. This is tied to the fact that national judiciaries form sluices through which international law, often derived from human rights conventions, is admitted to and can circulate through the domestic legal/political order.

The end of constituent power as a primary source of norms

In most contemporary polities, the space for *ex-nihilo* constitutional foundation is reduced, and national democratic agency loses significance as the founding source of legitimacy. Courts in fact now widely pre-define the scope and content of constituent power. In many cases, interactions between courts provide constituent power for polities, and polities conduct processes of constitutional foundation within constraints dictated by international norms. This means that constituted institutions exercise constituent power. Constituent power is often already constituted before it is asserted or exercised. The radically external source of legitimacy for the political system, which classical constitutional doctrine defined as the essence of democratic institution building and legitimation, is lost.[12]

Rights supplant constituent power

The primary basis for constituent power is derived from international rights conventions, applied by courts. Actors in national domains struggle to assert constituent power not derived from rights, and rights widely act as final points of normative regress for national law making – both founding and statutory. Rights distil the essence of constituent power, and this essence is transplanted across different jurisdictional divides by courts.

Transnational reconstruction of constituent power

Constituent power, which, if we accept the classical views of James Wilson, Alexander Hamilton and Emmanuel Joseph Sieyès, is the defining expression of the national will, is now constructed through a transnational normative mix. The original constituent will underpinning national polities and their constitutions is now largely asserted through a cross-national amalgam of institutions, many of a judicial nature, and the elements of constituent power which have a specific national character are limited.[13]

Overall, in summary, the first rise of mass-democracy typically saw a shift in power from legislatures to executives.[14] Recent political history, by contrast, has witnessed an unprecedented shift in power from legislatures and executives to judiciaries, whose power is partly a result of their openness to engagement with international bodies. This has promoted a model of *transnational judicial democracy* as the basic design for contemporary political structures. This model first became prominent in the post-authoritarian polities that were established, experimentally, after 1945. It then became more widespread through the democratic transitions from the 1970s to the 1990s. With variations, this model is now almost universal. There are some very extreme cases of this new model of democracy. For example, it finds extreme expression in polities subject to territorial administration by international organisations.[15] Such cases, however, are not wholly sui generis; they are simply unusually exaggerated manifestations of a relatively uniform basic phenomenon.[16] In fact, few polities are resistant to the growing bias towards transnational judicial democracy, and even those that historically had relatively weak judiciaries and low regard for any higher-order norms are increasingly transformed by this model. Today, the growth of judicial power, forming a nexus between the national and the extra-national dimensions of the political system, is able even to determine polities in which the immediate reception of international law has traditionally been obstructed. For instance, this model penetrates polities (e.g. the UK), which are constitutionally resistant to higher-order legal norms;[17] it penetrates polities (e.g. China),[18] which have not yet evolved fully enforceable democratic constitutions and which historically rejected international law as Western imperialist artifice; it penetrates polities, for example in Southern Africa, whose basic domestic legal order remains uncertain, pluralistic, often informal;[19] it even penetrates polities, for instance in North Africa, where historical and cultural reconditions pull against easy acceptance of universal international norms.[20] On this basis, the textbooks on democracy and the separation of powers ought to be re-written. Democracy only really began to take hold across the globe at a time when its basic design had moved outside the parameters set by classical definitions of democracy. The exponential growth of democracy over the last two decades has been accompanied by a deep shift in its substance, through which the power of the judicial branch, acting as a filter for international rights norms, exceeded all precedent or provision in classical conceptions of democratic will formation.

A sociological approach to transnational constitutional law

This new model constitutional democracy has attracted great scholarly interest. In legal inquiry, as discussed, judicial democracy is examined widely, and mainly affirmatively, in the literature on global constitutionalism. In addition, this model is often criticised in more established lines of constitutional reflection, by theorists located at very different points on the political spectrum.[21] A body of political-scientific literature has recently developed which examines the judicialisation of democracy from the perspective of international political economy.[22] There is now also a growing corpus of research that examines inter-elite motivations for binding states into the transnational legal domain through inter-judicial exchanges.[23] Of course, further, there is also a well-established body of legal/political-scientific inquiry into patterns of judicial cross-fertilisation.[24]

What is missing in this growing corpus of research, however, is a wide-angled sociological approach to the rise of rise of courts as primary constitutional subjects. To be sure, there is some important sociological research on transnational judicial power,[25] and there have been a few notable sociological interventions in the discussion about the reasons for the rise of courts in democratic polity building.[26] Naturally, recent years have also seen the growth of a very large body of sociological literature addressing the proliferation of international human rights norms. In fact, the increasing cross-border diffusion of international human rights conventions has put wind in the sails of sociological cosmopolitanism, which now takes the filtration of international human rights law into domestic legal practices as one of its primary objects of study.[27] Nonetheless, the simple sociological questions – *Why do national polities now normally derive the foundations of their legal order from international law? Why does constitutional law now typically possess a transnational basis?* – have not been widely posed. This is a most striking omission. On one hand, these questions can be seen as questions that clearly pertain to the core domain of classical institutional sociology. Indeed, if the absorption of international law in domestic legal practices is identified as part of a process of inner-societal institutional construction, it falls squarely within the framework of post-Weberian sociology. On the other hand, these questions are questions with first-rank sociological importance, and they touch on a deep transformation of the most elementary understandings and practices of contemporary political democracy.

My conjecture is that this omission in sociological inquiry results from the fact that most sociologists tend to follow more classical legalistic perspectives when observing the domestic impact of inter- or transnational norms in domestic politics. That is to say, implicit in sociologically inflected analyses of the rise of judicial power is the suggestion that international law originates *outside* national societies, and that it cannot be comprehended as an expression of inner-societal behaviours or dispositions. The original sociological scepticism towards international law, evident in the works of Weber and Ehrlich, thus re-surfaces in new form in approaches to global law.[28] To a large degree, however implicitly and reluctantly, sociological inquiries into the changing legal phenomena of global society move broadly within the framework of positivist legal observation: that is, they tend to proceed from an original construction of international society as a system of fully formed states, and they tend to perceive the growing force of international law as a process that is neutral, external or indifferent to deep-rooted socio-political interactions.[29] In fact, these inquiries tend to see the rise of international law, and its filtration into national law through courts, as a process that occurred at a historical juncture after the full formation of national societies and national states had been completed, and which thus subjects national societies and states to a logic of transformation which is not intrinsically an object for sociological explanation. In many cases, in fact, sociological approaches to new global legal phenomena examine the growth of transnational judicial power as a process, which, at least latently, restricts the autonomy of evolved national state institutions, and positions states within an abstracted normative order.[30] Even cosmopolitan theory, which comprehends itself as implacably critical of positivism in the classical sense, repeatedly replicates many ideas inherent in the positivist standpoint. Notably, the cosmopolitan literature identifies human rights norms as principles that are primarily constructed outside the national legal arena, and it posits the rising power of transnational norms as a block on the power of domestic state institutions.[31] Somewhat obscurely, in other words, in approaching the rise of global constitutional law, sociology usually forgets to think sociologically, it omits to trace the emergence of global norms to distinct inner-societal motivations, and it often accepts, against its own deepest methodological imperatives, an abstractly legalistic understanding of the origins of global law.

In my analysis, given above, of the three lines of interaction between national and international courts, however, we can find a framework in which the formation of global constitutional law can be re-situated firmly within the focus of sociological inquiry. On the basis of the above model, we can observe the rise of global constitutional law, not as an occurrence located in a domain completely removed from institutional formation in national settings, but as a process that is deeply interwoven with inner-societal trajectories of institution building, i.e. with the field of legal phenomena which classical sociology made its own. On this basis, we can begin to propose a more strictly sociological approach to the growth of global constitutional law. At an immediate level, of course, we can make a few conjectural comments about the first two lines of interaction. We can probably attribute the increase in direct engagement between courts to the simple fact that global society requires more and more law, and pre-debated norms borrowed from the international domain have the benefit that they authorise laws relatively simply and in a relatively uncontroversial fashion. Similar points might be suggested in relation to the increasing phenomenon of judicial borrowing.

It is in the third line of interaction, however, that a sociological approach to global constitutional law finds particular purchase. In addressing the national use of international law to address problems of national systemic differentiation, in fact, the growth of global constitutional law can clearly be approached and explained from a standpoint taken directly from classical historical sociology. That is to say, the impact of global constitutional law on national societies and their institutions is observable, not in the first instance as a process that is driven by forces or norms imposed externally on national institutions, but rather as expressions of a reflexive or adaptive dimension within these institutions, which play a vital role in their systemic formation and differentiation. To approach this point, it is necessary to make a series of preliminary observations:

1. The assumption that states possessing the legal title of sovereignty are real sovereign states is misleading (again due to positivism). Most states did not fully possess sovereignty, and they typically struggled to generate motivations for compliance across domestic society.
2. Historically, most states have relied, not on public order or legitimacy, but rather on privatism/patrimonialism to extend legal and power across society. In most settings, society's inclusionary structure has depended, not on fully articulated statehood or public law, but on privatism and patron–client relations.
3. Most states have struggled effectively to operate as states because they have encountered endemic and insurmountable *inclusionary crises* in applying law and power to their societies. This usually has two or three core causes:

    a. inability to reconcile class conflicts;
    b. inability to reconcile ethnic conflicts;
    c. inability to reconcile both class conflicts and ethnic conflicts at the same time.

4 In most cases, the inclusionary crises suffered by states gave rise to a *hyperpoliticisation* of the political system, and in fact of society more broadly, in which states are forced to trade public goods to obtain and secure societal support. This in turn usually gives rise to a condition of extreme privatism within the political system.

Implied in these claims is the sense that the common perception of global constitutional law as a normative apparatus that originates outside, or somehow constrains the power of, national states is both sociologically ill-tuned and unaccountably pre-figured by positivist concepts of statehood. If we scratch beneath the positivist construction of statehood, we can observe that in most societies statehood, until recently, did not exist, even remotely, as a fully consolidated phenomenon. To be sure, institutions assuming state-like functions evolved in most societies. However, as soon as these institutions began to penetrate deeply into society, they encountered sources of conflict and inclusionary pressures which, with rare exceptions, they were not autonomously able to resolve. Most states, usually more than once and in some instances cyclically, were beset by endemic and highly unsettling experiences of *inclusionary crisis*, resulting from their internalisation of deeply unsettling class conflicts and centre/periphery conflicts. As a result, most states forfeited a discernibly public structure in face of the pressures of inclusion which they confronted and the cycles of escalating politicisation which they consequently engendered. In fact, for similar reasons, nationhood is also a recent phenomenon. Few nations approached a condition of relatively even national inclusion until very recently. On this basis, then, we can observe that in most trajectories of nation and state building the precondition of statehood and nationhood has been that states tied their normative structures into a transnational order, and – albeit constructively and selectively – they assimilated international law into their own domestic fabric. Most states only came fully to operate as states – that is, as systems of *categorically public legal inclusion* – by virtue of the fact that they integrated international law into their domestic legal order in order to palliate problems that had historically impeded their effective public abstraction and differentiation. The establishment of statehood as a more or less reliable inclusionary structure within society was usually dependent on the convergence of national statehood and norms borrowed from the international domain. In fact, international law needs to be observed, sociologically, as an embedded element of national societies, by means of which these societies learned to compensate for their inclusionary crises, to soften the extreme politicisation resulting from inclusionary crisis, and to extract reasonably effective and differentiated institutions. Against this background, the contemporary transformation of constitutional law, often seen as eroding the autonomous powers of statehood, can equally be viewed as producing a transnational constitutional model through which states stabilise their autonomy against pressures which historically prevented them from conclusively acting as states.

The problem of statehood and the function of global constitutional law: examples

Hyperpoliticisation and class

Germany

In the interwar era, Germany existed as a state that was marked, unmistakeably, by the fact that it was committed to high degree of class inclusion: that is, it defined its legitimacy, constitutionally, as a result of its ability to mediate deep-lying class conflicts and to promote laws based in cross-class agreement. Notably, the early years of the Weimar Republic saw the promotion of a body of *corporatist labour law*, which was specifically intended to bind the legitimacy of the state to a class-transcendent consensus on key points of political-economic orientation. This inclusionary impulse began with legislation to regulate labour contracts (*Tarifvertragsordnung*) in the immediate wake of armistice in late 1918. It was consolidated in the Weimar Constitution of 1919, in which Article 165 made especial provision for collective regulation of the conditions of production. It culminated in the introduction (tellingly, by emergency decree) of related legislation in 1923, by means of which major industrial disputes were subject to mandatory state arbitration (*Zwangsschlichtung*), and the state was designated the final arbiter of (increasingly volatile) class conflicts.[32]

Each of these packages of corporate legislation meant that class conflicts were placed at the nervous centre of the state, and the state's operative legitimacy had to be constantly regenerated through the resolution of often extremely intensified conflicts, lying in different realms of society. In many cases, the political system contributed to the further intensification of these conflicts. By internalising economic conflicts, the state made itself porous to groups seeking to harden their economic positions in society, and it transformed its own offices into spoils to be monopolised by rival parties in the conflicts over distribution and production. Overall, the high levels of class inclusion in interwar Germany led to what we would now diagnose as a chronic *hyperpoliticisation* of the political system, in which the political system internalised and generated a mass of demands and obligations which it could not address, and which deeply eroded its legitimacy. Gradually, then, the political system lost its basic abstraction or differentiation against antagonistic social groups, it was invaded by organised and semi-organised interests who sought to use public office to secure collective private advantages, and the essential distinction between its own structure and the interest groups vying for a share in its power was critically unsettled.

Ultimately, as is well known, the democratic political system of interwar Germany collapsed, largely because of its lack of adequate inclusionary capacity to reconcile divergent class prerogatives. The self-description used by the regime that replaced the Weimar Republic is often taken literally in this context, and it is widely assumed that the post-1933 Germany was governed by a total or at least highly expansionist public order.[33] This ideological self-projection of the National Socialist regime, however, was really nothing more than a smokescreen. The political apparatus that developed in Germany between 1933 and 1945 can more properly be viewed as a systemic order marked, not by total politics, but rather by intense political-systemic crisis and structural dissolution. In this regime, public institutions, destabilised by pressures of class inclusion and hyperpoliticisation, haemorrhaged functional integrity and incrementally coalesced with, or lost its differentiated position in relation to, dominant private groups in society at large. Even Nazi insiders repeatedly observed that the apparatus of Hitler's regime was marked by extreme centrifugalism, so that, behind the veneer of totalitarian control, many offices were transacted as private goods, different regional and sectorial actors established local domains of semi-autonomy in the margins of the political system, and different administrative sectors and office holders vied for similar functions, thus creating a highly pluralistic and internally dispersed administrative order.[34] Even the use of the term 'state' to describe Hitler's regime is a matter of reasonable dispute. Hitler's regime could be equally well be defined as a fluid conglomerate of coercive functions, held together through a mixture of private interests, personal associations and systemic violence.[35] The creation of a 'unitary state' revolving around 'strongly centralized power' may have been a declared objective of the Nazi leadership. This, however, never became reality.[36]

Against this background, it is notable that the political system that developed first in post-1945 West Germany and then in post-1990 Germany as a whole was built, to a large degree, on inter-, or, more properly, on transnational law. On one hand, this was reflected in the fact that the legal order created in 1949 was avowedly friendly and open to international law.[37] However, this was also reflected in the fact that the newly established Constitutional Court began to act as a *transformer* of international law, translating rights enshrined under international conventions into objective institutions to be applied domestically and used structurally to shape German society.

This of course had a number of very varied results. Amongst its more notable outcomes, however, was the fact that the emergent democratic political system acquired a source of legitimacy which it was in itself not required endlessly to generate. Indeed, internationally projected human rights norms gradually became the dominant source of legitimacy for the production of legal norms in German society, and laws obtained primary legitimacy, not from objective conflict mediation or organic consensus obtained by acts of the state towards particular social agents, but from human rights, stored virtually within the political system and applied pervasively throughout society by the high judiciary. This impacted transformatively on the historical structural problems of the German state. It led, quite rapidly, both to a relative de-politicisation of class conflict, and, as a consequence, to a relatively clear abstraction or differentiation of the political system in its engagement with private organisations. In West Germany after 1949, trade unions were not subject to forcible state regulation, and industrial disputes were not subject to mandatory arbitration and were not fully internalised within the state.[38] Moreover, the force of monopolistic industrial enterprises was also diminished. Industrial de-concentration measures were imposed by the allies, and the debate about anti-cartel legislation remained a matter of pressing concern throughout the post-war era, and it culminated in Ludwig Erhard's anti-cartel laws of 1957/8. Overall, therefore, the state was – to some degree – split apart from class conflicts, and the capacity of private actors to utilise economic conflicts to invade the state was diminished. The fact that the state could avail itself of at least a *quantum of legitimacy*, which it was not forced to generate through external conflict mediation, proved vital to the stabilisation of the political system as a reasonably abstracted public order. In fact, the reference to international human rights law meant that the state was increasingly able to preserve its legitimacy as an internal resource, and this simplified and rendered less unsettling its interactions with potent private actors.

Naturally, it would not be accurate to observe Germany as an example of a seamless transition from depleted statehood to a conclusively stabilised state structure. However, it is notable that the gradual consolidation of the German political system relied on the fact that interactions between political and economic organisations could be located at a sub-executive level. This meant that a system of neo-corporatist political economy was able to develop, in which the executive positioned and legitimised itself above class disputes, yet possessed sufficient autonomy to bind industrial organisations selectively into the policy-making process. Arguably, in fact, whilst in post-1949 Germany class relations assumed renewed significance in the process of *legislation*, they preserved only limited importance in the process of *legitimisation*, and the most fundamental reserves of legitimacy for the political system were obtained through reference to rights. This re-location of legitimacy from class mediation to rights, we can conjecture, was the vital ingredient in the stabilisation, the abstraction, and above all, the relative de-politicisation of the German political system as it developed through the post-war era.

Argentina

The case of Argentina shows some similarities with that of Germany. After 1943, Argentina also unmistakeably assumed the features of a hyperpoliticised state, in which the endeavour to mediate class conflict led to acute malfunctioning, and egregious loss of public distinction, in the political system.[39] The first stage in this process of extreme politicisation was cemented in Perón's attempt, in 1949, to establish a corporate constitution, which brought the labour movement under the protection of the state, and placed entrepreneurial organisations under state jurisdiction. In this constitution, notably, Article 37 provided for a long catalogue of social rights. Article 38 declared that 'private property has a social function' and had to be subject to interests of common good, and it authorised the state to intervene in economic practices in order to stimulate development. Although he placed coercive restrictions on union activity, Perón's constitution and attendant policies brought about a significant downward redistribution of public wealth, and he sanctioned the forcible expropriation of hitherto potent and autonomous social groups. Notably, Perón's first administration (1946–55) witnessed the nationalisation of vital industrial sectors, and it saw a significant increase in wages and legal rights for organised labour.[40] As a result of these policies, however, those social groups that were placed at a disadvantage by Perón mobilised with extreme vehemence against his brand of corporatism, and they declared implacable hostility towards corporatism promoting the (semi-)consensual inclusion of organised labour.[41] Once installed in government, anti-Peronist factions normally sought support amongst actors tied to international capital markets, they introduced swingeing anti-union laws, and they heightened the porosity of the state to powerful industrial elites and their corporate lobbies. From 1943 up to 1983, in consequence, the political system of Argentina was polarised between two adversarial factions, each of which largely refused to accept the other as legitimate, and each of which sought to control the state through the permanent exclusion of the rival party. Throughout this period, in fact, government offices were treated as objects of conflict (that is, de facto, spoils) between two encompassing rival social groups, Peronists and anti-Peronists. In this conflict, each party aimed to mobilise social forces in order to annex the state to the interests of one distinct set of economic prerogatives and interests.[42]

Overall, this acute polarisation in Argentine political society situation triggered a hyperpoliticisation both of the state and of society as a whole, which, in turn, drained the state of autonomy, and left it vulnerable, repeatedly, to inner fragmentation and overthrow by politicised societal groups. In this process, rival actors endeavoured to control the state and to rigidify a distinct model of order strong enough permanently to exclude other social groups, and neither side in the socio-political conflicts refracted through the state was prepared to recognise the state as a publicly constituted order, normatively and functionally distinct from persons or groups holding office at one given moment. Clearly, this is exemplified by the periods of Peronist rule and by the weak dictatorship of the 1960s, in which the transparency of public office to private prerogatives is well documented. However, the military dictatorship which collapsed in 1983 can be seen as an extreme culmination of these processes. In fact, the last phase of the military dictatorship can be examined as a prime example of the privatisation of state power – or *state capture* – by rent-seeking groups, through which dominant actors were able use their societal positions to take control of state resources.[43] One analysis of the dictatorship claims simply that by the early 1980s the Argentinean state had forfeited 'autonomy vis-à-vis rent-seeking pressure groups such as the military, labour unions or certain business groups'. In consequence, 'the state had lost the power to act as a state'.[44] As in interwar Europe, therefore, in post-Peronist Argentina the centring of the state structure around class mediation ultimately eroded even the basic qualities of the state as a structure of differentiated public inclusion.

Against this background, it is notable that in Argentina the transition from military rule beginning in 1983 was impelled, to a not insubstantial degree, by human rights movements and initiatives. The process of democratic re-orientation at this time drew primary legitimacy from human rights norms, declared by organisations, commissions and judicial bodies, situated in part in the international domain. International human rights advocacy networks had played a prominent role in Argentina prior to the onset of the transition, and had done much to draw international attention to acts of regime violence.[45] The Inter-American Court of Human Rights had been constituted in 1979, and it began tentatively to promote supranational rights jurisprudence. Moreover, the UN had advocated an interventionist approach to rights-abusing states in Latin America throughout the later 1970s, and it had gained in confidence through the Carter administration beginning in 1977. During the preliminary stages of the transitional elections in 1983, the eventual president, Alfonsín, seized on the issue of human rights as a register in which he could give direction to the democratic transition. The vocabulary of rights, naturally, reflected a widespread array of political emotions in the wake of the collapse of military rule, and rights acquired symbolic and normative importance in a number of different social dimensions. At one level, rights created a register in which members of society could examine the military dictatorship, and construct a political system on new normative foundations. At a different level, however, the transition was marked by a deep intersection between national legal politics and international legal expectations, and the focus on rights was used to re-define national law and legally to assuage the state's traditional exposure to deep-lying traumatic tendencies in Argentine society: especially those impacting deleteriously on processes of structural abstraction and systemic differentiation.

Most notable in this regard was the fact Alfonsín used the vocabulary of international human rights because this created a diction of legitimacy, through which it was possible both to reject only military authority, but also to face down the claims of re-formed trade unions to serve as inner pillars of government.[46] Alfonsín's first legislative act (*Ley de Reordnamiento Sindical*, 1983) related to the status and structure of unions. This law clearly reacted against the violent suppression of unions under the military regime, and it gave express recognition to the freedom of trade unions, and reinstated the General Confederation of Labor. Nonetheless, this law was also designed to weaken the corporatist structure of trade union organisation, to de-couple the unions from the political system, and to offset tendencies to coercive organisation within unions: that is, to impose a pattern of single rights holding on units of economic organisation.[47] On that basis, Alfonsín was able – uniquely – to strip the state structure away from the trade unions without relying on the army to accomplish this. In fact, he was able to create a foundation for the legitimacy of the state which did not require the endless and systemically internalised conflict over conditions of labour, production and development. This shaped a wider move away from anti-individualistic political vocabularies (derived from corporatist populism, or Peronism),[48] and it promoted a growing de-collectivisation of society, a separation of public office from private power, and a (tentative) rise in the autonomy of the state in its engagement with powerful and traditionally privileged societal organisations.[49]

As in Germany, therefore, the integration of international norms into the domestic political system in Argentina acted to locate the political system on a new foundation of legitimacy. Primarily, it meant that the legitimacy for acts of legislation did not have to be extracted solely from factual processes for resolving concrete and unsettling conflicts in society. The fact that general political direction and specific acts of law making could be authorised through human rights meant that some element of legitimacy, at least as a residual quantity, could be presupposed – internally – within the political system. This led to a partial marginalisation of class as the basis of legitimacy, it offset tendencies towards excruciating levels of systemic politicisation, and it ultimately played an important role in the construction of the political system as a meaningfully *public* order. Of course, it would border on absurdity to say that through the transition Argentina was miraculously converted into a highly abstracted and differentiated political system.

However, incrementally, certain key indicators of growing systemic autonomy became apparent in the longer wake of the transition. These included, notably, that the political system could set policy directives in independence of established elite players, and that trade unions could re-define their position outside the state, without necessarily losing social influence.

Hyperpoliticisation and ethnicity: Kenya

Problems of state softness caused by high exposure to class inclusion and resultant hyperpoliticisation can be found, widely, in Sub-Saharan Africa. In fact, throughout the course of decolonisation most states in Sub-Saharan African were founded as corporatist states, committed to the mediation of class conflict, and they often proved incapable of sustaining a resiliently differentiated structure in face powerful societal actors. Indeed, most African states experienced problems of hyperpoliticisation close to, or even exceeding, those crises induced by class inclusion described above. In many Southern Africa states, however, problems caused by failed class inclusion proved less potent than a rather distinct (although often overlapping) pattern of hyperpoliticisation: hyperpoliticisation owing to pressures resulting from the failed inclusion of ethnic conflict.

Ethnic hyperpoliticisation can be observed in many or even most African societies. However, one especially important example of this is Kenya. In Kenya, the first post-colonial constitution (1963) had committed the new state to a federal system, recognising regional fault lines of ethnic and tribal autonomy: it endorsed *majimboism* as a compromise pattern of nation building.[50] However, the post-independence government led by Kenyatta soon effaced the federal design of the state. In fact, Kenyatta rejected all alternatives to unitary statehood, and the pluralistic plan for the Kenyan Republic never materialised.[51] After Kenyatta came to power, in fact, executive power was anchored strongly in a particular ethnic group, and the president secured his hold on executive competence by allocating goods to the ethnic population, and affiliated groups, from which he drew primary support. As a result of this, the foundation of the Kenyan state remained necessarily, in part, founded in partial, semi-private bargains between the president and ethnic elites, so that policy-making could not easily be directed by distinctively national – i.e. generally inclusive – interests and commitments. In particular, this promoted high levels of clientelism in the state, as the state, lacking a general substrate of legitimacy, was forced to manufacture a basis of working compliance in society by allocating public goods, as spoils, to different ethnic groups. Moreover, this meant that governments were reluctant to submit to multi-party elections because of the threat that they would release and give expression to uncontrollable ethnic tensions.[52] In consequence, further, governments were scarcely in a position to exercise inclusionary rule over all society. Alternative patterns of affiliation and obligations existed alongside, and often overrode, the loyalty of citizens to the laws of state.[53] As in cases of hyperpoliticisation through exposure to class conflicts, therefore, the Kenyan state appears as a model of ethnic hyperpoliticisation, which ultimately also provoked a damaging privatisation of state offices, resources and structure.

The complex and unmediated ethnic structure of Kenyan society then impacted on the more recent attempts at constitutional reform of the state. The first attempt at democratic transition in the early 1990s, driven in part by external pressures, was short-lived, and it resulted in presidential re-assertion of repressive measures against political opponents.[54] However, the late 1990s saw the beginnings of a long and more conclusive process of constitutional reform. In 1997, parliament introduced the Constitution of Kenya Review Act, which provided a basic framework for constitutional reform. Later, the Constitution of Kenya Review Commission was appointed, to prepare a draft constitutional reform bill for parliament. After much postponement, this also led to the convention of a National Constitutional Conference in 2003, which was charged, by parliament, with approving a new constitutional document. The resulting constitution was rejected in a referendum in late 2005. In fact, ethnic conflicts played a salient role in unsettling the constitution-making process at this time. Constitution writing often proved incendiary for ethnic rivalries, and it raised historically volatile questions regarding access of ethnic groups to state offices, resources and positions of directive influence.[55] Both the 2005 constitutional referendum and the elections held in 2007 saw high levels of ethnic violence. Notably, therefore, whereas other transitional societies in Africa, led by South Africa, had been able to extract certain pre-agreed principles to stabilise processes of constitutional-democratic transition, in Kenya the transition itself became an object of intensified politicisation, and the abstraction of stabilising norms was disrupted by the uneven inclusionary foundations of the polity.

On these grounds, Kenya might appear prima facie as a most unlikely case of state stabilisation by transnational judicial norms. In Kenya, in fact, conditions for the rise of judicial power and the reinforcement of human rights norms were singularly unfavourable. Kenya was traditionally regarded as a society with a highly dualist, post-Westminster judicial order. *Okunda* v. *Republic* (1970), in which international law was ruled subordinate to domestic law, long remained a leading case in that regard. During the pre-constitutional part of the transition, in fact, the Kenyan High Court repeatedly reiterated the view, in a suite of further high-profile cases, that international norms could not be directly translated into domestic law, and that the judiciary was required to prefer national to international norms and case law.[56]

Despite this, however, the Kenyan transition was also marked by the salience of judicial power, which at times played a vital role in stabilising the polity as a whole. During the constitution-writing process, the Kenyan High Court was called upon to intervene in constitutional foundation, and in so doing it developed a seminal body of constitutional jurisprudence. This became prominent, first, as, in *Njoya and Others* v. *Attorney General and Others* (2004), the authority of the Constitutional Conference to draft a new constitution was challenged before the High Court. This case remains very controversial, and it was plainly driven by political opposition to the draft constitution. In this case, the applicants argued that the parliament, acting via the Constitutional Conference, could not lay claim to exercise constituent power, and a new constitution could not be authorised by a sitting government. Further, the applicants protested against the parcellation of the Kenyan nation into separate regions during the writing of the constitution, which, they claimed, led to privileging of distinct ethnic groups, and was prohibited under terms of international law. Ultimately, the court found in favour of the applicants. The Justices argued that a new constitution needed to be activated by the *single and sovereign national people*, with authority to act, not in the style of Westminster as a parliamentary assembly, but as a primary constituent power. The court thus determined that a referendum should be held to endorse the constitution; only a referendum would serve to elevate the constitution above the will of a simple parliament, especially one quite manifestly in thrall to ethnic interests. In the first instance, the draft constitution was not accepted in the ensuing referendum, and a new democratic constitution was not finally ratified until 2010. In its 2004 ruling, however, the court spelled out certain vital principles. First, it designated *itself* as authorised to allocate political rights, and in fact to identify and to circumscribe the locus of national sovereignty. In this respect, the court assumed and established powers which were not yet constitutionally extant, and so it accorded itself *proprio motu* constitution-writing force.[57] Second, the court responded to the fragmented ethnic landscape of Kenyan society by defining a source of national agency standing above or behind different ethnic sub-groups, and by – albeit momentarily – locating that agency in the guardianship of the court. After 2008, this stabilising role of the judiciary remained prominent, and a special court was created to resolve disputes resulting from the process of transition.[58]

The constitution finally agreed in Kenya in 2010 ultimately reflected the intermittent judicial emphasis of the longer transition. In Article 160, the constitution accorded special weight to the need to preserve the autonomy of the judiciary in relation to the executive. Article 165(3) created a High Court, with authority in human rights cases, and Article 168 gave heightened protection to the independence and tenure of judges.[59] Article 259 accorded a distinctive purposive role to the judiciary, and it directed the judiciary to promote the values and purposes inherent in the constitution, and to develop law. Article 261(5, 7) implicitly assigned a mandate to the judiciary to order parliament to pass bills implementing constitutional values and provisions. These provisions were intended, at one level, to elaborate the law as a normative foundation for social life. But they were also intended to emphasise the transformative role of the judiciary in society. This judicial emphasis was accompanied by the fact that Article 2(5) stated that international law was to have direct and autonomous application in Kenya, so that, although Kenya remained a formally dualist state, the purposive duties of the courts were in part based on their assimilation of international law. This objective was taken very seriously by the Supreme Court, which consciously promoted the incorporation, although not the supremacy, of international law, and especially international human rights conventions, within the municipal legal system.[60] After the passing of the constitution, these tendencies continued with the introduction of a Judicial Service Commission to lead reforms, and with the implementation of a Judiciary Transformation Framework, to direct and consolidate the new role of the judiciary. In fact, the writing of the final constitution in Kenya was generally marked by an increasing openness of Kenyan law to international law, as the ethnic violence of 2007 brought Kenyan law and its deficiencies under scrutiny of the International Criminal Court, so that eventually international criminal law was systematically integrated into domestic law, in the International Crimes Act (2009).[61] Notably, this reception of international law has also given rise to the more consolidated promotion of regionalism and decentralisation, so that in some respects it marks a return of *majimboism*.

Naturally, we can only speculate what the final outcome of this process will be. However, we might base a prognosis on the fact that earlier constitutions which use courts to allow states to sidestep extreme exposure to class conflict generally contributed to the stabilisation of the state, and even to its construction as a public order. This may also be the case with constitutions that use courts to allow states to avoid extreme politicisation of ethnic conflict.

Outcomes of transnational law

These different examples could, with variations, be extended to include many more. However, even in this narrow selection of case we can observe that modern societies are in the process of producing a distinct genus of global or transnational constitutional law. This phenomenon can be explained in a strictly sociological framework, using methods characteristic of institution-sociological inquiry. The emergence of transnational constitutional norms is typical for societal settings in which states, or actors within state institutions, assimilate international law to resolve deeply rooted problems in the political system of national societies. In many such cases, international law, and especially that part of international law concentrated on human rights law, is applied to offset extreme cycles of hyperpoliticisation in the state, which often lead to a fragmentation and a general weak differentiation of the state's public authority. This occurs because the use of international law to authorise legislation means that one fraction of the state's legitimacy is imprinted and distilled *internalistically, within the state itself*, and it does not need to be objectively produced through external acts of mediation and conflict resolution. This means in turn that the state can insulate itself against the most intense inclusionary demands and conflicts in society, it can mobilise sources of legitimacy that are to some degree withdrawn from heightened political conflict, and it can preserve its own reality as a reasonably differentiated functional domain. The expenditure of legitimacy becomes separated from the process of its manufacture, and *legitimacy itself* becomes relatively depoliticised.

This has the implication, first, that the dualist distinction between international law and domestic law, or between international law and national sovereignty, is fictitious. International law has acquired perhaps its most abiding significance in the fact that it instils a highly internalised residue of legitimacy within national political systems, and this allows national political systems to emerge that are capable of applying inclusionary power and of building a consistently inclusionary structure across a national society. International law thus widely acts, not as an external constraint on, but as the internal foundation for, the meaningful exercise of sovereignty by state institutions. Indeed, it is a striking paradox of state formation that before the consolidation of a powerful domain of international law few states approached the condition of fully abstracted sovereignty (inclusionary autonomy) in their domestic settings. Of course, many states possessed the legal title of sovereignty under international law, but this was only rarely mirrored in their ability to exercise sovereign control of a national society. The transformation of international law into transnational law, adapted to pervasive pressures in the structure of national societies, has widely acted as the key to the abstraction of statehood. Far from contradicting national constitutional law, inter- or transnational law usually brings compensatory benefits to societies in which the abstraction of institutions founded in public law had, for historical reasons, proved difficult – or impossible.

This has the implication, second, that the emergence of a *transnational constituent power*, fusing legislative and judicial activity and supported by elements of national and elements of international law, would seem to lie at the heart of recent processes of state building and democratic foundation. Speculatively, in fact, we might observe that the formation of global constitutional law discloses a hidden secret in the history of nation and state building. Most nations and states were initially based on processes of institutional integration conducted through the factual inclusion of different social subjects via the resolution or at least the partial pacification of highly resonant or even dominant social conflicts. Few states and nations, however, managed effectively to regulate such inclusionary conflicts, and they remained both internally privatised and unable to apply law cohesively to their outer social environments as realised *nations*. What we now observe in the emergence of transnational judicial constitutionalism is the rise of an alternative process of systemic inclusion, occurring through the integration of citizens, not as factual agents in material or ethnic conflicts, but as judicially constructed holders of rights. Normative judicial integration thus supplants factual material integration as the foundation of society's structure of legal and political inclusion. The nation- and state-building force of transnational rights-based normative inclusion, instead of inclusion through material conflict mediation, appears prima facie likely to create more enduring, and in fact *more nationalised*, states and nations. Classical constitutional theory construed constituent power as the distillation of the will of the nation. It seems, however, that it is only through the supersession of this principle as the formula of constitutional legitimacy that nations are able to enter a condition of relative stable state- and nationhood.

Notes

1 Parts of this chapter were first presented at the University of Modena in May 2013. It was then presented more fully as a lecture to mark the opening of a new research centre on 'Law and Society in Global Context' at Queen Mary University, University of London. I wish to record my thanks to the organisers of both events, and to all participants in ensuing discussions. Most of the research for this chapter was funded by the European Research Council (Advanced Grant: 323656-STC).

2 For a selection of this literature see Thomas M. Franck, 'The Emerging Right to Democratic Governance'. *The American Journal of International Law* 86(1) (1992): 46–91. For a general cross-section of the global-constitutionalist literature, see Bardo Fassbender, 'The United Nations Charter as Constitution of the International Community'. *Columbia Journal of Transnational Law* 36(3) (1998): 539–619; Pierre-Marie Dupuy, 'The Constitutional Dimension of the Charter of the United Nations Revisited'. Max Planck Yearbook of United Nations Law 1 (1997): 1–33; Louis Henkin, 'Human Rights and State "Sovereignty"'. *Georgia Journal of International and Comparative Law* 25 (1995–6): 31–44; 39; Stefan Kadelbach and Thomas Kleinlein, 'International Law – A Constitution for Mankind? An Attempt at a Re-appraisal with an Analysis of Constitutional Principles'. *German Yearbook of International Law* 50 (2007). For a nuanced approach, see Anne Peters, 'Global Constitutionalism in a Nutshell', in Klaus Dicke, Stephan Hobe, Karl-Ulrich Meyn, Anne Peters, Eibe Riedel, Hans-Joachim and Christian Tietje (eds), *Weltinnenrecht. Liber amicorum Jost Delbrück* (Berlin: Duncker & Humblot, 2005), pp. 535–50; Ernst-Ulrich Petersmann, 'Human Rights and International Economic Law in the 21st Century: The Need to Clarify their Interrelationships'. *Journal of International Economic Law* 4(1) (2001): 3–39; 22; Mattias Kumm, 'The Legitimacy of International Law: A Constitutionalist Framework of Analysis'. *The European Journal of International Law* 15(4) (2004): 907–31; Laurence R. Helfer, 'Constitutional Analogies in the International Legal System'. *Loyola of Los Angeles Law Review* 37 (2003): 193–238; 237; Alec Stone Sweet, 'Constitutionalism, Legal Pluralism, and International Relations'. *Indiana Journal of Global Legal Studies* 16(2) (2009): 621–45; 637; Bruce Ackerman, 'The Rise of World Constitutionalism'. *Virginia Law Review* 83(4) (1997): 771–97; 777. For an overview, see Chapter 1 in Christine E.J. Schwöbel, *Global Constitutionalism in International Legal Perspective* (Leiden: Nijhoff, 2011).

3 This literature is of course not homogenous. Gunther Teubner's work on auto-constitutionalisation is much the most important. See Gunther Teubner, *Constitutional Fragments: Societal Constitutionalism and Globalization* (Oxford: Oxford University Press, 2012), pp. 160–61. The constitutionalist dimension in other theories of transnational law is visible in the assertions that transnational law can be construed as providing a system of 'transnational legal ordering', or an 'effective pluralistic conception of regulatory governance'. See Gregory Shaffer, 'Transnational Legal Ordering and State Change', in Gregory Shaffer (ed.), *Transnational Legal Ordering and State Change* (Cambridge: Cambridge University Press, 2013), pp. 1–10; 6; Robert Wai, 'Transnational Liftoff and Juridical Touchdown: The Regulatory Function of Private International Law in an Era of Globalization', *Columbia Journal of Transnational Law* 40 (2002): 209–74; 273–4. This constitutionalist dimension also appears in the claim that transnational private law might be viewed as a procedural constitution, able to provide normative structure against a background in which substantive concepts of justice and institutional models derived from the nation state increasingly forfeit their purchase. See Peer Zumbansen, 'Transnational Law', in Jan Smits (ed.), *Encyclopedia of Comparative Law* (Cheltenham: Edward Elgar, 2006), pp. 738–54; 747; Andreas Fischer-Lescano, 'Die Emergenz der Globalverfassung'. *Zeitschrift für ausländisches öffentliches Recht und Völkerrecht* 63 (2003): 717–60; 735, 751. This constitutionalist dimension is evident, further, in the fact that transnational legal theory often embraces human-rights norms as ineliminable principles of normative order, and it sees the coalescence of private and public law as a vital instrument for the protection and enforcement of human rights. All these positions are shaped by a perception of transnational legal order which defines the law of contemporary society as suspended from classical hierarchies and fixed normative structures, yet which nonetheless views the spontaneous emergence of transnational law as producing legal forms, albeit in highly contingent, systemically internalistic and rapidly adaptive fashion, which obtain a status close to the laws of classical constitutions. See Peer Zumbansen, 'Comparative, Global and Transnational Constitutionalism: The Emergence of a Transnational Legal-Pluralist Order'. *Global Constitutionalism* 1(1) (2012): 16–52; 50.

4 Philip C. Jessup, *The Use of International Law* (Ann Arbor: University of Michigan Law School, 1959), p. 63

5 See Antonio Cassese, 'Remarks on Scelle's Theory of "Role Splitting" (*dédoublement fonctionnel*) in International Law'. *European Journal of International Law* 1(1) (1990): 210–31; 212.

6 Peer Zumbansen, 'Transnational Legal Pluralism'. *Transnational Legal Theory* 1(2) (2010): 141–89; 152.

7 See Yuval Shany, *Regulating Jurisdictional Relations between National and International Courts* (Oxford: Oxford University Press, 2007), p. 27

8 See A.A. Cançado Trindade, *The Application of the Rule of Exhaustion of Local Remedies in International Law* (Cambridge: Cambridge University Press, 1983), pp. 55, 127.

9 The use of rights to mark spheres of discretion was formalised most clearly in the *Solange II* ruling of the German Constitutional Court in 1986, in which European law was allowed to take precedence over German national law as long as it was consonant with the basic human-rights norms enshrined in the West German constitution. Through this ruling, rights became a medium which made it possible for a national state to transfer 'sovereign powers' to inter-state institutions and generally to disperse judicial and legislative powers across the polity as a whole. See Rainer Hofmann, *Grundrechte und grenzüberschreitende Sachverhalte* (Berlin: Springer, 1993), p. 46. Although the 1986 *Solange* ruling resulted from a long history of conflict between the German Constitutional Court and the ECJ, this ruling, in essence, established a system of comity, in which different courts used rights to mark out boundaries of competence, deference, and mutual recognition. Rights thus formed a language of constitutional or in fact *constituent* dialogue between different tiers of a supranational political system. On the *Solange* rulings as a basis for comity see Gráinne de Búrca, 'The European Court of Justice and the International Legal Order after *Kadi*'. *Harvard International Law Journal* 51(1) (2010): 1–49; 43; Nikolaos Lavranos, 'The *Solange*-Method as a Tool for Regulating Competing Jurisdictions among International Courts and Tribunals'. *Loyola Los Angeles International and Comparative Law Review* 30 (2008): 275–334; 312; N. Türküler Isiksel, 'Fundamental Rights in the EU after *Kadi and Al Barakaat*'. *European Law Journal* 16(5) (2010): 551–77; 562.

10 Mohammed Bedjaoui, 'The Reception by National Courts of Decisions of International Tribunals', in Thomas M. Franck and Gregory H. Fox (eds), *International Law Decisions in National Courts* (Leiden: Brill, 1996), pp. 21, 31; Moritz Renner, 'Towards a Hierarchy of Norms in Transnational Law?' *Journal of International Arbitration* 26(4) (2009): 533–55; 554; André Nollkaemper, *National Courts and the International Rule of Law* (Oxford: Oxford University Press, 2011), pp. 12, 301; André Nollkaemper, 'The Internationalized Rule of Law'. *Hague Journal on the Rule of Law* 1(1) (2009): 74–8; 75, 77.

11 See Karen Knop, 'Here and There: International Law in Domestic Courts'. *New York University Journal of International Law and Politics* 32 (1999): 501–35; 525.

12 For the classical view of constituent power in nuce see Emmanuel-Joseph Sieyès, *Préliminaire de la constitution* (Paris: Baudouin, 1789), p. 20.

13 See my analysis in Chris Thornhill, 'Contemporary Constitutionalism and the Dialectic of Constituent Power'. *Global Constitutionalism* 1(3) (2012): 369–404, 'Rights and Constituent Power in the Global Constitution'. *International Journal of Law in Context* (2014) 3.

14 For contemporary observation see James Bryce, *Modern Democracies*, 2 vols (London: Macmillan, 1923), vol. 2, p. 374

15 See Philipp Dann and Zaid Al-Ali, 'The Internationalized *Pouvoir Constituant* – Constitution-Making under External Influence in Iraq, Sudan and East Timor'. *Max Planck Yearbook of United Nations Law* 10 (2006): 423–63.

16 See for comment Federico Fabbrini, 'Kelsen in Paris: French Constitutional Reform and the Introduction of *a posteriori* Constitutional Review of Legislation'. *German Law Journal* 9(10) (2008): 1297–312; Alec Stone Sweet, 'The Constitutional Council and the Transformation of the Republic'. *Yale Law School Faculty Scholarship Series* 79 (2008); Aileen Kavanagh, *Constitutional Review under the UK Human Rights Act* (Cambridge: Cambridge University Press, 2009), p. 275. For a more general picture, see Mitchel de S.-O.-L'E Lasser, *Judicial Transformations in the Courts of Europe* (Oxford: Oxford University Press, 2009), p. 24.

17 Since the *Factortame* cases, the UK national parliament is clearly, in part, subordinate to European law. See Anthony Bradley, 'The Sovereignty of Parliament – Form or Substance?' in Jeffrey Jowell and Dawn Oliver (eds), *The Changing Constitution*, 7th edition (Oxford: Oxford University Press, 2011), pp. 35–69; 56. Note also the force of the 1998 Human Rights Act as a 'constitutional statute'. See Roger Masterman, 'Taking the Strasbourg Jurisprudence into Account: Developing a "Municipal Law of Human Rights" under the Human Rights Act'. *International and Comparative Law Quarterly* 54(4) (2005): 907–31; 913.

18 Guobin Zhu, 'Constitutional Review in China: An Unaccomplished Project or a Mirage?' *Suffolk University Law Review* 63 (2010): 101–29; 109.

19 Henry Kwasi Prempeh, '*Marbury* in Africa: Judicial Review and the Challenge of Constitutionalism in Contemporary Africa'. *Tulane Law Review* 80 (2006): 1239–323; 1241, 1242. Generally, see Henry Kwasi Prempeh, 'Africa's "Constitutionalism Revival": False Start or New Dawn'. *International Constitutionalism* 5 (2007): 469–506; 505.

20 Mona El-Ghobashy, 'Constitutionalist Contention in Contemporary Egypt'. *American Behavioral Scientist* 51 (2008): 1590–610; 1613.

21 See Jeremy Rabkin, 'International Law vs. the American Constitution – Something's Got to Give'. *The National Interest* 55 (1999): 30–41; 39; Jeremy A. Rabkin, *Law without Nations? Why Constitutional Government requires Sovereign States* (Princeton: Princeton University Press, 2007), p. 70; Ernest A. Young, 'The Trouble with Global Constitutionalism'. *Texas International Law Journal* 38 (2003): 527–546; 536, 542. See also Dieter Grimm, *Die Zukunft der Verfassung* (Frankfurt am Main: Suhrkamp, 1991), p. 31; Martin Loughlin, 'In Defence of *Staatslehre*'. *Der Staat* 48(1) (2009): 1–27.

22 See Ran Hirschl, 'The New Constitutionalism and the Judicialization of Pure Politics Worldwide'. *Fordham Law Review* 75 (2007): 721–53; 723. More generally see, Ran Hirschl, *Towards Juristocracy: The Origins and the Consequences of the New Constitutionalism* (Cambridge, MA: Harvard University Press, 2004). Additionally, see John Ferejohn, 'Judicializing Politics, Politicizing Law'. *Law and Contemporary Problems* 65(3) (2002): 41–68; 41, 44; David Schneiderman, *Constitutionalizing Economic Globalization. Investment Rules and Democracy's Promise* (Cambridge: Cambridge University Press, 2008); Danny Nicol, *The Constitutional Protection of Capitalism* (Oxford and Portland: Hart, 2010), chapter 4.

23 Tom Ginsburg, 'Locking in Democracy: Constitutions, Commitment and International Law'. *New York University Journal of International Law and Politics* 38 (2006): 707–59.

24 Anne-Marie Slaughter, 'A Typology of Transjudicial Communication'. *University of Richmond Law Review* 29 (1995): 99–137; Anne-Marie Slaughter, 'A Global Community of Courts'. *Harvard International Law Journal* 44 (2003): 191–219.

25 César Rodríguez-Garavito, 'Toward a Sociology of the Global Rule of Law Field: Neoliberalism, Neoconstitutionalism, and the Contest over Judicial Reform in Latin America', in Yves Dezalay and Bryant G. Garth (eds), *Lawyers and the Rule of Law in an Era of Globalization* (Abingdon: Routledge, 2011), pp. 156–82; 165.

26 Sara Schatz, 'A Neo-Weberian Approach to Constitutional Courts in the Transition from Authoritarian Rule: The Mexican Case (1994–1997)', *International Journal of the Sociology of Law* 26 (1998): 217–44; Thomas Gawron and Ralf Rogowski, *Die Wirkung des Bundesverfassungsgerichts. Rechtssoziologische Analysen* (Baden-Baden: Nomos, 2007).

27 See for example Kate Nash, 'Human Rights, Movements and Law: On Not Researching Legitimacy'. *Sociology* 46(5) (2012): 797–812; 798, 807; Fuyuki Kurasawa, *The Work of Global Justice: Human Rights as Practices* (Cambridge: Cambridge University Press, 2007), p. 200; Boaventura de Sousa Santos, *Toward a New Legal Common Sense: Law, Globalization and Emancipation*, 2nd edition (London: Butterworths, 2002), chapters, 2, 5; Seyla Benhabib, 'Claiming Rights across Borders: International Human Rights and Democratic Sovereignty'. *American Political Science Review* 103(4) (2009): 691–704; 701.

28 See Max Weber, *Wirtschaft und Gesellschaft. Grundriß der verstehenden Soziologie* (Tübingen: Mohr, 1921), p. 18; Eugen Ehrlich, *Grundlegung der Soziologie des Rechts*, 4th edition (Berlin: Duncker & Humblot, 1989), p. 19.

29 As background to this definition of positivism see Mónica García-Salmones Rovira, *The Project of Positivism in International Law* (Oxford: Oxford University Press, 2013), p. 357

30 This is the overlying argument in Hirschl's work.

31 See Allan Rosas, 'State Sovereignty and Human Rights: Towards a Global Constitutional Project'. *Political Studies* 43 (1995): 61–78; 75.

32 See Josef Englberger, *Tarifautonomie im Deutschen Reich. Entwicklung des Tarifvertragswesens in Deutschland von 1870/71 bis 1945* (Berlin: Duncker & Humblot, 1995), pp. 153–4; Karsten Steiger, *Kooperation, Konfrontation, Untergang. Das Weimarer Tarif- und Schlichtungswesen während der Weltwirtschaftskrise und seine Vorbedingungen* (Stuttgart: Franz Steiner, 1998), pp. 132–5.

33 Ernst Forsthoff, *Der totale Staat* (Hamburg: Hanseatische Verlagsantalt, 1933), p. 24.

34 The lack of statehood under Hitler was admitted by Alfred Rosenberg, a leading ideologue of the NSDAP, who stated: 'The National Socialist state developed into a *legal centralism* and into a *practical particularism*' (quoted in Michael Ruck, 'Zentralismus und Regionalgewalten im Herrschaftsgefüge

des NS-Staates', in Horst Möller (ed.), *Nationalsozialismus in den Regionen* (Munich: Oldenbourg, 1996), pp. 99–122; 99). Similarly, Hans Franck, the chief jurist of the Hitler regime, claimed that National Socialism was based in a 'clear attack on the state'. See the account in Dieter Rebentisch, *Führerstaat und Verwaltung im Zweiten Weltkrieg. Verfassungsentwicklung und Verwaltungspolitik 1939–1945* (Stuttgart: Franz Steiner, 1989), p. 2. For similar reflections, see Peter Diehl-Thiele, *Partei und Staat im Dritten Reich. Untersuchungen zum Verhältnis von NSDAP und allgemeiner innerer Staatsverwaltung 1933–1945* (Munich: Beck, 1969), p. 21; Gerhard Schulz, *Die Anfänge des totalitären Maßnahmenstaates* (Frankfurt am Main: Ullstein, 1974), p. 294. See similar claims more recently in António Costa Pinto, 'Ruling Elites, Political Institutions and Decision-Making in Fascist-Era Dictatorships: Comparative Perspectives', in António Costa Pinto (ed.), *Rethinking the Nature of Fascism: Comparative Perspectives* (Basingstoke: Palgrave, 2011), pp. 197–226; 206–7. Classically, see the argument in Franz Neumann, *Behemoth: The Structure and Practice of National Socialism 1933–1944* (New York: Harper & Row, 1944), p. 467.

35 Note the telling comment on the 'essential difference between state and totalitarian rule' in Hans Buchheim, *Totalitäre Herrschaft. Wesen und Merkmale* (Munich: Kösel, 1962), p. 117.

36 Rebentisch, *Führerstaat und Verwaltung*, p. 97

37 Note the commitment to *Völlkerrechtsfreundlichkeit* [friendliness to international law] declared in Articles 24, 25, 26 and 100(2) of the *Grundgesetz*. The *Grundgesetz* also dramatically reduced expectations of social inclusion vis-à-vis organised labour, and it clearly separate trade-union activity from the state by sanctioning union rights of collective bargaining.

38 The Tarifvertragsgesetz of 1949 guaranteed the autonomy of unions and associations. See Veit Schell, *Das Arbeitsrecht der Westzonen und der jungen Bundesrepublik* (Bayreuth: P.C.O., 1994), p. 100. See further Wilhelm Rütten, 'Gewerkschaften und Arbeitsrecht nach dem Zweiten Weltkrieg (1945–1950/52)', in Bernhard Diestelkamp, Zentarô Kitagawa, Josef Kreiner, Junichi Murakami, Knut Wolfgang Nörr and Nobuyoshi Toshitani (eds), *Zwischen Kontinuität und Fremdbestimmung. Zum Einfluß der Besatzungsmächte auf die deutsche und japanische Rechtsordnung 1945 bis 1950* (Tübingen: Mohr, 1996), pp. 149–66; 160–62.

39 In 1943, organised labour first became a potent political force in the domestic politics of Argentina. See Joel Horowitz, *Argentine Unions, the State and the Rise of Peron, 1930–1945* (Berkeley: University of California Press, 1990), pp. 125, 180.

40 See James W. McGuire, *Peronism without Perón: Unions, Parties, and Democracy in Argentina* (Stanford: Stanford University Press, 1997), pp. 53–66, 783; Ruth B. Collier and David Collier, *Shaping the Political Arena* (Princeton: Princeton University Press, 1991), p. 342.

41 The dictatorship established in 1976 followed fascist models in replacing free union representatives with appointed trustees. See Gerardo L. Munck, *Authoritarianism and Democratization: Soldiers and Workers in Argentina, 1976–1983* (University Park: Pennsylvania State University Press, 1998), p. 77.

42 Munck, *Authoritarianism and Democratization*, p. 51

43 See Peter Ranis, *Argentine Workers: Peronism and Contemporary Class Consciousness* (Pittsburgh: University of Pittsburgh Press, 1992), pp. 38–9.

44 Silvio Borner and Markus Kobler, 'Strength and Commitment of the State: It Takes Two to Tango: A Case Study of Economic Reforms of Argentina in the 1990s'. *Public Choice* 110(3/4) (2002): 327–50; 340.

45 See generally Ellen L. Lutz and Kathryn Sikkink, 'International Human Rights Law and Practice in Latin America'. *International Organization* 3 (2000): 633–59.

46 Munck, *Authoritarianism and Democratization*, p. 155.

47 See Viviana Patroni, 'The Decline and Fall of Corporatism? Labour Legislation Reform in Mexico and Argentina during the 1990s'. *Canadian Journal of Political Science* 34(2) (2001): 249–74; 268; Ricardo Gaudio and Héctor Domeniconi, 'Las primeras elecciones sindicales en la transición democrática'. *Desarrollo Económico* 26(103) (1986): 423–54; 427.

48 See Enrique Peruzzotti, 'Towards a New Politics: Citizenship and Rights in Contemporary Argentina'. *Citizenship Studies* 6(1) (2002): 77–93; 82–3.

49 In support see Enrique Peruzzotti, 'The Nature of the New Argentine Democracy: The Delegative Democracy Argument Revisited'. *Journal of Latin American Studies* 33(1) (2001): 133–55; 142, 145. Close to my position, Peruzzotti sees the process of 'constitutionalization' in Argentina as expressed through a growing 'institutional differentiation between state and society', induced by the 'emergence of rights-oriented politics' (p. 148).

50 See for comment Stephen N. Ndegwa, 'Citizenship and Ethnicity: An Examination of Two Transition Moments in Kenyan Politics'. *The American Political Science Review* 91(3) (1997): 599–616; 605.

51 See David M. Anderson, '"Yours in Struggle for Majimbo". Nationalism and the Party Politics of Decolonization in Kenya, 1955–64'. *Journal of Contemporary History* 40 (2005): 547–64; 562; H.W.O. Okoth-Ogendo, 'The Politics of Constitutional Change in Kenya since Independence, 1963–69'. *African Affairs* 71(282) (1972): 9–34; 18; Donald S. Rothchild, *Racial Bargaining in Independent Kenya: A Study of Minorities and Decolonization* (Oxford: Oxford University Press, 1973), p. 140.
52 Ndegwa, 'Citizenship and Ethnicity', p. 610.
53 Ndegwa, 'Citizenship and Ethnicity', pp. 612–13.
54 Stephen N. Ndegwa, 'The Incomplete Transition: The Constitutional and Electoral Context in Kenya'. *Africa Today* 45(2) (1998): 193–211; 188.
55 See Bruce J. Berman, 'Ethnic Politics and the Making and Unmaking of Constitutions in Africa'. *Canadian Journal of African Studies* 43(3) (2009): 441–61; 449, 445; Laurence Juma, 'Ethnic Politics and the Constitutional Review Process in Kenya'. *Tulsa Journal of Comparative & International Law* 9(2) (2002): 471–532; 532.
56 See *Pattni & Another* v. *Republic*, *Mary Rono* v. *Jane Rono*. For comment see J. Osogo Ambani, 'Navigating Past the "Dualist Doctrine": The Case for Progressive Jurisprudence on the Application of International Human Rights Norms in Kenya', in Magnus Killander (ed.), *International Law and Domestic Human Rights Litigation in Africa* (Pretoria: Pretoria University Law Press, 2010), pp. 25–35.
57 See Laurence Juma and Chuks Okpaluba, 'Judicial Intervention in Kenya's Constitutional Review Process'. *Washington University Global Studies Law Review* 11 (2012): 287–364; 312.
58 Juma and Okpaluba, 'Judicial Intervention', p. 363.
59 See Migai Akech, 'Abuse of Power and Corruption in Kenya: Will the New Constitution Enhance Government Accountability?' *Indiana Journal of Global Legal Studies* 18(1) (2011): 341–94; 390.
60 See Tom Kabau and Chege Njoroge, 'The Application of International Law in Kenya under the 2010 Constitution: Critical Issues in the Harmonization of the Legal System'. *Comparative and International Law Journal of Southern Africa* 44(3) (2011): 293–310; 294–5.
61 Antonina Okuta, 'National Legislation for Prosecution of International Crimes in Kenya'. *Journal of International Criminal Justice* 7 (2009): 1063–76; 1072.

References

Ackerman, Bruce. 'The Rise of World Constitutionalism'. *Virginia Law Review* 83(4) (1997): 771–97.

Akech, Migai. 'Abuse of Power and Corruption in Kenya: Will the New Constitution Enhance Government Accountability?' *Indiana Journal of Global Legal Studies* 18(1) (2011): 341–94.

Ambani, Osogo. 'Navigating Past the "Dualist Doctrine": The Case for Progressive Jurisprudence on the Application of International Human Rights Norms in Kenya'. In *International Law and Domestic Human Rights Litigation in Africa*, edited by Magnus Killander, 25–35. Pretoria: Pretoria University Law Press, 2010.

Anderson, David M. '"Yours in Struggle for Majimbo". Nationalism and the Party Politics of Decolonization in Kenya, 1955–64'. *Journal of Contemporary History* 40 (2005): 547–64.

Bedjaoui, Mohammed. 'The Reception by National Courts of Decisions of International Tribunals'. In *International Law Decisions in National Courts*, edited by Thomas M. Franck and Gregory H. Fox, 21–31. Leiden: Brill | Nijhoff, 1996.

Benhabib, Seyla. 'Claiming Rights across Borders: International Human Rights and Democratic Sovereignty'. *American Political Science Review* 103(4) (2009): 691–704.

Berman, Bruce J. 'Ethnic Politics and the Making and Unmaking of Constitutions in Africa'. *Canadian Journal of African Studies* 43(3) (2009): 441–61.

Borner, Silvio, and Markus Kobler. 'Strength and Commitment of the State: It Takes Two to Tango: A Case Study of Economic Reforms of Argentina in the 1990s'. *Public Choice* 110(3/4) (2002): 327–50.

Bradley, Anthony. 'The Sovereignty of Parliament – Form or Substance?' In *The Changing Constitution*, 7th edition, edited by Jeffrey Jowell and Dawn Oliver, 35–69. Oxford: Oxford University Press, 2011.

Bryce, James. *Modern Democracies*. 2 vols. London: Macmillan, 1923.

Buchheim, Hans. *Totalitäre Herrschaft. Wesen und Merkmale*. Munich: Kösel, 1962.
Cançado Trindade, Antônio A. *The Application of the Rule of Exhaustion of Local Remedies in International Law*. Cambridge: Cambridge University Press, 1983.
Cassese, Antonio. 'Remarks on Scelle's Theory of "Role Splitting" (*dédoublement fonctionnel*) in International Law'. *European Journal of International Law* 1(1) (1990): 210–31.
Collier Ruth B., and David Collier. *Shaping the Political Arena*. Princeton: Princeton University Press, 1991.
Costa Pinto, António. 'Ruling Elites, Political Institutions and Decision-Making in Fascist-Era Dictatorships: Comparative Perspectives'. In *Rethinking the Nature of Fascism: Comparative Perspectives*, edited by António Costa Pinto, 197–226. Basingstoke: Palgrave, 2011.
Dann, Philipp, and Zaid Al-Ali. 'The Internationalized *Pouvoir Constituant* – Constitution-Making under External Influence in Iraq, Sudan and East Timor'. *Max Planck Yearbook of United Nations Law* 10 (2006): 423–63.
de Búrca, Gráinne. 'The European Court of Justice and the International Legal Order after *Kadi*'. *Harvard International Law Journal* 51(1) (2010): 1–49.
de S.-O.-L'E Lasser, Mitchel. *Judicial Transformations in the Courts of Europe*. Oxford: Oxford University Press, 2009.
de Sousa Santos, Boaventura. *Toward a New Legal Common Sense: Law, Globalization and Emancipation*, 2nd edition. London: Butterworths, 2002.
Diehl-Thiele, Peter. *Partei und Staat im Dritten Reich. Untersuchungen zum Verhältnis von NSDAP und allgemeiner innerer Staatsverwaltung 1933–1945*. Munich: Beck, 1969.
Dupuy, Pierre-Marie. 'The Constitutional Dimension of the Charter of the United Nations Revisited'. *Max Planck Yearbook* of *United Nations Law* 1 (1997): 1–33.
Ehrlich, Eugen. *Grundlegung der Soziologie des Rechts*, 4th edition. Berlin: Duncker & Humblot, 1989.
El-Ghobashy, Mona. 'Constitutionalist Contention in Contemporary Egypt'. *American Behavioral Scientist* 51 (2008): 1590–610.
Englberger, Josef. *Tarifautonomie im Deutschen Reich. Entwicklung des Tarifvertragswesens in Deutschland von 1870/71 bis 1945*. Berlin: Duncker & Humblot, 1995.
Fabbrini, Federico. 'Kelsen in Paris: French Constitutional Reform and the Introduction of *a posteriori* Constitutional Review of Legislation'. *German Law Journal* 9(10) (2008): 1297–312.
Fassbender, Bardo. 'The United Nations Charter as Constitution of the International Community'. *Columbia Journal of Transnational Law* 36(3) (1998): 539–619.
Ferejohn, John. 'Judicializing Politics, Politicizing Law'. *Law and Contemporary Problems* 65(3) (2002): 41–68.
Fischer-Lescano, Andreas. 'Die Emergenz der Globalverfassung'. *Zeitschrift für ausländisches öffentliches Recht und Völkerrecht* 63 (2003): 717–60.
Forsthoff, Ernst. *Der totale Staat*. Hamburg: Hanseatische Verlagsantalt, 1933.
Franck, Thomas M. 'The Emerging Right to Democratic Governance'. *The American Journal of International Law* 86(1) (1992): 46–91.
García-Salmones Rovira, Mónica. *The Project of Positivism in International Law*. Oxford: Oxford University Press, 2013.
Gaudio, Ricardo, and Héctor Domeniconi. 'Las primeras elecciones sindicales en la transición democrática'. *Desarrollo Económico* 26(103) (1986): 423–54.
Gawron, Thomas, and Ralf Rogowski. *Die Wirkung des Bundesverfassungsgerichts. Rechtssoziologische Analysen*. Baden-Baden: Nomos, 2007.
Ginsburg, Tom. 'Locking in Democracy: Constitutions, Commitment and International Law'. *New York University Journal of International Law and Politics* 38 (2006): 707–59.
Grimm, Dieter. *Die Zukunft der Verfassung*. Frankfurt am Main: Suhrkamp, 1991.
Helfer, Laurence R. 'Constitutional Analogies in the International Legal System'. *Loyola of Los Angeles Law Review* 37 (2003): 193–238.
Henkin, Louis. 'Human Rights and State "Sovereignty"'. *Georgia Journal of International and Comparative Law* 25 (1995–6): 31–44.

Hirschl, Ran. *Towards Juristocracy: The Origins and the Consequences of the New Constitutionalism*. Cambridge, MA: Harvard University Press, 2004.

———. 'The New Constitutionalism and the Judicialization of Pure Politics Worldwide'. *Fordham Law Review* 75 (2007): 721–53.

Hofmann, Rainer. *Grundrechte und grenzüberschreitende Sachverhalte*. Berlin: Springer, 1993.

Horowitz, Joel. *Argentine Unions, the State and the Rise of Peron, 1930–1945*. Berkeley: University of California Press, 1990.

Isiksel, Türküler. 'Fundamental Rights in the EU after *Kadi and Al Barakaat*'. *European Law Journal* 16(5) (2010): 551–77.

Jessup, Philip C. *The Use of International Law*. Ann Arbor: University of Michigan Law School, 1959.

Juma, Laurence. 'Ethnic Politics and the Constitutional Reform Process in Kenya'. *Tulsa Journal of Comparative & International Law* 9(2) (2002): 471–532.

Juma, Laurence, and Chuks Okpaluba. 'Judicial Intervention in Kenya's Constitutional Review Process'. *Washington University Global Studies Law Review* 11 (2012): 287–364.

Kabau, Tom, and Chege Njoroge. 'The Application of International Law in Kenya under the 2010 Constitution: Critical Issues in the Harmonization of the Legal System'. *Comparative and International Law Journal of Southern Africa* 44(3) (2011): 293–310.

Kadelbach, Stefan, and Thomas Kleinlein. 'International Law – A Constitution for Mankind? An Attempt at a Re-appraisal with an Analysis of Constitutional Principles'. *German Yearbook of International Law* 50 (2007): 303–48.

Kavanagh, Aileen. *Constitutional Review under the UK Human Rights Act*. Cambridge: Cambridge University Press, 2009.

Knop, Karen. 'Here and There: International Law in Domestic Courts'. *New York University Journal of International Law and Politics* 32 (1999): 501–35.

Kumm, Mattias. 'The Legitimacy of International Law: A Constitutionalist Framework of Analysis'. *The European Journal of International Law* 15(4) (2004): 907–31.

Kurasawa, Fuyuki. *The Work of Global Justice: Human Rights as Practices*. Cambridge: Cambridge University Press, 2007.

Lavranos, Nikolaos. 'The *Solange*-Method as a Tool for Regulating Competing Jurisdictions among International Courts and Tribunals'. *Loyola Los Angeles International and Comparative Law Review* 30 (2008): 275–334.

Loughlin, Martin. 'In Defence of *Staatslehre*'. *Der Staat* 48(1) (2009): 1–27.

Lutz, Ellen L., and Kathryn Sikkink. 'International Human Rights Law and Practice in Latin America'. *International Organization* 3 (2000): 633–59.

Masterman, Roger. 'Taking the Strasbourg Jurisprudence into Account: Developing a "Municipal Law of Human Rights" under the Human Rights Act'. *International and Comparative Law Quarterly* 54(4) (2005): 907–31.

McGuire, James W. *Peronism without Perón: Unions, Parties, and Democracy in Argentina*. Stanford: Stanford University Press, 1997.

Munck, Gerardo L. *Authoritarianism and Democratization: Soldiers and Workers in Argentina, 1976–1983*. University Park: Pennsylvania State University Press, 1998.

Nash, Kate. 'Human Rights, Movements and Law: On Not Researching Legitimacy'. *Sociology* 46(5) (2012): 797–812.

Ndegwa, Stephen N. 'Citizenship and Ethnicity: An Examination of Two Transition Moments in Kenyan Politics'. *The American Political Science Review* 91(3) (1997): 599–616.

———. 'The Incomplete Transition: The Constitutional and Electoral Context in Kenya'. *Africa Today* 45(2) (1998): 193–211.

Neumann, Franz. *Behemoth. The Structure and Practice of National Socialism 1933–1944*. New York: Harper & Row, 1944.

Nicol, Danny. *The Constitutional Protection of Capitalism*. Oxford and Portland: Hart, 2010.

Nollkaemper, André. 'The Internationalized Rule of Law'. *Hague Journal on the Rule of Law* 1(1) (2009): 74–78.

———. *National Courts and the International Rule of Law*. Oxford: Oxford University Press, 2011.

Okoth-Ogendo, Hastings W.O. 'The Politics of Constitutional Change in Kenya since Independence, 1963–69'. *African Affairs* 71(282) (1972): 9–34.

Okuta, Antonina. 'National Legislation for Prosecution of International Crimes in Kenya'. *Journal of International Criminal Justice* 7 (2009): 1063–76.

Patroni, Viviana. 'The Decline and Fall of Corporatism? Labour Legislation Reform in Mexico and Argentina during the 1990s'. *Canadian Journal of Political Science* 34(2) (2001): 249–74.

Peruzzotti, Enrique. 'The Nature of the New Argentine Democracy: The Delegative Democracy Argument Revisited'. *Journal of Latin American Studies* 33(1) (2001): 133–55.

———. 'Towards a New Politics: Citizenship and Rights in Contemporary Argentina'. *Citizenship Studies* 6(1) (2002): 77–93.

Peters, Anne. 'Global Constitutionalism in a Nutshell'. In *Weltinnenrecht. Liber amicorum Jost Delbrück*, edited by Klaus Dicke, Stephan Hobe, Karl-Ulrich Meyn, Anne Peters, Eibe Riedel, Hans-Joachim and Christian Tietje, 535–50. Berlin: Duncker & Humblot, 2005.

Petersmann, Ernst-Ulrich. 'Human Rights and International Economic Law in the 21st Century: The Need to Clarify their Interrelationships'. *Journal of International Economic Law* 4(1) (2001): 3–39.

Prempeh, Henry Kwasi. 'Marbury in Africa: Judicial Review and the Challenge of Constitutionalism in Contemporary Africa'. *Tulane Law Review* 80 (2006): 1239–323.

———. 'Africa's "Constitutionalism Revival": False Start or New Dawn'. *International Constitutionalism* 5 (2007): 469–506.

Rabkin, Jeremy A. 'International Law vs. the American Constitution – Something's Got to Give'. *The National Interest* 55 (1999): 30–41.

———. *Law without Nations? Why Constitutional Government requires Sovereign States*. Princeton: Princeton University Press, 2007.

Ranis, Peter. *Argentine Workers: Peronism and Contemporary Class Consciousness*. Pittsburgh: University of Pittsburgh Press, 1992.

Rebentisch, Dieter. *Führerstaat und Verwaltung im Zweiten Weltkrieg. Verfassungsentwicklung und Verwaltungspolitik 1939–1945*. Stuttgart: Franz Steiner, 1989.

Renner, Moritz. 'Towards a Hierarchy of Norms in Transnational Law?' *Journal of International Arbitration* 26(4) (2009): 533–55.

Rodríguez-Garavito, César. 'Toward a Sociology of the Global Rule of Law Field: Neoliberalism, Neoconstitutionalism, and the Contest over Judicial Reform in Latin America'. In *Lawyers and the Rule of Law in an Era of Globalization*, edited by Yves Dezalay and Bryant G. Garth, 156–82. Abingdon: Routledge, 2011.

Rosas, Allan. 'State Sovereignty and Human Rights: Towards a Global Constitutional Project'. *Political Studies* 43 (1995): 61–78.

Rothchild, Donald S. *Racial Bargaining in Independent Kenya: A Study of Minorities and Decolonization*. Oxford: Oxford University Press, 1973.

Ruck, Michael. 'Zentralismus und Regionalgewalten im Herrschaftsgefüge des NS-Staates'. In *Nationalsozialismus in den Regionen*, edited by Horst Möller, 99–122. Munich: Oldenbourg, 1996.

Rütten, Wilhelm. 'Gewerkschaften und Arbeitsrecht nach dem Zweiten Weltkrieg (1945–1950/52)'. In *Zwischen Kontinuität und Fremdbestimmung. Zum Einfluß der Besatzungsmächte auf die deutsche und japanische Rechtsordnung 1945 bis 1950*, edited by Bernhard Diestelkamp, Zentarô Kitagawa, Josef Kreiner, Junichi Murakami, Knut Wolfgang Nörr, and Nobuyoshi Toshitani, 149–66. Tübingen: Mohr, 1996.

Schatz, Sara. 'A Neo-Weberian Approach to Constitutional Courts in the Transition from Authoritarian Rule: The Mexican Case (1994–1997)'. *International Journal of the Sociology of Law* 26 (1998): 217–44.

Schell, Veit. *Das Arbeitsrecht der Westzonen und der jungen Bundesrepublik*. Bayreuth: P.C.O., 1994.

Schneiderman, David. *Constitutionalizing Economic Globalization: Investment Rules and Democracy's Promise*. Cambridge: Cambridge University Press, 2008.

Schulz, Gerhard. *Die Anfänge des totalitären Maßnahmenstaates*. Frankfurt am Main: Ullstein, 1974.

Schwöbel, Christine E.J. *Global Constitutionalism in International Legal Perspective*. Leiden: Nijhoff, 2011.

Shaffer, Gregory. 'Transnational Legal Ordering and State Change'. In *Transnational Legal Ordering and State Change*, edited by Gregory Shaffer, 1–22. Cambridge: Cambridge University Press, 2013.

Shany, Yuval. *Regulating Jurisdictional Relations between National and International Courts*. Oxford: Oxford University Press, 2007.

Sieyès, Emmanuel-Joseph. *Préliminaire de la constitution*. Paris: Baudouin, 1789.

Slaughter, Anne-Marie. 'A Typology of Transjudicial Communication'. *University of Richmond Law Review* 29 (1995): 99–137.

———. 'A Global Community of Courts'. *Harvard International Law Journal* 44 (2003): 191–219.

Steiger, Karsten. *Kooperation, Konfrontation, Untergang. Das Weimarer Tarif- und Schlichtungswesen während der Weltwirtschaftskrise und seine Vorbedingungen*. Stuttgart: Franz Steiner, 1998.

Stone Sweet, Alec. 'The Constitutional Council and the Transformation of the Republic'. *Yale Law School Faculty Scholarship Series* 79 (2008): 65–9.

———. 'Constitutionalism, Legal Pluralism, and International Relations'. *Indiana Journal of Global Legal Studies* 16(2) (2009): 621–45.

Teubner, Gunther. *Constitutional Fragments: Societal Constitutionalism and Globalization*. Oxford: Oxford University Press, 2012.

Thornhill, Chris. 'Contemporary Constitutionalism and the Dialectic of Constituent Power'. *Global Constitutionalism* 1(3) (2012): 369–404.

———. 'Rights and Constituent Power in the Global Constitution'. *International Journal of Law in Context* (2014): 357–96.

Wai, Robert. 'Transnational Liftoff and Juridical Touchdown: The Regulatory Function of Private International Law in an Era of Globalization'. *Columbia Journal of Transnational Law* 40 (2002): 209–74.

Weber, Max. *Wirtschaft und Gesellschaft. Grundriß der verstehenden Soziologie*. Tübingen: Mohr, 1921.

Young, Ernest A. 'The Trouble with Global Constitutionalism'. *Texas International Law Journal* 38 (2003): 527–46.

Zhu, Guobin. 'Constitutional Review in China: An Unaccomplished Project or a Mirage?' *Suffolk University Law Review* 63 (2010): 101–29.

Zumbansen, Peer. 'Transnational Law'. In *Encyclopedia of Comparative Law*, edited by Jan Smits, 738–54. Cheltenham: Edward Elgar, 2006.

———. 'Transnational Legal Pluralism'. *Transnational Legal Theory* 1(2) (2010): 141–89.

———. 'Comparative, Global and Transnational Constitutionalism: The Emergence of a Transnational Legal-Pluralist Order'. *Global Constitutionalism* 1(1) (2012): 16–52.

7 Constitutionalism and globalisation

A disputed relationship

Cesare Pinelli

Proposal

Several scholarships are engaged in affording a constitutional perspective to the vast phenomenon of 'globalisation'. Contrary to the assumptions of the decline of modern constitutionalism,[1] they maintain that 'a constitution beyond the state' is at least conceivable.

While sharing this hypothesis prima facie, I contend that current literature not only appears to be challenged by the contradictory effects of globalisation, namely the fragmentation of legal and political national orders and, on the other hand, the global financial market's attack on functional differentiation, but is also founded on gross misunderstandings, to the extent that it presents 'traditional constitutionalism' as a relic of the long-standing tradition of the sovereignty of the state.

I shall then argue that, irrespective of globalisation's future developments, attempts to provide a theoretical account of its relationship with constitutionalism require a more accurate narrative of the latter's legacy. In particular, I shall concentrate on its deep, albeit contested, pluralistic roots, which are likely to afford an alternative meaning to the 'constitution beyond the state' hypothesis.

The hypothesis of a constitutionalisation of international law

It was the establishment of the World Trade Organization (1994) that firstly posed the issue of whether an organisation significantly different from those of traditional international law might be 'constitutionalised'. Although regularly established by an international treaty, the WTO is in fact called upon to practise centralised jurisdiction through quasi-judicial panels and an Appellate Body for dispute settlement among member states adhering to the General Agreement on Tariffs and Trade (GATT), thus distinguishing itself from the International Court of Justice, which exercises jurisdiction to the extent that states have accepted its authority voluntarily. Furthermore, the broad interpretative authority given by the WTO agreement to the member states, acting by a three-quarter majority, and to its adjudicative panels has led to the conclusion that such law-making 'cannot help but alter the dynamics of domestic constitutional processes'.[2]

These features of the WTO agreement, together with its Preamble's references not only to the objective of 'expanding the production of and trade in goods and services', but also of those of 'ensuring full employment', 'raising standards of living' and 'sustainable development', have led to the suggestion that the agreement might be considered as if it were a constitution,[3] with the implication that the Appellate Body, as well as WTO officials, should interpret member states' trade obligations in harmony with their human rights obligations.[4]

In the same vein, some international lawyers tend to avoid a purely normative or a purely descriptive orientation towards global constitutionalism, rather researching 'what a constitutional international legal order could look like'.[5] They recognise that the constitutional features of the international order differ from those of the states, departing from the unfeasibility of a world constitution. However, the internal hierarchy between the *jus cogens* and the United Nations Charter, and the assimilation of the relationship between international law and domestic law to a federal structure, to the extent that the former is called upon to ensure the unity of the whole order, are considered symptoms of a gradual formal constitutionalisation of the international legal order.[6] Similarly, the worldwide expansion of the judicial protection of human rights and increasing international election monitoring in various states are likely to reflect such a trend on substantial grounds.[7] The WTO and the EU are viewed as pioneering examples,[8] while the EU's constitutionalisation is held to be a model for that of international law.[9]

These authors admit that the US claim to exceptionalism with regard to international law, starting from its military attack on Iraq in spring 2003, corresponds to an 'anti-constitutionalist trend', but assume that it can better be contrasted through a 'constitutional reading of current international law'.[10] Finally, they resist the objection that the flourishing of sectorial regimes, such as international environmental law, international trade law or international criminal law, might threaten the unity of international law, on the ground that even contemporary state constitutions no longer reflect the Enlightenment vision of the constitution as a planned order and unity of the state, and that a 'compensatory' approach to fragmentation 'might encourage rather than hinder the development of rules of conflict between the various and diverse subsystems'.[11] Rather than 'a project to interpret the world as constituted, held together in constitutional terms',[12] the hypothesis of a constitutionalisation of international law attempts to compensate for the 'de-constitutionalisation' of domestic orders with the advocacy of rules of conflict between the partial constitutions emerging from globalisation.

It is worthy of note that a compensation presupposes a zero-sum game: the good that has been lost can be gained through different means. In fact, the organisations and transgovernmental networks deriving from globalisation are depicted as 'partial constitutions', to the extent that they are likely to be connected through the development of rules of conflict. In practice, however, such organisations and networks are guided by their respective functional paradigms, which tend to enhance the fragmentation of international law.[13]

International lawyers are not at ease with fragmentation, namely the co-existence of several global regulatory regimes.[14] They tend to react to it with the hypothesis of the constitutionalisation of international law, which 'offers the perfect solution: it is flexible enough to take politics and economics into account, and at the same time provides ground for a strong normative framework. The appeal of a strong regulating framework that at the same time is realistic enough to take other (non-normative) forces into account is overwhelming'.[15]

Contrary to this view, 'global constitutionalism' should be understood as 'an on-going process, one with the potential to continually self-correct'.[16] But does such potential presuppose a break, or should it instead be connected to the legacy of constitutionalism? That question, as we shall see, requires historical and theoretical accounts that are lacking in the current literature.

The hypothesis of the emergence of a global administrative law

The issue of fragmentation appears to be no less crucial to scholars who advocate the emergence of a global administrative law (GAL). These argue that constitutionalist approaches are biased from a 'holistic vision' seeking 'to describe and develop a fully justified global order', in spite of the 'precarious legitimacy of transnational and global governance'.[17] None of the transnational institutions, so the argument goes, seems to satisfy democratic principles, nor do the classical ways of legitimising international institutions, such as a delegatory relationship with member states and the implementation of international decisions, 'guarantee significant national control over global governance institutions beyond the stage of their creation'.[18] GAL is expected to reveal a 'more limited ambition', being centred both on the 'mechanisms, principles, practices and supporting social understandings that promote or otherwise affect the accountability of global administrative bodies',[19] and on the standards and regulations arising from the networks connecting these bodies, which have a powerful impact on domestic regulation.[20]

The result of the GAL studies corresponds to this approach. Far from drawing a grand design, it recognises that 'the global legal order is made of a mosaic of legal systems, with different layers (local, national, regional, global) and a plurality of sectorial regulatory regimes. There is competition and overlapping, but there is also lack of communication and coordination. It is far from being a harmonious system of law', adding that the institutional setting of such a polity is characterised 'by atrophy of the legislative and the judicial branches', and by continuous negotiations between national administrations.[21]

Contrary to the 'constitutionalisation' hypothesis, the GAL does not imagine rules of conflict, and therefore an increasing interconnection, between the 'partial constitutions' emerging from globalisation. It registers fragmentation of transnational institutions and of their decision-making processes as a mere fact. Its ambition might thus be more limited than that of international lawyers, not because of its narrower scope, but because it does without a normative perspective.

This brings us to the issue of different disciplines competing with each other in the analysis of global governance. As has been observed, 'there is scant cross-fertilisation from the different points of departure, and what exchange does take place often appears to be the dialogue of the deaf'.[22] This may happen because 'it is always tempting in this sort of situation to imagine that each has hold of one piece of the elephant. They do, certainly. But they are also each proposing a different elephant. Each offers a vision, more or less in the mode of our conventional disciplines before them, which they claim to be a more complete account, a plausible total or ground level answer to the question of how we are governed, as a candidate to function as queen of the sciences when it comes to global governance'.[23]

In our case, it should only be added that the 'different elephant' drives us to the traditional dilemma between 'an anatomical account of the rule structure of an existing regime' and 'a normative theory of how things ought to be'.[24] In other words, either we content ourselves with describing the fragmented legal world resulting from globalisation, or we maintain a normative approach without giving a credible account of its feasibility.

The hypothesis of societal constitutionalism

While adapting Luhmann's theory of social systems to globalisation, Teubner's theory of 'societal constitutionalism' proposes an alternative picture of fragmentation. 'In functional differentiation', he argues, 'the experiment runs the risk of renouncing the unity of society and liberating a variety of fragmented social energies – each of which, since it is not limited by any in-built counter-principles, causes a massive internal growth-dynamic. The great achievements of civilisation in art, science, medicine, economics, politics and law only became possible by virtue of this process'.[25]

Far from creating a dilemma, fragmentation here becomes an opportunity for re-defining the constitutional problems of world society, leaving the idea of a globally unified constitution aside. Transnational regimes, particularly in the private area, are viewed as new constitutional subjects that compete with nation states in the global space: contrary to the 'obstinate state-and-politics-centricity of traditional constitutionalism', constitutional sociology projects the constitutional question not only onto the relationship between politics and law, but also onto the society as a whole, and believes that constitutionalism has the potential to counteract the expansionist tendencies of social systems outside the state, particularly the globalised economy, science and technology, and the information media, when they endanger individual or institutional autonomy.[26] The crucial point is that these social systems structure themselves into constitutions, in the sense of a body's *constitution*, namely the physical condition of that body.[27] This is the oldest meaning of constitution (constitution in the organic sense), as distinguished from its formal (or artificial) meaning.[28]

But the self-structuring of social systems into constitutions does not exhaust Teubner's account: 'In the course of functional differentiation, all sub-systems develop growth-energies, which, both in their productivity as well as in their destructivity, are highly ambivalent.'[29] And such a 'growth spiral' could accelerate 'to the point where it tips over into destructiveness by colliding with other social dynamics'.[30] These are potentially

> catastrophe moments, the constitutional moments which make possible collective learning experiences of self-limitation. 1945 is the paradigm. That was the constitutional moment for a worldwide proclamation of human rights in the wake of a political totalitarianism; the moment in which political power was willing, worldwide, to self-limit. Similarly, 1789 and 1989 were moments in which, in the wake of destructive expansion tendencies, politics limited itself by guaranteeing the separation of powers and fundamental rights within political constitutions.[31]

According to Teubner, 'catastrophe moments' require constitutional rules that, rather than being constitutive of the internal structure of each social system, should be limitative of its 'excessive growth processes'.[32] But these rules, no less than constitutive ones, should derive from self-limitation. External limitation, which would only result from state intervention, might in fact either engender a permanent subordination of the sub-systems to the state, which is no longer a valid option after the experiences of the last century's political totalitarianism, or prevent excessive growth processes through 'the external exercise of control, backed by massive sanctions', which are however 'bound to misfire'.[33]

According to the theory of societal constitutionalism, 'it is only possible to invent these limitations from within the system-specific logic, and not from the outside': external social forces – including state instruments of power, legal rules and civil society countervailing powers from other contexts, media, spontaneous protest, social movements, NGOs or trade union power – should rather 'apply such massive pressure on the function systems that internal self-limitations are configured and become truly effective'.[34]

While referring his theory to the current financial crisis, Teubner admits that societal constitutionalism here attempts 'to steer a difficult path between external interventions and self-steering'.[35] In particular, that path reflects an inner ambivalence, combining self-limitations of the sub-system with external pressures, including legal rules, that would at least be invented, if not imposed, from the outside.

Furthermore, irrespective of whether its solution will consist in a 'constitutional moment', the financial crisis already exhibits a danger for the theory of functional differentiation, namely 'the breakdown of the operative distinction between political and other forms of social rationality, such as economic rationality'.[36] Neo-liberalism, as well as other variants of political fundamentalism, aim at overcoming Luhmann's 'original sin' of functional differentiation 'through the submission of society in its entirety to a single form of rationality'.[37] Contrary to the totalitarian ideologies of the past, 'they paradoxically use a single universe which is external to the political system, such as economic, environmental, national or religious belief systems, as a vehicle for the attempt to submit society to a totalising political ideology'.[38] Therefore, 'an ideology such as neo-liberalism, which is seemingly aimed at reducing the reach of the political system as much as possible, can only achieve this through political means and within the framework of a political universe', with the consequence that 'the intention to submit society in its entirety to an economistic logic remains foremost a political objective, and only secondarily an economic one'.[39]

This attitude is demonstrated from a J.P. Morgan report, according to which the crisis of the Eurozone depends on

> deep-seated political problems in the periphery, which, in our view, need to change if EMU is going to function properly in the long run. The political systems in the periphery were established in the aftermath of dictatorship, and were defined by that experience. Constitutions tend to show a strong socialist influence, reflecting the political strength that left-wing parties gained after the defeat of fascism. Political systems around the periphery typically display several of the following features: weak executives; weak central states relative to regions; constitutional protection of labour rights; consensus-building systems which foster political clientelism; and the right to protest if unwelcome changes are made to the political status quo.[40]

Leaving aside the inaccuracy of this account, which goes so far as to attribute the crisis of the Eurozone to the constitutions of 'the periphery', namely of the EU's southern member states, the report demonstrates that the latter amount to a disturbing version of constitutionalism for authoritative protagonists of the global financial elite.

On the other hand, the de-regulation of the financial markets has been depicted

> as a move implying capture, in the sense that public regulators influenced by monetarist ideology were transformed from being the guardians of the public interest into being the servants of the financial industry, with the result that the relationship between operators and regulators increasingly became characterised by coalescence. This effectively undermined the value of the structural coupling between the economic and the political system, in the sense that the form of stability and restraint imposed by public regulation *vis-à-vis* economic processes was increasingly weakened. This had subsequent effects internally in the financial system because the differentiation between different functions, products and levels of risk collapsed, in the sense that the distinction between banks, investment banks and hedge funds became increasingly blurred.[41]

The assumption is that, notwithstanding its claim of setting exclusively economic benchmarks, the neo-liberal ideology is guided by political rationality that goes hand in hand with that of the coalescence between financial operators and regulators. Rather than its 'dark side', global markets should thus be at odds with functional differentiation.

Attempts of political reactions to the challenge of financial markets

In the light of these considerations, the heuristic capacity of the main theoretical accounts of global constitutionalism appears prima facie modest. Those pertaining to diverse legal disciplines are challenged by the fragmentation dilemma, while on the other hand tending to sidestep the important issue of financial markets. Societal constitutionalism is instead provided with analytical tools, such as those afforded by the theory of functional differentiation, which are likely to overcome the fragmentation dilemma. Conversely, the theory meets serious obstacles vis-à-vis the global financial market, whose 'growth excesses' are accompanied both by coalescence between regulators and operators and by the resort to a fundamentalist economic rationality that *inter alia* questions those versions of constitutionalism that are believed to run counter to its imperatives. The distinction thus appears to be blurred between internal self-limitation and external pressure, on which Teubner relies for formulating the hypothesis of a 'constitutional moment'.

These difficulties, however, affect societal constitutionalism's capacity to predict developments concerning the relationship between the financial market and political powers. A different question is that of how societal constitutionalism might be connected to versions of constitutionalism other than those centred on state sovereignty, with a view to display the challenge of globalisation regardless of its future developments.

In this respect, it is worth noting that, according to Teubner, 'partial societal constitutions' are not born with globalisation: these lived in a 'strange penumbra' under the nineteenth-century's political constitutions of liberalism and, after being submitted to the power of the state during the totalitarian epoch, were respected, although not officially recognised, by the constitutions of the late twentieth century, thus balancing state constitutionalism with constitutional pluralism.[42] This account appears far more accurate than the frequent opposition between a monistic and 'holistic' constitutionalism and the pluralistic trends that globalisation is believed to engender.[43] Contemporary constitutionalism is here simply traced back to the legacy of state sovereignty and opposed to pluralism. This point requires clarification.

Global finance and differentiation

Attention needs to be drawn to the post-totalitarian constitutional choices of recognising freedom of association without institutionalising economic and social pluralism. These choices reflected a decisive shift from the version of constitutionalism that prevailed in the aftermath of the French Revolution.

The revolutionary thinking of 1789 was affected by deep suspicion of the *corps intermédiaires*, namely the associations and professional groups that expressed the legacy of feudalism, which resisted the king's absolutist pretentions during the *ancien régime*. With the abolition of these entities (the 1791 *loi Le Chapelier*), nothing was left between the state and the individual, the former directly exerting its authority over the latter through an increasingly centralised administration. According to that institutional model, which was variously adopted in the rest of continental Europe, sovereignty was viewed in terms of omnipotence, with the effect that the individual's rights would depend either on the presumption that parliament, as the expression of the *volonté générale*, would ensure their best protection, or on self-limitations of the state, as in the German *Rechtsstaat*.

This led to the abstract nature of legislation and the disconnect between the public power and citizens, who were meanwhile entering into the public sphere due to the gradual extension of suffrage. Social and political conflicts followed and were exploited by leaders of totalitarian parties in an attempt to demonstrate the failure of the traditional legal order, whose formalism Carl Schmitt denounced, advocating a turn towards a 'concrete order'. The totalitarian regimes' concrete approach resulted in the abolition of every distance from citizens, to the point of conditioning their conscience. By no means limiting themselves to the repression of dissent, these regimes needed active consent from the people and managed to obtain it by the massive intrusion of propaganda into the realm of the individual.

The constituent assemblies that convened after the collapse of totalitarian regimes were therefore confronted with the issue of how to reverse the premises of totalitarianism without returning to the previous constitutional situations. The formers' concrete stance vis-à-vis ordinary citizens was of course the main threat to be avoided. But this was not a good reason for reverting to the abstract nature of parliamentarianism. Blending universal suffrage and majority rule together with the classical version of the separation of powers and the rule of law was thus felt to be inadequate for a post-totalitarian civilisation, which instead sought to achieve a fair equidistance between the public power and citizens.

While recognising the principle of human dignity, the constituent assemblies affirmed their 'never more' with respect to totalitarianism, in correspondence with the preamble to the 1949 Universal Declaration. But that recognisance was also intended to overcome the atomistic conception of freedom that characterised post-1789 constitutionalism: emphasis was put on the relational dimension of individual identity, as demonstrated both by the guarantee of freedom of association and by the promotion of pluralism in social, economic, cultural and religious spheres.

Pluralism, in turn, acquired the significance of enriching the notion of democracy. It is worth noting that, contrary to the economic and social councils provided for by some constitutions, which proved to be ineffective, informal or less institutionalised mechanisms were successfully adopted, such as the advice and consent given by economic and social groups in relation to public policies, agreements between parties conditioning the enactment of legislation and economic and voluntary enterprises taking over public functions previously carried out by elected authorities. Further democratic devices, such as referenda and the establishment of federal or regional structures, were intended to counterbalance the excesses of a purely representative democracy, impeding the formation of monolithic power by disseminating a pluralistic version of democracy. On the other hand, the introduction of a constitutional review of legislation introduced a sophisticated version of the rule of law that tended to override the myth of parliamentary sovereignty, with the aim of ensuring an effective protection of fundamental rights. While remaining at the centre of democratic life, parliament was no longer conceived of as the sole institution capable of granting fundamental rights: on the contrary, these rights were to be granted not only before administrative bodies, but also before statutory law.

The traditional combination between the rule of law and democracy was thus inserted within the framework of the principles and institutions mentioned previously, with the aim of setting new limits to the exercise of public power and, at the same time, providing it with further legitimacy. Without this framework, the constitution would have been simply superimposed on the other sources of law as the highest expression of the state's will. In that case, the pre-totalitarian system would only have been changed on formal grounds, but confirmed in its abstraction, with the effect of leaving the ultimate ends of the national community at the disposal of the state, the omnipotent sovereign of the continental tradition. In the perspective of post-totalitarian constitutionalism, on the contrary, every subject, including even the state, is prevented from determining the community's ultimate ends. These correspond to substantive principles enshrined in the constitution and intended to endure, regardless of the contingent expressions of public powers, including political decisions of the majorities in any given legislature. Instead, public powers are asked to protect or to promote these principles, according to whether the prevalence is given to the negative or to the positive side of constitutionalism.[44]

From this it follows that no organ enjoys either legal or political sovereignty, and that it is this lack that 'forces us to identify the people as the ultimate possessor of the sovereignty of their state. This does not mean that there is an entity "the people" that has an existence distinct from or prior to their constitution. On the contrary, they count as "a people" by virtue of the constitution that makes them so'.[45]

A further observation concerning pluralism is needed for the purposes of our inquiry. It is the recognition of pluralism in the diverse spheres of life that demonstrates that post-totalitarian constitutions are not expected to predict the social evolution of the respective countries, nor reflect the ambition of building an artificial order from above. Their principles are rather structured with the aim of orienting, and accompanying, social changes, on the assumption that the challenge of enduring through different generations distinguishes the constitution from ordinary legislation.

As a consequence, post-totalitarian constitutions admitted restrictions on national sovereignty, in the field of international relations, for the purpose of accepting the obligations deriving from membership in international organisations aimed at promoting peace and justice among nations. This constituted a turning point away from the holistic conception of sovereignty prevailing since the French Revolution, to the extent that the effects of these limitations on the national legal and political system are unpredictable, so that no harmonious order is likely to be established. That is why, although upsetting for traditional state constitutionalism, developments since the 1957 Treaty of Rome have not been alien to those countries' constitutions. In particular, while tensions arise between market competition and the state's role in providing social services, a variety of largely unpredictable factors contribute to the probability that diverse combinations are achieved among these elements. Rather than being planned by the will of the original authors of the constitutions in question, the quest for a fair equidistance between citizens and public power derives here from interactions between a plurality of the legal and political orders permitted by the constitution. EU law thus already built a bridge 'which poses the most pressing paradigm-challenging test to what we might call constitutional monism'.[46]

What is at stake for constitutional democracies?

The notion of contemporary constitutionalism as opposed to pluralism therefore amounts to a caricature of the former, in epistemological no less than in legal terms. 'That false opposition', it has been observed, sidesteps the central issue of 'the subject(s) of both the plurality of legal norms at stake and the plurality of corresponding constitutional constraints. It is not a matter of choosing the one over the many or *vice versa*, but of explaining who the many are and how they ought to relate in the absence of ultimate authority of the constituted orders'.[47] This moves in the same direction as the quest for an 'ordered pluralism', capable of dealing both with the growing complexity and fragmentation of legal and political orders, and with the forced uniformity pursued by the global financial market.[48]

However, it is precisely this double feature of globalisation that challenges constitutionalism. Heterarchical, rather than hierarchical, criteria may compose the conflicts arising between fragmented legal and political orders. But these, as demonstrated by the EU's reaction to the financial crisis, appear in any event to be too weakly organised to resist the financial system's 'growth excesses'.

Irrespective of further developments, this leads to the question of societal constitutionalism. The functional differentiation processes that lie at the core of this theory are indeed unchecked by the state's sovereign powers. On the other hand, as I have attempted to demonstrate, these processes stem from the very premises of constitutional pluralism. This origin should be borne in mind vis-à-vis the rise of any brand of fundamentalist ideology that tends to blur functional differentiation together with the achievements of civilisation that it has permitted. The question might thus be posed of whether there is any probability that the quest for a fair equidistance between citizens and public powers will be pursued in the seemingly turbulent conditions of our times.

Notes

1 D. Grimm, 'The Constitution in the Process of Denationalisation', *Constellations* 2 (2005): 460ff., and M. Loughlin, 'What is Constitutionalism?', in P. Dobner and M. Loughlin (eds), *The Twilight of Constitutionalism?* Oxford: Oxford University Press, 2010, 47ff.
2 E.A. Young, 'The Trouble with Global Constitutionalism', *Texas International Law Journal* 38 (2003): 535.
3 J.H. Jackson, 'The World Trade Organisation and the "Sovereignty" Question', *Legal Issues of European Integration* 1 (1996): 186.
4 E.-U. Petersmann, 'The WTO Constitution and Human Rights', *Journal of International Economic Law* 19 (2000). See also D.Z. Cass, *The Constitutionalisation of the World Trade Organisation: Legitimacy, Democracy and Community in the International Trading System*, Oxford: Oxford University Press, 2005.
5 C. Schwoebel, 'The Appeal of the Project of Global Constitutionalism to Public International Lawyers', *German Law Journal* 13(1) (2012): 1.
6 J.A. Frowein, 'Konstitutionalisierung des Voelkerrechts', in K. Dicke et al. (eds), *Voelkerrecht und internationales Privatrecht in einem sich globalisierenden internationalen System: Auswirkungen der Enstaatslichung transnationaler Rechtsbeziehungen*, Heidelberg: Mueller, 2000, 427ff.; A. Peters, 'Compensatory Constitutionalism: The Function and Potential of Fundamental International Norms and Structures', *Leiden Journal of International Law* 19 (2006): 598; E. De Wet, 'The International Constitutional Order', *International and Comparative Law Quarterly* 55 (2006): 57ff.
7 Peters, 'Compensatory Constitutionalism', 599ff., and De Wet, 'The International Constitutional Order', 67ff.
8 Peters, 'Compensatory Constitutionalism', 595 and De Wet, 'The International Constitutional Order', 52ff.
9 M. Kumm, 'The Legitimacy of International Law: A Constitutionalist Framework of Analysis', *European Journal of International Law* 15 (2004): 907.
10 Peters, 'Compensatory Constitutionalism', at 605.
11 Peters, 'Compensatory Constitutionalism', at 603.
12 D. Kennedy, 'The Mystery of Global Governance', *Ohio Northern University Law Review* (2008): 841.
13 E. De Wet, 'The Constitutionalisation of Public International Law', in M. Rosenfeld and A. Sajo (eds), *The Oxford Handbook of Comparative Constitutional Law*, Oxford: Oxford University Press, 2012, at 1223.
14 International Law Commission, *Fragmentation of International Law: Difficulties Arising From the Diversification and Expansion of International Law*, UN General Assembly, A/CN.4/L.682 13 April 2006.
15 Schwoebel, 'The Appeal of the Project of Global Constitutionalism', at 15.
16 Schwoebel, 'The Appeal of the Project of Global Constitutionalism', at 21.
17 N. Krisch, 'Global Administrative Law and the Constitutional Ambition', LSE Law, Society and Economy Working Papers 10/2009, 2.
18 Krisch, 'Global Administrative Law', at 5.
19 B. Kingsbury, N. Krisch and R. Stewart, 'The Emergence of Global Administrative Law', Institute for International Law and Justice Working Paper 2004/1.
20 S. Cassese, *The Global Polity. Global Dimensions of Democracy and the Rule of Law*, Sevilla: Global Law Press – Editorial Derecho Global, 2012, 23ff.
21 Cassese, *The Global Polity*, at 175.
22 N. Walker, 'Beyond the Holistic Constitution', in P. Dobner and M. Loughlin (eds), *The Twilight of Constitutionalism*, Oxford: Oxford University Press, 2012.
23 Kennedy, 'The Mystery of Global Governance', at 844.
24 M. Loughlin, 'The Nature of Public Law', in C. MacAmhlaigh, C. Michelon and N. Walker (eds), *After Public Law*, Oxford: Oxford University Press, 2013, at 20.

25 G. Teubner, 'A Constitutional Moment? The Logics of "Hitting the Bottom" ', in P.F. Kjaer, G. Teubner and A. Febbrajo (eds), *The Financial Crisis in Constitutional Perspective*, Oxford and Portland: Hart, 2011, 12.
26 G. Teubner, *Constitutional Fragments: Societal Constitutionalism and Globalisation*, Oxford: Oxford University Press, 2012, 7.
27 Teubner, *Constitutional Fragments*, 89.
28 For a recent account of these meanings, see Y. Hasebe and C. Pinelli, 'Constitutions', in M. Tushnet, T. Fleiner and C. Saunders (eds), *Routledge Handbook of Constitutional Law*, London and New York: Routledge, 2013, 9ff.
29 Teubner, 'A Constitutional Moment?', at 12.
30 Teubner, 'A Constitutional Moment?', at 10.
31 Teubner, 'A Constitutional Moment?', at 12.
32 Teubner, *Constitutional Fragments*, 75–6.
33 Teubner, 'A Constitutional Moment?', at 13.
34 Teubner, 'A Constitutional Moment?'.
35 Teubner, 'A Constitutional Moment?'.
36 P. Kjaer, 'Law and Order Within and Beyond National Configurations', in P.F. Kjaer, G. Teubner and A. Febbrajo (eds), *The Financial Crisis in Constitutional Perspective*, Oxford and Portland: Hart, 2011, 419–20.
37 Kjaer, 'Law and Order'.
38 Kjaer, 'Law and Order'.
39 Kjaer, 'Law and Order'.
40 J.P. Morgan, 'The Euro Area Adjustment: About Halfway There', *Europe Economic Research*, May 28, 2013, 12.
41 Kjaer, 'Law and Order', at 418.
42 Teubner, *Constitutional Fragments*, at 11.
43 See *inter alia* N. Krisch, *Beyond Constitutionalism: The Pluralist Structure of Postnational Law*, Oxford: Oxford University Press, 2010, and, with respect to multiculturalism, J. Tully, *Strange Multiplicity: Constitutionalism in an Age of Diversity*, Cambridge: Cambridge University Press, 1995.
44 On this see C. Pinelli, 'The Combination of Negative with Positive Constitutionalism in Europe: The Quest of a "Just Distance" between Citizens and the Public Power', *European Journal of Law Reform* 13 (2011): 1, 31ff.
45 N. MacCormick, *Questioning Sovereignty: Law, State, and Nation in the European Commonwealth*, Oxford: Oxford University Press, 1999, at 131. For a different account see Loughlin, 'The Nature of Public Law', at 23, according to which the relationships 'establishing the political unity of "the people" (or "the state") and the governing relationship between state and government . . . are not constituted by modern constitutions; they evolve from more basic political circumstances concerning the ways in which governing authority is continually acknowledged'.
46 N. Walker, 'The Idea of Constitutional Pluralism', *The Modern Law Review* 65 (2002): at 337.
47 S. Besson, 'The Truth about Legal Pluralism', *EuConst* 8 (2012): 358–9, reviewing Krisch, *Beyond Constitutionalism*.
48 M. Delmas-Marty, *Le pluralisme ordonné. Les forces imaginantes du droit*, 2, Paris: Seuil, 2010.

References

Besson, Samantha. 'The Truth about Legal Pluralism'. Review of *Beyond Constitutionalism, The Pluralist Structure of Postnational Law*, by Nico Krisch. *EuConst* 8 (2012): 358–9.

Cass, Deborah Z. *The Constitutionalisation of the World Trade Organisation: Legitimacy, Democracy and Community in the International Trading System*. Oxford: Oxford University Press, 2005.

Cassese, Sabino. *The Global Polity: Global Dimensions of Democracy and the Rule of Law*. Sevilla: Global Law Press – Editorial Derecho Global, 2012.

De Wet, Erika. 'The International Constitutional Order'. *International and Comparative Law Quarterly* 55 (2006): 51–76.

———. 'The Constitutionalisation of Public International Law'. In *The Oxford Handbook of Comparative Constitutional Law*, edited by Michael Rosenfeld and A. András Sajó, 1209–30. Oxford: Oxford University Press, 2012.

Delmas-Marty, Mirelle. *Le pluralisme ordonné. Les forces imaginantes du droit* (2). Paris: Seuil, 2010.

Frowein, Jochen A. 'Konstitutionalisierung des Voelkerrechts'. In *Voelkerrecht und internationales Privatrecht in einem sich globalisierenden internationalen System: Auswirkungen der Enstaatslichung transnationaler Rechtsbeziehungen*, edited by Klaus Dicke, Waldemar Hummer, Daniel Girsberger, Katharina Boele-Woelki, Christopher Engel and Jochen Frohwein, 427–88. Heidelberg: Mueller, 2000.

Grimm, Dieter. 'The Constitution in the Process of Denationalisation'. *Constellations* 2 (2005): 447–63.

Hasebe, Yasuo, and Cesare Pinelli. 'Constitutions'. In *Routledge Handbook of Constitutional Law*, edited by Mark Tushnet, Thomas Fleiner and Cheryl Saunders, 9–19. London and New York: Routledge, 2013.

International Law Commission. 'Fragmentation of International Law: Difficulties Arising From the Diversification and Expansion of International Law'. UN General Assembly, A/CN.4/L.682 13 April 2006.

Jackson, John H. 'The World Trade Organisation and the "Sovereignty" Question'. *Legal Issues of European Integration* 1 (1996): 179–87.

J.P. Morgan. 'The Euro Area Adjustment: About Halfway There'. *Europe Economic Research*, May 28, 2013.

Kennedy, David. 'The Mystery of Global Governance'. *Ohio Northern University Law Review* 34 (2008): 827–60.

Kingsbury, Benedict, Nico Krisch and Richard B. Stewart. 'The Emergence of Global Administrative Law'. Institute for International Law and Justice Working Paper 2004/1.

Kjaer, Poul. 'Law and Order Within and Beyond National Configurations'. In *The Financial Crisis in Constitutional Perspective*, edited by Poul F. Kjaer, Gunther Teubner and Alberto Febbrajo, 395–429. Oxford and Portland: Hart, 2011.

Krisch, Nico. 'Global Administrative Law and the Constitutional Ambition'. LSE Law, Society and Economy Working Papers 2 10/2009.

———. *Beyond Constitutionalism: The Pluralist Structure of Postnational Law*. Oxford: Oxford University Press, 2010.

Kumm, Matthias. 'The Legitimacy of International Law: A Constitutionalist Framework of Analysis'. *European Journal of International Law* 15(5) (2004): 907–31.

Loughlin, Martin. 'What is Constitutionalism?' In *The Twilight of Constitutionalism*, edited by Petra Dobner and Martin Loughlin, 47–69. Oxford: Oxford University Press, 2010.

———. 'The Nature of Public Law'. In *After Public Law*, edited by Cormac MacAmhlaigh, Claudio Michelon and Neil Walker, 11–24. Oxford: Oxford University Press, 2013.

MacCormick, Neil. *Questioning Sovereignty: Law, State, and Nation in the European Commonwealth*. Oxford: Oxford University Press, 1999.

Peters, Anne. 'Compensatory Constitutionalism: The Function and Potential of Fundamental International Norms and Structures'. *Leiden Journal of International Law* 19 (2006): 579–610.

Petersmann, Ernst-Ulrich. 'The WTO Constitution and Human Rights'. *Journal of International Economic Law* 19 (2000): 19–25.

Pinelli, Cesare. 'The Combination of Negative with Positive Constitutionalism in Europe: The Quest of a "Just Distance" between Citizens and the Public Power'. *European Journal of Law Reform* 13 (2011): 31–40.

Schwoebel, Christine. 'The Appeal of the Project of Global Constitutionalism to Public International Lawyers'. *German Law Journal* 13(1) (2012): 1–22.

Teubner, Gunther. 'A Constitutional Moment? The Logics of "Hitting the Bottom"'. In *The Financial Crisis in Constitutional Perspective*, edited by Poul F. Kjaer, Gunther Teubner and Alberto Febbrajo, 3–41. Oxford and Portland: Hart, 2011.

———. *Constitutional Fragments: Societal Constitutionalism and Globalisation*. Oxford: Oxford University Press, 2012.

Tully, James. *Strange Multiplicity: Constitutionalism in an Age of Diversity*. Cambridge: Cambridge University Press, 1995.

Walker, Neil. 'The Idea of Constitutional Pluralism'. *The Modern Law Review* 65 (2002): 317–59.
———. 'Beyond the Holistic Constitution'. In *The Twilight of Constitutionalism*, edited by Petra Dobner and Martin Loughlin, 291–308. Oxford: Oxford University Press, 2012.
Young, Ernest A. 'The Trouble with Global Constitutionalism'. *Texas International Law Journal* 38 (2003): 527–45.

8 'Cross-constitutionalism' and sustainable comparison

Michele Carducci

Introduction

In this chapter, I intend to discuss two questions:

a what can be the utility of comparative constitutional law in monitoring the new semantics of contemporary constitutionalism?
b what conception of constitutional comparison is spreading today in the light of the phenomena of 'global constitutionalism'?

By way of launching this discussion, I shall call attention to certain events that have taken place in recent years, since they are very significant in terms of contents, of the new semantics they seem to produce and of the responses they could help provide to the two questions.

I shall divide these events into three areas of geopolitical interest and describe them in brief, before then testing which methods of comparison are or can be used to analyse them.

For this purpose, I observe that the conception of constitutional comparison that prevails today is one of 'judicial dialogue': an approach that favours 'communication' about the pluralism of rights, but not necessarily 'information' about the complexity not only of the pluralism of rights, but also about the plurality of constitutional conceptions practised in the world, thus benefitting the maintenance of the socio-economic status quo and demeaning any use of comparison to likening models and experiences of 'good life': a comparison that might contribute to eliminating inequalities and to the survival of the entire 'geo-human system'.

News from Europe and North America

The first geopolitical area of interest is that of Europe and North America and includes the following four events.

1

In March 2013, the private bank J.P. Morgan published a document about the 'constitutional obstacles' to the revival of growth in Europe. This document states that the constitutions of the countries along Europe's southern fringe, starting with the Italian constitution, display a 'strong influence of socialist ideas', because of the 'great political strength achieved by the parties of the left after the defeat of Fascism'. It therefore follows that southern Europe's constitutional systems suffer from the following 'negative' characteristics: executives that are weak vis-à-vis parliaments, central governments that are weak vis-à-vis the regions, constitutionally protected workers' rights, methods of consensus building based on clientelism and a 'licence to protest' against any unpopular 'amendments to the status quo'.[1]

It is not hard to imagine what constitutes these 'amendments to the status quo' for J.P. Morgan. According to its document, the great and constantly[2] debated European issue of the 'constitutionalisation' of the right to work represents an 'obstacle' to the future of the European Union, while a constitutionalism without the right to work and without the right to protest would certainly be preferable, as it would be functional to the purpose of 'growth'.

This regressive idea of constitutional law (a law without the rights that were constitutionalised in the course of the twentieth century in Europe, from Weimar onwards) substantially reflects the ideology of austerity.[3] Yet it also expresses a method of comparison that is based on taking constitutional experiences out of their historical contexts (this is demonstrated by the absurdity of equating Europe's social constitutionalism solely with 'socialist ideas') and by standardising/neutralising legal models for managing social conflicts. We shall see that similar tendencies are typical of other events and news that have featured in recent years.[4]

For now, it is important to remember that the discussion currently taking place about the issue of 'global constitutionalism', construed as the need for a global normative constitution[5] or as the confirmation of a fragmentary system of plural and societal constitutionalism,[6] offers proposals alternative to this neo-liberal neutralisation.

2

Talks got under way in Washington in July 2013 on the Transatlantic Trade and Investment Partnership (TTIP), a free-trade agreement between the United States and the European Union, which the European Commission's website has described as 'the world's greatest trade agreement'. The procedure is surrounded by an aura of secrecy.[7] The Commission ensures us that the agreement's implementation will be accompanied by a regular flow of information to stakeholders (such as the business community, trade unions and consumer associations) and will follow the 'usual' procedures of consultation; but it stops short of specifying what these procedures will be and who will decide about them. In addition, the partnership also envisages a mechanism for solving conflicts between investors and the state, which will enable private concerns to take the state to an 'international court' if they suffer damage to their investments as a result of state regulations and policies. This would mean that Europe would also acquire a 'special' judicial organ separate from the European Court of Justice in Luxembourg, as a waiver to the Lisbon Treaty and to Articles 4.2 and 6 of Treaty of the European Union, which safeguard the 'democratic identities' of the member states and their 'shared constitutional traditions'. The European Union, too, would accept the criterion of splitting the rules between processes of integration and external relations, to the benefit of the principle of the 'speciality' of the rules,[8] as is already known in other contexts of regional integration,[9] and to the detriment of international parity between states.[10]

3

On 11 March, once again the European Union adopted European Parliament and Council of Ministers Regulation N° 235/2014, which establishes a financial instrument for promoting democracy and human rights in the world.

This regulation declares the equality of all states in international relations with regard to safeguarding not only individual rights, but also the social and political rights of participation, in the name of the rule of law and of democracy, as indicated in Articles 4 and 6 of the Treaty of the Union.

What, then, is European constitutionalism's current semantic? Is it that of the 'unconditional' and even 'global' promotion of human rights, including social rights and the rights of democracy, as would appear to certified by the 2014 Regulation, in compliance with the European Treaties? Or is it that of rights and 'democratic constitutional identities' being conditioned by economic interests and the multinationals, as premised by J.P. Morgan and by the EU–USA TTIP project?

4

Again in March 2014, the Law Society, the body that represents the interests of solicitors in England and Wales, published guidelines for drawing up the wills of Muslim clients who intend to bequeath their worldly goods in accordance with the laws of *Shariā*.

This document raised a lot of eyebrows in Europe, since the introduction of these guidelines could constitute a dangerous precedent for a multicultural Europe as a whole. To allow the use of the *Shariā* is to promote divisions between Muslims and non-Muslims, as well as within the Muslim community itself, favouring discriminatory practices against women, children and non-Muslims, in a perspective of a juridical pluralism based on the identity and free self-determination of each individual. The individual, seen in the context of his or her human rights, would ultimately be considered as a legal order per se, giving concrete form to what Vittorio Frosini once called the 'Robinsonian hypothesis' of pluralism.[11] Does it then follow that the future of European democratic pluralism will be based on the methodological neo-individualism of the 'personal status' of legal practices, endorsed by private associations of lawyers and consultants?

News from outside the European and North American context

Also in the geopolitical space outside Europe and North America, four innovations of constitutional significance can be identified.

1

The UNDP's 2013 report was dedicated to *The Rise of the South: Human Progress in a Diverse World*. It emphasised the protagonism of several states from the 'peripheral' or southern areas of the globe in promoting four strategic areas of the development of humanity as a whole: enhancing equity, including the gender dimension; enabling greater voice and participation of all citizens, including youth; confronting environmental pressures; and managing demographic change. This idea of the 'quadrilateral of development' discussed and launched in the southern part of the globe appears to differ from the analytical approach that first came into vogue several years earlier with the Brundtland Report and the Rio Conference on sustainable development: that approach remained anchored to the 'sustainability triangle', comprising the environment (the need to achieve a balance between the exploitation of natural resources and the conservation of biodiversity), the economy (the need for an efficient system of production and allocation for a stable growth of wealth and of accumulation) and society (the need for a subjective and territorial distribution of that wealth and accumulation).

In fact, when the UNDP calls attention to the need for 'enabling greater voice and participation of all citizens', it is adding a clearly 'constitutional' profile of development alongside the economic, social and environmental headings that distinguished the scientific and political debate about the issue in previous decades: the 'triangle' of environment, economy and society is now joined by a new (constitutional) 'angle' of participatory democracy in 'demographic change': the new frontier of a constitutionally harmonious and inclusive development that is neither technocratic, nor elitist.

So is there a nexus between sustainable development, human development and constitutional development? And what concept of constitutionalism underlies the 'quadrilateral of development' proposed by the UNDP?

2

A group of important peripheral and southern countries has also come together to inaugurate the BRICS. The acronym not only identifies today's large emerging new economies (Brazil, Russia, India, China and South Africa), but above all encapsulates a phenomenon of informal international relations that is producing commercial trade and related flows of policies and even of legal rules, something very different – in terms of its context of operations and methods of implementation – from the experiment of 'multilevel regionalisation' structured in the second half of the last century by Europe (EEC-EU) and by Latin America (SICA, CAN, CARICOM, MERCOSUR). The BRICS countries have reciprocally very different legal systems, political systems and cultural traditions: three are democracies growing towards consolidation (Brazil, India and South Africa) and two are systems with an authoritarian and oligarchic stamp (Russia and China).[12]

This means that the BRICS do not present us with a simple 'expansion' of a constitutional semantic that we already know (the supranationality legitimised by the theories of David Mitrany for the post-world-war world[13]). They are an 'elsewhere' that disorients us precisely because it marks the emergence of these co-ordinates.[14]

The BRICS' competitive edge over systems of regional supranational integration can be found, in fact, in its internal constitutional heterogeneity. This factor emerges clearly from a comparison with the European Union. Suffice to consider Articles 4.2 and 6 of the Treaty of the European Union after the Lisbon reform: the talk in Europe is about 'constitutional traditions common to the member states' and 'respect for national identities'. These two elements are known to have contributed to constructing the process of integration and to strengthening its 'constitutional synallagma'.[15] In the BRICS, on the other hand, there is no requirement of constitutional homogeneity, nor is there any 'constitutional synallagma', since the BRICS countries want to be competitive and alternative at world level, without having to impose structural conditions on their constitutional identities. Paradoxically, their very constitutional heterogeneity acts as a very sharp global competitive edge, because it does not produce the 'costs' of structural adaptation required for any process of integration.[16]

But the BRICS countries also benefit from a second global competitive edge: they can activate economic co-operation without any conditional clauses. This is another very marked difference from the current European context. As we know, the revision and simplification of Article 136 of the Treaty on the Functioning of the European Union, approved by the Council of Ministers on 25 March 2011, adds a paragraph that states that, for the member states in the Eurozone, 'the concession of any necessary financial assistance . . . shall be subject to strict conditions'. This means that the criterion of 'strict conditions' has found its way into the process of European integration. The mechanism has been described as 'a regional copy of the IMF' and ends up being completely intergovernmental, contributing to increasing the complexity of the Union's institutional structures as community integration and making it even more difficult to hold out any hope for a real federative and constitutional process.[17] How, then, will constitutionalism react in future to these two so different and distant models?

3

Among other things, one of the BRICS countries – China – never misses an opportunity to underscore its 'diversity' from the traditions of constitutionalism. At the end of the third plenary of its XVIII Congress, held in November 2013, the Chinese Communist Party made some operational decisions designed to improve the socialist system by means of the '3–8–3 Project' (three concepts, eight areas of reform and three correlated combinations), so as to progress to a new phase for managing the market more equitably, openly and transparently, but above all with more solidarity, relying on a guiding ideology of technical and scientific development, together with Marxism-Leninism, the thinking of Mao Zedong and the theories of Deng Xiaoping, in the perspective of a 'different pluralism' from the capitalist and democratic model of the West.[18]

The continent-state, which according to the *Financial Times* report on 30 April 2014 is now the world's leading economy, surpassing the primacy held by the United States since 1872,[19] intends to promote a constitutional semantic alternative to the one that has evolved in the last two centuries of history.

4

Without leaving Asia, a state with one of the more complex compositions in terms of linguistic and cultural identities is Kazakhstan, which is experimenting with a political and social dialogue unlike the models of representation and voting known from the West.[20] In 2008, the country introduced the Assembly of the People of Kazakhstan as its fourth constitutional organ, operating alongside the three traditional powers of the state and responsible for activities that cannot be classified under any of the liberal tripartite organisations of functions, because it aims to feed in constantly to legitimising the other powers not as a conflict between majority and minority, but as a shared approach to solving common problems of pluriethnic and multicultural cohabitation. Kazakhstan's pluralist model does not reproduce Western semantics and practices. On the contrary, it 'invents' new powers and new ways of communicating compared to the traditions of constitutionalism. Could this be applicable in Europe's multi- and inter-culturalism?

News from the world

The fact is that challenges to the traditions of constitutionalism are even being launched at planetary level. Here are four examples.

1

Following up in due course on the attempt to proclaim the 'Declaration of the Independence of Cyberspace', promoted by Jeff Barlow in the name of an unprecedented principle of the 'self-determination of information technology',[21] Google promoted the project for creating a 'constitutional cyberspace',[22] aiming to offer 350 thematic areas for writing or designing constitutional texts, by conducting a census of the words and the language used in all the constitutions of the world.[23]

This initiative, which appears to confirm the Internet's constituent strength compared to existing constitutional law, lends even more force to Günter Frankenberg's idea of 'IKEA constitutionalism':[24] the emergence of a global supermarket of 'empty rules',[25] where constitutional texts reduced to words with no space, no history, no state and no authorship are made available to any operation of 'constitutional borrowing'. After all, it is only in conditions of 'spatial atrophy'[26] that 'transplants' and 'transfers' can be made with no intellectual difficulty and above all with no 'political' commitment, transforming the process of 'constitution making' into one of 'constitutional design'[27] and abolishing the distinction between words and concepts or, as Husserl would have put it, between *noema* and *noesis*.

It is no coincidence that Google's aim is to 'democratise' access to the words of constitutionalism at the global level, but certainly not to promote global democracy.

2

On 28 January 2013, the twentieth Conference of Heads of State and Government of the African Union approved a proposal moved by Tunisia to formalise the call to establish an International Constitutional Court under the auspices of the United Nations.[28]

This initiative introduces the significant characteristic of connecting the idea of an International Constitutional Court not so much (or not only) to reinforcing the protection of human rights as individual and collective expectations, as above all to guaranteeing democracy as a form of government recognised universally for its distinctive characteristics that underlie peace between peoples and between individuals and, as such, is uniquely protectable by a single international organ with multiple modes of access.

It is this unprecedented experiment's African origins and inspiration that make it all the more noteworthy, because it shifts the mainstream of the debate about 'global constitutionalism', away from a dimension focused exclusively on safeguarding those human rights that have an individual content and only have a marginal influence on the political forms of cohabitation between individual state contexts, towards the dimension of the unique and universal justiciability of the democratic practices of deliberative participation and of social inclusion, for the purpose of constructing a fully-fledged 'right to democracy' as a unique and uniform access to justice for the effectiveness of all human rights, starting from political and social rights. Until now, the issue of the 'right to democracy' has been discussed under four headings: the first is more specifically philosophical and moral in nature and can be traced back to the approach adopted by John Rawls[29] and the discussion that took place about his theses;[30] the second discusses the qualification of the 'right to democracy' as an individual and collective human right with the potential to be justiciable;[31] the third develops on the nexus between the 'democratic credentials' of international institutions and the 'right to democracy';[32] while the fourth and last distinguishes between the right of self-determination and the 'right to democracy', qualifying the latter as a constituent element of a general principle of non-discrimination.[33]

What role could an international constitutional court play in this framework of theoretical elaborations? According to the African Union's intentions, the court's purpose would be to trigger a unique, unitary system for accessing constitutional justice, aimed primarily at safeguarding the practices of participation, social inclusion and non-elusion of all the fringe mechanisms of democratic deliberations (from the right to information and safeguarding minorities and oppositions to the transparency of funding, national and international lobbies and so on). In fact, it would appear to be rather implausible to call for an 'international constitutionalism' on the level of individual rights alone, if it were then to operate asymmetrically with regard to the homogeneity of the standards of political participation and of the procedures of democratic deliberation. In this sense, what is known as the 'judicial dialogue' still has very little of a cosmopolitan nature about it, as not only domestic constitutional courts, but also international judges, starting with the three courts that sit in appraisal of the human rights conventions (the European Court of Human Rights in Strasbourg, the Inter-American Court of Human Rights in San José and the African Court of Human and Peoples' Rights), which prefer to 'limit' the effects of their decisions on states' constitutional orders, use techniques that 'contextualise' the arguments and rules governing human rights. This can be demonstrated with a handful of examples: from the reference to the 'margin of appreciation' in the jurisprudence of the European Court of Human Rights,[34] to the Inter-American Court of Human Rights' justification – formalised explicitly in the *Gelman* v. *Uruguay* case in 2011 – of the 'control of the conventionality' of democratic deliberative procedures,[35] the *Tanganyika Law Society et al.* v. *Tanzania* case,[36] which was judged by the African Court of Human and Peoples' Rights in 2013 on the basis of the specific context of the individual country, and the decision N° 82/2001 of the Mexican Supreme Court (dismissing the application) about the participation of native communities in procedures of constitutional reform.[37]

The open door to universalism that seemed to have been established by the famous International Court of Justice case *Nicaragua* v. *USA* in 1986, towards stating a principle of the 'free choice of political, economic and social system', as a veritable 'constitutional autonomy' guaranteed by international judiciary,[38] has not yet produced any standardisation of rules and principles to underpin an effective universalisation of the contents and procedures of democracy in guarantee of rights.

The challenge is therefore radically innovative: from inter-state interference in internal constitutional questions, which was declared illegal by the International Court of Justice in 1986, the move would be towards socialising the principle of self-determination by providing widespread access to a 'universal judge of democracy'.

The idea of exercising political participation globally, starting with sharing democratic practices, also globally,[39] could thus open a door to the idea, already advanced by Frantz Fanon, of the 'sovereignty of the everyday life' of each member of the human race,[40] but it would probably also reinforce the aspirations of 'societal constitutionalism' against the authoritarian and oligarchic tendencies of global powers and the influences they bring to bear on the formally democratic decisions made by state powers.[41]

The African Union counters Google's proposal for decontextualising the 'constitutional cyberspace' with the idea of a universal safeguard for democracy as a material context common to the entire human race.

3

On the occasion of the American Geophysical Union's conference in 2012, the scientist Brad Werner presented a series of complex readings and projections in support of his argument that 'geo-human systems' have now become dangerously unstable. In a nutshell, the long-established harmony between humanity and nature has faltered.

In the same period, NASA was funding a study that was recently published by the University of Maryland's National Socio-Environmental Synthesis Center[42] and accredited by the important journal *Ecological Economics*, published by the Society for Ecological Economics. Unequivocally entitled *Human and Nature Dynamics (HANDY): Modelling Inequality and Use of Resources in the Collapse or Sustainability of Societies*, the study advocates a 'crisis of the civilisation' of consumption and of the exploitation of natural resources, which is also legitimised by the institutions that constructed it and by the global inequalities that have maintained it.[43]

Is there a link between the 'semantics' of constitutionalism and 'geo-human systems'? In the light of the theses published in *Human and Nature Dynamics*, the planet's ecological stability would appear to be put at risk by constitutional models that legitimise the primacy of the individual over nature, in which nature, as material and property, is seen as a function of society, but not of nature itself. In such a scenario, the relationship between constitutionalism, on the one hand – with its calls for freedom, justice and intergenerational equity – and nature as a 'geo-system' of human survival, on the other, now indicates an enormous paradox of civilisation: how is it possible to conceive of a world society that is more equitable, more just and more worthy in respect of rights and freedoms, if the states whose national constitutions pursue those 'values' do little or nothing to fend off the planet's self-destruction?

Constitutional law's Eurocentric *logos* has never faced up to this question, except in purely and exclusively anthropocentric terms (treating nature as an object, as an anthropic environment). This limit is now being denounced by the states that were once colonised by that *logos*. How?

Modern-day colonisation, led by England, the Netherlands and France from the seventeenth century onwards, was based on a concept – apparently new to mankind – that focused on the primacy of reason as the dominion over nature and a tool for constructing a society of equals.[44] This aim of equality established just one way forward for humanity: the triumph of reason over nature. The natural selection of the species has of course been accompanied by the Darwinism of those who have accepted the challenge of 'modernity' as synonymous with human 'progress'.[45]

This depiction of society and of constitutional law as the consequence of 'human rationality' provided the premises for a veritable 'dialectic of nature', which treated natural resources as goods with a definable value that are there to be exploited, and human beings as individuals to be adapted to the requirements of growth and development. Modernity (the relationship in which man exercises a rational dominance over nature) and modernisation (adapting mankind to the requirements of progress, growth and development) have hit the headlines as synonyms for the future of mankind as a whole. It was Friedrich Engels, in the work he wrote in 1873–82 (although it was only published posthumously in 1925) entitled *Dialects of Nature*, who denounced the ideology behind this assumption: the presumed 'rationality' of the nexus between nature, development and legal institutions is neither 'neutral' nor 'natural', but reflects relationships of dominion and hegemony internal to humanity.

It is now up to us, then, to become aware of these nexuses today, too, so as to avoid falling into the trap of irenic visions of the relationship between constitutional legality and social relations, regardless of the restriction constructed with nature and its resources. If the 'geo-human system' is truly in danger, then the time has now come to call for constitutionalism also for nature and not only for society

From this perspective, the 'constitutional cyberspace' propounded by Google appears to leave much to be desired.

4

That much said, however, when do constitutions speak explicitly of 'nature' and the 'geo-human system'? In general, constitutions may speak about intergenerational rights, development and the justice of distribution in time and space. If they refer to 'geo-human' survival, they do so imagining war to be the only instrument liable to cause the destruction of humanity (especially after Hiroshima) and peace as the only 'guarantee' of survival (on this, see Article 11 of the Italian constitution): an outlook that, as Carl Schmitt accurately points out in his still pertinent *Der Nomos der Erde*,[46] conceals the nexus between war and the accumulation of natural resources, that between peace and the exchange of natural resources[47] and that between constitutional rules and the property of natural resources.[48]

Constitutionalism does not therefore seem to have been an immediate synonym for safeguarding the survival of the 'geo-human system'.

This is why several recent experiences in the southern hemisphere, starting with what is known as 'new Andean constitutionalism' as identified by Ecuador's 2008 constitution and Bolivia's adopted in 2009, mark a radical change, at least with reference to these four areas:

- the constitution no longer serves only to guarantee individual and collective freedoms based on the primacy of the human being as a subject of history and of nature;
- the constitution is not restricted to influencing the social dialectic between freedom and authority, so as to guarantee rights, property, the use of goods and limits to abuses of power;
- the constitution's task is to be responsible also for the historical dialectic between man and nature, as elements simultaneously present in the 'geo-human' ecosystem;
- the constitution therefore not only repudiates war as the sole 'evil' afflicting humanity's survival, but must also repudiate the indiscriminate and interested exploitation of nature and of its ecosystem.

That is why the two Andean countries' constitutions make a statement about the primacy of 'Mother Nature'. The human being is not just society, but is primarily nature: we live *in* nature and *with* nature, so our relations with it cannot be left any more to the indifference of legality or to being regulated solely as a function of the interests and of the goods of individuals and communities.

This is a progression of major importance: nature has at long last been recognised as a constitutional subject since, *without* nature, no human being and no society can survive.

In addition, this 'constitutionalism of biodiversity' is based on five refusals and one claim, which distinguish it from the 'constitutionalism of risk' discussed in the European and North American context.[49]

These are the five refusals:

- the refusal of the paradigm of the sustainability of development as a logic functional to the interests of capitalism;[50]
- the refusal of the concept of citizenship as the legitimation of the individualism of the interests to be safeguarded;[51]
- the refusal to cede the state's economic sovereignty in the name of a supranational functionalism built on the logic of the pre-eminence of the market over nature;[52]
- the refusal of the constitutional postulate of the 'mandate to optimise rights' as the simple satisfaction of individual expectations, to the detriment of the 'ecological mandate' necessary to guarantee the future of humanity as a whole;[53]
- the refusal of the logic of 'risk' as a constituent element of public decisions and the basis for legitimising the balance between nature and private economic interests.[54]

The claim is implicit in the statement of the primacy of 'biodiversity', which in fact means constitutionalising the 'geo-human system', not only as a natural or cultural plurality of the human being, but above all as an element of living the 'good life' with nature (known in Latin America as *Buen Vivir*).[55]

A 'cross-constitutionalism' worth observing

Semantics old and new meet and interface in contemporary constitutional experiences. This is not so much a case of the emergence of a single 'global constitutionalism' as, more realistically and correctly, a call for the emergence of a form of 'cross-constitutionalism': a web of models, experiences, innovations, declarations and visions of natural and social life coming from all over the world and from all kinds of spaces, including the virtual spaces on the Internet, and imposing new geopolitical co-ordinates for observing even the constitutional culture whose matrix is European and North American.

In addition, this 'cross-constitutionalism' has elements not only of the transformation of twentieth-century constitutionalism, but also of the persistence of some of its original components, which many apologists of globalism too superficially consider to be in a critical condition: the issues of representation ('no taxation without representation'), of social democracy and of the central role played by the state in the survival of humanity.[56]

What tools and what methods can be used to monitor this complex panorama?

Two considerations come to mind.

a On the one hand, the issue of nature and the 'geo-human system' calls attention to the question of the 'eco-systemic/eco-logical' – and not only the 'eco-nomic' – sustainability of constitutionalism;
b on the other hand, the call for the 'right to democracy' within states demonstrates that globalisation cannot do without the state as a producer of democracy,[57] since only democratic and constitutional states can face up to the global challenge of the global survival of the 'geo-human system' by including all subjects and their relationships with nature.[58]

Democratic equilibrium and eco-systemic equilibrium are becoming the two new elements in contemporary cross-constitutionalism: they do not replace, but complement, the supranational and international dimension of safeguarding human rights and dignity.

The 'right to democracy' propounded by the African Union therefore appears to be complementary to the constitutional law of 'nature' enshrined in the two Andean countries' constitutions.

This perspective is very different from the paradigms of neo-liberal 'rationality' that has preached the extinction of the state and the sustainability of constitutionalism, primarily on the basis of the 'economic analysis of the law' (which states that everything has a 'cost' and so also a 'price' in its relations with nature[59]): from the various different versions of the theory of legal origins[60] and of the logic of legal standards of development[61] (based on the presumption that so-called development can be measured as the accumulation of data that can be quantified per capita),[62] to emphasising the rule of law as law that is efficient for the market[63] and global legal training[64] and ultimately arriving at the comparative constitutional law promoted by J.P. Morgan.

A discussion about whether visions of 'global constitutionalism', based on the primacy of society construed as the economy and the market, nourish phenomena of 'symbolic constitutionalism' or of 'simulacrum constitutions', as has happened at the level of individual states,[65] could make an excellent contribution of constitutional comparison for the future of the 'geo-human system'. It would help experiment with comparisons across a broader horizon: as an exercise in comparing models and experiences of the 'good life' for humanity as a whole, and not only as pluralism and individual rights functional to maintaining economic interests.[66]

Yet this does not appear to be the prevailing trend. There is a much more widespread idea that what we are facing is a 'global constitutionalism' that in fact favours the pluralism of rights in economic globalisation, via the privileged observatory of 'judicial dialogue'[67] and 'trans-judicial communications',[68] two phenomena that express the principle of 'ubiquitous' law[69] established by 'post-state' discursive practices and as such oblivious to the problems of economic and social underdevelopment, of indiscriminate exploitation of labour and of nature, and of the 'delegative' rather than 'deliberative' democracy of the majority of states around the world.[70]

This kind of comparison, in the name of 'global constitutionalism' and of the pluralism of rights guaranteed by judges, is based on six postulates:

1 each constitution is a fragment of the pluralism of global society, so each constitution cannot be understood any more as a stand-alone;[71]
2 each constitution must be analysed only as a part (a 'knot'[72]) in a global network of constitutions that express different rules, cultures and experiences;[73]
3 'judicial networks' are the pioneers of this process of opening constitutions up and circulating constitutional ideas;
4 in fact, the role of the judge is not focused on interpreting domestic law any more, but above all on legitimising the transnational network of constitutions;[74]
5 in this way, pluralism becomes the epistemological basis of constitutional theory, on the one hand delegitimising the utility of constitutional concepts whose foundations are exclusively national,[75] while on the other hand legitimising all the subjects and forms of intersubjective communications of global society;[76]
6 comparative constitutionalism is none other than the study of these forms of 'judicial dialogue' and of pluralist global communications,[77] itself becoming a dialogue and a reasoning[78] with a dual purpose: to 'constitutionalise' international law by 'internationalising' constitutional law[79] and to 'constitutionalise' all social orders, including economic orders.[80]

Ultimately, the transformation of comparison into 'judicial dialogue' is said to stand as a symptom of the end of comparative law based on the imperatives of the Westphalian system and on the primacy of national constitutional law.[81]

A closer analysis reveals that these postulates seem to suffer from certain conceptual lacunae.

a On the one hand, they reduce the concept of 'constitutionalisation' to a mere 'graft', brought about primarily by judicial means, of constitutional elements into any social order, whether local or global, public or private,[82] as though constitutionalisation were not historically and semantically a constitutional morphogenesis, i.e. the process of defining specific legal forms that the evolution and the development of social and legal transformations have highlighted tangibly.[83]
b On the other hand, they construe the concept of 'constitutionalisation' to mean simply 'interpretation' for the purpose of safeguarding human rights, and not to mean also 'decision' about the forms for rationalising power and exercising democracy,[84] thus emphasising an idea of 'legal' and 'judicial' or 'cultural' constitutionalism and not also of 'political' and 'general' constitutionalism'.[85] In fact, the strategic focus of this comparison-dialogue is on the erosion of the state's monopoly in the field of human rights,[86] which has three important consequences on the proposed comparison: the outlook concentrates on the

legal situation of individuals; the outlook is no longer based on the economic and social sphere of cohabitation, but on self-determination and on privacy; the idea of pluralism is explained as the difference between cultural self-determinations and not the difference between material socio-political conditions.

c Lastly, these postulates do not overcome the Hegelian approach in the Western – European and North American – memory and experience of constitutionalism,[87] because they imagine a flat reality, diversified in its premises (social and cultural pluralism outside the West), but convergent in its development aims (how Western judges interpret human rights),[88] and split, according to the heuristic logic denounced by Ferguson,[89] between modernity as *telos* (i.e. as the aim of a process that develops with time) and modernity as *status* (i.e. as the privilege of those who are *already* modern: obviously the European and North American West). In fact, what common or universal parameter might persist throughout this comparison-dialogue? The very same circuit of communications between judges?[90] But who decides how this circuit is triggered? Who has the last word? Is this really a spontaneous, unconditional, neutral, symmetrical circuit on a par for all the communicating actors, both in its premises (as 'incoming' comparison) and in its objectives (as 'outgoing comparison)? Do such multi-level dimensions really not accentuate asymmetries that influence dialogues and communications?[91] How many judges around the world (and inside states) actually practise comparison-dialogue? And what empirical checks are run on the everyday reality of 'global constitutionalism', as practised through the 'judicial dialogue'?[92]

For some,[93] 'trans-judicial communication' favours a non-scientific legal culture, so one that adopts a more tolerant attitude towards complexity and pluralism, regardless of its diffusion. For others,[94] precisely because it is independent of any empirical verification on a global scale, any such epistemology serves the purpose of re-legitimising relationships of (economic and political) strength between asymmetric cultural contexts and social situations, using the topic of pluralism to focus attention on cultural and religious differences, which are faced by asserting the primacy of the West, while at the same time concealing the social inequalities generated by the self-same West over the several centuries of its 'mission' of civilising colonisation: a strategy comparable, it might be added, with what happened in the course of history as a result of the evolution in international relations[95] and of diplomatic language, which are also based on transnational dialogue communications taken out of context and not subject to verification.[96]

Google and 'ad hoc comparison'

In addition, to describe constitutional comparison as a primarily judicial network would also generate consequences on the level of the ethos of legal education.[97] How many judges are really aware of this ethos? How many universities teach their students how to practise this ethos truly globally, in other words in ways that are independent of the 'methodological nationalism' of reproducing one's own legal system and of the 'parochialism' of one's own techniques of discussion?[98] After all, we know that the 'practice' of judicial decision-making does not always coincide with the 'doctrine' of the judge's function in the legal system.[99] And that is actually the reason why the 'judicial dialogue' has been defined correctly as a 'commonplace' assumption that enjoys very little confirmation from empirical verifications.[100]

Lastly, if constitutional comparison is reduced to the status of a mere 'dialogue', it is very unlikely to enable the complexity of differences, the historical causes of inequalities, the pre-comprehensions, interests and conditionings that motivate the preferences of legal and social actors to be understood.[101] This kind of comparison would appear to favour 'communication' to the detriment of 'information' about the complexity of pluralism and the plurality of visions of the 'good life'.

It follows that the communicative approach that is promoted by judicial decisions about human rights would be sufficient on its own to bring about a 'generic constitutional law',[102] but will never construct a general law which governments will be able to use to guarantee the quality of life to those they govern in an equal fashion all over the globe.

From this vantage point, our comparison-dialogue could cohabit happily with the 'constitutional cyberspace' proposed by Google: words of constitutional law to be assembled by means of communications. Nothing more.

This would end up ultimately as an 'ad hoc comparison'. But what does that mean?[103] Essentially, two things:

- firstly, it means that the law courts would be considered to be the preferential forum for comparing and composing pluralism and so for exercising comparison, forgetting that, even in the Common Law countries, judicial decisions have always been temporary – and never definitive – tools for declaring constitutionalism, above all vis-à-vis the prerogatives claimed by political representations;[104]
- secondly, it means reducing the law to the mere acquisition of knowledge functional to 'cases' and 'problems' found in a given space:[105] mere compared information about possible solutions, without taking into account the historical and semantic context of the society in question and of the plurality of spaces of public law.[106]

In other words, 'ad hoc comparison' deals with 'cases' (for example by comparing institutions, models, problems and solutions, adopting what could be termed a 'clinical' approach), but does not investigate the 'causes', so steers clear of considering the complexity of the histories of constitutionalism and of the geopolitical relationships of power and of knowledge that exist between the various legal systems,[107] as well as the economic and hegemonic conditionings at work in the relations between states.[108]

In this way, the very concept of 'legal system' would be set free of the prerequisite of 'statehood'.[109]

After all, as has been pointed out correctly,[110] the majority of global public law has been converted into an 'ad hoc-cracy', by virtue of the sectorialisation of the geopolitical and economic interests pursued by various different global and local actors. This sectorialisation diminishes the legal categories 'in the space' and threatens to underline the stability of people's rights and freedoms in their social relations 'in each space', over and above the safeguards of 'judicial networks'.[111]

This is demonstrated by the European supranational space: the offspring of functionalism and of the logic of 'spillover', it has witnessed the emergence of the 'judicial network' (known in German as the *Verfassungsgerichtsverbund*,[112] or network of constitutional courts) between the European Court of Justice in Luxembourg, domestic jurisdictions and the European Court of Human Rights in Strasbourg, for the purpose of providing multiple level safeguards for rights. Nevertheless, this 'judicial network' has never been enough, on its own, to legitimise the decisions of the supranational 'ad hoc-cracy', reinforcing all the uncertainties about the Union's democratic deficit.[113]

After all, solving 'cases' *in one* space, by virtue – also – of 'ad hoc comparison', does not necessarily translate into guaranteeing the stability of people's rights and freedoms *in all* spaces. And such an 'ad hoc comparison' *for one* space does not necessarily lead to extending the same results of stability *to other* spaces. As has been explained very effectively, the transnational dimension of the language of rights is not the place for political responses or community bonds: it only provides a premise based on the possibility to meet and communicate.[114]

In this perspective, it is hardly realistic to imagine that there is really any such thing as a transnational constitutionalism or even a cosmopolitan constitutional law.[115]

It may function – just about – in Google's 'constitutional cyberspace', as well as in the arguments employed in their decisions by certain judges. But nothing more.

Do we actually observe everything?

Considered in the light of an understanding of the phenomena and events, in Europe and in the rest of the world, mentioned earlier, the idea of comparison-dialogue would appear to be insufficient.

Maybe the human rights approach fuelled by 'judicial networks' is incapable of making a complete break away from the state approach.

After all, who are the ultimate decision-makers who settle the great questions of the future of humanity? The judges? Some social order? Or the states? Is it truly possible to imagine such a thing as 'global constitutionalism' based on the universalism of rights and on pluralism guaranteed by 'trans-judicial communication', when all it takes is for one state to express its veto (for example in the United Nations Security Council) to block or neutralise this circular process?[116]

Modern constitutionalism is not just a synonym for human rights and the limitation of the power of the state. It has also provided the foundation of that power and, as a consequence, the possibility to reform that power: any power. As a result, how is it possible to evoke a 'global constitutionalism', when the majority of international, global and supranational institutions (including Europe's), in addition to multinational economic orders, show themselves to be refractory to radical global reforms 'in the name' of constitutionalism? If the occasional reform is achieved from time to time, it is 'in the name' of (certain) human rights, and comparison-dialogue can certainly contribute to this change. Nevertheless, nothing has actually changed to date in the logic internal to international, global and supranational institutions. It is not at all separate from the states,[117] not even when it has to face the globalisation of financial capital:[118] it is always granted, regulated or limited by the states.[119] But, above all, the logic of international, global and supranational institutions is anything but constitutional: neither in its morphogenesis, nor in its evolution.[120]

So why does comparison-dialogue sound so convincing? There are five reasons.

1 Not infrequently, in the history of human thought, the *Ordo idearum* has been mistaken for the *Ordo rerum*.[121] And the *Ordo idearum* is always more enticing than the *Ordo rerum*, not just because, as Paul Valery wrote, language 'in the beginning was a fable',[122] but above all because it favours the use of 'magic formulae',[123] despite the risks of 'linguistic alienation' in their usage.[124] 'Transjudicial communication' is undoubtedly a formula for describing reality. But, equally undoubtedly, it also reflects only part of that reality, which is 'alienated' from the rest of the world by its own 'formula': maybe it is the most interesting part, but it is also the least problematic. If we forget this, we run the risk of telling a fable.
2 Thomas Kuhn associated four corollaries with the idea of the paradigm of scientific discovery:[125] exemplary metaphors, fundamental laws, shared values and a worldview. We also find these four corollaries in 'dialogic' comparativism,[126] as is actually acknowledged by those who deal with 'judicial dialogue' and 'constitutional borrowing': representing the world through metaphors exemplary of certain values.[127]

3 The 'judicial dialogue' fuels the idea of a 'common' global constitutional law: 'common' not in the sense of actually being present and practised all over the world in the same forms and with the same effects, but more in the sense of never being 'exceptional', i.e. of not containing any 'exception', or get-out clause, that could legitimise the rise of a global constituent power to decide about that 'exception'. This 'generic constitutional law' is therefore a 'pacific' constitutional law, but one that is also neutral with respect to the 'exception', reproducing Schmitt's 'non-political community'.[128]
4 It is no coincidence that the world circuit of judges is described as 'politically uncontaminated', since its connatural 'judicial candour'[129] is further strengthened by reciprocal communications of universally shared values.
5 Nevertheless, these shared values only concern human rights and certainly not conceptions of the state and its role in society. In other words, the supporters of comparison-dialogue share no common conception of 'statehood'.[130]

This consideration deserves to be developed a little more precisely. It is one thing to talk about 'states' and quite another to talk about 'statehood', i.e. about the forms in which state sovereignty is expressed. It is one thing to recognise that traditional elements, even private ones, can become constitutional subjects and quite another to deduce that this phenomenon confirms the existence of 'statehood'. If 'statehood' is construed as being no more than the monopoly of the system of sources and the exclusive right to produce rules and interpretations, it is clear that this concept has now almost completely disintegrated into the phenomena of global soft and hard law.[131] From this standpoint of 'interwoven hierarchies', 'global constitutionalism' certainly takes the shape of 'transconstitutionalism'[132] or 'constitution-network',[133] and probably also of co-operation between basically 'open' states.[134]

This observatory of contemporary constitutionalism is partial, however, since it overlooks the other historical expressions of statehood that are still fully applicable and effective today:[135] expressions that German doctrine has identified with the most accurate of linguistic formulae (*Souveränität*, *Staatsgewalt*, *Herrschaft*, *Volk*), so as to avoid limiting comparison to the mere production of rules and ignoring the semantics of constitutional phenomena in the historical significance of their manifestations.

If we then connect this perspective to the issue of the 'geo-human system', we notice just how much the concept of statehood continues to condition and limit global consideration of humanity's future as nature, survival and democratic cohabitation today. In other words, we notice that the topic of statehood crops up again in discussions about the issues tackled in the UNDP's 2013 Annual Report, about the proposal launched by the African Union and about the 'new constitutionalism' proposed by the Andean states. What system of sources will be capable of guaranteeing that the planet's resources and riches will be controlled at a time when its raw materials are diminishing? Who will decide about the demographic change of the world's population? On the basis of what democratic deliberations? Who will control climate change? On the basis of what democratic deliberations? And who will guarantee those democratic deliberations? All these are questions that are thoroughly attributable to the fields of *Souveränität*, *Staatsgewalt*, *Herrschaft* and *Volk*, all totally within the monopoly of states. And they are all constitutional questions. Hypotheses like the African proposal of an international constitutional court and the Andean model of nature as a constitutional subject seem to be aware of these challenges.

They seem to support the idea of a constitutionalism that is broader in scope than the mere 'discussion' between judges: an idea that appears to be reminiscent of the concept of the 'noosphere' theorised by Theilhard de Chardin[136] to state the need for a unit of information, methods and decisions capable of guaranteeing the future of humanity; an idea that concerns constitutionalism's 'genetic code' and not just its paradigms of observation.

Beyond constitutionalism's 'genetic code'

Modern constitutionalism is the offspring of European *Verweltlichung* (secularisation).[137] That is why its genetic code started life with an internal binary structure: no longer duties, but rights; no longer authority, but freedom. The human being was no longer a tool in the hand of another agent (the Church of God, or the sovereign in the name of God), but an autonomous focus of life in the world.

Has this secularised 'binary code' evolved without any pre-constituted, natural connective tissue: freedom *v.* authority? Rights *v.* duties? Or freedom *and* authority, rights *and* duties *v.* 'something in common'? In other words, for the very reason that it was emancipated from transcendence, it was fated to discover that it had no *Tertium* towards which to relate and justify the reasons of its binary nature. After all, as Paul Hazard explained,[138] medieval Europe's 'crisis of conscience' eventually ensured that the 'something in common' did not have to be considered as pre-existing anything at all, since it no longer derived from the will of God, nor any more so from the will of any sovereign: thenceforth, it was only to depend on consent or, in its absence, on anarchy.[139] The last four centuries of European history furnish the evidence.

In addition, this constitutionalism came to conceive of its binary dialectic as the 'natural' condition of human existence and, on this premise, it aspired to its universal vocation, in the process concealing its 'ethno-centric' – or exclusively European – matrix.

These two relations were to be captured with unusual intuition by J.J. Rousseau in his celebrated stag hunt dilemma (which he described in his *Discourse on the Origin and the Foundations of Inequality Among Men*, 1754): if the secular condition's genetic code is binary (freedom/authority), the problem inevitably arises of the conflict of individual interests between the individual's own immediate benefits of freedom and the benefits – common, but not immediate – of the greater collective interests that are in any case guaranteed by authority.[140] In addition, if social co-operation is fuelled by this dilemma, it will always be presented as identical to itself: it will be unable to experience exceptions to, or different visions of, the 'good life'.

In fact, the 'good life' was to derive from the combination between immediate individual benefits and common benefits guaranteed by authority. In the Middle Ages, these common benefits were identified as salvation (with the authority of the Church) and peace (guaranteed by the protection of the sovereign); moreover, in the Middle Ages, recognition of humanity was limited to Christian Europe alone.

The Europe that had its crisis of conscience was the same Europe that 'discovered' the New World and brought about the rift in Western Christendom, at the same time as it set out to experiment with salvation and peace as exclusively terrestrial dimensions, depending on agreement (between individuals as between states) and so on reciprocal trust. But that very reciprocal trust was the condition that could not pre-exist any more: in the absence of a divine certainty, it had to be experimented with as no more than a construct of reality.

Modern constitutions, as founding documents of the conditions of reciprocal trust[141] and so of the co-operation that replaced divine salvation to produce peace, have played the role of one of these constructs of reality produced by the Europe that suffered its crisis of conscience. Constitutions provided legitimation and guarantees for the 'Hobbesian public weal' of all members of society.[142]

These days, it is precisely this binary code of constitutionalism that is in a critical condition, but not because the state has given ground, as many of the supporters of global constitutionalism would have it. In reality, Rousseau's dilemma did not include the 'geo-human system'. Imagining society as a dialectic between freedom and authority, the genetic code of the rules of co-operation (and so in the first place of constitutionalism) has evolved outside the natural system.

The binary structure of constitutionalism's genetic code has therefore shown itself to be vulnerable on the very side of nature, which is reduced to an 'object' rather than treated as a 'subject' of the dilemma, as though it were not a biological element of human life processes. And with nature being treated as an 'object', constitutionalism has continued to legitimise the reasons of the *eco-nomy* and not those of *eco-logy*.

Outside the European and North American West, this 'colour of reason',[143] which has spent nearly three centuries lending its hue to the background of constitutionalism in its universal illusion, taken out of context by nature, has progressively been denounced as the cause of its own malaise. After all, outside that same West, its binary code, as Frantz Fanon already described it in *The Wretched of the Earth*, has been fuelled by 'inhuman humanism', not only during the colonial era, with its dichotomies between conquerors and conquered, between civilised and primitives and between rich and poor, but even during the so-called 'constitutional cycle' of independence and decolonisation, which hid behind 'constitutional façades'[144] while doing nothing at all to eliminate such dichotomies, simply because it ignored them and hindered the constitutional autocthonism of the oppressed, even though it was formally codified by many a proclamation of self-determination.[145]

These days, the examples mentioned in the previous paragraphs, drawn from Africa, from Asia and from Latin America, communicate a very important message for the future of constitutionalism. They tell us not to dwell immobile on Rousseau's dilemma, recycled in the dimension of global constitutionalism, in the name of only those human rights that defend the individual.

Just as it is surreal to imagine global constitutionalism outside the framework of Rousseau's dilemma, as a 'judicial dialogue' independent of the common benefits that are managed by the state authorities and by the democratic nature of their decisions, so it is equally surreal to think that global constitutionalism can survive outside the framework of the natural system.

So we are justified in wondering whether the vision of global constitutionalism, based on the sole paradigm of comparison-dialogue, really facilitates the process of observing global society, considering that it seems to be powerless against the risks of re-feudalisation of legal relations[146] and, above all, distracts our attention from the issues of the entire planet's ecological and democratic equilibrium.

If it is true that lawyers can contribute to determining the course of future events[147] and that there is an onus on those who observe world society to 'de-nationalise' the categories and the semantics of constitutional law,[148] then it is the responsibility of those lawyers to discuss and to promote hypotheses and forms of constitutional comparison that are not only 'dialogic', for the pluralism of rights, but above all 'sustainable', for the future of democracy and of the 'geo-human system': the two most important issues to be 'de-nationalised'.

Notes

1 J.P. Morgan, 'The Euro Area Adjustment: About Halfway There', *Europe Economic Research*, 28 May 2013, available at: www.jpmorganmarkets.com, 14.

2 H. Arthurs, 'The Constitutionalisation of Employment Relations: Multiple Models, Pernicious Problems', 19 *Social & Legal Studies*, 2010, 403; E. Tucker, 'Labour's Many Constitutions (and Capital's Too)', 33 *Comparative Labour Law and Policy Journal*, 2012, 355.

3 R.S. Turner, 'Neo-Liberal Constitutionalism: Ideology, Government and the Rule of Law', 1 *Journal of Politics and Law*, 2, 2008, 47; Aa.Vv. 'Special Issue. Austerity: The History of a Dangerous Idea', 6 *Comparative European Politics*, 11, 2013.

4 In the Italian debate, see G. Azzariti, *Il costituzionalismo moderno può sopravvivere?*, Roma-Bari, Laterza, 2013; M. Dani, *Il diritto pubblico europeo nella prospettiva dei conflitti*, Padova, Cedam, 2013; A. Carrino, *La giustizia come conflitto. Crisi della politica e Stato dei giudici*, Milano-Udine, Mimesis, 2011.
5 F. Rödl, 'Democratic Juridification without Statisation: Law of Conflict of Laws Instead of World State', in C. Joerges (ed.), *After Globalisation: New Patterns of Conflict and their Sociological and Legal Re-Constructions*, Oslo, Arena Report 4/11; S. Gill, 'Constitutionalizing Inequality and the Clash of Globalisations', *International Studies Review*, 2002, 47.
6 G. Teubner, *Constitutional Fragments: Societal Constitutionalism and Globalisation*, Oxford, Oxford University Press, 2012; 'Debate and Dialogue: Constitutionalizing Polycontexturality', 20 *Social & Legal Studies*, 2011, 209; and 'A Constitutional Moment? The Logics of "Hitting the Bottom"', in P. Kjaer, G. Teubner and A. Febbrajo (eds), *Financial Crisis in Constitutional Perspective: The Dark Side of Functional Differentiation*, Portland, Hart, 2011, 9.
7 A. Algostino, 'Transatlantic Trade and Investment Partnership: quando l'impero colpisce ancora?', 2014, available at: www.costituzionalismo.it.
8 A. Pizzorusso, *La produzione normativa in tempi di globalizzazione*, Torino, Giappichelli, 2008.
9 J. Roy (ed.), *Después de Santiago: integración regional y relaciones Union Europea-América latina*, Miami, Jean Monnet Chair, 2013.
10 M. Vellano, 'Verso il superamento del principio della parità formale degli Stati nel governo dell'economia mondiale', in A. Ligustro and G. Sacerdoti (eds), *Problemi e tendenze del diritto internazionale dell'economia, liber amicorum in onore di Paolo Picone*, Napoli, Editoriale Scientifica, 2011, 174.
11 V. Frosini, 'L'ipotesi robinsoniana e l'individuo come ordinamento giuridico', 3 *Sociologia del diritto*, 2011, 11.
12 Special Issue: International Workshop for Young Scholars 2012. 'The Future of Transnational Law: The EU, USA, China and the BRICS', 19 *European Law Journal*, 6, 2013, 705; M. vom Hau, J. Scott and D. Hulme, 'Beyond the BRICs: Alternative Strategies of Influence in the Global Politics of Development', 24 *European Journal of Development Research*, 2012, 187.
13 D. Mitrany, *A Working Peace System: An Argument for the Functional Development of International Organizations*, London, Royal Institute of International Studies, 1943.
14 See M. Carducci and A.S. Bruno, 'The Brics Countries between Justice and Economy: Methodological Challenges on Constitutional Comparison', 2 *Sociology and Anthropology*, 2, 2014, 45.
15 G. Martinico, 'Complexity and Cultural Sources of Law in the EU Context: From the Multilevel Constitutionalism to the Constitutional Synallagma', 8 *German Law Journal*, 2007, 205.
16 M. Bodenstein and H.W. Ursprung, 'Political Yardstick Competition, Economic Integration, and Constitutional Choice in a Federation', *Independent Institute Working Paper*, 37, 2001, 1.
17 M. Ruffert, 'The European Debt Crisis and European Union Law', *Common Market Law Review*, 2011, 1789.
18 E. Esposito Martino, 'Struttura costituzionale cinese tra tradizione e innovazione', *Osservatorio AIC*, 2014, 1.
19 http://blogs.ft.com/the-world/2014/04/does-size-matter-china-poised-to-overtake-us-as-worlds-largesteconomy-in-2014/.
20 D. Citati and A. Lundini, *L'unità nella diversità. Religioni, etnie e civiltà del Kazakhstan contemporaneo*, Roma, IsAG Fuoco edizioni, 2013.
21 https://projects.eff.org/~barlow/Declaration-Final.html.
22 http.//googleblog.blogspot.ca/2013/09/explore-worlds-constitutions-with-new.html.
23 G.L. Conti, 'La Governance dell'Internet: dalla Costituzione della rete alla Costituzione nella rete', in M. Nisticò and P. Passaglia (eds), *Internet e Costituzione*, Torino, Giappichelli, 2014, 117.
24 G. Frankenberg, *Autorität und Integration*, Frankfurt a. M., Suhrkamp, 2003, 124.
25 G. Frankenberg, 'Constitutions as Commodities: Notes on a Theory of Transfer', in G. Frankenberg (ed.), *Order from Transfer: Comparative Constitutional Design and Legal Culture*, Cheltenham and Northampton, Edward Elgar, 2013, 1.
26 K. Schlögel, *Im Raume lesen wir die Zeit. Über Zivilisationsgeschichte und Geopolitik*, München, Carl Hanser Verlag, 2003.
27 G. Frankenberg, 'Preface', in Frankenberg, *Order from Transfer*.
28 doc.Assembly/AU/12 (XX) Add.1.
29 John Rawls, *The Law of Peoples*, Cambridge, MA, Harvard University Press, 1999.

30 A.R. Bernstein, 'A Human Right to Democracy? Legitimacy and Intervention', in D. Reidy and R. Martin (eds), *Rawls's Law of Peoples: A Realistic Utopia?*, Oxford, Blackwell, 2006, 1; A. Buchanan, *Justice, Legitimacy and Self-Determination: Moral Foundations for International Law*, Oxford, Oxford University Press, 2004.
31 J. Cohen, 'Is there A Human Right to Democracy?', in Ch. Sypnovich (ed.), *The Egalitarian Conscience*, Oxford, Oxford University Press, 2006, 226–48, 233–43; J. Nickel (ed.), *Making Sense of Human Rights*, Oxford, Blackwell, 2006; J. Mandle, *Global Justice*, London, Polity Press, 2006.
32 D. Miller, *National Responsibility and Global Justice*, Oxford, Oxford University Press, 2007; Th. Franck, *Fairness in International Law and Institutions*, Oxford, Oxford University Press, 1996.
33 T. Miketiak, 'Nondiscrimination and the Human Right to Democracy', 12 *Gnosis*, 1, 2011, 30.
34 S. Greer, 'The Interpretation of the European Convention on Human Rights: Universal Principle or Margin of Appreciation?', 3 *UCL Human Rights Review*, 2010, 1.
35 J.M. Mocoroa, *Justicia transicional, amnistia y Corte Interamericana de derechos humanos: el caso 'Gelman' y algunas inquietudes*, in M. Carducci and P. Riberi (eds), *La dinamica delle integrazioni regionali latinoamericane. Casi e materiali*, Torino, Giappichelli, 2014, 88.
36 V. Piergigli, 'La Corte africana dei diritti dell'uomo e dei popoli giudica sulla violazione dei diritti di partecipazione politica e delle regole democratiche in Tanzania', 6 *Federalismi.it*, Focus Africa, 2014.
37 J.A. González Galván, 'La Corte y los indígenas', 107 *Boletín Mexicano de Derecho Comparado*, 2003, 725.
38 M. Kamto, 'Constitution et principe de l'autonomie constitutionnelle', in *Recueil des cours de l'Académie internationale de droit constitutionnel*, vol. 8, Tunis, Cedex, 2000, 127.
39 M. Walzer, 'Il governo mondiale è un sogno?', *Quaderni Costituzionali*, 2011, 187.
40 A. Hirsch, 'Sovereignty Surreal: Bataille and Fanon beyond the State of Exception', 13 *Contemporary Political Theory*, 2014, 287.
41 D. Sciulli, *Theory of Societal Constitutionalism: Foundations of a Non-Marxistic Critical Theory*, Cambridge, Cambridge University Press, 1992.
42 www.sesync.org/. . ./motesharrei-rivas-kalnay.pdf.
43 NASA has since partly disowned the contents of this research (www.nasa.gov/press/2014/march/nasa-statement-on-sustainability-study/#.Uy88d1fAkqw).
44 J.M. Headlay, *The Europeanization of the World*, Princeton, Princeton University Press, 2008.
45 L. Sanchez, 'Darwin, Artificial Selection, and Poverty: Contemporary Implications of a Forgotten Argument', 29 *Politics and the Life Sciences*, 1, 2010, 61.
46 C. Schmitt, *Der Nomos der Erde* [1950], Berlin, Duncker & Humblot, 1974.
47 W.F. Bello, *The Food Wars*, London, Verso, 2009.
48 D. Schneiderman, *Constitutionalizing Economic Globalization: Investments Rules and Democracy's Promise*, Cambridge, Cambridge University Press, 2008.
49 X. Kontiadis, 'La revisione della Costituzione greca e il neo-costituzionalismo del rischio', 2 *Diritto Pubblico Comparato ed Europeo*, 2005, 34, and *Verso il costituzionalismo del rischio?*, Italian translation, Lecce-Cavallino, Pensa, 2005; J. Rougier, S. Sparks and L.J. Hill (eds), *Risk and Uncertainty Assessment for Natural Hazards*, Cambridge, Cambridge University Press, 2012; A. Vermeule, *The Constitution of Risk*, Cambridge, Cambridge University Press, 2014.
50 O. Quijano Valencia, *Ecosimías. Visiones y prácticas de diferencia económico/cultural en contextos de multiplicidad*, Quito, UASB-UC, 2012.
51 E. Gudynas, 'Ciudadanía ambiental y meta-ciudadanías ecológicas: revisión y alternativas en América Latina', 19 *Desenvolvimento e Meio Ambiente*, 2009, 53.
52 H.W. Afonso and J.L. Quadros Magalhães, 'O Estado Plurinacional da Bolívia e do Equador: matrizes para uma releitura do direito internacional moderno', 17 *Revista Brasileira de Direito Constitucional*, 2011, 263.
53 E. Gudynas, *El mandato ecológico*, Quito, Corte Constitucional del Ecuador, 2009.
54 Quijano Valencia, *Ecosimías*.
55 M. Carducci, 'La Costituzione come "ecosistema" nel nuevo constitucionalismo delle Ande', in S. Bagni (ed.), *Dallo Stato del Bienestar allo Stato del Buen Vivir*, Bologna, Filodiritto, 2013, 11.
56 On this, see J.J. Gomes Canotilho's theory of 'interconstitutionality': *'Brancosos' e Interconstitucionalidade*, Coimbra, Almedina, 2006.
57 B. Wejnert, *Diffusion of Democracy: The Past and the Future of Global Democracy*, Cambridge, Cambridge University Press, 2014.

58 O. Höffe, *Demokratie im Zeitalter der Globalisierung*, München, Beck, 1999.
59 Consider the principle of 'the polluter pays', introduced by Art. 174 of the European Treaty of Amsterdam.
60 L.M. Firefax, 'The Legal Origins Theory in Crisis', *Brigham Young University Law Review*, 2009, 1571.
61 K. Pistor, 'Standardization of Law and its Effect on Developing Economies', 50 *American Journal of Comparative Law*, 2002, 97.
62 L. Pes, *Teorie dello sviluppo giuridico: dal movimento di* Law and Development *all'esperienza neo-liberale*, Trento, Tangram Edizioni, 2012.
63 H.P. Glenn, *Legal Traditions in the World: Sustainable Diversity in Law*, Oxford and New York, Oxford University Press, 2010, 288; P.G. Monateri, *Geopolitica del diritto. Genesi, governo e dissoluzione dei corpi politici*, Roma-Bari, Laterza, 2013.
64 M. Bussani, *Il diritto dell'Occidente. Geopolitica delle regole globali*, Torino, Einaudi, 2010.
65 M. Neves, *A constitucionalização simbólica*, São Paulo, Martins Fontes, 2007; L. Moreira, *A constituição como simulacro*, Rio de Janeiro, Lumen Juris, 2007.
66 M.C. Nussbaum, *Not for Profit: Why Democracy needs the Humanities*, Princeton, Princeton University Press, 2010, and *Creating Capabilities: The Human Development Approach*, Cambridge, MA, The Belknap Harvard University Press, 2011.
67 O. Frishman, 'Transnational Judicial Dialogue as an Organizational Field', *European Law Journal*, 19, 2013, 739.
68 A.-M. Slaughter, *A New World Order*, Princeton, Princeton University Press, 2004.
69 M.R. Ferrarese, *Diritto sconfinato*, Roma-Bari, Laterza, 2006; I. Turégano Mansilla, *Justicia global: los límites del constitucionalismo*, Lima, Palestra, 2010.
70 E. Somaini, *Geografia della democrazia*, Bologna, il Mulino, 2009.
71 M. Rosenfeld, *The Identity of the Constitutional Subject: Selfhood, Citizenship, Culture, and Community*, London, Routledge, 2010.
72 A. Kemmerer, 'The Normative Knot 2.0: Metaphorological Explorations in the Net of Networks', 10 *German Law Journal*, 2009, 439.
73 Ch. Thornhill, 'Niklas Luhmann and the Sociology of the Constitutions', 10 *Journal of Classical Sociology*, 2010, 1.
74 V. Jackson, *Constitutional Engagement in a Transnational Era*, Oxford, Oxford University Press, 2010.
75 M. Loughlin, *The Idea of Public Law*, Oxford, Oxford University Press, 2004, 72.
76 P. Zumbansen, 'Comparative, Global and Transnational Constitutionalism: The Emergence of a Transnational Legal-Pluralist Order', 1 *Global Constitutionalism*, 1, 2012, 16.
77 V. Perju, 'Constitutional Transplants, Borrowing and Migrations', in M. Rosenfeld and A. Sajó (eds), *The Oxford Handbook of Comparative Constitutional Law*, Oxford, Oxford University Press, 2012, 1324.
78 S. Baer, 'Verfassungsvergleichung und reflexive Methode: interkulturelle und intersubjektive Kompetenz', 64 *Heidelberg Journal of International Law*, 2004, 735.
79 J. Habermas, 'The Constitutionalization of International Law and the Legitimation Problems of a Constitution for World Society', 2008, available at: www.onlinelibrary.wiley.com; J. Klabbers, A. Peters and G. Ulfstein, *The Constitutionalization of International Law*, Oxford, Oxford University Press, 2009; J.L. Dunoff and J.P. Trachtman (eds), *Ruling the World? Constitutionalism, International Law and Global Governance*, Cambridge, Cambridge University Press, 2009; C.E.J. Schwöbel, *Global Constitutionalism in International Legal Perspective*, Leiden, Martinus Nijhoff, 2011; B.N. Mamlyuk and U. Mattei, 'Comparative International Law', 36 *Brooklyn Journal of International Law*, 2011, 385; A. Roberts, 'Comparative International Law? The Role of National Courts in Creating and Enforcing International Law', 60 *International & Comparative Law Quarterly*, 2011, 57.
80 L. Fucci Amato, *Constitucionalização Corporativa. Direitos Humanos Fundamentais, Economia e Empresa*, Curitiba, Juruá, 2014; S. Gill and A.C. Cutler, *New Constitutionalism and World Order*, Cambridge, Cambridge University Press, 2014.
81 M. Siems, 'The End of Comparative Law', 2 *Journal of Comparative Law*, 2007, 133; M. Reimann, 'The End of Comparative Law as an Autonomous Subject', 11 *Tulane European and Civil Law Forum*, 1996, 49; H. Muir-Watt, 'Further Terrains for Subversive Comparison: The Field of Global Governance and the Public/Private Divide', in P.G. Monateri (ed.), *Methods of Comparative Law: An Intellectual Overview*, Cheltenham and Northampton, Edward Elgar, 2012, 270.
82 O. Diggelmann and T. Altwicker, 'Is there Something like a Constitution of International Law? A Critical Analysis of the Debate on World Constitutionalism', 68 *ZaöRV*, 2008, 623.

83 M. Loughlin, 'What is Constitutionalisation?', in P. Dobner and M. Loughlin (eds), *The Twilight of Constitutionalism?*, Oxford, Oxford University Press, 2010, 47.
84 On this distinction, see E. Betti, 'Possibilità e limiti di un diritto di convivenza europeo', VI *Nuova Rivista di Diritto Commerciale*, 1953, 104.
85 For the current state of debate, see: J. Waldron, 'A Right-Based Critique of Constitutional Rights', 13 *Oxford J. Legal St.*, 1993, 18; M. Goldoni, 'Il ritorno del costituzionalismo alla politica: il "Political" e il "Popular" Constitutionalism', 4 *Quaderni Costituzionali*, 4, 2010, 733. The formula 'general constitutional law' was generated by Boris Mirkine-Guetzévitch, *Les nouvelles tendances du droit constitutionnel*, Paris, Giard, 1931.
86 R. Hirschl, 'Globalization, Courts, and Judicial Power: The Political Origins of the New Constitutionalism', 11 *Indiana Journal of Global Legal Studies*, 2004, 71; K.-H. Ladeur and L. Viellechner, 'Die transnationale Expansion staatlicher Grundrechte: zur Konstitutionalisierung globaler Privatsrechtsregimes', 46 *Archiv des Völkerrechts*, 2008, 42.
87 M. Carducci, 'Judicial Re-Use: "Codification" or Return of Hegelism? The Comparative Arguments in the "South" of the World', paper presented at the *Second Thematic Congress of the International Academy of Comparative Law* – NTU Campus, 24–26 May 2012, in II *Eunomia*, 2, 2013, 7.
88 U. Baxi, 'The Colonialist Heritage', in P. Legrand and R. Munday (eds), *Comparative Legal Studies: Traditions and Transitions*, Cambridge, Cambridge University Press, 2003, 49.
89 J. Ferguson, *Global Shadows: Africa in the Neoliberal Order*, Durham, NC and London, Duke University Press, 2006, 191.
90 S. Choudhry, 'Globalization in Search of Justification: Towards a Theory of Comparative Constitutional Interpretation', 74 *Indiana Law Journal*, 1999, 819; P. Häberle, *Rechtsvergleichung im Kraftfeld des Verfassungsstaates*, Berlin, Duncker & Humblot, 1992; Q. Camerlengo, *Contributo ad una teoria del diritto costituzionale cosmopolitico*, Milano, Giuffrè, 2010.
91 I. Camyar, 'Institutions, Information Asymmetry and Democratic Responsiveness: A Cross-National and Multi-Level Analysis', 49 *Acta Politica*, 2014, 313.
92 For several examples of empirical verification, see the world-level research co-ordinated Lucio Pegoraro (partially summarised in: *Los jueces y los profesores: la influencia de la doctrina sobre las decisiones de los Tribunales y Cortes constitucionales*, in *Annuario Iberoamericano Costituzionale*, Napoli, Editoriale Scientifica, 2014, 101); C. Bateup, 'The Dialogic Promise: Assessing the Normative Potential of Theories of Constitutional Dialogue', 71 *Brooklyn Law Review*, 2006, 1109; G. Betlem and A. Nollkaemper, 'Giving Effect to Public International Law and European Community Law before Domestic Courts: A Comparative Analysis of the Practice of Consistent Interpretation', 14 *European Journal of International Law*, 3, 2003, 569; M. Carducci and V. de Oliveira Mazzuoli, *Teoria tridimensional das Integrações supranacionais*, Rio de Janeiro, Forense, 2014; B. Flanagan and S. Ahern, 'Judicial Decision-Making and Transnational Law', 60 *International & Comparative Law Quarterly* 2011, 1; T. Groppi and M.-C. Ponthoreau (eds), *The Use of Foreign Precedents by Constitutional Judges*, Portland, Hart, 2013; A. Lollini, 'La circolazione degli argomenti', 1 *Diritto Pubblico Comparato ed Europeo*, 2007, 307; N. Sagües, 'El recurso al derecho y al intérprete externo en la interpretación e integración de la Constitución nacional', in *Memoria del X Congreso iberoamericano de Derecho constitucional*, vol. I, Lima, Idemsa, 2009, 95.
93 G. Samuel, 'Epistemology and Comparative Law: Contributions from the Sciences and Social Sciences', in M. van Hoecke (ed.), *Epistemology and Methodology of Comparative Law*, Portland, Hart, 2004, 35.
94 B. de Sousa Santos, *Toward a New Legal Common Sense*, London, Butterworths, 2002; Azzariti, *Il costituzionalismo moderno può sopravvivere?*, chapter IV.
95 A. Yakhlef, 'The Trinity of International Strategy; Adaptation, Standardization and Transformation', 9 *Asian Business and Management*, 2010, 47.
96 D. Kappeler, 'The Birth and Evolution of a Diplomatic Culture', in H. Slavik (ed.), *Intercultural Communication and Diplomacy*, Malta, DiploFoundation, 2004, 355.
97 W. Twining, 'Globalization and Comparative Law', *Maastricht Journal of European & Comparative Law*, 6, 1999, 217; G.M. Sanchez, 'A Paradigm Shift in Legal Education: Preparing Law Students for the Twenty-First Century: Teaching Foreign Law, Culture, and Legal Language of the Major U.S. American Trading Partners', *San Diego Law Review*, 34, 1997, 635; M.C. Daly, 'The Ethical Implications of the Globalization of the Legal Profession: A Challenge to the Teaching of Professional Responsibility in the Twenty-First Century', *Fordham International Law Journal*, 21, 1998, 1239; M. Carducci and A.S. Bruno, 'Studying the "Legal Flows" as a Multidisciplinary Method to Promote Constitutionalism as a Common Property of Mankind', 4 *European Scientific Journal*, 2013, 119.

98 About these issues, see: B. Markesinis and J. Fedtke, *Judicial Recourse to Foreign Law: A New Source of Inspiration?*, London, UCL Press, 2006.
99 N. Achterberg, 'Rechtsprechung als Staatsfunktion, Rechtsprechungslehre als Wissenschaftsdisziplin', *DVBl*, 1984, 1093.
100 G. de Vergottini, *Oltre il dialogo tra le Corti. Giudici, diritto straniero, comparazione*, Bologna, il Mulino, 2010.
101 D. Gerber, 'Globalization and Legal Knowledge: Implications for Comparative Law', 75 *Tulane Law Review*, 2000–1, 966.
102 D.S. Law, 'Generic Constitutional Law', 89 *Minnesota Law Review*, 2005, 652.
103 M. Carducci, 'Crítica de la comparación constitucional "ad hoc" ', 55 *Revista de Direito Administrativo & Constitucional*, 2014, 13.
104 M. Luciani, 'Costituzionalismo irenico e costituzionalismo polemico', *Giurisprudenza Costituzionale*, 2006, 1654.
105 N. Dorsen, M. Rosenfeld, A. Sajó and S. Baer, *Comparative Constitutionalism: Cases and Materials*, St. Paul, Thomson West, 2003, 8.
106 M. Zuleta, H. Cubides and M. Escobar (eds), *¿Uno solo o varios mundos? Diferencia, subjetividad y conocimientos en las ciencias sociales contemporáneas*, Bogotá, Universidad Central-Iesco, 2007.
107 M. Koskenniemi, 'International Law: Constitutionalism, Managerialism and the Ethos of Legal Education', *European Journal of Legal Studies*, 1, 2007, 2.
108 P. Picone, 'Diritto internazionale dell'economia e costituzione economica dell'ordinamento internazionale', XVI *Comunicazioni e Studi*, 1980, 137; E. Posner, *The Perils of Global Legalism*, Chicago and London, University of Chicago Press, 2009.
109 L. Pegoraro, *Diritto costituzionale comparato. La scienza e il metodo*, Bologna, Bononia University Press, 2014, 210.
110 S. Cassese, 'Il diritto costituzionale globale: un'introduzione', *Rivista Trimestrale di Diritto Pubblico*, 2005, 342, and *Oltre lo Stato*, Roma-Bari, Laterza, 2006, 16.
111 D. Chalmers, 'Post-Nationalism and the Quest for Constitutional Substitutes', *Journal of Law and Society*, 27, 2000, 192.
112 A. Voβkuhle, 'Multilevel Cooperation of the European Constitutional Courts: der Europäische Verfassungsgerichtsverbund', 6 *European Constitutional Law Review*, 2, 2010, 175.
113 T. Russo, 'Deficit e anti-deficit democratico nell'ordinamento dell'Unione Europea', 2 *Quaderni dell'Università degli Studi di Salerno*, 2011.
114 M. Ferrarese, *Il diritto al presente. Globalizzazione e tempo delle istituzioni*, Bologna, il Mulino, 2002, 169.
115 R. Pierik and W. Werner (eds), *Cosmopolitanism in Context: Perspectives from International Law and Political Theory*, Cambridge and New York, Cambridge University Press, 2010.
116 S. Vaccaro, *Globalizzazione e diritti umani. Filosofia e politica della mondialità*, Milano-Udine, Mimesis, 2004; L. Vecchioli, *Il rischio della sovranità globale*, Torino, Giappichelli, 2004.
117 P. Dardot and Ch. Laval, *La nouvelle raison du monde. Essai sur la societé néoliberale*, Paris, La Découverte, 2009.
118 J. Gray, *False Dawn: The Delusion of Global Capitalism*, New York, New York Press, 1998.
119 G. Krippner, *The Political Origins of the Rise of Finance*, Cambridge, MA, Harvard University Press, 2011; E.C. Raffiotta, *Il governo multilivello dell'economia. Studio sulle trasformazioni dello Stato costituzionale in Europa*, Bologna, Bononia University Press, 2013; P. Leon, *Il capitalismo e lo Stato: crisi e trasformazioni delle strutture economiche*, Roma, Castelvecchi, 2014; J. Best and A. Gheciu, *The Return of Public in Global Governance*, Cambridge, Cambridge University Press, 2014.
120 For a bibliography, see: C. Focarelli, 'Costituzionalismo internazionale e costituzionalizzazione della Global Governance: alla ricerca del diritto globale', 2 *Politica del diritto*, 2011, 207; L. Ronchetti, *Il nomos infranto: globalizzazioni e costituzioni. Del limite come principio essenziale degli ordinamenti giuridici*, Napoli, Jovene, 2007.
121 R. Luperini, *L'allegoria del moderno*, Roma, Editori Riuniti, 1990.
122 P. Valery, *Piccola lettera sui miti*, Italian translation in *All'inizio era la favola*, Milano, Guerini & Associati, 1988, 55.
123 R. Wiethölter, *Rechtswissenschaft*, Frankfurt a. M.-Hamburg, Fischer, 1968.
124 F. Rossi-Landi, *Significato, comunicazione e parlare comune*, Padova, Marsilio, 1961, and *Il linguaggio come lavoro e come mercato*, Milano, Bompiani, 1968.
125 Th.S. Kuhn, *The Structure of Scientific Revolutions*, second enlarged edition, Chicago, Chicago University Press, 1970, 43.

126 F. Ost, 'Os desvios de Babel: a tradução como paradigma', in E. Menezes de Carvalho and R. Greenstein (eds), *Integração normativa. O direito em um contexto multicultural e multilingue*, Rio de Janeiro, FGV, 2013, 68.
127 D. Westbrook, 'Theorising the Diffusion of Law: Conceptual Difficulties, Unstable Imaginations and the Effort to Think Gracefully Nonetheless', 47 *Harvard International Law Journal*, 2006, 489; N. Tebbe and R.L. Tsai, 'Constitutional Borrowing', 108 *Michigan Law Review*, 2010, 459.
128 H. Hofmann, *Legitimität gegen Legalität*, Berlin, Duncker & Humblot, 2010, 66.
129 D.L. Shapiro, 'In Defense of Judicial Candor', 100 *Harvard Law Review*, 1986–7, 731.
130 L. Cohen-Tanugi, *Le droits sans état: sur la démocratie en France et en Amérique*, Paris, PUF, 2007.
131 A. Voβkuhle, Ch. Bumke and F. Meinel (eds), *Verabschiedung und Wiederentdeckung des Staates im Spannungsfeld der Disziplinen*, Berlin, Duncker & Humblot, 2013.
132 M. Neves, *Transconstitucionalismo*, São Paulo, Martins Fontes, 2009.
133 R. Bustos Gisberg, *La Constitución Red*, Bilbao-Vitoria, IVAP, 2005.
134 P. Häberle, *Der kooperative Verfassungsstaat: aus Kultur und als Kultur*, Berlin, Duncker & Humblot, 2013.
135 A. Carrino: *La dottrina dello Stato e la sua crisi*, Modena, Mucchi, 2014, and *Il problema della sovranità nell'età della globalizzazione*, Soveria Mannelli, Rubettino, 2014; M. Barberis, 'Il custode delle fonti. Lo Stato dopo lo Stato e la sua legalità', 2 *Lo Stato*, 2, 2014, 11; M. Revenga Sánchez, 'Cinco grandes retos (y otra tantas amenazas) para la democracia constitucional en el siglo XXI', 12 *Parlamento y Constitución*, 2009, 25; W. Leisner, *Institutionelle Evolution. Grundlinien einer Allgemeinen Staatslehre*, Berlin, Duncker & Humblot, 2012; M. Troper, 'The Structure of the Legal System and the Emergence of the State', available at: www.nyustrauss.org, paper 6/2012.
136 P. Teilhard de Chardin, *La Formation de la Noosphère* (1947), and *L'essence de l'idée de démocratie* (1948), now in *L'Avenir de l'Homme*, Paris, Editions du Seuil, 1959. See: M. Arruda, *Globalization and Civil Society: Rethinking Cooperativism in the Context of Active Citizenship*, Rio de Janeiro, PACS, 1996.
137 E.-V. Böckenförde, *Der säkularisierte Staat*, Carl Friedrich von Siemens Stiftung, 2007.
138 P. Hazard, *La crise de la coinscience européenne*, Paris, Boivin, 1935.
139 Ch. Taylor, *The Secular Age*, Cambridge, MA, Harvard University Press, 2007.
140 B. Skyrms, *The Stag Hunt and the Evolution of Social Structure*, Cambridge, Cambridge University Press, 2004.
141 Ferrarese, *Il diritto al presente*, 17.
142 S.P. Hargreaves-Heap, M. Hollis, B. Lyons, R. Sugden and A. Weale, *The Theory of Rational Choice*, Cambridge, Blackwell, 1992, 193.
143 C. León Pesántez, *El color de la razón. Pensamiento crítico en las Américas*, Quito, UASB, 2013.
144 F.W. Riggs, 'Fragilité des Régimes du Tiers Monde', 136 *Revue Internationale des Sciences Sociales*, 1993, 235.
145 M. Herrero de Miñon, 'Autoctonía constitucional y poder constituyente', *Revista de Estudios Políticos*, 1970, 138, and *Nacionalismo y constitucionalismo. El derecho constitucional de los nuevos Estados*, Madrid, Tecnos, 1971.
146 A. Supiot, 'The Public-Private Relation in the Context of Today's Refeudalization', 11 *International Journal of Constitutional Law*, 1, 2013, 129.
147 M. Scheltema, *Le droit de demain*, The Hague, Hague Academica Press, 2005, 4.
148 R. Koselleck, *Begriffsgeschichten: Studien zur Semantik und Pragmatik der politischen und sozialen Sprache*, Frankfurt a.M., Suhrkamp, 2006, 369.

References

Aa.Vv. 'Special Issue. Austerity: The History of a Dangerous Idea'. *Comparative European Politics* 11 (2013).

Achterberg, Nach. 'Rechtsprechung als Staatsfunktion, Rechtsprechungslehre als Wissenschaftsdisziplin'. *DVBl* (1984): 1093.

Afonso, Henrique W., and José L. Quadros Magalhães. 'O Estado Plurinacional da Bolívia e do Equador: matrizes para uma releitura do direito internacional moderno'. *Revista Brasileira de Direito Constitucional* 17 (2011): 263–76.

Algostino, Alessandra. 'Transatlantic Trade and Investment Partnership: quando l'impero colpisce ancora?', 2014. Available at: www.costituzionalismo.it/articoli/469/.

Arruda, Marcos. *Globalization and Civil Society: Rethinking Cooperativism in the Context of Active Citizenship*. Rio de Janeiro: PACS, 1996.

Arthurs, Harry. 'The Constitutionalisation of Employment Relations: Multiple Models, Pernicious Problems'. *Social & Legal Studies* 19 (2010): 403–22.

Azzariti, Gaetano. *Il costituzionalismo moderno può sopravvivere?* Roma-Bari: Laterza, 2013.

Baer, Susanne. 'Verfassungsvergleichung und reflexive Methode: interkulturelle und intersubjektive Kompetenz'. *Heidelberg Journal of International Law* 64 (2004): 735–58.

Barberis, Mauro. 'Il custode delle fonti. Lo Stato dopo lo Stato e la sua legalità'. *Lo Stato* 2 (2014): 11–30.

Barlow, John P. 'A Declaration of the Independence of Cyberspace'. Available at: http://projects.eff.org/~barlow/Declaration-Final.html.

Bateup, Christine A. 'The Dialogic Promise: Assessing the Normative Potential of Theories of Constitutional Dialogue'. *Brooklyn Law Review* 71 (2006): 1109–20.

Baxi, Upendra. 'The Colonialist Heritage'. In *Comparative Legal Studies: Traditions and Transitions*, edited by Pierre Legrand and Roderick Munday, 46–58. Cambridge: Cambridge University Press, 2003.

Bello, Walden F. *The Food Wars*. London: Verso, 2009.

Bernstein, Alyssa R. 'A Human Right to Democracy? Legitimacy and Intervention'. In *Rawls's Law of Peoples: A Realistic Utopia?*, edited by David Reidy and Rex Martin, 278–98. Oxford: Blackwell, 2006.

Best, Jacqueline, and Alexandra Gheciu. *The Return of Public in Global Governance*. Cambridge: Cambridge University Press, 2014.

Betlem, Gerrit, and André Nollkaemper. 'Giving Effect to Public International Law and European Community Law before Domestic Courts: A Comparative Analysis of the Practice of Consistent Interpretation'. *European Journal of International Law* 14(3) (2003): 569–89.

Betti, Emilio. 'Possibilità e limiti di un diritto di convivenza europeo', *Nuova Rivista di Diritto Commerciale, Diritto dell'economia, Diritto sociale* (1953): 104–8.

Böckenförde, Ernst-Wolfgang. *Der säkularisierte Staat: sein Charakter, seine Rechtfertigung und seine Probleme im 21 Jahrhundert*. Carl Friedrich von Siemens Stiftung, 2007

Bodenstein, Martin, and Heinrich W. Ursprung. 'Political Yardstick Competition, Economic Integration, and Constitutional Choice in a Federation'. *Independent Institute Working Paper* 37 (2001): 1–28.

Buchanan, Allen. *Justice, Legitimacy and Self-Determination: Moral Foundations for International Law*. Oxford: Oxford University Press, 2004.

Bussani, Mauro. *Il diritto dell'Occidente. Geopolitica delle regole globali*. Torino: Einaudi, 2010.

Bustos Gisberg, Rafael. *La Constitución Red*. Bilbao-Vitoria: IVAP, 2005.

Camerlengo, Quirino. *Contributo ad una teoria del diritto costituzionale cosmopolitico*. Milano: Giuffrè, 2010.

Camyar, Isa. 'Institutions, Information Asymmetry and Democratic Responsiveness: A Cross-National and Multi-Level Analysis'. *Acta Politica* 49 (2014): 313–36.

Carducci, Michele. 'Judicial Re-Use: "Codification" or Return of Hegelism? The Comparative Arguments in the "South" of the World'. Paper presented at the *Second Thematic Congress of the International Academy of Comparative Law* – NTU Campus, 24–26 May 2012. *Eunomia* 2 (2013): 7–27.

———. 'La Costituzione come "ecosistema" nel nuevo constitucionalismo delle Ande'. In *Dallo Stato del Bienestar allo Stato del Buen Vivir*, edited by Silvia Bagni, 11–18. Bologna: Filodiritto, 2013.

———. 'Crítica de la comparación constitucional "ad hoc" '. *Revista de Direito Administrativo & Constitucional* 55 (2014): 13–24.

Carducci, Michele, and Anna S. Bruno. 'Studying the "Legal Flows" as a Multidisciplinary Method to Promote Constitutionalism as a Common Property of Mankind'. *European Scientific Journal* 4 (2013): 118–24.

———. 'The Brics Countries between Justice and Economy. Methodological Challenges on Constitutional Comparison'. *Sociology and Anthropology* 2 (2014): 46–58.

Carducci, Michele, and Valerio de Oliveira Mazzuoli. *Teoria tridimensional das Integrações supranacionais*. Rio de Janeiro: Forense, 2014.

Carrino, Agostino. *La giustizia come conflitto. Crisi della politica e Stato dei giudici*. Milano-Udine: Mimesis, 2011.

———. *La dottrina dello Stato e la sua crisi*. Modena: Mucchi, 2014.

———. *Il problema della sovranità nell'età della globalizzazione*. Soveria Mannelli: Rubettino, 2014.

Cassese, Sabino. 'Il diritto amministrativo globale: un'introduzione'. *Rivista Trimestrale di Diritto Pubblico* (2005): 342–56.

———. *Oltre lo Stato*. Roma-Bari: Laterza, 2006.

Chalmers, Damian. 'Post-Nationalism and the Quest for Constitutional Substitutes'. *Journal of Law and Society* 27 (2000): 178–92.

Choudhry, Sujit. 'Globalization in Search of Justification: Towards a Theory of Comparative Constitutional Interpretation'. *Indiana Law Journal* 74 (1999): 819–92.

Citati, Dario, and Alessandro Lundini. *L'unità nella diversità. Religioni, etnie e civiltà del Kazakhstan contemporaneo*. Roma: IsAG Fuoco edizioni, 2013.

Cohen, Jerry. 'Is there a Human Right to Democracy?' In *The Egalitarian Conscience*, edited by Christine Sypnovich, 226–48. Oxford: Oxford University Press, 2006.

Cohen-Tanugi, Laurent. *Le droits sans État: sur la démocratie en France et en Amérique*. Paris: PUF, 2007.

Conti, Gian Luca. 'La Governance dell'Internet: dalla Costituzione della rete alla Costituzione nella rete'. In *Internet e Costituzione*, edited by Michele Nisticò and Paolo Passaglia, 117–30. Torino: Giappichelli, 2014.

Daly, Mary C. 'The Ethical Implications of the Globalization of the Legal Profession: A Challenge to the Teaching of Professional Responsibility in the Twenty-First Century'. *Fordham International Law Journal* 21 (1998): 1239–95.

Dani, Marco. *Il diritto pubblico europeo nella prospettiva dei conflitti*. Padova: Cedam, 2013.

Dardot, Pierre, and Chistian Laval. *La nouvelle raison du monde. Essai sur la societé néoliberale*. Paris: La Découverte, 2009.

de Sousa Santos, Boaventura. *Toward a New Legal Common Sense*. London: Butterworths, 2002.

de Vergottini, Giuseppe. *Oltre il dialogo tra le Corti. Giudici, diritto straniero, comparazione*. Bologna: il Mulino, 2010.

Diggelmann, Oliver, and Tilmann Altwicker. 'Is there Something like a Constitution of International Law? A Critical Analysis of the Debate on World Constitutionalism'. *ZaöRV* 68 (2008): 623–50.

Dorsen, Norman, Michel Rosenfeld, Andras Sajó and Susanne Baer. *Comparative Constitutionalism: Cases and Materials*. St. Paul: Thomson West, 2003.

Dunoff, Jeffrey L., and Joel P. Trachtman (eds). *Ruling the World? Constitutionalism, International Law and Global Governance*. Cambridge: Cambridge University Press, 2009.

Esposito Martino, Elisabetta. 'Struttura costituzionale cinese tra tradizione e innovazione'. *Osservatorio AIC* (2014): 1–24. Available at: www.associazionedeicostituzionalisti.it.

Firefax, Lisa M. 'The Legal Origins Theory in Crisis'. *Brigham Young University Law Review* 6 (2009): 1571–618.

Ferguson, James. *Global Shadows: Africa in the Neoliberal Order*. Durham, NC and London: Duke University Press, 2006.

Ferrarese, Maria R. *Il diritto al presente. Globalizzazione e tempo delle istituzioni*. Bologna: il Mulino, 2002.

———. *Diritto sconfinato*. Roma-Bari: Laterza, 2006.

Flanagan, Brian, and Sinéad Ahern. 'Judicial Decision-Making and Transnational Law'. *International & Comparative Law Quarterly* 60 (2011): 1–28.

Focarelli, Carlo. 'Costituzionalismo internazionale e costituzionalizzazione della Global Governance: alla ricerca del diritto globale'. *Politica del diritto* 2 (2011): 207–38.

Franck, Thomas M. *Fairness in International Law and Institutions*. Oxford: Oxford University Press, 1996.

Frankenberg, Günther. *Autorität und Integration*. Frankfurt am Main: Suhrkamp, 2003.

———. 'Constitutions as Commodities: Notes on a Theory of Transfer'. In *Order from Transfer. Comparative Constitutional Design and Legal Culture*, edited by Günther Frankenberg, 1–26. Cheltenham and Northampton: Edward Elgar, 2013.

———. 'Preface'. In *Order from Transfer: Comparative Constitutional Design and Legal Culture*, edited by Günther Frankenberg, XII–XVI. Cheltenham and Northampton, Edward Elgar, 2013.
Frishman, Olga. 'Transnational Judicial Dialogue as an Organizational Field'. *European Law Journal* 19 (2013): 739–58.
Frosini, Vittorio. 'L'ipotesi robinsoniana e l'individuo come ordinamento giuridico'. *Sociologia del diritto* 3 (2011): 5–16.
Fucci Amato, Lucas. *Constitucionalização Corporativa. Direitos Humanos Fundamentais, Economia e Empresa*. Curitiba: Juruá, 2014.
Gerber, David J. 'Globalization and Legal Knowledge: Implications for Comparative Law'. *Tulane Law Review* 75 (2000–1): 949–75.
Gill, Stephen. 'Constitutionalizing Inequality and the Clash of Globalisations'. *International Studies Review* (2002): 47–65.
Gill, Stephen and A. Claire Cutler. *New Constitutionalism and World Order*. Cambridge: Cambridge University Press, 2014.
Glenn, H. Patrick. *Legal Traditions in the World: Sustainable Diversity in Law*. Oxford and New York: Oxford University Press, 2010.
Goldoni, Marco. 'Il ritorno del costituzionalismo alla politica: il "Political" e il "Popular" Constitutionalism'. *Quaderni Costituzionali* 4 (2010): 733–55.
Gomes Canotilho's, José J. *'Brancosos' e Interconstitucionalidade*. Coimbra: Almedina, 2006.
González Galván, Jorge A. 'La Corte y los indígenas'. *Boletín Mexicano de Derecho Comparado* 107 (2003): 725–33.
Google Official Blog. 'Explore the World's Constitutions with a New Online Tool'. Available at: http://googleblog.blogspot.it/2013/09/explore-worlds-constitutions-with-new.html.
Gray, John. *False Dawn: The Delusion of Global Capitalism*. New York: New York Press, 1998.
Greer, Steven. 'The Interpretation of the European Convention on Human Rights: Universal Principle or Margin of Appreciation?' *UCL Human Rights Review* 3 (2010): 1–14.
Groppi, Tania, and Marie-Claire Ponthoreau (eds). *The Use of Foreign Precedents by Constitutional Judges*. Portland: Hart, 2013.
Gudynas, Eduardo. 'Ciudadanía ambiental y meta-ciudadanías ecológicas: revisión y alternativas en América Latina'. *Desenvolvimento e Meio Ambiente* 19 (2009): 53–72.
———. *El mandato ecológico*. Quito: Corte Constitucional del Ecuador, 2009.
Häberle, Peter. *Rechtsvergleichung im Kraftfeld des Verfassungsstaates*. Berlin: Duncker & Humblot, 1992.
———. *Der kooperative Verfassungsstaat: aus Kultur und als Kultur*. Berlin: Duncker & Humblot, 2013.
Habermas, Jürgen. 'The Constitutionalization of International Law and the Legitimation Problems of a Constitution for World Society'. 2008. Available at: www.onlinelibrary.wiley.com.
Hargreaves-Heap, Shaun P., Martin Hollis, Bruce Lyons, Robert Sugden and Albert Weale. *The Theory of Rational Choice*. Cambridge: Blackwell, 1992.
Hazard, Paul. *La crise de la conscience européenne*. Paris: Boivin, 1935.
Headlay, John M. *The Europeanization of the World*. Princeton: Princeton University Press, 2008.
Herrero de Miñon, Miguel. 'Autoctonía constitucional y poder constituyente'. *Revista de Estudios Políticos* (1970): 29–122.
———. *Nacionalismo y constitucionalismo. El derecho constitucional de los nuevos Estados*. Madrid: Tecnos, 1971.
Hirsch, Alexander K. 'Sovereignty Surreal: Bataille and Fanon beyond the State of Exception'. *Contemporary Political Theory* 13 (2014): 287–306.
Hirschl, Ran. 'Globalization, Courts, and Judicial Power: The Political Origins of the New Constitutionalism'. *Indiana Journal of Global Legal Studies* 11 (2004): 71–108.
Höffe, Otfried. *Demokratie im Zeitalter der Globalisierung*. München: Beck, 1999.
Hofmann, Hasso. *Legitimität gegen Legalität*. Berlin: Duncker & Humblot, 2010.
Jackson, Vicki. *Constitutional Engagement in a Transnational Era*. Oxford: Oxford University Press, 2010.
J.P. Morgan. 'The Euro Area Adjustment: About Halfway There'. *Europe Economic Research*, 28 May 2013. Available at: www.jpmorganmarkets.com.

Kamto, Maurice. 'Constitution et principe de l'autonomie constitutionnelle'. *Recueil des cours de l'Académie internationale de droit constitutionnel* 8 (2000): 141–6.

Kappeler, Dietrich. 'The Birth and Evolution of a Diplomatic Culture'. In *Intercultural Communication and Diplomacy*, edited by Hanna Slavik, 353–9. Malta: DiploFoundation, 2004.

Kemmerer, Alexandra. 'The Normative Knot 2.0: Metaphorological Explorations in the Net of Networks'. *German Law Journal* 10 (2009): 439–62.

Klabbers, Jan, Anne Peters and Geir Ulfstein. *The Constitutionalization of International Law*. Oxford: Oxford University Press, 2009.

Kontiadis, Xenofon. 'La revisione della Costituzione greca e il neo-costituzionalismo del rischio'. *Diritto Pubblico Comparato ed Europeo* 2 (2005): 559–68.

———. *Verso il costituzionalismo del rischio?* Lecce-Cavallino: Pensa, 2005.

Koselleck, Reinhart. *Begriffsgeschichten: Studien zur Semantik und Pragmatik der politischen und sozialen Sprache*. Frankfurt am Main: Suhrkamp, 2006.

Koskenniemi, Martti. 'International Law: Constitutionalism, Managerialism and the Ethos of Legal Education'. *European Journal of Legal Studies* 1 (2007): 2–18.

Krippner, Greta R. *The Political Origins of the Rise of Finance*. Cambridge, MA: Harvard University Press, 2011.

Kuhn, Thomas S. *The Structure of Scientific Revolutions*, 2nd enlarged edition. Chicago: Chicago University Press, 1970.

Ladeur, Karl-Heinz, and Lars Viellechner. 'Die transnationale Expansion staatlicher Grundrechte: zur Konstitutionalisierung globaler Privatsrechtsregimes'. *Archiv des Völkerrechts* 46 (2008): 42–73.

Law, David S. 'Generic Constitutional Law'. *Minnesota Law Review* 89 (2005): 652–742.

Leisner, Walter. *Institutionelle Evolution. Grundlinien einer Allgemeinen Staatslehre*. Berlin: Duncker & Humblot, 2012.

Leon, Paolo. *Il capitalismo e lo Stato: crisi e trasformazioni delle strutture economiche*. Roma: Castelvecchi, 2014.

León Pesántez, Catalina. *El color de la razón. Pensamiento crítico en las Américas*. Quito: UASB, 2013.

Lollini, Andrea. 'La circolazione degli argomenti: metodo comparato e parametri interpretativi extra-sistemici nella giurisprudenza costituzionale sudafricana'. *Diritto Pubblico Comparato ed Europeo* 1 (2007): 479–523.

Loughlin, Martin. *The Idea of Public Law*. Oxford: Oxford University Press, 2004.

———. 'What is Constitutionalisation?' In *The Twilight of Constitutionalism?* edited by Petra Dobner, and Martin Loughlin, 47–69. Oxford: Oxford University Press, 2010.

Luciani, Massimo. 'Costituzionalismo irenico e costituzionalismo polemico'. *Giurisprudenza Costituzionale* 2 (2006): 1654–68.

Luperini, Romano. *L'allegoria del moderno*. Roma: Editori Riuniti, 1990.

Mamlyuk, Boris N., and Ugo A. Mattei. 'Comparative International Law'. *Brooklyn Journal of International Law* 36 (2011): 385–452.

Mandle, Jon. *Global Justice*. London: Polity Press, 2006.

Markesinis, Basil, and Jörg Fedtke. *Judicial Recourse to Foreign Law: A New Source of Inspiration?* London: UCL Press, 2006.

Martinico, Giuseppe. 'Complexity and Cultural Sources of Law in the EU Context: From the Multilevel Constitutionalism to the Constitutional Synallagma'. *German Law Journal* 3 (2007): 205–30.

Miketiak, Tara. 'Nondiscrimination and the Human Right to Democracy'. *Gnosis* 12(1) (2011): 30–40.

Miller, David. *National Responsibility and Global Justice*. Oxford: Oxford University Press, 2007.

Mirkine-Guetzévitch, Boris. *Les nouvelles tendances du droit constitutionnel*. Paris: Giard, 1931.

Mitrany, David. *A Working Peace System: An Argument for the Functional Development of International Organizations*. London: Royal Institute of International Studies, 1943.

Mocoroa, Juan M. 'Justicia transicional, amnistia y Corte Interamericana de derechos humanos: el caso 'Gelman' y algunas inquietudes'. In *La dinamica delle integrazioni regionali latinoamericane. Casi e materiali*, edited by Michele Carducci and Pablo Riberi, 88–102. Torino: Giappichelli, 2014.

Monateri, Pier Giuseppe. *Geopolitica del diritto. Genesi, governo e dissoluzione dei corpi politici*. Roma-Bari: Laterza, 2013.

Moreira, Luiz. *A constituição como simulacro*. Rio de Janeiro: Lumen Juris, 2007.

Muir-Watt, Horatia. 'Further Terrains for Subversive Comparison: The Field of Global Governance and the Public/Private Divide'. In *Methods of Comparative Law: An Intellectual Overview*, edited by Pier Giuseppe Monateri, 270–88. Cheltenham and Northampton: Edward Elgar, 2012.

Neves, Marcelo. *A constitucionalização simbólica*. São Paulo: Martins Fontes, 2007.

———. *Transconstitucionalismo*. São Paulo: Martins Fontes, 2009.

Nickel, James (ed.). *Making Sense of Human Rights*. Oxford: Blackwell, 2006.

Nussbaum, Martha C. *Not for Profit: Why Democracy needs the Humanities*. Princeton: Princeton University Press, 2010.

———. *Creating Capabilities: The Human Development Approach*. Cambridge, MA: The Belknap Harvard University Press, 2011.

Ost, François. 'Os desvios de Babel: a tradução como paradigma'. In *Integração normativa. O direito em um contexto multicultural e multilingue*, edited by Evandro Menezes de Carvalho and Rosalind Greenstein, 68–85. Rio de Janeiro: FGV, 2013.

Pegoraro, Lucio. *Diritto costituzionale comparato. La scienza e il metodo*. Bologna: Bononia University Press, 2014.

———. 'Los jueces y los profesores: la influencia de la doctrina sobre las decisiones de los Tribunales y Cortes constitucionales'. *Annuario Iberoamericano Costituzionale*, 101–21. Napoli: Editoriale Scientifica, 2014.

Perju, Vlad. 'Constitutional Transplants, Borrowing and Migrations'. In *The Oxford Handbook of Comparative Constitutional Law*, edited by Michel Rosenfeld and Andras Sajó, 1324–70. Oxford: Oxford University Press, 2012.

Pes, Luca. *Teorie dello sviluppo giuridico: dal movimento di* Law and Development *all'esperienza neoliberale*. Trento: Tangram Edizioni, 2012.

Picone, Paolo. 'Diritto internazionale dell'economia e costituzione economica dell'ordinamento internazionale'. *Comunicazioni e Studi* 16 (1980): 137–219.

Piergigli, Valeria. 'La Corte africana dei diritti dell'uomo e dei popoli giudica sulla violazione dei diritti di partecipazione politica e delle regole democratiche in Tanzania'. *Federalismi.it* Focus Africa 1 (2014). www.federalismi.itFocus Africa.

Pierik, Roland, and Wouter Werner (eds). *Cosmopolitanism in Context: Perspectives from International Law and Political Theory*. Cambridge and New York: Cambridge University Press, 2010.

Pistor, Katharina. 'Standardization of Law and its Effect on Developing Economies'. *American Journal of Comparative Law* 50 (2002): 97–130.

Pizzorusso, Alessandro. *La produzione normativa in tempi di globalizzazione*. Torino: Giappichelli, 2008.

Posner, Eric A. *The Perils of Global Legalism*. Chicago and London: University of Chicago Press, 2009.

Quijano Valencia, Olver. *Ecosimías. Visiones y prácticas de diferencia económico/cultural en contextos de multiplicidad*. Quito: UASB-UC, 2012.

Raffiotta, Edoardo C. *Il governo multilivello dell'economia. Studio sulle trasformazioni dello Stato costituzionale in Europa*. Bologna: Bononia University Press, 2013.

Rawls, John. *The Law of Peoples*. Cambridge, MA: Harvard University Press, 1999.

Reimann, Mathias. 'The End of Comparative Law as an Autonomous Subject'. *Tulane European and Civil Law Forum* 11 (1996): 49–72.

Revenga Sanchez, Miguel. 'Cinco grandes retos (y otra tantas amenazas) para la democracia constitucional en el siglo XXI'. *Parlamento y Constitución* 12 (2009): 25–44.

Riggs, Fred W. 'Fragilité des Régimes du Tiers Monde'. *Revue Internationale des Sciences Sociales* 136 (1993): 236–87.

Roberts, Anthea. 'Comparative International Law? The Role of National Courts in Creating and Enforcing International Law'. *International & Comparative Law Quarterly* 60 (2011): 57–92.

Rödl, Florian. 'Democratic Juridification without Statisation: Law of Conflict of Laws Instead of World State'. In *After Globalisation: New Patterns of Conflict and their Sociological and Legal Re-Constructions*, edited by C. Joerges, 17–46. Oslo, Arena Report 4/11.

Ronchetti, Laura. *Il nomos infranto: globalizzazioni e costituzioni. Del limite come principio essenziale degli ordinamenti giuridici*. Napoli: Jovene, 2007.

Rosenfeld, Michel. *The Identity of the Constitutional Subject: Selfhood, Citizenship, Culture, and Community*. London: Routledge, 2010.

Rossi-Landi, Francesco. *Significato, comunicazione e parlare comune*. Padova: Marsilio, 1961.

———. *Il linguaggio come lavoro e come mercato*. Milano: Bompiani, 1968.

Rougier Jonathan, Sparksve and Lisa J. Hill (eds). *Risk and Uncertainty Assessment for Natural Hazards*. Cambridge: Cambridge University Press, 2012.

Roy, Joaquín (ed.). 'Después de Santiago: integración regional y relaciones Union Europea-América latina'. Miami: Jean Monnet Chair, 2013.

Ruffert, Matthias. 'The European Debt Crisis and European Union Law'. *Common Market Law Review* 48 (2011): 1777–806.

Russo, Teresa. 'Deficit e anti-deficit democratico nell'ordinamento dell'Unione Europea'. *Quaderni dell'Università degli Studi di Salerno* 2 (2011): 589–608.

Sagües, Nestor P. 'El recurso al derecho y al intérprete externo en la interpretación e integración de la Constitución nacional'. In *Memoria del X Congreso iberoamericano de Derecho constitucional*, vol. I, 95–110. Lima: Idemsa, 2009.

Samuel, Geoffry. 'Epistemology and Comparative Law: Contributions from the Sciences and Social Sciences'. In *Epistemology and Methodology of Comparative Law*, edited by Mark van Hoecke, 35–77. Portland: Hart, 2004.

Sanchez, Gloria M. 'A Paradigm Shift in Legal Education. Preparing Law Students for the Twenty-First Century: Teaching Foreign Law, Culture, and Legal Language of the Major U.S. American Trading Partners'. *San Diego Law Review* 34 (1997): 635–79.

Sanchez, Luis. 'Darwin, Artificial Selection, and Poverty: Contemporary Implications of a Forgotten Argument'. *Politics and the Life Sciences* 29(1) (2010): 61–71.

Scheltema, Martijin. *Le droit de demain*. The Hague: Hague Academica Press, 2005.

Schlögel, Karl. *Im Raume lesen wir die Zeit. Über Zivilisationsgeschichte und Geopolitik*. München: Carl Hanser Verlag, 2003.

Schmitt, Carl. *Der Nomos der Erde*. Berlin: Duncker & Humblot, 1974. Originally published *in Der Nomos der Erde im Völkerrecht des Jus Publicum Europaeum* (Köln: Greven, 1950).

Schneiderman, David. *Constitutionalizing Economic Globalization: Investments Rules and Democracy's Promise*. Cambridge: Cambridge University Press, 2008.

Schwöbel, Christine E.J. *Global Constitutionalism in International Legal Perspective*. Leiden: Martinus Nijhoff, 2011.

Sciulli, David. *Theory of Societal Constitutionalism: Foundations of a Non-Marxistic Critical Theory*. Cambridge: Cambridge University Press, 1992.

Shapiro, Debra L. 'In Defense of Judicial Candor'. *Harvard Law Review* 100 (1986–7): 731–50.

Siems, Mathias M. 'The End of Comparative Law'. *Journal of Comparative Law* 2 (2007): 133–50.

Skyrms, Brian. *The Stag Hunt and the Evolution of Social Structure*. Cambridge: Cambridge University Press, 2004.

Slaughter, Anne-Marie. *A New World Order*. Princeton: Princeton University Press, 2004.

Somaini, Eugenio. *Geografia della democrazia*. Bologna: il Mulino, 2009.

Supiot, Alain. 'The Public-Private Relation in the Context of Today's Refeudalization'. *International Journal of Constitutional Law* 11(1) (2013): 129–45.

Taylor, Charles. *The Secular Age*. Cambridge, MA: Harvard University Press, 2007.

Tebbe, Nelson, and Robert L. Tsai. 'Constitutional Borrowing'. *Michigan Law Review* 108 (2010): 459–522.

Teilhard de Chardin, Pierre. 'La Formation de la Noosphère'. (1947). In *L'Avenir de l'Homme*, 201–31. Paris: Éditions du Seuil, 1959.

———. 'L'essence de l'idée de démocratie'. (1948). In *L'Avenir de l'Homme*, 307–16. Paris: Éditions du Seuil, 1959.

Teubner, Gunther. 'A Constitutional Moment? The Logics of "Hitting the Bottom"'. In *The Financial Crisis in Constitutional Perspective*, edited by Poul F. Kjaer, Gunther Teubner and Alberto Febbrajo, 3–41. Oxford and Portland: Hart, 2011.

———. 'Debate and Dialogue: Constitutionalizing Polycontexturality'. *Social & Legal Studies* 20 (2011): 209–52.

———. *Constitutional Fragments: Societal Constitutionalism and Globalisation*. Oxford: Oxford University Press, 2012.

Thornhill, Chris. 'Niklas Luhmann and the Sociology of the Constitutions'. *Journal of Classical Sociology* 10 (2010): 315–37.

Troper, Michel. 'The Structure of the Legal System and the Emergence of the State'. Available at: www.nyustrauss.org, paper 6/2012.

Tucker, Eric. 'Labour's Many Constitutions (and Capital's Too)'. *Comparative Labour Law and Policy Journal* 33 (2012): 355–78.

Turégano Mansilla, Isabel. *Justicia global: los límites del constitucionalismo*. Lima: Palestra, 2010.

Turner, R.S. 'Neo-Liberal Constitutionalism: Ideology, Government and the Rule of Law'. *Journal of Politics and Law* 1(2) (2008): 47–55.

Twining, William. 'Globalization and Comparative Law'. *Maastricht Journal of European & Comparative Law* 6 (1999): 217–43.

Vaccaro, Salvo. *Globalizzazione e diritti umani. Filosofia e politica della mondialità*. Milano-Udine: Mimesis, 2004.

Valery, Paul. 'Piccola lettera sui miti'. In *All'inizio era la favola*, 55–6. Milano: Guerini & Associati, 1988.

Vecchioli, Laura. *Il rischio della sovranità globale*. Torino: Giappichelli, 2004.

Vellano, Michele. 'Verso il superamento del principio della parità formale degli Stati nel governo dell'economia mondiale'. In *Problemi e tendenze del diritto internazionale dell'economia, liber amicorum in onore di Paolo Picone*, edited by Aldo Ligustro and Giorgio Sacerdoti, 153–74. Napoli: Editoriale Scientifica, 2011.

Vermeule, Adrian. *The Constitution of Risk*. Cambridge: Cambridge University Press, 2014.

Voβkuhle, Andreas. 'Multilevel Cooperation of the European Constitutional Courts: der Europäische Verfassungsgerichtsverbund'. *European Constitutional Law Review* 6(2) (2010): 175–98.

Voβkuhle, Andreas, Christian Bumke and Florian Meinel (eds). *Verabschiedung und Wiederentdeckung des Staates im Spannungsfeld der Disziplinen*. Berlin: Duncker & Humblot, 2013.

vom Hau, Matthias, James Scott and David Hulme. 'Beyond the BRICs: Alternative Strategies of Influence in the Global Politics of Development'. *European Journal of Development Research* 24 (2012): 187–204.

Waldron, Jeremy. 'A Right-Based Critique of Constitutional Rights'. *Oxford Journal of Legal Studies* 13 (1993): 18–51.

Walzer, Michael. 'Il governo mondiale è un sogno?' *Quaderni Costituzionali* 1 (2011): 187–98.

Wejnert, Barbara. *Diffusion of Democracy: The Past and the Future of Global Democracy*. Cambridge: Cambridge University Press, 2014.

Westbrook, David. 'Theorizing the Diffusion of Law: Conceptual Difficulties, Unstable Imaginations and the Effort to Think Gracefully Nonetheless'. *Harvard International Law Journal* 47 (2006): 489–505.

Wiethölter, Rudolf. *Rechtswissenschaft*. Frankfurt am Main and Hamburg: Fischer, 1968.

Yakhlef, Ali. 'The Trinity of International Strategy; Adaptation, Standardization and Transformation'. *Asian Business and Management* 9 (2010): 47–65.

Zuleta, Mónica, Humberto Cubides and Manuel R. Escobar (eds). *¿Uno solo o varios mundos? Diferencia, subjetividad y conocimientos en las ciencias sociales contemporáneas*. Bogotá: Universidad Central-Iesco, 2007.

Zumbansen, Peer. 'Comparative, Global and Transnational Constitutionalism: The Emergence of a Transnational Legal-Pluralist Order'. *Global Constitutionalism* 1(1) (2012): 16–52.

9 Towards the constitution of networks?

Karl-Heinz Ladeur

The law of the 'society of individuals'

The law that governs the liberal 'society of individuals' is not simply a set of barriers to which the subjects driven by their arbitrariness are obliged to be exposed (Rogozinski 1999: 111).[1] In particular, in civil law, the subjective right becomes the means for enforcing a trans-subjective collective legal order, whose concrete form evades both the subject's intention and the community's representation (see Thomas 1998).[2]

The law and its individuality

The law is necessarily detached from virtue – unlike in classical Greek law – because it cannot rely on a stable tradition of rules and customs. It enforces a distributed order that remains dependent on co-ordination between subjects, which is only possible in a paradoxical, self-transcending manner. The practical rules of co-operation and co-ordination can only evolve indirectly, as the temporary result of a spontaneous, lasting change to a process of reciprocal observation that brings possibilities and constrained connections with it. This process is supported epistemologically by the fact that experience as a type of knowledge conducts a paradoxical continuation – as does tradition – in a procedural way. The practice of legal transactions is construed as an 'application' of the law and as such is subordinated to it.

Legal doctrine has to retain the compatibility of the law's case orientation with the need to preserve the text of the law as a symbol of its validity (Luhmann 1993: 279, 289, 479f.; 1982). Similarly, 'deduction' as a favoured form of 'application' of the law by means of judicature, is also a doctrinal way of achieving compatibility between the unity of the law and changes in legal practice (for the traditional background, see: Kirchhof 1986: 11; further: Müller and Christensen 2009: Rn. 14, 86, 162). For the legal subject, this means that he must and can observe his interests (Hirschman 1987)[3] in the 'other's mirror' (Smith 1761: III.3–4: 137) and, as a result of this observation, specify his own person and not only his opportunities for action.

The individual and collective experience

The continuity of experience and its lasting change condense in the person as a permanent upheaval of observation, comparison and distinction (Parker et al. 2011: 1, 8, 14). The law in the private sphere constitutes a trans-subjective acentric order that maintains its motion by distributing subjective rights (Ladeur 2008: 109). It is underpinned by rules of knowledge whose impact extends beyond the openly institutionalised rules of proof and probability, and which 'institute' acknowledged practices (Blumenberg 2010: 240; Descombes 2013: 247; 2004: 442, 449), while putting operations that deviate from them under a higher burden of argumentation (Gaskins 1993: 19, 266f.).

Cavell formulates this paradox so that the paradigm of the 'experience' characterised here as the 'society of individuals' is the 'constitution of a reality' (Cavell 1990: 96) that establishes an 'unclosable distance' to our desire of a world for us. The 'conventional nature' of human knowledge (Laugier 2006: 23) over and above the reflected 'agreement' (see Descombes 2004: 442) is a reality that cannot be circumvented: the rule is itself a collective 'cognitive device' (Raymond and Richebé 2007: 10). Referring to operating with societal rules (in distributed practices, not only of the law), Quéré (1994: 18) speaks about a 'reflection without concept', so without a theoretical substructure. Knowing the rule is more than an effect than a cause of good practice: 'In rules, there are many more rules than we are led to believe' (Cometti 2013).

Lastly, this is a matter of a process that underpins historical change: that of the institutionalisation of how the paradoxes of the societal individuum before society (Markus Schroer) emerge and are protected: paradoxes that focus primarily on producing individuality in accordance with certain societal norms. Similarly, the complex rules that govern the justification and the infringement of 'privacy' were based in the past on the enforcement of social norms and the 'social control' of individuals. Observing and evaluating 'private' behaviour in spatially manageable communities has served the purpose of safeguarding and confirming social norms (Strahilevitz 2004).

The same applies equally to the public sphere, which is also a social construct subject to change, while its various different forms and forums for generating and reflecting collective cultural memory, processing shared issues in reference to a given forum of (state) decision-making, educating individuals publicly in schools over and above the education furnished by the family, taking part in associations, sharing the reading of canonised writings, etc. has also been subject to continuous change (Blickle 2008: 226, 270; Blanning 2006: 116).[4]

The constitutionalisation of the legal order and the juridification of the constitution

The juridification of the constitution and the constitutionalisation of the legal order are first set in motion when an organisation rises to the status of the legal actor. In the society of organisations, social norms and the law go their increasingly separate ways, inducing increasingly problematic relations between normativity and facticity. The rise of reflexive, explicit normation (standardisation) and of the strategic 'planning-oriented' design of long chains of action in and by organisations inserts a question against the autonomy of legal normativity and its structural performance for ordering facticity. This is also reflected in what is described as the historicisation of basic rights by Gauchet (1979: 451): the constitution of the society of organisations disengages from the concepts of a non-juridical, yet stable, constitution of the 'society of individuals'. The role of the society of individuals is more than that of a political constitution. It becomes the benchmark framework for preserving a 'collision order' that, with the aid of variable but compatible values (principles), seeks to co-ordinate strategies and groups with one another in individual cases and so admits no clear separation between normativity and facticity. It also crosses the border between public and private law and postulates that fundamental rights apply as private law. It is worth highlighting here that the first variants of the constitutionalisation of the legal order in the Weimar Republic date back to C. Schmitt (1932) focusing primarily on safeguarding a corpus of central legal norms as property or 'institutional guarantees' (in public law) against being amended by later (Weimar Republic) legislators.

The second variant of constitutionalisation, which developed after the Second World War, questioned the symbolic primacy of the explicitly durable order of the law and of political representation (which was underpinned by the stability of the implicit order of experience). It questioned also the thinking in stable borderline concepts (especially the distinction between public and private), as a result of the dynamic self-transformation of the medium of organisation: organisational decisions could neither be treated *ex ante*, as a mere durable variation of a stable matrix, nor justify *ex post* any expectation of a 'general compensation' (C.C. v. Weizsäcker) of the consequences of a liberal order. Benjamin had already described this change in the 1920s as a transition to trans-subjective 'groupings' of individuals and interests on the part of society and the state.

The constitution of the 'society of organisations'

The factual change of society, its accelerated self-transformation by aggregated effects of organised chains of actions and strategies of reflexive knowledge ('special knowledge') recoil on the state, which – as Ridder (1960) put it – becomes the 'societal state' and questions non-instrumental law. In the law, the forms assumed by change are firstly those already mentioned above that favour 'weighing up interests' rather than 'conceptual jurisprudence' in the 'free law school', and in the 1960s those of the rise of the 'balance of legally protected interests' and of the dissemination of the 'principle of proportionality' (Klatt and Meister 2012: 159; critically Reimer 2013: 27). In public law in England this principle incidentally rivals the higher recognition of administrative expert knowledge (Tomkins 2003: 273) – and other variations on proceduralising (Wollenschläger 2009), which are all cases of secondary remodelling of classical case-related doctrine. The concept of applying the law recedes behind the need to render the law 'concrete' to the case (Gadamer 1993: 446). Yet the persistence of the 'pouvoir instituant' (Descombes) of the law's self-dramatisation maintains the link to the '*Dogmatik*' (see in general Luhmann 1982).

Concretising the law

It is characteristic of the continuity of *Dogmatik* that the 'weighing up of interests' has been replaced with the formula of 'balancing interests protected by (constitutional) law' (starting with the German Constitutional Court decision BVerfGE 7, 198, 210 – Lüth). The correlation between the new doctrine and the observation of the equally altered organisationally 'instituted' facticity was rendered possible in legal theory by the Alexy School's 'theory of the principles' of law (Alexy 1986: 72; Klatt 2013; critically Reimer 2013: 27). In a 'bid for optimisation' constructed normatively (rather than merely by mixing facticity and normativity in the process of 'weighing up interests'), this 'theory of principles' furnishes a functional equivalent to separating legal norms and applying the law in individual cases (for an alternative of 'concretising the law' to suit the case, see Müller and Christensen 2009: 178). The judicature's previous self-orientation as an 'interpretation' and application of legal norms corresponds to the liberal, non-instrumental, functionality of the law. It is attuned to providing the societally distributed experimental order and the experience accumulated in the process with the forms of movement that enable uncertainty to be bound by rules.[5]

The law has to change, because the rules of social practices change. As shown, normativity always brings an epistemic model with it. At the same time, it needs a multiplicity of 'cases' for which it is possible to read off a new 'text' that can be used as the framework of reference for legal practice. (Incidentally, an objection to extending the competence of European courts can be deduced from this: they will always have too few cases for deserving such a procedure.) This could be described as a variation on what Cavell introduced with the paradox of 'finding as founding' (Cavell 1989: 77; Laugier 2011: 994), or what Descombes called the self-confirmation of a practice by its 'pouvoir instituant', to which a relational rationality of connections could be assigned, blurring normativity and facticity. Unlike in the case of the 'pouvoir instituant', it does not function *ex ante* as a 'foundation', but becomes manifest *ex post*, when its tracks are read and used to lay further tracks. Malabou (2005) expressed this in terms of a 'lecture plastic' (James 2012: 85) that starts from a fundamental process that implies the subject itself, forming and deconstructing the shapes of a text, practising a 'retreat of the substance' in reaction to what remains unpredictable and unexpected.

As an 'event' that cannot be deduced from a norm, the decision about an open 'situation' is more than a simple episode: its focuses 'awareness' from a heterarchical position (Crary 2002), receives a surplus that opens up new connecting possibilities for further 'cases'. This also makes for a sustainable 'suspicion' that not only does language as such not enable the legislator's transparency for himself but, on the contrary, it keeps non-decidability in the balance (Wetters 2008: 12). This leads to an instability on the part of (legal) language that is provoked by the emergence of novelty from 'outside', beyond the conceptually expressed 'control project' (James 2012: 2; Lyotard 1989: 13).

The balance of legally protected interests and its approach of observing and evaluating purposes in order to adjust the materialisation of the law – an approach that cannot very easily be calibrated to suit the other strategies of 'proceduralising' the law – leads to an underestimated evaluation of the distributed knowledge and to rules of supposition and knowledge that underpin it, as well as to the burdens of argumentation and of proof (e.g. when the concept of danger is superseded by that of risk in environmental law: Luhmann 1991; Ladeur 1993: 209). Also in the more complex formulation of the protection of personal privacy vis-à-vis the press and the implicit deontological rules governing the relationship between the public and private spheres, there are changes when new rules of presupposition are formulated to give right to the public interest (Ladeur and Gostomzyk 2011: 710). When 'materialisation' predominates in the form of the custom-designed 'requirement of optimisation' (Alexy 1986: 75) – i.e. when colliding 'basic rights positions' are co-ordinated – the problem of an unstructured balance of legally protected interests leads to a situation in which the possibilities available to the state are increased against the societally-based 'social epistemology' of basic rights. It is thus possible to make an instrumental ranking of relationships between different constellations of the usage of fundamental rights as the subject of the 'assessment' of the correspondent values and the situations (Reimer 2013: 35). This could be avoided if greater consideration were given to the moment of 'proceduralisation' and to the infrastructure of the changed law (e.g. the change in the determination of the relationship between privacy and the public sphere when establishing the limits of the freedom of the press).

Following Peirce (1931: 2.623), this could lead to the form of 'abduction' (after deduction) that is inclined to require rules when explaining or justifying social phenomena, but is also attuned to how rules change (Schurz 2008: 201, 208; also Reichman 2006: 28, 106, 261). It seeks to extend awareness of new phenomena in search of the 'best explanations' that at the same time question the rationality of acknowledged rules and matrices as little as possible. This stimulates a continuity corresponding to the function of the law in a form functionally equivalent to deduction. Legal theory shows that this thinking seems to be eminently well suited to the law, since it is capable, also on the side of facticity, of entering into a relationship of correspondence with the reflexive social normations (standards), as well as with the social compulsion to operate with risks. This enables a 'probable law' to be envisaged, that it will have to be improved upon (see also the decision of the German Constitutional Court BVerfGE 50: 290, 332 on participatory management), since the social rules to which it has to be attuned actually underpin the change themselves. This means neither that the bond of uncertainty through decision is waived, nor that the social consequences of deciding are included in the subject matter of the decision itself, but that the only thing that happens is the impact on a changeable constellation, which otherwise avoids the 'evaluation of consequences'. This could be reconciled with the law's function of safeguarding the certainty of expectations (Luhmann 1993: 154), since this is a question of observing more complex chains of actions which might generate more uncertainty on the part of organisations.

Changing the order of knowledge

The facticity of knowledge is changed by the fragmentary 'special knowledge' (Guéhenno 1999: 16) that relates reflexively to the concepts of normality based on experience (e.g. the 'state of the technik' vis-à-vis the environmental law (Wolf 1986)). As rules of knowledge become more reflexive for their part, they also allow for the representation of the law that only becomes concrete (and not interpreted) in individual cases as law. This also changes the actual practice of organisations and is followed by a more professional approach to knowledge generation and knowledge management. The normativity of a new 'collision order' (Joerges 2009: 309; Fischer-Lescano 2008: 167) contributes to shaping this better-organised knowledge infrastructure. By managing the heterarchical relations between cases and the juridical exclusion of other possibilities, an effect of control of uncertainty is brought about that is comparable to the conceptually-led and hierarchically determined deduction of 'applications' from the text of the law (see Scott and Sturm 2007: 565). This shift in the conceptually-based doctrine of the case-related balance of legally protected interests can be classified as a linguistic transition from deciding what words and terms mean 'from their usage in normatively prescribed contexts' to the awareness of the 'actual usage of words in the framework of living languages' (Groys 2012: 23), according to the structuralism of F. de Saussures and R. Jacobsons. However, their 'plastic' matrices (Malabou 2005) are again determined normatively.

That this is by no means obvious is visible from the fact that the different variants on the theme of the 'society of organisations' in the Western world contain some quite different approaches to legal institutionalisation. This can be seen, for example, in the English opposition to the European 'principle of proportionality': England has maintained a model of political constitutionalism (Bellamy 2011: 86) that conflicts with Germany's judicial constitutionalism (Bryde 2004: RN 67), which for German constitutionalists is something absolutely obvious. The English model leaves more space for parliamentary political discretionary shaping (Tomkins 2003: 273) and also for the technical administrative knowledge whose use is checked far more rigorously against the yardstick of proportionality in Germany. Representing the 'balance of legally protected interests', and practising the principle of proportionality law, is a product of the meanwhile reflexive practice of constitutional law, in particular of constitutional jurisdiction.

The freedom of opinion and its limits

One example of the form and consequences of the transition of the balance of legally protected interests to the law, and of the relations between normativity and facticity that this changes, is offered by the question that arises in media law about where to draw the borderline between the public and the private spheres: while in the society of individuals a relatively stable 'honourable order' made allowance in particular for protecting the 'honour' of a private individual, giving it priority over what was considered to be the private interest of the press (Ladeur 2007), in the society of organisations the relationship between the public and the private spheres calls for a continuous balancing act, intervening from one case to the next, as even the right to privacy cannot be outlined with clear rules. The borders of the public realm are determined by variable deontological rules and practices, which are developed from the observation of the variable economic impact of media on the 'attention' and how it relates to the superficial result of audience effects (H.U. Gumbrecht) (Ladeur and Gostomzyk 2011: 710).

The constitution of the 'society of networks'

The methods adopted by the law of the 'society of networks' now being constituted are still in a state of flux. In my opinion, the new difficulties encountered when developing a constitution for the 'society of networks' are related to the fact that the networks develop to a considerable extent beyond the mediation of the state's legal system. One far from negligible effect is that the development of suitable institutions is also at least partly blocked. Networks can be characterised negatively first by the fact that they circumvent the classical distinctions between inside and outside, between market and organisation, between public and private (Teubner 2004; Ladeur 2010: 143). In particular, the dynamic of disruptive technologies leads to the development of 'epistemic communities', where knowledge is generated and processed. It is accompanied by volatile institutions of self-organisation, because the state law is badly attuned to observing and shaping networks. In this respect, Gunther Teubner's analysis (2012) of the 'self-constitutionalisation' of inter-organisational co-operation etc. is exemplary.

How networks organise themselves

The unlimited way in which networks proceed corresponds to the rise of the concept of governance (Schuppert 2011). It indicates that the state and the law can rely less and less on 'decisions' as means of binding and dealing with uncertainty. On the other hand, the institutionalisation of networks also calls for new forms of reconciliation with state law, whose relatively stable institutions need to be adapted to an experimental mode of observing development trajectories *ex post*, how they are confused by the introduction of multiple possibilities (replacing guidance) and the increase in transparency. Only a few comments can be made about this here.

It could be said that not only is the law further fragmented by the compulsion to adjust to new hierarchical networks, but that the function of law itself is also fragmented: the law becomes more markedly experimental in character as it makes individual partial functions available, which may structure private and private–public procedures of normation, for example, but may also come unstuck in the process. This applies in public international law, for example, to the development of emerging legal reforms beyond the boundaries of the state (responsibility to protect, global administrative law; see Brunnée and Toope 2000: 19; Ku 2012: 13), or to the preparation of the ability to build issues in complex operative networks without any clear purpose (Jennejohn 2010: 173).[6] This includes new forms of mediation and conflict resolution, which also lead to the development of new law. These forms combine when, for example, new networks of evaluation (such as eBay) have to be taken into consideration by juridification and their productivity unsettled. This calls for new forms of monitoring and evaluation that open the law up systematically to a learning process. As a result, facticity and normativity are blurred in a new way. Juridification is called into play explicitly as a way of regulating private and private–public networks.

It does not make much sense to derive more extensive materials or formal demands of the law of networks from the principle of democracy if the state and administration are incapable of taking expertise into account. It would make rather more sense to integrate the demands on law-making formulated *ex ante* by mobilising the instrument of subsequent improvement, with whose assistance the suitability of decision-making procedures could be evaluated *ex post* (Ladeur 2012: 369).

The limits of the institutions

As the flipside of this change, the change in the individuality of the 'society of networks' must also be taken into consideration from a legal perspective. How can a cognitive, epistemic link be maintained in a society whose institutions are so volatile and fragmented? This calls for a new collective model of 'order apart from equilibrium' (Prigogine and Stengers 1990; Nicolis and Prigogine 1987: 77; Atlan 1979) that is also compatible with the law. In my opinion, its shortcomings are reflected not only in the field of data protection and the Internet, but also in the conflict about religion in the public realm (of school) and generally in the rise of a 'nomadically-inclined individualism', which rejects the influence of communications via third parties as illegitimate 'interference' and so hinders every process of the construction of institutions.[7]

Inside these networks, it is possible to discern signs of the development of a new relational person, who takes part in a variety of networks, e.g. in the Internet, relating together the interests of a variety of 'societies of mind' (Marvin Minsky), corresponding to the 'society of mind' that the cognitive sciences have observed in the human brain.

The changing cognitive infrastructure of the society of networks

The development of high knowledge in the epistemic communities of the society of networks is accompanied by a renewed and also methodically relevant mutation in the legal system. Suffice to mention, in this respect, the rise of new high technologies, such as biotechnology, neurological or cognitive sciences, information technology and nanotechnology.

Nanotechnologies and the cognitive sciences

Modelling nanotechnological processes no longer forms a generalisable connection that already exists prior to being depicted, but is blurred with the process of producing a certain effect itself: the image produces a connection that it first becomes possible to revise as a result of its depiction. Nanotechnological design is 'part of an object's emergence' (Daston and Galison 2007: 407). The depiction is part of a production process. Rheinberger (2007: 121; Kogge 2008: 939) argues that nanotechnology's hybrid character enables a 'space of possible traces to be generated . . . where the game of molecular epistemic objects' takes place without a hierarchical precedence over the practice of 'applications' (Loeve 2008: 10). This is a technological modification to which the new observations of a materiality goes beyond a prior scientific and conceptual construction, without every linguistic mediation (Harman 2013: 49).

In my opinion, the cognitive sciences are rightly related with information technology, nanotechnology and biotechnology ('NBIC'), in a connection, brought about by new cross-border contaminations, that is determined by 'de-substantialising' traditional separations (Malabou 2004). This applies to the distinction between life and inanimate nature, biology and physics, science and technology as the application of science. The advance of 'information' as the new all-encompassing benchmark (for the law, see Augsberg 2013; Vesting 2012: § 20) and of information technology as the new integration science is decisive. 'Information' is thus at one and the same time detached from the spirit's meaningful sovereignty and is blurred with a complex architecture of media, programs, protocols and hypertexts, which are used to process it – in practice, regardless of the material nature of its supports (Hayles 1999). The 'de-substantialisation of individuals', and thus the fragmentation of their identity, simultaneously paves the way for possible connections that rescind the separations of biology and of the culture of processing information, conveying them into a network of 'different milieus of subjectivisation' (Hörl 2011: 33). Knowledge becomes self-reflexive and 'operative', also in the sense that human nature's 'biological heritage' (R. Kurzweil) becomes a potential object of the self-modification of 'intelligence'. Over and above the quest for and application of 'laws' of nature (see Malabou 2004: 9), this allows for objectives and means of a blurring design of optional spaces in technologically determined 'experiential realms' that are liable only to an acentrically distributed reflexion and 'control'.

An example: the internet

Another variant can be seen in the discussions about the limits of Internet communications. The web communities tend to regard every legal barrier to Internet communications as an unacceptable interference in the individual's fundamental rights. This, too, is an example of the deterioration of a balance of legally protected 'groupings' of interests (W. Benjamin).

Against this background, which can only be illustrated summarily here, the development of Internet connections, from a perspective of both social and legal theory, must be seen as a challenge, as it rips right through the differentiated construction of the public sphere and of privacy, as well as of each one's relationship with the other.

Compared to this, forms of communication typical of the new media, such as blogs or social media posts, acquire a hybrid character.[8] In this context the factual, social and legal conditions of the differentiation of the relationship between the private and the public spheres are convulsed (Ladeur and Gostomzyk 2011: 710). In particular, individuals can communicate with large numbers of unknown participants electronically, or non-orally, and this derails the rules that govern the borderline between private and public issues. Electronic communications about 'private' issues take place in a potentially public manner, so that the participants in the communications frequently also quite unintentionally can reach a large number of people, without the person generating the message always being able to control this, as was hitherto the case with the mass media. It might even be said that mass media forms can be reproduced within hybrid Internet communications (by professional bloggers), but there are also the ambiguous figures of communicating individuals who themselves become semi-media when they set out to achieve mass dissemination of their communications and actually succeed in doing so.

In the past, the oral nature of communications used to set factual limits to the dissemination of the private individual's messages, while the public media's right to express themselves was limited by the law. On the other hand, examples can be used to show that 90–95 per cent of information that is of general interest at local level is produced by the traditional media, while the new media just distribute it. That is why issues that are much more specialised are now reproduced. This leads to the bundling function of the classical media focused on the civic public realm losing out in significance (FCC 2011: 124). A report from the United States' FCC calls this development 'the great unbundling' (127). The professionalisation of reporting standards and the centralisation of knowledge rules also benefitted the legal protection of third parties and enabled criteria to be developed for processing knowledge or maintaining or limiting non-knowledge or silence.

The Internet is changing the procedural rules of knowledge and non-knowledge fundamentally: communications now only appear to be disseminated horizontally, with no beginning and no end, to be brought into being without any standards that could be used for evaluating the proficiency of the knowledge they contain for the future (Herrenschmidt 2007). This also makes any legal control and monitoring of such standards more difficult. The most important battle fought by the American Civil Liberties Union (ACLU) against the chilling effects of juridification is symptomatic of the absence of any concept of a 'control project' for the Internet or of any overarching perspective.

Knowledge is still connected to a distributed heterarchical network that does not appear to leave any space for stable rules of responsibility to develop and be centralised. The attention paid to knowledge is generated virally or by being infected by matrices, for which there are no prior regularities and which allow no rules to develop to govern the social reflexion of the limits of knowledge and non-knowledge (secrecy). This is logical, to the extent that, as B. Groys puts it, in many of the new forms of communication on the Internet (in this case referring to Google), 'man no longer speaks in the traditional sense'. He becomes a 'user' who 'applies the various different linguistic contexts, topoi or terrains or makes new ones' (Groys 2012: 27). He lets 'words appear or disappear in different contexts – in a completely silent and purely operative extra- or metalinguistic form of practice' (Groys 2012: 27). The flow of the process itself becomes the framework of reference of the 'synaptic self' or of the 'neuronal personality' (Ledoux 2003; Malabou 2004), which is disturbed by 'censorship', i.e. the external interruption of the process of relating. It might be thought that the fact that Germany's Pirate Party has no political platform, together with the rising interest in 'direct' democracy, is a manifestation of the viral character of the Internet itself and thus of the heterarchical 'society of networks'. This corresponds to the emergence of a fleeting, oscillating subjectivity that is inherent to the immediate experience of fluctuating attention and refutes all forms of mediatisation, institutionalisation and representation of generalisable interests.[9]

New institutions for the 'society of networks'

The development of the Internet marks a break with the rules and the regularities that changes social communications on the borderline between the private and the public spheres. This calls for (complementary) new institutions of (alternative) conflict resolution that are attuned more to change and less to conservation (Ladeur and Gostomzyk 2011), so as to allow for 'learning by monitoring' (Jennejohn 2010). A practice of this kind can be observed in the 'relational (incomplete) contracts' of high-tech companies (Sabel and Zeitlin 2004: 388), in which conflicts are no longer soluble by external judges, but are more likely to be found in and submitted to modular procedural methods designed to enable the problem to be described and overcome in a context that goes beyond the traditional concepts of borderlines (Jennejohn 2010). This does not rule out the possibility of an external support, also from the state's courts. But their role changes in the dynamic of the Internet, with its focus on self-adjustment, that is on the ability of Internet communications to organise themselves.

Prospects

Paradoxically, as already mentioned, basic rights have had a rather political function in the society of individuals. Even in the United States, they acted primarily as a benchmark in constitutional conflicts between the states and the federation. The legal order is only constitutionalised when basic rights are 'historicised' (Gauchet 1979: 451), that is are converted into 'values' that judicial decisions 'concretise' and refer to different factual contexts. This once again changes in the 'society of networks': It is notable that, despite the expansion of constitutional jurisdiction in Germany, the country's Federal Constitutional Court plays no role in this process of evolution, with the exception of a handful of decisions about religious freedom and 'information self-determination', which unreflexively pursue a dissolution of these basic rights' collective trans-subjective dimension and do not reflect the fundamental change in constitutional law.

The new issue of fundamental rights in networks might consist in a further step beyond abduction, to be taken as a sort of hypertext: the law would embark on monitoring 'traces' not guided by an established text, whose matrices would subsequently be read off and tested for their normative self-stabilisation. This would be a variant on what Cavell, as already mentioned, has described with the paradox of 'finding as founding'.

Notes

1 This is stressed more clearly in the Jewish tradition of the law, see Ladeur and Augsberg (2010/11: 427).

2 The law cancels mankind's stable nature out through fictions (about the fiction of subjective law, see Ladeur 2008: 109; about the link between the law's emergence and the 'fictive' city: Gernet 1982: 155).

3 On the sublimation of the refinement of customs and the 'faculty of imagination' in eighteenth-century England, see Brewer (1997). The 'faculty of imagination' was not at all oriented at achieving political enlightenment in the public realm, but was thoroughly compatible with the requirements of developing trade and 'fine' goods.

4 About how the German Constitutional Court has focalised its understanding of the public sector on the state, see only BVerfGE 7, 198, 208; 5, 85, 205.

5 Operating with creative fictions means using a legally indeterminate 'case' to establish what should apply in future cases (Hardin 2003: 128).

6 The law only becomes *ex post* when, for example, an unstructured high-tech co-operation network (such as Silicon Valley) is 'translated' into a legal form, after the network's product has achieved a high market value: this is when the need arises to clarify what kind of legal relationship has actually come into being. The availability of fictions makes the law thoroughly suitable for this purpose.

7 The crucifix decision handed down by the German Constitutional Court (BVerfGE 93, 1) established the negative freedom of confession as the underlying norm of what is now known as Germany's 'religious constitutional law' (Walter 2006), an expression that is increasingly superseding the old term of 'state-church law'. This, too, is characteristic of how the relationship between religion and politics has been de-institutionalised and of how the freedom of conscience has become a personal matter, corresponding to a decline in the previously public status of the Christian churches in general, as well as of the collective and so also cultural dimension of religion as a whole. This collective dimension has been reflected in particular in the possibility of concluding treaties between the state and church about the public dimension of religion.

8 About the 'superficiality' of blog communications, see A. Sullivan (MERKUR) 2009: 103.

9 Post-structuralist philosophy's favour of 'singularity' ignores the correspondence between its observation of singularity and the new cult of immediacy in the society of networks. For more on this, see James (2012: 6).

References

Alexy, Robert. *Theorie der Grundrechte*. Frankfurt am Main: Suhrkamp, 1986.

Atlan, Henri. *Entre le cristal et la fumée*. Paris: Seuil, 1979.

Augsberg, Ino. *Informationsverwaltungsrecht*. Tübingen: Mohr i.E, 2013.

Bellamy, Richard. 'Political Constitutionalism and the Human Rights Act'. *International Journal of Constitutional Law* 9 (2011): 86–111.

Benjamin, Walter. 'Zur Kritik der Gewalt'. In *Gesammelte Schriften II/1*, 1921, 179–204. Frankfurt am Main: Suhrkamp, 1999.

Blanning, Timothy C.W. *Das Alte Europa (1660–1789)*. Darmstadt: Primus, 2006.

Blickle, Peter. *Das Alte Europa. Vom Hochmittelalter bis zur Moderne*. Munich, 2008.

Blumenberg, Hans. *Theorie der Lebenswelt*. Berlin: Suhrkamp, 2010.

Brewer, John. *The Pleasures of Imagination: English Culture in the 18th Century*. London: HarperCollins, 1997.

Brunnée, Jutta, and Stephen J. Toope. 'International Law and Constructivism'. *Columbia Journal of Transnational Law* 39 (2000): 19–74.

Bryde, Brun-Otto. 'Programmatik und Normativität der Grundrechte'. In *Handbuch der Grundrechte*, vol. 1, edited by Detlef Merten and Hans-Jürgen Papier, 679–706. Heidelberg: C.F. Müller, 2004.

Cavell, Stanley. *Cavell: This New Yet Unapproachable America*. Chicago: Chicago University Press, 1989.

———. *Conditions Handsome and Unhandsome*. Chicago: Chicago University Press, 1990.

Cometti, Jean-Pierre. 'On Standard and Taste'. *Aisthesis* 6 (2013): 5–15.

Crary, Jonathan. *Aufmerksamkeit und moderne Kultur*. Frankfurt am Main: Suhrkamp, 2002.

Daston, Lorraine, and Peter Galison. *Objektivität*. Frankfurt am Main: Suhrkamp, 2007.

Descombes, Vincent. *Le complément de sujet*. Paris: Gallimard, 2004.

———. *Les embarras de l'identité*. Paris: Gallimard, 2013.

Federal Communications Commission (FCC). *The Information Needs of Communities*. Washington, DC, 2011.

Fischer-Lescano, Andreas. 'Kritik der praktischen Konkordanz'. *Kritische Justiz* 41 (2008): 166–78.

Gadamer, Hans-Georg. *Wahrheit und Methode*, vol. 2, *Afterword* to the 3rd edition, 2nd new edition. Tübingen: Mohr Siebeck Verlag, 1993.

Gaskins, Richard H. *Burdens of Proof in Modern Discourse*. New Haven: Yale University Press, 1993.

Gauchet, Marcel. 'De l'avènement de l'individu à la découverte de la société'. *Annales* 34 (1979): 451–63.

Gernet, Louis. *Droit et institutions en Grèce antique*. Paris: Flammarion, 1982.

Groys, Boris. 'Google: Worte jenseits der Grammatik'. *100 Gedanken* 46 DOCUMENTA 46 (2012).

Guéhenno, Jean-Marie. *L'avenir de la liberté*. Paris: Flammarion, 1999.

Hardin, Russell. *Indeterminacy and Society*. Princeton: Princeton University Press, 2003.

Harman, Graham. 'Objektorientierte Philosophie'. In *Realismus Jetzt. Spekulative Philosophie und Metaphysik für das 21. Jahrhundert*, edited by Armen Avanessian, 122–36. Berlin: Merve, 2013.

Hayles, N. Katherine. *How We Became Posthumans*. Chicago: Chicago University Press, 1999.

Herrenschmidt, Clarisse. *Les trois écritures: Langue, nombre, code*. Paris: Gallimard, 2007.

Hirschman, Albert O. *Leidenschaften und Interessen*. Frankfurt am Main: Suhrkamp, 1987.

Hörl, Erich. 'Die technologische Bedingung: Zur Einführung'. In *Die technologische Bedingung*, 7–53. Berlin: Suhrkamp, 2011.

James, Ian. *The New French Philosophy*. Cambridge: Polity, 2012.

Jennejohn, Matthew. 'Contract Adjudication in a Collaborative Economy'. *University of Virginia Law and Business Review* 5 (2010): 223–35.

Joerges, Christian. 'Kollisionsrecht als verfassungsrechtliche Form'. In *Was bleibt vom Staat? Demokratie, Recht und Verfassung im globalen Zeitalter*, edited by Nicole Deitelhoff and Jens Steffek, 309–31. Frankfurt am Main and New York: Campus, 2009.

Kirchhof, Paul. 'Der Auftrag des Grundgesetzes an die rechtsprechende Gewalt'. In *FS der Juristischen Fakultät zur 600-Jahr-Feier der Ruprechts-Karls-Universität Heidelberg*, 11–37. Heidelberg: C.F. Müller, 1986.

Klatt, Matthias (ed.). *Prinzipientheorie und Theorie der Abwägung*. Tübingen: Mohr, 2013.

Klatt, Matthias, and Moritz Meister. 'Verhältnismäßigkeitsprinzip als universelles Rechtsprinzip'. *Der Staat* 51 (2012): 159–88.

Kogge, Werner. 'Technologie des 21. Jahrhunderts. Perspektiven der Technikphilosophie'. *Deutsche Zeitschrift für Philosophie* 56 (2008): 935–56.

Ku, Charlotte. *International Law, International Relations, and Global Governance*. Oxford: Routledge, 2012.

Ladeur, Karl-Heinz. 'Risiko und Recht'. In *Risiko und Gesellschaft*, 2 impression, edited by Gotthard Bechmann, 209–33. Opladen: Westdeutscher Verlag, 1993.

———. *Das Medienrecht und die Ökonomie der Aufmerksamkeit*. Köln: von Halem, 2007.

———. 'Das subjektive Recht als Medium der Selbsttransformation der Gesellschaft und Gerechtigkeit als deren Parasit'. In *Nach Jacques Derrida und Niklas Luhmann: Zur (Un-)Möglichkeit einer Theorie der Gerechtigkeit*, edited by Gunther Teubner, 109–24. Stuttgart: Lucius + Lucius, 2008.

———. 'Die Netzwerke des Rechts'. In *Netzwerke in der funktional differenzierten Gesellschaft*, edited by Michael Bommes and Veronika Tacke, 143–71. Wiesbaden: VS Verlag, 2010.

———. 'Die Herausbildung des globalen Verwaltungsrechts und seine Verknüpfung mit dem innerstaatlichen Recht'. *Die Öffentliche Verwaltung* 65 (2012): 369–78.

Ladeur, Karl-Heinz, and Ino Augsberg. 'The Letter Kills, But the Spirit Gives Life?' *Journal of Law and Religion* XXVI(2) (2010/11): 427–67.

Ladeur, Karl-Heinz, and Tobias Gostomzyk. 'Der Schutz vor Persönlichkeitsrechtsverletzungen in Blogs'. *Neue Juristische Wochenschrift* 61 (2011): 710–15.

Ladeur, Karl-Heinz, and Michael Wehsack. '"Jugendgefährdung" durch Medien'. *UFITA* 3 (2009): 695–714.

Laugier, Sandra. 'Politiques de la conversation ordinaire'. In *L'ordinaire et le politique*, edited by Claude Gautier and Sandra Laugier, 23–52. Paris: Presses Universitaires de France, 2006.

———. 'Mind and Matter: Cavell's (Concept of) Importance'. *Modern Language Notes* 126 (2011): 994–1003.

Ledoux, Joseph. *The Synaptic Self: How Our Brain Becomes What We Are*. London: Penguin, 2003.

Loeve, Sacha. 'Autour d'une définition des nanos'. In *Bionano-éthique: Perspectives sur les Bionanotechnologies*, edited by Bernadette Bensaude-Vincent, Raphaël Larrère, Vanessa Nurock and Sacha Loeve, 3–18. Paris: Vuibert, 2008.

Luhmann, Niklas. *Rechtssystem und Rechtsdogmatik*. Stuttgart: Kohlhammer, 1982.

———. *Soziologie des Risikos*. Berlin and New York: de Gruyter, 1991.

———. *Das Recht der Gesellschaft*. Frankfurt am Main: Suhrkamp, 1993.

Lyotard, Jean-François. *Differend: Phrases in Dispute*. Minneapolis: University of Minnesota Press, 1989.

Malabou, Catherine. *Que faire de notre cerveau?* Paris: Bayard, 2004.

———. *La Plasticité au soir de l'écriture*. Paris: Scheer, 2005.

Menke, Christoph. *Recht und Gewalt*. Berlin: August, 2012.

Müller, Friedrich, and Ralph Christensen. *Juristische Methodik*, vol. I. Berlin: Duncker & Humblot, 2009.

Nicolis, Pierre, and Ilya Prigogine. *Die Erforschung des Komplexen*. München: Piper, 1987.

Parker, Andrew, Austin Sarat and Martha Umphrey. *Subjects of Responsibility*. New York: Fordham University Press, 2011.

Peirce, Charles S. *Collected Papers*, vol. 2. Cambridge, MA: Harvard University Press, 1931.

Prigogine, Ilya, and Isabelle Stengers. *Dialog mit der Natur*. München: Piper, 1990.

Quéré, Louis. 'Le préjugé du monde objectif'. *Sociétés Contemporaines* 18/19 (1994): 17–41.

Raymond, Jean-Daniel, and Nathalie Richebé. 'Règles, Conventions et Valeurs'. *Revue Française de Sociologie* 48 (2007): 3–36.

Reichman, Ronen. *Abduktives Denken und talmudische Tradition*. Tübingen: Mohr, 2006.

Reimer, Philipp. '. . . und machet zu Jüngern alle Völker'. *Der Staat* 52 (2013): 27–57.

Rheinberger, Hans-Jörg. 'Wie werden aus Spuren Daten, und wie verhalten sich Daten zu Fakten?' *Nach Feierabend. Zürcher Jahrbuch für Wissenschaftsgeschichte* 3 (2007): 117–25.

Ridder, Helmut. *Zur verfassungsrechtlichen Stellung der Gewerkschaften im Sozialstaat nach dem Grundgesetz für die Bundesrepublik Deutschland*. Stuttgart: Fischer, 1960.

Rogozinski, Jacob. *Le don de la loi*. Paris: Presses Universitaires de France, 1999.

Sabel, Charles F., and Jonathan Zeitlin. 'Neither Modularity nor Relational Contracting: Interfirm Collaboration in the New Economy'. *Enterprise and Society* 5 (2004): 388–403.

Schmitt, Carl. 'Inhalt und Bedeutung des zweiten Hauptteils der Reichsverfassung'. In *Handbuch des Deutschen Staatsrechts*, vol. 2, edited by Gerhard Anschütz and Richard Thoma, 572–683. Tübingen: Mohr, 1932.

Schuppert, Gunnar Folke. *Governance und Rechtsetzung*. Baden-Baden: Nomos, 2011.

Schurz, Gerhard. 'Patterns of Abduction'. *Synthese* 164 (2008): 201–34.

Scott, Joanne, and Susan P. Sturm. 'Courts as Catalysts: Rethinking the Judicial Role in New Governance'. *Columbia Journal of European Law* 13 (2007): 565–94.

Smith, Adam. *The Theory of Moral Sentiments*, III.3–4, 2nd edition. London: Millar, 1761.

Strahilevitz, Lior. 'A Social Networks Theory of Gossip'. *University of Chicago Public Law. Working Paper* No. 79 (2004).

Sullivan, Andrew. 'Warum ich blogge'. *MERKUR* 717 (2009): 103–14.

Teubner, Gunther. *Netzwerk als Vertragverbund*. Baden-Baden: Nomos, 2004.

———. *Verfassungsfragmente*. Berlin: Suhrkamp, 2012.

Thomas, Yan. 'Le sujet de droit, la personne et la nature'. *Le Débat* 100 (1998): 85–107.

Tomkins, Adam. 'Of Institutions and Individuals: The Enforcement of EC-Law'. In *Law and Administration in Europe: Essays in Honour of Carol Harlow*, edited by Paul Craig and Richard Rawlings, 273–95. Oxford: Oxford University Press, 2003.

Vesting, Thomas. 'Die Bedeutung von Information und Kommunikation für die verwaltungsrechtliche Systembildung'. In *Grundlagen des Verwaltungsrechts*, vol. 2, 2nd edition, edited by Wolfgang Hoffmann-Riem, Eberhard Schmidt-Aßmann, and Andreas Voßkuhle, § 20 1–35. München: Beck, 2012.

Walter, Christian. *Religionsverfassungsrecht*. Tübingen: Mohr, 2006.

Wetters, Kirk. *The Opinion System: Impasses of the Public Sphere*. New York: Fordham University Press, 2008.

Wolf, Rainer. *Der Stand der Technik*. Opladen: Westdeutscher Verlag, 1986.

Wollenschläger, Burkard. *Wissensgenerierung im Verfahren*. Tübingen: Mohr, 2009.

10 Standards of 'good governance' and peripheral constitutionalism

The case of post-accession Romania

Bogdan Iancu

Introduction

Starting in the 1990s, first as a result of conditionalities attached to various international development programmes (IMF, World Bank) and later as a consequence of the expansion of international cooperation organisations (OECD, UNDP) or 'constitutionalisation' of international structures (most notably the EC/EU, but also the Council of Europe system), the notion of 'good governance' arose as a somewhat fuzzy umbrella concept of 'best practices' related to administration and government. As a direct consequence, 'peripheral jurisdictions' were increasingly coaxed or compelled into adopting various 'good governance' reform projects.

Prima facie, at a superficial level of inquiry, good governance appears to be a form of surrogate constitutionalism. To wit, the notion of 'good governance' as such and the various standards attached to proposals or yardsticks related, for instance, to transparency, anticorruption measures, the inclusion of 'civil society' stakeholders and the like, seem to equate to, or at least resonate with, established constitutional ideals related to limited, effective and accountable government.

Nonetheless, a closer look reveals the rift and tension between these two paradigms. Unlike the paradigm of classical constitutionalism, which is dominated by inherently normative values and procedural criteria, the logic of 'good governance', albeit not devoid of ostensibly normative connotations, is primarily driven by instrumentalism and the pursuit of 'Pareto efficient', calculable efficiency. The fact that the language of (often open-ended) normativity and the pursuit of effectiveness are fused at the hip in 'good governance' programmes renders the efficacy of such programmes hard to assess. Moreover, as a side effect, the proliferation of this quasi-constitutional discourse gradually displaces, i.e. falsifies by oversimplification or substitutes, the competing values and solutions of classical constitutionalism and good (i.e. constitutional) government.

This chapter inquires into the antinomies brought about by this paradigm clash, using the case study of Romanian judicial/rule of law and anticorruption reforms prior to and after the country's accession to the EU.

Anticorruption

Since the beginning of accession negotiations, and at a pace that accelerated increasingly after January 2007, the date of the country's entry into the European Union, Romanian anticorruption legislation and judiciary organisation laws have undergone a series of overhauls. As a result of the conditions of membership imposed by the EU, an autonomous anticorruption prosecutor's office and an integrity agency were established.[1] The integrity agency is an autonomous administrative authority[2] with attributions regarding the monitoring and enforcement of asset verification, incompatibilities and conflicts of interest rules. The National Anti-corruption Directorate (NAD) is a network of prosecutors' offices (a territorial structure comprising 15 services, with residences in the cities where Courts of Appeal are located and a central office in the capital, Bucharest) under the direction of a Chief Prosecutor. Although the latter is formally subordinated to the General Prosecutor of Romania, the symmetrical modes of appointment and tenures of both the General Prosecutor and the Chief Prosecutor of the NAD in practice guarantee the functional autonomy of the anticorruption prosecutorial office from the Public Ministry.[3] High- and medium-level corruption (gauged according to the quality of the accused or – alternatively – the value of the bribe or the assessed prejudice to the public interest) fall under the exclusive jurisdiction of the NAD.[4] The justice system as such, in its entirety, was 'immunised' from political influences in 2003, by constitutionally entrenching a high judicial council (Superior Council of the Magistracy (SCM)).[5] This SCM is composed primarily of elected members, i.e. judges and prosecutors elected by their peers, in a double ballot system at local and national levels. The body is charged constitutionally with extensive responsibilities for professional training, appointments, promotions and disciplinary measures. These legislative and institutional reforms have generated significant systemic changes and ripple effects in the entire Romanian political-constitutional landscape, to the effect that local politics started to be increasingly dominated by two mutually and circularly reinforcing topics: 'corruption' and 'judicial independence'.

In the last 10 years, corruption, which, as opposed to e.g. lustration or decommunisation, was not a major political debate issue in the 1990s,[6] has started being presented increasingly as the cause of a congeries of dysfunctions. By the same token, the autonomy of the justice system from external influences, i.e. any form of political or social control and accountability, has correlatively appeared as the axiomatic *sine qua non* of successful anticorruption strategies. These two themes polarise and colour recent electoral campaigns, to the virtual exclusion of almost all other substantive issues. The new terms of debate often lead to unusual or paradoxical situations.

For instance, the main supporter of the anticorruption rhetoric in the 2014 presidential campaign, Klaus Iohannis, was himself the target of an incompatibility appeal lodged by the National Integrity Agency with the High Court of Cassation and Justice. As this chapter was being written, the incompatibilities provision as such pended, by virtue of an exception of unconstitutionality, on the docket of the Romanian Constitutional Court. Both court sessions were scheduled for terms falling after the election returns of the second round of the presidential election, in which Iohannis, the runner-up of the first ballot, was a candidate. The High Court session was initially tabled for 18 November, precisely two days after the second round, whereas the Constitutional Court was due to hold hearings on 9 December. In practice this meant that, should the candidate have won the ballot, a newly-elected president could potentially be found incompatible immediately after the elections and would have to step down, unless the provision was held unconstitutional. In the meantime, Iohannis won the presidency, whereupon the High Court adjourned once again, without deciding on the merits, while various experts and analysts incessantly debated the constitutional implications and consequences that a hypothetical incompatibility judgment would bring to bear on a newly-sworn president.[7]

Conspiratorial mythologies have flourished recently, as anticorruption prosecutions have increasingly relied on surveillance and as a result of frequent leaks of wiretap transcripts in the press. To be sure, conspiracy theories have been a resilient pastime of the public sphere in the post-communist Balkans, but the recurrent leaks in the media, the fact that the execution of wiretap warrants is by law the prerogative of the internal intelligence service (SRI) and hazardous declarations made by anticorruption prosecutors do little to alleviate such proclivities or dispel such scenarios. To the question, posed by an Austrian journalist, whether her office was becoming the local equivalent of the American NSA, given the widespread wiretapping paranoia (*Schreckgespenst*), the current head of the anticorruption prosecutors, Laura Codruţa Kövesi, retorted: 'Not at all. For that we do not have sufficient resources, either in terms of personnel or of funding.'[8] The subsequent observation, that wiretap warrants could only be issued by a court, seemed to be something of an afterthought. In the course of the same interview, Ms Kövesi also observed that some matters could be resolved preventively, since 'the cure of corruption in the education and health systems could not be the arrest and prosecution of all teachers and doctors'.[9] One possible implication of this assertion would be that corruption (rather than, say, lack of funding, bad legislation, brain drain, bad allocation of public/private responsibilities, etc.) was the main problem of the education and health systems and could be eradicated by arresting all doctors and teachers. To be sure, most instances of corruption in the health care and education systems are small-scale and would fall outside the material competence of the NAD in any case. But the remarks as such are indicative and exemplary of a widespread new phenomenon. Matters of substantial constitutional debate and legislative policy have increasingly taken a distant second place or are discussed in terms of or by reference to anticorruption and judicial independence. It sometimes appears that significant portions of the anticorruption camp perceive politics as such, including constitutional politics, as putatively corrupt and in principle suspect.

In the extreme, Manichean rhetoric opposes demonic narratives of corrupt politics to heroic tales of anticorruption.[10] Revealingly, the title of a recent volume, a collection of interviews with high-ranking anticorruption magistrates, the president of the National Integrity Agency, and one anticorruption 'expert', is *I vote DNA!*[11] DNA, the Romanian abbreviation for the National Anticorruption Directorate (*Direcţia Naţională Anticorupţie*, the autonomous prosecutors' office charged with combatting high-ranking corruption), is an acronym everyone in the country has come to know. In recent years, anticorruption prosecutions have resulted in high-stake imprisonment sentences handed out to previously untouchable public figures (among them, one former prime minister, the leader of a government coalition party and the brother of the incumbent President), along dozens of lesser notables and hundreds of public servants. To the European Commission (the main promoter and supporter of the anticorruption reforms), the anticorruption agencies and the social and political actors who support or, respectively, run on the anticorruption ticket, these are irrefutable proofs of success (quantified in high-stake convictions) and impartiality (as no political party appears to have been spared by the tide of arrests, indictments and convictions). Conversely, the anti-anticorruption camp accuses 'televised' and 'telephone' justice prompted by occult, behind-the-scenes motives and cabals. Neither of these affirmations can be either proved or disproved, either factually or in a normative, legal key. In point of fact, indictment and sentencing statistics lead to logics of quantification, which, if taken to the extreme, would seem to require impartiality in the form of 'non-partisan' convictions on a par with political representation over time, so that equal numbers of sitting and former MPs, ministers, mayors, aldermen, etc., representing all political factions, would be convicted to proportionally comparable sentences. Normatively speaking, the quantification logic, along with the occasional transcript leak, seems somewhat at odds with general constitutional reflexes regarding the rights of the defendant and formal equality before the law. Since all the local institutions involved in anticorruption monitoring and law enforcement – namely, the National Anti-corruption Directorate, the National Integrity Agency, the Superior Council of the Magistracy and the Romanian Intelligence Service – are by design autonomous, it is impossible to assign responsibility for decisions in the majoritarian, political accountability-driven fashion of democratic politics. Moreover, local 'neutral institutions' are on the whole a postmodern novelty, recently and hastily parachuted by the needs of EU accession and monitoring into an unconsolidated 'post-post-communist' constitutional system. Naturally, the functioning of these new 'independent agencies' is poorly understood and relatively unassimilated, even at the level of constitutional adjudication. The complexities associated with the place of such institutions in their Western jurisdictions of origin (trade-offs between accountability and independence, the role of expertise in legitimising independence, etc.) are much harder to digest in systems where the 'fuzzy concepts'[12] underlying the functioning of these institutions (impartiality, autonomy/independence, etc.) are perceived, at best, as imported slogans, a new wooden tongue of sorts. In this environment, once 'the political [and social] demands of scandal politics'[13] have been quenched by a sufficient number of high-profile arrests, the recourse to cloak-and-dagger explanations for the functioning of politically opaque processes is a natural reflex, a complexity-reduction heuristic.

Changes of such tectonic proportions inevitably affect constitutionalism and constitutional law. In the remainder of this chapter, I shall inquire into the antinomies brought about by this recent paradigm shift, using Romania's pre- and post-accession anticorruption and rule of law reforms as a case study, insofar as these have affected the constitutional status of the judiciary. My argument proceeds upon a number of assumptions. Constitutionalism, the philosophy and traditions of limited government over time, consists of a deeply normative or normativised set of principles, concepts and practices. From the early 1990s, a counter-vocabulary started appearing in the discourse and practices of international organisations: the language of 'good governance'. Unlike constitutionalism, good governance mixes loosely normative concepts with efficiency and effectiveness-driven criteria. Unlike that of constitutionalism, the logic of good governance is essentially instrumental. The interaction between the criteria of good governance and constitutional systems produces paradigm shifts in constitutionalism itself. These mutations occur both at a conceptual level (good governance influences the meanings of inherited constitutional categories, by distortion and oversimplification) and at the direct phenomenal level, that of the context in which constitutional practices operate. Such tendencies are more visible in the European Union, an international organisation with a highly dense juridical structure, approximating to, albeit not fully equating, that of a federal state, an evolutionary path that is often referred to as 'constitutionalisation'. Contradictory effects deriving from this inchoate, governance-induced constitutionalism can be discerned at the level of the Union, in terms of mandate bootstrapping. For instance, the fluid terms of reference implicit in 'good governance' *qua* constitutionalism provide the Commission with a justification for overreaching and stealthily extending its competence. By the same token, tensions arise when older constitutional concepts, translated and reinterpreted at the level of the EU, collide with the constitutional and conceptual traditions of nation states: witness the consistently obstinate resistance of Germany's Federal Constitutional Court.[14] Such effects are even more directly noticeable at the level of the newer member states, over whose constitutional systems the Union has more direct leverage, by way of conditionalities, including political-constitutional conditionalities.

My more limited argument is that the use of these good governance criteria in the monitoring process has produced important mutations in Romanian constitutionalism, due to the way in which the anticorruption and rule of law discourses have reinforced each other and affected actual constitutional changes, including constitutional interpretations of local fundamental law provisions. Even though the 2007 accession states were subject to a form of post-accession monitoring that has not been replicated elsewhere thus far (in the case of Croatia, the newest entrant, there is no *ex-post* Mechanism of Co-operation and Verification in force), these metamorphoses are not of purely idiosyncratic interest. Conversely, the general trends described here, epitomised by the Romanian example, evidence shifts of competence within European constitutionalism itself and stand as predictors for future constitutional evolutions at the level of the Union.

Government, governance, 'good governance'

Etymologically, the word 'government' in the sense of 'the action of ruling; continuous exercise of authority over the action of subjects or inferiors; authoritative direction or regulation; control, rule' superseded 'governance', its older English counterpart, around the late sixteenth century.[15] This was roughly the time when the phenomenon that the word denoted, the modern state, was consolidated in England. According to the etymological chart in the *Oxford English Dictionary* entry on 'government', the first documented use of the word is found in a 1566 translation from French of Pierre Boaistuau's *Theatrum Mundi*: 'A king or prince that hath under his government so manye thousands of men.'

'Governance' resurfaced in the late twentieth century as a concept initially used in economics and business management (see 'corporate governance'). More recently, the notion has also seeped into the public sphere, as an ostensibly neutral umbrella term for sets of good practices in administration, compiled by international organisations for the purposes of assessing structural adjustment programmes to be implemented by borrowing countries.[16] According to a study on the emergence and implications of the concept of governance in public law, the World Bank was the first entity to shift from a purely descriptive to a loosely normative usage of this term, i.e. 'good' vs. 'bad' governance, in a 1989 report on sub-Saharan Africa.[17] The use of 'good governance' by international institutions gave rise in turn to a body of social science literature on the concept and its relevance, which has grown almost exponentially since the early 2000s.[18]

Strangely enough, the proliferation of the normative use of 'governance' has evolved in inverse lockstep with the concept's analytical coherence.[19] Even though the World Bank, the IMF, the OECD, the UNDP, the Council of Europe and, more recently, the European Union developed various sets of good governance criteria, white papers, codes of good practice and the like, at an ever more vigorous pace in the 1990s and early 2000s, and although one notices intense cross-fertilisation and hybridisation tendencies among these structures, the concept and its purported practical applications have remained for the most part elusive. In other words, it has been increasingly hard to detach a stable and reliable normative core from the laundry lists of criteria and ideals proffered by international organisations as yardsticks for 'good governance': anticorruption, the rule of law, accountability, administrative efficiency, participation of 'stakeholders' (sometimes, of 'civil society') in decision-making processes and transparency. Moreover, how these values were to be relatively ranked and implemented was unclear from the onset.

To wit, the 1996 Declaration of the IMF Board of Governors' Partnership for Sustainable Global Growth Interim Committee listed anticorruption, accountability, efficiency and the rule of law among the essential pillars of a successful good governance project and declared that an IMF priority would be: '[p]romoting good governance in all its aspects, including by ensuring the rule of law, improving the efficiency and accountability of the public sector and tackling corruption, as essential elements of a framework within which economies can prosper.'[20] A more coherent and widely-cited definition by the World Bank Research Institute describes governance as 'The traditions and institutions by which authority in a country is exercised. This includes (1) the process by which governments are selected, monitored and replaced;

(2) the capacity of the government to effectively formulate and implement sound policies; and (3) the respect of citizens and the state for the institutions that govern economic and social interactions among them'.[21] In 1996, the World Bank started reporting Worldwide Governance Indicators (WGI) for 215 economies, an individual and aggregate set of perception-based data based on 'a variety of survey institutes, non-governmental organisations, international organisations and private sector firms'. These indicators are structured in six categories, namely 'Voice and Accountability', 'Political Stability and Absence of Violence', 'Government Effectiveness', 'Regulatory Quality', 'Rule of Law' and 'Absence of Corruption'.[22] The ambiguities and tensions implicit in such slightly haphazard lists reflect the inescapable problems of applying 'neutral' efficiency-driven criteria to complex and wildly diverse constitutional-political settings. Some of the governance variables seem to evoke or approximate constitutional ideals, as evidenced for instance by the inclusion in various lists of the rule of law, accountability and participation, whereas some notions and definitions appear to concede a certain leeway to the inherited categories of nation-state constitutionalism ('the traditions and institutions by which authority in a country is exercised').

In constitutionalism, however, such notions and concerns are enmeshed in a very complex structure of normative justifications, institutions and procedures. Moreover, even though there are core accepted understandings in the traditions of liberal constitutionalism at the level of general principles and even – albeit to a much more limited extent – of specific practices, no wholesale transpositions of institutions or transplants of norms across jurisdictions are conceivable without great concessions, respectively in terms of conceptual and contextual reductionism.[23] For instance, even though judicial independence or constitutional supremacy are generally accepted corollaries of the rule of law, no particular institutional solution in terms of constitutional review or judicial organisation is dictated as orthodoxy ('standard practice') by simply conjuring the concept of the 'rule of law'. The translation as such of the analogous French and German concepts of 'État de droit' and 'Rechtsstaat' is a generous approximation. This is not to deny that notions such as the rule of law or accountability serve important heuristic or polemical purposes in the constitutionalist tradition: it is only to observe that, at these rarefied levels of abstraction and generality, few directly prescriptive consequences can be derived legitimately from conjuring them.[24]

Moreover, in the logic of the governance discourse, normatively laden terms such as the rule of law are melded with effectiveness-driven criteria, such as anticorruption. These cornucopian aggregates are subsequently tendered as Pareto efficient cures to a congeries of complex (governmental, social, political) evils.[25] It was inevitable that, in order for good governance to have any reliable practical bite for the purpose of coming up with precise policy-making guidelines or benchmarks for purposes of external evaluation and with express proposals for legislative and institutional reform, some of the initial dimensions would have to be detached and overemphasised, thus gaining the definitional upper hand over the others.

Indeed, more recent positions of the IMF appear to consider corruption as an independent variable, namely, as a leading cause of bad governance.[26] The World Bank's increased focus on corruption in the late 1990s and early 2000s similarly 'yielded a very comprehensive and sweeping vision of good governance, which is presumably what corruption corrodes'.[27] Once a group of policy-makers associated with the World Bank had created Transparency International in 1993, annual perception indices compiled by the local chapters started providing a 'civil society' platform and an apparently objective reference point for the expansion of the anticorruption discourse and the fledgling global crusade against corruption.[28] Although the World Bank governance indicators and the Transparency perception indices are essentially loosely compiled statistical surveys of subjective opinions (perceptions), the recourse to methodology, the reliance on empirical data and the sheer scope of both endeavours evoke objectivity and implicitly claim a breezily neutral, quasi-scientific authority. As a fringe benefit and apparently paradoxically in view of the rejections of cultural relativism explicit in the formulation of these new standards, the rankings routinely mirror and reinforce stereotypical representations about proper hierarchies and established divides of 'geographical morality'.[29]

At a practical level, the rise of good governance with anticorruption as its conceptual lodestar has generated a sophisticated systemic ratchet effect, inasmuch as international organisations and the global industry of anticorruption civil society players (NGOs, experts, etc.) co-operate both at the immediate practical level, promoting treaties and monitoring ratification and implementation at the national level, and at the meta-constitutional level, imposing an increasingly influential quasi-constitutional discourse.[30] Insofar as politically autonomous government bodies (prosecutors' offices or integrity commissions or agencies) are created to enforce anticorruption measures, patterns of co-operation and networking emerge in which domestic institutions develop overlapping national and transnational loyalties and dependencies.

These general developments inevitably influence nation-state constitutionalism, insofar as they both sometimes directly affect constitutionally-relevant norms and institutions and – more importantly – produce significant mutations with respect to the practical and discursive context in which national constitutionalism functions and evolves. For instance, 'soft law' criteria of good governance adopted or promoted by international organisations (codes of good practice or recommendations) can lead to unmeditated and often controversial institutional transplants.[31] Furthermore, since elements of open-ended normativity (rule of law, accountability) and the instrumental pursuit of efficiency and effectiveness (anticorruption) are fused at the hip in global 'good governance' campaigns, the proliferation of this quasi-constitutional discourse gradually displaces, i.e. falsifies by oversimplification or substitutes, the competing values and solutions of classical constitutionalism and good (i.e. constitutional) government.

The impact of constitutional experiments with 'good governance' is considerable in transitional or developing jurisdictions, which are, from both a civilisational and an economic standpoint, unprepared to resist or properly assimilate international pressures.[32] Moreover, while such civilisational tendencies operate in subtler, primarily persuasive ways in most jurisdictions,[33] the conflicts between good governance and constitutional government are formalised and more sharply evidenced in the case of the European Union. The Union itself has oscillated continuously between a form of neutral administrative co-operation and recurrent attempts at borrowing or mimicking elements of state-centred constitutional government traditions. In the case of newer entrants, the political conditionality element of the Copenhagen criteria is an authoritative mandate for the export of quasi-constitutional good governance principles and institutions. The political criteria as such are formulated in a way that could in theory be interpreted and applied in a more limited manner, consistent with generally accepted standards of constitutional civility and openness. As will be shown, however, the introduction of anticorruption among these standards has led to a peculiarly expansive dynamic in the case of the 2004 entrants, a tendency accelerated during the last accessions to the Union.

Governance and constitutionalism in the union: putting corruption in its place

In the European Union itself, according to the Commission's 2001 White Paper on European Governance, the 'basis of good governance' entails compliance with five principles, which, if followed, would bring the citizens closer to the EU institutions: openness, participation, accountability, effectiveness and coherence.[34] Corruption, somewhat counter-intuitively in view of recurrent graft scandals dating back to the collective resignation of the Santer Commission in 1999 over fraud and nepotism,[35] was not considered for inclusion in the White Paper, at least not with regard to the EU's own governance.

Good governance nevertheless played an important role for the purposes of exporting civilisation, insofar as some of the standards of democratisation lumped together by the political conditionality acquis and imposed on new candidate countries are essentially notions of good governance translated into quasi-constitutional language. The element of political conditionality in the Copenhagen criteria does not explicitly include the fight against corruption, cryptically indicating that a candidate state must ensure 'the stability of institutions guaranteeing democracy, the rule of law, human rights and respect for and protection of minorities'. The terms are generous enough to warrant a good measure of flexibility in their implementation by the Commission, including the postulate that corruption threatens institutional stability, the rule of law, democracy and human rights.

Before Lisbon, however, there was little if any justice and home affairs acquis[36] on the matter: the 1995 Convention on the Protection of the European Communities' Financial Interests came into force, together with the additional protocols, in October 2002, just days after the Commission recommended closing negotiations with the 2004 new member states.[37] This lack of a legal basis did not prevent the Commission from listing a litany of anticorruption treaties to which accession countries had to accede, among them the OECD Convention on Combatting Bribery of Foreign Public Officials in International Business Transactions and the two Council of Europe anticorruption conventions regarding civil and criminal law matters, respectively, even though many of the older member states were not at the time parties to the same. For instance, only Finland and Sweden had ratified both Council of Europe conventions, in 2002 and 2004, whereas six of the 15 member states (Austria, France, Germany, Italy, Luxembourg and Spain) had ratified neither by the end of 2004.[38] After December 2003, when it was opened for signature, the UN Convention against Corruption was added to the list.

Due to the lack of a substantive acquis basis, the EU Commission could only treat anticorruption policies as a political and constitutional matter at the time of the 2004 and 2007 expansions, although the crucial 'how' and 'why' issues remained underspecified. As a part of the political acquis, long discussions of 'anticorruption measures' in pre-accession progress reports on Romania were included in the 'democracy and the rule of law' category, after the paragraphs on 'institutions' and before the part of the reports monitoring evolutions related to 'human rights'. Few documents explained this inclusion as a part of the political acquis other than cursorily and implicitly, usually in stereotypical iteration, as for instance in the 2002 Progress Report on Romania: '[C]orruption remains a widespread and systemic problem in Romania that is largely unresolved.'[39] In the main, the link appears to be a cause–effect correlation, corruption being presented as the main culprit behind dysfunctional democratic institutions: 'International reports and surveys indicate that corruption in Romania continues to be widespread and affects all aspects of society. It undermines the effectiveness and legitimacy of state institutions and restricts Romania's economic development.'[40] Sometimes, references were made to perception indices (without citing either Transparency International or Eurostat) as the reliable referential of the reforms' impact, although the Commission also complained about the lack of successful high-level corruption prosecutions.[41] In many reports, the Commission incorporated by reference IMF agreements or GRECO recommendations, 'which [Romania was] strongly encouraged to [*sic*] follow-up'.[42] Corruption was also included in the much more limited scope of the-then pillar three chapter on justice and home affairs co-operation and was treated cross-referentially, in tandem with the monitoring of the political acquis, an artifice which correspondingly extended the leeway with respect to the justice and home affairs chapter.

The rise of the fight against corruption in EU law has slowly generated an interesting bootstrapping effect, not only with respect to the monitoring competences of the EU commission vis-à-vis newer European hinterlands but also – and more surreptitiously – in terms of the competences of the EU itself.[43]

Now, the general theme is much better entrenched in the Lisbonised 'area of freedom, security and justice' (the former third pillar), right between justice and fundamental rights. The pertinent part of Chapter 23, 'Judiciary and fundamental rights', reads as follows:

> Legal guarantees for fair trial procedures must be in place. *Equally, Member States must fight corruption effectively, as it represents a threat to the stability of democratic institutions and the rule of law. A solid legal framework and reliable institutions are required to underpin a coherent policy of prevention and deterrence of corruption.* Member States must ensure respect for fundamental rights and EU citizens' rights, as guaranteed by the acquis and by the Fundamental Rights Charter. [my italics][44]

On the face of it, by squeezing a grand policy imperative between a standard element of judicial independence (fair trial guarantees) and a reference to fundamental rights as guaranteed by the acquis and the Charter, the formulation strikes a rather odd chord. Guarantees of a fair trial ('natural justice') as elements of a due judicial process have stable meanings and a genealogy that predates the rise of anticorruption by centuries, whereas guarantees of fundamental rights can be related to more constrained, punctual issues of EU law. Corruption as such can be associated with these separate issues (fundamental rights and the judiciary) only in an instrumental or consequentialist key, which requires a leap of faith unwarranted by the discrete constitutional genealogies of the two concepts. Be that as it may, this change has been translated into a more effective monitoring, based on a formalised, explicit acquis chapter. Current progress reports on candidate countries have kept corruption within the scope of the political conditionality, where the matter is expedited in a paragraph, whereas effective monitoring proceeds on the basis of the 'area of freedom, security and justice' judiciary and human rights acquis.[45] The acquis as such includes few hard EU law instruments (for instance the EU Convention on the fight against corruption involving officials of the European Communities or officials of the EU member states, which came into force on 28 September 2005, or the Framework Decision 2003/568/JHA on combatting corruption in the private sector, adopted in 2003). Consequently, much of the integrity crusade led by the Commission is still based primarily on network constitutionalism (references to other international organisations and bodies) and campaigns for democratisation targeting candidates and associated states. The 2011 Communication from the Commission to the Parliament, the Council and the Economic and Social Committee (entitled 'Fighting Corruption in the EU') premises these efforts on perception indices and cites an actual figure of 120 billion euros per year, 1 per cent of the EU's GDP, that is allegedly lost to corruption. This is an estimate based on estimates by 'specialised institutions and bodies, such as the International Chamber of Commerce, Transparency International, the UN Global Compact, the World Economic Forum and Clean Business is Good Business', which apparently suggest that 5 per cent is lost globally to graft.[46] Once a percentage can be conjured, although the Commission admits in small print that the sum total was arrived at by way of an approximation of an approximation, the figure can still be presented as a fact and a bootstrapping mandate ('It is not acceptable that an estimated 120 billion Euros per year . . . is lost to corruption'.) and can be cited for future reference as a relatively well established fact.[47]

The language of good governance and its composites (insistence on corruption as the cause of a bevy of evils, reliance on anticorruption policies, insistence on 'judicial(-prosecutorial) independence' writ large as a means to the end of corruption, a strong tendency towards depoliticisation, and a related preference for lighter participatory substitutes – 'civil society' – for majoritarian politics) is now a mainstay of Union constitutionalism and can be brought to bear on new accession countries under the Copenhagen criteria.

Due to the pliability of the terms of reference and the unstructured nature of the implementation of the political acquis, the end results will naturally differ from one country to another. These asymmetries of impact reflect both the differential leverage of the Commission on candidate countries and the degree of local receptivity (and interest) in adopting some parts or some versions of the EU conditionality recommendations. As a result, although the general discourses are the same and important changes do occur at the level of all new member states, there is as yet no institutional synchronicity. For instance, Croatia has instituted an autonomous prosecutor's office (the USKOK), whose attributions are however less focused on high (political) corruption than those of its Romanian counterpart; entering the EU in 2013, the country is under no post-accession monitoring. Bulgaria has adopted significant judicial independence reforms, which have resulted in a loftier relative domestic status of the judicial system, but was loath to implement effective anticorruption policies. Good governance criteria have noticeably started to crystallise in institutional patterns and ideological uniformities. Nevertheless, in spite of these emergent orthodoxies, the chances are that the ensuing normative and institutional grafts will still produce differential impacts and generate different forms of adaptation and resistance in the context of different constitutional systems.

The Romanian case is ideal-typically exemplary not of general statistical trends, but of the expansive potentialities of the influence of 'good governance' and the capacity of this malleable discourse to justify unforeseen mutations and manipulations of classical constitutional concepts and institutions. In this respect, it is not important to show whether the metamorphoses described below will result in structures that are effective in strictly instrumental terms, e.g. whether the new settings actually reduce public graft. What the Romanian example nonetheless reveals is the propensity of this quasi-constitutional language and new type of instrumentalism to translate the old concepts and reference frameworks of constitutionalism into a new, less normatively tractable jargon.

The corruption of judicial independence

Romania's 1991 post-communist Constitution provided for a High Judicial Council (SCM) composed of 'magistrates' (the notion encompasses both judges and prosecutors) elected for four-year terms by a joint session of the Parliament. The Council nominated magistrates to be appointed by the President and served as a 'disciplinary council' for judges (Arts. 132–3, Romanian Constitution (1991)). Neither the number of Council members nor the ratio of prosecutors to judges represented were specified, which meant in practice that crucial functional elements were left to the decision of the Parliament and relegated to the domain of organic legislation.[48] This arrangement reflected both the early post-communist lack of interest in a strong judiciary and the ambivalence regarding the proper constitutional status of prosecutors. The latter, despite being considered to be magistrates, constitute a hierarchical structure with recognisable executive features, expressly placed by the Constitution 'under the authority of the Minister of Justice' (Art. 131 (1) Romanian Constitution (1991)).

In preparation for Romania's accession and in furtherance of repeated Commission Reports recommending more 'judicial independence', the fundamental law was amended in 2003.

According to the amended Article 133(1) (previously Article 132), the Council 'shall guarantee the independence of justice'. The terms of office were extended to six years, whereas the composition was now specified in the constitutional text: 14 elected magistrates (nine judges, five prosecutors), two representatives of 'civil society', elected by the Senate, and three *ex officio* members (the Minister of Justice, the President of the High Court of Cassation and Justice and the Prosecutor General). According to the revised version of Article 134(2), the new SCM 'perform[s] the role of a court of law' in disciplinary decisions regarding prosecutors and judges. Disciplinary proceedings are tried in the two sections; appeals against their decisions can be lodged with the administrative review section of the High Court. *Ex officio* members are not entitled to vote in disciplinary proceedings, whereas the 'civil society' representatives can only take part in plenary sessions. These changes turned the initial logic of checks and balances on its head and converted an insignificant institution into one of the most powerful judicial councils in the world.[49]

Romania had essentially transplanted an extreme version of the French-Italian judicial model of organisation, under the influence of the EU. A council composed predominantly of elected magistrates, patterned on a bowdlerised version of the Italian and French prototypes, was initially recommended as an international good practice by the Association of European Magistrates for Democracy and Freedom's 'Palermo Declaration' and incorporated by reference, starting with 1994, in Council of Europe recommendations to its members.[50] Interestingly, the jurisdictions of origin do not correspond to the template translated as an international 'best practice' into the Romanian context. On the contrary: membership of the French *Conseil Supérieur de la Magistrature*, as reconfigured by the 2008 amendments to the 1958 Constitution, now conspicuously comprises more non-elected members (a Councillor of State, a member of the bar and six 'external personalities' appointed by the President and the Speakers of the two Houses, respectively) than elected magistrates. Even in the Italian case, the epitome or 'ideal-typical' apex of corporatist autonomy, the ratio of elected to appointed members is two-thirds to one-third.

In spite of comparative evidence to the contrary, the position of the Romanian SCM was further entrenched after 2003. By the same token, all attempts to change this newer status quo were fended off internally in the name of 'judicial independence', whereas the understanding as such of 'judicial independence' was extended as time went on, in the name of European standards and integrity imperatives. The phrase as such has increasingly gained an axiomatic value, to the point where simply invoking the principle appears to function as an informal gag rule. To be sure, this has been a two-way process from the beginning. On the one hand, the local judiciary, once entrenched, has used the phrase to deflect all attempts at institutional change; on the other hand, the EU Commission has legitimised all corporative judicial positions conducive to more autonomy, since the insulation of the judicial system from political and social influences was perceived as an indispensable means for pursuing effective anticorruption policies. These conjoined developments generated a dynamic, systemically self-referential process. For instance, matters of constitutionality were not included in post-accession monitoring. In spite of this formally limited scope, the Constitutional Court, which exercises vital gatekeeping functions with respect to amendments and the constitutional interpretation of legislation governing the judicial organisation, was gradually 'co-opted' by the Commission and brought under the umbrella of the Cooperation and Verification Mechanism. The Mechanism itself was initially created for a limited timeframe (three years after the accession), to ensure the timely post-accession implementation of pending or ongoing judicial reforms and anticorruption measures. But, under the influence of the dialectical corruption/independence logic described above, judicial reform and the fight against corruption were related to the rule of law and judicial independence, constitutionality was defined as the foundation of the rule of law and the Constitutional Court as a part of the justice system, broadly understood. More recent reports by the Commission include sub-sections on 'the Romanian constitutional system' under the judicial reform heading and are replete with holistic references such as this: 'Though not strictly a part of the judiciary, the Constitution and the Constitutional Court are at the heart of the rule of law.'[51] At the more practical level, Commission delegations liaise with the constitutional justices, to discuss issues related to the 'rule of law' and the future optimal course of adjudication.[52]

The logic of transnational institutional networking and conceptual transitivity impacted locally to generate a more creative range of interpretive cross-references. In 2011, the Constitutional Court rendered an opinion on a presidentially sponsored initiative to amend the Constitution. At the time, the proposal was to modify the composition of the Council, adding four more civil society representatives, three more Presidential appointees and three more elected by the Parliament, and to reduce the number of elected judges correspondingly, from nine to five. At this point, the Court considered that the proposed amendments were conducive to the 'annihilation of the constitutional guarantee of judicial independence', due to the fact that an increase in the number of the politically-appointed members, in conjunction with a proportional decrease in the number of elected magistrates (from 14 to 10), would have led to 'an alteration of the representation proportion in the Council [to the detriment of career magistrates], susceptible to produce negative effects on the activity of the judicial system'.[53] To be sure, according to the Constitution, the civil society representatives must be lawyers with extensive experience and of 'good professional and moral reputation'. Yet, the Court's argument was valid in its own terms. It could be admitted in principle that the possibility given to political appointees to outvote elected magistrates, in the circumstances pertaining to Romania, might have brought nefarious political influences to bear on disciplinary proceedings. The reasoning advanced in 22011 included a brief foray into comparative law: the Spanish, Portuguese and Italian models were somewhat selectively presented in support of the holding. No reference was made to the contrary example offered by France's 2008 amendments.

In *obiter*, the Court sought to allay fears and reservations concerning a perceived lack of transparency and accountability, noting that, in accordance with the organic law of the Superior Judicial Council, 317/2004, elected magistrates 'are accountable to their peers with regard to the performance of their mandates'. The recall procedure under Law 317/2004 provides that a member of the council can be revoked with the votes of two-thirds of the judges or prosecutors corresponding to his or her representational and jurisdictional tier (trial court, tribunal, appeals court, High Court of Cassation and Justice). The Court's argument reduced the constitutional guarantees of judicial responsibility to the legislative safeguards of corporate accountability. Yet, the reference corresponded at least to the internal logic of the decision's reasoning ('judicial independence means that the judicial system is primarily governed by magistrates, elected and controlled predominantly or exclusively by their peers') and could be accepted or not under the terms of a normative key of constitutional interpretation.

In 2013, by virtue of an exception of unconstitutionality, the Court was called on to render a decision on the recall provision whose application had been implicitly portrayed in 2011 as the main guarantee of accountability within the judicial system. According to Article 55 of the law, any general assembly of prosecutors or judges can trigger the recall procedure to revoke a SCM member representing its jurisdictional hierarchy level for 'not accomplishing or faultily carrying out the attributions for whose execution he was elected to the Council'. Once a given general assembly adopts the proposal by a two-thirds vote, the results are notified to the SCM. The Council then verifies that the formal procedural conditions were complied with and forwards the decision to all assemblies represented by that Council member. A countrywide recall ballot is then held and, once votes in favour of revoking the Council member have reached the requisite qualified majority (two-thirds), the procedure is stopped and the result is announced, whereupon the Council takes note of the results, vacates the seat and organises a by-election.

One member of the Council, recalled by his peers, appealed against the Council's administrative decision, raising an exception of unconstitutionality in the course of the administrative appeal. Deciding on the exception, the Constitutional Court declared the recall provision unconstitutional and ordered the incumbent's reinstatement. In a defence of the free mandate redolent of the 'Letters to the Electors in Bristol', the Court noted that electors do not 'charge [SCM members] with specific attributions', since the members' attributions are of a legislative and internal administrative nature. Moreover, the Court opined, the 'electorate' could at any rate not know how such attributions are individually discharged, since voting is secret in the Council. Furthermore, according to the justices, the reference to the neglect or faulty discharge of 'attributions' in the article presupposed professional misconduct, which in turn implied a punitive measure. Once a recall procedure has been (mis)characterised as roughly equivalent to a criminal sanction, as the Court did, all the trappings of judicial proceedings come into play (the existence of a reasoned indictment, based on a precise and clear rule, rights of defence, guarantees of a fair trial, etc.).[54] The Court recommended that the legislator take stock of these considerations when remedying the situation. In view of the reasoning and keeping in mind that even 'corporative recall' is – *mutatis mutandis* – a majoritarian, referendum-like decision-making process, it is very hard to imagine what kind of norm and procedure would satisfice the procedural hurdles intimated by the Constitutional Court.[55]

More recent decisions concerning the judicial system seem to have relinquished normative rationales altogether. In 2013, the Parliament made an abortive attempt to amend the Constitution. Initially, various proposals were aired, regarding the reconfiguration of the Council, including the creation of two separate councils for prosecutors and judges. In the end, a timid proposal to raise the number of civil society representatives from two to four found its way into the revision bill. In its 2014 *ex ante* decision on the constitutionality of this revision bill, the Court did not find it necessary to review the older arguments and simply stated that any increase in the number of the external members would in and of itself change the proportion of representation and affect the independence of justice:

> The current proposal leaves the number of magistrates [sitting in the Council] unchanged, while nonetheless increasing the number of civil society representatives, a fact that determines an alteration of the relative representation proportions. Thus, the considerations that underpinned the [2001 decision] subsist, due to the fact that a modification of representation rates by increasing the number of members in the Council recruited from outside the judicial system is of a nature to jeopardise the activity of the judiciary.[56]

The brief reference to the 2011 amendment initiative papered over the essential differences: in 2011, the argument underlying the unconstitutionality finding was that a significant decrease in the number of elected judges corresponding to a threefold increase in the number of appointed external members, so that the votes of the latter could have overpowered those of the former in disciplinary proceedings, endangered judicial independence. In 2014, any increase in the number of civil society representatives, provided that it is not accompanied by a corresponding increase in the number of magistrate members, was presented as imperilling the independence of the judiciary. Yet, the 2014 Constitutional Court found an analysis of the new norm and hypotheses, referring cavalierly to the 2011 reasoning, the alleged identity of reasons, and the overarching value of judicial independence.

The roughly simultaneous (January 2014) European Commission CVM report took up the challenge and raised the stakes. The report admonished Romania to consult the SCM in future amendment processes affecting judicial independence and intimated that general consultations with both the Venice Commission and the EU Commission would be in good order:

> With the Constitutional debate expected to return this year, it will be important to ensure that the Superior Council of the Magistracy has the opportunity to comment on all areas relevant to the judiciary. In particular, care will be needed to exclude changes which increase the opportunity for politicians to influence the judicial leadership or challenge judicial independence or authority. For this reason, the commitment of the government to consult the Venice Commission in particular is an important sign of Romania's commitment to base any future Constitutional change on European norms. The Romanian authorities have also made clear their intention to keep the European Commission informed.[57]

Conclusion

The vocabulary of good governance, as international and supra-national institutions have recently promoted it, contrasts national constitutionalism with an influential quasi-constitutional paradigm. Even when the syntactic and semantic articulations of this new idiom of 'constitutionalism beyond the state' use the words of classical traditions of fundamental law, the inherent dynamics of good governance are prone to alter the meanings and implications of what is being said. Otherwise put, good governance and classical constitutionalism speak different languages, even when the same words appear to be uttered.

The Romanian evolutions described above as epiphenomenal of these changes show how, in the name of a postulated 'European' or 'international' standard of 'judicial independence', local and European institutions have mutually reinforced their actions and created a fully idiosyncratic kind of autonomous social and political structure. From the crucially important external perspective, that of the Union, this development was justified, not only in its own 'best practice' terms, but also in an instrumental key, namely, the successful pursuit of anticorruption campaigns, with which judicial reforms have coalesced, both in the particular case of this country and at the formal level of evolutions in the EU acquis.

It is too early and perhaps impossible to tell whether or not corruption will be combatted more effectively and eventually eradicated in this way. The alteration of concepts differs from the corruption of people. For example, unlike successful bribery, undue benefits or conflict of interest prosecutions or convictions, the implications of conceptual paradigm shifts cannot be quantified in statistical terms. From a normative standpoint, however, one may wonder whether the corruption of concepts and frameworks of reference will not eventually produce generous possibilities for manipulation and thus open avenues for, albeit more insidious, equally detrimental forms of corruption.

Notes

1 In the case of Romania and Bulgaria, the two countries are also subject to post-accession conditionalities, through the Mechanism for Co-operation and Verification. In the case of Romania, the four benchmarks of the Mechanism are concerned essentially with anticorruption and judicial reforms. Even though the instrument was initially supposed to be lifted after three years (in 2010), according to

the Act of Accession of Romania and Bulgaria (Art. 37), CVM monitoring has been since extended – for both member states – *sine die*.

2 'Autonomous administrative authority' (a term by which the Romanian Constitution denotes 'independent agencies') can be created outside the formal executive hierarchy (Art. 116 (2)).

3 Both the Chief Prosecutor of the DNA and the General Prosecutor of the Prosecutor's Office attached to the High Court of Cassation and Justice are appointed by the President, at the recommendation of the Minister of Justice, upon receipt of the high judicial council's advisory opinion on the nominee, for three-year terms of office, renewable once.

4 To fall under the *ratione materiae* prosecutorial jurisdiction of NAD, the value of the bribe or prejudice has to exceed 10,000 and 200,000 euros, respectively. *Ratione personae*, the institution has jurisdiction over corruption crimes committed by enumerated categories of public officials, according to Law 78/2000 on the prevention, investigation and sanctioning of corrupt acts.

5 The initial setting, that of the 1991 Constitution, provided for a High Judicial Council with more limited responsibilities (it served as a disciplinary committee for judges only and nominated magistrates for appointment by the President) and whose autonomy was much more restricted (initially, all members were elected by the two Houses of the Parliament, in joint session).

6 Passive and active bribery, undue influence and the receipt of undue benefits were criminalised under the provisions of the 1968 Criminal Code. The first special anticorruption law dates back to 1996 (Law 115/1996 regarding the declaration and control of assets belonging to officials, public servants and magistrates, as well as other persons in positions of authority) and was passed in the aftermath of a short-lived corruption scandal. Due to the cumbersome mechanism initially provided for its enforcement, these provisions went virtually unapplied until 2005.

7 Iohannis, a former mayor of the Transylvanian city of Sibiu, was accused of breaching incompatibility provisions in Law 161/2003, as he represented the municipality in a public utility's general assembly of shareholders, while serving as mayor.

8 'Keinesfalls. Dazu hätten wir keine ausreichenden Ressourcen, weder in puncto Personal noch bei der Finanzierung. Auch muss eine Erlaubnis von einem Richter vorliegen'. Interview of 12 August 2014 in the Austrian newspaper *Der Standard*, http://derstandard.at/2000004252427/Rumaenien-Gesetz-ist-mittlerweile-fuer-alle-gleich (last accessed 4 November 2014).

9 Ibid. 'Unter anderem müsste es einen deutlicheren politischen Willen zur Bekämpfung der Großkorruption geben und mehr Präventivmaßnahmen – es kann nicht sein, dass die DNA alle Ärzte oder Lehrer verhaften muss, bevor wir gegen die Korruption im Gesundheitssystem oder im Bildungswesen vorgehen.'

10 Laura Ştefan, 'Eroii de lângă noi' (The Heroes Among Us), *Revista 22*, 12 August 2014, www.revista22.ro/eroii-de-lnga-noi-46359.html (last accessed 4 November 2014).

11 Cristian Ghinea, *Eu votez DNA! De ce merită să apărăm instituţiile anticorupţie* (Bucureşti: Humanitas, 2012).

12 András Sajó, 'Neutral Institutions: Implications for Government Trustworthiness in East European Democracies', in Susan Rose-Ackerman and János Kornai (eds), *Building a Trustworthy State in Post-Socialist Transition* (New York: Palgrave Macmillan, 2004), pp. 29–51.

13 James B. Jacobs, 'Dilemmas of Corruption Control', in András Sajó and Stephen Kotkin (eds), *Political Corruption in Transition: A Skeptic's Handbook* (Budapest: CEU Press, 2002), pp. 81–90, at p. 90.

14 For a recent example, see the decision (Second Senate) dated 26 February 2014, 2 BvE 2/13, regarding the 3 per cent electoral threshold in the Law Governing European Elections, which essentially argued that an electoral hurdle would be unconstitutional in the case of European Parliament elections, unlike the case of national democracy. The majority held that, since the European Parliament was not a democratically representative institution in the sense of national legislatures, such as the Bundestag, restrictions on the franchise and on party equality, for instance electoral thresholds, would be fully unwarranted at EU level.

15 *Oxford English Dictionary*, entry on 'Government': 'In the main, this word may be considered to have superseded "governance".'

16 Bo Rothstein, 'Good Governance', in David Levi-Faur (ed.), *The Oxford Handbook on Governance* (Oxford: Oxford University Press, 2012), pp. 143–54.

17 Lorenz Engi, 'Governance-Umrisse und Problematik eines staatstheoretischen Leitbildes', *Der Staat*, 47/4 (2008), pp. 573–87, at p. 574.

18 The recent literature on governance is enormous. See, generally, the recent reference handbook edited by Levi-Faur.

19 Engi, 'Governance-Umrisse und Problematik eines staatstheoretischen Leitbildes'. See also Christoph Möllers, 'European Governance: Meaning and Value of a Concept', *Common Market Law Review* 43 (2006), pp. 313–36.
20 www.imf.org/external/np/sec/pr/1996/pr9649.htm#partner
21 D. Kaufmann, A. Kraay and P. Zoido-Lobáton, 'Governance Matters', Policy Research Paper No. 2196, Washington DC, World Bank Institute, 1999, p. 1.
22 http://info.worldbank.org/governance/wgi/index.aspx#home.
23 Witness the enormous body of literature on legal transplants or methodology in comparative law.
24 Indeed, such notions may serve these discursive purposes precisely because they are indeterminate: 'Concepts such as "democracy", "justice" and "rule of law" are widely popular in part because they are so open to interpretation'. David S. Law, 'The Myth of the Imposed Constitution', in Denis J. Galligan and Mila Versteeg (eds), *Social and Political Foundations of Constitutions* (New York: Cambridge University Press, 2013), pp. 239–68, at p. 251.
25 Rothstein, 'Good Governance', p. 151: '[N]either the absence of corruption, nor representative democracy, nor the size of government, nor the rule of law, nor administrative efficiency captures what should be counted as good governance. Searching for a definition, it is notable that the conceptual discussion has largely been detached from normative political theories about social justice and the state. It should be obvious that when terms like "good" are placed in political contexts, it is impossible to refrain from entering the normative issues that are raised in political philosophy.'
26 'Governance is a broad concept covering all aspects of the way a country is governed, including its economic policies and regulatory framework, as well as adherence to the rule of law. Corruption – the abuse of public authority or trust for private benefit – is closely linked: a poor governance environment offers greater incentives and more opportunities for corruption.' IMF Factsheet dated 18 March 2014, www.imf.org/external/np/exr/facts/gov.htm
27 Mlada Bukovanski, 'The Hollowness of Anti-Corruption Discourse', *Review of International Political Economy* 13/2 (2006), pp. 181–209, at p. 191.
28 Padideh Ala'i, 'The Legacy of Geographical Morality and Colonialism: A Historical Assessment of the Current Crusade Against Corruption', *Vand. J. Transnat'l L.* 33 (2000), p. 877.
29 András Sajó, 'Corruption, Clientelism and the Future of the Constitutional State in Eastern Europe', *E. Eur. Const. Rev.* 7 (1998), at p. 42: 'To call the transition economies "corrupt" remains . . . a therapeutic means of preserving Western self-esteem, of maintaining its sense of moral superiority. The cheapest form of such therapy consists in disdain for "the countries in the East".'
30 Steve Sampson, 'The Anti-Corruption Industry: From Movement to Institution', *Global Crime* 11/2 (2001), pp. 261–78. See also, Luís de Sousa, Peter Larmour and Barry Hindess, *Governments, NGOs and Anti-Corruption: The New Integrity Warriors* (London and New York: Routledge, 2009).
31 Note the successful promotion by international organisations of the model of judicial councils whose membership includes a majority of judges elected by their peers, in spite of the dearth of evidence as to the efficiency of such institutions in providing quality of justice and in the face of tremendous context-related complexities entailed by judicial reforms. *See* Nuno Garoupa and Tom Ginsburg, 'Guarding the Guardians: Judicial Councils and Judicial Independence', *Am. J. Comp. L.* 57 (2009), p. 103.
32 Kevin L. Cope, 'South Sudan's Dualistic Constitution', in Galligan and Versteeg, *Social and Political Foundations of Constitutions*, pp. 295–321, at p. 312: '[Internationally drafted constitutional templates] are most likely to emerge in developing countries (which are, perhaps, in relatively weak positions to refuse international pressure, and thus more susceptible to that international template).'
33 The persuasiveness of soft law criteria of good governance is enhanced, however, by substantial resource allocations. According to a 2006 estimate, the World Bank alone had funded 330 'rule of law' projects with $2.9 billion since 1990 (David Trubek, 'The "Rule of Law" in Development Assistance: Past, Present and Future', in David Trubek and Alvaro Santos (eds), *The New Law and Economic Development* (New York: Cambridge University Press, 2006), pp. 74–94, at p. 74).
34 European Governance: A white paper, COM (2001) 428 final, Official Journal C 287 of 12.10.2001.
35 www.economist.com/news/europe/21601287-european-unions-inexplicable-fear-exposing-corruption-dragon-room.
36 Chapter 24 at the time.
37 Peter W. Schroth and Ana Daniela Bostan, 'International Constitutional Law and Anti-Corruption Measures in the European Union's Accession Negotiations – Romania in Comparative Perspective', *Am. J. Comp. L.* 52 (2004), pp. 636–637. The authors comment extensively on the disparities with

respect to the imposition of anticorruption measures and the related ambiguities in 'creeping EU "competence" '.

38 Ibid., at p. 639 (chart on disparities between the EU Member States and the 'Class of 2004') regarding the ratification of the CoE conventions.

39 2002 Regular Progress Report on Romania's Progress Towards Accession, COM (2002) 700 final, at p. 26, http://ec.europa.eu/enlargement/countries/strategy-and-progress-report/index_en.htm.

40 2003 Regular Report.

41 'Although significant efforts were made during the reporting period to intensify the fight against corruption there has been no reduction in perceived levels of corruption and the number of successful prosecutions remains low.' 2004 Regular Report, COM (2004) 657 final, at p. 21.

42 2002 Regular Report, COM (2002) 700 final, at p. 28.

43 I am loosely paraphrasing Jon Elster, 'Constitutional Bootstrapping in Philadelphia and Paris', in Michel Rosenfeld (ed)., *Constitutionalism, Identity, Difference, and Legitimacy: Theoretical Perspectives* (Durham, NC: Duke University Press, 1994), pp. 57–83, at p. 57.

44 http://ec.europa.eu/enlargement/policy/conditions-membership/chapters-of-the-acquis/index_en.htm.

45 See, e.g., 2013 Progress Report on Montenegro, COM (2013) 700 final.

46 COM (2011) 308 final, FN 3.

47 See EU 2014 Anticorruption Report (Report of the Commission to the Council and the European Parliament, COM (2014) 38 final).

48 In the Romanian constitutional systems, specified subject matters (the organisation of important institutions, criminal law, referenda, etc.) fall into the domain of organic legislation, a category similar to the French or Spanish organic laws and functionally analogous to Hungary's 'cardinal acts'. Organic laws, unlike ordinary legislation, require an absolute majority to pass through the decision-making House of Parliament.

49 For an elaboration of the context and initial implications of the 2003 amendments, see Bogdan Iancu, 'Post-Accession Constitutionalism with a Human Face: Judicial Reform and Lustration in Romania', *European Constitutional Law Review* 6/1 (March 2010), pp. 28–58.

50 Garoupa and Ginsburg, 'Guarding the Guardians'.

51 2014 CVM Monitoring Report on Romania.

52 www.ccr.ro/noutati/COMUNICAT-DE-PRES-134.

53 Decizia Nr. 799 din 17 iunie 2011, M.Of. Nr. 440 din 23.06.2011.

54 Decizia Nr. 196 din 4 aprilie 2013, referitoare la excepţia de neconstituţionalitate a dispoziţiilor art. 55 alin. (4) şi (9) din Legea nr. 317/2004 privind Consiliul Superior al Magistraturii, publicată în M.Of. nr. 231 din 22.04.2013.

55 The Parliament has not yet amended the law. Since the two paragraphs declared unconstitutional in 2013 (Art. 55, pars. 4 and 9) are void, the recall procedure is inoperative.

56 Decizia Nr. 80 din 16 februarie 2014 asupra propunerii legislative de modificare a Constituţiei României, M.Of. Nr. 246 din 07.04.2014.

57 Report from the Commission to the European Parliament and the Council on Progress in Romania under the Co-operation and Verification Mechanism, COM (2014) 37 final.

References

Ala'i, P. 'The Legacy of Geographical Morality and Colonialism: A Historical Assessment of the Current Crusade Against Corruption', *Vanderbilt Journal of Transnational Law* 33 (2000), 877–932.

Bukovanski, M. 'The Hollowness of Anti-Corruption Discourse', *Review of International Political Economy* 13/2 (2006), 181–209.

Cope, Kevin L. 'South Sudan's Dualistic Constitution', in Galligan, D.J. and Versteeg, M. (eds), *Social and Political Foundations of Constitutions* (New York: Cambridge University Press, 2013), 295–321.

Elster, J. 'Constitutional Bootstrapping in Philadelphia and Paris', in Rosenfeld, M. (ed.), *Constitutionalism, Identity, Difference, and Legitimacy: Theoretical Perspectives* (Durham, NC: Duke University Press, 1994), 57–83.

Engi, L. 'Governance-Umrisse und Problematik eines staatstheoretischen Leitbildes', *Der Staat* 47/4 (2008), 573–87.

Galligan, D.J., and Versteeg, M. (eds). *Social and Political Foundations of Constitutions* (New York: Cambridge University Press, 2013).

Garoupa, N., and Ginsburg, T. 'Guarding the Guardians: Judicial Councils and Judicial Independence', *American Journal of Comparative Law* 57 (2009), 103–34.
Ghinea, C. *Eu votez DNA! De ce merită să apărăm instituțiile anticorupție* (București: Humanitas, 2012).
Iancu, B., 'Post-Accession Constitutionalism with a Human Face: Judicial Reform and Lustration in Romania', *European Constitutional Law Review* 6/1 (2010), 28–58.
Jacobs, James B. 'Dilemmas of Corruption Control', in Sajó, A. and Kotkin, S. (eds), *Political Corruption in Transition: A Skeptic's Handbook* (Budapest: CEU Press, 2002), 81–90.
Kaufmann, D., Kraay, A. and Zoido-Lobáton, P. 'Governance Matters', Policy Research Paper No. 2196, Washington DC, World Bank Institute, 1999.
Law, David S. 'The Myth of the Imposed Constitution', in Galligan, D.J. and Versteeg, M. (eds), *Social and Political Foundations of Constitutions* (New York: Cambridge University Press, 2013), 239–68.
Levi-Faur, D. (ed.). *The Oxford Handbook on Governance* (Oxford: Oxford University Press, 2012).
Möllers, C. 'European Governance: Meaning and Value of a Concept', *Common Market Law Review* 43 (2006), 313–36.
Rothstein, Bo. 'Good Governance', in Levi-Faur, D. (ed.), *The Oxford Handbook on Governance* (Oxford: Oxford University Press, 2012), 143–54.
Sajó, A. 'Corruption, Clientelism and the Future of the Constitutional State in Eastern Europe', *East European Constitutional Review* 7 (1998), 37–46.
———. 'Neutral Institutions: Implications for Government Trustworthiness in East European Democracies', in Rose-Ackerman, S. and Kornai, J. (eds), *Building a Trustworthy State in Post-Socialist Transition* (New York: Palgrave Macmillan, 2004), 29–51.
Sajó, A. and Kotkin, S. (eds). *Political Corruption in Transition: A Skeptic's Handbook* (Budapest: CEU Press, 2002).
Sampson, S. 'The Anti-Corruption Industry: From Movement to Institution', *Global Crime* 11/2 (2001), 261–78.
Schroth P.W. and Bostan, A.D. 'International Constitutional Law and Anti-Corruption Measures in the European Union's Accession Negotiations – Romania in Comparative Perspective', *American Journal of Comparative Law* 52 (2004), 625–711.
de Sousa, L., Hindess, B. and Larmour, P. (eds). *Governments, NGOs and Anti-Corruption: The New Integrity Warriors* (London and New York: Routledge, 2009).
Ştefan, Laura. 'Eroii de lângă noi' (The Heroes Among Us), *Revista 22*, 12 August 2014.
Trubek, David. 'The "Rule of Law" in Development Assistance: Past, Present and Future', in Trubek, D. and Santos, A. (eds), *The New Law and Economic Development* (New York: Cambridge University Press, 2006), 74–94.
Trubek, D.M., and Santos, A. (eds). *The New Law and Economic Development* (New York: Cambridge University Press, 2006).

Bogdan Iancu Associate Professor (Comparative Constitutional Law and Constitutional Theory), Faculty of Political Science, University of Bucharest. Research for this article was supported by and undertaken in the framework of the research project PN-II-ID-PCE-2011-3-0115, "Governance/ Government – The Constitutional Semantics of Autonomy." A prior version of the argument was presented at the Fermo Summer School "Constitutionalisms and Legal Cultures", August 25–29, 2014. I thank the participants to the workshop for their comments and suggestions. The usual disclaimers apply.

11 The organisation of market expectations beyond legality

An Argentinian case

Matías Dewey

Introduction

The importance of the sociology of law in Niklas Luhmann's intellectual concerns and work can hardly be overstated. Equally true is the fact that, after Luhmann's death, developments in the field of the theory of systems have also considered the law as a central topic. Both in Luhmann's work and in subsequent studies based on the same theoretical architecture, the law (*das Recht*) is understood in the same way: the structure par excellence governing the counterfactual stabilisation of normative expectations (Luhmann 1987: 43; Luhmann 1993: 135). Conflicts arising from opposed expectations should provoke the reaction of the legal system: '[the legal system] uses a mode of information processing that functions precisely when conflicts arise', wrote Luhmann in his book *Social Systems* (Luhmann 1995a: 375). At the core of the legal system, this task, i.e. the protection of expectations as the result of codifying the reality according to the distinction legal/illegal, remains uncontested in all subfields of the theory, including in studies of the world legal system, constitutionalism and criminal law (Fischer-Lescano and Teubner 2006: 34; Jakobs 2000). In any of these cases, it is assumed that law acquires general significance in society due to specific procedures – legislative, court and administrative – that have the ability to restructure participants' expectations by producing a 'social climate', the main outcome of which is the limitation of options. Procedures limit alternatives, little by little, step by step, until at the end of the procedure, the only way out is the acceptance of the decision. Several types of procedures – even at the level of world society – are responsible for bringing about the belief in the legality of binding decisions. Procedures are designed to breed the legitimacy of legality (Luhmann 1983). In other words, the theory of systems operates under the assumption that legitimacy, produced by procedures, is always related to legality.

The idea of the pre-eminence of the legal system as a guarantor of normative expectations in modern society has had remarkable consequences, even within the theory of systems itself. The significance of the law is not only a diagnosis of modern society, it is even more; a structural component of the whole theoretical architecture itself. A clear example of the status of the law as an integral part of the theory is the 'dividing-function' (*Trennfunktion*), as Luhmann himself stated, of the legal system among the subsystems, above all between the economy, politics and law (Luhmann, introduction in Neves 1992). Or, using other terms, the legal system as structure plays a decisive role in the intersystem structural couplings. Insofar as the political system is coupled with the legal system through the constitution (the text in which role expectations are defined by specifying rights and obligations), the politics analysed by the theory of systems is the official, formal politics (Luhmann 2005: 373ff.). A similar line is taken regarding the topic of this chapter. Insofar as the economy is coupled with the political system by means of taxes and policies, and coupled with the legal system by means of property rights and contracts, the economy analysed by the theory of system is the official, formal economy (Luhmann 1988: 92ff.).

For any empirically informed sociologist, the obstacles posed by such theoretical dispositions are enormous. The absence of a clear distinction between the legitimacy of established law and the legitimacy of other normative orders led the theory of systems to the automatic exclusion of traditional sociological fields. It would be exceedingly difficult to ignore – even in the context of a world society – the importance for sociology of phenomena that go beyond the formal economy or the formal politics. I mean here: political clientelism, informal labour, organised crime, illegal markets, or social settings in which the expectation that the state will re-stabilise broken norms is contested or simply does not exist and, as a replacement, the belief in legitimacy is attached to other instances. Thus, by observing legitimacy exclusively as the acceptance of decisions made in the context of legal procedures, the legitimacy of informal normative frameworks – either in economic or political realms – appears as a marginal, usually also imperfect phenomenon.[1] What sociologists or political scientists nowadays refer to as informal politics (Helmke and Levitsky 2006) is represented in Luhmann's theory of systems as corruption or solidarity networks, problems mostly of peripheral societies that short-circuit the autopoietic functioning of operative closed systems.[2] At stake here is not the problem of the status given to the different sources of legitimacy, both legal and illegal. More important seems to be that the latter, the informal sources of legitimacy, are not considered in the theory, neither in the realm of politics nor of economics. Social systems are structures assembled by the legitimacy of legality. Accordingly, the theory has reserved for other sources of legitimacy the side of exclusion, the place where 'nothing happens' (*Nichtereignis*) (Stichweh 2000: 96). Good examples of attempts to overcome this theoretical blind spot are the conceptual suggestions made in the field of theory of systems by scholars concerned with phenomena such as clientelism, corruption networks and non-democratic regimes. Episodic de-differentiation of the legal system, i.e. the replacement of legal communication by political communication is, for example, what Aldo Mascareño suggests for the Latin American case (Mascareño 2012). Marcelo Neves, on the contrary, readily rejects one the basic pillars of Luhmann's theory, the concept of autopoiesis, and introduces the notion of allopoiesis, meaning an asymmetric intervention, usually political, in the self-reference of the legal system (Neves 1992).

In this chapter, my point of departure will be a functioning, empirically verifiable illegal market. On this basis, this research will not suggest, as other studies have done, a new interpretation of the problems with the functional differentiation. For the meantime, this discussion will be set aside. In this chapter, I am interested in the way alternative normative orders reach a certain degree of stability. Hence I suggest the analysis of a paradox: how, in a social space where the law is de-coupled from the economy, i.e. a space in which contracts and property rights are not backed by law, are contracts fulfilled and property rights recognised? This paradox would not be possible without the informal intervention of politics in the space of exclusion, meaning that political actors foster the emergence of political brokers, who in turn enforce informal contracts and property rights.

In this chapter, there is no intention to deal with issues such as the functional differentiation of society or the system's operative closure. Instead, I aim to devote the analysis to what happens within the 'exclusion-side', a space that remains silent and unexplored in the theory of systems. A space that was strikingly defined as 'a negative fact [*Sachverhalt*], a not-occurrence [*Nichtvorkommen*], a non-event [*Nichtereignis*], an expulsion' (Stichweh 2000: 96). By shedding light on a social context characterised by informality, and the illicit trade of counterfeit clothing, attention is focused on operations outside the legal system and, therefore, on the constitution of alternative normative expectations. In so doing, the theory gains new momentum, since we do not discuss the vicissitudes of (legally structured) systems (their level of differentiation or their closure), but the constitution of parallel structures of expectations.

This task is best achieved by focusing on a basic process, commonly found in Luhmann's work on the sociology of law, and a constitutive element of every system: the formation of expectations of expectations, i.e. structures that orient communications and social action. Hence, I will contend here that the aforementioned paradox – a counterfactual re-stabilisation of normative expectations related to contracts and property rights in a social space where the legal system plays no role – is explained by the appearance of 'third parties' that manage normative expectations (Luhmann 1987: 66; 1995a: 395). More precisely, the challenge posed by the irrelevance of the legal system for the 'double contingency' problem in certain social settings is solved by the emergence of third parties acting as arbitrators of conflicts and enforcers of norms. Ultimately, my analysis offers a point of access to the distinction between legitimate and illegitimate, an issue absent from the theory of systems.[3]

The chapter is divided as follows: firstly, I will show in detail what I consider a blind spot in Luhmann's theory of systems and, drawing on his work, I will develop my main argument. Secondly, I will allude to the case study that shows the emergence of a third instance ordering of normative expectations. In this section, I will first describe 'La Salada', the informal and illegal market located on the periphery of the city of Buenos Aires. Following this, I will show a well-established structure that functions as a third party organising normative expectations attached to contracts and property rights.

The primacy of legitimation by procedures

According to Luhmann, the transition from a segmentary to a modern society not only means the emergence of systems – structures of expectations orienting communication in very specialised forms – but also means a fundamental transformation in the way authority is legitimised. In fact, following Luhmann, the positivisation of the law in the nineteenth-century in conjunction with the ongoing systemic differentiation forces the question: if the decision-makers are few, how could the generalisation of law's binding force or the generalisation of conviction regarding the correctness of the law be possible? (Luhmann 1983: 27).

It is quite clear that Luhmann's idea of modern society assumes that norms regulating expectations and behaviour in each system are codified and enforced by the legal system. In his book devoted to the legitimation of binding decisions, *Legitimation durch Verfahren*, there are no references to alternative forms of domination [*Herrschaft*]. Traditional norms (traditional domination) and norms introduced by charismatic leaders (charismatic domination), both discussed by Max Weber, seem nevertheless to be outdated forms of legitimation that are not characteristic of modern society. The legal system is thus considered an evolutionary achievement of modern society and is, as such, only a guarantor of those normative expectations – those norms – present in each system (Luhmann 1995a: 374). In simplified terms: social systems are criss-crossed by the legal system and develop their functions on the back of its authority. This statement is especially apt for the economy and politics. The ability to pay (economy) or the availability of power (politics) both assume that legal norms regulate economic transactions as well as power struggles.[4]

When the law is considered to be the defining structure orienting social expectations and behaviours in modern society, the question of the legitimacy governing modern society is only weighed in relation to official rules, i.e. the law. The problem is thus reduced to the legitimation of legal norms. The answer is, accordingly, the idea of legitimation by procedures. Procedures are social systems whose function is the generation of expectations and their transformation:

social systems that, based on a set of roles and pre-programmed proceedings, are able to create a social climate and allow a generalised disposition towards the acceptance of decisions made within the procedure to emerge (Luhmann 1983).

One type of procedure is, for instance, a political election. Different actors intervening in the production of these political devices – voters, candidates, mass-media, marketing agencies, political parties, etc. – recreate a particular climate. Their contributions lead to the appearance of new topics, mainly boosted by opinion polls, news, scandals, statements, etc. that capture the public's attention. Whilst involved in such a climate, actors are waiting for a result. All agree that there will be an outcome, a final decision, and that it will result in winners and losers. Where one will accept the result without any problem, another must accept it even against her will because there is no leeway for protest – she would only deepen her social discredit. Thus the generalisation of acceptance takes place, a crucial issue in Luhmann's early work.

Although the idea of legitimation by procedures constitutes a major step forward in the comprehension of the way beliefs towards the legitimacy of distant and abstract official codes are formed, this theory is also in some respects limited. In effect, the idea that procedures are the only mechanisms with a legitimacy-generation capability and, more pertinently, that this capability is only linked to legality, leaves aside several traditional sociological research topics, as well as characteristics of modern society.

The most distinctive consequence of this lack of alternative ways of legitimation is that the theory itself loses its ability to capture phenomena such as economic informality, illegal markets or informal political institutions, and to convert them into research topics. In this way, almost by default, Luhmann's theory of systems has reserved for these phenomena the exclusion side, i.e. a place outside of the systems. Whereas the system is the place of inclusion par excellence, to be outside of the system means to be excluded. It is true, however, that the theory reflects an undeniable feature of our society: the enormous obstacle that forms the barrier built between the inclusion (system) and exclusion (out of system) sides. The description of the exclusion side as a space of 'Nichtsereignis', a negatively-integrated space, also seems plausible. However, this kind of integration needs to be explained and specified; the black box needs to be opened. One example where the black box remains firmly closed can be found in a book published just a few years ago in which, by adopting the perspective of the theory of systems, a well-known and prevalent phenomenon such as the informal economy is totally absent (Baecker 2006).[5]

Third parties and the stabilisation of alternative normative frameworks

How we can get out of this straitjacket? I suggest that our first clue is to be found in Luhmann's writings themselves. If the basic difference between informal and formal normative expectations (norms) does not lie in their qualities (in both cases a resistance against reality takes place), but in the fact that the latter has legitimacy provided by the state, we can assume that the constitution and institutionalisation processes are in both cases the same. In this case, we need only to return to a central element of these processes, an element very much present in Luhmann's sociology of law: the appearance of third parties mediating and administrating normative expectations (Esslinger 2010; Luhmann 1987: 66).

The process of formation of expectations of expectations starts with the possibility of an uncontrolled irritability: a state of uncertainty without any possibility that 'expectations could rely on expectations of expectations of third instances' (Luhmann 1987: 67). Uncertainty is the result of a lack of experience (*erleben*) of such instances; a situation in which one cannot expect the stabilisation of expectancies by a third party after a case of disappointment. On the contrary, this stabilisation becomes a real possibility once an 'unknown, anonymous third, whose assumed opinion embodies the institution' intervenes.[6] Luhmann emphasised the function of thirds: 'Originally, a third does not occupy a specially created role of a watcher tasked with watching; instead, a third is occupied with other things, but could nevertheless be called upon at an instant to co-experience, co-judge, co-condemn and co-act. One is not a third at the moment of his or her own expectation and action, but becomes such in the horizon of expectations of those currently orienting themselves towards potential co-experiencers' (Luhmann 1987: 66).[7]

Without a doubt, the lower institutionalisation and differentiation degree of informal norms also means fewer possibilities for the limitation of contingency and therefore a greater level of insecurity of expectation.[8] However, the appearance of third parties such as political brokers or groups imposing power by force (as described by Charles Tilly (1985)), provides an initial solution to the problem at the root of the institutionalisation norms: a fulcrum in the face of a limited capacity for attention.[9] Third parties, already established as instances of stabilisation of expectancies, are also meaningful building blocks since they introduce a consensus regarding acceptable and unacceptable behaviours. Present in Luhmann's sociology of law and also well-known as 'generalised others' in the pragmatist tradition (Mead 1973; Dodds et al. 1997), such a consensus is critical for the coordination of illegal exchanges; market actors act under the assumption that this consensus exists and is real.

The identification of third parties ordering normative expectancies in social sectors where the legal system does not have the relevance that Luhmann supposed allows the differentiation – besides legal and illegal – between legitimate and illegitimate normative orders, a distinction notably absent from Luhmann's theory of systems. This is a fundamental distinction since it allows existing alternative, normative orders that coexist with the legal system to be considered. Making this distinction helps to expose the different levels of law's social relevance, as well as whether other types of (extra-legal) norms are equally relevant in terms of guiding behaviours and social expectations. Accordingly, this distinction breaks from the idea that legally structured procedures are the only mechanisms capable of producing legitimation of norms; on the contrary, my main argument highlights the significance of third parties capable of managing and enforcing normative expectations. Thus, while it is still possible to hold that belief in the legitimacy of legality is generated through procedures, third parties are also in charge of generating belief in the legitimacy of alternative norms.

In the second part of this chapter, I will show how a third party structures economic expectations in the context of an informal and illegal market. The third adopts the form of an informal tax system or state-sponsored protection racket that orders the expectations of sellers of clothing produced in sweatshops as well as those of buyers. The belief in the legitimacy of norms originates in this kind of informal taxation system, a structure dependent on strong informal leaders chiefly active in informal politics and in charge of enforcing the conditions within the market.

Emerging thirds outside the legal system

A third is someone who is able to manage and enforce normative expectations. In the case of illegal markets, however, there are producers, sellers and buyers willing to trade prohibited products or services. On the other hand, there are authorities representing the state. At least in principle, both have opposed interests. Thirdly, we have actors taking an intermediate position between the state and market players. The latter are brokers, mediators and managers of the interface between legality and illegality. Relevant for them is the satisfaction of expectations of both state and market actors. The available literature on informal and illegal markets conceptualises the state/third (broker, mediator) relation as corruption. Here is meant the exchange of favours that are usually intended for the personal enrichment of state agents. Contrary to the literature on corruption, studies on the relationship between thirds acting as mediators and market actors are scarce. Only recently have scholars become aware of the fact that in certain social spaces the state has lost influence and relevance as a mediator appearing in the horizon of possibilities when conflicts arise. These new thirds, a sort of functional equivalent of the state, are called new sovereignties, or extra-legal governance (Arias 2006; Centeno and Portes 2006; Clunan and Trinkunas 2010).

The following depiction is a case of new sovereignty governed by several actors functioning as mediators between the state on one side, and producers, sellers and buyers of clothing manufactured in sweatshops on the other. The final outcome of this configuration of actors is a well-functioning informal and illegal garment market. As I will show, operations in this market are governed by an informal taxation system (or state-sponsored protection rackets) imposed by informal managers with strong roots in local and national level politics in Buenos Aires. Such a taxation system differs from bribery due to its high level of organisation and institutionalisation but also due to the fact that the money collected goes above all to state agencies. This institutionalisation reduces the need to impose order through violence; after an initial violent period, the institutionalised system later functions more or less peacefully. The thirds, mediating between the inclusion and the exclusion side, offer an explanation as to how the aforementioned paradox is possible, that is, a social space where contracts are fulfilled and property rights are recognised despite the de-coupling of the law from the economy. In other words, this informal taxation system controlled by managers linked to politics becomes an organised way of managing market expectations. The threat of violence is without doubt a resource used by power holders in these spaces to legitimate norms. However, as recent research shows, the assumption that illegal markets are violent per se is contested (Reuter 2009; Dewey 2014). Through this system, access to and expulsion from the market is controlled, costs of production are set and, in general, social relationships are framed. But the most important effect of this taxation system is the expectation created by the managers that the law will be not enforced. Acting as intervening thirds, managers assure that authorities will not enforce the law by transferring a portion of the collected money to them. Regarding the question of how order in the market is produced, the expectation that the law will not be enforced is a crucial factor. The absence of enforcement opens up a future for producers, sellers and buyers; they will engage in coordinated market actions and save the energy they would otherwise devote to avoiding law enforcement agencies. Other than social relationships regulated by the legal system, the expectations of actors in the case presented here are managed and enforced in the context of an illegal taxation system. It is a case of illegal but legitimised authority guaranteeing the fulfillment of contracts and the recognition of property rights.

A short description of the market

Fifteen kilometres away from the city of Buenos Aires, the marketplace of La Salada is at the heart of an informal economy that has become the primary means of acquiring clothing for the lower and middle classes of Argentina as well as of neighbouring countries. It covers 18 hectares on the banks of the Riachuelo, one of the most polluted rivers in the world, and is composed of 7,822 stalls almost exclusively selling garments. The bulk of these stalls are comprised of shed-markets and the relevance of this immense garment-oriented economy lies in its wholesale nature. On average, 200 long-distance buses and thousands of cars arrive at the marketplace three times per week. Massive quantities of jeans, jackets, underwear, socks, shorts, caps, bags, sport shoes and t-shirts are bought in La Salada and resold in other provinces and neighbouring countries. High quality counterfeit Adidas, Puma and Disney items are cheaper than their official counterparts, even taking into account transport costs for retailers going on to resell items thousands of kilometres away from Buenos Aires.

Today, 2,915 stalls outside (on the street) and 4,907 inside (within the sheds) are rented per day to those entrepreneurs looking to sell their wares. Hence, by renting a stall within La Salada, producers shorten the commercialisation chain, becoming dealers able to offer cheaper products. To protect stallholders from the punishment for their illegal activity, which would discourage potential tenants, keeping the authorities sweet is therefore one of the main tasks for the managers. As I mentioned before, the main tool used in this regard is the informal taxation system that, as will be shown, plays an essential role in preventing possible disturbances.

Contrary to the rest of the country's economic climate, La Salada reached its peak in 2001. In the following years until the present day, this marketplace has consolidated to become the main low-cost garment supplier for the Argentinian lower and middle classes. Around the central market, several secondary markets emerged which are basically responses to different demands or needs of stallholders and clients. For instance, the informal real estate market gained newfound momentum in light of the stallholders' demand for a space where goods can be safely stored between the market's opening days. In this way, hundreds of properties close to the sheds and the streets of wire-mesh stalls increased in value and gave rise to the profitable business of warehousing. In the same fashion, a demand for the services of cart-pullers arose, since there was a need to move large containers full of garments from the warehouses to the stalls both inside the sheds and in the streets. Currently, each shed-market has a fixed number of cart-pullers, a situation that, given the high demand for jobs among young people, increases aspirations to 'belong' to such an exclusive group of workers. The aspirational component associated with this job also provided an outlet for the managers' political opportunism. In fact, a requirement of being a member of a group of cart-pullers is to participate in political demonstrations organised by the parties with which the managers have aligned themselves.[10]

La Salada is a good example of the Argentinian garment industry's transformation. The informality of the economy centred in La Salada covers all sectors, from the production stage in thousands of sweatshops that have sprung up throughout Greater Buenos Aires, to the commercialisation stage in the marketplace and the reselling that occurs in the outer provinces. The systematic avoidance or circumvention of established fiscal, labour and security rules marks La Salada as an economy completely detached from the formal economy. Among other things, this means a disconnection from formal financing sources and, consequently, that the trade around La Salada is fed only with cash. Adherence to official regulations that do exist is rare. Overall, the economy centred in La Salada shows that legality and, even more so, informality and illegality live side by side. As will be shown later, there is a convergence of the interests of a state sector and of other important actors in this economy, i.e. managers, entrepreneurs/stallholders and consumers. A clear example of such a convergence of interests can be found in the uncontested informal tax system in La Salada, established after a few years of conflict between the security forces (unofficially demanding protection rackets), and the Bolivian community refusing any state regulation. In 2001, the Bolivian leader of the biggest shed-market at that time was officially accused and found guilty of illegal trading and counterfeiting, charges that ultimately resulted in a prison sentence. A few days after the verdict, he was found dead in his cell having reportedly committed suicide. This suspicious incident marks the beginning of the established, uncontested tax system described below.

Managing and enforcing agreements through informal taxation

At La Salada, stalls are open for business three times per week. Entrepreneurs from several locations around Greater Buenos Aires and south of the city attend the market in order to sell their products. These entrepreneurs – many of them sweatshop owners – are responsible for buying fabric, designing patterns, cutting fabrics, and carrying out some of the final sewing work. The remaining tasks, which are mainly the sewing, are outsourced to other sweatshops. Conservative estimates indicate that a total number of 31,288 sweatshops are linked to the garment business with its epicentre at La Salada.

What are the factors managing and reinforcing market actors' expectations? Or, what is the explanation for the continued significant growth of La Salada, a marketplace to which thousands of sweatshops bring their products and the mainstay of the informal garment industry? To answer these questions, we need to consider the aforementioned taxation system that, acting as an intervening third, set in motion an extra-legal normative framework guiding the decisions made by entrepreneurs, workers, transport companies and security forces. Such a framework is particularly important given that this type of garment production and commercialisation involves economic activities without any kind of support from the law. Bearing this in mind, alternative regulatory mechanisms become decisive for market actors.

An informal taxation system

The 7,822 stalls are distributed between five sheds and along the nearby streets, which are permanently occupied by wire-mesh stalls. Besides the infrastructure, the main difference between the sheds and the wire-mesh stalls on the street is the way they are controlled: the sheds have managers with an extended and efficient network of informants at all levels. As shown by Table 11.1, between 40 and 60 per cent of the stalls (depending on location) sell counterfeit clothing with brands such as Adidas, Puma, Nike, Disney and many others. It is worth pointing out that around half of the garments sold in La Salada do not violate trademark law. However, regardless of the quality of the copy, each stall on which garments with brand logos are displayed has to pay a tax known as 'brand' (*marca*). Those who do not sell any

Table 11.1 Number of stalls and taxes collected by marketplace (sheds and streets) in La Salada

Markets	*Sheds*					*Street*	*Total*
	Red	*Yellow*	*Green*	*Blue*	*Violet*		
Number of stalls	1,102	2,210	1,254	171	170	2,915	7,822
Number of stalls selling 'brands'	440	875	512	69	72	1.049	3.017
Amount of the tax (Argentine pesos)	150	150	200	100	100	35	
Monthly tax collection (Argentine pesos)	793,440	1,575,360	1,228,800	82,800	86,400	440,580	4,207,380
Monthly tax collection (US dollar, exchange rate as at 14 July 2013)	145,578	289,042	225,456	15,191	15,852	80,836	771,955

Source: author's calculation based on an individual stall-count and interviews conducted with stallholders from each marketplace.

'branded' garments do not pay this tax. It is interesting from an organisational perspective that the 'brand' tax has to be paid every time a garment with a logo is exhibited on the stall and a debt is recorded if, for whatever reason, the stallholder fails to pay. The shed markets have tax collectors who walk through the aisles collecting the 'fixed tax' sums. Without such structured organisation, but equally as effective, the Argentinian police are responsible for illegally collecting tax directly from the street-market vendors. Due to their centralised administration, the shed markets also centralise tax collection, whereas the police, without any apparent intermediaries, collect taxes from the street markets.

The collectors justify levying such taxes to the stallholders by referring to the need to pay compensation either to the authorities, or even to the companies whose rights have allegedly been violated. In the shed markets, there is no bargaining when it comes to the amount of the tax, which shows just how highly organised and institutionalised the practices are. In the street markets, however, there is some scope to negotiate a discount, though this comes with the disadvantage that, in comparison to dealing with one sole tax-collector as in the sheds, stallholders on the street must contend with a number of people collecting money, all identifying themselves as police officers. Stallholders selling counterfeit garments – usually entrepreneurs who own sweatshops – take this tax into account when calculating their production expenses. According to several interviews, it is accepted that this tax is the price they must pay in order to increase their sales. Equally significant is the widespread acceptance of this kind of taxation, that is to say, the absence of protest surrounding the issue. This lack of resistance to taxation is based not only on the considerable demand for the counterfeit garments (which increases profit and reduces the significance of the taxation) but, even more importantly, stems from the fear of the consequences of refusing to pay, which is particularly true of the street markets where stallholders are more exposed to a variety of dangers.

The total tax sum collected from both the shed and street markets – US$771,955 each month – is distributed between at least eight state agencies at both national and provincial levels, as well as a portion going to the Municipality of Montañitas. An ex-employee of a shed market recounted his experience as a tax collector:

> We went and collected inside. Going through the aisles, gathering money. She went and collected. [When I asked whether they are women] Yes, there are a lot, they go and collect for . . . say Delitos y Estafas [the Crime and Fraud Agency], la Brigada de Mitre [the Mitre Police Service], Narcotráfico [the Anti-Narcotics Agency], la Distrital and the Departamental [District and Departmental Offices]. The [shed] market also gives money to the coach drivers, around 20 pesos and pays for their breakfast [When I mentioned that the shed market manager denies such practices] I don't know what it's like now, but Pepe [the manager] went to have lunch with Ordaz [a Police Chief] every market day. You have no idea! Sometimes we had plastic bags full of money and then the members of the Police Service came to collect the money and I joked with them telling them that we were recording them. I didn't like them because they took advantage of people.

A current manager of one shed market confirmed that this is indeed the way the police forces collect taxes. As a direct witness of this phenomenon, he stressed that the people collecting money are police officers demanding payment independently without any connection to the market administration:

> Nobody tells me the true story. Who would do? The police come and surround you. On weekends they know you have [the collected] money from the 'brand' tax and they come

to pick it up. I know who I have to give it [the collected tax money] to. There are around 10 of them [state agencies, police]. The Federal, ehhh, you have to give it to everyone. Because otherwise they stop the vans [of stallholders or buyers] when they enter [La Salada]. They took the vans when they were arriving and they really fucked me up.

Finally, a public servant currently working for the Montañitas Municipality who used to be the right-hand man of one of the shed-market managers goes further when he describes the final stage of tax collection and the relationship between La Salada and the government:

> In La Salada markets, and I'm not only speaking of the Yellow Market, I also mean in Larroque and Turdera, the guy who has a stall and sells 'brand' has to pay 450 bucks, and those who don't sell 'marca' pay 300. The difference is because of the fact that people go and buy branded clothing. But also because part of this tax goes to the companies [that own the violated trademarks], which might cause a problem. Do you understand? If I were Adidas, I would kick up a big fuss! I would close down the stalls; judicially, I would kick the market people up the ass! I would close the markets down. What do they do? So, in order for this not to happen, Adidas goes every month and takes the money, Nike takes the money, Topper takes the money: everyone takes the money. Do you understand how it works? Do you understand what I'm saying to you? Nobody knows that. In this district there are 300 organisations. All of them received bags with 30 pairs of shoes. Brand new. Nike, Adidas, and so forth. Do you know where they came from? From La Salada. It's called 'Ropa para Todos'. I warn you, if you repeat what I'm saying tomorrow, I don't know you.

The second tax is not imposed on stallholders, but on the buyers traveling to the markets by long-distance bus. This is collected by a federal security force and is similar to a bribe because the collection is made at random and does not involve fixed amounts or register the amount charged. However, similar to the 'brand' tax, the function of the payment is to suspend law enforcement. Therefore, the economic activity is not abolished but taxed instead. A former Chief of the National Gendarmerie claims:

> But it isn't in anyone's interest [that the security forces stop buses at La Noria Bridge or on the highways]! Nobody would agree. Because otherwise the circus is over. Look, it isn't convenient for any authority that buses don't come any more . . . because they regularly leave an ovule [*sic*, tax]. If the business is over, we are fucked. I take you and call you 'stupid! [He imitates a senior policeman speaking with a junior officer who has stopped a bus] What are you doing? I told you, stop the buses from time to time; of 20 [buses] you stop one. If you take 100 pesos from each passenger . . . with 50 passengers . . . you do the math!' It is not that they don't check; they make arrangements for everything. Do you think that if I see a bus on the highway I don't know it's coming from La Salada? They even have the money ready! The passengers themselves say 'guys, we should put the money there'.

With these taxes – particularly the 'brand' tax – the state has access to resources that allow political control, strengthen patronage networks, and enable it to address issues regarding administration and the state budget. Such taxes ensure the functioning of an essential market: the garment market. On the one hand, political control over the population comes from the ability of the state to assure a certain level of income by creating jobs that are insecure and against official regulations. On the other hand, political stability is achieved by promoting consumption and also assures access to garments.

Conclusion

In summary, this research identifies the role of thirds as instances through which normative expectations can be structured beyond the reach of the legal system. This approach to the legitimation of norms outside the legal system is based on a critical reading of Niklas Luhmann's conception of legitimation processes. According to Luhmann, the mechanisms oriented towards the legitimation of authorities are procedures, and these procedures are understood to be the keystones in the production of law, which is to say the structuring of normative expectations. In other words, normative system expectations are, for Luhmann, the consequence of law-based, successful procedures. Problems arise, however, as soon as we try to analyse the legitimation of norms in spheres such as the informal or illegal economy. Based on this reading, I argued that illicit markets emerge when third instances (e.g. mediators, brokers) appear and those thirds are able to manage expectations. This chapter also provides strong empirical evidence providing the emergence of a third party and explains how this structures La Salada market, an arena of informal and illegal exchange that emerged in Argentina in the 1990s. The evidence reveals a third party that takes the form of an informal tax system run by powerful informal actors.

By illustrating the level of institutionalisation of this tax system, the involvement of state agencies at various levels, and the volume of resources that flow around the system, this chapter shows that third parties do indeed have the ability to frame expectations and enable a well-functioning and geographically widespread system of exchange to exist.

Notes

1 At this point, it is necessary to state that I am completely aware that the distinction between legal/illegal or legitimate/illegitimate do not have any relevance in Luhmann's theory of systems. Luhmann's main interest lies in observing complex structures. There are, however, several reasons that allow me to maintain my criticism. In Luhmann's theory, the mechanisms oriented towards the legitimation of authorities are procedures. They are understood to be the keystones in the production of law, i.e. the structuring of normative expectations. Other than to Max Weber, charisma and tradition do not play a role. For Luhmann, normative system expectations are the consequence of law-based, successful procedures. Therefore, in Luhmann's terms, legitimation processes should be understood in relation to the production of legality. Supporting this perspective, the only book devoted to the topic of legitimation does not allude to other types of legitimation. In my view, therefore, the question is: how do we understand the structuring of normative expectations beyond the scope of the legal system?
2 Two good examples are Luhmann 1995b and 2008.
3 The study of social spaces governed by logics other than those present in the systems, i.e. a self-reproduction based on its own elements, offers the same possibilities of social criticism as those practised by the *Kritische Systemtheorie* (Amstutz 2014). In fact, to shed light on social sectors excluded by the systemic logic allows the exclusive and disruptive character of some systemic logics to be observed.
4 This statement is, however, less clear in the case of the education system and even less so in the cases of religion and love.
5 Luhmann refers to the problems of informality and illegality only in regard to the organisational level. See Luhmann (1965: 114).
6 Luhmann (1987: 66) ('unbekannten, anonymen Dritten, deren vermutete Meinung die Institution trägt').
7 'Man ist Dritter ursprünglich nicht in einer eigens dafür geschaffenen Rolle, als ein mit Zuschauen beschäftigter Zuschauer, sondern als jemand, der mit andern Dingen beschäftigt ist,

aber möglicherweise für ein aktuelles Miterleben, Miturteilen, Mitverurteilen, Mithandeln zu gewinnen ist. Man ist nicht Dritter in der momentanen Aktualität seines Erwartens und Handelns, sondern im Erwartungshorizont derer, die sich aktuell an möglicherweise Miterlebenden orientieren.'

8 Interestingly, we can see here that Luhmann's understanding of anomie, a meaningful notion in functionalist thought, means insecurity of expectancy. In this sense he states: 'insecurity of expectancies is much more intolerable than the experience [*erleben*] of surprises and disappointments. Anomie in terms of Durkheim concerns the insecurity of expectancies and not facts regarding others' behavior. It is true: to expect and to behave stabilize each other but norms produce a great deal of security while expecting, something which is justified with behaviors. This is the specific contribution of norms to the autopoiesis of communication in society' (Luhmann 1993: 152).

9 Besides Husserl's phenomenology, the limited capacity for attention of human beings – an element already present in Arnold Gehlen's anthropology – is a constitutive principle of systems. In fact, the function of systems and the reduction of complexity, comes from this anthropological requirement.

10 In fact, those cart-pullers who do not attend political demonstrations receive suspensions; usually two workdays. Additionally, the high demand for jobs gives rise to a curious phenomenon: the position of cart-puller has a price. Since there is a fixed number of cart-pullers working for the sheds and each has an ID-number, there is a possibility to sell the positions (or numbers). In 2013, the price of one position was around 4,000 US dollars.

References

Amstutz, Marc. 2014. *Kritische Systemtheorie Zur Evolution Einer Normativen Theorie*. Bielefeld: transcript Verlag. Available at: www.myilibrary.com?id=630885.

Arias, Enrique Desmond. 2006. 'The Dynamics of Criminal Governance: Networks and Social Order in Rio de Janeiro'. *Journal of Latin American Studies* 38(2): 293.

Baecker, Dirk. 2006. *Wirtschaftssoziologie*. Bielefeld: Transcript-Verl.

Centeno, Miguel Angel, and Alejandro Portes. 2006. 'The Informal Economy in the Shadow of the State'. *Out of the Shadows: Political Action and the Informal Economy in Latin America*, 23–48.

Clunan, Anne L., and Harold A. Trinkunas. 2010. *Ungoverned Spaces: Alternatives to State Authority in an Era of Softened Sovereignty*. Stanford: Stanford Security Studies.

Dewey, Matías. 2014. *Taxing the Shadow: The Political Economy of Sweatshops in La Salada, Argentina*. 14/18. MPIfG Discussion Paper. Available at: www.econstor.eu/handle/10419/104712.

Dodds, Agnes E., Jeanette A. Lawrence, and Jaan Valsiner. 1997. 'The Personal and the Social Mead's Theory of the "Generalized Other"'. *Theory & Psychology* 7(4): 483–503.

Esslinger, Eva. 2010. *Die Figur des Dritten : ein kulturwissenschaftliches Paradigma*. Frankfurt am Main: Suhrkamp.

Fischer-Lescano, Andreas, and Gunther Teubner. 2006. *Regime-Kollisionen: zur Fragmentierung des globalen Rechts*. Frankfurt am Main: Suhrkamp.

Helmke, Gretchen, and Steven Levitsky. 2006. *Informal Institutions and Democracy: Lessons from Latin America*. Baltimore: Johns Hopkins University Press.

Jakobs, Günther. 2000. 'Strafrechtliche Zurechnung Und Die Bedingungen Der Normgeltung'. *ARSP-BEIHEFT-* 74: 57–72.

Luhmann, Niklas. 1965. *Grundrechte als Institution; ein Beitrag zur politischen Soziologie*. Berlin: Duncker & Humblot.

———. 1983. *Legitimation Durch Verfahren*. Frankfurt am Main: Suhrkamp.

———. 1987. *Rechtssoziologie*. Opladen: Westdeutscher Verlag.

———. 1988. *Die Wirtschaft der Gesellschaft*. Frankfurt am Main: Suhrkamp.

———. 1993. *Das Recht der Gesellschaft*. Frankfurt am Main: Suhrkamp.

———. 1995a. *Social Systems*. Stanford: Stanford University Press.

———. 1995b. 'Kausalität Im Süden'. *Soziale Systeme* 1: 7–28.

———. 2005. *Die Politik der Gesellschaft*. Frankfurt am Main: Suhrkamp.

———. 2008. *Die Soziologie Und Der Mensch*. 3rd edn. Wiesbaden: VS Verl. für Sozialwiss.

Mascareño, Aldo. 2012. *Die Moderne Lateinamerikas Weltgesellschaft, Region und funktionale Differenzierung*. Bielefeld: Transcript.

Mead, George Herbert. 1973. *Self, Language, and the World*. Austin: University of Texas Press.

Neves, Marcelo. 1992. *Verfassung und Positivität des Rechts in der peripheren Moderne: eine theoretische Betrachtung und Interpretation des Falls Brasilien*. Berlin: Duncker & Humblot.

Reuter, Peter. 2009. 'Systemic Violence in Drug Markets'. *Crime, Law and Social Change* 52(3): 275–84.

Stichweh, Rudolf. 2000. *Die Weltgesellschaft: Soziologische Analysen*. Auflage: 3. Frankfurt am Main: Suhrkamp Verlag.

Tilly, Charles. 1985. 'War Making and State Making as Organized Crime'. In *Bringing the State Back In*, by Dietrich Rueschemeyer and Theda Skocpol, 169–91. Cambridge University Press.

12 De-constitutionalising Latin America

Particularism and universalism in a constitutional perspective

Aldo Mascareño

Introduction

The tension in transnational constitutional theory between emerging constitutional orders in social systems and national constitutions is well-known (Teubner 2012, Neves 2013, Kjaer 2014). The dogmatic unity of domestic political constitutions, the hierarchy of norms and courts and the politicisation of conflicts in terms of local interests contrast with a rather weak institutionalisation of transnational norms, with the decentralised functioning of (mostly arbitral) courts and with the mainly technical character of conflicts in the transnational arena. The consequence is multiple collisions between transnational normative orders and domestic political imperatives in which state interests meet private actors in fields such as commerce, finance, sports and the Internet.

In the European region, supranational codifications in different social systems, harmonisation projects in critical areas and a complex structure of multilevel governance have been developed to deal with these collisions (Scharpf 2010). Certainly, this means neither a declining degree of conflict between transnational sectors and national interests, nor a state of harmony and total coherence. Instead, there is probably an increase in problems of co-ordination concerning the proliferation of solution-oriented systems of negotiation. Politically-guided co-ordination efforts have induced the European region to construct intermediate mechanisms, in which conflicts between emerging constitutional norms and politically-constituted domestic orders can be processed and decided not only politically but also technically – and, if not decided, at least publicly exposed as attributed responsibility. There is nothing comparable to this supranational architecture in others regions of world society – though systems operate globally and interact positively with culturally differentiated regions.

Latin America, for example, has a two-centuries-long constitutional tradition and an even longer process of integration to the systemic structures of world society – particularly in commerce, law, politics, education, art and even technology (Mascareño 2012). Nonetheless, there are definitely no supranational operating structures capable of co-ordinating nascent transnational sectors with national politics and domestic legal orders. As there is no *Latin American region* in a policy-based institutional sense, without intermediate regional institutions, state constitutionalism is less persuaded by transnational constitutionalism.

My hypothesis for explaining this fact is that normative particularism has prevailed in Latin American domestic constitutionalism. This particularism (emerging from political elites with a conservative or populist inspiration that aim to secure positions of political and economic power) collides with the normative universalism of sectorial constitutionalisation, suppressing any opportunity for a constructive institutional interpenetration and producing processes that de-differentiate systemic operations at local level. A dual approach is necessary to deal with this problem: on the one hand, the de-constitutionalisation of domestic normative particularism and, on the other, constitutive normative interpenetration with universalistic norms in emerging transnational constitutions.

My approach to describing the crucial stages of this argument starts with a broad characterisation of Latin America's entry into world society, aiming to illustrate its prevailing normative particularism, and continues with the consequences of that particularism for Latin American constitutional arrangements. Contrasting with this, I reconstruct the relationship between the necessary normative particularism of systemic closure and the universalistic character of sectorial constitutionalism by means of what I call *moments of universality*. Bearing this framework in mind, I then illustrate the problems of constitutional particularism and the collisions between national and transnational orders, using two politically opposed examples: the cases of Venezuela and of Chile. Finally, I present some concluding remarks.

Normative particularism in Latin American functional differentiation

Colonial institutions are at the root of how Latin America interpreted functional differentiation and the central definitions for the state-building process in the nineteenth century and put them into effect. On the one hand, the centralised decision-making structure in the colonial period promoted increasingly complex political and legal structures (procedures, rules, administrative specialisation, supervision mechanisms) that, on the other, guided the emerging functional differentiation, particularly in the economy, law and education (Pietschmann 1980, Véliz 1980, Ansaldi and Giordano 2012, Mascareño 2012). The centralisation of social operations in an incipient system of political functions calls in turn for the exclusion of competitive alternatives. We know that stratification prevailed during the colonial period as a generalised form of societal differentiation. That meant that the differentiation of privileges was institutionalised, decisions were concentrated at the higher levels and no differentiation was drawn between religion dogmatics and socially generalised normative principles – in a word: extended normative particularism.

Colonial particularism is rooted in a contractual mechanism developed by the Spanish monarchy to control the mediaeval *Cortes* and centralise power. The mechanism was called *pactismo*:

> *Pactismo* described a constitutional regime in which the monarchy obtained licence to legislate by acknowledging in contractual fashion certain private legal and judicial privileges existing in society, in which the passing of particular laws was tied to clear preconditions and redress of particular grievances, and in which delegates of privately privileged groups granted taxes to the monarchy in return for singular acts of redress and for the preservation of particular customary rights.
>
> (Thornhill 2011: 113)

In this sense, the *Cortes* were not representative bodies. Rather, they 'acted primarily as a particularistic bargaining agent and source of judicial arbitration' (Thornhill 2011: 114). Reforms introduced by the Bourbon kings in the eighteenth century aimed to normalise this political particularism, at least administratively, and to achieve the indifferentiation of politics and religion by means of a traditional legal pluralism (Bethell 1991, Benton 2005). However, the political and symbolic density of the Catholic Church and the pressures brought to bear by particular groups on the foundations of the social order prevailed through informal networks and mechanisms for co-opting representatives. As a consequence, particularism succeeded as a political force, since it defined a style of political action. In Thornhill's view: 'the monarchy did not succeed in elevating itself above its late-feudal structure of residual particularism, and a high level of governmental privatism remained a feature of Spanish government until the twentieth century' (Thornhill 2011: 116).

Nonetheless, in Latin America, the Bourbon reforms became relevant to integrating local economic operations in global commerce, albeit with particularistic precautions. The *Reglamento para el Comercio Libre de España y las Indias* (Rules of Free Trade Between Spain and the Indies 1778) promoted free trade, instituting Latin America as an economic region for the Crown. The aim was not the welfare of the Indies, but to counter England's power in colonial trade. There were certainly no significant commercial advantages accruing from this peripheral position, yet inclusion in world economic relations connected concrete operations to expectations of monetised interchange that were crucial for the differentiation of an autonomous economic system in Latin America, particularly during the Republican period in the nineteenth century. Publicists such as D.F. Sarmiento (2003), J.B. Alberdi (1957) and A. Bello (1995), highly influential intellectuals in the political and legal organisation of the state in Latin America, have supported free trade as a means for welfare and the progress of civilisation. Nonetheless, the construction of legal systems remains a key element in the process of state building and the operation of functional differentiation in Latin America.

The nineteenth-century's revolutionary processes did not deconstruct the concentration of political and economic power inherited from the colonial period. The Latin American countries experienced no bourgeois revolution, but a movement of political elites (*criollos*, a generation of European offspring born in Latin American territory) driven mainly by particularistic economic motives. Well equipped with the political semantics of modern Europe (liberty, equality, the rule of law, democracy), the emerging nation-states confronted a *constitutional moment* without the concrete experiences from which these political concepts stem (Mascareño 2013a). The origins of symbolic constitutionalisation (Neves 2007) – namely, a constitutional text expressing universal contents but without factual efficacy – can be found here. In this case, the circle of the co-originality of political power and law, which characterises democratic states and stabilises universalistic normative expectations, is not completed. Politics and law are always open to particularistic influences coming from cultural communities, local networks and religious interests. Elsewhere (Mascareño 2010, 2012), I have interpreted this as a process of de-differentiation of political power upon legal validity. By constituting the core element of the Republican period, this operational openness of politics and law towards non-proceduralised external influences led to a concentric organisation of functional differentiation in Latin America. That means:

a the instrumentalisation of the state's apparatus by particularistic interests and groups;
b the extra-political dissemination of particularistic power towards non-political sectors (arts, education, science, family);
c episodic obstructions of the emerging systemic autonomy in non-political sectors and subordination to particularistic politics;
d the development of stratification and reciprocity networks that constrain public access to the outcomes of functional differentiation; and
e an increasing tension between national particularistic politics and transnational operations of autonomous functional systems.

This offers a two-sided depiction of the Latin American region. On the one hand, the events of world society include Latin America mainly by means of commerce and the circulation of universalistic political ideas. On the other, this inclusion in world society features particular traits that define the institutional form of the state and how Latin America deals with functional differentiation, i.e.:

a oligarchic elites create a constitutional state with low political participation and high rates of exclusion;
b the constitutional order is hamstrung by tension between universalistic expectations (inclusion, democratic participation, republican virtues) and the state's capture by the hegemonic particularistic interests of the elites; and
c as a consequence, the differentiation of social systems has to deal with the extra-political dissemination of particularistic power aimed at instrumentalising the outcomes of multiple social systems by means of stratification and reciprocity networks.

Constitutional consequences

This complex socio-historical setting produced three main constitutional conceptions in nineteenth-century Latin America:

a conservative models;
b populist models; and
c liberal constitutions (Gargarella 2004).

Although they are certainly ideal types, in the origins of Latin American constitutionalism they match rather well with the concrete constitutional projects of the nascent states and, in so doing, also express different forms of normative particularism.

The conservative model focuses on the political defence of a particular conception of good provided by Catholicism. In this setting, the coercive power of the state is employed to preserve a particular moral ordering of society, to the exclusion of alternative views. Modern human rights are deemed to be adaptable to the natural value scale held by Catholic elites, who consider themselves to be the representatives of higher moral values and consequently argue that 'the majority of the people are not adequately prepared to realize those valuable conceptions of the good life' (Gargarella 2004: 144). The constitutional order is therefore built on a fundamental exclusion of different values and practices, or – at best – they are categorised in a scale of substantive moral correctness. Institutionally, this implies a centralised power structure without the interference of excluded or subordinated sectors, namely: weak parliaments, a strong presidential figure and a senate of landowners. The Chilean Constitutions of 1823 and 1833, the Ecuadorian Constitutions of 1842 and 1851 and the constitutional conventions held in Mexico (1857) and Argentina (1853) can be identified with this conservative constitutional conception. In the twentieth century, a paradigmatic case of conservative constitutionalism is provided by the Chilean Constitution of 1980.

While the conservative model defends Catholic particularism, the populist model preserves the particularism of the *pueblo*. Here, the *pueblo* is the ultimate principle of legitimacy and authority, in whose name other democratic institutions are deemed to be of secondary relevance (the senate, the executive and the judiciary). Even bicameral legislation is suspected of dividing popular will (Gargarella 2004: 147). Checks and balances are not part of the vocabulary of populist constitutionalism. The particularism of Latin American populist constitutions lies precisely in the unilateral view of the decision-making process and the symbolic and practical identification of the will of the majority with the will of the populist leader. The infallibility of the *volonté générale* becomes the infallibility of a man (or a woman). In this sense, the populist constitutional model finds common ground with European totalitarianism (Germani 1981). Latin American cases of this constitutional programme include Mexico's first Constitution (1814) and its revolutionary Constitution of 1917, the Cuban Constitution of 1976 and the reforms of 1992, as well as the Venezuelan Constitution of 1999 and in some respects also the Bolivian Constitution of 2009.

The liberal model comes closer to universalistic values and democratic institutional settings, which may explain why it is far from easy to find concrete expressions of this constitutional practice in Latin America. Liberal constitutionalism promises an autonomous though interdependent institutional setting, a neutralisation of the public sphere from moral particularisms and a limitation of state power, particularly with regard to the paradoxical mechanism of the *constitutional state of exception*, applied mostly in conservative settings as a way of preserving elitist privileges under unstable political conditions (Gargarella 2004, Loveman and Lira 2002). The first Venezuelan Constitution of 1811, the Peruvian Constitutions of 1856 and 1867 and the modern Brazilian Constitution of 1988 are good examples of liberal programmes.

In comparing Latin American with US constitutionalism, M. Schor (2006) elaborates an interesting argument explaining the roots of Latin American constitutional particularism:

> The elites or framers who shaped Latin America's constitutions believed that economic development had to occur before the masses could be allowed to participate in democracy. As a consequence, these elites opted for malleable constitutions . . . The formal rules of the game had to be malleable if elites were to retain power, but the consequences have been, as Madison surmised, 'calamitous'. Every change in political leadership is a potential constitutional crisis if the selection of new leaders means that the fundamental rules of the game might be changed with the adoption of a new constitution.
>
> (Schor 2006: 7)

In Schor's view, nineteenth-century Latin American elites were aware of problems of exclusion at the beginning of the Republican period – and were also aware of the potential political conflicts that might emerge from the dissolution of the institutionalised privileges of the colonial period. For that reason, and in order to prevent social turbulence, stratification (the concentration of power and money in the higher strata) had to be preserved somehow. The method chosen was strong presidentialism, supported by political and economic elites. However, strong presidentialism fails to stabilise normative constitutional structures for the very reason that it depends more on political (and personal) interests than on rules. Constitutional rules become an instrument for exercising and maintaining power rather than a force for curtailing political excess. The high number of constitutions enacted in the various countries of Latin America in the last two centuries reveals the primacy of political will over constitutional rules (15 constitutions in Peru, 18 in Bolivia, 20 in Ecuador, 16 in Venezuela). Instead of adapting political practice to universalistic rules, constitutions are adapted to particularistic political interests.

As a consequence, the relationship between publicly generalised normative expectations and the constitution weakens: 'The people had little trust in constitutions that could be changed so readily. Without popular support, the constitution could not provide the institutional matrix needed for political accommodations to be reached' (Schor 2006: 19). Trust in particularistic networks with the power and connections to bypass the law – or even promote and enforce a new constitution – seems to be far more efficient than institutional trust.

Constitutional particularism in Latin America thus has substantial historical roots. It is not a question of an essentialist cultural identity of *being Latin American*, as some scholars have argued (see Véliz 1994, Morandé 1987, Parker 1996), but a sociological one. The paradox is that particularism is at odds with constitutionalism in terms of promoting and sustaining universal values. Considering the pre-eminence of particular political interests over a government of rules, Latin American constitutionalism is more inclined to mean the de-constitutionalisation of the social order, i.e. the primacy of coercive power rather than universalistic rules as a means for managing contingencies and reducing complexity. This explains the continuous politicisation of functional systems in most Latin American countries, the obstacles to building up regional structures for supranational co-ordination and the problems encountered in dealing with the universalistic normative principles of emerging transnational sectorial constitutionalisation.

Normative universalism in transnational sectorial constitutions

There is no doubt about the problems that beset functional differentiation in the construction of a socially integrated world society. N. Luhmann warned about this succinctly and lucidly:

> Today, the problem is much worse than before. We may continue with our habits and resort to moral claims that are as justified as ever. But who will hear these complaints and who can react to them, if society is not in control of itself? And what can we expect when we know that the very success of the function systems depends upon neglect? When evolution has differentiated systems whose very complexity depends upon operational closure (and the paradigmatic case is, of course, the human brain), how can we expect to include all kinds of concerns into the system? . . . The point is that we are not in a phase of *posthistoire* but, on the contrary, in a phase of turbulent evolution without predictable outcome.
>
> (Luhmann 1997: 74–5, 76)

If the success of systemic functioning depends upon neglect, then we are confronted with a major problem of systemic integration and, consequently, with the highest barrier that transnational sectorial constitutionalisation has to overcome. Co-ordination by systemic indifference (negative co-ordination) is helpful up to the point where the symbolic production of a given system exceeds its own mechanisms for controlling the environmental consequences of its functioning (Willke 2014). Beyond that point, only the stop-rules against transferential operations of over-productive systemic practices may have positive results in affected systems. However, these stop-rules are developed unevenly in different systemic settings. The economy reacts to political interventions quiet powerfully and efficiently, but science has to adapt itself to the politically-defined funding agenda. Intimate relations have increasingly developed barriers against religious internal control (at least in Western societies and even for religious people), but little can be done against the fact that most of the daily communications in families deal with money issues, followed by events in the media.

Systemic indifference is definitely a powerful mechanism for systems to become autonomous. It enables environmental noises to be discarded, so that systems can focus on their own operations. However, this turns out to be problematic, as 'noises' also arise from crises in other systemic practices. The economy may remain indifferent to inequity, as long as the wealthy few are able to point to the positive value of the economic code and the non-wealthy majority watches passively. Equally, politics may also be indifferent to mafia networks, as long as these preserve some order in their territories, reduce unemployment with their illegal activities and pay bribes to politicians. By looking the other way, systems continue with *business as usual*, while the crisis in the environment develops slowly but surely.

The only intermediate conclusion that can be drawn from this is that of particularism as a normative mode of systemic operation. As a socio-political concept, particularism has a well-defined meaning:

> 'Particularism' describes the attitude [Mentalität] upon which political values and programmes of single social or political groups, belonging to a political or social whole, are based. Such groups defend and concede priority to autonomy, independence and singular interests of the parties rather than to general interests, though they are seldom prepared for a real disengagement (separatism).
>
> (Brunner et al. 2004: 735)

Certainly, I am considering systems here neither as social groups, nor as promoters of political intentions, but at a semantic level they definitely construct normative orders that concede priority to their own autonomy: the autonomy of the Central Bank in finance, judicial independence in law, sovereignty in state politics, the inviolability of the private sphere in personal relations, of sources in the media, of confession in religion, originality in the arts and knowledge production in science. For each system, normative expectations in other fields (or in society as a whole) are irrelevant or, at least, of secondary significance when compared with their own internal reproduction. This code obviously applies universally: the economy functions wherever money pays, politics works wherever decisions find acceptance, but a system's normative construction focuses primarily on defending (and expanding!) its borders counterfactually: systems react against external intervention (negative freedom) and promote the symbolic growth of their own semantic discourses and operational practices (positive freedom). This normative construction functions as a means for justifying their autonomy in semantic terms, for elaborating the substantial, value-loaded dimension of programmes, for motivating the selection of individuals and for excluding alternative concerns or redirecting them towards the system's own operational code.

It is true that clashes between systems do not originate in norms, but in colliding operations. Norms are a by-product of systemic operations and not the other way around. Yet, the expressive side of each conflict has to be performed through norms: Should a journalist reveal her sources when uncovering a political scandal? Should the authorities of Central Banks be criminally liable for financial crises? Is a politician's private sexual life significant when he is running for public office? Such conflicts are normally presented as ethical problems and consequently treated with ethical solutions that usually leave the fundamental operational problems untouched. The blind spot of ethical reflections is that particularistic norms in conflict are in fact operational collisions between autonomous systems. The constitutional question aims to deal with these problems in an operative and universalistic normative fashion.

The difference between universalism and particularism in sociology has been described originally by Talcott Parsons, in action-theoretical terms, as a contingency problem:

> In confronting any situation, the actor faces the dilemma whether to treat the objects in the situation in accordance with a general norm covering *all* objects in that class or whether to treat them in accordance with their standing in some particular relationship to him or his collectivity, independently of the objects' subsumibility under a general norm. This dilemma can be resolved by giving primacy to norms or value standards which are

> maximally generalized and which have a basis for validity transcending *any* specific system of relationships in which ego is involved, or by giving primacy to value standards which allot priority to standards *integral* to the *particular* relationship system in which the actor is involved with the object.
>
> (Parsons and Shils 1962: 81–2)

By calling the difference an 'actor's dilemma', Parsons emphasises the fact that the selection of norms in a given system is contingent upon an actor's decision: that both alternatives are neither impossible nor necessary. That is to say that particularistic norms emerging from operational closure can be countered by universalistic normative expectations, 'which' in Parson's words, 'have a basis for validity transcending *any* specific system of relationships'. In transnational constitutionalism this is the role of law:

> Social systems are never entirely autonomous: there are always points of heteronomy. If this externalization now occurs with the help of constitutions, the moment of heteronomy comes when the social system refers to law. The 'self' of the social system is defined heteronomously by legal norms and it can then define itself autonomously thereby. While the unity of a social system develops through the concatenation of its own operations, its identity is created in its constitution through the re-entry of external legal descriptions into its own self-description.
>
> (Teubner 2012: 65)

By means of interpenetration (not coupling!), law provides the system with universalistic normative expectations, helping it to construct its own identity. As the system has no inbuilt fundamental norm that can do this, the problem is confronted with an expansion of fundamental rights into autonomous systems (Habermas 2001, Höffe 2004, Ladeur and Viellechner 2008). In state politics, fundamental rights protect individuals against the de-differentiating power of state interventions, thus preserving functional differentiation (Luhmann 1991, 1999, Corsi 2002, Thornhill 2010). In systemic politics, two considerations are crucial. Firstly, systems should 'counteract self-destructive tendencies and [secondly] limit damage to their social, human and natural environments' (Teubner 2012: 10). By solving the first problem, the system equalises its own risks; by solving the second one, it protects its own conditions of possibility. Achieving this results in (self-)transcending normative particularism and encountering a norm for general interest, inside the system, yet provided externally. This can be called a *moment of normative universalism* (Mascareño 2013b), meaning, on the one hand, the construction inside the system of general normative principles that are applicable to every social context, even globally, and, on the other, the specification of those principles to the problems arising from the self-destructive tendencies of a particular system and their consequences for the environment.

Certainly, the existence of universal normative expectations inside the system is not enough for either preventing or controlling damage: institutionalisation by law is required (Teubner 2012: 126). Yet institutionalisation demands a prior recognition of the generalised correctness enclosed in the universal norm. Universal principles such as *good faith and fair dealing* in the field of transnational commerce, for example, can be translated into legal operations easily; however, they do not arise from legal operations, but from reflexive processes in commercial practices aiming to stabilise the self-destructive tendency of commerce of taking unfair advantage of the other party (Mascareño and Mereminskaya 2013). *Prudence* plays a comparable role in finance: in its simplest and most original form, 'only profits made at the balance sheet date may be included' (Hulle 1996: 377). Cases such as Enron and the subprime crisis show how important the norm is, while also revealing the significance of the modern difference between a micro-prudential approach – preventing the high costs of default of individual financial institutions – and a macro-prudential one which 'recognizes the importance of general equilibrium effects and seeks to safeguard the financial system as a whole' (Festl-Pell 2012: 16). *Fair play* is the equivalent norm in sports, aiming to set limits to potential extreme manifestations of sport's code of competition and its endangering consequences for itself and particularly the human environment (doping, corruption, violence). While sport's morality was based on honour in ancient societies (Dunning 1971), it is grounded on fairness in modern society – and has been at least since the nineteenth century. In this vein, fairness in sports reflects the political principle of equality, namely, 'that everyone shall have the opportunity to compete, and that the conditions for competition should be the same for all contestants' (Renson 2009: 7).

For transnational constitutionalisation to come into existence, these universal principles need to be validated by legal decisions, but there would be nothing to validate without a sense of universal correctness inside the system. This sensitivity is not transferred into the system by law, but developed incrementally in systemic practices connecting their own operations with relevant events in the environment as a consequence of functional needs (Kjaer 2012). In other words, systems learn cognitively to act normatively or, at least, to hold this expectation in some fundamental respect involving their own self-endangerment and some major environmental consequences of their functioning. Systems thus learn to act counterfactually, as long as they become constitutionalised:

> Counterfactual objectives are universal in nature, such as the striving toward the realization of non-discriminatory free trade, free and uncensored global access to the Internet, basic worldwide access to health, and not only a formal, but also a *de facto* inclusion of all humans under the umbrella of the human rights regime.
>
> (Kjaer 2013: 799)

In doing this, the interpenetration between the *specific system* and the *law system* contributes new expressions of normative universalism to the law, while law in return provides the validation of normative discourses to the particular system. The most relevant consequence is that the specific system and the sectorial constitutionalisation become normatively entangled – by means of those moments of normative universalism – with constitutional democracy (via fundamental rights), with universal principles of the international system of states (through norms of *jus cogens*) and with the supranational level of the members of the human species (by means of human rights).

The question now is what happens when this systemic global setting of particularistic constitutive norms and self-limiting universalistic constitutionalisation meets the particularistic social contexts of Latin American constitutionalism.

Constitutional particularism in Latin America

Considering the constitutional models in Latin America (conservative, populist and liberal) discussed above and the normative constructions in transnational constitutionalism, I shall now examine the consequences on functional differentiation and transnational constitutionalisation of two paradigmatic cases: the Venezuelan case, as a model of populist constitutionalism and politicisation of the social order, and the Chilean case, as an example of the monetisation of functional differentiation through a neoliberal model that combines conservative values and individualistic liberal perspectives on economic organisation.

Venezuela

On 25 April 1999, three months after Chávez was sworn in as president, Venezuelan citizens had to answer a simple but crucial question: 'Do you want a National Constituent Assembly for the purpose of transforming the state and creating a new legal order guaranteeing the effective functioning of a participatory and social democracy?' Of the whole electoral register, 37.6 per cent took part in the referendum, and 87.7 per cent of those expressing a vote answered yes. After electing representatives for the National Constituent Assembly, the new organ dissolved the National Congress, which had been elected in 1998, and introduced two new state-powers: the Citizen and the Electoral. The new Constitution came into force on 15 December 1999 (Arráiz 2012).

Since then, transformations for Venezuelan society have been profound and convoluted – institutionally, politically (see Díaz 2012) and semantically (see Torres 2011). The new Constitution replaced the liberal Constitution of 1961, which had no mechanisms for a radical constitutional change, but only for amendments. For this reason, the Venezuelan Supreme Court of Justice was called upon – with Chávez already in office – to pronounce on his call for a Constituent Assembly. Needless to say, the Court's decision was reached under strong political pressure from the populistic new government. On the other hand, the judges had to face public opinion that had generally lost faith in the old institutional model in force since 1961. Against this backdrop, two major points in the Court's decision are indicative of things to come:

a the Court established that the constituent power (the *pueblo*) was 'prior and superior to the juridical order'; and
b that its power is not exhausted by transferring competencies to institutions or government (Colón 2011: 371).

The first argument raised authority to a mystical status beyond any positive law, as in totalitarian regimes, while the second argument introduced the possibility of a permanent change of the constitutional order. For a government aiming to reconstruct the whole social order, this swept away all restrictions on the permanent politicisation of social spheres without any institutional balances. The best method for achieving this was the so-called 'enabling acts', a sort of licence (a state of exception) issued by the National Assembly to the President, allowing him to rule by decree for a defined period (between six and 18 months). The National Assembly passed five such enabling acts from 1999 to 2013.

A good example of this mechanism is the 2007 Act, which authorised the President to intervene in the following areas:

a the structure of the state;
b popular participation;
c values in public functions;
d the economy, aiming to create a new economic and social model;
e finance and taxes;
f public protection and the police;
g science and technology;
h territorial organisation;
i national security and defence;
j infrastructure, transport and services; and
k energy (República Bolivariana de Venezuela 2007).

The 2013 Act, when Nicolás Maduro was already President, introduced, among others, the fight against corruption and the promotion of socialist ethics and morality, the fight against foreign powers aiming to 'destroy the homeland' economically, politically and through the media, the consolidation of social justice in order to achieve a good life and happiness for the Venezuelan people and the strengthening of the planned, rationalised and regulated character of economic and financial matters (República Bolivariana de Venezuela 2013).

This concentric, constitutionalised form of politicisation of the whole social order is at odds with the decentralised character of functional differentiation and transnational constitutionalisation. This can be analysed both operationally and normatively. Operationally, while the transnational constitutionalisation of functional differentiation stresses law's primacy over systemic politics, in constitutional populism that primacy is conferred on politics by means of a self-enacting, non-procedural form of authority. There is no interpenetration between law and politics that could validate political decisions. Validity does not come from the law, but from a semantic construction generated in politics itself: the mystical authority of the *pueblo*. By drawing on this, politics condenses and de-differentiates the symbols of power and validity, thus instrumentalising legal operations via political decisions. There is no way to escape from this artificial self-completeness, for constituent power is just the symbol of constituent politics and government puts this into effect beyond any positive form of law.

At the normative level, this operational unity of power and law leads to radical particularism. There are no external parameters – such as legally sanctioned fundamental rights that might erect barriers against politicisation – to confront and counter decisions. On the contrary, the particularism of *nation and pueblo* is constructed and presented as an external, superior value, against which political decisions can be assessed. Yet there is no *pueblo* outside politics. The universalism of the *pueblo* is much like religious universalism: it claims to be universal without considering that it has no universal acceptance from outside. That is why normative acceptance must be enacted forcefully in constitutional populism: by expropriating companies in the name of a widespread 'social interest' (Azzellini 2009), by closing or controlling corporate media (Dinneen 2012), or by using schools, organisations and workplaces to instruct Venezuelans in socialist values that reject the 'individualistic ideology of capitalism' (Burbach and Piñeiro 2007).

It follows that several incompatibilities arise when constitutional populism meets transnational constitutionalism:

a between a nation state's politically centralised operations and the polycontextural autonomous operations of social systems;
b between the unpredictable particularism of the *pueblo*'s social interest and the substantive and procedural universalism of transnational constitutionalism;
c between the unilateralism of decisions in populist constitutionalism and the interpenetrating balancing act of legal universalism and systemic self-limitation in transnational constitutionalisation; and
d between the politicisation of functional differentiation at national level and the constitutionalisation of systemic particularisms in the transnational arena.

Expropriations, aggressive speeches against 'foreign powers', the aspiration of controlling global information flows and the revival of the semantics of 'endogenous development' proposed by Cepal in the mid-twentieth century as a means for countering the uneven global distribution of wealth are all ways of expressing the incompatibilities between Venezuela's constitutional populism and the transnational constitutionalisation of functional systems.

In these circumstances, the only way out seems to be to de-constitutionalise the particularism of the unity between *pueblo* and government, so that the relationship between politics and law can evolve from indifferentiation to interpenetration. The Chilean case adds new insight into this.

Chile

The present Chilean Constitution was promulgated in 1980 under Pinochet's dictatorship (1973–90). As in the Venezuelan case, Chilean citizens also 'approved' this Constitution in a fraudulent referendum held on 11 September 1980 with 67.5 per cent voting 'yes' and 29.6 per cent no. After the coup d'état against Salvador Allende's constitutional government on 11 September 1973, the military junta (whose members were three generals of the armed forces and the director general of the police) assumed that the Constitution in force until 1973 (the 1925 Constitution) was the root of the political decay that led to the coup. For this reason, the junta commissioned a select group of right-wing conservative jurists to formulate the draft for a new Constitution that would change not only the country's political organisation but also its whole social order. The text was called a 'draft' because prior to its promulgation it had to be revised, modified and approved by the junta and, as planned, submitted to popular decision in a referendum. Nevertheless, the junta did not act in a legal vacuum from 1973 to 1980. In 1974, it passed the Estatuto Jurídico de la Junta de Gobierno (Legal Statutes of the Government Junta), which invested the dictator as 'Supreme Chief of the Nation' and head of the executive and the legislative. Yet it was the 1980 Constitution that reframed Chile institutionally in a founding act, turning the military junta into a (counter-)revolutionary constituent power (Valenzuela 1997, Garretón 2000).

The social transformations produced by the dictatorship and its Constitution pointed in precisely the opposite direction to the Venezuelan case. While Venezuela's pre-Chávez 1961 institutional framework was designed to exclude left-wing politics, the Chilean coup reacted against the socialist project of Allende's government by imposing an apparently contradictory, two-sided depiction of social relations: conservative Catholicism in the value system and neoliberalism in the economic system. In normative terms, the Chilean constitution is a paradigmatic case of Gargarella's (2004) conservative model: the coercive power of the state is used to promote and defend the particularistic worldview of the conservative elite. As stated in the Declaration of Principles of the Military Junta in 1974 (a preliminary basis for the constitutional draft), 'the Chilean government respects the Christian conception of man and society . . . Man has natural rights prior to the state, rights that arise from the very nature of human beings, namely, from the Creator' (Gobierno de Chile 1974). This rather mediaeval conception of Christianity is expressed in the Constitution in terms of naturalised forms of authority (hierarchical authority, protected democracy), legitimacy (strong presidentialism, the restriction of pluralism), family (as the 'fundamental core of society'), property (as a natural right) and human beings (as equals in dignity and rights) (Bassa and Viera 2008). Politically, however, neither the centrality of human beings nor the significance of the family were of any service in avoiding torture, persecution and murder. Instead, the dictatorship 'drew on Catholic political thought both to justify the coup and to argue that the regime's attempts to privatize and decentralize the economy were applications of papal social principles, particularly the principle of subsidiarity enunciated by Pope Pius XI in 1931' (Sigmund 1986: 33).

The principle of subsidiarity is of crucial significance in explaining both a sort of invisibility of transnational orders in Chilean politics and the adoption of neoliberal policies in the economic field. The original Catholic version of the principle reads as follows: 'That which individuals can make on their own and with their own strength should not be taken away and given to the community; the same shall apply to smaller and lesser societies or groups with respect to their relationship with larger and higher societies or groups' (Pius 1931: §XX). In this view, a 'higher society' means the state. The Catholic version rests on a hierarchical conception of an ordered society in which the family is the first social unit and the state the major one. The state thus includes families and intermediate organisations, co-ordinating them as a whole and fulfilling the functions they cannot perform. As Pius himself argued in his encyclical, this classical corporatist conservative view is authoritarian at heart: 'Therefore, those in power should be sure that the more perfectly a hierarchic order is kept among the various associations, in observance of the principle of "subsidiary function", the stronger will be authority and social efficiency and the happier and more prosperous the condition of the State' (Pius 1931: §80).

A state-controlled social order has no time for transnationality: it aims to keep the autonomy of social systems within limits and to control it heteronomously with compulsory membership and comprehensive regulations (Teubner 2012). In this vein, there is neither a chance to give serious consideration to the formation of private regimes, nor the possibility to acknowledge that the validity of normative orders that apply beyond the state may influence intermediate associations within the state. No room can therefore be expected to be made for the legitimacy of collisions between national and transnational orders to be accepted. There is always just one and the same solution: the supremacy of the state prevails. Yet Chile's authoritarian corporatism did foster a certain degree of autonomy for lower levels in the realms of 'less important things' that would otherwise have distracted the state from its main functions (internal and external security). This paved the way for liberalism in the economic arena.

The Chilean case was characterised by a peculiar combination of authoritarian politics in the area of public affairs (controlling the media and unions, proscribing political parties, instituting political persecution and torture, banning dissident art, intervening in universities, controlling community associations) and liberal policies in the economic field. As Hilbink argues: 'While this model had roots in Catholic, corporatist thought, its "non-partisan" pretence and its focus on order and stability fit nicely with the mindset and need of the neoliberal economists that were empowered to restructure the economy' (Hilbink 2009: 790). For the right-wing civilians supporting the coup and the dictatorship (and clearly for the military), the socialist experience of Allende's government was considered traumatic. In addition to political and ideological reasons, the intensification of the agrarian reform, the nationalisation of industries, price control and the general ambition to build a planned economy were viewed as the main causes for Chile's economic stagnation. The coup was the opportunity for a radical change in economic matters. In this sense, between 1973 and 1989, Chilean society came close to reproducing the conditions of a controlled experiment, with no opposition of subjects, coercive eradication of deviant behaviour, a 'fresh start' in politics and the economy and a constitutionally established hypothesis: the less the state intervenes, the more efficient the economy.

Chile's constitution thus amounted to an economic constitution, with an *economic public order*. The economy's autopoiesis could develop freely, not only nationally but also transnationally, contradicting the structure of authoritarian corporatism and producing a radical move away from the trend of inward development and imported substitutive industrialisation that had held sway in Latin America since 1930. The constitutionalisation of the economy as an autonomous system was also an innovation in constitutional doctrine: 'the fact that the new constitutional charter would include not just political aspects, but also social and economic ones, would make it the first *full constitution* (*constitución plena*) Chile ever had. After all, every previous constitution had been *only political*' (Couso 2011: 408). Transferring crucial aspects of economic operations into constitutional terms grants the economy not only protection against political interventions (negative freedom), but also massive symbolic power to explore alternatives of interpenetration with the environment (positive freedom). The problem, however, was that the *full constitution* was not really full: other social fields were not constitutionalised, since they lacked both the constitutional protection and symbolic incentives to look for interpenetrations with the environment. Indeed, the problem was not the constitutionalisation of the economy itself, but the fact that, in the absence of the constitutionalisation of other sectors, the symbolic expansionist tendencies of economic communications was free to act without restraint on non-constitutionalised systems such as education (primary, secondary and superior), health care, basic services, social services, transport systems and pension systems. The consequence of this asymmetric constitutionalisation of social systems was the monetisation of society.

When society is monetised it means primarily that the symbolic medium of money defines access, but also crucial operations in non-economic systems. Concretely, monetisation took the form of the execution of an extensive programme of privatisation and deregulation of health care, pensions, schools and universities, telecommunications, public transport, basic services and even public order, with private guards in private and public places (see Meller 1992, Teichman 2001, Schamis 2002). In all these sectors, access to services and particularly their quality depends on payments made by individuals or families. The more they pay, the better the system operates in terms of efficiency (costs/benefits), efficacy (achieving its goals) and opportunity (timing its outcomes). Prices thus become a medium for operational quality in different social systems, triggering alternative operational procedures that result in clearly stratified outcomes of the same general kind.

This leads to two main consequences. On the one hand, if the quality of outcomes depends on payments and economic functioning is constitutionalised, then the most relevant social effect of this is the constitutional legitimation of stratification. As in stratified societies, privileges are legally and semantically institutionalised, the asymmetric constitutionalisation of social systems produces stratification by monetising both the operational quality of particular functions and personal access to its outcomes. Inequality thus becomes constitutionalised indirectly, by means of the constitutionalisation of the economy and of the constitutionally legitimised de-differentiation of other systems. On the other hand, Chile's constitutionalisation of the economy collided with sectorial constitutionalisation in terms of the restrictive dimension of transnational economic constitutions. Restrictive mechanisms in transnational constitutions ought to restrain both excessive systemic growth and damage to the social, natural and human environment. When tackling the case of Chile, we are dealing with a national constitution that sets no barriers against economic expansion.

Certainly, the transnational economic practice of the Chilean economy has been 'civilised' in recent decades, particularly by international agreements, contracts and the country's membership of global economic fora. On the other hand, since the political system returned to democracy in 1990, selected regulations and supervisory instances have provided at least a procedural framework for dealing with the *economic public order*. But the constitutional character of the economy and the weaknesses of its restrictive functions still remain. Envisioned constitutional changes should, therefore, include the de-constitutionalisation of particularistic Catholic values and, if not a de-constitutionalisation of the economy, at least a constitutionalisation of the universalistic normative expectations protecting other systems' autonomy, as well as a sensitivity to damage in the social, natural and human environment.

Conclusion

Like most of the Western world, Latin America embarked on the process of functional differentiation as a colonial periphery. Its position was a paradox: the region became part of world society, but played a subordinated role in it. This produced a permanent double tension between the global differentiation of functional systems and the regional concretisation of systemic operations, on the one hand, and between universalistic norms of world society and normative particularism of local and regional provenience on the other. In colonial structures, this tension had been solved in favour of a concentration of political power in the hands of Spanish elites and their particular semantic worldviews. The transition to independent states in the nineteenth century reproduced these patterns, but changed the actors, as the Spanish elites were replaced by local oligarchic elites that, in structural terms, built a highly exclusionary state with strong presidentialism and low political participation and, in normative terms, captured the state's apparatus with their hegemonic particularistic interests.

Constitutionalism does not sit well with strong presidentialism or with normative particularism. On the one hand, while constitutionalism aims to achieve a government of rules, presidentialism relies on political will and short-term interests. Accordingly, public trust is redirected from structures to persons, so that constitutions are not in a position to represent publicly generalised normative expectations. As a consequence, their legitimisation weakens. On the other hand, particularistic commitment becomes an alternative when universal constitutional norms have a limited or definitely no practical efficacy. In fact, normative particularism prevails in Latin American constitutionalism, in conservative Catholic constitutions or in populist constitutions. Liberal constitutionalism is a rather unusual experience in Latin American politics.

The question arises as to whether there is any chance that transnational constitutionalism can tackle Latin America's particularistic constitutionalism. There is no doubt about the particularism of its social systems: the code has primacy over environmental considerations that take priority over their own autonomy. Clashes and collisions between systems originate predominantly in this indifference towards the environment. The constitutional question reacts to this from a universalistic point of view, aiming to build an interpenetrating relationship between colliding systems and law so as to avoid both the self-destructive tendencies of functional systems and the damage they cause to their social, natural and human environment.

By elaborating on the cases of Venezuela (populist constitutionalisation) and Chile (conservative-liberal constitutionalisation), I have shown that the universalistic normative expectations in transnational sectorial constitutionalisation can hardly be reconciled with a particularistic domestic constitutionalisation. In Venezuela, constitutional populism identifies power and law with government, thus producing a strong *politicisation* of the whole society that depends on a particularistic political will correspondingly fictionalised and managed by the semantic of the *pueblo*. In the Chilean case, a complex and contradictory constitutional structure is observed. On the one hand, conservative authoritarian corporatism does not recognise normative orders beyond the state that influence domestic affairs; transnational constitutionalism thus becomes a rather fictitious problem. On the other hand, the national constitutionalisation of the economy produces an asymmetric interplay between different functional systems, resulting in a *monetisation* of the whole society and a constitutionalisation of social inequalities. The restrictive function of the transnational economic constitution – which is actually incompletely developed at present – has little chance against this.

Certainly, the restrictive function of constitutions is not limited to transnational constitutionalisation. Limiting political power by means of fundamental rights has been always the main goal of constitutionalisation. However, achieving this demands the effective translation of universalistic normative expectations into valid law. When constitutions are captured by particularistic interests and normative worldviews of political elites from a populist-authoritarian or conservative background, as in the cases of Venezuela and Chile, the restrictive function turns into a limitation of universalistic norms. That means a severe restriction in the ability of functional systems to incorporate the consequences of their own functioning for the social, natural and human environment. Without universalistic principles acting inside the system, indifference and neglect are the normal condition.

In this sense, a de-constitutionalisation of constitutional particularism is required in order to co-ordinate functional autonomy with environmental concerns. The continuous production of major social crises and catastrophes is an indicator of how far away that goal remains. Crises are definitely a normal condition in contemporary complex world society. As long as constitutional structures at national or transnational level can effectively stabilise their restrictive function, they will provide a significant antidote against escalating crises turning into catastrophes that alter the whole social order. A stable constitutional setting helps put a stop to crises before this tipping point is reached. The example of the current financial crisis illustrates the dramatic consequences of the absence (or at least weakness) of this restrictive constitutional function in global finance.

In a historical perspective, Latin America has undergone many crises covering a wide range. Revolutions, military coups, major economic crises, radical economic transformations, rent-seeking and corruption, ongoing inequality and deep-seated structural exclusion are common features in contemporary Latin American history. This means on the one hand that constitutional structures have difficulty in accomplishing their restrictive function, while on the other being a long way from co-ordinating the functional autonomy of social systems with environmental concerns. If the hypothesis of the capture of constitutional structures by particularistic interests and norms is accurate, then a de-constitutionalisation of particularism and a re-constitutionalisation through universalistic normative expectations would be a useful strategy both for achieving a systemic self-limitation (particularly in politics and the economy) and for addressing environmental concerns. Although the pressures coming from emerging transnational constitutionalising processes may be very helpful in accomplishing this task – as long as they are not absorbed by the gravitational field of Latin American conservative and populist particularism – the main efforts and struggles in combining systemic autonomy and multilateral non-intrusive interpenetration with the environment still remain at the domestic level.

References

Alberdi, Juan B. *Bases y puntos de partida para la organización política de la República Argentina*. Buenos Aires: Editorial Jackson, 1957.

Ansaldi, Waldo, and Verónica Giordano. *América Latina. La construcción del orden*. Barcelona: Ariel, 2012.

Arráiz, Rafael. *Las constituciones de Venezuela (1811–1999)*. Caracas: Editorial Alfa, 2012.

Azzellini, Dario. 'Venezuela's Solidarity Economy: Collective Ownership, Exproriation, and Workers Self-Management'. *The Journal of Labor and Society* 12 (2009): 171–91.

Bassa, Mercado J., and Álvarez Viera, C. 'Contradicciones de los fundamentos teóricos de la Constitución chilena con el estado constitucional: Notas para su reinterpretación'. *Revista de Derecho* 21(2) (2008): 131–50.

Bello, Andrés. 'Las repúblicas hispanoamericanas'. In *Fuentes de la cultura latinoamericana*, edited by Leopoldo Zea. México DF: Fondo de Cultura Económica, 1995: 187–89.

Benton, Lauren. *Law and Colonial Cultures*. Cambridge: Cambridge University Press, 2005.

Bethell, Leslie. *Historia de América Latina*. 7 vols. Barcelona: Crítica, 1991.

Brunner, Otto, Werner Conze and Reinhart Koselleck. *Geschichtliche Grundbegriffe. Band 4*. Stuttgart: Klett-Cotta, 2004.
Burbach, Roger, and Camila Piñeiro. 'Venezuela's Participatory Socialism'. *Socialism and Democracy* 21(3) (2007): 181–200.
Colón, Joel I. 'Carl Schmitt and Constituent Power in Latin American Courts: The Cases of Venezuela and Colombia'. *Constellations* 18(3) (2011): 365–88.
Corsi, Giancarlo. 'Sociologia da constituição'. *Revista Juridica UNIGRAN* 4(8) (2002): 97–116.
Couso, Javier. 'Trying Democracy in the Shadow of an Authoritarian Legality: Chile's Transition to Democracy and Pinochet's Constitution of 1980'. *Wisconsin International Journal* 29(2) (2011): 393–415.
Díaz, Luis C. *Golpe al vacío*. Caracas: Lugar Común, 2012.
Dinneen, Mark. 'The Chávez Government and the Battle over the Media in Venezuela'. *Asian Journal of Latin American Studies* 25(2) (2012): 25–53.
Dunning, Eric. 'The Development of Modern Football'. In *The Sociology of Sport: A Selection of Readings*, 133–51. London: Frank Cass, 1971.
Festl-Pell, Diana. 'Applying Macro-Prudence in Financial Standard Setting'. *ACRN Journal of Finance and Risk Perspectives* 1(1) (2012): 15–31.
Gargarella, Roberto. 'Towards a Typology of Latin American Constitutionalism, 1810–60'. *Latin American Research Review* 39(2) (2004): 141–53.
Garretón, Manuel. A. *Política y sociedad entre dos épocas*. Rosario: HomoSapiens, 2000.
Germani, Gino. *The Sociology of Modernization*. London: Transaction Books, 1981.
Gobierno de Chile. *Declaración de Principios del Gobierno de Chile*. Santiago: República de Chile, 1974.
Habermas, Jurgen. *Zeit der Übergänge*. Frankfurt: Suhrkamp, 2001.
Hilbink, Lisa. 'The Constituted Nature of Constituents' Interests: Historical and Ideational Factors in Judicial Empowerment'. *Political Research Quarterly* 62(4) (2009): 781–97.
Höffe, Otfried. *Wirtschaftsbürger, Staatsbürger, Weltbürger. Politische Ethik im Zeitalter der Globalisierung*. München: C.H. Beck, 2004.
Hulle, Karel van. 'Prudence: A Principle or an Attitude'. *The European Accounting Review* 5(2) (1996): 375–82.
Kjaer, Poul. 'Legitimacy Through Constitutionalism'. In *Legitimization in World Society*, edited by Aldo Mascareño and Kathya Araujo, 99–114. Surrey: Ashgate, 2012.
———. 'Transnational Normative Orders: The Constitutionalism of Intra- and Trans-Normative Law'. *Indiana Journal of Global Legal Studies* 20(2) (2013): 777–803.
———. *Constitutionalism in the Global Realm*. Oxon: Routledge, 2014.
Ladeur, Karl-Heinz, and Lars Viellechner. 'Die transnationale Expansion staatlicher Grundrechete: zur Konstitutionalisierung Privatrechtsregimes'. *Archiv des Völkerrechts* 46(1) (2008): 42–73.
Loveman, Brian, and Elizabeth Lira. *Arquitectura política y seguridad interior del Estado: Chile, 1811–1990*. Santiago: Dirección de Bibliotecas, Archivos y Museos, LOM Ediciones, 2002.
Luhmann, Niklas. 'Verfassung als evolutionäre Errungenschaft'. *Rechtshistorisches Journal* 9 (1991): 176–220.
———. 'Globalization or World Society: How to Conceive of Modern Society?' *International Review of Sociology* 7(1) (1997): 67–79.
———. *Grundrechte als Institution*. Berlin: Duncker & Humblot, 1999.
Mascareño, Aldo. *Diferenciación y contingencia en América Latina*. Santiago: Ediciones Universidad Alberto Hurtado, 2010.
———. *Die Moderne Lateinamerikas Weltgesellschaft*, Region und funktionale Differenzierung. Bielefeld: transcript, 2012.
———. 'Sattelzeit y transición. Fundamentos estructurales y semánticos de la modernidad en América Latina'. In *América Latina moderna*, edited by Adelaida Strück. Caracas: Ediciones Universidad Central de Venezuela, 2013a: 1–44.
———. 'Justicia global y justicia sectorial en la sociedad mundial. Momentos de universalidad en la lex mercatoria'. *Dilemata* 13 (2013b): 45–68.

Mascareño, Aldo, and Elina Mereminskaya. 'The Making of World Society Through Private Commercial Law. The Case of the Unidroit Principles'. *Uniform Law Review* 18(3–4) (2013): 447–72.

Meller, Patricio. 'A Review of Chilean Privatization Experience'. *Working Paper* 93(6), *Texas Papers on Latin America*, Austin: University of Texas, 1992.

Morandé, Pedro. *Cultura y modernización en América Latina*. Madrid: Ediciones Encuentro, 1987.

Neves, Marcelo. *A constitutionalização simbólica*. São Paulo: Editora Acadêmica, 2007.

———. *Transconstitutionalism*. Oxford: Hart Publishing, 2013.

Parker, Cristián. *Otra lógica en América Latina*. México DF: Fondo de Cultura Económica, 1996.

Parsons, Talcott, and Edward Shils. *Toward a General Theory of Action*. Cambridge, MA: Harvard University Press, 1962.

Pietschmann, Horst. *Die staatliche Organisation des kolonialen Iberoamerika*. Stuttgart: Klett-Cotta, 1980.

Pius XI. *Encyclia Quadragessimo Anno*. 1931. Available at: www.vatican.va/holy_father/pius_xi/encyclicals/documents/hf_p-xi_enc_19310515_quadragesimo-anno_en.html (accessed December 2013).

Renson, Roland. 'Fair Play: Its Origin and Meanings in Sport and Society'. *Kinesiology* 41(1) (2009): 5–18.

República Bolivariana de Venezuela. 'Ley que autoriza al Presidente de la República para dictar decretos con rango, valor y fuerza de ley en las materias que se delegan'. *Gaceta Oficial* 38 (2007).

———. 'Ley que autoriza al ciudadano Presidente de la República para dictar decretos con rango, valor y fuerza de ley en las materias que se delegan'. *Gaceta Oficial* 40.297 (2013).

Sarmiento, Domingo F. *Facundo: Civilisation and Barbarism*. London: University of California Press, 2003.

Schamis, Hector E. *Re-Forming the State: The Politics of Privatization in Latin America and Europe*. Michigan: Michigan University Press, 2002.

Scharpf, Fritz W. *Legitimacy in the Multi-Level European Polity*. Oxford: Oxford University Press, 2010.

Schor, Miguel. 'Constitutionalism Through the Looking Glass of Latin America'. *Texas International Law Journal* 41(1) (2006): 1–37.

Sigmund, Paul E. 'Revolution, Counterrevolution, and the Catholic Church in Chile'. *Annals of the American Academy of Political and Social Science* 483 (1986): 25–35.

Teichman, Judith A. *The Politics of Freeing Markets in Latin America*. Chapel Hill: The University of North Carolina Press, 2001.

Teubner, Gunther. *Constitutional Fragments*. Oxford: Oxford University Press, 2012.

Thornhill, Chris. 'Niklas Luhmann and the Sociology of the Constitution'. *Journal of Classical Sociology* 10 (2010): 315–37.

———. *A Sociology of Constitutions*. Cambridge: Cambridge University Press, 2011.

Torres, Ana T. *La herencia de la tribu*. Caracas: Editorial Alfa, 2011.

Valenzuela, Samuel J. 'La Constitución de 1980 y el inicio de la redemocratización en Chile'. *Working Paper* 242, The Hellen Kellogg Institute for International Studies, September 1997.

Véliz, Claudio. *The Centralist Tradition of Latin America*. Princeton: Princeton University Press, 1980.

———. *The New World of the Gothic Fox: Culture and Economy in English and Spanish America*. Berkeley: University of California Press, 1994.

Willke, Helmut. *Regieren*. Wiesbaden: Springer VS, 2014.

13 Paradoxes of transconstitutionalism in Latin America*

Marcelo Neves

Introduction: from constitutional inflation to transconstitutionalism

Towards the end of the last century, scholars of constitutional law from different theoretical traditions and a wide array of different countries, but all strongly linked to the study of state constitutions, began to concern themselves with the new challenges of cross-border constitutional law relevant to other legal orders, including non-state orders. In the United States, for example, Bruce Ackerman acknowledged that 'American practice and theory have moved in the direction of emphatic provincialism' and stressed that 'we should resist the temptations of a provincial particularism'.[1] Later, in a paper delivered to the Hague Institute for the Internationalisation of Law, Mark Tushnet spoke of 'the inevitable globalisation of constitutional law',[2] clarifying that he was concerned with domestic constitutional law and not with the 'separate question of . . . whether there is something fairly called a constitution of the international order or a global constitution'.[3] On the other side of the Atlantic, J.J. Gomes Canotilho, basing his argument on Lucas Pires, referred to 'interconstitutionality', albeit restricted to the relationship between the legal order of the European Union and the constitutional orders of EU member states.[4] Meanwhile, in Germany, Ingolf Pernice has also developed a model of 'multilevel constitutionalism', mainly taking experience in Europe into account.[5]

Outside the circle of constitutional lawyers working in the tradition of national law, it has become commonplace to use the term 'constitution' in other disciplines to refer to widely differing situations: the Constitution of Europe,[6] the Constitution of the International Community,[7] 'global civil constitutions',[8] and so on. This inflation in the use of the term has led to considerable vagueness, such that the term 'constitution' has begun to lose much of its historical, normative and functional meaning. In this context, 'the importance of being called a Constitution'[9] has taken the spotlight, resulting in the persistence of the mistake of nominalism to which Ackerman refers in his analysis of comparative constitutional law: 'Important differences are frequently obliterated by loose talk invoking a common label.'[10]

Thus, the concept of constitution discussed here is not a historical-universal one.[11] Normally this concept is encountered at the empirical level, showing that every society or state has basic structural power relations that also determine juridical forms. According to this conception, which is to be found in authors as disparate as Engels, Lassalle and Weber,[12] the presence of a constitution cannot be excluded from any social order, including archaic societies, since basic structures of 'diffuse power'[13] exist there too. But the historical-universal concept is also found in the idea of a constitution in the material sense, as a set of supreme positive legal norms,[14] since a supreme normative nucleus can be detected in any legal order. A concept of this type could exclude primitive legal orders, insofar as they lack the secondary rules of organisation, especially the ultimate rule of recognition, considered as a constitution in the material sense;

nevertheless, for each and every state there must be a constitution (ultimate rules of recognition).[15] It is very hard to analyse the specificity of the meaning and function of a constitution as one of the few 'achievements of modern civilisation' that are 'the result of intentional planning',[16] when the analytical tools to be used are these historical-universal concepts.[17]

I aim to avoid the tendency to invoke the creation of a new constitution whenever a legal order, institution or organisation emerges in contemporary society. Starting from the solid notion that the meaning of 'constitution' in the strictly modern sense is linked to the constitutionalism that resulted from the liberal revolutions of the eighteenth century in France and the United States, as well as from British political and legal history, albeit atypically so in the latter case, I intend to identify the problems that constituted a condition for the historical possibility of the emergence of the constitutional state. Having determined the problems, it is relevant to ask what functional and normative answers were intended to be embodied in the constitutions of modern states. It is precisely this relationship between problems and solutions that enables the concept of constitution resulting from constitutionalism to be fixed.

Two problems were of vital importance to the appearance of constitutions in the modern sense: on the one hand, the emergence of demands for fundamental or human rights in a society of increasing systemic complexity and social heterogeneity; on the other, and associated with this, the organisational question of the limitation and internal and external control of power (including the participation of the governed in procedures, especially those involved in determining the composition of government bodies), which also related to the question of the growing specialisation of functions, a condition for greater efficiency of state power. As world society has become more integrated, it has recently become impossible for any single national legal order to deal with these problems within its territory alone. Problems of human or fundamental rights and the limitation or control of power are increasingly becoming relevant to more than one legal order at the same time; many of these are non-state orders, but they, too, are called upon to offer solutions to such problems. This entails permanent cross-cutting relationships among legal orders revolving around shared constitutional problems. Constitutional law is thus set free from the state, in which its foundations were originally located, not exactly because a multitude of new constitutions has appeared, but because other legal orders are directly involved in resolving basic constitutional problems, frequently prevailing over the orientation of the legal orders of the respective nation-states. Furthermore, permanent direct relations are formed between states to deal with the constitutional problems they have in common. The exception has become the rule in both cases.

To address this situation I introduce the concept of transconstitutionalism. On the one hand, transconstitutionalism is not to be confused with mere transjuridicism, such as, for example, in relations between legal orders in medieval pluralism, especially between canon law (including Roman law), urban law, royal law and feudal law,[18] since medieval experience did not involve constitutional problems in the modern sense. Thus it was not a matter of fundamental rights, or of the legal limitation and control of power, much less of various claims for the self-referentiality of the foundations of law (ultimately the law had sacred foundations[19]).

On other hand, I am not discussing international, transnational, supranational, national or local constitutionalism. The concept of transconstitutionalism points precisely to the development of legal problems that cut across the various different types of legal order. A transconstitutional problem entails an issue that may involve national, international, supranational and transnational courts or arbitration tribunals, as well as native local legal institutions, in the search for a solution. In discussing transconstitutionalism, I refer to Wolfgang Welsch's concept of 'transversal reason',[20] although I keep my distance somewhat from this ambitious concept, to analyse the limits and possibilities of the existence of 'transversal rationalities' (or 'bridges of transition'), both between the legal system and other social systems (transversal constitutions) and among legal orders within the law as a functional system of world society.

Moreover, in discussing transconstitutionalism, I do not consider it merely as a functional requirement and normative claim for transversal rationality among legal orders, but also take into empirical consideration the negative aspects of transconstitutional entanglements, such as cases where the problem involves situations of anti-constitutional orders or practices, i.e. those which counteract the protection of human and fundamental rights, or which counteract the control and limitation of power. Similarly, I address the question of anti-constitutional practices found within the orders of typically constitutional states.[21] It is therefore worth distinguishing transconstitutionalism (genus), which includes relations between constitutional and anti-constitutional orders, from interconstitutionalism (species), which comprises only relations between legal orders to fulfil constitutionalist requirements.

Transconstitutionalism does not take any single legal order or type of order as a starting point or *ultima ratio.* It rejects nation-statism, internationalism, supranationalism, transnationalism and localism as privileged spaces for solving constitutional problems. Instead, it points to the need to build 'bridges of transition', to promote both 'constitutional conversations' or 'dialogue'[22] and 'constitutional collisions' and to strengthen constitutional entanglements among the various legal orders, be they national, international, transnational, supranational or local. The transconstitutional model avoids the dilemma of 'monism versus pluralism'. From the standpoint of transconstitutionalism, a plurality of legal orders entails a complementary relationship between identity and alterity. The orders involved in solving a specific constitutional problem continuously reconstruct their identity at the level of their self-referential foundations by means of transconstitutional entanglement with another order or orders: identity is articulated on the basis of alterity. Thus rather than seeking a 'Herculean Constitution', transconstitutionalism points to the need to tackle the many-headed Hydra of constitutional problems by articulating reciprocal observations among the various legal orders of world society.

In the first section, the central topic is addressed more directly to a discussion of the diversity of transconstitutionalism between legal orders.

The second section looks at transconstitutionalism not just between two legal orders (of the same or different types), but also among several legal orders in a multicentric world system characterised by entangled hierarchies.

The prospects for transconstitutionalism are the focus of the third section. Its limits and possibilities are examined, taking into account both the empirical conditions for its materialisation and development, and the fact that it appears to be a functional requirement and normative claim of today's world society.

Lastly, I present a brief reflection on the theoretical implications of the argument in a final comment.

Diversity of transconstitutionalism between legal orders

Transconstitutionalism between public international law and state law

Juridico-constitutional problem cases arise with increasing frequency in the relations between international legal orders and state legal orders, and the various orders involved all have a concurrent interest in their solution. These are situations in which more than one court is invoked to settle the case without there necessarily being norms for resolving conflicts of jurisdiction or, when such norms exist, without there being a convergence on them among the courts involved.

From the vantage-point of the state order, the increasing involvement of constitutional courts in these issues, where the classical ratification model has gradually lost ground, heightens the tendency for them to be considered constitutional problems relating to human or fundamental rights, or to the limitation and control of power, involving claims that transcend the specific sphere of validity of the domestic order. From the vantage-point of the international order, this entails the incorporation of constitutional issues into the sphere of competence of its courts, which are beginning to claim the jurisdiction to make decisions that are immediately binding on agents and citizens of states.

Several cases from outside Latin America could be analysed here, such as the relations between the European Court of Human Rights (ECHR) and the legal cultures consolidated in the constitutional orders of the respective European states that are parties to it. For present purposes, however, it is pertinent to consider examples of Latin American experience.

Transconstitutional entanglements between international and state orders are developing in the relations between the 'inter-American Human Rights System', introduced by the American Convention on Human Rights, and the constitutional orders of the signatories that have ratified it.[23] In this context, it is not simply a matter of imposing the decisions of the Inter-American Court of Human Rights (IACHR), created and structured by Chapter VIII (Articles 52–69) of the Convention, on national courts with constitutional competence. The national courts are also reviewing their jurisprudence in the light of the Court's decisions. Both the IACHR and state courts have displayed a willingness to enter into a 'dialogue' on common constitutional issues relating to the protection of human rights, so that the application of conventional law by domestic courts is being extended.[24]

An interesting case deals with the collision between Article 7.7 of the American Convention on Human Rights and Article 5.LXVII of the Brazilian Constitution. While the latter provision allows civil imprisonment for indebtedness in the case of an unfaithful trustee, the above-mentioned provision of the American Convention prohibits it. In judging three cases on 3 December 2008 (RE 466.343/SP, RE 349.703/RS and HC 87.585/TO), a majority of the Brazilian Supreme Court ruled that treaties and conventions on human rights, when not approved in accordance with the procedure stipulated in Article 5, § 3, of the Brazilian Constitution (identical to the procedure for passing a constitutional amendment),[25] have supralegal but infraconstitutional standing.

These cases sparked a broad debate about the incorporation of human rights treaties by the Brazilian legal order.[26] One tendency in analysis of the case has been to advocate a solution based on the idea of unlimited internal validity for the above-mentioned provision of the American Convention on Human Rights, given that this norm would lead to an extension of the rights established in the Brazilian Constitution and that the law contained in it would therefore be in harmony with Article 5, § 2, of that Constitution.[27] However, even the restrictive interpretation of the provision's internal validity does not exclude a positive solution that extends fundamental rights in practice: the argument in favour of the ratified Convention's supralegal and infraconstitutional validity served as a basis for a decision that, since the Constitution only allows unfaithful trustees to be imprisoned for debt,[28] infraconstitutional law could therefore decide freely on permission or prohibition and, if so, the Convention had primacy over the Brazilian Civil Code.[29] Only maintenance of the orientation that had predominated previously in Brazilian legal tradition, i.e. the principle that ratified international acts have the same level of validity as ordinary law, could lead to an insuperable conflict between the Supreme Court of Brazil and the IACHR, since the Brazilian Civil Code came into force after ratification of the treaty, and the maxim *lex posterior derogat priori* would therefore apply.[30] If it had maintained that position, the Supreme Court would have broken off the constitutional 'dialogue' with the

IACHR on their respective understandings of human and fundamental rights. The discussion that did take place, however, appears to have foregrounded an effort to form a transversal rationality that can prove acceptable to both the legal orders involved.[31]

On the side of the IACHR, it is important to note the decision in *YATAMA* v. *Nicaragua*, a case which dealt with the right to democratic participation by members of the indigenous community belonging to YATAMA, a political party, who were forbidden to stand in the municipal elections of 5 November 2000, by a ruling of Nicaragua's Supreme Electoral Council.[32] The IACHR not only ordered the State of Nicaragua to pay compensation for pecuniary and non-pecuniary damages, but also ordered Nicaragua to reform the electoral law in question. This is a clear example in which a norm of the international order is invoked to settle a dispute and support the extension of constitutionally ordained fundamental rights: the application of internal law regarding active citizenship, an intrinsically constitutional matter, is linked to international norms and becomes dependent on the interpretation of an international court.

However, there are experiences in the opposite direction, where the international norm of human rights protection to be invoked can be presented as a restriction to fundamental rights as covered by a state constitution. Examples include the collision between the Brazilian Constitution and the Rome Statute of the International Criminal Court, which was adopted on 17 July 1998 and entered into force in the international order on 1 July 2002. Brazil ratified it via Legislative Decree 112 (2002). Whereas under Article 77, § 1 (b), of the Rome Statute the International Criminal Court may impose a 'term of life imprisonment, when justified by the extreme gravity of the crime and the individual circumstances of the convicted person', this penalty is prohibited under Article 5.XLVII (b) of the Brazilian Constitution. Although Article 5, § 4, of the Brazilian Constitution, introduced by Constitutional Amendment N° 45 in 2004, establishes that 'Brazil shall be submitted to the jurisdiction of the International Criminal Court, to whose creation it has expressed agreement', the matter remains problematic because, according to Article 60, § 4.IV of the same Constitution, the ban on life imprisonment included in the catalogue of individual rights and guarantees cannot be abolished because it is an 'entrenched clause'.[33]

On the one hand, the understanding of human rights in international public law focuses on concern with scandalous and shocking crimes against humanity. On the other, the starting-point for the Brazilian constitutional understanding of fundamental rights is that life imprisonment infringes human rights. A unilateral solution is not adequate in this case.

Precedent suggests a tendency in the Brazilian constitutional jurisdiction to require a specific condition to be fulfilled for the extradition of an alleged criminal for trial or of a convicted criminal by the International Criminal Court: he or she will be handed over only if life is commuted to a maximum of 30 years.[34] Although in the hypothesis of an international court it is not strictly speaking a matter of extradition, since the concept of extradition refers to relations between states, this solution could be adopted for applications to Brazil to *hand over* criminals, defendants or indicted persons to the International Criminal Court.[35] This is an intermediate solution which, while not entirely compatible with the Rome Statute, might be supported by the International Criminal Court in a constructive, learning-disposed position.

The issue could become more problematic if the Supreme Court considers the hypothesis equivalent to 'extradition' and affirms its jurisprudence contrary to extraditing Brazilians in accordance with Article 5.LI of the Brazilian Constitution. In this case, resolving the normative conflict would not be so straightforward. However, as already mentioned, it does not seem correct to extend this principle semantically so that the prohibition would also apply to handing over a criminal, defendant or indicted person to the International Criminal Court, since extradition refers to relations between states. Undoubtedly, even if this interpretation of the concept of extradition were accepted, there would be other problems, due to the invocation of Article 60, § 4.IV of the Brazilian Constitution, which prohibits the abolition of guarantees of fundamental rights ('entrenched clauses' – *see* note 11). Developments in this normative context appear to be moving in an open direction. Nevertheless, a willingness to learn on both sides, via the formation of a constructive transversal network, i.e. transconstitutionalism, is the key to success in this area of collision. According to this hypothesis, internationalism and nationalism could lead to destructive attitudes for human or fundamental rights.

These examples of transconstitutionalism between international and state orders point to the need to transcend the provincial treatment of constitutional problems by states, without this leading to a belief in the *ultima ratio* of international public law: not only the former but also the latter may make mistakes when faced with constitutional issues, including issues of human rights.

Transconstitutionalism between supranational law and state law

If the legal concept of supranationality is restricted to an organisation grounded in a treaty that attributes broad legislative, administrative and jurisdictional competences in the personal, material, territorial and temporal spheres of validity to its own bodies, with direct binding force on the citizens and bodies of the member states, the European Union can be considered the only experience of supranationality,[36] although it is also possible to see supranationality developing in the sphere of the Andean Community.[37] Another example is the Central American Court of Justice, which is competent, among other things, for settling disputes between the powers of any of the states under its jurisdiction.[38] However, both experiences are limited in practice to the dimension of judicial competence. That is why in this chapter I will not discuss examples of Latin American experience with transconstitutionalism between state orders and supranational orders.

Transconstitutionalism between state legal orders

A transconstitutional 'conversation' is developing more frequently among courts in various nation-states via reciprocal references to decisions of courts in other states.

Several cases of transconstitutionalism between state legal orders, besides those of Latin America, could be cited, as discussed in my book. Examples worth mentioning here include *Lawrence* v. *Texas* and *Roper* v. *Simons* in the United States; *Harvard College* v. *Canada* in Canada; *State* v. *Makwanyane* in South Africa; and *Derbyshire County Council* v. *Times Newspapers Ltd.* in the United Kingdom, among others. For the purposes of this chapter, however, Latin American experience is of particular interest.

In Latin America, there is also a long-standing tradition of reference to foreign constitutional provisions, case law and doctrine. Although the influence of the United States has long prevailed, especially by virtue of the strong influence of its constitutional model on the origins of Latin American constitutionalism, European constitutional law and court jurisprudence are increasingly invoked. German constitutionalism, in particular, has exerted significant influence more recently. It is true that, historically speaking, references to foreign constitutional texts, doctrine and precedents have largely been an expression of '*bacharelismo*',[39] figuring in 'rhetorical' judges' opinions as proof of erudition, without relevant links to the merits of the case in question. Recent case law, however, displays a tendency to include references to foreign constitutional texts and precedents as both *obiter dicta* and part of the *ratio decidendi.*

In more recent Brazilian experience, transconstitutionalism with other legal orders has developed conspicuously in the Federal Supreme Court. In important decisions relating to fundamental rights, foreign constitutional case law is cited not only in the opinions of individual justices, but also in case dockets as part of the *ratio decidendi*. In upholding an appellant's conviction on charges of racism for publishing a book with anti-Semitic content (Holocaust denial) in the historic *Ellwanger* case (Habeas Corpus 82.424/RS, 17 November 2003), for example, references to foreign constitutional precedents played a fundamental role in the reasoning used by the Plenary of the Supreme Court.

In their written opinions, the justices conducted a detailed discussion of jurisprudential precedents, constitutional provisions and legislation in foreign states, with relatively little reference to domestic and international case law.[40]

A great many other examples could be given of Supreme Court judgments that cite foreign cases, although they do not always do so as part of the *ratio decidendi*, but as a contribution to the underlying reasoning.

Transconstitutionalism between state and transnational legal orders

One of the most intriguing dimensions of transconstitutionalism is the relationship between state legal orders and legal orders that are transnational in the strict sense, i.e. normative orders constructed primarily not by or from states, but by private or quasi-public actors or organisations.

Several cases of transconstitutionalism between state and transnational legal orders on a worldwide scale could also be analysed here, such as the entanglements concerning *lex mercatoria*, *lex sportiva* and *lex digitalis*. For present purposes, however, it is again pertinent to consider examples of Latin American experience.

A typical example is the ruling of the Court of Arbitration for Sport (CAS; 17 May 2007), which based its move on the merits of the case when it overturned a decision taken by a national court.[41] In this case, the World Anti-Doping Agency (WADA) appealed two rulings, one by the Disciplinary Committee of the Mexican Football Federation (FMF) and the other by CAAD (Comisión de Apelación y Arbitrage del Deporte), a governmental sports regulation and arbitration body in Mexico. Both had failed to act on a positive doping test from a WADA-accredited lab (UCLA Olympic Analytical Laboratory). CAS both dismissed the ruling of the FMF's Disciplinary Committee and declared that CAAD's decision 'has no effect on the system of sanctions established under the FIFA Statutes and Regulations'.[42] Thus, in the light of the fact that the player had twice been convicted of using the same prohibited substance (the first time he had been suspended for a year), CAS declared him 'ineligible with immediate and lifetime effect' from taking part in any competition governed by FIFA.[43]

In judging the case and ruling against a state arbitration tribunal, CAS invoked analogous grounds to those used in the decision analysed above: equality of treatment for athletes involved in transnational sports. CAS categorically dismissed the argument that 'the most favourable laboratory' should be considered, which had been proposed by the player on the grounds that he had obtained a negative test result from a lab not accredited by WADA. While this decision by CAS overruled the ruling by CAAD, a state body, regarding the need to ensure the 'equal and consistent treatment of all participants in a sport',[44] it is important to note that this is also the root of the potential collision between the constitutional principle of equality asserted by the transnational sports legal order and the right to legal remedy with full defence based on the internal order of the constitutional state and implicitly invoked by the player. This is thus an issue that falls entirely within the sphere of transconstitutionalism, requiring constructive 'conversations' between transnational and state legal orders.

Finally, it is worth noting that transconstitutional entanglements between transnational and state orders do not usually occur in isolation. Given the wide range of different types of transnational orders, many of which are, moreover, informal, they are typically involved in transconstitutional problems with multiple types of orders at the same time (state, international, supranational and local). In addition, because they interface with various different kinds of legal order, transnational orders in the strict sense are intrinsically involved more directly with transconstitutionalism in a tangled 'multilevel' world legal system.

Transconstitutionalism between state legal orders and extra-state local orders

Another side of transconstitutionalism points to the problematic relationship between state legal orders and extra-state orders of native collectivities, whose anthropological and cultural assumptions are not compatible with the model of state constitutionalism. In this case, it is evidently a matter of archaic orders that do not have principles or secondary rules of organisation and therefore do not fit into the reflexive model of constitutionalism. Strictly speaking, they do not admit juridico-constitutional problems of human rights and legal constraints on power. When normative orders of this kind collide with institutions of a state's constitutional legal order, a 'unilateral transconstitutionalism' of tolerance and, to some extent, learning is required.

Latin American experience is rich in juridico-constitutional problems deriving from entanglements between native normative orders and state constitutional orders, especially with regard to fundamental rights.

One of the most delicate recent cases involved relations between the Brazilian state legal order and the normative order of the Suruwaha people who live in Tapauá, a municipality located in Amazonas State, and remained voluntarily isolated until the end of the 1970s.[45] Under Suruwaha customary law, children born unhealthy or disabled must be killed. Another case involved the Yawanawa living in Acre on the border between Brazil and Peru, among whom a customary normative order required the killing of one newborn twin. In this context, it also became public that practices of this kind were common among the Yanomami and other indigenous groups. This situation led to controversy, since it involved a practically irresolvable conflict between the right to cultural autonomy and the right to life.

The impact of this case on public opinion led Congressman Henrique Afonso, representing the state of Acre, to draft a bill that would have criminalised this practice in indigenous communities (Projeto de Lei 1057/2007). The hypotheses specified in the bill correspond to practices observed to take place among the indigenous communities located in the territory of the Brazilian state. The Human Rights Committee held a public hearing to discuss the bill in the Chamber of Deputies, Brazil's lower house.[46] While the measure was not taken further, the context in which it was drafted and the discussion to which it led constituted a unique instance of transconstitutional 'dialogue' between the state legal order and the local normative orders of indigenous communities.

The bill's drafters and advocates took as their basic starting-point the idea of the absolute primacy of the individual's fundamental right to life in accordance with Western, Christian morality. Secondarily, the mother's fundamental right to motherhood also contributed to the proposition behind the bill. This unilateral advocacy of individual rights to the detriment of the cultural autonomy of indigenous communities did not seem adequate to those who took part in the debate from a broader anthropological perspective. Moreover, straightforward criminalisation of indigenous practices in the name of protecting the right to life can be seen as tantamount to cultural genocide and destruction of the community via the destruction of its most deeply held beliefs.

Rita Laura Segato is one of the anthropologists who participated intensely in the debate, including the public hearing held on 5 September 2007 in the Chamber of Deputies.[47] Her remarks were of great help in clarifying the implications of this collision, pointing to the need for a transversal communication between normative orders in terms that can be considered appropriate to a constructive model of transconstitutionalism. In the context of the debate, Segato acknowledged that she was faced with 'the ungrateful task of arguing against this bill, but at the same time I would wager strongly on a change in customs'.[48] Her contribution included a report on empirical research showing that there were 16 births, 23 suicides, two homicides of newborns (referred to as 'infanticide' by the anthropologists but not in the same technical sense as the legal definition used in the Penal Code) and one death from disease among 143 Suruwaha between 2003 and 2005. Thus while 7.6 per cent of all Suruwaha deaths in the period were due to 'infanticide', 57.6 per cent were due to suicide.

This situation points to an understanding of life that differs starkly from the Christian one predominant in the West. The view traditionally held by indigenous peoples is that a good life is a life without excessive suffering for both the individual and the community. In other words, it makes sense to live only if life is placid and enjoyable. Thus, infant homicide is justified in certain cases.[49] According to this view, the meaning of life and death for the Suruwaha deserves as much respect as the meaning attributed by Christianity: 'We also found a complex, sophisticated vision of great philosophical dignity that owes nothing to Christianity.'[50] The argument is fortified by reference to Yanomami practice giving women absolute autonomy to decide whether their children should live. The mother withdraws into the forest to give birth, so that delivery occurs outside the context of social life, leaving the choice to the mother:

If she does not touch the newborn child or welcome it into her arms, but leaves it on the ground where it fell, that means it has not been accepted into the world of culture and social relations. It is therefore not human. Thus it is cannot be said that a homicide has occurred from the viewpoint of this indigenous group, since one who remains on the ground is not a human life.[51]

This very different idea of human life genuinely entails a delicate problem, which I also consider incompatible with the mere imposition of external conceptions of life and death by means of what in another context I have paradoxically called 'human rights imperialism'.[52] This is valid not only from an anthropological-cultural or anthropological-legal standpoint, but also from the specific constitutional law perspective that is sensitive to transconstitutionalism.

In this context, it is fundamental to consider the collision between two distinct perspectives on rights while endeavouring to avoid 'injustice' by imposing one, the order of the strongest, on the other, the order of the weakest. On one side is the right to collective autonomy, on the other the right to individual autonomy. Simply submitting the former, considered the expression of an ethical way of life, to the latter, considered the expression of universal morality as the basis for human rights,[53] does not seem to be the most appropriate solution in a model of transconstitutionalism. On the contrary, in this context of radical collision between the state's legal order and indigenous normative orders, it is necessary to consider and weigh the relative importance of 'the individual subject's right to life and the collective subject's right to life', as Segato argues.[54] The 'ultracriminalisation' of homicide practised against newborn children within indigenous communities proposed by the above-mentioned bill (Projeto de Lei 1057/2007) could lead to 'ethnocide by eliminating cultural values indispensable to the biological and cultural life of a people'.[55] Such a legal solution, moreover, would have implications that it would be hard to render compatible with the constitutional order of the Brazilian state.[56] Under such circumstances, a search for a different route would appear necessary.

The proposal that appears best suited to transconstitutionalism resides in guaranteeing 'ethnic jurisdiction or an ethnic forum', so that each indigenous community can 'settle its disputes and work out a solution to internal dissent in its own way'.[57] This does not simply mean tolerance by the most powerful, or even tolerating the intolerant,[58] but rather the ability to acknowledge the autonomy of others, i.e. of the sphere of communication, of the different language game or the different life form of indigenous people, without submitting them to the models of state constitutionalism. It is even less appropriate to speak of 'decent' and 'indecent' societies, or societies that are worthy or unworthy of 'dialogue' with the 'liberal' societies of the constitutional democratic state,[59] as if we were not all in the same world society with collisions and conflicts between domains of communication and language games. Nevertheless, it is necessary to bear in mind that, not just from an anthropological standpoint, but also from that of transconstitutionalism, faced with dissent and disputes within indigenous communities, not least with regard to the practice of killing infants,

> the role of the state, in the person of its agents, must be to be available to supervise, mediate or intervene with the sole aim of ensuring that the internal process of deliberation can take place freely, without abuse by the most powerful individuals in that society.[60]

In this regard, the transconstitutional stance aims to place a legal limit on abusive power inside the community. This is because if there is manipulation of community decisions by the most powerful, without legitimacy in the respective normative order, the result is the disappearance of the ethnic autonomy that is the starting-point for a constitutional 'dialogue'. Hence, it can be seen that no form of presentation of autonomy for social spheres, including those constructed by indigenous communities that are not functionally differentiated, is absolute: all are relative in the context of today's world society.

This delicate problem is not confined to the dilemma between ethical relativism (oriented to particular cultures) and moral universalism (oriented to human rights). It also points to the possibility of coexistence between legal orders based on distinct historical experiences,[61] requiring moderation, especially on the part of the constitutional state, with regard to their claim to concretise their specific norms when these collide with the norms of indigenous communities with essentially different cultural foundations. Discretion and self-restraint seem in this case to be the right way to go about engaging in constructive 'conversations' capable of stimulating internal self-transformation by indigenous communities, so that they have less conflictual relationships with the state order. An attempt to pursue internal models of optimisation in accordance with the theory of principles could be disastrous under these circumstances. Instead, when dealing with the 'other', with the different order of indigenous peoples, it is advisable to adopt a transconstitutional stance of self-containment with regard to the fundamental rights whose optimisation could lead to disintegration of life forms, with destructive consequences for the minds and bodies of the members of the communities involved.[62]

Transconstitutionalism in a 'multilevel' or multicentric world legal system

Multiangle transconstitutionalism between orders of the same kind and orders of different kinds

Transconstitutionalism between two legal orders, be they of the same or of different kinds, is not restricted to the forms discussed previously. Besides these, it is possible to envisage the entanglement of constitutional problems between two international orders, between two transnational orders, between an international order and a transnational order, between an international order and a local order, between a transnational order and a local order, between transnational orders and supranational orders, between local orders, between a supranational order and a local order, and prospectively between supranational orders in the strict sense. As a rule, however, transconstitutionalism tends to involve more than two legal orders, which may be of the same or different kinds. These complex situations point to a 'multilevel' world legal system, in which pluridimensional transconstitutionalism occurs as a result of the simultaneous relevance of one and the same juridico-constitutional problem to a range of legal orders.[63]

This reference to a 'multilevel world legal system', an expression that has become a commonplace and originates in the concept of a 'multilevel policy system',[64] calls for prior clarification regarding the term 'levels', in order to avoid any suspicion that what is being expounded here entails a pyramidal or hierarchical model of the legal orders of world society. Nor is this expression as used here intended to affirm a division of labour between these orders, which would imply a plane of supraordination, making a discussion of the delicate problems of transconstitutionalism superfluous. Much less is it a matter of linking the notion of a 'multilevel' system with the inflationary concept of a relation between plural (and complete) constitutions. Nevertheless, the expression 'multilevel system' appears to have been used predominantly in this sense of a hierarchy and division of labour, especially when constitutional issues are involved. The following assertion by Pernice is a good example:

> The outcome is a *tiered connecting of complementary constitutions*, a system with multiple levels of public power in which the respective material spheres have limited competence to perform the public tasks with which they are entrusted, in accordance with the division of labour.[65]

Moreover, as evidenced by this passage, the emphasis has been placed on the 'public' and the political ('power'), rather than the relations between legal orders in the entanglement of public and private.

The use made here of the expression 'multilevel world legal system' is intended to stress a plurality of orders whose structural types, forms of differentiation, models of self-comprehension and modes of concretisation are sharply distinct and peculiar, a multiplicity that leads to entanglements in which none of the orders can present itself legitimately as the holder of the discursive *ultima ratio*. The phenomenon in question is thus a *multicentric* system in which heterarchical relations prevail between orders, although there is hierarchy within each order. The circular nexus between orders admits only the notion of 'tangled hierarchies', which is incompatible with a 'tiered connecting' between them.[66] In this context, there is entanglement among various legal orders, each of which claims self-grounding to a greater or lesser extent and which are confronted by juridico-constitutional problems that are equally relevant to all.

In the light of the above, transconstitutional entanglements may be found simultaneously between state, supranational, international, transnational and local orders whenever a juridico-constitutional problem arises that is relevant to them in a particular case. As a rule, not all types of order are faced by the same constitutional problem concurrently, but it is usual for more than two legal orders, which may or may not be of different types, to establish a transconstitutional connection via legal cases that are relevant to them all simultaneously.

An interesting example involving the Brazilian legal order is the case of imports of retreaded tyres by Brazil. This dispute touches on Brazilian constitutional law, the legal orders of Uruguay and Paraguay, the laws of Mercosur and the legal order of the WTO. On 17 December 2007, the WTO Dispute Settlement Body (DSB), in adopting the WTO Appellate Body Report of 3 December 2007, which modified the Panel Report of 12 July 2007, upheld an appeal by Brazil to ban imports of retreaded tyres from the EU based on arguments relating to protection of the environment. However, this decision established that the Brazilian policy of continuing to import retreaded tyres from Paraguay and Uruguay entailed discrimination and should therefore be abolished, and the DSB did not accept the Brazilian claim that the number of retreaded tyres imported from Paraguay and Uruguay was insignificant.[67] Later, the European Union requested binding arbitration. An arbitration award by a WTO-appointed arbitrator determined that the reasonable period for Brazil to implement the recommendations and rulings of the DSB was 12 months from the adoption of the Panel Report and Appellate Body Report on 17 December 2007, i.e. by 17 December 2008.[68]

The problem posed by the DSB's decision was that the Mercosur Permanent Review Court had previously ruled against a petition from Argentina requesting a ban on imports of retreaded tyres from Uruguay, reaffirming earlier decisions, based on the understanding that such a ban would infringe Mercosur legal principles.[69] Brazil initially attempted to circumvent both decisions by proposing to cap the number of retreaded tyres imported from Paraguay and Uruguay, leading to simultaneous conflict with the norms of Mercosur and the WTO, in diametrically opposite directions. However, conflict between the administrative bodies that established norms banning imports of retreaded tyres and judicial bodies that declared the norms in question to be unconstitutional led to dissent and strife concerning the issue within the Brazilian state apparatus.

The situation became more complicated when a claim of non-compliance with a fundamental precept deriving from the Constitution (as provided for by Article 102, §2) was put before the Supreme Court by the Office of the Presidency on 29 September 2006 (ADPF 101/2006). The Court was asked to declare unconstitutional and illegal judicial decisions that had admitted the importation of retreaded tyres based on the argument that the infraconstitutional norms that prohibit this practice were unconstitutional. The core reasoning underlying this motion was the claim that these decisions infringed Article 225 of the Constitution, which states: 'Everyone has the right to an ecologically balanced environment, which is a public good for the people's use and is essential to a healthy life. The Government and the community have a duty to defend and preserve it for present and future generations.' Given the significance of this issue, a public hearing was held on 27 June 2008.[70]

Although the Supreme Court ruled partially in favour of the motion, prohibiting imports of retreaded tyres in general but allowing for some exceptions when such imports were based on Mercosur laws and guaranteeing *res judicata*,[71] the situation points to the pressing problems of combating provincial constitutionalism in the Brazilian case. At the same time, it evidences the great difficulty of achieving a satisfactory solution for all the orders involved.

Pluridimensional transconstitutionalism of human rights

From the cases analysed in the previous sections, it can be inferred that transconstitutionalism in a 'multilevel' or multicentric world legal system relates directly or indirectly to problems of 'fundamental rights' or 'human rights'.

The question of human rights, which arose as a juridico-constitutional problem in the state sphere, now pervades all types of legal orders in the multicentric world legal system: state, international, supranational, transnational and local. It is a central issue in transconstitutionalism. Controversy about human rights derives from the possibility of different interpretations of the concept, the conflict-ridden plurality of interpretations/concretisations of related norms and the practical incongruence of different types of human rights. The situation worsens when in the light of the fact that the various orders of the multicentric world legal system have significantly different understandings of human rights questions. Indeed, many are averse to the idea of human rights as rights that claim to be valid for every single person. It is in this context that the pluridimensional transconstitutionalism of human rights takes on special significance, by cross-cutting legal orders of every kind and stimulating both co-operation and collisions.

In Brazil, not only is foreign law often cited in human rights cases but, in terms of pluridimensional transconstitutionalism, it is also usual to refer to conventional norms of international law and the jurisprudence of international courts. In the above-mentioned *Ellwanger* case (Habeas Corpus 82.424/RS),[72] in which the Plenary of the Supreme Court (STF) upheld an appellant's conviction on charges of racism for publishing a book with anti-Semitic content (Holocaust denial) and ruled against application of the statute of limitations, in addition to numerous references to foreign law, the justices also cited countless acts and norms of international public law and invoked *Jersild* v. *Denmark*, judged by the ECHR in September 1994.[73] In many other judgements, the STF has displayed evidence of its readiness to join a transconstitutional 'dialogue' in the multicentric system where various legal orders are concomitantly articulated to solve constitutional human rights problems. This is not a matter of adopting a simple 'Convergence Model' based on Article 5, paragraph 2, of the Federal Constitution, and later on paragraphs 3 and 4 of the same article, introduced by Constitutional Amendment N° 45 in 2004.[74] Much less is it a retreat to a 'Resistance Model' based on a provincial interpretation of these constitutional provisions.[75] The most suitable path in human rights issues appears to be the 'Engagement Model',[76] or rather a transversal entanglement among legal orders, whereby all orders would be capable of permanent reconstruction by learning from the experience of other orders concomitantly interested in solutions to the same constitutional legal problems of fundamental or human rights. The absolute alternative 'convergence or resistance' carries respectively potential elements of self-destruction for the constitutional order or heterodestruction of other legal orders.

Besides the invocation of norms and precedents from other legal orders, especially when the national courts cite foreign and international laws and jurisprudence, it is important to note cases relating to fundamental and human rights in which courts hand down binding judgements that cut across various legal orders. In this regard, it is worth paying particular attention to the approach taken by the IACHR in judging *Yakye Axa* v. *Paraguay* and *Sawhoyamaxa* v. *Paraguay*,[77] regarding property rights to the territories of the Yakye Axa and Sawhoyamaxa indigenous communities, located in Paraguay. In these interesting cases, the IACHR decided not in accordance with the technical and legal concept of private property defined in terms of state constitutional law, but primarily taking into account the cultural notion of 'ancestral property', which is traditional in such communities. Pushing a fundamental right that is constitutionally assured in the *state* sphere into the background, the IACHR found in favour of the right of an *extra-state local* community to its territory in order to protect human rights guaranteed in the international sphere. This multiangled entanglement around human and fundamental rights would not be possible without the willingness of the various orders, especially the state order, to give ground to the perspectives of other normative orders with regard to the significance and applicability of colliding rights.

Problems of pluridimensional entanglement around human rights also arise in cases involving indigenous communities where the killing of newborn babies is considered legitimate, as discussed above in connection with transconstitutionalism between state orders and extra-state local orders. In this context, it is relevant to note ILO Convention 169 concerning Indigenous and Tribal Peoples in Independent Countries,[78] which states in Article 8, paragraph 2: 'These peoples shall have the right to retain their own customs and institutions, where these are not incompatible with fundamental rights defined by the national legal system and with internationally recognised human rights.' This provision further complicates the collision between native local orders and the order of state fundamental rights and international human rights. A literal reading of the provision, applied to absolute protection of the lives of newborns, would tend to lead to ethnocide against the respective indigenous communities. In such cases, it is necessary but not sufficient to engage in a complexly suitable re-reading of the norms both of state fundamental rights and of international human rights. A superficial universalism of human rights, based in linear fashion on a certain Western ontological conception of such rights, is incompatible with a constitutional 'dialogue' with indigenous orders that do not correspond to this model. On the contrary, a refusal to engage in a constructive 'dialogue' with indigenous orders on this issue is itself a violation of human rights, since it would entail the 'ultra-criminalisation' of the entire community of perpetrators of the acts concerned, indiscriminately affecting their bodies and minds by means of destructive interference. In such cases, what is required in the name of positive transconstitutionalism is the willingness of state and international orders to experience the surprise of reciprocal learning from the experience of the other, the indigenous community in its self-understanding.

The examples presented here regarding the pluridimensional transconstitutionalism of human rights seem to me to corroborate the idea that, while it is not possible to relinquish classical constitutional state law, generally linked to a constitutional text, constitutionalism is opening up to spheres beyond the state, not exactly owing to the emergence of other (non-state) constitutions, but rather because eminently constitutional problems, especially those relating to human rights, intersect simultaneously with several legal orders that entangle with each other in their search for solutions. Thus, transconstitutionalism can be said to be the constitutional law of the future, requiring a higher degree of interdisciplinarity. In this sense, it is vitally important to construct a specific methodology for transconstitutionalism.

Outlines of a methodology of transconstitutionalism

Transconstitutionalism depends on a method that does not focus on a blind identity. Isolated legal orders are evidently led to consider their own identity first and foremost, especially through their supreme or constitutional courts, since they are otherwise diluted as orders that are not differentiated from their environments. If, however, they are confronted by common problems, especially when these are constitutional in nature, alterity simply has to be taken into consideration, on pain of becoming reciprocally blocked. Thus it is vitally important for the construction of a methodology of transconstitutionalism to perceive the permanent reconstruction of 'constitutional identity' by virtue of a permanent consideration of alterity to be indispensable.[79] This does not mean negating identity as in an innocent model of pure convergence: it means being prepared to open up not just cognitively, but also normatively, to other entangled orders in concrete cases. The results will remain uncertain, of course, but only if this readiness exists will it be possible to absorb the original dissent. The alternative would lead to reciprocal blockage and the impossibility of resolving significant constitutional problems in fundamental and human rights, in respect of the organisation (control and limitation) of power.

As already noted, if application of the 'optimising balancing' model[80] is already problematic within a given constitutional order, it becomes especially debatable when applied to relations between legal orders regarding fundamental rights in the sphere of transconstitutionalism. The tendency to 'optimise' relations between radically different 'constitutional identities' may lead not just to illusions, but also to reciprocal 'narcissistic' paralysis. The key in this case is to construct mechanisms that serve to articulate identity via observation of the solution offered to a given problem by the other order. Rather than affirming optimisation, it is appropriate to speak of containment as the first step in the transconstitutional method.[81] But this containment is not an end in itself: it relates to double contingency, to the ability to be surprised by others, to acknowledge the possibility of an open future, which cannot be predetermined by any of the orders entangled in the case.[82] A willingness to seek out the normative 'findings' of others is crucial,[83] in order to fortify one's own capacity to offer solutions to common problems.

The starting-point for the method of transconstitutionalism cannot therefore be a given legal order, let alone the orders of the most powerful, but must instead be the constitutional problems with which the various orders are entangled.[84] From the initial disconnection between orders imprisoned in their respective identities, transconstitutionalism enables rules and principles to articulate reciprocally in seeking a solution to the case. In this perspective, the development of a method of transconstitutionalism opens up the possibility of constructing a transversal rationality in the relations between the principles and rules of different legal orders. This entails considering three levels of relations between the principles and rules of different legal orders: each of these levels is entangled with the others in circular fashion – principle–principle, rule–rule, principle–rule (if more than two orders are involved, the situation becomes still richer in possibilities for entanglement). An understanding of the multiple interfaces can offer new insights, not least into the theory of the relations between principles and rules.[85]

A model that emphasises alterity and entails a constant search for ways to articulate identity vis-à-vis the other evidently has its limits in the 'multilevel' or multicentric world legal system. Some legal orders are not disposed to engage in a transconstitutional 'dialogue', yet this does not mean they should be methodologically excluded from transconstitutionalism. Above all with regard to such orders, transconstitutionalism faces a delicate challenge: how to offer methods that lead to internal transformation through reciprocal inducements? If straightforward 'imposed constitutionalism'[86] is excluded, this entails a certain capacity for finding the elements in the other's order that can serve its self-transformation as a first step in the transconstitutional 'dialogue'. This initial limitation is problematic and at times it will not even be possible to begin a transconstitutional rapprochement.

Nevertheless, in a world of common constitutional problems for a plurality of legal orders, the transconstitutional method seems better suited to the passage from a simple situation of unstructured fragmentation to one of constructive differentiation among legal orders in the plane of their respective self-groundings than definitive linear hierarchical methods, be they international, state, supranational, transnational, or even local juridico-anthropological. Based on a methodology of transconstitutionalism, we must therefore reject both a hierarchical methodological model and the mere affirmation of the fragmentation of law without any methodological horizon at all. Faced with fragmentation, the transconstitutional method must develop in search of the construction of 'bridges of transition' that enable more constructive (or less destructive) relations to be fostered among legal orders, via the pluridimensional articulation of their principles and rules, to address common juridico-constitutional problems that require solutions acceptable to all the orders involved, without an ultimate decision-making instance. Rather than authority, transconstitutionalism requires method.

Limits and possibilities of transconstitutionalism in terms of empirical conditions, functional requirement and normative claim

Empirical conditions: transconstitutionalism versus asymmetry of the forms of law

There are relevant negative empirical conditions for the realisation of transconstitutionalism in today's world society. It can also be said that transconstitutionalism bears within itself a positive dimension, the development of transversal rationality among legal orders, and a negative dimension, blocking and destructive relations among them. Thus its limits are not only determined from outside the legal system via the superimposition or 'colonisation' of legal orders by social systems that instrumentalise the law: in addition, from the legal order's internal standpoint, transconstitutionalism is self-blocked by the asymmetries of the forms of law, although these asymmetries are conditioned by the above-mentioned external factors.

First, however, I should clarify my use of the expression 'forms of law' (in the plural). The 'form of law' ['*Rechtsform*'] is a term used in the Marxist tradition, analogously to the concept of commodity form,[87] but it is used in the singular by Marxists.[88] In both cases, the term refers to a distance between structural forms of society (in law and the economy) and concrete subjects, i.e. to forms of 'alienation' ['*Entfremdung*']. My intention in referring to 'legal forms' in the plural is to disconnect my arguments from this tradition to a certain extent. I thus consider the various ways in which the primary code difference of law (legal/illegal) relates in the temporal, social, material and territorial dimensions to the legal programmes and criteria for judging and resolving conflicts (particularly constitutional, statutory and customary norms, judicial and administrative rulings, private juristic acts, doctrinal models and judicial precedents). Speaking of multiple manifestations of the 'form of law' would be appropriate if it were a matter of adhering to the Marxist tradition. However, using the expression 'forms of law' is more suitable to emphasise plurality.

The asymmetries of legal forms create obstacles or impairments to transconstitutionalism by virtue of the fact that, in certain contexts, one is stronger than another and ignores the other's claims and demands. This superimposition of one legal form over another does not imply the formation of a hierarchical order or organisation in the traditional sense of a stepped structure, but instead leads to diffuse mechanisms of oppression or negation of the autonomy of some legal forms by others.

Transconstitutionalism is a scarce resource of world society. Stable transconstitutional entanglements among legal orders have so far occurred only in very limited portions of the 'multilevel' world system in territorial or functional terms. The outlook remains unfavourable to positive developments. Nothing could be more illusory than the idea that experiences of transversal rationality in transconstitutionalism among legal orders are generalised or in a position to become so in the short or medium term: these experiences are part of the privileges of some legal spheres in an acutely asymmetrical world society.

In summary, it can be seen that strong forms of law are superimposed oppressively on fragile forms of law in the 'multilevel' world system.

Functional requirement: beyond constitutional utopia and fragmentation – promoting a 'differentiated communication order' (system integration)

In the area of research into public international law and transnational legal orders, use of the term 'fragmentation' has become a commonplace to designate the lack of unity of law in today's world society.[89] In this theoretical context, when fragmentation is not recognised, the alternative presented is 'constitutional utopia'.[90] From the standpoint of a systemic functional approach, mere affirmation of teleological utopias or simple recognition of fragmentation does not constitute an alternative, but indicates respectively excess of normativism or realism in addressing the legal problems of world society.

In this respect, from the standpoint of the legal system, transconstitutionalism serves as *one* structural model of functional connection among the fragmented functional spheres of world society. This is because what is lacking in mere fragmentation is structure.[91] Mere fragments internal and external to the legal system find in transconstitutionalism, from the partial standpoint of law, the constitutional elements that can contribute to its structural connection and hence help promote 'a differentiated communication order'.[92]

The question, therefore, concerns the need to 'promote' the stable structures of a differentiated communication order by connecting the fragments transversely. This is achieved neither by teleological 'constitutional utopias', nor by ultimate normative orders, but by models that offer conditions for an 'interweaving' of the fragments. By promoting 'dialogue' among legal orders on constitutional issues and linking identity to alterity in their relations, transconstitutionalism fosters differentiated communication both between the legal system and the outside world, and within the legal system itself.

Normative claim: beyond hegemony and community – promoting inclusion ('social integration')

Although the normative dimension is not totally disconnected from the functional dimension, it is necessary to distinguish between the plane of functional requirements (relations between problems and solutions) and that of normative claims, which has to do with expectations that are stabilised counterfactually in the sphere of world society. From this derive elementary normative structures related to the highly complex multicentric society.[93] Transconstitutionalism takes the form of a basic normative counterpoint to both the expansionary primacy of the cognitive *structures* of world society (linked to the economy, technology and science) and the *semantics* of the control of information (and knowledge) by the mass media.

One tendency in critical studies of legal internationality or transnationality is the affirmation of the hegemonic nature of law.[94] Thus Koskenniemi argues that public international law is a 'hegemonic technique'[95] and points to the professional capacity to distinguish between 'hegemonic and counter-hegemonic narratives'.[96] In this context, 'community' is presented as the alternative in the following terms.[97]

The hegemony model, developed most completely in the work of Gramsci,[98] becomes vague if used without specific contours. Plural relations between hegemony and counterhegemony are inherent in any 'political community' and can be transcended only in the 'utopia' of a purely moral community. Thus it is not appropriate to posit an alternative between hegemony and community.

Beyond this, however, the concept of 'political community' applied to the 'international world' is inadequate, since the concept of community implies a type of social relationship of membership, as well as solidarity grounded in the sharing of common values. The notion of political community serves to describe pre-modern forms of society.[99] In its turn, under contemporary conditions of differentiation between society and organisation, membership refers to belonging to a given organisation. The 'international world' is not an organisation. For world society, indeed, any attempt to use the rhetoric of community is rather a rhetorical expression of the hegemonic discourse. What we do have are communication systems, language games, different groups and individuals, in a heterogeneous confluence of interests, values and expectations in general. Indubitably there are community formations within today's world society (or 'international world'), but understanding the term as 'political community' is both a theoretical and a practical disaster.

What is required for today's world society is the promotion of inclusion, via the reduction of the growing exclusion sector. In this regard, Luhmann warns of the danger of an 'avalanche of exclusion', as welfare states are dismantled even in the most developed parts of the world.[100] This relates to social integration in the sense used by systems theory: 'a person's chance to achieve social consideration'.[101] Strictly speaking, inclusion means access to the benefits of functional systems, while exclusion entails lack of access to such benefits.

A fundamental assertion falls into place at this point: what is required in the sphere of transconstitutionalism is not membership or community, but the promotion of generalised inclusion, or better still the reduction of increasing primary exclusion, especially with regard to law, in the context of a heterogeneous and differentiated communication structure. Hence the importance of perceiving that not only is systemic corruption a moral problem of today's world society, but also the associated exclusion of huge swathes of world society from the elementary benefits of functional systems. If moralisation in today's world society only has a meaning for functional systems in pathological cases,[102] then it must be concluded that the goal of transconstitutionalism's normative claim is to affirm itself counterfactually against the 'pathologies of normalcy'.[103]

Final comment: the other can see your blind spot

The constitution provides the basic instance of normative self-grounding for the state as a territorial politico-legal organisation. As the basic criterion for the state legal order's self-understanding, the constitution cannot be put aside by interpreters and enforcers of the constitutional order, nor by those upon whom it is incumbent to concretise it as an order with normative force, especially constitutional judges and courts. In this sense, it constitutes an 'inviolate level' (in Hofstadter's sense) of the legal order of the constitutional state. But in the dynamic constitutional game the 'inviolate level' may be involved (tangled) with other levels, forming a 'supertangled level'.[104] In our context, this means that although the constitutions of constitutional states normatively bind their concretisers, especially constitutional courts and judges, they are permanently reconstructed via interpretation and application by those same concretisers. This is the paradox of tangled hierarchies: a constitutional ruling is normatively subordinated to the constitution and affirms what is constitutional by concretising the constitution.

However, this paradox presents nothing special with regard to any act of constitutional jurisdiction. What transconstitutionalism evidences above all is the profound change that has taken place under the conditions prevailing in today's world society, whereby provincial or parochial constitutionalism is being transcended. This change should be taken seriously: the state has ceased to be a privileged locus for solving constitutional problems. Albeit fundamental and indispensable, it is only one of several loci for co-operation and competition in pursuit of solutions to such problems. The increasing system integration of world society has led to the de-territorialisation of juridico-constitutional problem cases, which, as it were, have emancipated themselves from the state. This situation, however, should not lead to new illusions, such as a search for definitive 'inviolate levels': internationalism as *ultima ratio*, in a new absolute hierarchisation; supranationalism as a legal panacea; transnationalism as fragmentation to cast off the shackles of the state; localism as the expression of a definitively inviolate ethicality.

Against these tendencies, transconstitutionalism entails the recognition that the various legal orders entangled in the search for a solution to a constitutional problem case that is concomitantly relevant to all of them – involving fundamental or human rights and the legitimate organisation of power – must pursue transversal forms of articulation in order to develop such a solution, each observing the others in an effort to understand its own limits and possibilities for contributing to the solution. Its identity is thereby reconstructed as long as it takes alterity seriously, always observing the other. In my view, this is productive and enriching for identity itself, since every observer has a 'blind spot' and hence limited vision, due to being in a certain position or observing from a certain vantage point.[105] However, while it is true, considering the diversity of vantage points from which alter and ego observe, that 'I see what you do not see',[106] it should be added that what is unseen by one observer owing to this 'blind spot' can be seen by another. In this sense, it can be stated that transconstitutionalism entails the recognition of the limits to observation of any given order and acknowledges the alternative: *the other can see your blind spot*.

Notes

* This article is based on my book *Transconstitutionalism* (Oxford: Hart, 2013), published originally in Portuguese: *Transconstitucionalismo* (São Paulo: WMF Martins Fontes, 2009).
1 Ackerman, 1997, 773 and 794.
2 Tushnet, 2008.
3 Tushnet, 2008, 2, note 7.
4 Canotilho, 2006, 265ff.; Pires, 1997, 101ff.
5 Pernice, 1999; 2002.
6 Weiler, 1999, among many.
7 See, e.g., Fassbender, 1998; Tomuschat, 1995, 7.
8 Teubner, 2003 [English trans. 2004].
9 Maduro, 2006, 335ff.
10 Ackerman, 1997, 794.
11 Canotilho, 1991, 59. This historical-universal concept holds to the formula 'no state without a constitution' (Biaggini, 2000, 447). Writing from the perspective of a history of the constitution, Koselleck (2006) extends the concept to include 'all legally regulated institutions and their forms of organisation, without which a social community of action is not politically capable of acting'. And he clarifies this as follows: 'My proposal that the history of the constitution should encompass all domains characterised by repeatability by virtue of legal rules is therefore designed to bridge the gap between pre-modern histories of law and modern histories of the constitution so as to include not just interstate but also post-state and to some extent suprastate phenomena of our times' (2006, 370f.). Thornhill (2011) also proposes a historical-universal concept of constitution 'in terms that can be applied to many societies in different historical periods', although limiting his view of constitution to 'the fact that it refers primarily to *the function of states* [in general, not the modern states – MN], and it establishes a legal form relating to the use of power by states, or at least by actors bearing and utilising public authority' (11). Unlike what Thornhill (9f.) suggests, I think that this discussion must not be confused with the issue whether there is a 'formally written constitution'.
12 Engels, 1988 [1844], especially 572ff.; Lassalle, 1987 [1862], 130; Weber, 1985 [1922], 27.
13 Burdeau, 1949, 249–51.
14 Kelsen, 1960, 228–30; 1946, 124f.; 1925, 251–3.
15 See Hart, 1994, 91–123ff., especially 107. Hart also speaks of 'constitutional matters' in respect of the secondary rules for alteration (1994, 60).
16 Luhmann, 1990a, 176.
17 See Luhmann, 1990a, 212. Unlike what Thornhill (2011, 9) asserts, Luhmann has not 'accepted latitude in the definition of constitution', rather he has proposed a very strict concept of constitution: 'My theses will be that the concept of constitution – contrary to the first impression – responds to a differentiation between law and politics, even more: to a separation of these both functional systems *and to the need arising therefrom for linkage*' (Luhmann, 1990a, 179–80).

18 See Berman, 1983, Fig. 2, 522–6.
19 See Neves, 2009, 8–10 and 16, note 63 [English trans. 2013, 9–11 and 14, note 63].
20 Welsch, 1996; 2002, 295–318.
21 See, e.g., Scheppele, 2006; Roach, 2006; Gross, 2006.
22 I use 'dialogue' and 'conversation' not in the sense of understanding- or consensus-oriented discourse, but rather to refer to forms of communication designed to absorb dissent, assuming double contingency (see below, p. 243), although I am well aware that these words are not usually deployed with such meanings. Between different legal orders, especially on the plane of constitutional problems, these terms point to transversal communications, implying reciprocal instigations.
23 This Convention was adopted on 22 November 1969, at San Jose, Costa Rica, and entered into force on 18 July 1978, in accordance with Article 74, N° 2. On this subject, see Burgorgue-Larsen, 2009; Ortiz, 2009; on the discussion in Brazil, see de Oliveira, 2007, highlighting the preface by Trindade, 2007. For an analysis of the jurisdiction of the Inter-American Court of Human Rights (IACHR), see Ramírez, 2008.
24 See Ortiz, 2009, 273ff.; Burgorgue Larsen, 2009, 309ff.
25 Article 5, paragraph 3, of the Brazilian Constitution reads as follows: 'The international treaties and conventions on human rights approved by each house of Congress in two rounds by three-fifths of all members shall be equivalent to constitutional amendments.'
26 RE 466.343/SP, RE 349.703/RS, HC 87.585/TO, 03/12/2008, TP, DJe 5 and 26 June 2009.
27 Position defended by Justice Celso de Mello, leading the dissent, with support from Piovesan, 2008a, 51–77; Mazzuoli, 2001, 147–50; 2007, 682–702. Mello (2001, 25f.) goes further to argue that treaties and conventions on human rights are supraconstitutional. Article 5, paragraph 2, of the Brazilian Constitution reads as follows: 'The rights and guarantees expressed in this Constitution do not exclude others deriving from the regime and from the principles adopted by it, or from the international treaties to which the Federative Republic of Brazil is a party.'
28 Article 5.LXVII of the Brazilian Constitution reads as follows: 'There shall be no civil imprisonment for indebtedness except in the case of a person responsible for voluntary and inexcusable default on an alimony obligation and in the case of an unfaithful trustee.'
29 Position defended by Justice Gilmar Mendes, in an opinion leading the majority. In this sense, see Mendes et al., 2007, 665ff.
30 Jurisprudence consolidated by the Brazilian Supreme Court (STF) in the decision of RE 80.004/SE, Judgement of 1 June 1977, DJ 29 December 1977. On this jurisprudence, see Mendes et al., 2007, 659ff. This is also the position taken by Dimoulis and Martins (2007, 50) for treaties not approved in accordance with Article 5, §3, of the Brazilian Constitution. Pontes de Miranda (1960, 225), while arguing that treaties are hierarchically equivalent to ordinary law, states that 'the Constitution cannot affect a prior treaty unless said treaty is valid in international law and contains provision for its denunciation or abrogation of its rules. Thus the primacy of international law is unquestionable . . . In this regard, the framers committed grave errors due to careless assimilation of treaties prior to and subsequent to the Constitution'.
31 I invoke here Wolfgang Welsch's concept of 'transversal reason' (Welsch, 1996), although I take my distance somewhat from this ambitious concept by using the expression 'transversal rationality'. See Neves, 2009, 38ff. [English trans. 2013, 28ff.].
32 *YATAMA* v. *Nicaragua* – Series C No. 127 [2005] IACHR 9 (23 June 2005).
33 Article 60, § 4.IV, of the Federal Constitution of Brazil reads as follows: '§ 4 – No proposal of amendment shall be considered if it aims to abolish [...] IV – individual rights and guarantees'.
34 Confirming precedents in more recent jurisprudence, see the following extradition applications, all decided unanimously by the Plenum of the Supreme Court STF: Ext. 1.104/UK – Reino Unido da Grã-Bretanha e da Irlanda do Norte (United Kingdom of Great Britain & Northern Ireland), 14 April 2008, DJe 23 May 2008; Ext. 1.103 – Estados Unidos da América (United States of America), 13 March 2008, DJe 7 November 2008; Ext. 1.060/PU – Peru, 15 October 2007, DJe 31 October 2007; Ext. 1.069/EU – Estados Unidos da América (United States of America), 9 August 2007, DJe 14 September 2007.
35 See Maliska, 2006, 188f., also admitting the hypothesis of handover to the ICC without these conditions (189), which to me seems incompatible with Brazilian jurisprudence and precedent, not to mention the fact that it would infringe an entrenched clause. On this, see Sabadell and Dimoulis, 2010.
36 In this sense, Langer (1995, 50) states that 'practically speaking, it is correct only in the case of the European Union to speak of a "supranational organisation" '. Similarly, Grimm (2008, 161): 'So far

there has been no supranational arrangement of the same density [as the European Union] either outside of Europe or on a global scale.'

37 On the affirmation of the Andean Community's legal supremacy or primacy over national law, see the following judgements, among many, of the Court of Justice of the Andean Community: Case 1-IP-87; Case 50-IP-2008; Case 67-IP-2008. On the significance of this court, see Perotti, 1998; Toledo, 2009.

38 See Perotti, 2002.

39 *Bacharelismo* refers to a predominance of *bachareis* (university-educated professionals, especially lawyers), in political and cultural life. It is also used to refer to a preference for rhetoric over research, not only among lawyers, but also among doctors, engineers, economists and other members of the liberal professions (Chacon, 1969, 21). According to Birman and Lehmann, '*bacharelismo* is a rhetorical style associated with useless knowledge of little practical value'; 'a type of rhetoric, a style of writing, oracular and archaic, which was prevalent in politics and high culture' (Birman and Lehmann, 1999, 163, notes 13 and 14). For a critique of the generalised and simplistic use of the term with regard to Brazilian jurists, see Saldanha, 1978. On the various conceptions of *bacharelismo*, see Venancio Filho, 1977, 271ff.

40 HC 82.424/RS, judgement of 17 November 2003, TP, DJ 19 March 2004.

41 Award N° 2006/A/1149 and no. 2007/A/1211, extract and commentary by Loquin, 2008, 259–72.

42 In: Loquin, 2008, 270.

43 Loquin, 2008.

44 In: Loquin, 2008, 262.

45 Segato, 2011, 363.

46 Convened by the Human Rights Committee of the Chamber of Deputies in August 2007, the hearing took place on 5 September 2007 (see Segato, 2011, 357 and 369). Major alterations to this bill later reduced it to generic declarations and promises of support for the respective communities.

47 See Segato, 2011, 370ff.

48 Segato, 2011, 358.

49 Segado, 2011, 364f.

50 Segato, 2011, 364.

51 Segato, 2011, 365.

52 Neves, 2005, 23 and 27 [English trans. 2007, 432 and 436].

53 Klaus Günther, while arguing that '[t]he appropriate application of legitimate norms may not harm forms of life *without reason*' (my emphasis), actually appears to be in favour of this approach, insofar as he claims that 'conflicts between principles of justice and orientations of the good life at the post-conventional level can only be resolved universalistically, that is, in favour of justice' (1988, 196 [English trans. 1993, 153]). It should be noted, however, that in the terms of Habermas' theory of communicative action and discourse, which Günther espouses, the collision in this case would be between post-conventional and pre-conventional morality. On the levels of development of moral consciousness in Habermas' theory of social evolution, see Neves, 2006, 25ff.

54 Segato, 2011, 367. At the above-mentioned public hearing, Segato explained what she understood by 'the expression "right to life"' in this context: 'This expression can indicate two different types of right to life: the individual's right to life, i.e. protection for the individual subject of rights; and the right of life of collective subjects, i.e. to protection for the life of peoples in their condition as peoples' (Segato, 2011, 372).

55 Botero, 2006, 156, also cited by Segato, 2011, 367.

56 Specifically Article 231 of the Federal Constitution: 'Recognition is hereby granted to the social organisation of the Indians, their customs, languages, beliefs and traditions, and their original rights to the lands which they have traditionally occupied. The federal government shall demarcate those lands, and shall protect and ensure respect for all of their possessions.'

57 Segato, 2011, 375 and 377.

58 Rawls, 1990 [1972], 216–21.

59 Rawls, 1999, 4f. and 59ff.

60 Segato, 2011, 375. On this point, Segato adds: 'Nor it is appropriate to demand the withdrawal of the state, because as evidenced by the many demands for public policy in this matter raised by indigenous peoples on the basis of the 1988 Constitution, after the intense and pernicious disorder created by contact, the state can no longer simply abstain. It must remain permanently available to offer guarantees and protection when called upon to do so by members of the communities, provided that such intervention involves a dialogue between representatives of the state and representatives of the

community in question. Its role in this case can be none other than to promote and facilitate dialogue between the powers of the village and its weakest members' (2011, 375f.).

61 See Segato, 2011, 375–7; see also 2006 for a broader treatment. On the intrinsic relationship between universalism and difference, see Neves, 2002.

62 By having destructive effects on bodies and minds, the optimisation of fundamental rights violates human rights understood as 'intended guarantees of the integrity of mind and body' (Teubner, 2006, 175 [English trans. 2006, 338]).

63 In this sense, the situation is more complex than that presented in the 'glocalisation of law' model (Randeria, 2003; see Robertson, 1995).

64 Specifically in connection with Europe, see Scharpf, 1994, especially 17f.; 2002. In this context, another expression found in the literature is 'multi-layered global governance' (Held and McGrew, 2002, especially 9). For reception in the legal sphere, see among many others Pernice, 1999; 2002; Joerges and Petersmann, 2006; Petersmann, 2008; Joerges, 2003. On interjudicial conflicts, see Sauer, 2008.

65 Pernice, 2006, 511f.

66 In this sense, Hofstadter also uses the term 'level', especially in his discussion of 'tangled hierarchies'. See 1979, 684ff.

67 WT/DS332/AB/R; WT/DS332/R.

68 WT/DS332/16, of 29 August 2008. For more on this case, see Perotti, 2009.

69 Award 1/2005 of 20 December 2005; Award 1/2007, of 8 July 2007; Award 1/2008 of 25 April 2008.

70 See the official site of the Supreme Court (STF): www.stf.jus.br/portal/cms/verTexto.asp?servico=processoAudienciaPublicaAdpf101 (last visited on 24 November 2008).

71 ADPF 101/DF, judgement of 24 June 2009, TP, DJe 4 June 2012. This was a majority decision, with only Justice Marco Aurélio dissenting.

72 HC 82.424/RS, judgement of 17 November 2003, TP, DJ 19/03/2004.

73 *Jersild* v. *Denmark* (Application no. 15890/89), judgement of 23 September 1994.

74 For a 'Convergence Model', see Mello, 2001; Trindade, 2000; Piovesan, 2008a, 51ff.; Mazzuoli, 2001, 33ff.; 2005; 2007, 682ff.; Galindo, 2005. More cautiously, Sarlet (2001, 77–95 and 132–5; 2006; 2010) and Gomes (2008, especially 189) relativise the 'Convergence Model', albeit displaying a preference for this model. Uniquely, Tavares (2005, 47f.) argues for the reception of human rights treaties prior to Constitutional Amendment N° 45/2004 as constitutional norms with the entry into force of this amendment.

75 Dimoulis and Martins (2007) strangely opt for a 'Resistance Model' in relation to international human rights norms (40–51), but enthusiastically support a 'Convergence Model' with regard to foreign law, especially the jurisprudence of Germany's Federal Constitutional Court (261ff.).

76 On 'convergence model', 'resistance model' and 'engagement model', see Jackson, 2005.

77 *Comunidad Indigena Yakye Axa* v. *Paraguay*, judgement of 17 June 2005, Series C No. 125 (for an analysis of this case, see Ramírez, 2005); *Comunidad Indígena Sawhoyamaxa* v. *Paraguay*, judgement of 29 March 2006, Series C No. 146 (for summaries of both cases, see Piovesan, 2008b, 71–3).

78 On this Convention, see the brief exposition by Wolfrum, 1999.

79 From an entirely different perspective grounded in psychoanalytical assumptions, Rosenfeld (1998, 144ff.) associates the 'identity of the constitutional subject' with the viewpoint of 'the other'.

80 Alexy, 1986, especially 71ff. [English trans. 2002, 44ff.], who developed his sophisticated model from Dworkin, 1991 [1977], especially 16–80.

81 It is relevant to note here the tendency for the various social spheres or discourses to maximise their own rationalities to the detriment of other's rationalities, as stressed by Fischer-Lescano and Teubner (2006, 25ff.). See Teubner, 2008, 32f. [English trans. 2009, 33].

82 See Neves, 2009, 166, note 128, and 270ff. [English trans. 2013, 105, note 130, and 169ff.].

83 See Waldron, 2005.

84 See Baudenbacher, 2003, 523.

85 Thus what is being proposed here is not a retreat to the classical rules model. Principles such as norms of norms are reflexive instances that are indispensable to the legal system, serving to demarcate and construct rules in the process of concretisation (on reflexive mechanisms or reflexivity, see Luhmann, 1984; 1987, 601 and 610–16 [English trans. 1995, 443 and 450–55]).

86 See Schauer, 2005; Feldman, 2005; Sunder, 2005; Levinson, 2005; Choudhry, 2005; Chesterman, 2005; Janis, 2005.

87 See Marx, 1988 [1863–7], especially 24 and 27.

88 See Buckel, 2008.
89 See Fischer-Lescano and Teubner, 2006; 2007; Teubner, 2006, 175ff. [English trans. 2006, 338ff.]; 2012 [English trans. 2012]. Fischer-Lescano, 2005, 187ff.; Koskenniemi and Päivi, 2002; Koskenniemi, 2004, 205f.; 2006a; 2006b; 2008, 70ff. Ladeur and Viellechner (2008, 60) rightly point out, however, that tendencies towards fragmentation already exist within national states themselves.
90 See Koskenniemi, 2006a.
91 Luhmann has this to say on the concept of structure: 'Structures anchor a fragment of the possible as expectable' (Luhmann, 1987, 41). Later he adds: 'Structures are indeed necessary since they restrict the space for adequate connections among operations so broadly that the development of one operation after another is feasible. It might also be said that they are a necessary reduction of complexity' (Luhmann, 1997, vol. 1, 437).
92 Luhmann, 1965, 25, associating fundamental rights with the maintenance of a 'differentiated communication order'.
93 On the distance he takes from normative theories of society, Luhmann explains: 'This sceptical abstinence vis-à-vis norm-centred theory does not, of course, imply that one can imagine a possible societal life without norms. Binding oneself to norms or values is a pervasive aspect of social life' (1987, 444 [English trans. 1995, 325f.]).
94 On this subject, see Koskenniemi, 2004; Buckel and Fischer-Lescano, 2008; 2007.
95 Koskenniemi, 2004, 198.
96 Koskenniemi, 2004, 202.
97 Koskenniemi, 2004, 214.
98 Gramsci, 1999, distinguishing between hegemony (civil society) and domination (state) (especially 145).
99 Hence the distinction between community (ancient, traditional) and society (modern) deriving from Tönnies (1979, especially 3–6, 34, 73ff. and 106ff.), via Weber (1985, especially 21–3). See Neves, 1992, 11ff.
100 Luhmann, 2000, 427f.
101 Luhmann, 1997, vol. 2, 620.
102 See Luhmann, 1997, vol. 2, 1043.
103 At this point, I quote Fromm (1956, 12ff.) with respectful irony.
104 See Hofstadter, 1979, 686ff.
105 Von Foerster, 1981, 288f.
106 Luhmann, 1990b.

References

Ackerman, Bruce. 'The Rise of World Constitutionalism'. *Virginia Law Review* 83 (1997): 771–97.

Alexy, Robert. *Theorie der Grundrechte*. Frankfurt am Main: Suhrkamp, 1986 (English translation: *A Theory of Constitutional Rights*. Oxford: Oxford University Press, 2002).

Baudenbacher, Carl. 'Judicial Globalization: New Development or Old Wine in New Bottles'. *Texas International Law Journal* 38 (2003): 505–26.

Berman, Harold J. *Law and Revolution: The Formation of the Western Legal Tradition*. Cambridge, MA and London: Harvard University Press, 1983.

Biaggini, Giovanni. 'Die Idee der Verfassung – Neuausrichtung im Zeitalter der Globalisierung?' *Zeitschrift für Schweizerisches Recht* 141 (119 in the new series) (2000): 445–76.

Birman, Patricia, and David Lehmann. 'Religion and the Media in a Battle for Ideological Hegemony: The Universal Church of the Kingdom of God and *TV Globo* in Brazil'. *Bulletin of Latin American Research* 18(2) (1999): 145–64.

Botero, Esther S. *Entre el Juez Salomón y el Dios Sira. Decisiones interculturales e interés superior del niño*. Bogotá: Universidad de Amsterdam y Unicef, 2006.

Buckel, Sonia. '"Judge without a Legislator" – Transnationalisierung der Rechtsform'. In *Rechts-Staat: Staat, internationale Gemeinschaft und Völkerrecht bei Hans Kelsen*, edited by Hauke Brunkhorst and Rüdiger Voigt, 269–81. Baden-Baden: Nomos, 2008.

Buckel, Sonja, and Andreas Fischer-Lescano. *Hegemonie gepanzert mit Zwang: Zivilgesellschaft und Politik im Staatsverständnis Antonio Gramscis*. Baden-Baden: Nomos, 2007.

———. 'Emanzipatorische Gegenhegemonie im Weltrecht'. In *Transnationale Verrechtlichung. Nationale Demokratien im Kontext globaler Politik*, edited by Regina Kreide and Andreas Niederberger, 114–33. Frankfurt am Main and New York: Campus, 2008.
Burdeau, Georges. *Traité de Science Politique*, vol I, 2nd edition. Paris: Librairie Générale de Droit et de Jurisprudence, 1949.
Burgorgue-Larsen, Laurence. 'El Sistema Interamericano de Protección de los Derechos Humanos: Entre clasicismo y creatividad'. In *¿Integración suramericana a través del derecho? Un análisis multidiciplinario y multifocal*, edited by Armin von Bogdandy, César L. Arroyo and Mariela M. Antoniazzi, 287–338. Heidelberg: Max Planck Institute for Comparative Public Law and International Law/ Madrid: Centro de Estudios Constitucionales, 2009.
Canotilho, José J.G. *Direito constitucional*, 5th edition. Coimbra: Almedina, 1991.
———. *'Brancosos' e interconstitucionalidade: Itinerários dos discursos sobre a historicidade constitucional*. Coimbra: Almedina, 2006.
Chacon, Vamireh. *Da Escola do Recife ao Código Civil (Artur Orlando e sua geração)*. Rio de Janeiro: Simões, 1969.
Chesterman, Simon. 'Imposed Constitutions, Imposed Constitutionalism, and Ownership'. *Connecticut Law Review* 37(4) (2005): 947–54.
Choudhry, Sujit. 'Old Imperial Dilemma and the New Nation Building: Constitutive Constitutional Politics in Multinational Polities'. *Connecticut Law Review* 37(4) (2005): 933–45.
De Oliveira, Márcio L. (ed.). *O sistema interamericano de proteção dos direitos humanos – interface com o direito constitucional*. Belo Horizonte: Del Rey, 2007.
Dimoulis, D., and L. Martins. *Teoria geral dos direitos fundamentais*. São Paulo: Revista dos Tribunais, 2007.
Dworkin, Ronald. *Taking Rights Seriously*. London: Duckworth, 1991.
Engels, Friedrich. 'Die Lage Englands. II. Die englische Konstitution'. In *Werke*, 15th edition, vol. I, edited by Karl Marx and Friedrich Engels, 569–92. Berlin: Dietz Verlag, 1988 (first published in *Vorwärts!*, no. 75, 18 September 1844).
Fassbender, Bardo. 'The United Nations Charter as Constitution of the International Community'. *Columbia Journal of Transnational Law* 36(3) (1998): 529–619.
Feldman, Noah R. 'Imposed Constitutionalism'. *Connecticut Law Review* 37(4) (2005): 857–89.
Fischer-Lescano, Andreas. *Globalverfassung: Die Geltungsbegründung der Menschenrechte*. Weilerswist: Velbrück, 2005.
Fischer-Lescano, Andreas, and Gunther Teubner. *Regime-Kollisionen: Zur Fragmentierung des globalen Rechts*. Frankfurt am Main: Suhrkamp, 2006.
———. 'Fragmentierung des Weltrechts: Vernetzung globaler Regimes statt etatischer Rechtseinheit'. In *Weltstaat und Weltstaatlichkeit: Beobachtungen globaler politischer Strukturbildung*, edited by Mathias Albert and Rudolf Stichweh, 37–61. Wiesbaden: VS Verlag, 2007.
Fromm, Erich. *The Sane Society*. London: Routledge & Kegan Paul, 1956.
Galindo, George R.B. 'A reforma do judiciário como retrocesso para a proteção internacional dos direitos humanos: um estudo sobre o novo § 3° do artigo 5° da Constituição Federal'. *Cena Internacional* 7(1) (2005): 83–102.
Gomes, Luiz F. 'Direito internacional dos direitos humanos: vigência, validade e operacionalidade do princípio *pro homine*'. In *20 anos de Constituição Cidadã*, edited by Zulmar Fachin, 179–90. Rio de Janeiro: Forense/São Paulo: Método, 2008.
Gramsci, Antonio. *Selections from the Prison Notebooks*. Edited and translated by Quintin Hoare and Geoffry N. Smith. London: ElecBook, 1999.
Grimm, Dieter. 'Constitution in the Process of Denationalisation'. In *Constitutionalism: New Trends*, edited by Nergelius Joakim. Leiden and Boston: Martinus Nijhoff, 2008.
Gross, Oren. '"Control Systems" and the Migration of Anomalies'. In *The Migration of Constitutional Ideas*, edited by Sujit Choudhry, 403–30. Cambridge: Cambridge University Press, 2006.
Günther, Klaus. *Der Sinn für Angemessenheit: Anwendungsdiskurse in Moral und Recht*. Frankfurt am Main: Suhrkamp, 1988.

Hart, Herbert L.A. *The Concept of Law*, 2nd edition. Oxford: Clarendon Press, 1994 (1st edition 1961).

Held, David, and Anthony McGrew. 'Introduction'. In *Governing Globalization: Power, Authority and Global Governance*, edited by David Held and Anthony McGrew, 1–21. Cambridge: Polity Press, 2002.

Hofstadter, Douglas R. *Gödel, Escher, Bach: An Eternal Golden Braid*. Hassocks: The Harvester Press, 1979.

Jackson, Vicki C. 'Constitutional Comparisons: Convergence, Resistance, Engagement'. *Harvard Law Review* 119(109) (2005): 109–28.

Janis, Mark W. 'Human Rights and Imposed Constitutions'. *Connecticut Law Review* 37(4) (2005): 955–61.

Joerges, Christian. 'On the Legitimacy of Europeanising Europe's Private Law: Considerations on a Law of Justi(ce)-fication (Justun Facere) for the EU Multi-Level System'. *EUI Working Paper: Law* 3. San Domenico, Florence: European University Institute, 2003.

Joerges, Christian and Ernst-Ulrich Petersmann (eds). *Constitutionalism, Multilevel Trade Governance and Social Regulation*. Oxford and Portland: Hart, 2006.

Kelsen, Hans. *Allgemeine Staatslehre*. Bad Hamburg v. d. Höhe, Berlin and Zurich: Gehlen, 1925.

———. *General Theory of Law and State*. Translated by Anders Wedberg. Cambridge, MA: Harvard University Press, 1946.

———. *Reine Rechtslehre*, 2nd edition. Vienna: Franz Deuticke, 1960.

Koselleck, Reinhart. 'Begriffsgeschichtliche Probleme der Verfassungsgeschichtsbeschreibung'. In *Begriffsgeschichten*, 365–401. Frankfurt am Main: Suhrkamp, 2006.

Koskenniemi, Martti. 'International Law and Hegemony: A Reconfiguration'. *Cambridge Review of International Affairs* 17 (2004): 197–218.

———. 'The Fate of Public International Law: Constitutional Utopia or Fragmentation?' Paper presented at Chorley Lecture, London School of Economics and Political Science, 7 June 2006a.

———. 'International Law: Between Fragmentation and Constitutionalism'. Lecture presented at Canberra, 27 November 2006b.

———. 'Formalismus, Fragmentierung, Freiheit – Kantische Themen im heutigen Völkerrecht'. In *Transnationale Verrechtlichung. Nationale Demokratien im Kontext globaler Politik*, edited by Regina Kreide and Andreas Niederberger, 65–89. Frankfurt am Main and New York: Campus, 2008.

Koskenniemi, Martti, and Leino Päivi. 'Fragmentation of International Law? Postmodern Anxieties'. *Leiden Journal of International Law* 15 (2002): 553–79.

Ladeur, Karl-Heinz and Lars Viellechner. 'Die transnationale Expansion staatlicher Grundrechte: Zur Konstitutionalisierung globaler Privatregimes'. *Archiv des Völkerrechts* 46 (2008): 42–73.

Langer, Stefan. *Grundlagen einer internationalen Wirtschaftsverfassung – Strukturprinzipien, Typik und Perspektiven anhand von Europäischer Union und Welthandelsorganisation*. Munich: Beck, 1995.

Lassalle, Ferdinand. 'Über Verfassungswesen'. In *Reden und Schriften*, edited by Hans-Jurgen Friederici, 120–47. Cologne: Röderberg, 1987. Originally published 1862.

Levinson, Sanford. '"Imposed Constitutionalism": Some Reflections'. *Connecticut Law Review* 37(4) (2005): 921–32.

Loquin, Eric. 'Tribunal Arbitral du Sport: 2 Chronique des sentences arbitrales'. *Journal du Droit International Clunet* 1 (2008): 233–309.

Luhmann, Niklas. *Grundrechte als Institution. Ein Beitrag zur politischen Soziologie*. Berlin: Duncker & Humblot, 1965.

———. 'Reflexive Mechanismen'. In *Soziologische Aufklärung 1: Aufsätze zur Theorie sozialer Systeme*, 5'th edition, 92–112. Opladen: Westdeutscher Verlag, 1984 (first published in *Soziale Welt* 17 (1966): 1–23).

———. *Soziale Systeme: Grundriß einer allgemeinen Theorie*. Frankfurt am Main: Suhrkamp, 1987. (English translation: *Social Systems*. Stanford: Stanford University Press, 1995).

———. 'Verfassung als evolutionäre Errungenschaft'. *Rechtshistorisches Journal* 9 (1990a): 176–220.

———. 'Ich sehe was, was Du nicht siehst'. In *Soziologische Aufklärung 5: Konstruktivistische Perspektiven*, 228–34. Opladen: Westdeutscher Verlag, 1990b.

———. *Die Gesellschaft der Gesellschaft*, vol. 2. Frankfurt am Main: Suhrkamp, 1997.
———. *Die Politik der Gesellschaft*. Edited by André Kieserling. Frankfurt am Main: Suhrkamp, 2000.
Maduro Miguel P. *A Constituição plural: constitucionalismo e União Européia*. Cascais: Principia, 2006.
Maliska, Marcos A. *Estado e século XXI: A integração supranacional sob a ótica do direito constitucional*. Rio de Janeiro and São Paulo: Renovar, 2006.
Marx, Karl. *Ökonomische Manuskripte: 1863–1867: Text – Teil I*. In Karl Marx and Friedrich Engels, *Gesamtausgabe* (*MEGA*), vol. IV, part 1. Berlin: Dietz, 1988.
Mazzuoli, Valério de Oliveira. *Direito internacional: tratados e direitos humanos fundamentais na ordem jurídica brasileira*. Rio de Janeiro: América Jurídica, 2001.
———. 'O novo § 3° do art. 5° da Constituição e sua eficácia'. *Revista da AJURIS* XXXII(98) (2005): 303–31.
———. *Curso de direito internacional público*, 2nd edition. São Paulo: Revista dos Tribunais, 2007.
Mello, Celso D. de Albuquerque. 'O parágrafo 2° do artigo 5° da Constituição Federal'. In *Teoria dos direitos fundamentais*, 2nd edition, edited by Ricardo L. Torres, 1–33. Rio de Janeiro: Renovar, 2001.
Mendes, Gilmar F., Inocêncio M. Coelho and Paulo G.G. Branco. *Curso de direito constitucional*. São Paulo: Saraiva/IDP: Brasília, 2007.
Neves, Marcelo. *Verfassung und Positivität des Rechts in der peripheren Moderne: Eine theoretische Betrachtung und eine Interpretation des Falls Brasilien*. Berlin: Duncker & Humblot, 1992.
———. 'Gerechtigkeit und Differenz in einer komplexen Weltgesellschaft'. *Archiv für Rechts- und Sozialphilosophie* 88 (2002): 323–48.
———. *Entre Têmis e Leviatã: uma relação difícil – o Estado democrático de direito a partir e além de Luhmann e Habermas*. São Paulo: Martins Fontes, 2006.
———. 'A força simbólica dos direitos humanos'. *Revista Eletrônica de Direito do Estado* 4 (2005): 35. (English translation: 'The Symbolic Force of Human Rights'. *Philosophy & Social Criticism* 33(4) (2007): 411–44).
———. *Transconstitucionalismo*. São Paulo: WMF Martins Fontes, 2009 (English translation: *Transconstitutionalism*. Oxford: Hart, 2013).
Ortiz, Pía C. 'El Sistema Interamericano de Derechos Humanos: democracía y derechos humanos como factores integradores en Latinoamérica'. In *¿Integración suramericana a través del derecho? Un análisis multidiciplinario y multifocal*, edited by Armin von Bogdandy, Césae Landa Arroyo, and Mariela Morales Antoniazzi, 231–85. Max Planck Institute for Comparative Public Law and International Law/ Madrid: Centro de Estudios Constitucionales, 2009.
Pernice, Ingolf. 'Multilevel Constitutionalism and Treaty of Amsterdam: European Constitution-Making Revisited?' *Common Market Law Review* 36(4) (1999): 703–50.
———. 'Multilevel Constitutionalism in the European Union'. *European Law Review* 27 (2002): 511–29.
———. 'Artikel 24 [Übertragung und Einschränkung von Hoheitsrechten]'. In *Grundgesetz-Kommentar*, 2nd edition, vol. 2, edited by Horst Dreier, 501–31. Tübingen: Mohr, 2006.
Perotti, Alejandro D. 'Los Tribunales comunitarios en los procesos de integración: El caso del Tribunal de Justicia de la Comunidad Andina'. *Revista Jurídica del Perú* XLIII(17) (1998): 282–314.
———. 'Tribunales supranacionales. La Corte Centroamericana de Justicia'. *Revista Costarricense de Derecho Constitucional* III (2002): 153–252.
———. '¿Quién paga los costos del incumplimiento de las sentencias del Tribunal Permanente de Revisión (MERCOSUR)? Responsabilidad del Estado por violación del Derecho de la integración'. *El Derecho* – ED, Suplemento de Derecho Administrativo (2009): 1–8.
Petersmann, Ernst-Ulrich. 'Multilevel Constitutionalism and Judicial Protection of Freedom and Justice in the International Economic Law of the EC'. In *Continuity and Change in EU Law: Essays in Honour of Sir Francis Jacobs*, edited by Anthony Arnull, Piet Eeckhout and Takis Tridimas, 338–53. Oxford: Oxford University Press, 2008.
Piovesan, Flávia. *Direitos humanos e o direito constitucional internacional*, 9th edition. São Paulo: Saraiva, 2008a.
———. 'Igualdade, diferença e direitos humanos: perspectivas global e regional'. In *Igualdade, diferença e direitos humanos*, edited by Domingo Sarmento, Daniela Ikava and Flávia Piovesan, 47–76. Rio de Janeiro: Lumen Juris, 2008b.

Pires, Francisco L. *Introdução ao direito constitucional europeu (seu sentido, problemas e limites)*. Coimbra: Almedina, 1997.
Pontes De Miranda, Francisco C. *Comentários à Constituição de 1946*, vol. I. Rio de Janeiro: Borsoi, 1960.
Ramírez, Andrés D. 'El caso de la comunidad indígena *Yakye Axa vs. Paraguay*'. *Revista IIDH/Instituto Interamericano de Derechos Humanos* 41 (2005): 349–64.
Ramírez, Sergio Garcia. 'Cuestiones de la jurisdicción interamericana de derechos humanos'. *Anuario Mexicano de Derecho Internacional* (2008): 187–221.
Randeria, Shalini. 'Glocalization of Law: Environmental Justice, World Bank, NGOs and the Cunning State in India'. *Current Sociology* 51(3/4) (2003): 305–28.
Rawls, John. *A Theory of Justice*. Oxford: Oxford University Press, 1990 (first edition 1972).
———. *The Law of Peoples, with 'The Idea of Public Reason Revisited'*. Cambridge, MA and London: Harvard University Press, 1999.
Roach, Kent. 'The Post-9/11 Migration of Britain's Terrorism Act 2000'. In *The Migration of Constitutional Ideas*, edited by Sujit Choudhry, 373–402. Cambridge: Cambridge University Press, 2006.
Robertson, Roland. 'Glocalization: Time-Space and Homogeneity-Heterogeneity'. In *Global Modernities*, edited by Mike Featherstone, Scott M. Lash and Roland Robertson, 25–44. London: Sage, 1995.
Rosenfeld, Michel. 'The Identity of the Constitutional Subject'. In *Law and the Postmodern Mind: Essays on Psychoanalysis and Jurisprudence*, edited by Peter Goodrich and David G. Carlson, 143–74. Ann Arbor: The University of Michigan Press, 1998.
Sabadell, Ana L., and Dimitri Dimoulis. 'O Tribunal Penal Internacional em face da Constituição brasileira e a questão da ineficácia social dos direitos fundamentais'. In *Transnacionalidade do direito: novas perspectivas dos conflitos entre ordens jurídicas*, edited by Marcelo Neves, 157–86. São Paulo: Quartier Latin, 2010.
Saldanha, Nelson. 'O chamado "bacharelismo" brasileiro: ensaio de revisão'. *Convivivm* XVII(21) (1978): 477–84.
Sarlet, Ingo W. *A eficácia dos direitos fundamentais*, 2nd edition. Porto Alegre: Livraria dos Advogados, 2001.
———. 'A reforma do judiciário e os tratados internacionais de direitos humanos: observações sobre o § 3.° do art. 5.° da Constituição'. *Interesse Público* VIII(37) (2006): 49–64.
———. 'Direitos fundamentais e tratados internacionais em matéria de direitos humanos: revisitando a discussão em torno dos parágrafos 2.° e 3.° do art. 5.° da Constituição Federal de 1988'. In *Transnacionalidade do direito: novas perspectivas dos conflitos entre ordens jurídicas*, edited by Marcelo Neves, 73–99. São Paulo: Quartier Latin, 2010.
Sauer, Heiko. *Jurisdiktionskonflikte in Mehrebenensystem: Die Entwicklung eines Modells zur Lösung von Konflikten zwischen Gerichten in vernetzten Rechtordnungen*. Berlin and Heidelberg: Springer, 2008.
Scharpf, Fritz W. 'Community and Autonomy: Multilevel Policy-Making in the European Union'. *EUI Working Paper RSC* (94) 1. San Domenico, Florence: European University Institute, 1994.
———. 'Regieren im europäischen Mehrebenensystem – Ansätze zur einer Theorie'. *Leviathan: Berliner Zeitschrift für Sozialwissenschaft* 1/2002 (2002): 65–92.
Schauer, Frederick. 'On the Migration of Constitutional Ideas'. *Connecticut Law Review* 37(4) (2005): 907–19.
Scheppele, Kim L. 'The Migration of Anti-constitutional Ideas: The Post-9/11 Globalization of Public Law and the International State of Emergency'. In *The Migration of Constitutional Ideas*, edited by Sujit Choudhry, 347–73. Cambridge: Cambridge University Press, 2006.
Segato, Rita L. 'Que cada pueblo teja los hilos de su historia. El pluralismo jurídico en diálogo didáctico con legisladores'. In *Justicia y diversidad en América Latina. Pueblos indígenas ante la globalización*, edited by Victoria Chenaut, Magdalenao Gómez, Héctor Ortiz and Maria T. Sierra, 357–81. México, DF: CIESAS/Quito: FLACSO, 2011.
Sunder, Madhavi. 'Enlightened Constitutionalism'. *Connecticut Law Review* 37(4) (2005): 891–905.
Tavares, André Ramos. *Reforma do judiciário no Brasil pós-88*: *(des)estruturando a justiça. Comentários completos à Emenda Constitucional n.° 45/04*. São Paulo: Saraiva, 2005.

Teubner, Gunther. 'Globale Zivilverfassungen: Alternativen zur staatszentrierten Verfassungstheorie'. *Zeitschrift für ausländisches öffentliches Recht und Völkerrecht* 63(1) (2003): 1–28. (English translation: 'Societal Constitutionalism: Alternatives to State-Centred Constitutional Theory?' In *Transnational Governance and Constitutionalism*, edited by Christian Joerges, Inger-Johanne Sand, and Gunther Teubner, 3–28. Oxford: Hart, 2004).

———. 'Die Anonyme Matrix: Zu Menschenrechtsverletzungen durch "private" transnationale Akteure'. *Der Staat* 45(2) (2006): 161–87 (English translation: 'The Anonymous Matrix: Human Rights Violations by 'Private' Transnational Actors'. *Modern Law Review* 69 (2006): 327–46).

———. 'Selbstsubversive Gerechtigkeit: Kontingenz- oder Transzendenzformel des Rechts'. *Zeitschrift für Rechtssoziologie* 29(1) (2008): 9–36 (English translation: 'Self-Subversive Justice: Contingency or Transcendence Formula of Law?'. *Modern Law Review* 72 (2009): 1–23).

———. *Verfassungsfragmente: gesellschaftlicher Konstitutionalismus in der Globalisierung*. Berlin: Suhrkamp, 2012 (English translation: *Constitutional Fragments: Societal Constitutionalism and Globalisation*. Oxford: Oxford University Press, 2012).

Thornhill, Chris. *A Sociology of Constitutions: Constitutions and State Legitimacy in Historical-Sociological Perspective*. Cambridge: Cambridge University Press, 2011.

Toledo, Ricardo V. 'La contribución del Tribunal de Justicia Andina al proceso de integración suramericana'. In *¿Integración suramericana a través del derecho? Un análisis multidiciplinario y multifocal*, edited by Armin von Bogdandy, Césae Landa Arroyo, and Mariela Morales Antoniazzi, 397–412. Max Planck Institute for Comparative Public Law and International Law/Madrid: Centro de Estudios Constitucionales, 2009.

Tomuschat, Christian. 'Die internationale Gemeinschaft'. *Archiv des Völkerrechts* 33 (1995): 1–20.

Tönnies, Ferdinand. *Gemeinschaft und Gesellschaft: Grundbegriffe der reinen Soziologie*. Darmstadt: Wissenschaftliche Buchgesellschaft, 1979.

Trindade, Antônio A.C. *A proteção internacional dos direitos humanos e o Brasil (1948–1997): as primeiras cinco décadas*, 2nd edition. Brasília: UnB, 2000.

———. *Tratado de direito internacional dos direitos humanos*, 2nd edition, vol. I. Porto Alegre: Fabris, 2003.

———. 'Prefácio. A Corte Interamericana de Direitos Humanos: um testemunho para a história'. In *O Sistema Interamericano de Proteção dos Direitos Humanos: interface com o direito constitucional*, edited by Márcio Luís de Oliveira, XVII–XLIII. Belo Horizonte: Del Rey, 2007.

Tushnet, Mark. 'The Inevitable Globalization of Constitutional Law'. Paper presented at the seminar 'The Changing Role of Highest Courts in an Internationalizing World', sponsored by the Hague Institute for the Internationalisation of Law, 23–24 October 2008. Available at: http://ssrn.com/abstract=1317766.

Venancio Filho, Alberto. *Das arcadas ao bacharelismo: 150 anos de ensino jurídico no Brasil*. São Paulo: Perspectiva, 1977.

Von Foerster, Heinz. 'On Constructing Reality'. In *Observing Systems*, 288–309. Seaside: Intersystems Publications, 1981.

Waldron, Jeremy. 'Foreign Law and the Modern *Ius Gentium*'. *Harvard Law Review* 119(1) (2005): 129–47.

Weber, Max. *Wirtschaft und Gesellschaft: Grundriß der verstehenden Soziologie*, 5th edition. Edited by Johann J. Winckelmann. Tübingen: Mohr, 1985 (1st edition 1922).

Weiler, Joseph H.H. *The Constitution of Europe: 'Do the New Clothes have an Emperor?' and Other Essays on European Integration*. Cambridge: Cambridge University Press, 1999.

Welsch, Wolfgang. *Vernunft: Die zeitgenössische Vernunftkritik und das Konzept der transversalen Vernunft*, 2nd edition. Frankfurt am Main: Suhrkamp, 1996.

———. *Unsere postmoderne Moderne*, 6th edition. Berlin: Akademie Verlag, 2002.

Wolfrum, Rüdiger. 'The Protection of Indigenous Peoples in International Law'. *Zeitschrift für ausländisches öffentliches Recht und Völkerrecht* 59 (1999): 369–82.

Appendix

14 The constitution in the work of Niklas Luhmann

Giancarlo Corsi

To understand how Luhmann studied the constitution, a premise is necessary. The systems theory is actually based on the idea that modern society is a functionally differentiated system. This means that subsystems are distinguished on the basis of the functions they fulfil, and have a de facto monopoly of their specific functions. This also applies to the system of law as well as to the system of politics: they are distinct systems, with different functions, structures and codes. This is a statement that would probably still not meet with the orientation of several researchers today and that already raised many an eyebrow in the 1960s (see Luhmann 2005: 272). All we can do here is recall that the law's function, for the systems theory, is not to regulate behaviour, but to create, maintain and generalise expectations of behaviour established by norms or in some other way traceable to legal factors. The function of politics, on the other hand, is to exercise power to make collectively binding decisions, these days through democratically-organised state structures.

It is important to remember this position adopted by the systems theory, because the constitution is a text that has played a pivotal role in both politics and law and, as we shall see, Luhmann holds that the meaning it has acquired in the last two hundred years actually derives from its relationship with these two different subsystems.

With regard to Luhmann's research on the constitution, his later writings only include one essay devoted explicitly to the topic (1990, but this was preceded by another back in 1973). In addition, he discusses the constitution in the two main books he devoted to the law (*Das Recht der Gesellschaft*, 1993, translated into English as *Law and a Social System*, 2004) and to politics (*Die Politik der Gesellschaft*, 2000). He also mentions the topic occasionally in other essays and books (see the references at the end of this chapter). It may be worth bearing in mind that he only dedicates a handful of lines to the constitution in his first book devoted to the law (*Rechtssoziologie*, 1972, translated into English as *A Sociological Theory of Law*, 1985), while analyses of the issue can be found in some of his writings about political sociology.

The following paragraphs are concentrated on Luhmann's research into the constitution in the political sense and in the legal sense, and will conclude with the argument that was crucial to his analyses, i.e. that the constitution's primary function is to enable the relations between the two systems of politics and of the law. The key term here will be structural coupling.

From a political standpoint, Luhmann sees the constitution primarily as the modern solution to the classical problem of political theory, i.e. the legitimation of power. The problem cannot be solved because it is structurally based on a paradox: it is impossible to justify and legitimise a situation in which some exercise power over others, except by having recourse to semantic artifices, such as today's constitutional state and/or popular sovereignty (Luhmann 2000: 33).

That society's underlying structural problems, like those of all its subsystems, take the form of a paradox is typical of the systems theory. In the case of politics, the paradox is that the legitimation sought can only come from the power itself: in other words, the legitimation in question is always self-legitimation (Luhmann 1981). But that is the very reason why the power has to find a way to 'externalise' its legitimation, thus concealing the paradox and making the difference between those who hold the power and those who are subject to it acceptable.

While the sovereign in the pre-modern tradition was legitimised by a divinity or by reference to natural law, modernity brought the political theory that initially put its trust in the doctrines of contract, in a much more complex and refined approach. In any case, the apex of the political system has always had blurred outlines, which in one way or another end up pointing at arbitrariness, so to something that cannot be justified.

Luhmann's arguments about the political constitution are inspired by the characteristics of the modern state, above all by the division of powers, which enables the judiciary to control and limit the political power, this latter being a factor that from the very beginning legitimised the need for the constitution. The development of modern politics led to its democratisation, which for Luhmann means primarily the legitimation of the opposition, so that the apex of the exercise of power is now split along the lines of government vis-à-vis opposition (Luhmann 1989). In parallel, the figure of the sovereign also changes: it is the people. Yet popular sovereignty is only another version of the underlying paradox, deriving from the idea of a people that governs itself, of a people that decides to be governed (Luhmann 2000: 141).

Many other aspects typical of constitutions are related to these political developments, including the relevance of interests (mediated by political parties), the protection of minorities, the fundamental rights, to which Luhmann devotes some important works (Luhmann 1965, 1973). From a political standpoint, Luhmann holds that fundamental rights and the values in which they are condensed are a form of legitimation of the constitution, a sort of 'civil religion' (Luhmann 2000: 141). Nevertheless, constitutional values are politically important not as ideals to be approached as closely as possible, but because they enable politics to create a specific uncertainty of its own (Luhmann 2000: 177–80), being not always mutually compatible as for instance the two values of freedom and equality: the very fact that they clash is the reason why they could be the lasting benchmark of nineteenth-century ideologies.

Ultimately, Luhmann holds that the constitution and the transformation of the liberal state into a constitutional state enable the political system to set its own internal and external boundaries: internally by organising the control and the division of powers, and externally by means of fundamental rights. In both directions, politics outlines its own possibilities and becomes autonomous as a differentiated subsystem within modern society. The control of what is politically permissible is thus not entrusted to supreme organs, but to the law and to justice on the one hand and to public opinion on the other.

From a legal standpoint, Luhmann sees the constitution as the modern tool that enables the law to manage its autonomy in a functionally differentiated society. In this context autonomy means above all positivisation of the law.

Luhmann stresses this point repeatedly in several works, as he believes it to be the decisive turning point for achieving the complete differentiation of a system of law (Luhmann 1970; 1972: 190–205; 1988). The question is still being discussed, although there is no doubt that the traditional distinction drawn between *jus naturale* and *jus positum*, natural law and positive law, which dominated the classical tradition until the beginning of the modern era, loses out in significance with functional differentiation. Luhmann notes that modern law is entirely positive law, in the sense that it is the result of decisions and can be created, amended or abolished by means of decisions.

This evolutionary process in the law is clearly visible in the birth of the United States. After the revolution, when the newly independent colonies set about creating territorial states and their new nation, one of the most important problems they had to face was how to bridge the normative gaps deriving from their independence. The need to reorganise their legal material on foundations that were certainly traditional, but that would make allowance for a thoroughly unprecedented situation, suggested that the entire normative apparatus could be reviewed, reconsidered and potentially adapted and changed. In short, there was nothing that could be considered to be immune to potential revision: everything could be rearranged and reorganised in whatever way was most suitable. The constitution was an ideal solution for this purpose, and the consequences were of the utmost relevance 'A Law repugnant to the Constitution is void', as Marshall stated in the *Marbury* v. *Madison* case in 1803 (about the birth of the American constitution, see Luhmann 1990).

Luhmann focuses his interest on the formal and structural aspects of the constitutional text. The systems theory, as already mentioned, attributes pivotal importance to the circularity of communication in all its forms, especially to paradoxes and to tautologies. The law is an exemplary case: if all law were to become positive, how could the problems of self-control, of self-limitation and of change based on internal criteria be managed?

Luhmann returns repeatedly to the double distinction that has characterised the law since the invention of the constitution: the code of *Recht/Unrecht*[1] is not alone, but is also joined by 'the additional coding constitutional/unconstitutional' (Luhmann 1993: 120; here as in the following quotations see the English translation). This gives us 'a second level, where everything is different from the normal level' (Luhmann 2005: 232). While the rule that normally applies in the law is 'new law breaks old law', in the case of the constitution, it is the opposite rule that applies and this leads to the need for rules governing collisions and to the question of limits on the changeability of constitutional norms. It is then also possible to end up in a situation where norms or decisions may comply with the law, but be in breach of the constitution: a 'very unusual thing' (Luhmann 2005: 232).

The problems whose nature is more or less one of logic do not end here. For example, the constitution must include itself in itself, establishing rules for its own amendment and criteria and forms for judging constitutionality; in addition, the constitution proclaims itself, stating that it draws its legitimacy from God or from the people, thus externalising its own circularity (Luhmann 1993: 406). Alternatively, to mention another example, constitutions sometimes establish norms that establish other norms that have not to be changed. But since this prohibition could be changed, the whole thing ends up with a recourse to infinity (Luhmann 1993: 126–7). The law is therefore entrusted to a political evaluation, thus avoiding the issue of the paradox ending up blocking the law. Luhmann's interest in the constitution from a legal standpoint springs from historical analyses that attempt to answer the question: why does modern law need a constitution and what is its function?

It is no coincidence that the only essay that Luhmann devoted explicitly to the constitution is entitled 'Verfassung als evolutionäre Errungenschaft' (1990, 'The Constitution as an Evolutionary Achievement'). The fact that Luhmann places the constitution within an evolutionary process enables him to disregard its inventors' intentions: in other words, the constitution is the result of a process that has manifested its potential in a way that goes well beyond those intentions. According to the meaning given to it by the systems theory, the expression 'evolutionary conquest' stands for a social form that not only has to be compatible with the context in which it comes about (in our case, that of law and politics), but must also be advantageous, enabling internal complexity to be increased in order to reduce external complexity, as Luhmann constantly formulated it in his writings (lastly in *The Theory of Society*, 1997: 505–16). In this sense, we can see that the constitution represents the structural coupling between law and politics.

The concept of structural coupling, revived by Humberto Maturana, becomes necessary to describe the relationships that systems succeed in establishing with their environment. If we start from the premise that systems are autopoietic, i.e. operationally closed, and if we therefore rule out the possibility that exchanges or input–output relationships take place between a system and its environment, then we need to understand how the environment becomes relevant for the system in terms of its possibilities of survival. And the answer is in fact structural coupling, i.e. very specific and extremely selective relationship between the system and particular sectors of its environment. On the one hand, the system must be able to remain indifferent to almost everything that happens in its environment, but on the other it must be open to being 'irritated', 'perturbed' and 'disturbed', albeit only to a very limited extent. Any communication, for example, is not sensitive to anything of what happens or exists outside social systems. Natural differences (temperature, radiation and waves of all kinds), including differences produced by individuals' bodies and minds, are inaccessible to communication (this is what the systems theory means by 'operational closure'). But at the same time communication has to be liable to irritation and in fact can only be irritated by those who take part in the communication through very specific forms of structural coupling, such as language.

Luhmann's thesis is that the constitution fulfils the function of structural coupling between the political system and the legal system, once modernity enables the two systems to achieve complete differentiation. In other conditions the relationships between law and politics did not require any such structure: law recognised society's class order and the nobility prevailed in cases of legal conflicts, while any problems between the normative order and structures of dominion were regulated contractually (Luhmann 1993: 450). But this involved extensive integration between the two systems that limited their development.

With the invention of the constitutional state, strict limits were imposed on the possibilities of reciprocal influence between law and politics, excluding such classical forms and customs as for example the 'exploitation of legal positions in the economic system (wealth, legal control of politically important options) in order to achieve political power, or political terrorism or political corruption' (Luhmann 1993: 404). The two systems' dynamic actually increase as a result of this limitation, while the reciprocal influences are limited to the fact that 'positive law is the instrument of choice for political organisations and, at the same time, constitutional law is a legal instrument for the disciplining of politics' (Luhmann 1993: 404).

This generates an enormous potential for reciprocal irritability that translates into an equally high degree of structural variability. Consider the developments in modern politics, about which Luhmann argues that 'democracy is a consequence of the positivisation of law and of the ensuing possibilities of changing the law at any time' (Luhmann 1993: 404). The function of structural coupling is concealed by the symbolic emphasis attributed to constitutions, as though they were a unitary, superior form, while from a sociological point of view – and in particular from that of the systems theory – they are only a form 'that can be read two ways and can be tackled differently from two sides, without insoluble political conflicts continuously arising as a result' (2000: 392). Luhmann closes this argument saying that those who do not see this difference of perspective can only generate confusion (2000: 392). The meaning of the constitution from the point of view of systemic sociology is rather different from that usually attributed to it by law and politics and by the theories that these systems have developed. The interpretative framework is offered here in more abstract terms by the systems theory that enables the subsystems of modern society to be compared to one another, providing the structures necessary for solving specific problems, such as the issue of structural coupling between operationally closed systems. This permits the constitution to be compared with the other forms of structural coupling that came about with functional differentiation, such as the institution of property and those of contract for regulating relations between law and the economy, of qualifications and degrees for regulating relations between the economy and education, of the central banks for regulating relations between politics and the economy and so on: a theoretical approach and a scientific methodology that are decidedly unusual in the panorama of a fragmented sociology.

Note

1 Luhmann defines the code of law in terms of the two poles *Recht/Unrecht*, which are usually translated into English as legal/illegal. It is worth noting that this translation does not render the full meaning of the two terms *Recht/Unrecht*, which are hard to translate into any other language. The problem is that the law is not limited to dealing with questions of legality or illegality: it is safe to assume that this distinction came along relatively late, as a consequence of elaborate – if not already written – legal codes. *Recht* and *Unrecht* are far more generic terms that refer to any case that calls for an intervention to solve a conflict. As a matter of fact, even today, not all conflicts that end up in court or that have some form of legal solution concern questions of legality/illegality. When he was speaking in English, Luhmann himself on many occasions used the words right/wrong.

Selected Luhmann's works about the constitution

Grundrechte als Institution. Ein Beitrag zur politischen Soziologie, Berlin, 1965, 3rd edition 1986.

'Positivität des Rechts als Voraussetzung einer modernen Gesellschaft', *Jahrbuch für Rechtssoziologie und Rechtstheorie* 1 (1970): 175–202.

Rechtssoziologie, 2 vols, Reinbek, 1972; 2nd extended edition, Opladen, 1983. English translation: *A Sociological Theory of Law*, London: Routledge, 1985.

'Politische Verfassungen im Kontext des Gesellschaftssystems', *Der Staat* 12 (1973): 1–22 and 165–82.

'Selbstlegitimation des Staates', in Norbert Achterberg and Werner Krawietz (eds), *Legitimation des modernen Staates, Beiheft 15 des Archivs für Rechts- und Sozialphilosophie*, Wiesbaden, 1981, pp. 65–83.

'Positivität als Selbstbestimmtheit des Rechts', *Rechtstheorie* 19 (1988): 11–27.

'Theorie der politischen Opposition', *Zeitschrift für Politik* 36 (1989): 13–26.

'Verfassung als evolutionäre Errungenschaft', *Rechtshistorisches Journal* 9 (1990): 176–220.

Das Recht der Gesellschaft, Frankfurt/M.: Suhrkamp, 1993. English translation: *Law as a Social System*, Oxford: Oxford University Press, 2004.

'Metamorphosen des Staates', *Information Philosophie* 4(22) (1994): 5–21.

Die Gesellschaft der Gesellschaft, Frankfurt/M.: Suhrkamp, 1997. English translation: *Theory of Society*, vol. 1, Stanford: Stanford University Press.

Die Politik der Gesellschaft, Frankfurt/M.: Suhrkamp, 2000.

Einführung in die Theorie der Gesellschaft, Wiesbaden: Carl-Auer Verlag, 2005.

15 The issue of the constitution in Luhmann's card index system

Reading the traces

Johannes F.K. Schmidt

Introduction

Niklas Luhmann, as already mentioned in Chapter 14, started discussing the issue of the constitution at a very early stage in his academic career: his first established publication in this field was his 1965 work, *Fundamental Rights as an Institution*, in which he already discussed from a standpoint of societal theory, referring to political sociology in the subtitle, but which also addressed jurists. This was followed in 1973 by his comprehensive approach to the *Political Constitution in the Context of the Social System*, which focused on the question of the constitution's function for the political system, but also still addressed an audience interested in legal theory. Following the autopoietic turnaround in the underlying system theory in the 1980s, the question about the constitution was raised once again in this changed theoretical framework, especially in his historically argued 1989 essay 'The Constitution as an Evolutionary Achievement' and notably in his 1993 monograph on the functional system *Law as a Social System*. It is therefore possible to speak of an ongoing, though maybe not exactly continuous, interest in the topic of the constitution on the part of the sociologist Luhmann. This chapter starts out against a background and on the basis of a preliminary inspection of Luhmann's card index system to ask what traces of the constitutional issue can be found in the unique collection of jottings pieced together by Luhmann from the 1950s onwards and which eventually totalled nearly 90,000 notes by the middle of the 1990s.

Luhmann's card index system

In Niklas Luhmann's description of the theory project he pursued purposefully and applied universally for over 35 years, his card index system constitutes a factor that cannot be ignored (namely, Luhmann 1981a; 1987): without the specific method of the notes he already started jotting down even before he started out on his actual academic career, the better to provide the results of his excessive and broadly interdisciplinary reading with a systematic organisation, as Luhmann tells us himself, the great number and thematic diversity of his publications would have been inconceivable. By organising his research in this way, he tapped into a system of knowledge management that had developed to keep pace with the rapidly increasing number of publications available since the sixteenth century (see Zedelmaier 1992, 22ff., 36ff., 99ff.), using a quite specific storage and retrieval system to perfect the possibilities of systematic knowledge generating offered by the card index system (see Krajewski 2002).

The card index system in Luhmann's academic estate comprises two largely separated collections:

a an early collection dating to the period 1951–62, based primarily on his readings in the areas of administrative and political sciences, organisational theory and philosophy and consisting of some 24,000 notes; and
b a later collection dating to the period 1963–96, featuring a clear sociological slant and consisting of some 66,000 notes.

As a rule, Luhmann did not put excerpts directly into his file system, but was far more likely to take notes while reading, then use them in a second stage to generate comments, which he then oriented in particular to relate to the other notes already contained in the system. He assumed that it would only be possible to decide at a later stage how meaningful a note would be, by seeing how it related to other notes.

Luhmann himself described his filing system on the one hand as a 'tool for thinking' that provided the groundwork that enabled him to think in a structured, link-oriented 'manner that works differences in': this brought all the 'ideas' and 'chances of (his) reading' into his collection, leaving the decision about how to link it all up internally to a later stage (ZK II: 9/8g, 9/8a2, 9/8i).[1] On the other hand, he said that his filing system was a 'second memory' that constituted not so much a simple archive of knowledge as a partner in a process of communication, so that he himself was surprised by the information furnished by the system (Luhmann 1981a, 225). The reason why the difference of his system of storage and use could be productive was because the collection's internal structure enabled some quite different combinations of several notes to be compiled in response to individual questions, making it largely independent of the original intention when the note was first drawn up.

Talking about his filing system, Luhmann (1981a, 224f.) based his approach on the unusual structure of the note collection, which he maintained explained his unusual productivity. In a section devoted to the card index system itself,[2] he describes the collection as 'a cybernetic system' in the shape of a 'combination of order and disorder, of coagulating and unpredictable combinations achieved by accessing it at random' (ZK II: 9/8). The precondition for this was that he had to accept the need to do without any predetermined order. But even though the note collection has no systematic structure, it nevertheless contains an accumulation of many notes about certain terms and individual issues. Correspondingly, there is a first level of order and sections that is thoroughly differentiated by topics. In the earlier of the two collections, this structure still bears clear signs of the (individual) processing of previously determined (and external) areas of knowledge, which are listed and processed in 108 sections. The core issues in this case are found in the area of legal and political sciences, of the science of administration and of organisational theory, but there are also sections on questions concerned with epistemology, as well as some individual sociological issues. The second and later collection was organised from the very beginning with a focus on identified issues and betrays a genuinely sociological grasp. Here there are only 11 main topics, while their respective sections contain several thousand cards each:

1 organisational theory
2 functionalism
3 decision theory
4 officialdom

5 formal/informal order
6 sovereignty/state
7 individual terms/problems
8 economics
9 random notes
10 archaic societies
11 high cultures.

It is easy to see that this is neither a mere list, nor a structural order with a preconceived system. Instead, this structure is very clearly the product of Luhmann's reading and research interests, as recorded in the course of time. This applies both to the first level of ordering and to the additional subsections that follow on them, which are at least loosely related to the original issue. Within these thematic blocks, each card is then the subject of a specific ordering principle that does not lead the respective first thematic stipulation to an obligatory monothematic succession, but often introduces it to a cascade of issues that take it further and further away from the point where the considerations started. As a result, the functionalism section, for example, contains not only thoughts about the concept of function, but also about that of system, the relationship between systems and the world, social theory and stratification, among other things.

This structure derives from the underlying idea behind Luhmann's card index system, that a card only needs to relate to the previous one and does not necessarily need to take a preconceived superior thematic structure into account. This corresponds to a specific way of generating notes, in which Luhmann followed up on secondary thoughts that triggered his interest, jotting down additional notes about a thought that had already occurred to him on a card that he would then place here in the filing system, so that he would retain a sequence of cards that led further and further away from the original issue or enabled the card index system to grow 'inwardly'. But placing individual cards in the collection was not the only product generated by Luhmann's reading interests in the course of time. The collection itself is also the consequence of the frequent difficulty he encountered when he tried to classify a question unequivocally under one and only one (superior) issue. Luhmann solved this problem by treating it as an opportunity: by adopting the principle that each the entry only has to relate to the previous entry, he adhered to the computer technology principle, already known in the 1950s, of 'multiple storage', so that notes about one issue can be found in quite different places in the card index system.

There is a constitutive relationship between the storage technique thus sketched and the special numbering system used for the notes. The principle behind it all derives necessarily from the decision to do without an explicit thematic order, which then leads to the question of how to retrieve a certain card once it has been filed. The solution is in each card's fixed location and a corresponding numbering system, which at the same time tackles the question of how to insert the new card into the existing index without causing havoc with the original numbering system. This idea was put into practice with a very simple expedient: in each of the major sections listed above, Luhmann first always applied a simple numerical sequence that reflected the moment when each entry was made. The section number comes before the actual sequential number, so 1/1 is followed by 1/2, 1/3 and so on. Cards that were then generated later on and pursue a single issue that is jotted down on card 1/1 are then identified by a corresponding numerical sequence of their own, so that card 1/1a is inserted between card 1/1 and card 1/2. The next card after that may return to a single issue with 1b or pursue the previous sequence further with 1/1a1: this latter card is inserted between card 1/1a and card 1/1b and so on. This procedure means that the space between two thematically related cards that were originally generated one directly next to another, so could also be found one directly next to the other, may end up being occupied by hundreds of cards generated later, whose numerical sequence can have combinations of up to 13 numerals and letters. This card index therefore features a thoroughly idiosyncratic 3D structure, which Luhmann described in his explanation of his filing system as an 'internal branching capacity' (1981a, 224).

A further need arises from the storage system sketched out above, and especially its principle of multiple storage: all the cards in the collection that are related to one another thematically or conceptually must also refer to one another, by means of a reciprocal notation of their respective card numbers. For this reason, individual references at the beginning of a thematic subsection are often accompanied by an introductory card with collective references, which develop systematically on the thematically related fields in the card system. Luhmann himself called this reference system network a 'spider-shaped system' (1987, 143). Test samples enable us to assume that there are about 20,000 references in the earlier collection and about 30,000 in the later one.

Lastly, in order to ensure that this network of references would always remain accessible, Luhmann drew up a list of keywords with about 4,000 entries. This list of keywords was the vital tool for using the index, as it was the only way in which notes about a given topic could be retrieved with certainty. Unlike a corresponding index in a book, this list of keywords lays no claim to achieving a complete compilation of the locations in the collection that tackle each concept. Instead, Luhmann generally only made of a record of at most three places in his system where the concept in question could be found. The underlying idea was that he could then use the internal system of cross-references to find the other relevant places very quickly.

In summary, we can say that not only was Luhmann's original approach to reading and note-taking crucial for his collection to function, but also the relationships between the notes that were created on the one hand by his special method of storage and on the other by his method of (selective) reference. The difference between the structure of the issues put down (more or less at random) in the course of time and the structure of references generated with every subsequent new entry thus became sometimes more available when the collection was consulted at a later date than had been intended with the original note. The collection's structural organisation ensures that any access to a conceptually pertinent place in the collection that is managed via the list of keywords does not restrict the search to that single location, quite the contrary: profiting from the specific approach adopted for inserting the cards and the structure of references, it opens the gates to a web of notes, so that the combination of the search question addressed to the list of keywords and the principle of placing the cards and the reference system systematically brings (theoretically or conceptually controlled) chance into play. With his principle of multiple storage and a method of references reminiscent of today's hyperlinks – and despite using an analogue storage system, Luhmann was already simulating a modern computer-aided databank system as early as the 1960s, to which he then resorted with increasing frequency for the purpose of generating his manuscripts, once he had achieved a critical mass of notes at the beginning of the 1970s. This by no means indicates that the relationship between the card index and Luhmann's publications was in any way one-sided, far from it: the basic assumption should be one of reciprocity, in which on the one hand the texts were initiated by consulting the card index and by asking it specific questions, so as generate a combination of a variety of findings from different places, while on the other hand the thoughts thus generated also found their way back into the card index in their own right (see Schmidt 2012, 10f.). Similarly, not (only) was verified knowledge entrusted to the collection's function as a tool for thinking, but a process of theory generation was also recorded, including potential mistakes and red herrings, which were revised by later entries, but not eliminated, as once a card had found its way into the index, it stayed there.

After this introduction, it is now time to ask what traces the constitutional issue left in the card index and whether the system's functionality as described above is confirmed for this topic.

The constitution in the card index system

The fact that Luhmann focused intensively on law as a subject matter throughout his entire academic career can of course be traced back to the circumstance that, as a jurist who first took an interest in constitutional law, he also had a special affinity for this field later in his career, as a sociologist. To this extent it comes as no surprise that his card index system contains a large number of notes about the law. To be sure, it should be noted from the start that this only applies to a limited extent for the issue of special interest to us here now: that of the constitution.

Card index I: the concept of constitutional law

From 1956 to 1962, Luhmann worked as an advisor in the Lower Saxony Ministry of Culture, although at the same time he was already pursuing advanced academic interests, with a special focus firstly on constitutional law and administrative studies, which already at this time led not only to extensive reading, but also to his first more comprehensive manuscripts. Thus does his estate include not only the manuscript of a practically complete, but never submitted, dissertation about *The Organisation of Government Advisory Bodies*, dated 1955, in which he discusses the question of submitting advisory relations to a process of normation under (organisational) law, but also further, albeit incomplete, manuscripts about political science and about a theory of the contemporary state dated to the late 1950s.

This primary perspective of political and administrative sciences, on which Luhmann was only to expand by taking an increasing and decided interest in organisational studies from the beginning of the 1960s,[3] already becomes clear in the structure he gave to the collection, which, compared to the second card index, still shows the signs of the (individual) processing of previously largely determined and relatively compartmentalised areas of knowledge: in particular in the earlier part of the collection, the majority of these still reflect a juridical approach.[4] Yet the fact that Luhmann's relationship to sociology is still rather distant here is not clear from the thematic priorities. Rather, the collection contains repeated formulations that demonstrate the jurist's lingering mistrust of what, from his point of view, was the conceptually less disciplined discussion about sociology. In a similar vein, the few references to the constitution are primarily expressed from an internal legal viewpoint. They can be found in the section on the constitution, section 27, which comes between section 26, 'Power', and section 28 on 'The Nature of Organisation'. When it comes, though, the topic's explicit treatment is certainly very clear: on no more than 13 cards (making this one of the shortest sections in the collection), Luhmann approaches the topic from a decidedly constitutional angle.

Already the literature that Luhmann noted at the beginning of the section derives practically exclusively from the juridical discussion (of political and administrative science and public law): in the notes that followed, he had evidently taken his cue in particular from Hermann Heller's 1934 political science. In addition to a majority of legal literature, he also took note of several works of legal history and just one sociological text, Helmut Schelsky's 1949 essay 'On the Stability of Institutions, Especially Constitutions' (Schelsky 1952). However there are no traces in the notes that follow of any reading of this text, which focuses primarily on discussing from a standpoint of cultural anthropology and institutions theory.

A short definition provides the introduction: the concept of the constitution is not 'phenomenologically traceable sociological circumstance', but a legal concept generated with certain historical and political intentions, whose meaning resides in 'being a self-made, supreme basic law that can be shaped, reshaped and amended to suit its purpose'. That is why its typical form is the written constitution, whose ultimate legitimation is the 'free will of the people' (ZK I: 27,1). The constitution is treated – in a still very old-European vein of legal theory – as an attempt on the part of 'Western man . . . to take possession of the state': it is part of the 'essence of the state . . . to be available and that means that it has a constitution'. In the process, Luhmann observes that 'this is not all explained by the sociological situation of the emerging citizenry that seeks its system of government' (27,2). As a consequence of the basic order guaranteed by the constitution becoming available, there is the rise of a need for the constitution to be safeguarded against amendments. This leads to:

a the problem of how to protect the constitution; and
b the question of putting barriers in the way of amending or altering the constitution (27,2).

However both of these points are only followed by a few references to the literature but no further discussion of contents.

For modern constitutional thinking, as Luhmann then continues, it is of decisive significance to the constitution not only that it is a manufactured fact, but also that it is homogeneous, meaning that it has

1 an external homogeneity, since it is set out in a single written document; and
2 an internal, material homogeneity, since it is the result of a closed, systematic plan (27,4).

In this vein, it is not the material content of the codification in itself that is characteristic of a modern constitution, so much as how it is systemised and rationalised. It is a necessary precondition for this that the state has a monopoly of law-making. In this context, Luhmann issues a demand (but takes it no further) for a theory of constitutional law-making to tackle the issue of a pre-constitutional subject, since the loss of belief in the divine establishment of the overall political order is of underlying significance for the modern constitution.

In conclusion, a short reference to Hans Freyer's 1925 work *Der Staat* (*The State*, although it is not quoted in the original, only as a secondary source) then accompanies a short comment on the paradoxical material content that the constitution is a 'system of axioms that stands unproven and unprovable at the beginning, but for its part lends their truth in the system to all true sentences' (27,6). This perception of the constitution's unjustifiable self-justification was to be crucial to Luhmann's later understanding in the 1980s, although nothing more is added to it in the earlier collection, as the section is simply discontinued here.

In the late 1950s and early 1960s, then, Luhmann took note of this issue, primarily in the framework of the established constitutional viewpoint, but no more than that: compared to other issues found in the first card index, this one is treated as marginal and no interpretation of his own is yet recognisable, to say nothing of a sociological one. Then there is the fact that there are absolutely no references to be found in this section that would lead to networking with other fields in the card index. In addition to this section, the only other reference in the list of keywords is one at point 10 'Organisation as Imagination and Reality', where there is just a note mentioning that the written constitution can be construed as a bridge between ideological state doctrine and reality. Since an examination of other, potentially more pertinent sections, such as on the Concept of State (ZK I: 9), on the Relationship between Organisation (State) and the Law (12) and on Politics and Law (14,6) has also turned up no additional findings, the first card index displays extensive ignorance of the constitutional issue, despite its focus on legal science.

Card index II: a social theory appreciation of the constitution

This tends to change in the second (sociological) card index collection, which Luhmann started at the beginning of the 1960s. Nevertheless, it must be said that the number of notes relative to constitutions that Luhmann generated in this collection, now with a primary focus on considerations of social theory, is comparably negligible here, too.

This applies in particular in the light of the fact that this collection contains an extensive block denominated 3414 'Legal Order', with some 2,500 cards, following the areas of 'Ideology', 'Authority' and 'Rules' in section 3 on 'Decision Theory'. In this block, a large number of more comprehensive sub-topics can be identified, which cover Luhmann's known concepts of the sociology of law and legal theory and follow one another more or less non-systematically, corresponding to the principle of information storage sketched out above: the function of the law, the concept of justice, the question of the generalisation of expected behaviour, the relationship between the sociology of law and legal theory, the positivisation of the law, basic rights, legal decision theory (conditional programming, legal doctrine, subjective rights), the differentiation of the legal system, the limits of enforceability of the law, justice/injustice, the legal system as a closed self-referential system. The names of these sub-topics already hint at Luhmann's various related publications. Although the block contains both earlier and later entries, there is a clearly identifiable focus datable to the 1970s.

The constitution as a legal institution

The legal section of the card index contains decidedly scanty notes about the constitution:

1 There is nothing substantial among the approximately 200 cards that make up the sub-topic 3414/6 'The Positivisation of the Law', except a few short comments about the possibility that positive law may stipulate the irreversibility of the law under the heading of 'constitutional amendments' (ZK II: 3414/6c6): here Luhmann makes a concrete reference to the relevant articles of several European countries' constitutions and then emphasises that the problem was originally not so much one of the possibility as far more of the impossibility of amending the constitution, because it is enacted as a positive law and is supposed to apply as such (3414/6c6a).

2 The most extensive notes can be found in the approximately 100 cards that make up the section 3414/10 'Basic Rights'. However just as in Luhmann's 1965 book on Basic Rights, whose preparation probably furnished the context for the majority of these notes, this section contains hardly any systematic considerations about the concept of the constitution itself. Again, just as in the book, which starts by mentioning only the difference between segments of constitutions that deal with basic rights and with organisation, as well as the question of their rationale in natural law, while focusing no particular attention on the concept of the constitution itself,[5] against the background of the thesis of the (latent) function of preserving a differentiated social order, the section ventures immediately (ZK II: 34141/10a) into a discussion of a variety of basic rights: rights of freedom, rights of

franchise, rights of property, rights of association, freedom of opinion, freedom of conscience, equality and freedom of religion. These are then followed by just two very short general comments about the constitution:

a Basic rights have the function not only of preserving a differentiated social order as a whole, but also of organising how the state reaches its decisions, since they organise their environment in such a way as to enable a political system to be differentiated. When basic rights are anchored in the constitution, this enables the state's decision-making system to concentrate on a specific function (3414/10f).

b At the same time, in the interests of encountering a differentiated social order in the form of basic rights, technology relieves the constitution of over-high interdependences: as a result, legal questions are differentiated by sector, even when a majority of basic rights may be affected 'in isolated cases' (3414/10f2).

3 Finally, section 3414/13 'Law and Power' contains an even more marginal observation: instead of assuming that the law is the code of political power, Luhmann finds it more sensible to ask what it means when the code of a medium – in this case political power – is placed contingently following on social development. According to his reading, only the law can be considered for controlling the contingency of the code of political power. This obliges on the one hand constitutions to be juridified and on the other the law to be positivised (3414/13f1).

In the last notes mentioned, it is striking that Luhmann here already abandoned the perspective originally focused on the law and adopted the dual perspective of law and politics that was to be a constituent factor of his later approach (see below).

Looking through the remaining notes about the law in the second collection in search of further supposedly pertinent places – for example in the sections on natural law (3414/3b), on the legal order and hierarchy (3414/9), on the sources of the law (3414/12) and on the differentiation of the law (3414/14), including its sub-topic on the legal system and political system (3414/14k10), on the law as a self-substituting order (3414/32), on the applicability of the law (3414/38b) or on the basic principles of the law (3414/48) – there are no entries of any kind that refer to the constitution.

Consulting the list of keywords, it soon becomes clear that Luhmann did not place the issue of the constitution in the block of notes about the law in the second card index, but in two places with notes about politics, in sections 35 'The Organisation of Decisions' and 7/54 'The Welfare State'. This thematic classification under politics can be explained by looking at the history of his works and is ultimately already applied in his book on basic rights, whose notes Luhmann nevertheless had still filed under the law (see above): the notes mentioned were probably first generated in the context of his 1973 essay on the constitution, which targeted an audience of legal theorists, although it focused on the function for politics; the second section is related to his 1981 book on the theory of the welfare state (1981b).

The constitution between politics and the law

Starting from the filing number 35/5g5, there are some 40 cards that tackle this issue in the sub-topic 35/5 'Administration as a System of Decision-Making', which can be found among the 700 cards that make up the large section 35 'The Organisation of Decisions', most of them dating to the 1970s, the rest to the 1980s. In this case, the focus or system reference is primarily on politics, something that is not necessarily surprising, in the light of the sequence in this section about decision-making, before then changing over from a political to a legal perspective, although without making any great fuss about it.[6] As a general rule, these notes tend to be fundamental and sometimes programmatic in character, i.e. they seldom go into detail and are scarcely co-ordinated in terms of theory, which indicates that they were jotted down over a considerable period of time.[7] Similarly, it is possible to identify several different approaches to determining functions and some only loosely related structural descriptions.

Limiting and increasing political power

This starts by defining the modern state as a decision-making organisation that, unlike the *res publica*, is no longer perceived as a continuation of an inherited order, but is legitimised rationally by a political formula made to measure especially for the purpose. Establishing that the decision is binding in nature and so legitimising it is the task of the constitution (ZK II: 35/5ga), while it is essential for a modern understanding of the constitution that there can only be *one* constitutional law (35/5g5a13), as this is the only way that the connection to the social function of politics is guaranteed after the unifying concept of civil society, i.e. of an ethically and politically constituted society, has dissolved (35/5ga1). In this connection we find a first, still very general definition of the concept: 'The constitution can be described as those structures in a system that are institutionalised *multifunctionally* and so cannot be separated from the point of view of a specific function. Any change in them makes it necessary to stabilise the entire system all over again and is correspondingly difficult' (35/5ga1). To be sure, Luhmann later added a question mark to this passage and noted only a little later that, in addition to this aspect of multifunctionality, which does not exclude enough, it was also necessary to consider the question of especially focal or essential connections that are placated by constitutions. With this in mind, he continued by noting two proposals:

a Constitutions are written for the purpose of limiting political power. This thesis is offered in the context of cybernetic thinking, typical of the perspectives of the 1970s, about how an increase in power becomes possible as a result of a decrease in power (35/5g5a3): while the old European model set out to draw distinctions between the rulers and the ruled, the modern model of power construes the constitution as a structure that enables power to increase as a result of restricting, so there is a need to draw distinctions between an internal limitation of political power in the form of checks and balances in the organisational part of the constitution and an external limitation achieved by natural laws, underlying values or basic rights (35/5g5a2–3). Luhmann thus considers the constitutional model's most important function to be to ensure that the limitations of power do not detract from the power itself. As the barriers to the power are not restricted to its ability to enforce, it is only possible to set conditions to relationships of power if they can then in turn become the object of politics (35/5g5a4). This is no longer just a question of applying the law to the state, but of the state regulating the conditions governing the guarantee of the law. Similarly, constitutionalism uses the constitution as a central tool of transformation (35/5g5a7), without there being any scope for still talking about using political means to achieve an intentional change of society: instead, we should assume that social development displays the form of evolution (35/5g5a10).

b For Luhmann, constitutions' second function is to reformulate the conditions of social compatibility for the political subsystem (35/5g5d), against the background of the general assumption that the constitution governs the relations between the system and its environment (35/5g5b). This function is linked to the observation that the planes of interaction, organisation and society that constitute society are pulling away from one another with increasing centrifugal force.[8] These social preconditions can no longer be taken for granted in a sovereign state, nor are they moralised any more, i.e. transferred from the model of interaction to the life of the state, but have to be reformulated.

The constitution as the deparadoxisation of the law

Alongside these notes, which are typical of Luhmann's approach to the dual perspective of politics and law, are others that concern themselves with the constitution's idiosyncrasies as a self-referential law to govern the law, prompting questions of law's self-imposed asymmetry and also including some historical observations.

The thesis that the constitution is construed as an installation in the system of a description of the system explains the high share of concepts of difference in constitutional semantics, both from a system-environment perspective (basic rights) and through an internal differentiation (the separation of powers) (ZK II: 35/5g5a9).

It is in this area that we find comments on the constitution's paradoxes. For example, that the problem was already diagnosed in the seventeenth century that no law can establish its own immutability, since it actually cannot exclude the possibility that the very clause that establishes immutability will itself be amended one day (35/5g5a11); similarly, the order of succession was still a crucial component of the pre-revolutionary understanding of the constitution (35/5g5a11g). Since more recent constitutional thinking no longer relies on a cosmologically inspired hierarchy of laws, it is confronted with the realisation that positive law requires immutability and hierarchies to be established (35/5g5a12).

Similarly, the need for constitutions is ascribed to positive law's idiosyncrasy of being circular in composition and having a tautological description (35/5g5k+k1–3): constitutions serve the purpose of breaking this circle by establishing hierarchies in the sources of the law and so concealing the fact that the law itself is the sole source of the law. Only in the legal system itself can and must a constitution be treated as a natural exigency. This brings Luhmann to a concept of the constitution that is based on a strictly functional definition with regard to a problem that first arose in history from the differentiation of the legal system in the course of the differentiation of society. This leads to a series of research questions, which Luhmann noted down here, although without following them up in his card index:

a he believed it was no coincidence that that the constitutional movement coincided with the demise of the case for natural law;

b according to his approach, constitutional problems in developing countries can be attributed to the fact that no premises had been created there for the problem that the constitutions set out to solve, i.e. the self-referentially closed nature of the various social subsystems arrived at by means of differentiation, so that the observable semantic borrowings from Europe could promise little in the way of success;[9]

c the 'beauty spots' that can be discerned in all constitutions in the form of unsupressible self-references called Luhmann's attention to the fact that all methods used to erase tautologies must proceed impurely, e.g. by anchoring corresponding plausibilities in the canon of basic values,[10] by delegating to organisation in the process of the separation of powers,[11] by a specifically juridical perception of the constitution as a natural exigency and by borrowing from logical analyses that demonstrate that it is impossible to achieve a logical conclusion[12] or by accepting a limited extent of self-reference at a higher level.[13]

It is notable here that none of the points mentioned results in a reference to other sections in the card index that might be pertinent in this respect: in each case, the only reference is outside the card index to other literature.

The constitutional state and the welfare state

The second more extensive heading mentioned in the list of keywords, to which reference is also made in the section just described, is also located in the area of political theory. Of the approximately 150 cards that make up the section 7/54 on the 'Welfare State', 20 come under the sub-topic 7/54b of 'The Welfare State/Constitutional State'.

In the context of the thesis of politics overstretching itself that we know from his 1981 book *Political Theory in the Welfare State* (1981b), Luhmann starts by using the feedback concept to compare the welfare state and the constitutional state (ZK II: 7/54b1–9). The welfare state relies on the principles of a positive feedback: any deviation from the condition as given is favoured, after which information is sought. The theories of the constitutional state, on the other hand, aim primarily to counter the abuse of power and are therefore formulated in terms of a negative feedback: they aim at acquiring information that indicates deviations from the morally and legally required condition, so that mechanisms can be introduced to recuperate the status quo. In a constitutional state with this kind of conception, Luhmann focuses primarily on two viewpoints, but without going into any greater detail:

1 sovereignty, in the sense that it is impossible to enforce a binding decision to solve every conflict; and
2 precautionary measures against the abuse of power.

Luhmann then considers the constitutional state's historical development into the (constitutionally based) welfare state as an example of how social evolution takes place on the plane of functional systems (7/54b5): although the constitutional state was stabilised by the law and so by a negative feedback, so could wait for conflicts, it introduced an evolutionary non-identical reproduction that can then be perceived to be the welfare state. Admittedly, the reference found here to a corresponding location in the more extensive section of the card index that deals with evolution (ZK II: 54/14kg) leads largely into the wilderness: there is only a short note commenting that when evolution is described in this case as non-identical reproduction, it means that all political decisions always contain a reference to the structure, especially to the state constitution, and that processes of variation and selection could come about here (54/14kgC1).[14]

Finally, in one note that was inserted at a very late stage and stands isolated in the section, Luhmann points out that the relationship between the constitutional state and the welfare state can be understood as the transformation of the basic paradox of a system's identity and its description of itself (ZK II: 7/54b10 f): in the constitutional state, there is a difference between the body of constitutional norms and the problem of the re-entry of the difference between the state and society in that state. In the welfare state, there is a comparable difference between superficial structures and deeper structures: the surface structure is described as a phenomenon of escalation (more social activities and commitments, more impact on society, more financial burdens, more juridification, more bureaucracy, etc.). As a result, it is programmed into the crisis of the state, as no escalation is in fact possible. The basic paradox is then in the consequence that the political system is thus occupied with more and more problems that it actually created for itself, so needs new forms of re-entry rationality. In this respect, Luhmann mentions the social diagnostic suspicion that the welfare state therefore has 'the more contemporary problems', so that the constitutional state loses out on thematic relevance and is not tackled (ZK II: 7/54b4).

Any search in the remaining political sections of the second card index for any additional notes comes up with thoroughly negative results: in the place actually reserved for this in the card index, section 533/15 on 'Politics', where the majority of the approximately 800 cards decidedly dedicated to political theory are collected as a sub-heading of the section 533 on 'Peer Groups, Problems of Consensus and Consensus Formalisations', most of which date to the 1970s and 1980s, there are no observations of any kind. And that despite the fact that Luhmann discusses the 'Relationship to Other Subsystems' there in a separate section 533/15t, in the process quoting economics, science, religion, the educational system and the family and tackling them under individual, sometimes quite extensive, sub-headings. In vain does one search for notes on the law, however. In this respect, there is nothing more than a reference in an introductory overview of the various different constellations of systems to publications on basic rights – here, too, then, to material outside the collection, but not to the relevant section described above – as well as to the location 3414/14k10 already mentioned above, with a glimpse at the constitution, although it is not exactly pertinent.

Likewise, there are no findings in the older, primary notes contained in the section 353 on 'Power and Influence' dating back to the 1960s and 1970s, on which Luhmann presumably drew when preparing his 1975 book on power. The same also applies for the fourth place in the system with a decided affinity to politics, which is located in the block 6 'Sovereignty and the State', drawn up in the 1970s and 1980s and comprising approximately 150 cards, although an introductory mention is made here of the legal side of the sovereignty paradox in the form of freedom and obligation (ZK II: 6/1,3 f) and of the reflexivity of applicable law (6/1e). However, there are no references that develop any further on the theme of the role played by the constitution in this process of the differentiation of the political system, which Luhmann describes from a historical perspective, save one short note that the theory of the constitutional state[15] as a theory of reflection provides an answer to the question of whether all conflicts can be solved politically and discusses the nature of the non-arbitrary use of political force (6/11).[16] The same also applies in the case of the extensive section on the concept of the state (6/3).

To make a provisional appraisal, it has to be said that also the second card index only tackles the issue of the constitution rather marginally: most of the notes in the pertinent sections are no more than rapid sketches, while the presence of argumentatively more comprehensive considerations arrayed in sequence is rather sparse. The cohesion of the theses mentioned is mostly poor, just as the notes are evidently altogether a documentary record of a rather long period of time and a correspondingly unsystematic search process, in which nothing seems to have been attached purposefully to any particular location in the card index system. Instead, the majority of Luhmann's actual theoretical and conceptual work took place outside the card index, with a first focus especially in his 1965 book on basic rights, whose main emphasis is nevertheless still on the controversy with political science and legal theory. Also in the case of his 1975 essay on 'Political Constitutions in the Context of the System of Society', which spelled out the general thesis that the constitution plays a regulatory role for the political system's relationship with its environment and which goes much further than the available notes, Luhmann seems to have made practically no use of his card index or at the most used his notes as no more than sources of keywords. Lastly, something similar applies to his 1981 publication about the welfare state. Since the notes in the collection are rather rudimentary in character, it is also impossible to use the formulation that was so popular with Luhmann with reference to his publications, i.e. that the card index even exceeded his output of learned texts. On the contrary, only a few of the discussions crucial to these publications found their way into the card index, so that in this particular case not only is the linkage between the card index and the book at best a loose one, but in addition it can be stated that Luhmann mostly refrained from transferring the considerations he had developed in the process of developing his manuscript into the card index, unlike what he often did when producing other manuscripts, since he intended to develop their themes further.

A quest for the reasons for this finding leads in particular to two reciprocally related causes. On the one hand, the constitution probably achieves such scanty consideration in the card index because the issue was both an early and a late developer in Luhmann: he had already tackled the issue comprehensively at a very early stage with his 1965 book on basic rights and his 1973 essay on the constitution, without having been able to fall back on any substantial numbers of existing notes in his card index at that stage. Correspondingly, all we find in the card index are the outlines he had prepared in the framework of the practical preparatory work for these publications, whereas the majority of the work he put into developing the arguments for this purpose took place outside the card index, directly during the preparation of the manuscripts. On the other hand, despite his enduring interest in the law, much of Luhmann's attention was evidently drawn to other fields by the work he started doing on his other publications in the mid-1970s, so that there were at first very few concrete opportunities for any further notes.[17] In addition, as already mentioned before, the comparatively few outlines are scattered across several different places in the card index. This feature of how the card index is composed on the basis of the principle of multiple storage reflects the circumstance that Luhmann went against the grain of the constitutional presumption of a fusion between politics and the law, proceeding from an operative difference between the two and so from a dual perspective also of the constitution. Nevertheless, in the sketches dating to the 1970s, this dual perspective leads to notes that are mostly unconnected to their neighbours, some of them adopting the political standpoint, others the legal or constitutional perspective.[18] Paradoxically, it was only when he transposed the general theory of social systems onto the model of operational closure that the possibility of a new theoretical conception was revealed, one that was capable of taking both perspectives into consideration at the same time. Yet this late development was based primarily on the essentials, so that its development in terms of material records on the issue of the constitution could not really draw on the card index.

The constitution as a structural bond between politics and law

After a certain period of respite, the problem of the theoretically conclusive treatment of inter-system phenomena concomitant with the concept of autopoiesis (Luhmann 1982) led Luhmann at the end of the 1980s to introduce the general theoretical concept of structural coupling, which enables the reciprocal irritation in closed systems to be modelled.[19] In the context of this development, he then also achieved a theoretical reformulation of the concept of the constitution, which is construed as a structure in the social subsystems of law and politics that operate not only separately from one another, yet refer reciprocally to each other, but in addition as a mechanism that at the same time ensures a close correlation between the two functional areas.

The relationship implicit in this between politics and the law was first subjected to preliminary development at the end of the 1980s in the corresponding concept of the state based on the rule of law, which in its turn was derived from a reading of the state as the political system describing itself. The development of this theory is recorded in parts of the approximately 80 cards about the state based on the rule of law that date back to the 1970s and 1980s and can be found in the second collection under 35/5j6, in the same main section 35 'The Organisation of Decisions' as the subsection on the constitution, although there is no direct reference to this section, despite a corresponding note to that effect.[20] The concept of the state based on the rule of law hinging on the reciprocal relationship between the law and politics that was adopted by Luhmann from the very beginning (1971), and espoused against the political science that held sway in the 1960s and 1970s, eventually blossomed into the thesis that the state based on the rule of law itself constitutes the borderline between the law and politics, where both sides only ever see their own potential, just as in a mirror. This concept then manifested itself again in the essay published in 1988, 'The Two Sides of the State Based on the Rule of Law': this essay's development either drew on some of the notes contained in the section mentioned above or was the occasion for others to be added.

The corresponding constitutional concept reacts to the diagnosed need for the completely separated system to be connected, as Luhmann notes in his essay 'The Constitution as an Evolutionary Achievement' (1990, 180; 193). The thesis of the constitution achieving the structural coupling between politics and the law was eventually lexicalised in Luhmann's monograph on the legal system (1993, 440ff.), although in the card index the constitution is merely noted as a candidate for this theoretical figure: as already mentioned previously, the sub-heading on differentiation from the legal system contains a small sequence of cards on the legal system and politics (ZK II: 3414/14k10 ff) which, while it does refer to the above-mentioned section 35/5j6 on the state based on the rule of law, does not refer to the constitution, but merely makes a brief statement to the effect that the relationship between the law and politics can be formulated anew on this basis. The corresponding place in the system for the theoretical concept of structural coupling can be found in the larger block about the concept of function (ZK II: 21/8v). Arranged at the end of the 1980s, the 35 cards that make up this subsection are not particularly comprehensive, nevertheless they include not only primarily conceptual and terminological clarifications, but also evidence of their application. Along with others, the constitution is mentioned twice as this kind of mechanism of structural coupling (21/8v2 and v12): as in other cases specific to functional systems, however, this thesis is merely hinted at in the card index, while the actual developments on the theme are reserved for the author's corresponding publications.

With reference to the works he published in the field of the law from the mid-eighties onwards, it has to be said that Luhmann evidently decided to do largely without providing his card index with a documentary record of the latest theoretical developments. The reason why this is worth mentioning is because he continued to generate more extensive notes for other topics right up to the 1990s, among others for his 1991 book on risks (ZK II: 21/3d18c60o9 ff) and the 1995 volume on art (ZK II: 32/3g13k ff and 11/13 ff). Yet this does not apply to the topic of the law in general, nor in particular to Luhmann's 1993 monograph on the legal system. So it follows that the conceptual stipulations that were only first developed in this framework were no longer worked systematically into the card index. Similarly, the essay about the constitution published in 1990, with its wealth of material content, also has no immediately discernible corresponding section in the card index.[21] Luhmann appears to have found it much easier to develop his text conventionally in the case of law than in other cases, where he first had to work on the topic's material content himself,[22] with the result that this, too, led to no further new entries. Correspondingly, the card index also only contains relatively few notes that were first generated in the framework of the preparation for the monograph *Law, Justice, Society*.[23] Section 3414/18, which is supposedly pertinent, since it bears the same title, comprises precisely one card, although this one card dates not from the end of the 1980s, but from the beginning of the 1970s, reacting to the evidence of a crisis in the law – in the sense of a crisis in legal consciousness – and containing a reference to the approximately 150 cards that make up another, older block, 3414/14 on 'Law in a Differentiated Social Order', that first of all links to Durkheim and his theory of using the law to integrate a differentiated social order, then adds observations about contemporary legal development and the differentiation of the law, yet contains only selectively newly-inserted cards (as in the case of section 3414/6 on the positivisation of the law). Meanwhile, the section 3414/38 on 'Law as a Self-Referential Closed System' was drawn up in the framework of Luhmann's later socio-legal thinking. Admittedly, it contains only about 40 cards, but they include his well-known observations about the concept of law's operational closure, validity, codification and the jurisprudence of interests, which he had developed and extended on in essays published in the journal *Rechtstheorie* in the 1980s and while preparing the ground for the 1993 monograph on the Legal System, although none of this generated any feedback worth mentioning in the card index. The fact that the section that covers the concept of validity contains a reference of content (to 3414/38b1) 'elaborated in *Law, Justice, Society* (Ms 89)' indicates that the card index was no longer Luhmann's primary dialogue partner at this stage, just as, vice versa, it had not yet been at the earlier time when he drew up his book on basic rights.

Conclusion

To summarise, it must therefore be stated that the card index was no particularly original dialogue partner for Luhmann when it came to his work in the area of the constitution. Since Luhmann's interest in the topic of the constitution was first reflected in early corresponding publications, as time went on this led to very few follow-up entries in the card index, so that it is possible to observe a phenomenon, with regard to these notes, that Luhmann described in his own appraisal of the card index as a process of trickling and of patchy growth (1981a, 225): although the sections with notes about the law and politics grew continuously in the 1970s and 1980s, the process was neither even nor applied across the entire scope of the theme. Similarly, Luhmann's late development of his newer, decidedly bifocal understanding of the constitution could not link up to any already existing larger body of notes. As it was probably predictable for Luhmann at the end of the 1980s that these were likely to be his last publications about the law, so that in that sense there was no longer any need for the collection to be tailored to keep up what was in practice an intrinsically future-oriented attitude, he was gradually converted to producing his texts more conventionally when his card index still featured no corresponding contents, as a result of which he also did without any feedback into it.[24]

The small number of cards about the issue of the constitution is closely related – and this is far more important for the functionality of the card index – to the small rate of references in the available notes. Within the card index, they contradict what ought to be the very *raison d'être* of their networking principle by being relatively isolated: the few references that are made are also overwhelmingly circular, so that original new perspectives are seldom found in the card index. And the few references that do venture outside the theme's traditional grounds end up referring to discussions that are then taken no further in the card index, such as on the evolution of politics and the law as cases where a general theory of evolution is applied. Correspondingly, no internal network of references could be set in motion with regard to the issue of the constitution and the card index could also not act as a generator of surprise links, in accordance with the general principle sketched out by Luhmann. This makes it clear that there are not only opportunities intrinsic to the principle of reference, but also risks, as Luhmann pointed out himself: 'Every note is just an element that only achieves quality from the network of references and cross-references in the system. A note that is not linked in to this network gets lost in the card index: the card index forgets it. Its rediscovery is a matter of chance and also of the fortuitous circumstance that it will be rediscovered at a moment when the occurrence happens to mean something' (1981a, 225).

It would be exaggerated to argue that the notes about the constitution were forgotten in the card index, but no critical mass of observations, of the kind that could have triggered a process of new combinations of notes, ever came about, with the result that the card index was unable to act as a productive second memory for the issue of constitutionalism. In the case of the newer definition of the constitution, this led to the situation that Luhmann's theoretical work no longer took place in the card index, but only in his publications themselves, as can easily be discerned, for example, by comparing how the two monographs on the law and on politics (published in 1993 and 2000, respectively, but developed in close succession) handled the issue of the state and the constitution: they both illustrate his theory as work in progress, a state of affairs that in other fields tended to be recorded in the card index itself. In this respect, the card index was certainly not Luhmann's favourite tool of thought for the issue of the constitution: at best, it could be a source of keywords.

Notes

1 In this chapter, references to the notes in the filing system are identified with the numbers given to them by Luhmann himself, 'ZK I' or 'ZK II', as the two collections have substantially separate numbering and are independent of one another (ZK is an acrynom for 'Zettelkasten', German for card index system).
2 This may have been drafted in connection with the 1981 article mentioned above.
3 It was also at this time that Luhmann spent a sabbatical at the Harvard University School of Government, where he first came into contact with Talcott Parsons: this led to Luhmann to apply himself more vigorously to sociology.
4 Such as the issues of the state, equality, planning, the right of veto, power, the constitution, emergency, government and the majority principle. Subsequently, the topics (among others the division of labour, hierarchy, roles and integration) then enable a gradual orientation towards organisational studies – and thus also as a consequence to sociology – to be detected.
5 This can be explained by the fact that this feeds directly into the constitutional discussion – so the concept of the constitution is ultimately consolidated – from whose interpretation of basic rights Luhmann then dissociates himself, however, with his functional questioning. The social theory grounding for the concept of the constitution that is still largely missing here then followed in the 1973 essay mentioned above.
6 It is worth recalling the fact mentioned above that a card's location in the index was ultimately determined by the principle of how it would relate to the previous card, not by how it would relate to the overall topic.
7 Further indicators in favour of this theory are the changing handwriting and the different types of paper used for the cards.
8 The thesis of an increasing difference between the planes of interaction, organisation and society is developed further at note ZK II: 21/3d27f.
9 This topic was discussed by Marcelo Neves in his dissertation *Constitution and the Positivity of the Law in Peripheral Modern Societies*, whose manuscript is also mentioned here by Luhmann.
10 Without Luhmann referring here to the relevant sections in his card index.
11 Luhmann mentions Hermann Heller by name, but without naming the relevant location in his system in card index ZK I.
12 Luhmann here merely makes fleeting mention of 'Gödel and successors'.
13 This card contains a literature reference to Lars Löfgren, but without any subsequent reference to sections relevant to self-reference (ZK II: 21/3d26g98) or to paradox (21/3d26g70m).
14 Luhmann then developed this point further in the 1990s, when he wrote his monograph on politics as a functional system (2000, 422f.).
15 A reference is also made to this location from the section 7/54 mentioned above.

16 The reference found here to the location 533/15z/e on 'Political Theory' goes no further here.

17 In this respect, it is worth mentioning that Luhmann's book on basic rights was edited repeatedly without amendment once every decade, which can be read as evidence that the author felt that the publication had not been superseded.

18 In his book on basic rights, on the other hand, Luhmann construes the benchmark issue to which basic rights react as regarding society as a whole: the conservation of a functionally differentiated society.

19 The concept of structural coupling was first introduced in a 1989 manuscript about the relationship between the law and the economy, which was then reflected in the relevant section in Luhmann's monograph on the functional system of the law (1993, 452ff.).

20 'The state based on the rule of law is the notion that the political system determines its essence as a "state" in accordance with the constitution, i.e. in a nutshell, the law is established and determined by the law. The state is defined in its particular form by the constitution, i.e. by a law. This is underscored emphatically as the victory of the law over the power, so over politics; and, thus, of reason over arbitrariness. All power must therefore take the form of competences' (ZK II: 35/5j6i).

21 Unlike the short, rather sketched 1988 essay 'The Two Sides of the State Based on the Rule of Law'.

22 The legal scholar's 'insider perspective' leads correspondingly to clearly higher expectations of reception from sociologists, which can easily be discerned in the relevant 1972 publication (of particular note alongside the book on basic rights is the manuscript on contingency and law that has since been published (2013)), which was produced in parallel to and as an extension of his *A Sociological Theory of Law* (1972).

23 Which incidentally also devotes comparatively little space to the issue of the constitution (see in particular 1993, 470ff.).

24 Luhmann also tells us that this was the procedure he used increasingly during a late phase of the theory in an interview he gave in 1997: 'I now have an alternative [to the card index], what you might call half-finished book manuscripts, which are stored in boxes under my desk . . . When I now discover anything interesting about "sovereignty", I can put it directly into the manuscript, where "state" and "sovereignty" are dealt with'. (Hagen and Luhmann 2004, 107). What he does not say is that was accompanied by a fundamental change in his way of producing theories and texts.

References

Freyer, Hans. *Der Staat*. Leipzig: Rechfelden, 1925.

Hagen, Wolfgang, and Niklas Luhmann. 'Die Realität der Massenmedien. Niklas Luhmann im Radiogespräch mit Wolfgang Hagen'. In *Warum haben Sie keinen Fernseher, Herr Luhmann? Letzte Gespräche mit Niklas Luhmann*, edited by Wolfgang Hagen, 79–107. Berlin: Kadmos, 2004.

Heller, Hermann. *Staatslehre*. Edited by Gerhart Niemeyer. Leiden: Sijthoff, 1934.

Krajewski, Markus. *Zettelwirtschaft. Die Geburt der Kartei aus dem Geiste der Bibliothek*. Berlin: Kulturverlag Kadmos, 2002.

Luhmann, Niklas. *Grundrechte als Institution. Ein Beitrag zur politischen Soziologie*. Berlin: Duncker & Humblot, 1965.

———. 'Gesellschaftliche und politische Bedingungen des Rechtsstaats'. In *Politische Planung. Aufsätze zur Soziologie von Politik und Verwaltung*, 53–65. Opladen: Westdeutscher Verlag, 1971.

———. *Rechtssoziologie*, 2 vols. Reinbek b. Hamburg: Rowohlt, 1972 (A Sociological Theory of Law. London et al.: Routledge and Kegan Paul, 1985).

———. 'Politische Verfassungen im Kontext des Gesellschaftssystems'. *Der Staat. Zeitschrift für Staatslehre, Öffentliches Recht und Verfassungsgeschicte* 12 (1973): 1–22, 165–82.

———. 'Kommunikation mit Zettelkästen. Ein Erfahrungsbericht'. In *Öffentliche Meinung und sozialer Wandel*, edited by Horst Baier, Hans M. Kepplinger, and Kurt Reumann, 222–8. Wiesbaden: Westdeutscher Verlag, 1981a.

———. *Politische Theorie im Wohlfahrtsstaat*. Munich and Vienna: Olzog, 1981b (Political Theory in the Welfare State, in: N. Luhmann, Political Theory in the Welfare State. Berlin et al.: de Gruyter, 1990, 21–115).

———. 'Autopoiesis, Handlung und kommunikative Verständigung'. *Zeitschrift für Soziologie* 11 (1982): 366–79.

———. 'Biographie, Attitüden, Zettelkasten'. In *Archimedes und wir. Interviews*, edited by Dirk Baecker and Georg Stanitzek, 125–55. Berlin: Merve, 1987.

———. 'Zwei Seiten des Rechtsstaates' (1988). In *Conflict and Integration. Comparative Law in the World Today: The 40th Anniversary of The Institute of Comparative Law in Japan*, 493–506. Tokyo: Chuo University Press, 1989 (Two Sides of the State Founded on Law, in: N. Luhmann, Political Theory in the Welfare State. Berlin et al.: de Gruyter, 1990, 187–202).

———. *Wirtschaft und Recht: Probleme struktureller Kopplung*. Bielefeld: unpublished manuscript, 1989.

———. 'Verfassung als evolutionäre Errungenschaft'. *Rechtshistorisches Journal* 9 (1990): 176–220.

———. *Das Recht der Gesellschaft*. Frankfurt am Main, Suhrkamp, 1993 (Law as a Social System. Oxford et al.: Oxford University Press, 2004).

———. *Die Politik der Gesellschaft*. Edited by André Kieserling. Frankfurt am Main: Suhrkamp, 2000.

———. *Kontingenz und Recht. Rechtstheorie im interdisziplinären Zusammenhang*. Edited by Johannes F.K. Schmidt. Berlin: Suhrkamp, 2013.

Neves, Marcelo. *Verfassung und Positivität des Rechts in der peripheren Moderne. Eine theoretische Betrachtung und Interpretation des Falls Brasilien*. Berlin: Duncker & Humblot, 1992.

Schelsky, Helmut. 'Über die Stabilität von Institutionen, besonders Verfassungen. Kulturanthropologische Überlegungen zu einem rechtssoziologischen Thema'. *Jahrbuch für Sozialwissenschaften* 3(1) (1952): 1–21.

Schmidt, Johannes F.K. 'Luhmanns Zettelkasten und seine Publikationen'. In *Luhmann-Handbuch. Leben – Werk – Wirkung*, edited by Oliver Jahraus, Armir Nassehi, Mario Grizeli, Imhild Saake, Christian Kirchmeier and Julian Müller, 7–11. Stuttgart: Metzler, 2012.

Zedelmaier, Helmut. *Bibliotheca Universalis und Bibliotheca Selecta. Das Problem der Ordnung des gelehrten Wissens in der frühen Neuzeit*. Cologne, Weimar and Vienna: Böhlau Verlag, 1992.

Index

For Product Safety Concerns and Information please contact our EU
representative GPSR@taylorandfrancis.com
Taylor & Francis Verlag GmbH, Kaufingerstraße 24, 80331 München, Germany

www.ingramcontent.com/pod-product-compliance
Ingram Content Group UK Ltd.
Pitfield, Milton Keynes, MK11 3LW, UK
UKHW050054200926
475702UK00019B/2826

* 9 7 8 1 1 3 8 4 9 7 5 6 6 *